Select an attractive format for your data using AutoFormat; see page 485 in Chapter 16.

Format your data with the Formatting toolbar; see page 464 in Chapter 16.

Create formulas that calculate new values from existing values; see page 556 in Chapter 19.

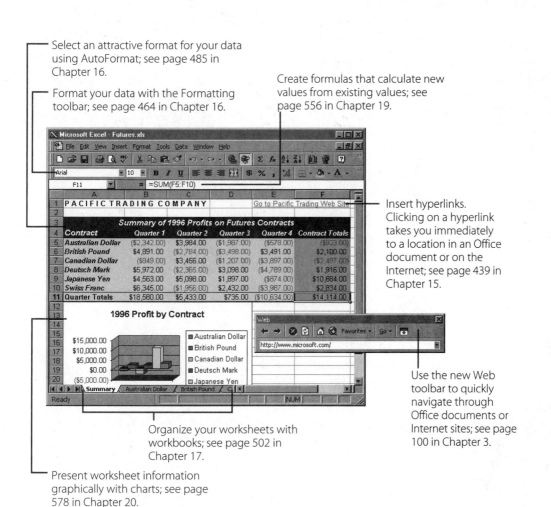

Insert hyperlinks. Clicking on a hyperlink takes you immediately to a location in an Office document or on the Internet; see page 439 in Chapter 15.

Use the new Web toolbar to quickly navigate through Office documents or Internet sites; see page 100 in Chapter 3.

Organize your worksheets with workbooks; see page 502 in Chapter 17.

Present worksheet information graphically with charts; see page 578 in Chapter 20.

About the Authors

Michael Halvorson worked for Microsoft Corporation from 1985 to 1993, where he was employed as a technical editor, acquisitions editor, and localization manager. He received a B.A. in computer science from Pacific Lutheran University and an M.A. in history from the University of Washington.

In 1996, Michael received a Merit Award for technical writing from the Society for Technical Communication, and the Thomas M. Power Award for excellence in historical writing.

Michael is the author of *Microsoft Visual Basic 5 Step by Step* and *Learn Visual Basic Now,* and coauthor (with Chris Kinata) of *Microsoft Word 97/ Visual Basic Step by Step,* all published by Microsoft Press.

Michael J. Young is an author of books on using and programming computers, a contributor to several computer magazines, and a freelance programmer. He has written 15 computer books, including *Visual Basic—Game Programming for Windows* for Microsoft Press, and he has used and written about Microsoft Office applications for almost a decade. Michael graduated from Stanford University and was a member of the ANSI committee on the standardization of the C language. His Web page is at http://ourworld.compuserve.com/homepages/mjy; you can send him e-mail at 75156.2572@compuserve.com.

RUNNING
Microsoft® Office 97

Michael Halvorson
and Michael Young

PUBLISHED BY
Microsoft Press
A Division of Microsoft Corporation
One Microsoft Way
Redmond, Washington 98052-6399

Library of Congress Cataloging-in-Publication Data
Halvorson, Michael.
    Running Microsoft Office 97 / Michael Halvorson, Michael Young.
        p. cm.
    Includes index.
    ISBN 1-57231-322-6
    1. Microsoft Office. 2. Microsoft Word. 3. Microsoft Excel
(Computer file) 4. Microsoft PowerPoint (Computer file)
5. Microsoft Access. 6. Word processing. 7. Business--Computer
programs. 8. Electronic spreadsheets. 9. Business presentations-
-Graphic methods--Computer programs. 10. Internet (Computer
network) I. Young, Michael, 1948- . II. Title.
HF5548.4.M523H355 1997
005.369--dc21   96-44022
                                   CIP

Printed and bound in the United States of America.

2 3 4 5 6 7 8 9 QFQF 2 1 0 9 8 7

Distributed to the book trade in Canada by Macmillan of Canada, a division of Canada Publishing Corporation.

A CIP catalogue record for this book is available from the British Library.

Microsoft Press books are available through booksellers and distributors worldwide. For further information about international editions, contact your local Microsoft Corporation office. Or contact Microsoft Press International directly at fax (206) 936-7329.

Acquisitions Editor: Kim Fryer
Project Editor: Lucinda Rowley
Manuscript and Technical Editing: Labrecque Publishing

Chapters at a Glance

Table of Contents

Acknowledgments

To some of you, preparing a 1000-page computer book might seem like publishing a giant cookbook or a one-volume encyclopedia. In other words, it might seem like steady, respectable work—something people do between Nine and Five with plenty of time for coffee breaks and reflection. Publishing this book didn't work that way. Like a team of scholars decoding ancient hieroglyphics or a rally crew driving across the Sahara, countless publishing literati labored late into the night to bring this book to you. The Running Office team scrutinized each new release of the Office 97 software, worked tirelessly to develop clear and useful examples, and expertly implemented a book design that blends dozens of useful and interesting elements.

Our warmest thanks go to Lucinda Rowley, who served as the book's acquisitions editor and project editor; Mark Woodworth, for his intelligent copy editing; Lisa Auer and Curtis Philips, for their skillful technical editing; Lisa Bravo, for creative page composition; Andrea Fox, for eagle-eyed proofreading; and Lisa Labrecque, for managing the project at Labrecque Publishing. Many thanks also to Ina Chang and Kim Fryer at Microsoft Press, for moving the project along in its final stages.

Finally, a word of thanks to all the editors, compositors, proofreaders, and artists who worked on the previous edition of Running Office. Their efforts last time made this title a pleasure to revise.

Introduction

We're glad you've chosen this book to get the inside scoop on Microsoft Office 97—Microsoft's newest integrated software suite. The 1997 model year builds on "old reliable" by introducing a number of powerful and entertaining software features. With Microsoft Office 97, you get a complete set of software tools that every business and home can use. And if you're looking to leverage your work on the Internet, just power up your modem, sit back, and relax: We'll show you all the Web tricks right here.

Microsoft Office 97, Standard Edition, contains Microsoft Word, Microsoft Excel, and Microsoft PowerPoint, plus a new information management program called Microsoft Outlook. If you have the Professional Edition of Office, you also have Microsoft Access. This book shows you how to get the most from these best-selling applications and describes ways that you can use them together to create professional-looking reports, presentations, financial models, and databases. We have designed this book to help get you up and running quickly, learn the basics of the Office applications, and then build on your new skills by exploring advanced concepts. If you follow the tips, tutorials, and examples in this book, you'll be creating and printing documents the very first day you use the Office software! As you gain experience with Office, you can also use the book as a reference to the advanced features and capabilities of your applications. A comprehensive index, the table of contents, and our cross-referencing system will guide you instantly to the solutions you need.

How This Book Is Organized

Because Microsoft designed the applications in the Office suite to be used together, you'll be pleased to find that many of the skills you learn in one application will be useful in another. Rather than simply listing the features of each Office application, this book shows you how to accomplish *useful* work with the Office tools. When it's advantageous to do so, we show you how to use your Office applications in concert to build a special document or create a report. To structure the presentation, we have divided the book into six major parts.

Part I of the book shows you how to *master essential skills* using the Office software. You'll learn how to start and use each Office application, how to manage programs with the Microsoft Office Shortcut Bar and the Windows taskbar, and how to perform essential skills such as navigating windows, completing dialog boxes, naming and saving files, and printing documents. You'll also learn how to open, share, and search Office documents on the Internet World Wide Web (a mouthful we'll simply abbreviate as "the Web"). If you're new to Office applications or the Internet, this is the place you can learn the fundamental skills used in all Office documents.

Part II of the book covers *Microsoft Word,* the word processing application that you can use to create memos, newsletters, reports, and other desktop publishing projects. The first few chapters in this part introduce Word and its newest features; the remaining chapters teach Word's intermediate and advanced features, including document formatting, using styles and templates, designing columns and pages, creating mailing lists, customizing Word, and working in workgroups. If you're an avid user of Word, this could be the only product documentation you ever need.

Part III of the book presents *Microsoft Excel,* the electronic spreadsheet that you can use to create ledgers, invoices, charts, and powerful financial models. If you're new to spreadsheets, you can learn the basics in Chapter 15, "Building a Worksheet." After this foundation chapter, Part III introduces you to the depth and breadth of Excel. You'll learn how to use workbooks to organize information, build sophisticated formulas and functions, create presentation-quality charts, manage database information with lists, customize Excel to suit your needs, analyze business data with "what-if?" scenarios, and increase your productivity with Visual Basic macros. Check out Chapter 22, "Analyzing Business Data," if you've never used Excel's Solver feature, and learn how easily you can apply it to help you make complex quantity and pricing decisions.

Part IV of the book deals with *Microsoft PowerPoint,* the essential presentation tool for slide shows, overhead presentations, automated demonstrations, and multimedia expositions. If you're like most PowerPoint users, you're an expert in your own field but have little formal experience with desktop presentation software—so you want to create and finish your presentation quickly and get on to more important things. In Part IV, we teach the basic PowerPoint skills in short, concise chapters to get you up and running as quickly as possible. Then, for those who have more time, we move on to advanced topics such as creating special effects and adding variations to the show. Whether you want to learn the PowerPoint basics or explore the newest features in electronic presentation, this part of the book is for you.

Part V of the book covers *Microsoft Access,* the database application that you can use to create and manage customer lists, data-entry forms, product inventories, and other collections of organized information. For those who are new to databases, a quick introduction explains how to design and build a database effectively. (This is easier than ever, because of a collection of stellar database wizards.) If you're already an Access user, you'll find techniques to improve your skill as you work with forms, design queries, and reports.

Part VI of the book focuses on *using the Office applications together* to prepare reports, presentations, and other projects that benefit from integrated use of the Office tools. In this part of the book, you'll learn how to share data among Office applications, use the Office Binder to store several files in one convenient location, and use Microsoft Outlook to manage both electronic mail and your personal schedule and appointments.

Who This Book Is For

Running Microsoft Office 97 is for active business professionals who create or use electronic documents as part of their job. We designed the book to teach fundamental skills to beginners and to provide ongoing, essential information for experienced users of the Office software. Most Microsoft Office users are familiar with one or two applications, but are less familiar with the remaining programs. To cover all the possibilities, we start from the beginning in each section, and then move quickly to intermediate and advanced topics that will be helpful to readers with a variety of skills.

The book contains step-by-step instructions and examples that cover the breadth of each Office product, so that you can use this book as either a tutorial or a reference. After you learn the skills you need, we hope that you'll keep the book by your computer to consult when you have a question about your software or want the challenge of using advanced options to make your work product even more professional and attractive. To give you many entry points to the material, we've included sidebars, tips, notes, warnings, and cross-referencing information to help you get the most from your purchase. By the time you finish using this book, your colleagues might think of you as some sort of "Office guru."

Conventions Used in This Book

This book contains concise descriptions of the commands and features in Office, plus step-by-step instructions (often beside a picture of an actual application window) that you can follow to complete a task or solve a problem. Most of the instructions rely on mouse actions, so you'll see the directives "click," "double-click," "right-click," and "drag" a good deal. If you're not familiar with the mouse or with running commands in Windows 95, we recommend that you read *Introducing Microsoft Windows 95*, the user's guide that comes with the retail version of Windows 95, or a similar short tutorial about working in the Windows 95 operating environment.

Occasionally, we give you shortcut key combinations for running commands in Office applications. For example, Ctrl+S means that you hold down one of the Ctrl keys on your keyboard and press the letter *S*. If we have important information or a helpful tip to show you, we'll include it in a shaded box that has a "Tip" icon. Finally, wherever you encounter the "See Also" icon, you find references to other sections in the chapter or the book that provide additional, related information.

Installing and Maintaining the Office Software

Before you get started with Chapter 1, verify that the Microsoft Office 97 software is installed on your system. The easiest way to do this is to click the Start button, point to the Programs folder, and verify that the Microsoft Word, Microsoft Excel, Microsoft PowerPoint, and Microsoft Outlook icons are present. (If you have the Professional Edition of Office, you'll also see the Microsoft Access icon.)

If you haven't installed the Office software yet, open the Control Panel folder (by clicking the Start button, choosing Settings, and clicking Control Panel) and then double-click the Add/Remove Programs icon. Click the Install button on the Install/Uninstall tab. When the Install Program From Floppy Disk Or CD-ROM dialog box appears, insert your Office Setup disk into the appropriate drive. (If you're using floppy disks, insert Setup Disk 1 into drive A.) Click the Next button to have the Control Panel locate the Setup program. If the Setup program isn't found, make sure that the disk is in the proper drive and either try again or use the Browse button to locate the Setup program yourself. To start the Office Setup program, click the Finish button.

During the setup process, you get a chance to specify which components of the Office software you want installed. You'll probably want to specify the Typical installation option, but if you have less than 121 megabytes of free disk space (the amount required for a Typical installation of the Professional Edition), you might want to install with the Compact option or remove a few of the nonessential components, such as the file converters, filters, or Office tools.

To run Microsoft Office under Microsoft Windows 95, you need a VGA or higher resolution adapter, a Microsoft Mouse or compatible pointing device, and 8 megabytes of memory to run two Office applications simultaneously. If you plan to use Access for serious database work, you need 12 to 16 megabytes of memory. And don't forget a printer if you want to create hard copy that you can share with your colleagues. You can also profitably run Microsoft Office on systems running the Microsoft Windows NT operating system. For more information, see the system requirements listed on the Office software box.

After you install Office, you can run the Office Setup program again to add applications and components to your Office installation, or to remove them. For example, you might want to install one or more of the optional Excel add-in programs (such as the Solver) when you create "what-if?" models in Chapter 22, "Analyzing Business Data." To add or remove programs, double-click the Add/Remove Programs icon in the Control Panel, select Microsoft Office 97 from the list of programs on the Install/Uninstall tab, and then click the Add/Remove button. Make sure your Office disk is inserted in the correct drive and click OK when prompted. Next click the Add/Remove button in the Microsoft Office 97 Setup dialog box, and select the components that you want to add or clear the components that you want to remove. If you need to remove all the programs in your Office installation, click the Remove All button in the Microsoft Office 97 Setup dialog box. Be sure to keep your Office Setup disks handy—you'll need them if you decide to add new components in the future.

Using the Companion CD-ROM

Bound into the back of this book is a CD-ROM disc. The companion CD contains an online, HTML version of this book; Microsoft Internet Explorer; and the book's sample files.

Installing Microsoft Internet Explorer 3.0

While you can use most Web browsers to view the online version of this book, the text is best viewed in Microsoft Internet Explorer 3.0. For this reason, a copy of Internet Explorer 3.0 is included on the CD.

When you run the installation program, you will be able to add some extras to your browser, such as NetMeeting; Comic Chat; Microsoft Internet Mail & News; and ActiveMovie.

To install Internet Explorer from the CD, choose Run from the Start menu, and then type *d:\IE30\setup.exe* in the Run dialog box (where *d* is the drive letter of your CD-ROM drive). Then follow the instructions for installation as they appear.

When you run Internet Explorer after installing it, you will see the Internet Connection Wizard. This wizard helps you set up an account with an Internet service provider or establish a connection to your current service provider. (You do not have to be connected to a service provider to use the files on the CD.)

Viewing the Online Version of the Book

The online version of *Running Microsoft Office 97* provides easy access to every part of the book, and the powerful search feature will help you find the information you're looking for in record time.

You can use Internet Explorer (or another browser if you prefer) to view the book on line. Access the CD's home page by choosing Run from the Start menu and entering *d:\contents.htm* in the Run dialog box (where *d* is the drive letter of your CD-ROM drive). This will display the *Running Microsoft Office 97* home page in your default browser, from which you can choose to view the book on line.

Accessing the Book's Sample Files

You can use the book's sample files for hands-on exploration or as templates for your own work. You can either install the sample files on your hard disk or access them directly from the companion CD.

To install the sample files on your hard disk, be sure the companion CD is in your CD-ROM drive. Choose Run from the Start menu, and then type *d:\samples\setup.exe* (where *d* is the drive letter of your CD-ROM drive). Then follow the instructions for installation as they appear.

If you prefer, you can use the sample files directly from the CD without installing them on your hard disk. Note, however, that you cannot update any of the sample files directly on the CD. If you want to make changes to the data, use the Setup program to copy the samples onto your hard disk.

Note that you can also access the sample files from the CD's home page. (See the instructions on the previous page.)

Additional Information

In addition to providing access to the online version of this book and to the book's sample files, the CD's home page offers access to the Microsoft Knowledge Base, the Microsoft Press home page, and e-mail links to the authors.

If you have comments, questions, or ideas regarding this book or the companion CD, please write to Microsoft Press at the following address:

Microsoft Press
Attn: Running Series Editor
One Microsoft Way
Redmond, WA 98052-6399

You can also send feedback to Microsoft Press via electronic mail at mspinput@microsoft.com. Please note that product support is not offered through this e-mail address.

PART I

Getting Started with Microsoft Office

A Quick Tour of Microsoft Office

Microsoft Office 97, Professional Edition, is a state-of-the-art application suite containing five Windows 95 application programs and several powerful utilities that will make you more productive at home and in the office. In this chapter, you'll learn what you can do with the applications included in Microsoft Office and how to launch them with the Start button. You'll also learn how to switch between Office applications using the Windows taskbar and how to use the Office Help system when you have a question or need a little guidance. After you get the lay of the land, you'll be ready to explore a few essential skills that are useful in *all* Office applications.

Introducing Microsoft Office

Welcome to Microsoft Office 97 for Windows, Microsoft's best-selling application suite containing the latest versions of Microsoft's most popular business software products. If you're like most users, you've probably had some experience using one or more of the applications in Office. For this release, each program has been enhanced with new features and fine-tuned to access information on the Internet. If you have the Professional Edition of Office 97 (the software described in this book), you have the following application programs:

- Microsoft Word 97

- Microsoft Excel 97

- Microsoft PowerPoint 97

- Microsoft Access 97

- Microsoft Outlook 97

If you have the Standard Edition of Microsoft Office, your application suite doesn't include the database program Microsoft Access.

In a nutshell, you might ask, what are the benefits of Microsoft Office 97? By combining Microsoft's flagship programs into one unified application suite, Microsoft has created a general-purpose tool that can handle virtually all of the data processing, forecasting, and scheduling activities of a modern business or organization. Each Office application shares common commands, dialog boxes, and procedures, so that once you learn how to use one application, you'll have gone a long way to learning them all. In addition, the Office applications have been designed to work together, enabling you to combine text from Word, a chart from Excel, and database information from Access into one compelling presentation. Office applications also support a variety of file formats, present similar formatting tools and macro languages, and include full support for electronic mail and workgroup activities, so that you don't have to reinvent the wheel each time you start a new project. In short, Microsoft Office 97 is designed to adapt itself to the way *you* work.

What's New in the Software?

If you've used a previous version of the Office software, you'll notice that there are a number of new features and improvements in Office 97. New utilities, including shared drawing tools, the helpful Office Assistant, and a desktop information manager named Microsoft Outlook will make your workday more productive and enjoyable. Essential toolbars, menus, and workgroup tools have been standardized across applications, making Office programs even more accessible and easy to use. Finally, each application in the Office software suite has been redesigned to support the Internet and utilize advanced Internet technology. When you're ready to share your documents with a colleague down the hall or a friend on the other side of the world, Office 97 will make it as simple as clicking a button.

Here's a list of the new Office features:

Microsoft Office 97

Microsoft Outlook

A desktop information management application that helps you and your workgroup organize information and communicate with others. Outlook features electronic mail, contact management tools, scheduling software, a planning calendar, and "Explorer-like" document management.

Internet Support

You can now create hyperlinks between documents with the Insert Hyperlink command, including those on the World Wide Web. You can also use the new Web toolbar to navigate your way around new and familiar Internet sites.

Drawing Tools

A shared set of drawing tools will allow you to create professional, appealing graphics in all Microsoft Office applications. Compelling new graphical effects include multicolored gradient fills, textured fills, adjustable autoshapes, Bézier curves (for smooth, free-form curves), and impressive 3-D effects.

Office Assistant

A friendly, animated character that provides help, advice, and guidance in Office 97 applications. If you get stuck, you can ask Office Assistant for help, using your own words.

Improved IntelliSense Technology

A collection of technical improvements resulting from recent advances in natural-language processing. By using IntelliSense, the Office software can automate your routine tasks and simplify complex ones.

Microsoft Word

AutoText

A context-sensitive toolbar for adding content to documents and reusing text. By using AutoText, you can paste almost anything into documents—whether paragraphs, figures, directions, artwork, or other information you use often.

Letter Wizard

A single, easy-to-use interface for creating, changing, and removing the structural elements of a letter. Perfect for starting new letters or adding classy formatting touches.

Background AutoFormat

An IntelliSense feature that works in the background to apply appropriate formatting to the content of your document *after* you type it. Create numbered lists, bulleted lists, borders, tables, and headings without stopping to think about how you do it!

Long-Document Improvements

A series of improvements related to the creation and maintenance of book-length documents, including Table of Contents, Table of Authority, Cross-References, Footnotes, and Annotations.

Workgroup Enhancements

Enhancements designed for users who share documents on a network, including collaboration, online navigation, hypertext, and mail support.

Visual Basic for Applications

A new, industry-standard macro language that replaces WordBasic. Now all Office applications speak the same language.

Microsoft Excel

Page Break Preview

A new worksheet view that lets you examine and fine-tune your page breaks before printing.

Charting

Five new chart types and a streamlined charting wizard help you create worksheet charts more easily and more quickly.

Shared Workbooks

Enhancements for users who share their workbooks with others over the Internet or a network. A new Track Changes submenu makes it easier to resolve conflicts that result from multiuser editing sessions.

Multiple Levels of "Undo"

Like Microsoft Word, Excel now lets you reverse or "undo" many or all of the commands you issued in your editing session.

Conditional Formatting

You can now apply formatting to worksheet cells, depending on the value in those cells. For example, make a special cell blue if it falls below a certain value.

Input Validation

A new Validation command lets you control the type of data users enter into worksheet cells. Let users "discover" your requirements by leaving pop-up comments and custom error messages.

Rotate Text 360 Degrees

A new option in the Alignment tab allows users to rotate their text and borders anywhere along a 360-degree circle.

Microsoft PowerPoint

Redesigned Menus and Tools

Microsoft streamlined the PowerPoint menu structure in this release, making existing commands more consistent with Word and Excel, and adding a Slide Show menu with several new presentation tools.

Animation Options

An improved collection of animation options make slide transitions and special effects more exciting than ever.

More Multimedia

New Action Buttons let you create interactive buttons in your presentations, and your ability to add movies, sounds, and supporting artwork have been greatly improved.

Formatting Enhancements

Add comments, symbols, and enhanced Drawing objects to your slides. Crop pictures and expand one slide into several with a quick series of mouse clicks.

Web Home Page Tools

New templates help you quickly design the ultimate home page for work or home. Create Internet links between business presentations and jump quickly between Web sites with the new Web toolbar.

More Presentation Options

Special templates and formatting options make it easy to create kiosk shows, HTML documents, multimedia demonstrations, and remote conferences. Record voice narration to go with your slides and create a custom show from a standard set of presentation slides.

Microsoft Access

Make Hyperlinks of Fields

Assign a field the "hyperlink" data type, so that the field can be used to store the location of another database object, an Office document (such as a Word document or an Excel worksheet), or a page on the World Wide Web. You can then open the target object, document, or Web page simply by clicking the hyperlink in the field.

Make Hyperlinks of Database Objects

You can now make an Access database object the target of a hyperlink in another Office document, such as a Word document or an Excel worksheet. This enables you to quickly update information and verify the source of your data.

Convert Datasheets or Reports to HTML Files

You can convert an Access datasheet or report to a file created in the Hypertext Markup Language, enabling you to display it on the Web.

New Form Design Controls

Use new controls to design forms, such as a Tab Control for displaying separate tabs of information on a form (like the tabbed dialog boxes used in Office applications).

Choosing an Office Application

The following table shows you the purpose of each Office application and the program icons that appear next to Office applications in the Programs menu when you click the Start button. You'll want to remember the icons—you'll use them to start Office applications later in this chapter. The tasks performed by the Office applications fall into several general categories, such as word processing and database management, though in many cases you'll find that you can best solve a particular problem by using more than one program. To give you additional information about each application, this chapter contains five Application Spotlight sidebars to describe the documents you can create with the five Office applications. You'll learn considerably more about each of these programs as you work through the chapters in this book.

Program Icon	Office Application	Purpose
W	Microsoft Word	General-purpose word processor and desktop publishing tool
X	Microsoft Excel	Electronic spreadsheet with high-end data analysis, charting, and analytical functions
▣	Microsoft PowerPoint	Presentation graphics software for slide, overhead projector, and multimedia presentations
⚷	Microsoft Access	Relational database management system with query, reporting, and mailing list management features
▤	Microsoft Outlook	Information management software for electronic mail, document management, calendar scheduling, meeting planning, and resource management

Using the Office Shortcut Bar

The Office Shortcut Bar is your "remote control" for the Microsoft Office 97 application suite. You can use the Office Shortcut Bar to start Office applications, open predesigned Office templates, customize the Office software, or start other applications and utilities on your system (such as Windows Explorer). The Office Shortcut Bar is a set of toolbars with customizable buttons that appears along the top, bottom, or side edge of your screen. The Office Shortcut Bar can also appear as "floating" on the desktop. The Shortcut Bar works a lot like the toolbars do in each of the individual Office applications—you simply click the button on the Shortcut Bar for the program you want to run or the folder you want to open.

If you installed the Office Shortcut Bar when you ran Setup, it opens on your screen whenever you start your computer. (If the Office Shortcut Bar does not appear, run Setup again and choose the Microsoft Office Shortcut Bar option under Office Tools.) The appearance of the Shortcut Bar depends on how it has been configured. It might appear docked on the right side of your screen, as shown in Figure 1-1, or

FIGURE 1-1.
The Office Shortcut
Bar appears on your
screen when you start
your computer.

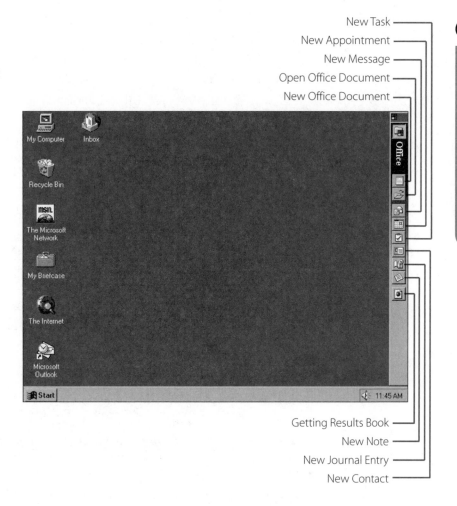

New Task
New Appointment
New Message
Open Office Document
New Office Document

Getting Results Book
New Note
New Journal Entry
New Contact

it may appear along one of the other three sides of the screen, as a
floating toolbar in the middle of the screen, or as a smaller toolbar at
the top of the screen. If you don't see the Office Shortcut Bar, you can
start it by clicking the Start button, pointing to the Programs folder,
selecting StartUp, and then clicking the Microsoft Office Shortcut Bar.
To run a command or application listed on the bar, simply click the
button representing the tool you want to use. If you're unsure what
a particular button does, hold the mouse pointer over it and you'll
see a ScreenTip describing the feature. The list of buttons is fully customizable, so that you can add, delete, or rearrange the applications

represented by buttons on the Shortcut Bar as you see fit. To customize the settings in the Shortcut Bar or to add other toolbars, double-click the background of the toolbar (not a button) and use the four tabs in the Customize dialog box to create your favorite configuration.

Moving the Shortcut Bar

Once the Microsoft Office Shortcut Bar starts, it remains on the screen at all times—even when you're working in an application. Microsoft designed the Office Shortcut Bar this way so that you could easily jump

Application Spotlight: Microsoft Word

Microsoft Word handles complex reports, multicolumn newsletters, and desktop publishing as easily as it does simple memos, letters, and party invitations. Word lets you mix words, charts, pictures, and tables on the page with a few straightforward mouse clicks and commands, and includes useful spelling, thesaurus, and grammar tools to help you improve your writing. Word also includes support for many popular word processor file formats, so if you have documents created in another word processor, such as WordPerfect, you can continue working with them in Word. Many people also use Word to create and maintain mailing lists and to compose electronic mail messages. The figure below shows a multi-column newsletter created with the Newsletter Wizard in Word.

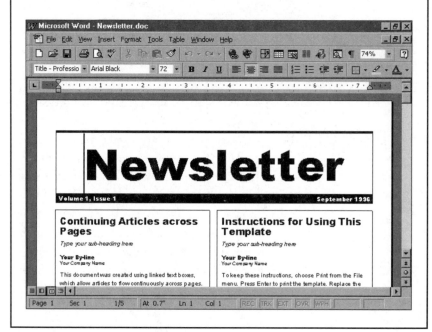

 SEE ALSO
To learn how to use Microsoft Word, read the chapters in Part II, "Microsoft Word."

from one task to another and create documents using several Office applications. The Office Shortcut Bar even contains a few special buttons that place you exactly where you want to be in an application. For example, the New Appointment button (the button with the picture of a calendar on it) starts Microsoft Outlook when you click it, and then opens an Appointment window set to the current date. Using this shortcut button, you could update your schedule while working in another application, and then return immediately to what you were doing.

To move the Office Shortcut Bar to another place on the screen, you simply drag it to a new location with the mouse. The Office Shortcut Bar can attach itself to the top, bottom, right, or left edge of the screen, or it can float on the desktop. By default, the Office Shortcut Bar always appears on top of everything in the Windows desktop, giving you access to it at all times.

> By *drag*, we mean positioning the mouse pointer over an object in the Windows environment (such as the Office Shortcut Bar), holding down the left mouse button, moving the object to a new location, and releasing the mouse button. This procedure is also known as *drag and drop*.

To move the Office Shortcut Bar, follow these steps:

1 Position the mouse over an empty spot on the Office Shortcut Bar (not over a button).

2 Drag the bar to a new location. (You can select one of the four edges of the screen, or a place in the middle, for your new location.) As you drag the Office Shortcut Bar, an outline of the bar appears, to help you place the bar.

3 Release the mouse button to place the Shortcut Bar. If you get tired of the Shortcut Bar's being where it is, just drag it to another location!

Customizing the Shortcut Bar

If you use several Windows-based applications each day, you might find it easiest to add them to your Microsoft Office Shortcut Bar and start them from there. The Office Shortcut Bar makes launching

Application Spotlight: Microsoft Excel

Microsoft Excel is a multipurpose electronic spreadsheet designed for record keeping, tax planning, general accounting, charting, and financial analysis. If you need to keep track of facts and figures in your business, Excel is the application for you. Excel documents, called worksheets, consist of cells organized in rows and columns containing values that can be added, formatted, or sorted with the click of a mouse. Typical worksheets created in Excel include general ledgers, expense reports, sales summaries, data consolidation, and "what-if" scenarios. As a bonus, Excel lets you create charts from the data in worksheets in a variety of shapes and sizes. The figure below shows a worksheet created by the Excel Invoice template.

 SEE ALSO

To learn how to use Microsoft Excel, read the chapters in Part III, "Microsoft Excel."

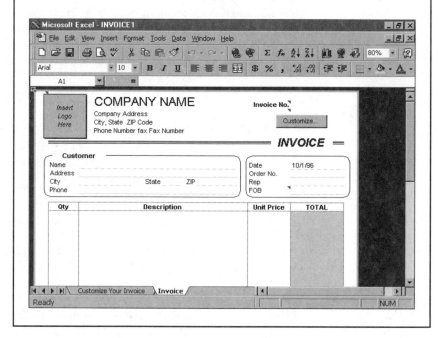

programs *fast*, because the bar is conveniently placed on the screen and you can start any application on it with a mouse click. Before you can start an application from the Office Shortcut Bar, however, you must add a button for the program. For example, to add Windows Explorer to the Office Shortcut Bar, double-click the Shortcut Bar in one of the background areas between the buttons. The Customize dialog box appears, as shown here:

1 Click the Buttons tab.

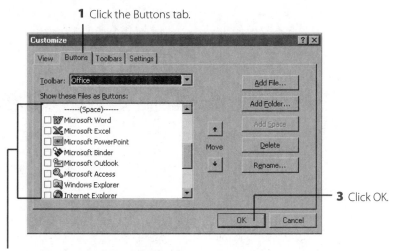

3 Click OK.

2 Locate the Windows Explorer application and then click on the check box next to the Explorer program name.

Optimize Your Workspace

To display more vertical lines in your Office application, place the Shortcut Bar on the right or left edge of the screen. To display more horizontal columns, place the bar on the top or bottom edge of the screen. If you need to maximize the length and width of the screen, but have room in the middle of your document, place the bar inside your document. The AutoFit Into Title Bar Area option on the View tab of the Customize dialog box saves space by allowing the Shortcut Bar to appear at the right side of your application's title bar. You can choose to turn off the Always On Top option, allowing your application to cover the Shortcut bar, or you can turn on the Auto Hide Between Uses option so that the Shortcut Bar isn't visible until you move the mouse pointer over the edge of the screen where it's docked, making it reappear.

After adding the Windows Explorer button, your Office Shortcut Bar should look similar to the following:

The Windows Explorer button

To remove an application's button from the Shortcut Bar, open the Buttons tab of the Customize dialog box and turn off the check box next to the name of the application.

Application Spotlight: Microsoft PowerPoint

Microsoft PowerPoint is a presentation graphics program designed to create slides, transparencies, handouts, and speaker notes for business presentations. The program lets you build your presentation from a collection of predefined formats, or lets you create your own content with the PowerPoint presentation tools and data from Word, Excel, or Access. Typical uses for PowerPoint include sales presentations, company-meeting slides, technical overviews, keynote addresses, and multimedia demos. In addition, a number of third-party vendors will convert your PowerPoint files into slides or color transparencies, letting you hit the road with a minimum of effort and a maximum of pizzazz. The figure below shows a strategy recommendation template in PowerPoint.

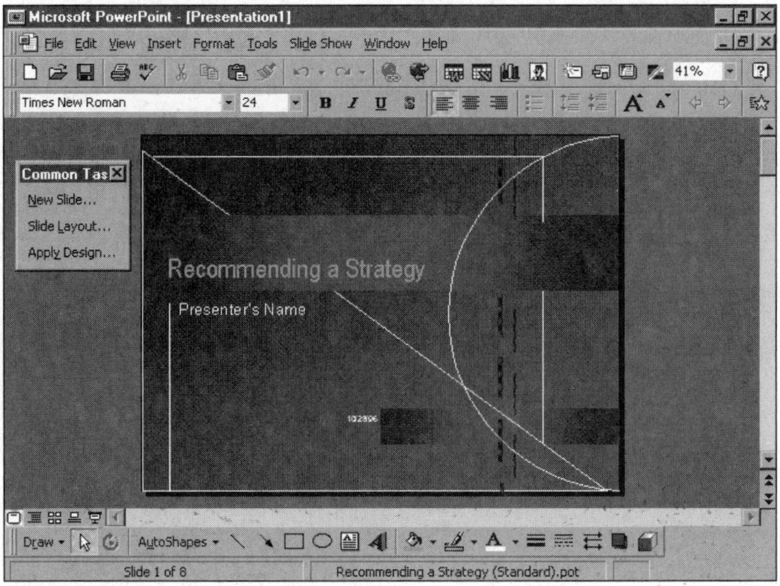

? SEE ALSO

To learn how to use Microsoft PowerPoint, read the chapters in Part IV, "Microsoft PowerPoint."

Getting Started

Add Your Favorite Toolbars

You can also use the Customize dialog box to add and customize additional toolbars. Open the Customize dialog box by double-clicking on the background of the Office Shortcut Bar, click the Toolbars tab, and then select a toolbar from the list or click the Add Toolbar button to create a new, blank toolbar or to make a toolbar for an existing folder. You can use the other tabs of the Customize dialog box to add or remove buttons or customize other settings for the new toolbar. You can have several toolbars open, though only one will be visible at a time. Each open toolbar will have a corresponding button visible at one end of the Office Shortcut Bar. To switch to another open toolbar, click its button.

Disabling the Shortcut Bar

By default, Microsoft Office installs the Office Shortcut Bar in your system's StartUp folder, so that the bar appears automatically each time you start Windows. If you don't want the Office Shortcut Bar started each time, you can remove it from the StartUp folder by following these steps:

1 Click the Start button and then point to the Settings folder.

2 Click Taskbar and then click the Start Menu Programs tab.

3 Click Remove and then click on the plus sign (+) to the left of the StartUp folder. (If the StartUp folder already lists its contents, you don't need to click on the symbol to the left of its name.)

4 Click the Microsoft Office Shortcut Bar program and then click Remove.

5 Click Close and then OK to close the Taskbar Properties dialog box. The next time you start your computer, the Office Shortcut Bar won't appear.

Bring Back the Shortcut Bar at Startup

To add the Office Shortcut Bar to the StartUp folder at a later time, follow steps 1 and 2 on the preceding page, but then click the Add button. In the first dialog box, locate and select the Microsoft Office Shortcut Bar program (in your Microsoft Office folder under Program Files) and click Next. In the second dialog box, locate and select the StartUp folder and then click Next. To finish adding the Office Shortcut Bar to your StartUp folder, click Finish and then click OK.

Application Spotlight: Microsoft Access

Microsoft Access is a relational database management system designed to store and manipulate large amounts of business information. An Access database can contain information of any kind, from inventory and tax records for your business and lists of customers and contacts, to the compact discs in your music collection. Access includes special tools that enable you to enter data, search for database records, create consolidated reports, build charts, and print mailing labels. Access is also compatible with most popular database formats, such as Paradox, dBASE, Oracle, and SQL Server. The figure below shows a typical database in Access created using the Address Book Wizard.

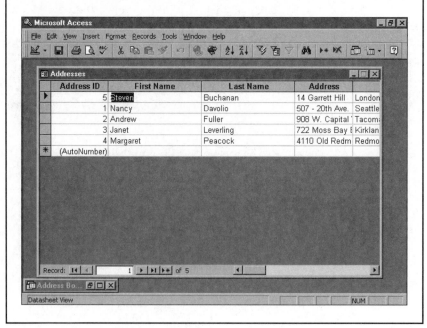

SEE ALSO

To learn how to use Microsoft Access, read the chapters in Part V, "Microsoft Access."

Closing the Shortcut Bar

It isn't necessary for you to close the Office Shortcut Bar before you shut down Windows, because the program doesn't make use of temporary files or other active utilities. However, if you want to close the Shortcut Bar to free up memory or make room on your desktop, double-click the tiny Office icon in the upper left corner of the Shortcut Bar, as shown below. The shortcut menu that pops up when you click this icon (rather than double-clicking) includes commands that configure the Shortcut Bar and provide documentation for the Office Shortcut Bar.

Double-click this icon to
close the Shortcut Bar.

Running Office Applications

You can *launch* (start) Microsoft Office applications with a new document in any of four ways:

- By clicking the Start button and then clicking the program's name in the Programs shortcut menu

- By clicking the program's icon on the Office Shortcut Bar

- By opening a document template

- By double-clicking a document's filename in Microsoft Outlook or Windows Explorer

We'll discuss each technique in this section.

Clicking the Start Button

The most straightforward way to start an Office application is to click the Windows Start button, point to the Programs folder containing the Office 97 programs, and then click the Office application you want to start. (If you're humming "Start Me Up" by the Rolling Stones now, you've got the right idea—Microsoft spent a considerable sum to link this popular song to the Windows Start button in its Windows 95 marketing campaign.) The Start button appears at the bottom of the screen on the taskbar, and is the recommended method for starting all programs in the Windows 95 operating system. (You can also place shortcut icons on the Windows desktop to launch your programs.)

For example, to start Microsoft Word with the Start button, follow these steps:

1   Click the Start button on the taskbar. (The Start button is in the lower left corner of the screen.)

Application Spotlight: Microsoft Outlook

Microsoft Outlook is a new information management system provided with Office 97. Outlook combines several important productivity tools into one application, allowing you to complete most of your work—including running Office documents—right from the Outlook environment. Outlook includes an electronic mail system; daily, weekly, and monthly schedule planners; a contact database you can use to track lists of names, addresses, and phone numbers; a "Tasks" list tool for prioritizing tasks and managing your time; and a document management system. Outlook even allows networked users to share their schedules, plan meetings, and book conference rooms—all with a few simple mouse clicks. The figure below shows a typical electronic mail Inbox in Outlook.

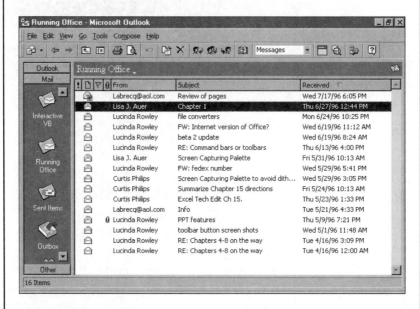

 SEE ALSO
To learn how to use Microsoft Outlook, read Chapter 41, "Managing Information with Microsoft Outlook."

2 Point to the Programs folder, and then locate the Microsoft Word program. The programs appear in alphabetical order.

3 Click the Microsoft Word program. The Microsoft Word application starts in a window, as shown in Figure 1-2.

FIGURE 1-2.
Microsoft Word launched with the Start button.

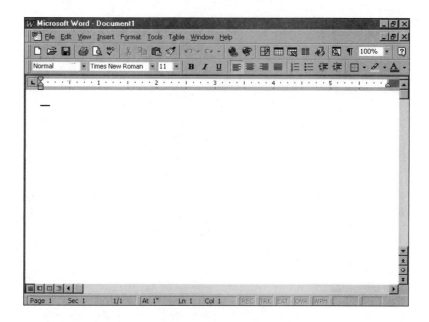

Clicking a Program Icon on the Office Shortcut Bar

? SEE ALSO

For more information about operating and customizing the Office Shortcut Bar, see "Using the Office Shortcut Bar," page 10.

Alternatively, you can start applications by clicking a program icon in the Office Shortcut Bar. (We covered this technique in the last section.) If the program you want to start isn't on the Office Shortcut Bar, add it with the Buttons tab or add a new Programs toolbar with the Toolbars tab.

Creating Files with a Document Template

If you need to create a specific business document, but you're not sure what Office application to use, you can click the New Office Document command on the Start menu or the New Office Document button on the Office Shortcut Bar to browse through a variety of predesigned document types, or *templates,* and open exactly the document you need. Templates let you focus on the information you want to present in your document, eliminating time-consuming design and formatting. Each

Office application includes a number of useful document templates, and you can open all of them directly with the New dialog box.

Start an Office application using a document template this way:

? SEE ALSO
You'll learn essential skills for working with Office applications in Chapter 2, "Learning the Basics: Windows, Toolbars, and Printing," and Chapter 3, "Managing Documents: From Your Hard Disk to the Internet."

1 Click the Start button and then click on New Office Document (or click the New Office Document button on the Office Shortcut Bar). The New Office Document dialog box appears with several tabs, each corresponding to a different type of document template. The dialog box also contains a preview window, which displays a small picture of the template currently highlighted in that dialog box, if one is available.

2 Click the tab corresponding to the type of document you want to create. For example, to see a list of the fax templates available, click the Letters & Faxes tab. Figure 1-3 shows a typical list of templates. You can see the template file size, type of file (including the associated application), and date the file was last modified if you click the Details button in the dialog box.

3 Double-click the template you want to open, and Windows 95 will start the application associated with it and load the template so that you can use it. For example, to create a fax based on the Professional Fax template, double-click the Professional Fax icon on the Letters & Faxes tab of the New Office Document dialog box. When the template you specify opens as a new untitled document, add your information to the document and save the information under a new filename to protect the original template (you'll want to use it again later). Most templates include basic instructions that tell you how to create the document, as shown in Figure 1-4.

Using a Wizard: A Special Type of Template

Did you notice the icon named Fax Wizard in Figure 1-3? A *wizard* is a special, automated document with features that guide you through the process of creating a business document, one step at a time. Wizards provide a handy alternative to templates because they let you change the style or format of a document as you create it. (Templates, by definition, always contain the same format.) For example, the Fax Wizard

FIGURE 1-3.

The New Office Document button lets you start Office applications with document templates. Each tab contains a different group of templates. (You might not see the filename extensions, depending on how your Windows options have been set up.)

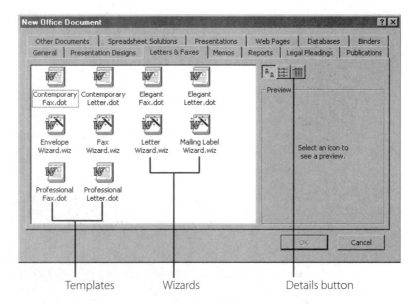

Templates   Wizards   Details button

FIGURE 1-4.

Templates are predesigned business forms with instructions. Simply enter your information and print.

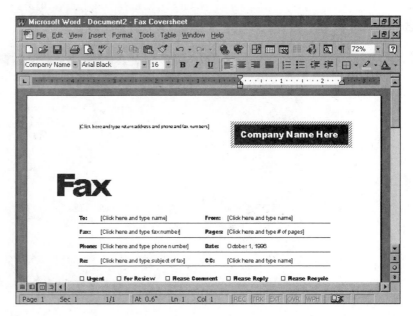

lets you create customized name, address, and phone number fields (locations) in your fax and add several types of artwork to your document. You'll find useful wizards on many of the tabs in the New Office Document dialog box.

To use a wizard to create a customized Office document, follow these steps:

1 Click the Start button and then click on New Office Document (or click the New Office Document button on the Office Shortcut Bar). A dialog box with document template tabs appears.

2 Click the tab corresponding to the type of document you want to create. For example, to use a wizard to create a fax, click the Letters & Faxes tab.

3 Double-click the wizard you want to use. For example, to create a fax using a wizard, double-click the Fax Wizard icon in the Letters & Faxes tab of the dialog box. Windows 95 opens the wizard you select and runs it in the associated Office application. Figure 1-5 shows the opening screen of the Fax Wizard. To complete a wizard procedure, simply answer the questions the wizard asks by choosing option buttons, entering information, or clicking the wizard control buttons.

FIGURE 1-5.
Wizards are special documents that automatically create a new document based on your preferences.

Opening Documents with Microsoft Outlook

In Office 97, you can also open documents with a new information management program named Microsoft Outlook. Outlook was designed for those people who are constantly dealing with information that originates from a variety of sources. Accordingly, Outlook lets you manage your electronic mail, appointment calendar, project "To-Do" list, business contacts, and important documents—all from one application! In Chapter 41, "Managing Information with Microsoft Outlook," we'll show you how to get the most out of Outlook in your daily activities. (You can turn to this chapter at any time—there are no learning prerequisites.) In this section, however, we describe an essential technique you can use to open existing Office documents from project folders in the Outlook application. (Before you follow these steps, start Microsoft Outlook with the Start button.)

To open your Office documents in Microsoft Outlook, follow the steps shown in Figure 1-6.

FIGURE 1-6.
Microsoft Outlook lists documents by name so that you can open them while working on electronic mail or other tasks. Unlike Windows Explorer, Outlook lists files with useful document properties such as comments and keywords, helping you learn more about the files you're examining.

1 Click the Other button. A collection of icons and folders appears in the folder pane, including My Computer, My Documents, and Favorites.

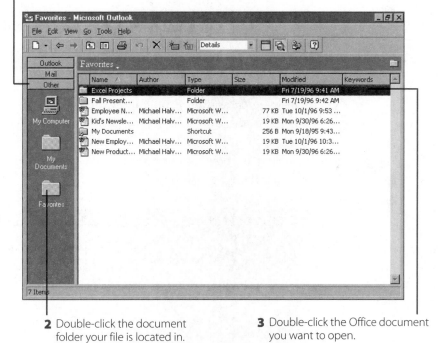

2 Double-click the document folder your file is located in.

3 Double-click the Office document you want to open.

Switching Between Office Applications

Microsoft designed Windows 95 specifically to be a multitasking operating system, capable of running several large applications at once. In plain English, this means that you can run two or more Office applications at the same time and quickly switch between them as your work requires. For example, you can run Microsoft Outlook, Microsoft Excel, and Microsoft Word all at the same time, using the programs jointly to build a report, or individually to create stand-alone documents. As you learned earlier, you start Office applications by using the Start button. To switch between open applications, you use the taskbar, located at the bottom of the screen.

Figure 1-7 shows a typical taskbar, with a button identifying each application that is running (currently three applications—Outlook, Excel, and Word). The current, or *active,* application (Microsoft Outlook) is highlighted on the taskbar, and, if you look, you'll see that the active application's title bar is also highlighted on the screen. (Often the title bar appears in a different color and contains a document name.) While all the programs running under Windows can perform useful work, the active, or *foreground,* application is the program that is currently ready to receive your input. If this application contains a cursor, it will probably be blinking now—a sign that the program is ready for work. In a multitasking environment, it's important to know the difference between a foreground application (the highlighted application) and the remaining *background* applications (the programs running behind the scenes) so that you can keep track of your programs and know which one's receiving input. The visual clues provided on the taskbar make this easy. To move from one task to the next, simply click the appropriate button on the taskbar.

FIGURE 1-7.
This taskbar shows three programs at work. The active application appears "pressed in."

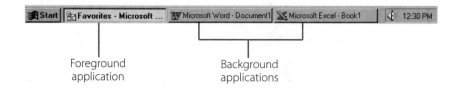

Foreground application

Background applications

Using the Taskbar

To switch from the active Windows application to a program that's running in the background, simply click the button on the taskbar associated with the program you want to use. For example, to switch from Microsoft Outlook to Microsoft Excel, click the Microsoft Excel button on the taskbar. This will move the selected application in front of any others, and (typically) will hide the other applications from view. The selected application becomes the new foreground application, standing ready to receive your input.

Increase the Taskbar's Size

If you have more than three or four programs running under Windows, you can make more room for taskbar buttons by increasing the height of the taskbar. To do this, move the mouse pointer toward the top edge of the taskbar until it changes into the sizing pointer (a double-headed arrow), and then drag the top edge up until the taskbar doubles in height. The number of programs you can run under Windows is limited by the amount of random access memory (RAM) and hard disk space you have, so use some discretion when loading full-size applications into memory. (The specific limit depends on both the hardware you have and the size of your programs.) If you get a warning message from Windows about low memory or resources, you'll know it's time to close a few programs.

Using the Help System

If you've used computer software for any length of time, you've probably had plenty of experience using an online (actually, on-screen) Help system. Office 97 takes online Help to new heights in this release, adding the personable Office Assistant help program to its already impressive collection of Help utilities. You'll find the following tools in each Office application:

- *Contents tab*—A handy "tree" of Help topics, featuring text-based articles, graphic learn-by-example documents, and computer-based training (CBT) tutorial programs.

- *Find and Index tabs*—Two search dialog boxes you can use to find specific information about a topic of interest.

- *Context-sensitive Help pointer*—A question-mark icon you can drop on an application feature to learn more about it.

- *Office Assistant*—A friendly and animated guide to each application in Office. Behind Office Assistant's kindly exterior is a powerful, natural-language search database containing answers to thousands of the most vexing Office application questions.

Microsoft Word and Microsoft Excel contain useful online information for users familiar with WordPerfect and Lotus 1-2-3, respectively. Check the Word and Excel online Help menus for information if you're making the transition from one of these products.

The Help Menu

Each Office application contains a Help menu with a standard list of commands that access the application's Help system. To get a general listing of Help topics for an application, click the Help menu, and then click the Contents And Index command on the Help menu. (This is usually the second command on the menu.) After a moment, you'll see a dialog box with tabs resembling those of labeled file folders. This dialog box gives you access to the different parts of the Help system. (Typical Windows 95 Help tabs include Contents, Find, and Index.) To access a Help topic, simply click the tab you want and fill out the dialog box. The following sections describe the most important Office Help features.

The final command on the Help menu (About) contains copyright and version information for the program you're using. The About dialog box also includes a System Info button, which you can click to display information about your computer's hardware and software configuration, plus a Tech Support button, which you can use to contact Microsoft Product Support. Office applications also have a Help-menu command called Microsoft On The Web, which you can use to exchange information with Product Support personnel and communicate with other owners of the product.

Using the Contents Tab

To get an overview of the Help topics available in the application you're using, click the Contents tab in the Help Topics dialog box. Each Office application has a different Contents tab, and the Help topics cover the entire feature set of the product, from basic skills to Visual Basic programming. Figure 1-8 shows the list of topics that

FIGURE 1-8.
Help topics appear in a tree structure on the Contents tab. To open a Help article, double-click one of the question marks.

Double-click on a closed book icon to see the list of subtopics.

An open book icon indicates that all of the subtopics are displayed.

The question mark icon indicates Help articles. Double-click to display the text.

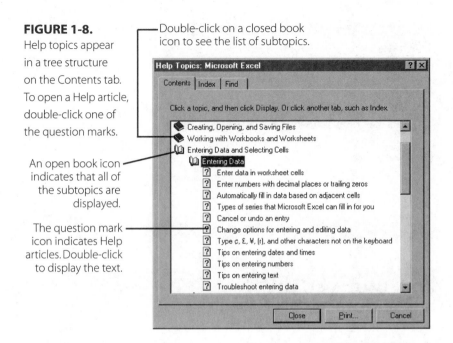

appears when you click the Contents And Index command on the Excel Help menu and then click the Contents tab. Notice that each main topic (marked with a book icon) contains a list of related topics beneath it, while the actual Help articles appear in the list marked with question marks. (Help topics are organized in a "tree" structure, similar to the way Windows Explorer displays folders and files.)

Help articles appear in several different formats—some in text-based dialog boxes, others in point-and-click windows with graphics and artwork. To close a Help article, click the Close button (the X) in the upper right corner of the Help window.

Using the Index Tab

To search for a specific keyword in the Help system, click the Index tab in the Help Topics dialog box, and then type the name of the word you want to find in the first text box. Figure 1-9 on the following page shows how you can search for the keyword *footnotes* in Microsoft Word. (To try this example, you have to start Word first and open its Help file.) As you enter a Search keyword in the first text box, watch the list of Help topics change as you type each character. The Index lists all its Help topics alphabetically, so that you can narrow your search significantly by typing

FIGURE 1-9.
The Index tab lets you search for a particular keyword in the Help system.

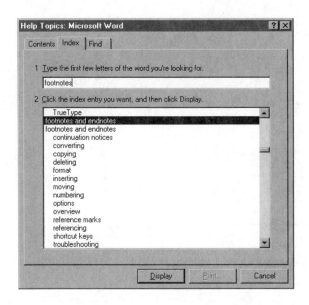

several characters. When you see the article you want to read in the second list box, simply double-click the topic to open it.

Most Help articles listed on the Index tab are text based and appear in a simple window with scroll bars and a few navigation buttons. Words underlined with a dotted line are Glossary topics, and when you click these terms, a short definition appears in a text box. To close the definition when you've finished reading it, click the text box. Some text boxes have a list of additional topics under a What Do You Want To Do heading at the bottom of the box. If you click one of these items, you'll move immediately to a related article in the Help system. Figure 1-10 shows the Help article for creating footnotes in Word. To move to an article you looked at previously in the Help system, click the Back button. To display the Index tab again, click the Help Topics button. To close the Help window, click the Close button on the window's title bar.

Using the Find Tab

The Find tab is a special Windows 95 feature. As with the Index tab, when you click it, it opens a Search dialog box that displays Help articles after you enter a Search keyword. Unlike the Index, however, the Find tab lists *every* Help article in your application that contains the keyword you're looking for, not just a predefined list of Help topics.

FIGURE 1-10.

A typical text-based Help article selected from the Index tab.

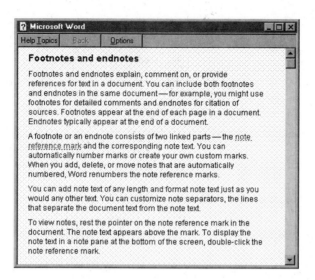

For example, if the Find Setup Wizard were in your office right now, searching through your bookcase to find an article about Leonardo da Vinci, it would search through every sentence on every page of every book to find the artist's name—*not* just through the book titles. This awesome process obviously takes some time, so the Find Setup Wizard does something clever the first time you select the Find tab—it builds a database of words that it can later search through very quickly.

To use the Find tab to search for a Help article, follow these steps:

1 Start the Office application you want to use. From the Help menu, choose Contents And Index.

2 Click the Find tab in the Help Topics dialog box. If this is the first time you're using Find in this application, you'll be prompted to build a database for the Find tab, using the Find Setup Wizard. We recommend that you choose the Customize Search Capabilities option if you're interested in how the Search database is created—it's quite fascinating.

3 When the word list is complete, type a search phrase in the first text box. For example, to find information about using toolbars in your application, type *toolbar*. Find displays the Help topics that match your phrase, including any special spellings.

4 To refine the search, click the word closest to the topic you want to look at in the second text box. Words in all capital letters usually identify a programming term, so avoid these topics unless you want to learn more about Visual Basic programming.

5 Finally, double-click the article you want to read in the third text box. Help articles appear in a text window equipped with standard scroll bars and navigation controls. When you're finished with the article, click the Close button on the window's title bar.

Using the What's This? Feature

Another useful Help feature in Office applications is an object called the *Help pointer*. The Help pointer appears when you choose What's This? from the Help menu or when you click the Help button that appears in the upper right corner of dialog boxes next to the Close button, which changes the mouse pointer to a question mark. After the transformation, your mouse works just like an alchemist's magic wand—when you move the Help pointer and click a menu item, toolbar button, or window element, the Help pointer displays a Help window showing you exactly what the object does. It's a Help feature designed for tactile people who want to poke and prod while they learn.

Figure 1-11 shows the Help button on a dialog box title bar. The figure also shows what the mouse pointer looks like after the button is clicked. There's no time limit with the Help pointer, but you only get one mouse click before you need to click the Help button again. This feature stops you from getting "stuck" in Help pointer mode.

 TIP

Call for Keyboard Help

You can also use the Help pointer to get help with keyboard combinations. To try this useful feature, choose What's This? on the Help menu, and then press the key or keys you want to learn about. For example, click the Help pointer and press Ctrl+B, the keyboard shortcut for bold formatting in Microsoft Word. The Help system will display a Help article related to the keys you press.

FIGURE 1-11.
The Help pointer lets
you click on elements
in the user interface
and read related Help
documents.

Help button

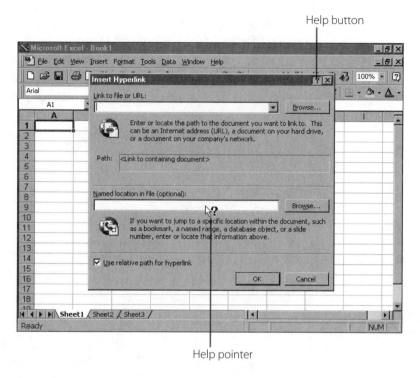

Help pointer

Office Assistant

A new player in Office 97 is Office Assistant, a friendly Help tool that
uses animation, humor, and a database containing thousands of tips,
techniques, and solutions to help you learn how the Office software
works. Office Assistant is not a simple dialog box, but rather an on-
demand "genie" that pops up when you need it to solve your problem
or give some advice. If you don't want the Office Assistant, fine—send
her (or him? or it?) away until you need her again (she won't bug you
or get in your way). Best of all, you can customize the Office Assistant
to appear just as you like, particularly if you don't care for the default
character (a snappy paper clip named Clippit).

Office
Assistant

You start Office Assistant by choosing the first command on the Help
menu, or by clicking the Office Assistant button on your application's
toolbar. As with the other Help features, the information provided by

Getting Started

Office Assistant is specific to the active application. For example, if you open Office Assistant in Microsoft Outlook, all the solutions provided will be related to Outlook. On the other hand, if you are in Word, the same question results in solutions specific to Word. A few of the animation antics created by the default Office Assistant look like this:

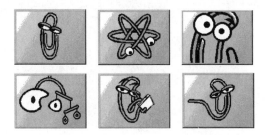

Clippit, the default Office Assistant, is a lively helper. To view some of its animation routines, right-click Office Assistant and choose the Animate! command.

As you work in your application, Office Assistant will periodically offer tips to streamline the commands you are using. Office Assistant doesn't just blurt out its advice (how rude!), but instead advertises its services by discreetly displaying a light bulb in its window pane, as shown here:

If you click this light bulb, you get to see the tip. For example, if you use the AutoSum button in Excel to create a subtotal, Office Assistant might recommend the following shortcut:

Office Assistant also provides detailed information about running certain commands and wizards in Office applications, such the Function Wizard in Excel. If Office Assistant appears in a situation like this, you'll have the opportunity to get more information by clicking labeled buttons, or by typing questions into a search or other dialog box. Since Office Assistant is fully integrated into the Office help system, you'll have access to the same information provided by Office's more traditional help tools. When you're finished using Office Assistant, simply click the Close button in the upper right corner of the Office Assistant window, and it'll disappear. You can also click Office Assistant with the right mouse button and choose the Hide Assistant command to give Office Assistant the afternoon off.

Customizing Office Assistant

If you get bored with Clippit, you can choose another electronic helper by clicking on Office Assistant with the right mouse button, and then selecting the Choose Assistant command on the shortcut menu that pops up. When you make this selection, the Office Assistant dialog box appears with the Gallery tab open, as shown in the following illustration:

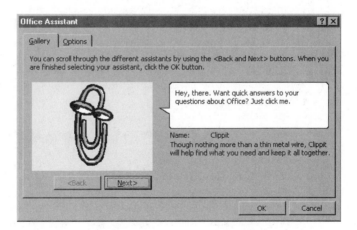

Each time you click the Next button in this dialog box, a new Office Assistant appears, ready to do your bidding. If you prefer a chatty human companion, you might like William Shakespeare, shown in the illustration on the following page.

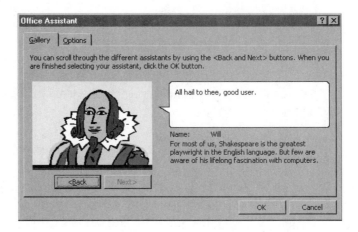

Drama lovers may enjoy receiving their advice from the Bard.

Finally, you can customize the capabilities of Office Assistant by clicking the Options tab in the Office Assistant dialog box. The Options tab contains a collection of check boxes that enable and disable features in Office Assistant. Simply adjust the settings and, presto, Office Assistant has a new personality! (Wouldn't it be great to be able to do this with people at work?) A few of the options we like are Only Show High Priority Tips, which stops Office Assistant from recommending nonessential shortcuts, and Move When In The Way, which forces Office Assistant to relocate on the screen if it's blocking a dialog box or important data. When you're done customizing Office Assistant, click OK to close the Office Assistant dialog box.

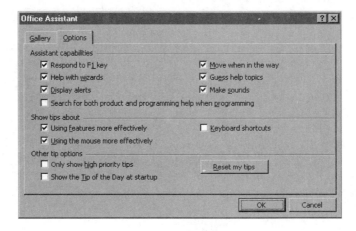

Quitting Office Applications

Whenever you're finished working with an Office application, you should close your documents or spreadsheets and exit the program before you shut down Windows and turn off your computer. If you don't exit applications properly, rest assured that you *won't* damage your system, though you *might* leave a few temporary files on your hard disk that will waste disk space. You could also lose the edits you made in your document since you last used the Save command. Fortunately, however, all Office applications ask you to save your changes whenever you try to exit a program with an unsaved file. (You'll learn more about saving documents in the next chapter.)

To quit an Office application, do *one* of the following:

- From the application File menu, choose the Exit command.

- Click the Close button on the application title bar. (The Close button is the X in the upper right corner.)

- Press Alt+F4.

- Click the application name on the taskbar with the right mouse button, and then click the Close command in the shortcut menu.

If you have any unsaved changes in your document, you'll be prompted to save them. (If Office Assistant is running, you'll see a dialog box similar to the one shown in Figure 1-12.) If you click Yes when prompted to save, your changes will be stored under the current filename. (If you haven't established a filename, you'll be given a chance to enter one.) If you click No, all the changes you made since your last save will be discarded. If you click Cancel, the dialog box will close without any changes being made, and you'll return to your application.

FIGURE 1-12.
A Save dialog box appears if you try to exit an application with unsaved changes.

CHAPTER 2

Learning the Basics: Windows, Toolbars, and Printing

When you work with the screens, dialog boxes, menus, and commands in a Windows application, you're using the program's user *interface*. In the Microsoft Office application suite, all five programs share the same basic user interface. The information displayed by each application appears in one or more standard windows that can be scrolled, resized, or in some cases split into two views. Programs present commands in standard menu bars, dialog boxes, and toolbars that share many common features. In addition, each Office application contains uniform printing commands that you can use to configure your printer, preview a document, and create a printout. In this chapter, you'll learn how to use each of these common application features. As you work with Office programs in the future, you'll find that you make use of these basic skills every time you create, modify, or print a document.

Working with Application Windows

When you start an Office application, the program appears in one of three states—minimized (as a button on the taskbar), maximized (to fill the entire screen), or in a Normal window (which appears to float on your screen). Maximizing your application provides the most workspace. Minimizing your application moves it out of the way while leaving it instantly available. Working with your application in a Normal window gives you the ability to change the window size so that you can work with more than one application on the screen at a time (as shown in Figure 2-1).

When working with a Normal window, you can change the size and shape of the window or move it to another location on your desktop. To change the size of a Normal window, position the mouse pointer over the window edge you want to stretch or shrink, and drag the edge to the new location with the sizing pointer. To move a window, drag the title bar from one location to another. Note that you can't change the size or the position of a window that has been minimized to a button on the taskbar nor one that is maximized to fill the entire screen.

When an application has been minimized to a button on the taskbar, you can either click it to restore it to a window or right-click it to display a shortcut menu with choices for restoring it to a window or maximizing it to fill the entire screen. When an application is within a Normal window or appears maximized, you can use the control buttons on the right side of the application's title bar to minimize the window to a button on the taskbar, maximize the window to fill the entire screen, restore the application to a Normal window, or close the window.

 TIP

Shortcuts Are a Mouse Click Away

Many times the next action you want to perform can be found on the special shortcut menu that appears when you press the right (or secondary) mouse button. The menu changes with the context of your actions, so check it often for possible shortcuts to accomplish your tasks more quickly.

FIGURE 2-1.

By sizing and moving application windows, you can position more than one Office application on the screen.

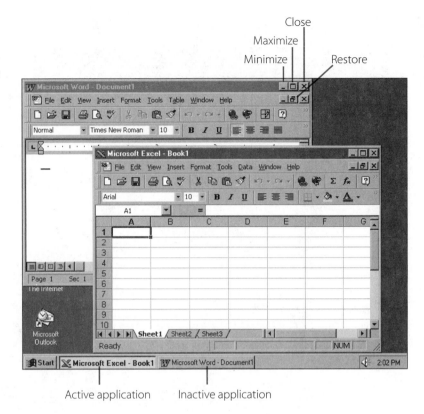

Close
Maximize
Minimize
Restore

Active application   Inactive application

Understanding the Workplace

The user interface elements you see when you run an Office application—the menu bars, toolbars, status bars, and windows—are known as the *workplace* of the program. Each Office application uses a different metaphor for its workplace; Word documents resemble typewritten pages, Excel documents resemble accounting spreadsheets, PowerPoint documents resemble slide presentations, Access documents resemble data entry forms, and Outlook documents resemble calendars and "To-Do" lists. The trick to learning how to use each Office application is understanding how to create documents that are in sync with the metaphor being used.

Figure 2-2 on the following page shows the workplace of Excel, a typical Office application. Along the top of the application window is the *title bar*, a rectangle containing the program name, and the *control buttons* used to size and close the window. If the document window is maximized, the title bar also includes the document name. Below the

FIGURE 2-2.

The user interface features shared by all Microsoft Office applications.

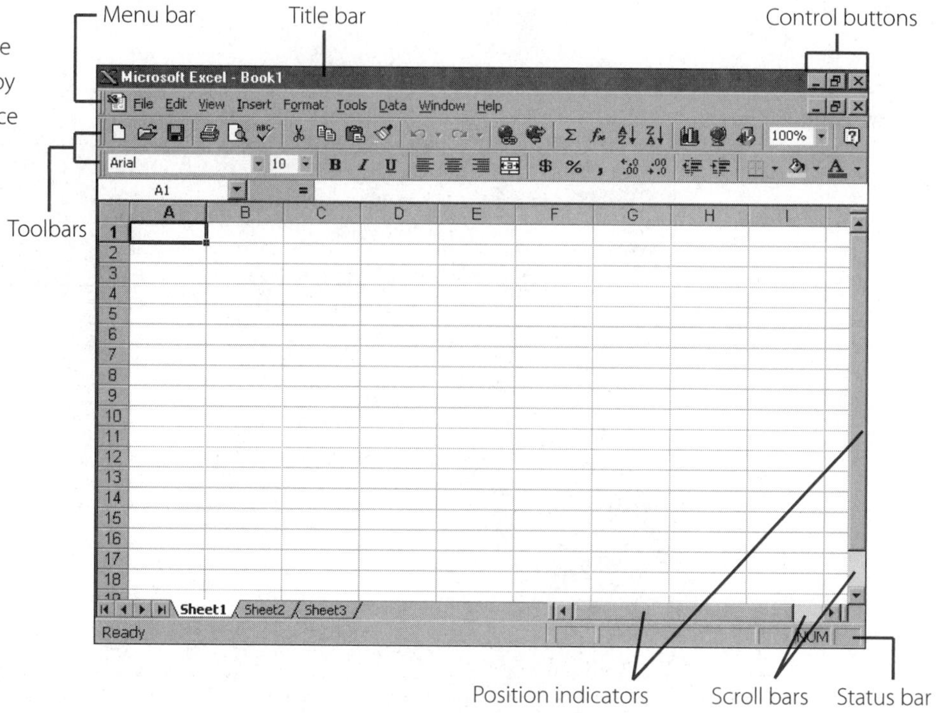

title bar is the *menu bar*, containing commands you click to perform the work of the program. Further down are one or more collections of buttons called *toolbars*. Toolbar buttons are typically shortcuts to commands on the menu bar (hence their synonym *command buttons*); to run a command on the toolbar you simply click the button.

Below the toolbar is the document area unique to each Office application. In Microsoft Excel, documents are called *worksheets*, ledgers divided into rows and columns to hold text, numbers, and charts. Each Office application uses a slightly different type of document. For example, the Word workplace contains word processing documents while the PowerPoint workplace contains the slides of a presentation, though *all* Office workplaces contain a set of common features you can use to complete work in your program. Finally, each Office application includes horizontal and vertical *scroll bars* to navigate each document window, plus a *status bar* (located at the bottom of the window) containing information about the toggle keys in use (Num Lock and Insert) and other details specific to each application.

? SEE ALSO

For information about unique workplace features of each Office application, read the opening sections of Parts II through V in this book.

A list of common workplace features is shown in Table 2-1.

TABLE 2-1.   Workplace Elements and What They Do

Workplace Element	Description
Title bar	Rectangular bar at the top of the application window containing the Office application name, the document name (if documents are maximized), and the control buttons.
Control buttons	Minimize, Maximize, Restore, and Close buttons for the application window and each document window.
Menu bar	The area under the title bar containing the menu names. Each menu opens to provide access to a group of application-specific commands.
Toolbars	One or more rows of drop-down list boxes and command buttons beneath the menu bar.
Scroll bars	Horizontal and vertical bars at the bottom and right edge of the window, used to view parts of a document not currently displayed in the window.
Status bar	Indicators for the Num Lock and Insert toggle keys, plus any application-specific data (such as page numbers or cell contents).

Navigating Document Windows

If a document is too large to be displayed completely in a document window, Office adds vertical and horizontal scroll bars to the window to give you access to the entire file. Figure 2-2 shows the scroll bars on a typical Excel worksheet. Scroll bars let you move through your document at your own pace, and include the following navigation options:

- You can move up or down one line or row by clicking the top or bottom arrow on the vertical scroll bar.

- You can move right or left a small amount (one column in an Excel worksheet) by clicking the right or left arrow on the horizontal scroll bar.

■ You can move in larger increments (approximately one page at a time) by clicking the horizontal or vertical scroll bar itself.

■ You can move to a specific location in the document by dragging the vertical or horizontal position indicator on the scroll bars. The position indicator gives you a visual clue of your place in the document.

> You can also scroll through a document window by pressing and holding the Up, Down, Right, or Left arrow keys or the Page Up and Page Down keys.

Working with Several Document Windows

Word, Excel, and PowerPoint let you open more than one document window at a time so that you can compare related documents, exchange information between files, and work on a multidocument report or presentation. When working with documents in separate windows, each open document window has its own title bar, control buttons, and scroll bars, as shown in Figure 2-3. (The Arrange All command on the Windows menu created this effect, as you'll see below.)

FIGURE 2-3.

Microsoft Word with two open documents.

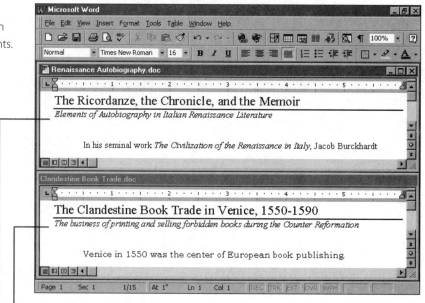

Clandestine Book Trade document

Renaissance Autobiography document

> Excel further organizes document windows by grouping worksheets into collections called *workbooks*. You can scroll through the worksheets in a workbook by clicking the tabs at the bottom of each document window.

To control how document windows are activated and displayed, Word, Excel, PowerPoint, and Access include a Window menu on their menu bars. Figure 2-4 shows Word's Window menu with two open documents. At the bottom of each menu in Word, Excel, and PowerPoint are the names of the open documents in the application. (A check mark appears next to the active or highlighted document.) To switch between open documents, click the name on the Window menu corresponding to the document you want to display, or type its number.

FIGURE 2-4.
Click the Window menu to open it and see a list of your open files.

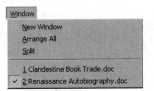

At the top of the Window menu are the commands you can use to open new windows and to arrange existing windows. In Word, Excel, and PowerPoint, the New Window command opens a new document window and displays the active document in it. This lets you have more than one window displaying the same document. Each of the different windows showing the same document is identified with a number following the document name.

In Word, below the New Window command on the Window menu is the Arrange All command, which divides the workplace evenly between all the open document windows. (Figure 2-3 shows the results of the Arrange All command.) Use Arrange All if you want to compare the documents you currently have open. If part of a document is no longer visible on the screen after you choose Arrange All, then use the scroll bars to bring it into view. Arranging documents with the Arrange All command is often called *tiling*, because you fit them together side by side like floor tiles. PowerPoint also offers an Arrange All command, while Excel and Access offer similar commands that give you greater control over how the windows are arranged.

The Split command, available in only Word and Excel, is similar to the New Window command, but rather than creating a new window, it simply splits the screen to give you different views of the active document. In Word, when you select the command, a shaded split line appears, which lets you specify how you want the window divided up. Click the document in the place you want the border to appear (the middle of the document usually works best), and then scroll each window until you see the information you want to compare. (You can fine-tune the split by dragging the middle window border with the mouse.)

You'll find the Split command most useful when you want to edit different parts of a document at once within a single window, or when you want to read the instructions in one part of a document while you work on the other. For example, you might want to read the template instructions at the top of a document while filling in the blanks below. Note that the Split command keeps track of the edits you make, so that changes in one window are automatically reflected in the second window. When you're finished using the Split command, choose the Remove Split command from the Window menu.

Resizing and Closing Document Windows

Just like application windows, individual document windows can be moved, resized, minimized, maximized, and closed. The commands used to manage document windows are located on the document Control menu, which appears when you click the Control-menu icon on the left side of an active document's title bar. Figure 2-5 shows an open Control menu for a document in Microsoft Word.

⭐ **TIP**

> The Control-menu icon only appears on the active document window—you must select a window before you can access its Control menu.

You can also minimize, maximize, restore, or close a document window by clicking the buttons on the right side of a document's title bar, which control the type of window you're using. These buttons work just like the ones on an application's title bar, and you'll usually find that using them is the quickest way to resize or close a document window. Note that if you minimize a document window, however, it

FIGURE 2-5.
Each document
window contains
a Control menu,
which you can open
by clicking the tiny
Control-menu icon.

Control-menu icon

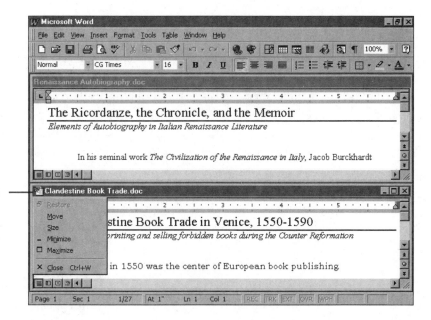

Getting Started

doesn't appear on the Windows taskbar. Rather, it appears as a small title bar at the bottom of the application's workspace. To restore the minimized document to its normal size, simply double-click the title bar or use the control buttons. (If the control buttons aren't visible, click once on the title bar of the minimized document to activate it.)

If you work with multiple document windows often, you might also find the keyboard shortcuts given in Table 2-2 useful.

TABLE 2-2.   Useful Keyboard Shortcuts for Document Windows

Keyboard Shortcut	Purpose
Ctrl+F4 *or* Ctrl+W	Close the active document window.
Ctrl+F5	Restore the active document to a window.
Ctrl+F6	Switch between open documents.
Ctrl+F7	Move the active document window.
Ctrl+F8	Resize the active document window.
Ctrl+F10	Maximize the active document window.
Alt+hyphen (-)	Open the active document's Control menu.

Using Menus and Dialog Boxes

As you've already learned, you can run commands in Office applications either by clicking a command name on the menu bar or by clicking a toolbar button. If the program needs additional information before it can run the command, it displays a *dialog box* in which you "talk" to the program by filling in the blanks or choosing from a list of preset options. This section describes some of the typical options found on Office menus and in dialog boxes. Because Office applications share many of the same features, you'll be able to apply what you learn here to the menus and dialog boxes in Word, Excel, PowerPoint, Access, and Outlook.

Menu Conventions

As you learned in the last section, three Office applications maintain a Window menu with nearly identical commands. However, all five Office applications have File, Edit, and Help menus with many of the same commands—so once you learn how to use these menus in one Office application, you'll be able to use them in all Office applications. In addition, each program follows a series of conventions for the presentation of commands, buttons, and information on menus and in dialog boxes. Table 2-3 lists the most important menu bar conventions. (You'll learn about dialog boxes in the next section.)

TABLE 2-3. Important Menu Bar Conventions

Menu Item	Convention	Example
Dimmed command	The menu command isn't currently available.	Paste Ctrl+V
Ellipsis (...)	Choosing the menu item will display a dialog box.	Borders and Shading...
Checked command	A command indicating an option that's currently active (these commands can be either on or off). Selecting a checked command removes the check and turns the option off; selecting an unchecked command turns it on.	✓ Formatting
Cascading menu (or submenu)	Pointing to this menu item will display more menu choices.	Macro ▶

(continued)

TABLE 2-3. *continued*

Menu Item	Convention	Example
Keyboard shortcut	A keyboard alternative for executing the menu command.	Select All Ctrl+A
Underlined letter	Pressing the underlined letter (often a mnemonic, as in S for Save) will run the command.	Header and Footer
Toolbar shortcut	A toolbar alternative for executing the menu command.	Print Preview

Dialog Box Options

Figure 2-6 on the following page shows a typical dialog box from an Office application. (This dialog box appears when you choose the Print command from Word's File menu.) Dialog boxes present you with one or more command options through list boxes, buttons, and other components. To complete a dialog box, you simply indicate your preferences and then click the OK button. To move from one item to the next in a dialog box, simply click the item, or use the Tab key until the item is highlighted. Many dialog boxes don't require you to fill every blank. If you have second thoughts about using the command after you see the dialog box, you can cancel the command by clicking the Cancel button or by clicking the Close button on the dialog box's title bar. You can also get help by clicking the Help button on the title bar, and then clicking the item you want to learn more about.

Figure 2-6 illustrates the following items and how to use them.

- *Drop-down list boxes* present a list of choices for you to select from, with a default setting (the built-in setting at program startup) typically recommended.

 TIP

Key to Your Choice in a List Box

To move quickly through a list box, press the letter on your keyboard that corresponds to the first letter of the list item you want to select. The first item beginning with that letter will be immediately displayed. You can then fine-tune your selection by using the Up and Down arrow keys. Then press Enter to make your choice.

■ *Text boxes* let you type text, numbers, or other characters into the dialog box. The format required by each text box changes from dialog box to dialog box.

Pressing the Tab key lets you cycle through the elements in a dialog box, and pressing Spacebar lets you select the highlighted element. To cycle in reverse order, press Shift+Tab.

■ *Option buttons* let you select one option from a group of choices—you can only pick one at a time.

■ *Check boxes* are similar to option buttons, though you can select more than one check box from a group, or none at all.

■ A *scroll box* is a navigation control next to a text box that lets you use the mouse to specify a number in a text box.

FIGURE 2-6.
Dialog boxes have several mechanisms for accepting user input.

Your selection appears in the drop-down list box.

Click the down arrow to display the list and then click an item to select it.

Help button

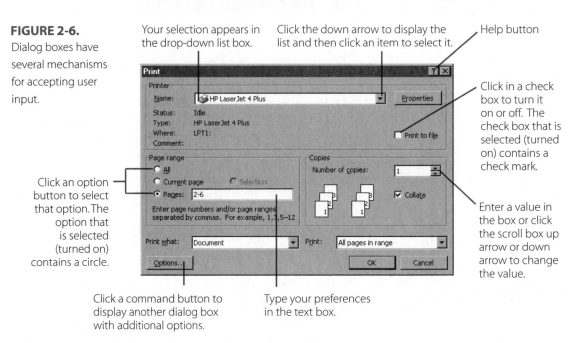

Click in a check box to turn it on or off. The check box that is selected (turned on) contains a check mark.

Click an option button to select that option. The option that is selected (turned on) contains a circle.

Enter a value in the box or click the scroll box up arrow or down arrow to change the value.

Click a command button to display another dialog box with additional options.

Type your preferences in the text box.

■ *Command buttons* determine how a command will be executed or present optional command settings.

> If you need to see document information displayed beneath a dialog box, move the dialog box out of the way by dragging its title bar.

You'll also see small panes called *tabs* near the edges of some Office dialog boxes. These tabs let you display other command settings to further customize your workplace. Figure 2-7 on the following page shows an example of a dialog box with four tabs related to printing.

Using the Right Mouse Button

If you've used the Windows operating system for a while, you know that before Windows 95, few applications provided complete support for the *right* mouse button. Although most pointing devices have two or even three mouse buttons, the left button has traditionally been the only button you could click in a Windows-based application. With the advent of Windows 95, however, the right mouse button has finally been put to use. The following list shows a few important uses for the right mouse button in Office applications:

■ To resize or close an Office application, right-click the application's title bar, and then click the window command you want on the shortcut menu that pops up.

■ To edit or format selected text in a document, right-click the text, and then click the formatting command you want on the shortcut menu.

■ To add, remove, or customize an Office application toolbar, right-click the toolbar, and then click the toolbar you want to view or hide, or click Customize to edit a toolbar.

■ To close an application from the taskbar, right-click the application's taskbar button, and then click the Close command.

FIGURE 2-7.
Dialog box tabs give you quick access to related options and property settings.

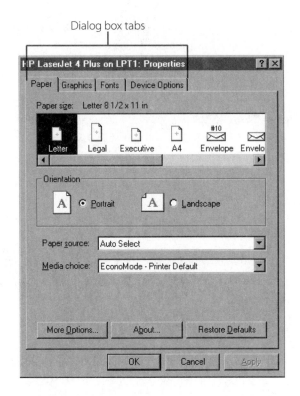

Dialog box tabs

Using Toolbars

A *toolbar* is a customizable set of buttons, commands, and drop-down list boxes, located below the menu bar of an Office application. Toolbars will likely become your favorite screen elements in Office, for they provide rapid access to the most common commands and procedures of an application. The buttons on Office toolbars typically have command equivalents on the menus of the applications, but are easier to remember than command names because they contain *icons*—graphic representations of the tasks they accomplish. Toolbar buttons are also easier to use because they require only one click to get them started. (Menu commands require a minimum of two clicks.)

 NOTE

In Office 97, toolbar buttons appear next to some of the menu commands, depicting graphically the functional overlap between toolbars and menus.

Figure 2-8 shows the default toolbars displayed in the Microsoft Excel workplace. The Standard toolbar, the toolbar with the most useful Excel commands, appears directly below the menu bar in the default (preset) Excel configuration. Below the Standard toolbar is the Formatting toolbar, a popular toolbar with drop-down list boxes and buttons used for formatting the cells in a worksheet. Microsoft Excel includes a total of 12 toolbars, and you can display none of them or all of them, or you can customize your own toolbars—it's completely up to you.

FIGURE 2-8.
Memorize these essential toolbar buttons.

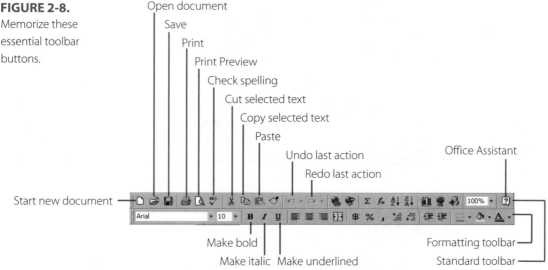

The labels in Figure 2-8 highlight the most popular Office toolbar buttons. (You'll find them, perhaps arranged in slightly different order, in virtually all Office applications.) If you're not sure what a toolbar button does, hold the mouse pointer over the button for a moment to see the button's name. This Help feature is called a ScreenTip. You can also click What's This? on the Help menu and then click a toolbar button to learn how to use it.

🔴 **TIP**

Get to Know Your Buttons
You'll save lots of work time if you memorize the functions of the toolbar buttons described in Figure 2-8. If Office 97 were a car, these would be the familiar knobs and buttons on your dashboard, and for your ease of driving and safety, you'd want to know what they do.

Moving Toolbars

If you'd like to make more room for data in your application workplace, you can move one or more toolbars to a different location on the screen. Most Office toolbars can be placed at the top of the application window (the default position for most toolbars), or at the bottom, or on either side—or even in a floating palette anywhere in the application window. To move an Office toolbar, simply click an empty place on the toolbar (the left edge works best), and then drag the toolbar to a new location. As you drag the toolbar, a shaded rectangle moves with your mouse pointer to help you place the buttons. If you move toolbars on top of each other, they will snap into place or *dock* in a position that partially obscures many of the buttons. (Tiny double arrows at the end of the toolbar will help you identify this useful state.) When you're ready to restore the toolbar, simply drag it back to its original position.

Figure 2-9 shows the Word workplace after the Formatting toolbar has been moved to the bottom of the window and the Standard toolbar has been floated in the upper right corner of the document window. Note that "floating" toolbars always remain above the document so that you can use them. After a toolbar has been positioned as a floating palette, you can also move it (drag its title bar) or resize it with the mouse (drag any of its edges to shrink or expand it).

FIGURE 2-9.
Office applications let you move toolbars from one place to the next to match your preferences.

Standard toolbar (as floating palette)

Formatting toolbar relocated

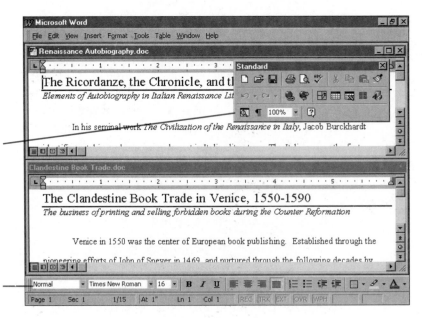

If you decide to use a floating toolbar palette, we recommend that you place it in the upper right corner of your screen. It's less likely to get in the way there when you type.

In Office 97, you can move the menu bar around the workplace just like the toolbars. Try this special customization option if you want to really fine-tune your user interface!

Adding and Removing Toolbars

When Microsoft designed the applications in Office, it conducted usability tests to determine which commands and procedures were run most often by Office users. From the results of these tests, Microsoft created a collection of toolbars for each Office application that provide access to the commands and procedures users found most helpful for a particular task. The most popular buttons were placed on the Standard toolbar, the buttons related to document formatting were placed on the Formatting toolbar, and so on. Microsoft also created several application-specific toolbars to help you achieve the most effective use of the unique features and capabilities of each Office application. In this section, you'll learn how to organize your workplace by adding and removing these toolbars.

Since Outlook is an application that manages mail messages and tasks, rather than documents, it contains only two toolbars. But the remaining Office applications include many more.

When you first start an Office application, you'll see one or two toolbars at the top of the application window. For example, Word and Excel display the Standard toolbar and the Formatting toolbar when you first start them. To see a list of the common toolbars supported by an application, simply click one of the toolbars with the right mouse button. (You can click anywhere on the toolbar.) When you do, a list of the available toolbars appears in a pop-up window, as shown in Figure 2-10 on the following page.

FIGURE 2-10.
To see a list of the
available toolbars
in an application,
click a toolbar with the
right mouse button.

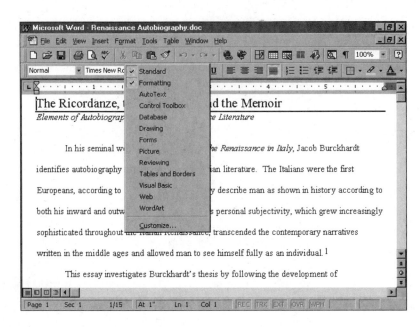

 SEE ALSO

To learn how to cus-
tomize toolbars in
Word and Excel, see
"Customizing Toolbars,
Menus, and Shortcut
Keys," page 407 and
"Customizing Toolbars,"
page 531.

The active toolbars in the list (the toolbars currently displayed) appear in
the list with a check next to them. Below the toolbar names is a special
command named Customize that lets you change the content and style of
the toolbars in the list. You can also use Customize to add new toolbars
or reset toolbars you've changed, back to their default configurations.

To add a toolbar to your workplace, simply click the name of the toolbar
you want to add on the toolbar shortcut menu. To remove an active
toolbar, click the toolbar name you want to hide; the check mark next to
its name on the menu will disappear and so will the toolbar itself from
the application workplace. Your Office application will immediately configure the workplace based on your request. Figure 2-11 shows Microsoft
Word after the Tables And Borders toolbar and the Drawing toolbar have
been added to the workplace.

⭐ **TIP**

Adding extra toolbars to your screen can be fun, but don't get too carried away
or you won't have any room left for your documents! We recommend that you
limit your workspace to three toolbars or fewer.

FIGURE 2-11.
The Word workplace with four toolbars visible.

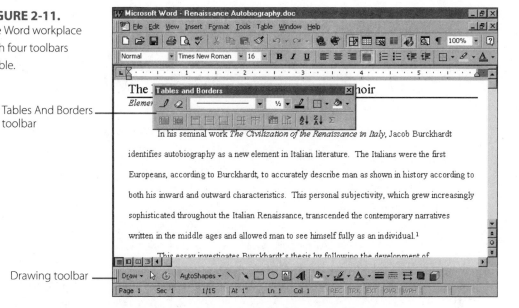

Tables And Borders toolbar

Drawing toolbar

Getting Started

Printing Documents

? SEE ALSO

To learn how to distribute documents in a networked workgroup or over the Internet, see Chapter 3, "Managing Documents: From Your Hard Disk to the Internet."

Although you might choose to distribute Office documents electronically from time to time—as files sent over the Internet or through electronic mail (e-mail)—you'll probably create most of your work with a final, hard-copy printout in mind. Fortunately, the printing process is straightforward and nearly identical in each of the five Office applications. In this section, you'll learn how to preview a document, print all or part of a document, and control the unique printing options of your printer.

Using Print Preview

? SEE ALSO

For more information on Print Preview in Word, see "Previewing and Printing Documents," page 330.

As you work on a document—an essay in Word, for example—you might not be interested in how wide the margins are, how long the essay runs, or where the page breaks occur. But when it comes time to print the document, each of these items becomes important. You might be printing on letterhead paper where specific margins need to be set, or you might need to hold the finished document to a certain number of pages. Fortunately, each Office application gives you the opportunity to see your completed document in electronic form before you print so that you can make any necessary adjustments. In Word, Excel,

Access, and Outlook, the command used to view your document in its final state is called Print Preview.

> PowerPoint doesn't have a specific Print Preview command.

Print
Preview

To open the Print Preview window in Word, Excel, Access, or Outlook, choose the Print Preview command from the File menu or click the Print Preview button. Figure 2-12 shows the window that appears in Word when a 15-page memo is the active document. (The Print Preview windows in Excel, Access, and Outlook will look slightly different.) Print Preview allows you to zoom in on parts of your document, and you can adjust the margins and other page setup options before printing.

FIGURE 2-12.
Print Preview lets
you examine your
document before
printing.

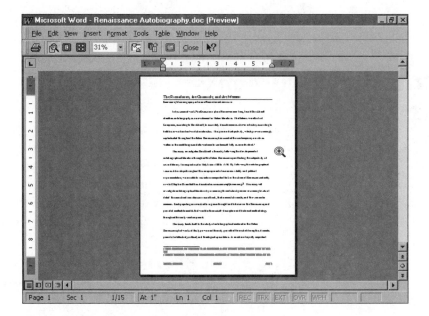

Using the Print Command

After you've examined your document with Print Preview and have made any last-minute adjustments, you're ready to print your work using the Print command. Each Office application has a Print command that sends output to an attached printer via special connectors called *ports* on the back of your computer. Your printer might be attached to your computer via a short parallel or serial cable, or through a long (and perhaps mysterious) series of network routers, cables, and connectors. In either case, your printer needs to be on line and ready to go before you print. In addition, you need to have the correct printer driver installed in the Windows Printers folder to take full advantage of the features of your printer.

Print

To start printing, choose the Print command from the File menu or click the Print button. Figure 2-13 shows the dialog box that appears when you choose Word's Print command from the File menu. The Name drop-down list box contains the set of installed printers and devices to which you can send your printer output. The name currently showing in the list box is the default printer, the printer that will receive your output unless you select a different printer. If you're on a network, you might have the ability to send documents to printers set up for different purposes by your workgroup. For example, you might be able to send memos and letters to a printer with letterhead in it and official documents to a printer with legal-sized paper in it. To find out about your options, ask a co-worker or the system administrator in charge of your network, and then do some experimenting.

For more information about installing printer drivers and setting the unique features of your printer, see the Microsoft Windows 95 documentation or the manual that came with your printer.

FIGURE 2-13.
The Print command lets you specify printing options.

Name list box   Printer Properties

Page range options

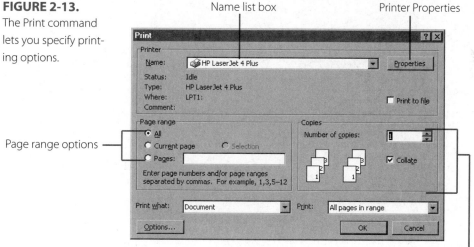

Multiple copies options

The Print button on the toolbar is the fastest way to print the entire document in an Office application. However, it doesn't let you choose the print range, the number of copies, or other special conditions.

Fax Directly from Office

If you have a fax modem in your computer, you can also fax Office documents (with or without a cover page) by selecting the Microsoft Fax device in the Printer Name list box. As long as Microsoft Fax is the default printer, your documents will be sent out over the phone lines. (You'll be prompted each time for the name and fax number of the recipient.)

Setting Printer-Specific Options

The Properties button in the Print dialog box lets you control the unique features of your printer, such as font resolution, paper type, and double-sided (duplex) printing. Figure 2-14 shows the dialog box that appears when you click the Properties button and a Hewlett-Packard LaserJet 4 Plus is the selected printer. The LaserJet 4 Plus Properties dialog box has four tabs of information related to the unique features of this particular

FIGURE 2-14.
The Properties dialog box lets you control the unique characteristics of your printer.

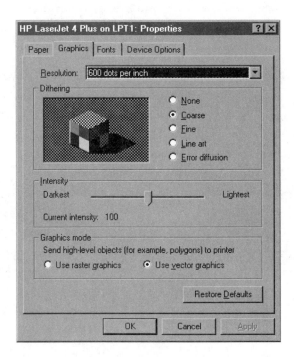

laser printer. The Paper tab lets you identify the kind of paper that is currently installed in the printer and select the orientation (or direction) you want text to appear on the page. The Graphics tab (shown in the figure) lets you select the font resolution and toner intensity, while the Fonts tab lets you choose the type of fonts you want to use. Finally, the Device Options tab lets you control unique characteristics of your printer, including print quality and how your printer's memory is used. The contents of the tabs in your Properties dialog box will vary depending on the type of printer you have. If you don't understand how a particular feature is used, be sure to use the Help pointer. In many cases, the Properties dialog box was designed specifically for you by the manufacturer of your printer and is automatically added to your Office programs when you install the printer.

TIP

> To get the best performance out of your printer, learn to use its control panel (if it has one) in *addition* to the printing options in your application. Sometimes you can get better performance by controlling the fonts, paper size, and copies printed with the buttons on your printer.

Setting the Page Range and Number of Copies Options

Finally, you might want to set the page range or the number of copies options before you send your document to the printer. The page range setting will vary depending on the application you're using. For example, in Word and Excel you can specify the number of pages you want printed, but in PowerPoint you specify the quantity in slides. In either case, the general procedure is the same—simply click the button next to the options you want and enter a page or slide range if necessary. When you're finished, click the OK button to send your document to the printer. (For example, to print pages 3 through 5 and page 7 in Word, turn on the Pages option button in the Print dialog box, and then type *3-5, 7* in the text box.)

To print more than one copy of a document, specify the number of copies with the Number Of Copies scroll box. If you do print more than one copy, be sure the Collate check box is marked if you want the copies printed in contiguous sets. Otherwise, your application will print all the copies of the first page, all the copies of the second page, and so forth.

Printing the Document and Watching the Print Queue

When you're finished setting printing options, click OK to send your document to the printer. After a moment, you'll see a message box indicating that your document has been submitted. (If you've turned on the Background Printing option in Word, you won't see this message box.) To help manage printing problems (such as out-of-paper error messages) and to get you back to your document as fast as possible, Windows stores all printing jobs in a printing *queue* until they've been entirely transferred to your printer's memory or stored in the Windows

Printer Troubleshooting

Since the printing process involves so many variables—printer drivers, ports, cables, paper, toner, and the mechanical process of transferring an electronic image to paper—it's likely you'll experience a few minor printing problems from time to time. If you're working on a network, you should be especially conscious of the things that can go wrong when you send documents to a shared printer. Since your files are sent to a remote network printing queue, rather than your own system's print queue, you probably won't see an error message if something goes wrong. To give you a hand, here's a list of solutions you can try if you run into trouble. For more information, check your printer documentation or talk to your system administrator.

■ If Windows displays an error message when you try to print, read the message carefully and try to resolve the problem. The most common errors are printers with the power off, printers with no paper or a missing tray, or printers that are off line. Check your printer first to be sure it's on and has the correct type of paper and has no paper jam, and then verify that your printer cables are properly connected. An error message typically looks something like this:

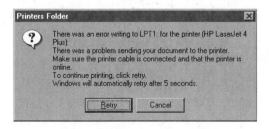

95 printing queue. If you ever need to look at your system's printing queue—for example, if you need to cancel or pause a printing job—simply double-click the printer icon that appears on the right side of the taskbar when the printing queue is active. The window that appears will show you all the pending printing jobs, and if you select a document in the list, you can use the commands on the Document menu to pause or cancel the printing job. You shouldn't need to monitor the printing queue often, but if you have to do some troubleshooting, it's nice to know how.

Printer Troubleshooting   *continued*

- If your printer control panel (if it has one) displays an error message, check your printer documentation for the specific meaning. The most common message is "paper jam," meaning one or more pieces of paper have wedged themselves into the printing mechanism. Turn off your printer, unplug the power cord, and then open the printer and address the problem. If you're using a laser printer or ink-jet printer, you'll also need to clean it periodically to remove loose bits of toner or ink. If you can't fix the printer problem, call your printer's manufacturer for techical support, or call an authorized dealer for advice or service.

- If you're printing on a network, you might not receive an error message when something goes wrong. On occasion, the network server that controls your workgroup printer might fail and will need to be restarted by the system administrator. However, the most common problem with printers used by a workgroup is that there is no paper in the tray, or the wrong type of paper is loaded. (For example, a close friend of ours—you know who you are!—loves to put a special letterhead in the tray and then leave it for others to "discover" that it's decorating their documents.)

- If your document doesn't look on the page the way it did on the screen, you need to verify that you have the correct printer driver installed. Check the Name list box in the Print dialog box. You should also be careful about printing a document from a computer other than the one you created it on. Although different versions of Office applications are compatible, the new computer might have a different collection of fonts or page settings. In addition, each printer model produces slightly different results.

CHAPTER 3

Managing Documents: From Your Hard Disk to the Internet

A *file* is an electronic storage container on disk used to hold valuable information permanently. Files let you retain important data between computing sessions, so that you can work on a report one day, and then pick up where you left off the next day. In the Windows 95 operating system, files are stored in folders, and each file has its own unique *pathname*. (The pathname is the list of folders that describes the path taken from the first level of folders on the drive down to the current folder.) When you save information in a Microsoft Office application, you create a file or *document* on disk that can be used again later or shared with others. In this chapter, you'll learn how to open documents, save them, and close them in Microsoft Office applications. You'll also learn how to search for documents on your hard disk, share them over the Internet, and use properties to add tracking information to a document. Although each Office application creates documents in a slightly different format, the process of working with documents is the same, so we can teach it to you in one place. After you read this chapter, you'll be prepared to work through the application-specific sections in this book.

Opening an Existing Document

Open

You can use four techniques for opening Office documents on your system. If an Office application isn't running, the fastest method is to click the Open Office Document command on the Start menu, or click the Open Office Document button on the Office Shortcut Bar. If you're working in an Office application, your best bet is to choose the Open command from the File menu, or click the Open button on the Standard toolbar. Figure 3-1 shows the dialog box that appears when you open a document in Microsoft Word. (A similar dialog box appears in each Office application.)

FIGURE 3-1.
The Open dialog box contains several features you can use to find and open Office documents.

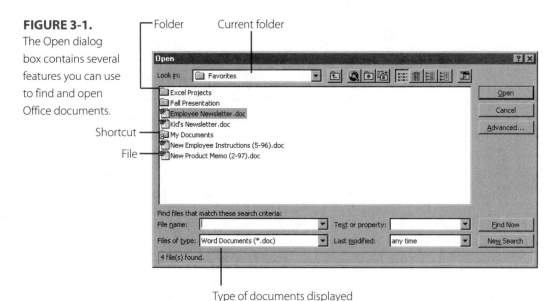

The Open dialog box displays the files and folders in the last folder you used in your application. (The last folder is often called the *current* folder, because that's the place Office puts your files by default.) The name of the current folder is displayed in the Look In box at the top of the dialog box, and the files and folders located in the

Getting Started

current folder are displayed below in a list box. Office documents are identified with the icons shown below. Application files are identified by a tiny application icon next to the filename, and folders are identified by a folder icon. To open a document file displayed in the list box, simply double-click the filename, and it will appear ready for work in your Office application.

Because a typical computer hard disk holds dozens of folders and thousands of files, the Open dialog box includes several features you can use to locate and open a particular document. For example, you can control the type of files that are displayed in the dialog box by choosing an entry in the Files Of Type drop-down list box. Figure 3-1 shows a typical Open dialog box in Word, in which the Word Documents option is selected in the Files Of Type list box. This particular setting means that only files identified as being created by Microsoft Word will appear in the list.

Icon	Represents Documents Created By
	Microsoft Word
	Microsoft Excel
	Microsoft PowerPoint
	Microsoft Access
	Link to the Internet
	Microsoft Binder
	Windows Shortcut

There are probably other files in this particular folder, such as programs and data files, but the criterion of displaying only files identified as Word Documents prevents them from appearing. Narrowing the display criteria with the Files Of Type drop-down list box is especially helpful if you have many files in a folder. If you have dozens of unrelated files and utilities in a folder, it will take you longer to find the file you want to open.

 TIP

Use All Files to See Everything

The options in the Files Of Type drop-down list box changes from application to application. If you want to see all the files in a particular folder, select the All Files criterion.

Opening Your Most Recently Used Files

In addition to using the Open command, you can open the last few files you've modified by simply clicking the file's name at the bottom of the File menu or typing the underlined number. This technique is quicker than using the Open command, because you bypass searching for the file with the Open dialog box. Figure 3-2 shows four recently used Word files at the bottom of the Word File menu. The file in the first position is the last document you used in the active application, the file in the second position is the second to last document you used, and so on. Each time you open a new file, the new name is added to the top of the list, and the file at the bottom is dropped off. The filename also includes a *pathname* to the file, unless the file is located in the current folder. The pathname lists the subfolders containing the file (space permitting), which can help you locate the file later if you need to.

Another way to open a recently used file is to click the Start button on the taskbar, point to Documents, and then click on the filename you wish to open. The Documents shortcut menu that pops up shows recently used files from Microsoft Office applications as well as many other programs. Clicking on the filename will open the associated application if the program isn't already running.

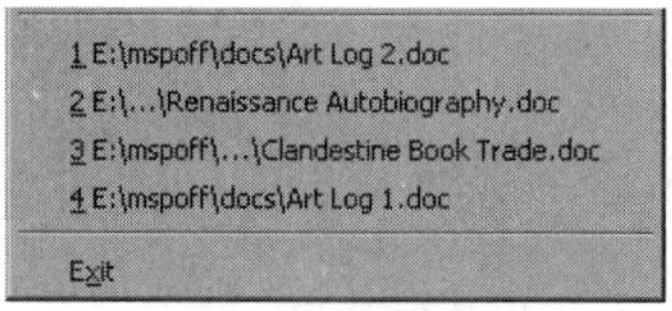

FIGURE 3-2.
The fastest way to open a file is to select it from the list of recently used files on the File menu.

```
1 E:\mspoff\docs\Art Log 2.doc
2 E:\...\Renaissance Autobiography.doc
3 E:\mspoff\...\Clandestine Book Trade.doc
4 E:\mspoff\docs\Art Log 1.doc

Exit
```

Browsing Through Folders

You can locate files in different folders by browsing through your computer's drive and folder structure using controls in the Open dialog box. Each computer has its own set of disk drives that are used to store and retrieve files located on different types of storage media. Typical computers have one or two floppy disk drives, a hard disk drive, a CD-ROM drive, perhaps a tape-backup drive, an Internet connection, and, in many cases, a connection to one or more network drives. You can look for files on different drives by clicking the Look In drop-down list box, and then clicking the disk drive you want to examine. Figure 3-3 shows the available disk drives for one of the computers we used to write this book.

FIGURE 3-3.
To look for a file in a different drive, click the Look In drop-down list box and click the drive.

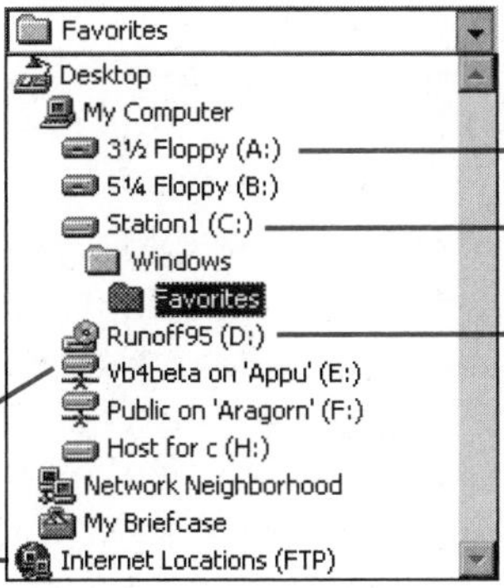

Favorites
Desktop
My Computer
3½ Floppy (A:) ——————— Floppy drive
5¼ Floppy (B:)
Station1 (C:) ——————— Hard drive
Windows
Favorites
Runoff95 (D:) ——————— CD-ROM drive
Vb4beta on 'Appu' (E:)
Public on 'Aragorn' (F:)
Host for c (H:)
Network Neighborhood
My Briefcase
Internet Locations (FTP)

Network drive

Internet connection

After you select a disk drive in the Look In list box, the list of folders and files in the dialog box is updated to match those on the disk you selected. You can examine the files and subfolders contained in a folder by double-clicking the folder in the list box. Each time you open a new folder, its contents are displayed in the list box. (Some users call this process "drilling down" into the directory structure of a disk.) To move back "up" to the folder on the previous level, simply click the Up One Level button in the dialog box. Remember that at any time you can open a file you find by double-clicking the filename in the dialog box, or by highlighting the file and clicking the Open button.

Up One
Level

Search
The Web

Hook Up to the Internet

If you'd like to create a link to information on the Internet right from the Open dialog box, click the Internet Locations (FTP) entry in the Look In drop-down list box, and then double-click the item named Add FTP Location. Office will display a dialog box asking you for the name of the Internet (FTP) site you want to use, plus the password required to connect. After you establish the Internet connection once, your site will appear in the Open dialog box under the Internet Locations (FTP) entry, and you can jump to the Web anytime you want!

You can also click the Search The Web button in the Open dialog box to open the Search page of your Internet browser.

To open a file in a folder that isn't currently displayed in the Open dialog box, follow these steps:

1 Click the Look In drop-down list box in the Open dialog box, and then click the disk drive you want to search. When you select a disk drive, a list of files and folders appears in the list box matching the contents of the disk. If the disk you want to search is already selected, you don't need to click it again.

2 Double-click the folder you want to search. Folders are organized in a "tree" structure, with large branches forking off to subsidiary branches (subfolders), so you might need to open several folders before you find the one you want. If the folder you want is above the current folder, click the Up One Level button in the dialog box.

3 Double-click the file you want to open when it appears in the list box.

Previewing Files with the Open Dialog Box

As you browse through files and folders in the Open dialog box, you might see a document you'd like to look at more closely. Fortunately, the Open dialog box contains four file view buttons you can use to learn more about a file's size, type, and contents *before* you open it. Using these preview features, you can avoid wasting time by opening the wrong file. (See Figure 3-4 for a description of the buttons.)

Figure 3-4 shows the Open dialog box after the rightmost button (Preview) has been selected. Notice that an extra window appears in the dialog box to display the contents of the document highlighted in the list box. The Preview button is very useful—it gives you a quick look at a document (though in condensed form) so that you can decide if you want to open it. (Sometimes the filename alone doesn't give you enough information.)

FIGURE 3-4.
Four buttons in the Open dialog box let you display different information about files before you open them.

Click the List button to display files and folders in a simple list.

Click the Details button to display the file size, document type, and date and time the file was last modified.

Click the Properties button to display document properties of the selected file, including title, template, and revision.

Click the Preview button to display a preview image of the file (if a preview exists).

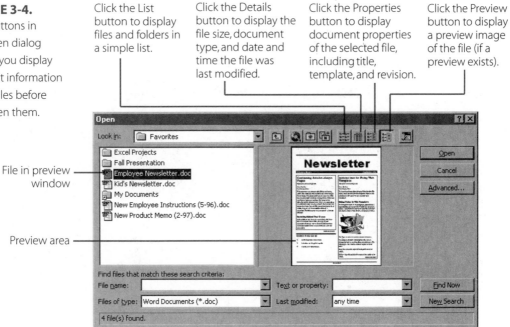

File in preview window

Preview area

To quickly preview all the documents in a folder, click the Preview button and then press the Down arrow key once for each file. The Down arrow key works more quickly than clicking with the mouse.

Performing an Automated Search for a File

The Open dialog box gives you several methods for locating a file on your own. If you still can't find the document you want to open, the

Open dialog box can search for it automatically using one or more search criteria. Open lets you use one or more of the following characteristics when looking for a file:

■ Part or all of a file's name

■ The document type of the file (that is, Word, Excel, or Access)

■ One or more words (called a text string) in the text of the file or in the file's property sheet

■ The amount of time elapsed since the file was last modified

■ The folder and subfolders to search

The following sections describe each of these search features.

TIP

Use the Nifty Find Utility

In addition to searching for files in Office applications with the Open dialog box, you can also use a separate utility program called Find that's included with Windows 95. To run the Find utility to search for files, click the Windows Start button, point to Find, and click the Files or Folders command. You can even click the Using Microsoft Outlook command on the Find shortcut menu to search for words or phrases in your electronic mail messages or Office documents. For more details, see Chapter 41, "Managing Information with Microsoft Outlook."

Searching for a Filename

SEE ALSO

In the section "Searching Subfolders" on page 77, you'll learn how to extend this search to multiple folders on your hard disk.

If you don't know where a particular file is located on disk, but you *do* remember part of its name, you can quickly track it down with the File Name box in the Open dialog box. For example, to list all the files in the current folder that have the word "Newsletter" in their name, type *Newsletter* (or the partial word *newslet* or even *newsl*; since case does not matter you can include partial spellings) in the File Name box, and press Enter. (You can click Find Now rather than pressing Enter if your hand is on your mouse.) Figure 3-5 shows the results of such a search in the Favorites folder. To open one of these documents, simply double-click the filename.

FIGURE 3-5.
The File Name text box lets you search for a file using part or all of its name.

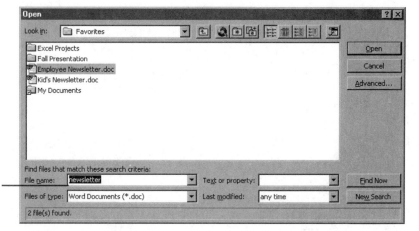

Type all or part of the filename here.

Searching for a Document Type

As you learned earlier, you can also search for a particular class of document by using the Files Of Type drop-down list box. By default, each Office application sets the file type in this box to the type of document it creates. For example, Microsoft Word automatically sets the Files Of Type list box to Word Documents. But at times you'll want to change this value. For example, to view all the text files in a folder, you would select Text Files in the Files Of Type list box. (Microsoft Word can open and edit text files, which are unformatted documents with the TXT filename extension.)

> To view all the files in a particular folder, select All Files in the Files Of Type list box. This is equivalent to typing *DIR* *.* (for wildcard characters) in MS-DOS.

Searching for Text or a Property

If you don't remember the name of the file you want to open, but you *do* remember some of the text in the file—one or more unique words, for example—you might try searching for the file with the Text Or Property text box. When you use this text box, Office searches at blazing speed through each file in the current folder for the words you specified. For example, if you type the words *book of the year* in this text box and press Enter, Office will search the current folder for that exact combination of words and display any matches in the list box. (Case does not matter in searches.) After the search, you can preview the file you're interested in by clicking the Preview button, or you can open the file by double-clicking it. You'll find the results of a search for the words "book of the year" in Figure 3-6.

FIGURE 3-6.

The Text Or Property text box lets you search for keywords in a document.

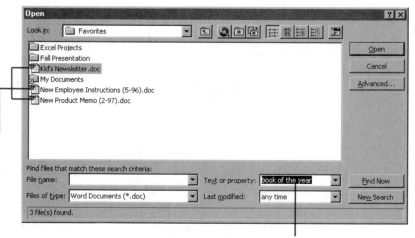

Three documents contain the specified text.

Type your search text here.

When you use this feature, Office also searches each document's properties to find a match for the words you entered. A property sheet is a collection of facts and statistics about a document file, including the document's title, the author of the document, the number of words in the document, and so on. (To examine and adjust the settings in a document's property sheet, open the document, choose the Properties command from the File menu, and then move through the tabs in the Properties dialog box.) For example, to use the Open dialog box to search for documents written by Michael Young, you would type *Michael Young* in the Text Or Property box and press Enter. For more information about property sheets, see the section "Working with Property Sheets" on page 88.

Searching for Recent Documents

If you still can't find the file you want, take advantage of the Last Modified drop-down list box, a very useful feature in the Open dialog box. The Last Modified drop-down list box lets you select a time frame for when a document was created or last modified so that you can track

Getting Started

down a file based on when you used it last. The list box contains several handy time periods for you to choose from, including Today, Yesterday, Last Week, Last Month, and Any Time (the default). For example, to search for all the files in the current folder that were modified during the last calendar week (not the last seven days), choose Last Week in the Last Modified list box and press Enter. Note that if you're using this search option, you'll probably also find it useful to click the Details button in the Open dialog box, which lists the time and date each file in the list was last modified.

Advanced Searching

The Open dialog box also contains an Advanced button that you can use to compose searches using several search criteria or to search multiple folders. When you click the Advanced button you'll see a dialog box similar to the one shown in Figure 3-7.

FIGURE 3-7.
The Advanced Find dialog box lets you search for files using more complex criteria.

2 To add a new criterion, select the property setting for which you want to search.

3 Select the comparison you want to make.

4 Enter the value you're testing.

1 First check the default criteria for the search (taken from the settings in the Open dialog box) in this window.

5 Click And to search for files that meet *all* the specified criteria. Click Or to search for files that meet *any* one of the specified criteria.

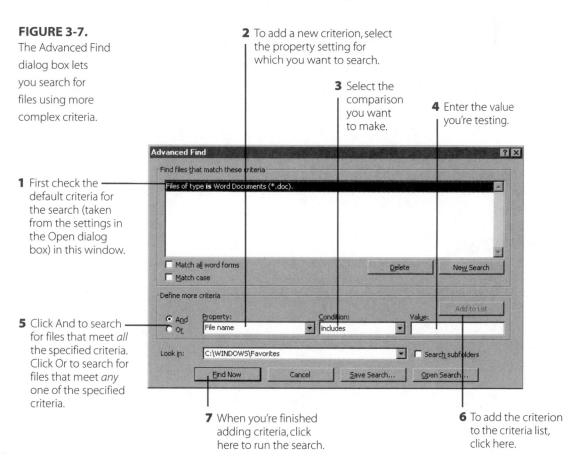

7 When you're finished adding criteria, click here to run the search.

6 To add the criterion to the criteria list, click here.

If you wanted to search for all the Word documents in the current directory containing at least 5,000 words, you would complete the Advanced Find dialog box as shown in Figure 3-8.

When you run the search, the Advanced Find dialog box closes and Office rapidly examines the files in the current folder for matches to your search criteria. The matching files appear in the list box as usual, and you can double-click any file to open it in your application.

FIGURE 3-8.
Completing the Advanced Find dialog box.

1 Choose Number Of Words.

2 Choose At Least.

3 Type *5000*.

5 The added criterion will be displayed here.

Advanced Find

Find files that match these criteria

Files of type **is** Word Documents (*.doc).

☐ Match all word forms
☐ Match case

Delete   New Search

Define more criteria

○ And ○ Or

Property:
Number of words

Condition:
at least

Value:
5000

Add to List

Look in: C:\WINDOWS\Favorites   ☐ Search subfolders

Find Now   Cancel   Save Search...   Open Search...

6 When you're finished adding criteria, click to start the search.

4 Click to add the criterion to the criteria list.

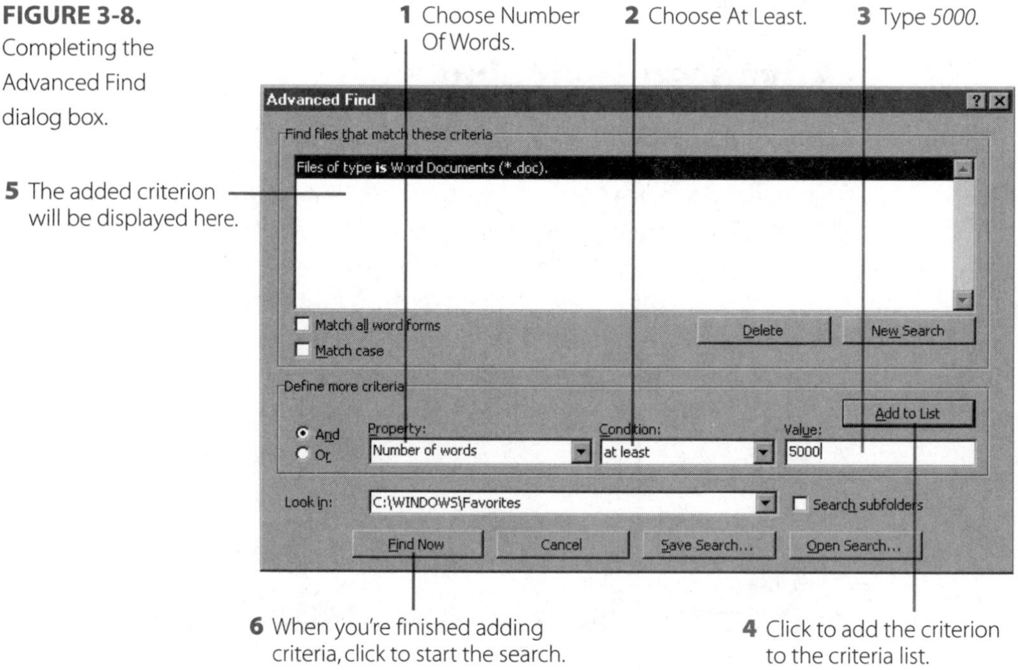

▷ NOTE

The criteria you select in the Advanced Find dialog box remain active until they're changed or cleared. If you want to compose a search without the Advanced Find search criteria, you need to clean the slate by clicking the New Search button.

NOTE

> If you have a particularly complex combination of search criteria in the Advanced Find dialog box, you can save the search for later use by clicking the Save Search button and entering a search name (say, *5000 Words*). When you're ready to use the search criteria again later, click the Open Search button and in the Open Search dialog box click the search you want to run, and then click the Open button.

Searching Subfolders

In our opinion, the most important feature of the Advanced Find dialog box is the Search Subfolders check box at the bottom right, which forces Office to search all the subfolders of the current folder for the search criteria you create (see Figure 3-9). This simple feature lets you search dozens of folders automatically for the file you want to open. Best of all, you can specify the starting point for the search by clicking the drive or folder name in the Look In drop-down list box before you start the search. With the Search Subfolders check box, you can plow through hundreds of files in seconds.

FIGURE 3-9.
Turn on the Search Subfolders check box and specify a starting point in the Look In box to search several folders for a file.

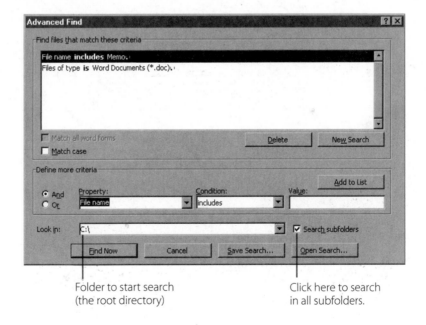

Folder to start search
(the root directory)

Click here to search
in all subfolders.

Getting Started

The Search Subfolders option is also available on the Open dialog box, although it isn't obvious. To locate the Search Subfolders option, click the Commands And Settings button in the Open dialog box. A menu appears with several useful commands and settings for controlling your search.

Commands
And Settings

To display all the files on your hard disk (drive C) that include the word *Memo* in their name, complete the Open dialog box as shown here:

1 Click here, and then click the icon representing your hard disk—probably the one with (C:) after its name.

3 Click the Commands And Settings button to display the menu.

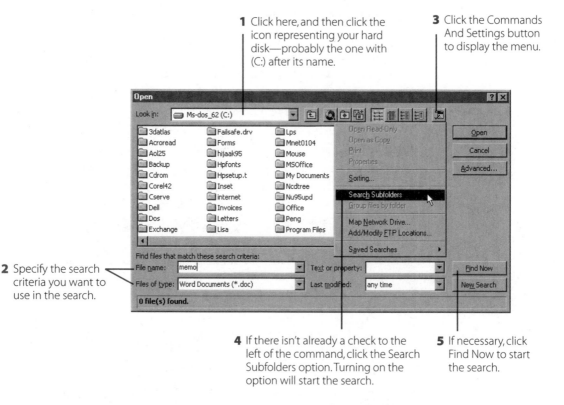

2 Specify the search criteria you want to use in the search.

4 If there isn't already a check to the left of the command, click the Search Subfolders option. Turning on the option will start the search.

5 If necessary, click Find Now to start the search.

When you find the file you want to open, double-click the filename to open it in your application.

Your hard disk is a big place, so searches that include all its subfolders will take a little while to run, especially if you select wide-ranging criteria.

Deleting Files, Renaming Files, and Creating Shortcuts with the Open Dialog Box

An extremely useful feature of the Open dialog box is the ability to delete and rename files in the current folder and create document short-cuts in the Favorites folder. This lets you do some on-the-fly hard disk management as you work in Office applications, obviating the need to run Windows Explorer every time you need to delete or rename a file.

The simplest procedure is deleting a file. To remove a file from the current directory, simply highlight the file, press the Delete key, and then click Yes when you're asked to confirm your deletion.

To rename a file, with the keyboard or mouse highlight the file you want to rename, and then click the filename. (Take care not to *double-click* the file, or you'll open it. If you're using the mouse, pause a moment between clicks.) When you rename a file, Office places a rectangle around the filename and highlights it, as shown in Figure 3-10. You can then start typing to delete the current filename, or press the Right or Left arrow key to move the cursor to a particular location in the name to correct it or add to it. When you're finished making your changes, press Enter to write the new name to disk.

FIGURE 3-10.
The Open dialog box also lets you delete files, rename files, and create shortcuts.

Click a highlighted file to rename it.

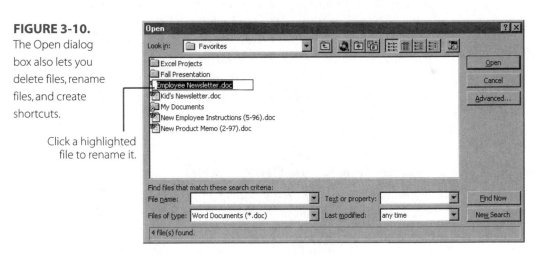

The Open dialog box also allows you to add shortcuts to files in a special folder on your hard disk, called Favorites. This folder is intended to give you one easy-to-remember way to locate the Office documents you use the most. (Favorites is a good place to keep your essential files, and you can also create subfolders in Favorites to organize specific projects.) To create a shortcut to a file in the Favorites folder, highlight the file you want to add, and then click the Add To Favorites button in the Open dialog box. From the pop-up menu, select whether you want to add the selected file (or files) or the folder that contains the file (or files). To view the files in the Favorites folder at a later time, click the Look In Favorites button. In addition to these three file-management techniques, you can also click files with the right mouse button to get a shortcut menu full of useful options.

Add To
Favorites

Look In
Favorites

Saving a File

After you open a file in an Office application, you can add to it or revise it based on your needs and interests. When you're ready to save a version of your document to disk permanently, you must *save* the file. Saving a file is an important step, because the changes you make to your document are only stored in temporary memory (RAM) until you transfer them to disk. If you should accidentally pull the power plug on your computer, or if your power fails in a thunderstorm, the changes you made since your last save will be lost. (This thorny problem is the dark side of personal computing, but you'll learn how to plan for this rather unlikely event later in the chapter.) In this section, you'll learn how to save Office files with two useful commands located on the File menu: Save and Save As.

Using the Save Command

If your file already has a name, you can update it on disk by choosing the Save command from the File menu. The Save command copies the Office document you're working on from computer memory to disk, preserving it in a transferable form and safeguarding it from loss if your application closes suddenly due to power failure or other problems. It's a good idea to save your editing changes to disk every ten minutes or

Save

so, either by choosing the Save command or by clicking the Save button on the toolbar. The Save command doesn't display a dialog box unless your file needs a name. In that case, Office displays the Save As dialog box, which we'll discuss in the next section.

The keyboard shortcut for the Save command is Ctrl+S. If your document doesn't have a filename yet, you'll be prompted for one.

Using the Save As Command

To assign a filename to your Office document, choose the Save As command from the File menu. The Save As command lets you specify the filename, disk location, and folder location of the file, and also lets you set a variety of application-specific options, including the document format of the file. Figure 3-11 shows the dialog box that appears when you use the Save As command in Microsoft Word. (Word has suggested the filename *Summer Picnic*, because those are the first words in the document. It also added the extension DOC, to mark it as a Word document.) If you worked through the section covering the Open dialog box earlier in this chapter, you'll recognize several of the remaining dialog box options.

FIGURE 3-11.
The Save As dialog box lets you assign a name to your document and save it to disk.

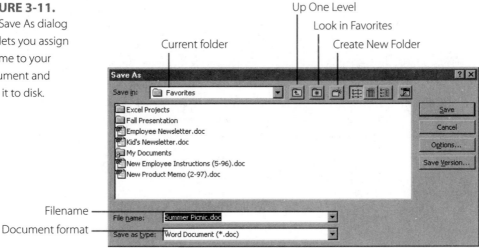

The Save In drop-down list box lets you specify the disk and folder location for your file. Office places your file in the current folder (the folder displayed in the list box) unless you specify a different location. You can open a folder in the list box below by double-clicking the folder icon next to the folder name. If you want to move up a level in the folder hierarchy (or "tree"), click the Up One Level button. Alternatively, you can move to the Favorites folder by clicking the Look In Favorites button. (See "Deleting Files, Renaming Files, and Creating Shortcuts with the Open Dialog Box" on page 79 for an explanation of the Favorites folder.) As you browse through the folders in your system, feel free to use the three view buttons at the top of the dialog box (List, Details, and Properties) to get more information about the files you see.

Get Organized with New Folders

If you want to create a new folder for your file, click the Create New Folder button in the Save As dialog box, and then type a unique folder name. Creating folders is a great way to get organized, especially if you're working with hundreds of documents. We recommend that you create a new folder for every dozen files or so (but put related files in the same folder).

After you set the disk and folder location for your document, you can assign a name to it with the File Name text box. Each file must have its own unique name in the folder, so that it can be differentiated from other files and referenced by name. A temporary name will automatically appear highlighted in the File Name text box when you open the Save As dialog box. (In Word, the temporary name comes from the first line in your document.) To place your own filename in the File Name text box, type in the new name. (Be sure to pick a descriptive phrase that reflects the file's contents.) Because your Office applications were written specifically for Windows 95, you can type up to 255 characters for your filename, with a few typographic caveats. (See the "What Name Do I Choose?" sidebar.) When you're ready to save the file to disk, click the Save button or press Enter.

What Name Do I Choose?

Naming a file is not as challenging as naming a baby, though there are some important rules you should follow to get it right. First, give your file a name related to its contents that you can easily remember later. In other words, don't type the first thing that comes into your head, but choose a few words that will quickly distinguish the file from the other documents in your system. (We think it's a good idea to include names and dates in filenames, so that later you can tell similar files apart.) Fortunately, Windows 95 filenames are no longer limited to the eight-character restriction imposed by MS-DOS, so that you can type up to 255 characters and include spaces, uppercase letters, and lowercase letters. We recommend that you make filenames two to four words long using 10 to 30 characters so that each filename fits well in dialog boxes. Valid filenames can include letters, numbers, and all but the following symbols:

/ \ < > * ? " | : ;

For example, the following filenames are appropriate for typical Office documents:

Current Status Memo (2-97)

Fall Comdex '96 Slide Presentation

2nd Quarter '97 Report

Fortune 500 Customers

New Hires [Probationary] @4-15-97

Saving in a Different Document Format

After you specify the name and folder location for your file, you might want to change the format you're using to save the document. Each Office application uses its own unique document format to translate the words and pictures on the screen into a document that can be printed on paper and stored on disk. Accordingly, you can't move documents from one word processor to another until you pick a format both applications can read. Fortunately, Microsoft Office applications allow you to save documents in a variety of different formats, so that you can open your work in many other applications.

To specify a different document format, click the Save As Type drop-down list box in the Save As dialog box, and then click the format you want to use. Each Office application supports a different list of document formats, so you'll have to experiment a little to see which applications you can use. (If you can't find the format you need, try Text Only, which removes all document formatting.) With some experimenting, you can learn to use the Save As Type feature to exchange files between many different programs; for example, you might share an important Microsoft Excel worksheet from your office with Lotus 1-2-3 users at another office. Figure 3-12 shows the Save As Type drop-down list box in Microsoft Word.

FIGURE 3-12.
The Save As Type drop-down list box lets you save your file in other formats.

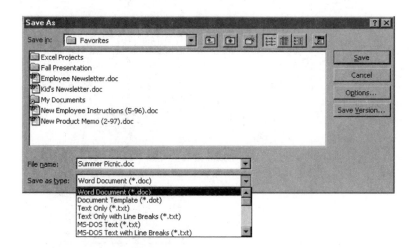

The Save AutoRecover Option

We think the most useful feature in the Save dialog box that appears when you click the Options button in the Save As dialog box in Word is the Save AutoRecover Info option, which directs Office to automatically save a recoverable copy of your document at a time interval you can specify. Save AutoRecover Info Every [X] Minutes helps you avoid losing unsaved changes in your document because of a system "crash," power outage, or other electronic disaster that terminates your application before you save your document. When you enable the Save AutoRecover Info feature, Office saves a copy of your document to the temporary directory on your hard disk at the specified time interval. By default, Office updates this temporary file with your changes every 10 minutes, though you can adjust this interval with the scroll box in the Save dialog box. Note, however, that automatic saves don't affect the document you create with the Save command—this file is always separate and only contains the information you specifically save.

> **NOTE**

Both Word and Excel have the AutoRecover feature, but they implement it differently. In Word (described above), you start the AutoRecover feature by turning on the Save AutoRecover Info option either in the Save dialog box that appears when you click the Options button in the Save As dialog box or on the Save tab of the Options dialog box opened by choosing Options from the Tools menu. In Excel, you start this feature by choosing the AutoSave command from the Tools menu. (If AutoSave doesn't appear on the Tools menu in Excel, choose Add-Ins from the Tools menu and then in the Add-Ins dialog box turn on the AutoSave option.)

Recovering from a Crash

If you do encounter a power loss, a system freeze, a program failure, or another problem that causes you to "crash" (lose unsaved data), start your application again and Office will automatically recover the files that were active when your program crashed. (You'll have one file for each open document.) If the recovered files look correct, save them to disk formally with the Save As or Save command and you'll be back in business. Of course, this only works if you actually enabled the AutoRecover feature before your application bombed. Even then, you'll probably lose the data you entered since your last automatic save. But if you're a little lazy about saving on your own, this "airbag" feature might save you hours of frustration down the road. (Aren't your files *worth* it?)

> **WARNING**

The AutoRecover feature isn't available in PowerPoint or Outlook. Also, Access handles saving information quite differently than Word and Excel.

Other Save Options

If you're using Word or Excel, you'll see an Options button in the Save As dialog box that lets you control additional features in the saving process. Figure 3-13 on the following page shows the Save dialog box that appears when you click the Options button in Word. (The dialog box in Excel will look slightly different.) Both give you a number of saving options, including the ability to create a separate backup copy of your file each time you save (strongly recommended), and the chance to control access to the file with a password (important in a multiuser office). If you're working on confidential documents in a workgroup setting, you might want to consider adding password protection to particular documents, but be advised that if you forget your password, you won't be able to open your documents again.

FIGURE 3-13.
The Save dialog box in Word gives you access to the automatic save feature.

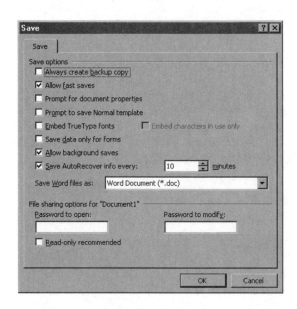

 TIP

Pick Your Format, and Keep Things Simple

To save files in a format that can be used by another application, click the Save As Type drop-down list box and specify the format you want to use. Be sure to select the specific version you want, if it's available, and don't use any advanced or incompatible features in your document that aren't available in the program you'll be transferring to. (The formatting commands and macro languages used by every product are different.)

Creating a New Document

SEE ALSO
Creating a new database in Microsoft Access is a different endeavor, and you'll need to follow slightly different steps. For more information, see Chapter 32, "Databasics."

When Office applications start, they typically present you with a new, empty document to work in. (The exception to this is Outlook, which displays either your personal planning calendar or your electronic mail Inbox.) Often you'll start working with this blank document, customizing it to match your preferences, or you'll open an existing file and start adding to it. However, at times you'll want to create additional blank documents to work in. Perhaps you'll want to split one document into two, or, after working on one project, you'll remember that you need to start another. If this happens, you can quickly open a new file in your Office application. The following section shows you how.

To open a new document in Word, Excel, or PowerPoint, choose the New command from the File menu. When you choose the New command in Word, for example, you'll see the dialog box shown in Figure 3-14.

FIGURE 3-14.
The New dialog box in Microsoft Word.

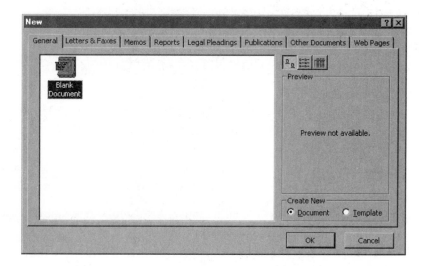

The New dialog box presents a series of tabs with standard document templates (preformatted documents) you can choose from. Highlight the template you want the new document to be based on, and then click the OK button. If you want to create a new, blank document based on the default template (without first seeing the New dialog box), click the New button located on the left side of the Standard toolbar.

New

 **TIP**

> You can also open a new document by selecting the New Office Document command on the Start menu or by clicking the New Office Document button on the Office Shortcut Bar. The New Office Document dialog box you'll see presents templates for all the Office applications organized on separate tabs.

Closing a Document

When you're finished working with a document, you can close it with the Close command on the File menu or by clicking the document's

Close button (be careful not to click the application's Close button by mistake). If you have any unsaved changes in the document, you'll see the dialog box shown in Figure 3-15, prompting you to save your changes. (If Office Assistant is running, you'll see a slightly different dialog box.) If you click Yes, your changes will be saved to disk under the current filename, and Office will close the document.

FIGURE 3-15.
Office warns you if you try to close a file with unsaved changes.

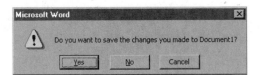

If the document doesn't yet have a filename, the Save As dialog box appears. If you click No, your changes will be discarded and your document will close (*take care not to click this button by mistake*, or you could lose important data). If you click Cancel, the Close command will be canceled, the dialog box will close, and you'll be returned to your document.

The Close command is most useful when you have several documents open, and you want to close one to get it out of the way. (In addition to removing the clutter, closing unneeded files can help you save system resources, or memory.) The Close command operates only on the active or *current* document, so it only closes the file in the highlighted window. Alternatively, if you're ready to quit your application, choose the Exit command from the File menu to close any open documents and quit the application in one step. Like Close, the Exit command also prompts you to retain unsaved changes (if you have any).

Working with Property Sheets

If you've used Windows Explorer to look at the files on your hard disk, or if you've clicked the Details button in the Open or Save As dialog box, you know that Windows 95 stores information about the size, document type, and modification date for each file in the system. These useful facts will probably give you enough information to open your files and keep them organized, though at times you might require additional information to determine a file's origins or make the best use of its contents. Microsoft Office addresses this need by attaching a unique set of *properties* to each file as it's created. A property sheet contains information about the content, revision history, author, and attributes of a document, as well as other information unique to the originating application. Some of the fields in the property sheet, such as the file size, application name, and revision dates, are created automatically by the Office application, while others are added independently by you, the user.

To display a property sheet in an Office application, choose the Properties command from the File menu. (In Microsoft Access, the command is called Database Properties.) Figure 3-16 shows the property sheet for a document in Word.

FIGURE 3-16.
The Properties command displays useful summary information about the active document.

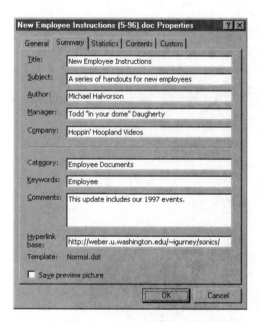

This particular sheet has five tabs of information, which you can access by clicking the tab names at the top of the dialog box. Most of the information on the Summary tab pertains to the content and author of the document, and is typically entered by the author. If you take the time to complete these fields, the members of your workgroup (if you have one) will better understand your goals for creating the document. Summary information could be especially helpful a few years down the road, say when the author of the documents has moved on.

 **TIP**

Take care to use standard, memorable words in your property sheets, so that you can search for them later with the Text Or Property box in the Open dialog box. And watch your spelling, because a search can only find exact word matches (for example, if you type *Grey* in the subject box, a search won't find *Gray*).

The most useful Property tab for people who work with text a lot (such as writers, editors, and desktop publishing specialists) is the Statistics tab, shown in Figure 3-17. The data on the Statistics tab is created entirely by your Office application; it features the file's creation date, modification date, author name, revision number, and the total editing time elapsed in the document. The tab lists other important statistics related to the file, including the number of pages, paragraphs, words, and characters in the file. If you're writing an essay or article that needs to be a certain length, the Statistics tab will probably be very helpful to you.

 **TIP**

If you write articles for a living, use the Statistics tab to track how many words you write and how much time you spend doing it.

FIGURE 3-17.
The Statistics tab displays useful information about the file's origin, editing history, and length.

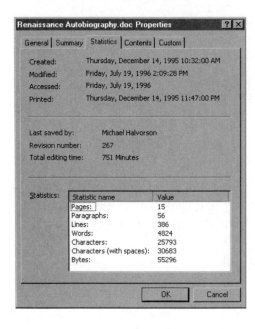

Using Property Sheets to Manage Your System

In the Windows 95 operating system, most files, objects, and devices have property sheets that you can display by clicking the item with the right mouse button, and then clicking the Properties command. (It's up to software developers to create the property sheets, so not all documents and devices have them.) Learning to use these property sheets will help you configure your system quickly. For example, you can configure the display properties of your monitor by clicking the Windows desktop with the right mouse button, and then clicking the Properties command. Figure 3-18 shows the property sheet you'll see when you configure the Windows desktop. The Display Properties property sheet lets you adjust the pattern and wallpaper used for the desktop, the settings for your screen saver, the appearance of your windows, and the colors on your screen.

FIGURE 3-18.
Windows 95 objects have property sheets that you can access with the Properties command.

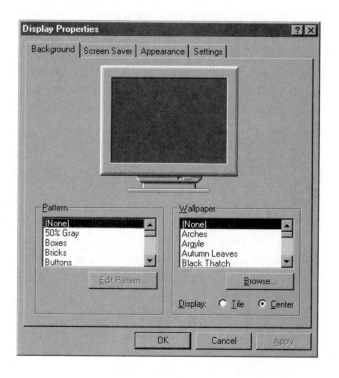

The information in a property sheet is stored in a file with the document it describes, but the data doesn't appear on the screen when you work with the document or on paper when you print. However, it's always available by way of the Properties command to everyone who uses your file, so be aware that when you give your file to others, those users will have access to all the information presented in the property sheet. (For example, it might be embarrassing to charge a magazine client for a business article of 10,000 words, when the client can see from your summary sheet that you wrote only 8,780.) Be sure to use this feature to your own advantage, too. If you have a question about the origin of an Office document you're looking at—a file on the Internet, for example, or a document on a disk you just received—open the file and use the Properties command to learn everything you can about the document. Property sheets are excellent sources of information, especially in workgroups.

 TIP

> To print the information contained in a property sheet for a Word document, choose the Print command from the File menu, select the Document Properties option in the Print What drop-down list box, and then click OK.

Sharing Documents in a Workgroup

As you create documents on your computer, you should do your best to organize them intuitively in folders and copy them regularly to backup disks for safekeeping. If you work in a *workgroup*—a networked collection of computers sharing files, printers, and other resources—you should also make some of your documents available electronically to your colleagues. You might share floppy disks from time to time, but if your co-workers are using Windows 95, the Office 97 applications, and networking software, you can distribute your documents quickly and effectively right from your Office applications. The following section describes a few ways you can accomplish this on a local area network (LAN). In the next section, we discuss sharing documents on the global network of computers known as the Internet.

Saving and Retrieving Files on a Network

Let's say you just completed a new marketing plan, and you want to send it out electronically to your co-workers, both down the hall and across town, so that they can comment on it and revise it. One option for you is to place the marketing document on a shared network drive to which everyone in your workgroup has access. Network drives are typically maintained by the workgroup system administrator, who monitors the free space on the drive, manages the network hardware, and provides support and training. Ask a co-worker or your system administrator what network drives are available to you and how you can establish a connection. A useful tool for browsing the network and moving files back and forth is Windows Explorer, shown in Figure 3-19.

FIGURE 3-19.

You can copy your workgroup documents to the network with Windows Explorer.

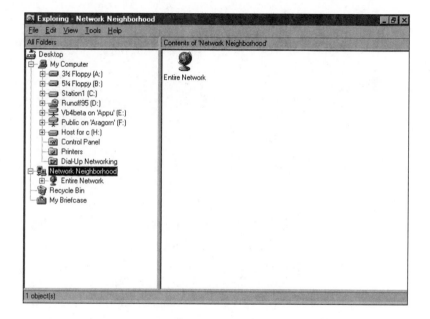

To use Windows Explorer to copy a file to the network, follow these steps:

1 Close your Office document (you can't copy open files), and then start Windows Explorer by clicking the Start button, pointing to Programs, and then clicking Windows Explorer. Locate the Office document you want to copy to the network by browsing through the All Folders list box, and then right-click the file to open the shortcut menu.

2   Choose the Copy command from the shortcut menu to copy the file to the Clipboard.

3   Scroll to the top of the Folders list box on the left side, and then click the network drive you want to use. (The name of this drive will vary from system to system.) Browse through the folders on the network drive until you find the folder in which you want to place the file. (This should be a folder to which everyone in your workgroup has access.)

4   From the Explorer Edit menu, choose the Paste command. A copy of the file appears on the network drive (at the bottom of the file list), ready for review.

 TIP

Notify your workgroup that the file has been posted (via electronic mail or other method), and tell them how you want them to work with the file. To copy the revised document back to your hard disk at a later time, simply reverse these steps. (You might also want to give the revised file a new name to differentiate it from the original file.)

Routing Files Through Microsoft Exchange

If you want to route your document to a specific list of users in your workgroup, you can use the Routing Recipient command to send the document along a specific path. This lets you set up a review chain that leverages the skills of each person in the workgroup. This feature uses Microsoft Exchange to send your file from user to user over the network, complete with routing instructions. To route a document:

1   Choose Send To from the File menu and then choose the Routing Recipient command from the submenu. You'll see a dialog box that lets you specify which users should receive the document and the order in which they should receive it.

2 To add users, click the Address button in the dialog box, and then select the names of users from your personal address book. Figure 3-20 shows a sample routing slip created in Microsoft Excel. You can include a brief message with the routing slip, and adjust several routing options, including the distribution order, routing status, and return method.

3 When you're ready to route your document, click the Route button and Office will send your file to the first recipient via Microsoft Exchange. If you turn on the Return When Done option, your document will return to you automatically after everyone reviews it.

FIGURE 3-20.
You can route a document to users in a particular order with the Routing Recipient command.

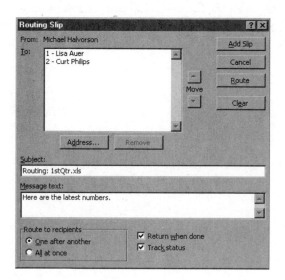

Sending Files via Electronic Mail

The slickest way to distribute Office documents over the workgroup network is to embed them in electronic mail messages. This approach has the advantage of sending files immediately to a set list of users in your workgroup, and allows you to type a longer, more stylized message than you can with the Routing Recipient command. To send a file via electronic mail, simply create your document, and then point to Send To on the File menu and click the Mail Recipient command on the submenu.

The Mail Recipient command starts your mail editor and displays a dialog box you can use to compose your electronic mail message. Office places an icon in your message to represent the file you've included, and when your co-workers receive the message, they can double-click the icon to review the document and edit it on their own system.

Figure 3-21 on the following page shows a sample message created with the Mail Recipient command in Microsoft Excel.

FIGURE 3-21.
You can send copies of your document through electronic mail with the Send To command.

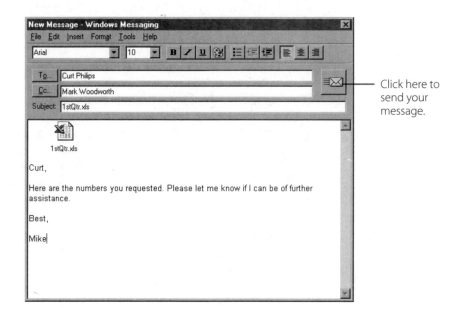

Click here to send your message.

Notice how users in the workgroup are identified by their real names in the To and Cc (for "carbon copies," now thoroughly antiquated) text boxes, and how the Excel worksheet (1stQtr.xls) appears as an icon in the body of the message. The composition window includes scroll bars so that you can type a long message and then format it using toolbar buttons or commands from the Format menu. When you're finished composing the message (be sure to include review instructions), click the Send button on the toolbar to distribute it. If you decide to cancel the message, click the Close button on the title bar (the button with an "X" in it), and the message will be canceled. Note that the Send command doesn't route one document and return a copy to you; rather, it simply sends a copy to everyone on the list. It's a less formal, but more storage-intensive, way to distribute documents in a workgroup environment.

Accessing the Internet

Perhaps the most exciting feature of Office 97 is the ability to access the Internet quickly and seamlessly while you work. The Internet is a global network of computers that are linked together by a collection of efficient and standardized communication protocols. In plain English, this means that you can share information with business colleagues, former teachers, political leaders, and family members all around the world at lightning speed. For many users, the most interesting component of the Internet (other than electronic mail, or e-mail) is an information service known as the World Wide Web (WWW for short, or simply the Web). The Web utilizes a formatting technology known as *hypertext*, which presents information through a rich combination of audio, video, and textual *links*. Now you can view hypertext sites or *home pages* on the Web right from your Office 97 applications!

In this section, you'll learn how to connect to the Web in your Office applications, and you'll learn how to navigate a series of hypertext links with the new Web toolbar. We'll provide additional information about using the Internet in the application-specific parts of this book.

Linking Up with the World Wide Web

Connecting to the Web in Office 97 applications is very simple—so simple, in fact, that you might be wondering what all the fuss is about. You just select a word or cell in your document that you want to act as the doorway or *hyperlink* to the Web, and then you format it by choosing the Hyperlink command from the Insert menu of most Office applications or by clicking the Insert Hyperlink button. (The Hyperlink command is included in Word, Excel, PowerPoint, and Access.) Hyperlink prompts you for the location of your file, which can be a document on your hard disk, or a valid Internet address, such as the home page for

Insert
Hyperlink

your business. (For example, the address for the Microsoft Press Home Page is *http://www.microsoft.com/mspress*.) Hyperlinks appear as underlined words in a special color and you activate them by clicking the word in your document. By default, the hyperlink first appears in blue and then when you activate it, it changes color. When you activate a Web hyperlink, Office starts your Internet browser and makes the connection using an attached modem, fax modem, ISDN line, or other communication device. Once the connection is established, the Web toolbar (described below) appears, to let you switch back and forth between your open connections.

Creating a Link to the Web from a Document

Create a link to the Web from your Office 97 documents by following these steps:

1 Select the word or cell in your document that you want to associate the hyperlink with. It usually works best if that word or phrase describes the purpose of the link, so that users can see what they're connecting to (for example, "Microsoft Press Home Page" or "Volcanoes on the Internet").

2 From the Insert menu, choose Hyperlink or click the Insert Hyperlink button. The Insert Hyperlink dialog box appears, prompting you for the name of the file that will open when the hyperlink is activated. If you wish, you can specify a particular location in the file that should appear on the screen; if not, the document simply opens at the beginning.

3 Type the address of the Web page in the Insert Hyperlink dialog box, or click the Browse button to search for an Internet shortcut on your hard disk. Addresses usually are in the format *http://www.xxxx.com*, where *xxxx* is the name of the business or service provider. For example, the address of Microsoft's new electronic magazine about politics and culture, called *Slate*, is *http://www.slate.com*.

Creating hyperlinks on the Web is an excellent way to share business documents with other users. To establish an Internet location for shared documents, contact your company's network administrator.

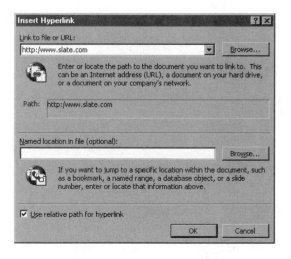

4 Click OK to add the hyperlink to your document. When the Insert Hyperlink dialog box closes, the highlighted text appears in underlined type and a different color.

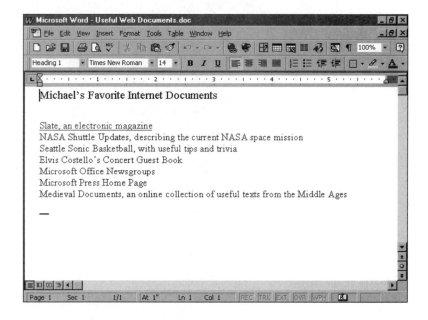

5 When you activate a hyperlink in a document, Office automatically starts the application associated with the document, displays the Web toolbar, and loads the linked document. If the hyperlink contains an Internet address, Office will start the default Internet

SEE ALSO

For more information about creating hyperlinks in Word, see "Inserting and Navigating with Hyperlinks," page 161. For details on creating Internet hyperlinks in Excel worksheets, see "Inserting Hyperlinks," page 439.

browser on your system and ask you for a username and password. After you complete the necessary connection details, you'll see the Internet document you requested. The following illustration shows the home page for *Slate*, an electronic magazine that author Michael Halvorson typically accesses from a Word hyperlink:

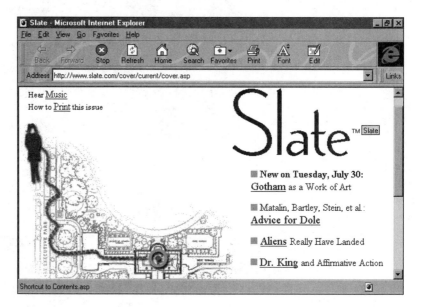

Using the Web Toolbar

After you create or activate a hyperlink in Office, a special Web toolbar appears on the screen, which lets you switch back and forth between open hyperlinks, establish additional Internet connections, or run special network-related commands. You don't have to use the Web toolbar when switching between hyperlinks (you can use your application's Window menu instead), but in many cases you'll benefit from doing so. Figure 3-22 shows the Web toolbar and identifies the purpose of its buttons.

 **TIP**

Web
Toolbar

To close the Web toolbar, click the Close button on the toolbar's title bar or click the Web Toolbar button on the Standard toolbar.

FIGURE 3-22.

The Web toolbar acts like a remote control for your Internet connections. Browse back and forth between open documents with the click of a button.

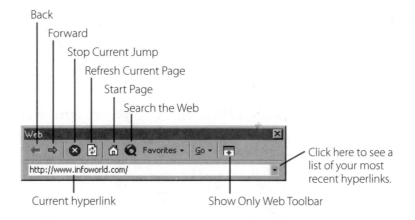

Back
Forward
Stop Current Jump
Refresh Current Page
Start Page
Search the Web

Click here to see a list of your most recent hyperlinks.

Current hyperlink
Show Only Web Toolbar

Getting Started

Browsing Your Connections

The most basic features of the Web toolbar are the hyperlink naviga-tion buttons. To display the last open document or Web page, click the Back button. To display the next open document or Web page, click the Forward button. If you want to add the open hyperlink to your favorites collection, click the Favorites button and then click Add To Favorites. (You can recall favorite hyperlinks at any time by clicking the Favorites button and then clicking Open Favorites.) Finally, if you wish to stop the current hyperlink connection (useful when a number of graphic files are opening and you want to halt the process), click the Stop Current Jump button. If you ever want to download the most current version of a document or Web page, click the Refresh Current Page button. (We often use the Refresh Current Page button in tandem with the Stop Current Jump button.)

Using Hyperlink History

In addition to managing your open hyperlink connections, you can click the Go button on the Web toolbar and choose Open History Folder to display a list of the hyperlinks you've used in previous sessions on your computer. A list of your past Internet activity appears (along with other hyperlinks you've used), and you're given the opportunity to open hyperlink history files stored in the History folder on your hard disk. Take advantage of this feature if you create Web hyperlinks often—by leveraging the past, you can often save time and effort in the present.

You can also use the down arrow next to the Address list box to display your most recent Internet connections. To reestablish one of the connections listed, simply click the address.

Picking a New Start Page for Your Browser

If you're currently using Microsoft Internet Explorer or a compatible browser, you can also change the start page that appears when you open your browser by using the Go button on the Web toolbar. This gives you the ability to customize your browser setup without actually starting the Explorer program. Our favorite technique is to use a Word or PowerPoint document as our Internet Explorer start page, and then add hyperlinks to the document so that we can make jumps to the Web or any of our critical files on disk.

NOTE

Your start page must have hyperlinks in it to be considered a valid start page. If your start page document doesn't contain a least one hyperlink, Office 97 will not enable the Set Start Page command.

To set a new browser start page, follow these steps:

1 Open the Office document you want to use as your new start page and customize it with hyperlinks and descriptive text, as necessary.

2 If the Web toolbar is not already visible, display it by clicking the Web Toolbar button on the Standard toolbar, and then click the Go button on the Web toolbar and click the Set Start Page command. You'll see the following dialog box:

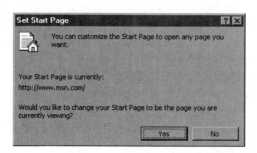

3 Click Yes to set the current open document as the start page for the Internet Explorer.

From now on, your custom start page will open every time you start your browser program.

PART II

Microsoft Word

CHAPTER 4

Getting Started with Word

Welcome to Microsoft Word! This chapter introduces you to Microsoft Word, a general-purpose word processing program that provides an unprecedented number and variety of features. The tasks you can perform using Word range from writing simple documents, such as memos and letters, to producing the camera-ready materials for professional-looking publications, such as newsletters and books.

Yet Word is relatively easy to use. First, Word's visual tools—that is, its menus, toolbars, and mouse interface—eliminate the need to memorize an extensive set of keyboard commands. Also, Word provides many predefined templates and styles that can assist you in producing attractive and effective documents. Finally, Word fully automates many important tasks, such as creating new documents, formatting paragraphs, and correcting text. You can compare Word to a sophisticated modern camera, which has automatic settings for you to use to take quick snapshots as well as manually adjustable settings with which you can achieve particular effects. With Word, not only can you choose "automatic" or "manual" methods to control virtually any feature of the

documents you create, but you can also customize the Word tools themselves—that is, the menus, toolbars, shortcut keys, and the way you
view and work with documents.

A Tour of the Word Workplace

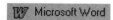

To run Word and take a short tour of its most basic features, click the
Start button on the taskbar, point to the Programs folder, and then click
on the Microsoft Word program icon.

As you saw in Chapter 1, you can also start Word by opening a document template, using the Office Shortcut Bar, or by double-clicking on
a shortcut icon for the program.

When Word first begins running, it automatically opens a new, empty
document. Figure 4-1 shows the Word program window displaying a
typical set of components. Because Word is so highly customizable,
your window could be quite different. If you are missing any of the
components shown in Figure 4-1, you can display them as follows: To
display the ruler, choose the Ruler command from the View menu. (You

FIGURE 4-1.

The Word window.

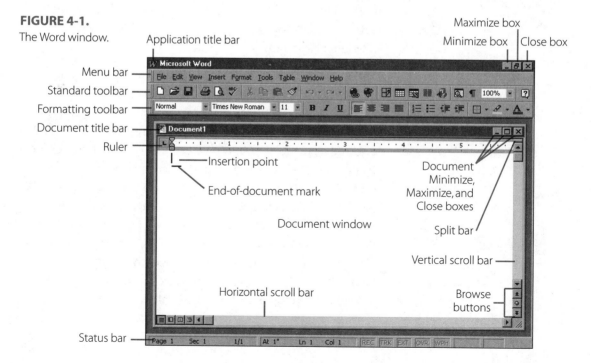

can also display the ruler temporarily, by simply placing the mouse pointer over the horizontal gray bar at the top of the document window.) To show either the Standard or the Formatting toolbar, point to Toolbars on the View menu—or place the mouse pointer over the menu bar or over a toolbar and click with the right mouse button—and then choose the Standard or Formatting option from the submenu that appears:

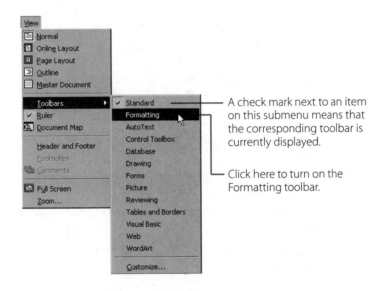

A check mark next to an item on this submenu means that the corresponding toolbar is currently displayed.

Click here to turn on the Formatting toolbar.

Microsoft Word

⭐ **TIP**

Shortcuts Are a Click Away

Many times the next action you want to perform can be found on the special shortcut menu that appears when you press the right (or secondary) mouse button. The menu changes with the context of your actions, so check it often for possible shortcuts to accomplish your tasks more quickly.

To show the horizontal and vertical scroll bars and the status bar, choose Options from the Tools menu, click the View tab in the Options dialog box, if it is not already selected, and turn on the corresponding items. (See Figure 4-2 on the following page.)

The document window shown in Figure 4-1 is in *Normal view*. A view is a way of displaying and working with a document; the different Word views will be explained near the end of the chapter. If the interior of your document window does not appear as shown in the figure, a different view might be active. To switch to Normal view, choose

FIGURE 4-2.

Displaying the horizontal and vertical scroll bars and the status bar using the Options dialog box.

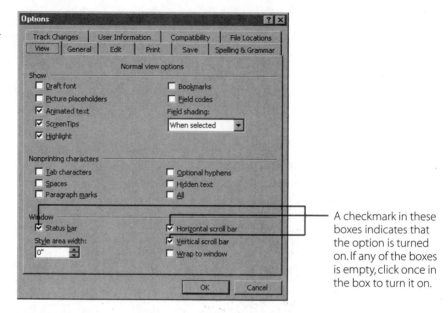

A checkmark in these boxes indicates that the option is turned on. If any of the boxes is empty, click once in the box to turn it on.

Normal from the View menu. Finally, the document window in the figure is displayed in its normal size—that is, it is neither minimized nor maximized. Maximized and minimized document windows are shown in Figures 4-3 and 4-4.

The Standard toolbar in Word lets you perform a variety of tasks, such as opening and saving documents, printing, copying text or formats, and obtaining help. The Formatting toolbar is typical of a special-purpose Word toolbar; it is used for modifying the *format* (that is, the appearance) of characters and paragraphs. In the following chapters, you'll learn how to use the buttons on these toolbars, as well as how to display, use, and even customize or create other specialized Word toolbars to suit your preferences.

 SEE ALSO

For general information about working with toolbars, see "Using Toolbars," page 52.

The ruler below Word's toolbars and title bars allows you to use the mouse to change the document margins and also to set the indents and tab stops for individual paragraphs. The vertical and horizontal scroll bars permit you to use the mouse to scroll through a document that is too large to fit within the document window. You can drag the split bar (see Figure 4-1 on page 108) down from the top of the vertical scroll bar to divide the document window into two panes; you can then view

FIGURE 4-3.
A maximized docu-
ment window fills
the entire Word work-
space, and its title bar
is merged with the
Word title bar.

Click the document window Restore box to
restore to a normal-sized document window.

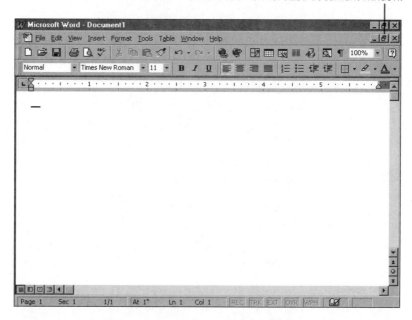

FIGURE 4-4.
A minimized document
window is reduced to
a small bar within the
workspace.

The minimized
document window

Click the document window Restore box to restore to a
normal-sized document window.

Microsoft Word

a different portion of the same document within each pane. The four buttons at the left end of the horizontal scroll bar permit you to change the document view, as explained later in this chapter in the section "Changing the Way You Display Documents," page 121. The three buttons at the bottom of the vertical scroll bar let you browse through the document; they are discussed in "Using the Browse Buttons," page 159.

To learn the purpose of a button (either on a toolbar or on the left end of the horizontal scroll bar or at the bottom of the vertical scroll bar), simply place the mouse pointer over the button *without* clicking the mouse. Word will display a brief description of the button's action, known as a *ScreenTip*, next to the button.

If ScreenTips don't appear, you can enable them by choosing the Customize command from the Tools menu, clicking the Options tab in the Customize dialog box, and turning on the Show ScreenTips On Toolbars option.

The Word *status bar* provides information about the operation of the program. The first six items indicate the current position of the *insertion point* within the document; the insertion point is the flashing vertical line that is displayed at the position where the characters you type appear in the document. The next five items indicate the status of various program features; if any of these items is displayed in dark print, the corresponding feature is active. Word uses the final two items to display appropriate icons when the program is engaged in various operations such as as-you-type spell checking, saving a document, or printing a document. The status bar items are labeled in Figure 4-5; the significance of each item will become clear when the related Word feature is discussed later in the book.

⭐ **TIP**

Use the Status Bar to Issue Some Commands
You can double-click on the status bar to quickly issue certain Word commands. For example, double-clicking the left half of the status bar activates the Go To command (discussed in Chapter 5), and double-clicking one of the program mode indicators toggles the selected mode on or off. If you have enabled ScreenTips, place the mouse pointer over any part of the status bar to have Word display the effect of double-clicking that part of the status bar.

FIGURE 4-5.
The Word status bar.

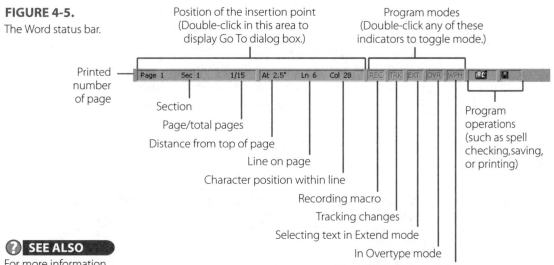

Printed number of page

Position of the insertion point
(Double-click in this area to
display Go To dialog box.)

Program modes
(Double-click any of these
indicators to toggle mode.)

Section

Page/total pages

Distance from top of page

Line on page

Character position within line

Recording macro

Tracking changes

Selecting text in Extend mode

In Overtype mode

WordPerfect Help enabled

Program operations (such as spell checking, saving, or printing)

SEE ALSO
For more information about starting and quitting Office applications, see Chapter 1, "A Quick Tour of Microsoft Office." To learn about working with document windows, see "Working with Application Windows," page 40.

Although Figure 4-1, page 108, shows only a single open document, you can simultaneously open several documents in Word, each document appearing in its own document window within the Word workspace. At a given time, only one document window is *active*; the document in the active window receives your keyboard input and is affected by the commands you issue.

Creating and Printing a Document from Start to Finish

In this section, you'll open, edit, format, print, and save a very simple Word document. All the techniques touched on here—as well as many others—are explained in detail in the chapters that follow.

NOTE

When you start Word, the program automatically opens a new, empty document based on the Normal template, which is called Document1 until you save it and specify a filename. You can immediately begin typing in this document, or you can open another new document using the procedures described in this section.

Microsoft Word

The first step in creating a new document is to choose the New command from the File menu. Word will display the New dialog box, which allows you to choose a template or a wizard for generating the kind of document that you want to compose. Figure 4-6 shows the completed New dialog box for creating a standard, general-purpose document. Word will base the new document on a template named Normal and open a new, empty document window. (You can close the document that was automatically created when you first started Word, or you can simply ignore it.)

FIGURE 4-6.
Creating a new document based on the Normal template.

1 Click the General tab, if not already selected.

2 Click on the Blank Document icon, if not already selected.

3 Click OK.

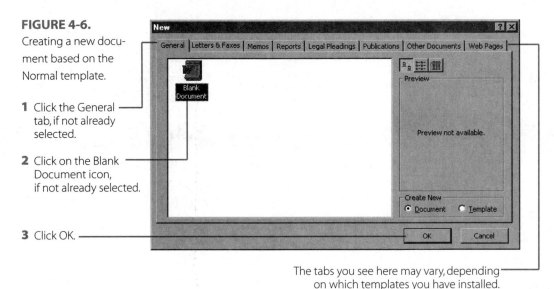

The tabs you see here may vary, depending on which templates you have installed.

As a shortcut, you can create a new document based on the Normal template by simply clicking the New button on the Standard toolbar or by pressing Ctrl+N.

New

Create a Word Document with the Office Shortcut Bar

You can also create a new Word document by clicking the New Office Document button on the Office Shortcut Bar or by choosing the New Office Document command from the Windows Start menu, as described in Chapter 1, "A Quick Tour of Microsoft Office." The resulting New Office Document dialog box will display templates for creating documents using various Office programs. If you choose a Word template or wizard (identified by a *W* on the icon), Word will start (if it is not already running), and the new document will open.

② SEE ALSO

For information about using the Office Short-cut Bar to create and open documents, see "Running Office Applications," page 19, and "Using the Office Short-cut Bar," page 10.

If you want to use a wizard or a template other than Normal, you must choose the New command from the File menu, as described.

After you have opened the new document, the next step is to enter the document text. Your document will consist of a heading followed by two paragraphs of body text. Begin by typing your heading at the top of the document window (for example, *My Summer Vacation*). If you reach the end of the line while you are still typing the heading, do *not* press the Enter key (as you would on a typewriter); rather, just keep typing and Word will automatically move the insertion point (along

---

Templates and Wizards

Word templates and wizards can give you a head start in creating your documents. The New dialog box allows you to choose from a large variety of professionally designed templates and wizards, each of which is tailored to fit a particular type of document.

A *template* serves as a blueprint for a document. It stores formatting styles and sometimes also document text and graphics (as well as several other features). When you create a new document based on a template, your document acquires a copy of the template's contents. You can then modify your document as necessary and add your own text and graphics.

For example, if you want to write a memo, you could choose the Contemporary Memo template (on the Memos tab in the New dialog box). Your new document would then contain the basic text and layout for a memo; you would need only to fill in some details and add your message.

If none of the special-purpose templates is suitable for the document you want to create, you can choose the most general template, Normal, which is labeled as Blank Document on the General tab of the New dialog box and stores a basic set of styles with *no* document text. Templates are discussed in detail in Chapter 7, "Customizing Styles and Templates."

Some of the items in the New dialog box are *wizards*. The name of a wizard generally contains the word "Wizard," and has the extension WIZ (rather than DOT, which is the extension for standard templates; note that you'll see these extensions only if you've chosen to display file extensions in Windows 95). When you create a new document based on a wizard, Word automatically guides you through a series of steps in which you choose the document features you want and enter some or all of the document text. After Word generates and opens the new document, you can manually make any necessary modifications. For example, if you want to produce a memo using a wizard, you could choose the Memo Wizard (also on the Memos tab in the New dialog box) and follow the instructions.

with any characters in the current word) down to the beginning of the next line, and the new characters will appear on the new line. Also, don't end the heading with a period. (If a line ends with a period, the Word automatic formatting feature won't recognize it as a heading.)

> **Install More Templates and Wizards to Suit Your Needs**
> The selection of templates and wizards available to you varies depending on the installation options you chose when setting up Microsoft Office. If you didn't specify the Complete installation option, you may want to install additional templates and wizards by running the Office Setup program again. For more information, see "installing Word components" in the online Help Index.

> If the Check Spelling As You Type or Check Grammar As You Type option is enabled, Word will mark spelling or grammar errors with wavy underlines. These features are discussed in Chapter 9, "Using Word's Proofing Tools."

If you make a mistake or want to make a change, you can use the following simple editing techniques:

1 Use the arrow keys to move the insertion point to the position in your text where you want to make the change.

2 To delete text, press the Backspace key to remove the character to the left of the insertion point, *or* press the Delete key to remove the character to the right of the insertion point. You can hold down either key to erase more than one character.

3 To add text, simply type it. If there are existing characters to the right of the insertion point, Word will move them to make room for the new characters you type. (You must be in the Insert editing mode. If the OVR indicator in the status bar is darkened, double-click it to switch from Overtype mode to Insert mode.)

When you have finished typing the heading, press the Enter key. The insertion point will move to the beginning of the following line, and the next characters you type will belong to a new *paragraph*. A Word document consists of a series of paragraphs; each paragraph (except the first one) is started by pressing Enter. (In Chapter 5 through Chapter 8 you'll learn about the properties of Word paragraphs.) Type several lines of text within the new paragraph. Again, when you reach the end of a line, simply let Word automatically wrap the text to the next line, rather than pressing Enter.

When you have finished typing the paragraph, press Enter to create another new paragraph. As you are typing this paragraph, you'll change the format of some of the characters. First, enter some **bold-face** characters by clicking the Bold button on the Formatting toolbar.

Bold

Type the characters, and then click the Bold button again to turn off the bold format.

Italic

Similarly, you can *italicize* text by clicking the Italic button on the Formatting toolbar, typing the characters, and then clicking the Italic button again.

In this example, shown in Figure 4-7, the document now consists of three paragraphs: a heading and two paragraphs of body text. Notice that if you insert or erase characters, Word moves all the following words within the same paragraph—if necessary—so that the text fits within the paragraph margins; this is one of the important properties of paragraphs. (You might want to experiment with it using the editing techniques given above.)

FIGURE 4-7.
An example Word document, before formatting.

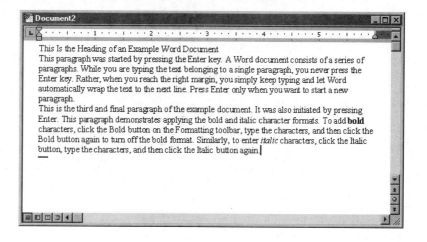

Microsoft Word

As you can see in Figure 4-7 on the preceding page, the document is not very attractive or even readable; it is difficult to distinguish both the heading from the body text, and one paragraph from the next. To improve this situation, the next step is to format the document—that is, to adjust the appearance of the document's characters and paragraphs.

To do this, choose the AutoFormat command from the Format menu. In the AutoFormat dialog box, make sure the AutoFormat Now and General Document options are selected and click the OK button.

Word will automatically format the entire document. Figure 4-8 shows the result of formatting the document shown in Figure 4-7.

FIGURE 4-8.

The example Word document of Figure 4-7 after automatic formatting.

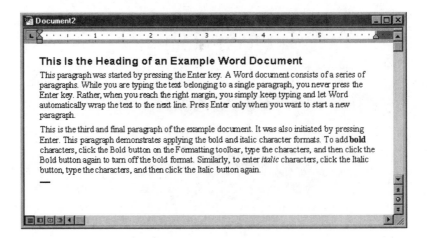

Word formatted the document by applying an appropriate *style* to each paragraph. A Word style contains a set of formatting features that is suitable for a particular type of text. The style that Word applied to the first paragraph (named "Heading 1") assigned the characters a large, bold font and added extra space above and below the paragraph. The style that Word assigned to the two paragraphs in the document body (named "Body Text") added space below the paragraphs to separate them. Styles are one of the most useful Word features. As you'll learn later in the book, you can manually apply styles to individual paragraphs or to blocks of characters, and you can even modify styles or create new ones.

As you'll also learn, you can apply to a paragraph various individual formats (such as centered text) that override the formats defined by the style.

You should now proofread your document. You could do it yourself, either on screen or using a paper printout, but why not have Word help? To have Word check your spelling and grammar, click the Spelling And Grammar button on the Standard toolbar. If Word finds a spelling or grammatical error, a dialog box will appear with suggestions and options for correcting the error.

Spelling
And
Grammar

(If Word doesn't check your grammar when you click the button, you can enable this function by choosing Options from the Tools menu, clicking the Spelling & Grammar tab in the Options dialog box, and turning on the Check Grammar With Spelling option.) Checking spelling and grammar will be discussed in detail in Chapter 9.

Print
Preview

Just before printing the document, you should check the appearance of the full printed page (or pages) by choosing the Print Preview command from the File menu, or clicking the Print Preview button on the Standard toolbar.

Figure 4-9 on the following page shows the example document (reduced to fit in the document window) as it is displayed by the Print Preview command. (You can close Print Preview by clicking the Close button or by pressing Escape.) To print the document using the default printer and print settings, simply click the Print button on the Print Preview or Standard toolbar.

Print

Finally, save your document by choosing the Save command from the File menu, or by clicking the Save button on the Standard toolbar.

Save

The first time you save a new document, Word will display the Save As dialog box, which lets you choose the name and location of the file in which the document is to be stored. When working on a longer document, you should save the document frequently, rather than waiting until you have printed it. Remember this: If the power goes out or your computer fails, you'll lose all the work you have done since the last time you saved!

FIGURE 4-9.
The example document from Figure 4-8 as displayed by the Print Preview command on the File menu.

Click here to return the document to Normal view.

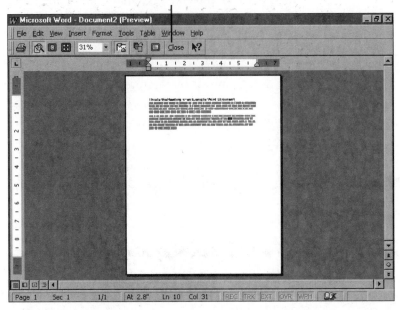

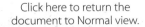

⭐ **TIP**

Protect Your Documents with AutoRecover
You can have Word automatically save information on the contents of your document at regular intervals. If Word is inadvertently terminated, it will use this information to restore the document. To set this feature, choose Options from the Tools menu, click the Save tab, turn on the Save AutoRecover Info Every option, and enter the desired number of minutes between saves into the adjacent text box.

You can now close your document by choosing the Close command from the File menu, or by simply clicking the Close box in the document window. (See Figure 4-1, page 108.) You can later reopen the document by choosing the Open command from the File menu, or by choosing the Open Office Document command from the Windows 95 Start menu, or by using the Office Shortcut Bar. If you have worked with the file recently, you can also reopen it by choosing the filename from the list at the bottom of the File menu.

❓ **SEE ALSO**

For more information about creating, opening, saving, and closing documents from within an Office application, see Chapter 3, "Managing Documents: From Your Hard Disk to the Internet."

To exit Word, you can choose the Exit command from the File menu or simply click the Close box in the upper right corner of the Word window.

Creating Web Pages

If you installed the "Web Page Authoring (HTML)" component of Word when you ran the Setup program, you can use Word to create pages that can be displayed on the World Wide Web of the Internet.

First, you can easily convert an ordinary Word document to a Web page. For example, you could convert the document you created in this chapter to a Web page so that you could post it on your Web site. To do this, open the document, choose the Save As HTML command from the File menu, and in the Save As HTML dialog box specify a name for the file and the location where you want to store it. Word will convert the document file to an HTML (hypertext markup language) file, which is the standard format required for Web pages, and it will assign this file the HTML extension. You then need to upload the HTML file to your Web site, using the appropriate procedure for the Internet server on your network or for your Internet service provider.

Also, you can create a new document that's designed specifically as a Web page. To do this, choose the New command from the File menu, and click on the Web Pages tab of the New dialog box. Then either double-click the Blank Web Page icon to create your own Web page from scratch, or double-click the Web Page Wizard icon to run a wizard that will assist you in designing your Web page. Word will then open either a blank Web page or—if you ran the wizard—a Web page with preliminary contents, and it will provide a set of menu and button commands that are appropriate for adding the text, graphics, and hyperlinks that you want to include in your page. For an explanation of hyperlinks, see the section "Inserting and Navigating with Hyperlinks," page 161. (The new document will be based on a template named HTML, which provides commands, styles, and other features helpful for creating Web pages.) To save your page, choose the Save command from the File menu or click the Save button, and Word will automatically store the document in HTML format. (To save the file in a different format, choose the Save As or Save As Word Document command from the File menu instead.)

II

Microsoft Word

Changing the Way You Display Documents

Word provides many options that affect the way you display and work with documents. Table 4-1 on the following page lists display options, briefly describes each, and identifies the chapters where you can find fuller discussions of each one.

TABLE 4-1. Display Options

View	Description	Chapter
Normal	General-purpose view for efficient editing and formatting. Does not show margins, headers, or footers.	4
Page Layout	Displays characters and text as they will appear on the printed page, including margins, headers, and footers. All editing and formatting commands are available, but Word runs somewhat more slowly than in Normal view.	10
Online Layout	Displays document in a format that is easy to read on the screen. The text is shown without page breaks, small fonts are enlarged, and you can assign an attractive background design to the window.	10
Print Preview	Displays an image of one or more printed pages, and lets you adjust the page setup.	10
Outline	Shows the organization of the document. Lets you view various levels of detail and rapidly rearrange document text.	12
Master Document	Displays the outline view for a *master document* along with the tools for managing its subdocuments. A master document consists of a collection of separate Word documents (the subdocuments), and is useful for managing a long manuscript, such as a book.	12

To switch into any view except Print Preview, choose the appropriate option from the View menu:

To switch into Print Preview, choose the Print Preview command from the File menu, or click the Print Preview button on the Standard toolbar. Also, you can switch into Normal, Online Layout, Page Layout, or Outline view by clicking a button at the left end of the horizontal scroll bar.

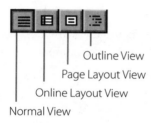

Outline View

Page Layout View

Online Layout View

Normal View

In addition to changing the basic view, you can also set a variety of options that affect the way a document is displayed within the current view. (Some of these options affect only certain views.)

First, you can change the size of the characters or graphics on the screen by using the Zoom Control on the Standard toolbar

or by choosing Zoom from the View menu. With either method, you specify the character size you want as a percentage of the normal size. Zooming is available in all views. Rest assured that zooming does *not* change the actual size of the text or graphics that are printed and stored in the document; rather, it affects only the level of magnification at which you view the document in the window.

? SEE ALSO

For information about other ways to customize Word, see Chapter 14, "Automating and Customizing Word."

Second, you can expand the Word workspace to fill the entire screen and hide all menus, toolbars, and other tools by choosing the Full Screen command from the View menu (the menu bar will appear, however, if you move the mouse pointer to the top of the screen). This command also affects all views. To restore the normal Word window, press the Escape key or click the Close Full Screen button that Word displays on its own toolbar:

II

Microsoft Word

Finally, you can set a variety of viewing options by choosing Options from the Tools menu and clicking the View tab. The particular options you can set depend on the current document view; Figure 4-10 shows the options for the Normal document view.

FIGURE 4-10.
Setting view options through the Options command on the Tools menu.

For an explanation of a particular view option, click this Help button and then click the option.

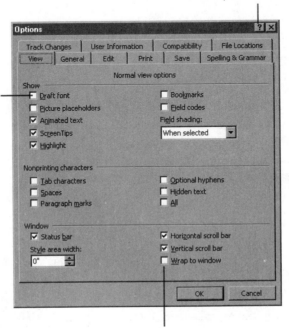

This option (available in Normal, Outline, and Master Document views only) causes Word to display a uniform font without formatting (formatted characters are merely underlined). This can speed up your editing and make it easier to read the document on the screen.

This option (not available in Page Layout view or Print Preview) causes Word to extend all lines of text to the right window border, rather than displaying them as they will be broken on the printed page. This lets you see more of the document text in the window.

 **TIP**

Prevent Eyestrain with the Blue Background, White Text Option
You can have Word display document text in white characters on a blue background by clicking the General tab in the Options dialog box and turning on the Blue Background, White Text item. This option affects all views except Print Preview, and can help prevent eyestrain (some Windows users find looking at a white screen similar to trying to read the wattage on a burning light bulb).

CHAPTER 5

Entering and Editing Text in a Word Document

Now that you know the basics of running Word, this chapter focuses on the *content* of a Word document—that is, the characters, words, sentences, and paragraphs that compose a document. You'll learn about the many ways to add, edit, and find document text. The next chapter focuses on the *format* of a Word document—that is, the appearance of the characters and paragraphs. These two topics are treated separately to make your learning task easier, not to imply that you must finish editing the entire document before you begin formatting it. Typically, you'll use formatting techniques *as* you are entering and editing the text.

Entering Text

As you learned in Chapter 4, to enter text you simply move the insertion point to the location you want in the document and type the text. (The methods you can use for moving the insertion point are discussed in the "Moving the Insertion Point" section of this chapter, page 138.) Word provides two editing modes: *Insert* and *Overtype*. In Insert mode (the most common mode), any existing characters beyond the insertion point are moved ahead in the document as you type. In Overtype mode, the new characters you type replace any existing characters. When Overtype mode is active, the OVR indicator in the status bar is darkened. To switch between the two modes, double-click the OVR indicator.

> **Create a New Line Within a Paragraph by Pressing Shift+Enter**
>
> To create a new line within a paragraph, press Shift+Enter. "Why not just press Enter and create a new paragraph?" you might ask. Some paragraph formatting affects only the first or last line in the paragraph, such as an initial indent or additional space above or below the paragraph. By pressing Shift+Enter, you can create a new line without introducing this formatting.

As you also learned in Chapter 4, you press Enter to create a new paragraph. Word marks the end of each paragraph by inserting a *paragraph mark*. A paragraph mark (¶) is one of the nonprinting characters that may be contained in a Word document. Nonprinting characters never appear on the final printed copy of the document. Normally, they are also invisible on the screen. You can, however, make them visible on the screen by clicking the Show/Hide ¶ button on the Standard toolbar.

Show/Hide ¶

The following is an example of some document text on the screen after nonprinting characters have been made visible:

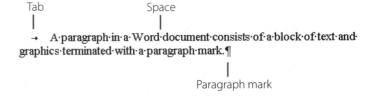

> ## ⓧ CAUTION
>
> Avoid deleting a paragraph mark unintentionally. (It can be deleted whether or not it is visible.) Doing so will merge the paragraphs on either side of the mark, and any paragraph formatting assigned to the second paragraph will be lost. (Paragraph formatting will be discussed in the next chapter.)

You can also display or hide specific nonprinting characters by choosing Options from the Tools menu, clicking the View tab, if it is not already selected, and turning on the appropriate options in the Nonprinting Characters area.

Inserting Special Characters

You can use the Symbol command on the Insert menu to insert into your text a variety of symbols and foreign characters that you won't find on your keyboard. For example, if you want to add a copyright symbol (©), choose Symbol from the Insert menu, and complete the Symbol dialog box, as shown in Figure 5-1. The symbol will appear in your document at the position of the insertion point, just as if you had typed it. You can leave the Symbol dialog box open while you work in your document. After you've inserted the symbols you need, click the Close button to close the dialog box.

The Symbol dialog box displays all the characters belonging to the font selected in the Font list at the top of the dialog box. If you don't immediately see the symbol you want, you may be able to find it by selecting various fonts. Note that the (Normal Text) item at the top of the Font list displays the characters common to all standard text fonts (such as Times New Roman and Courier New). Also, if you click the Special Characters tab in the Symbol dialog box, Word will display some additional characters that you can insert.

FIGURE 5-1.

Inserting the copyright symbol using the Symbol command on the Insert menu.

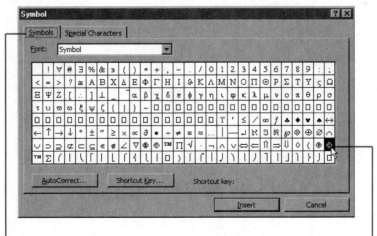

1 Click the Symbols tab, if not already selected.   **2** Double-click here to insert ©.

Many of the symbols have shortcut keys assigned to them. Word displays the available shortcut keys in the Symbol dialog box (on the Special Characters tab, and on the Symbols tab if you choose the (Normal Text) font). You can press the shortcut keys to quickly insert a symbol without opening the Symbol dialog box. For example, you can insert the copyright symbol by pressing Alt+Ctrl+C, and you can insert the foreign character á by pressing Ctrl+' and then typing *A*.

> **Set Up Shortcut Keys for Symbols You Frequently Use**
>
> You can define your own shortcut key for a symbol by opening the Symbol dialog box, clicking the symbol, and then clicking the Shortcut Key button.
>
> You can also define a character or group of characters—such as "(ae)"—that Word will *automatically* replace with a specified symbol such as æ. To do this, select the symbol in the Symbol dialog box and click the AutoCorrect button. The AutoCorrect feature will be discussed later in the chapter (in the section "Using the AutoCorrect Feature," page 135).

Finally, you can insert the current date and time into your document by choosing Date And Time from the Insert menu, and in the Date And Time dialog box choosing the desired format. (See Figure 5-2.)

FIGURE 5-2.
Inserting the current date and time using the Date And Time command on the Insert menu.

Click on the desired format.

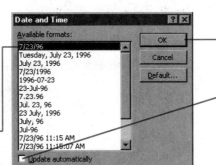

Click OK to insert the date into your document.

If you turn on the Update Automatically option, Word will update the date and time whenever you print the document; otherwise, the date and time will remain the same as when you inserted it.

Automatic Writing

This section is not about a spiritualist activity, but rather discusses several ways that you can have Word automatically insert text into your document.

Using the Repeat Command

First, if you have just typed some text, you can have Word place that *same* text at any location in a document as follows:

1 Type the original text.

2 Move the insertion point to the location where you want to repeat the text (in the same or in a different document).

3 Issue the Repeat command by choosing Repeat Typing from the Edit menu, or by pressing the Ctrl+Y key combination or the F4 key. Word will automatically insert the text that you originally typed. You can issue the Repeat command repeatedly to insert multiple copies of this text.

The Repeat Typing command reinserts all text that you have typed since the last time you performed any editing or formatting action *other than* simply moving the insertion point. If you don't like the result, you can reverse it by immediately choosing Undo Typing from the Edit menu, pressing Ctrl+Z, or clicking the Undo button on the Standard toolbar. (The Undo command will be described later in the chapter.)

> The Repeat command repeats *any* editing or formatting action, not simply text that you've typed. Word indicates the action that will be repeated in the caption for the Repeat command on the Edit menu. For example, if you have deleted a word (by pressing Ctrl+Del), the menu caption will read Repeat Delete Word and choosing the command will delete another word. As explained later in the chapter, this command will also *redo* an action that you have just reversed by using the Undo command.

Using the AutoText Feature

A second way to automate the insertion of text is to use the AutoText feature, which allows you to save commonly used blocks of text (or graphics) as *AutoText entries* and lets you quickly insert one of these blocks wherever you need it.

To create an AutoText entry, do the following:

1 Type into a document the block of text that you want to save. You should type the text into a paragraph that has the same style as the paragraphs into which you will later insert the text (styles are discussed in Chapter 6); the AutoText entry you create will be linked to this paragraph style (as you'll see later, this allows Word to list entries that are relevant to the style of the paragraph you are working on.)

2 *Select* (that is, highlight) the block of text. One way to select text is to hold down the Shift key while pressing the appropriate arrow key. Selection methods are discussed later in the chapter.

3 Point to AutoText on the Insert menu, and choose New from the submenu that appears. Alternatively, you can simply press Alt+F3. Word will display the Create AutoText dialog box.

4 Type a name for your AutoText entry into the text box and click OK. (Word proposes a name based on the selected text, but you'll probably want to invent a name of your own.) Make the name short because you'll need to type it every time you insert the entry. Note that if you type the name of an existing entry, Word will ask whether you want to redefine that entry; click Yes to replace the original text for the entry or No to choose a new name.

Figure 5-3 shows an example.

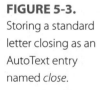

FIGURE 5-3.
Storing a standard letter closing as an AutoText entry named *close*.

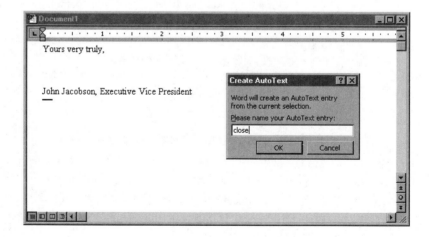

After you create an AutoText entry, it will be stored permanently. You can *insert* an AutoText entry in a document as follows:

1 Place the insertion point at the position in your document where you want to insert the text.

2 Type the name of the AutoText entry as a separate word. This means that you must type the name at the beginning of a line or following a space, tab, or punctuation symbol.

A Shortcut for Inserting AutoText Entries

If the Show AutoComplete Tip For AutoText And Dates option is enabled, as you begin typing an AutoText entry name into a document, Word will display the entry text (or part of the text) in a box near the insertion point. You can then insert the text by simply pressing Enter or F3, without typing the complete entry name. To turn this option on or off, point to AutoText on the Insert menu and choose the AutoText command from the submenu that appears. (Word will display the AutoText tab, which is discussed in the following section.)

Note that the AutoComplete option will also work whenever you begin typing the current date into a document.

3 Press F3 or Ctrl+Alt+V. If the AutoComplete tip is shown, you can also simply press Enter. Word will immediately replace the entry name with the entry text. For example, if you had defined the AutoText entry shown in Figure 5-3, at the end of a letter you could simply press Enter, type the word *close*, and then press Enter or F3:

Press Enter or F3 here.

Word would replace the word *close* with your standard letter closing:

Yours very truly,

John Jacobson, Executive Vice President

As an alternative to steps 2 and 3, you can point to AutoText on the Insert menu. Word will display a submenu listing the names of all

Microsoft Word

AutoText entries that are linked to the style of the paragraph currently containing the insertion point. Simply choose the entry you want from this list. (If *no* entries are linked to the style, the list will display *all* Autotext entries, which will include a set of predefined entries provided by Word. You can always force Word to display all AutoText entries by holding down the Shift key when you choose the AutoText item on the Insert menu.)

TIP

Change an AutoText Entry

To *modify* the contents of an AutoText entry (without having to delete it and reenter it), simply insert the text in the document (using one of the methods just described), make the changes you want, and then use the procedure given at the beginning of this section to save the text again as an AutoText entry, using its original name. You must answer *yes* when Word asks if you want to redefine the entry.

Using the AutoText Tab of the AutoCorrect Dialog Box

You can use the AutoText tab of the AutoCorrect dialog box to create AutoText entries, to view their contents, or to delete them. You can open this tab using *either* of the following methods:

- Point to AutoText on the Insert menu and choose the AutoText command from the submenu that pops up.

- Choose AutoCorrect from the Tools menu and click the AutoText tab in the AutoCorrect dialog box. (The other tabs in the AutoCorrect dialog box will be discussed later in the book.)

To create an AutoText entry, do the following:

1 Select the document text you want to save.

2 Open the AutoText tab using one of the methods given above.

3 Type a name for the AutoText entry into the Enter AutoText Entries Here box. Note that if you type the same name as an existing entry, the existing entry will be overwritten.

4 In the Look In list select the template in which you want to store the AutoText entry. If you select All Active Templates or Normal.dot (Global Template), the entry will be stored in the Normal template and *all* Word documents will have access to it. (You'll only see the DOT extension if you've chosen to display file extensions in Windows 95.) If the current document is attached to a template other than Normal and if you select the name of that template in the Look In list, then the entry will be stored in the attached template and it will be available *only* to documents attached to this same template. (Chapter 7 explains how templates are attached to documents, and shows how to copy AutoText entries from one template to another as well as how to rename them.) Note that your selection in this list will also affect the location in which AutoText entries are stored when you create entries using the New command on the AutoText submenu, as described in the previous section.

5 Click the Add button.

Figure 5-4 shows the completed AutoText tab just before clicking the Add button.

FIGURE 5-4.
Creating an AutoText
entry using the
AutoText tab of
the AutoCorrect
dialog box.

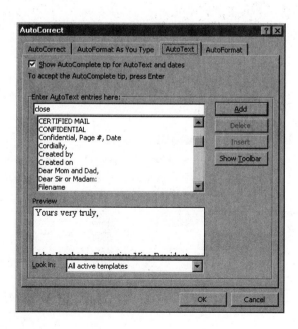

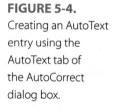

To view the contents of an AutoText entry, or to delete an entry, do the following:

1 Open the AutoText tab using one of the methods given above.

? SEE ALSO

For information on loading templates, see "Changing the Template Attached to a Document and Loading Global Templates," page 221.

2 Select a template in the Look In list. Word will list only the AutoText entries that are stored in the template you select. Note that if you choose All Active Templates, Word will list all entries stored in the Normal template, in the template attached to the document (if other than Normal), *and* in any other loaded templates. Note that if you select All Active Templates or Normal, Word will include the predefined entries that are provided by Word.

Your selection in the Look In list will also affect the AutoText entries that are subsequently displayed on the AutoText submenu of the Insert menu, as well as those that are displayed through the AutoText toolbar that is described in the next section.

? SEE ALSO

For a discussion on formatting, see Chapter 6, "Formatting a Word Document." For instructions on printing AutoText entries, see "Previewing and Printing Documents," page 330. For information on using a special AutoText entry named *Spike* to move blocks of text, see "Using the Spike," page 150.

3 Select the name of an AutoText entry in the Enter AutoText Entries Here list. You can now do one of the following:

- You can view the current contents of the entry in the Preview area.

- You can delete the entry by clicking the Delete button.

- You can insert an entry into your document by clicking the Insert button. (This is a useful feature because it allows you to preview the contents of any entry immediately before inserting it.)

Displaying the AutoText Toolbar

If you use AutoText frequently, you can save time by displaying the AutoText toolbar, which is shown in Figure 5-5. To display it, point to

FIGURE 5-5.
Using the AutoText toolbar.

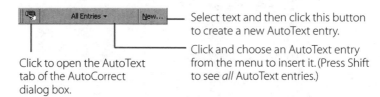

Select text and then click this button to create a new AutoText entry.

Click and choose an AutoText entry from the menu to insert it. (Press Shift to see *all* AutoText entries.)

Click to open the AutoText tab of the AutoCorrect dialog box.

Toolbars on the View menu *or* right-click the menu bar or a toolbar, and then choose the AutoText option from the submenu that pops up. You can also display the toolbar by clicking the Show Toolbar button on the AutoText tab.

 **NOTE**

> If you have defined AutoText entries for the style of the paragraph currently containing the insertion point, the middle button on the AutoText toolbar will be labeled with the name of the paragraph style rather than All Entries. When you click this button, the drop-down menu will display only the AutoText entries linked to that style. If you want to see all AutoText entries, hold down the Shift key while clicking on the button.

Using the AutoCorrect Feature

A final way to automate text insertion is to use the AutoCorrect feature, which is similar to the AutoText feature. The primary difference between the two is that after you have typed the name of an AutoCorrect entry followed by a space or a punctuation symbol, Word *automatically* replaces the name with the entry text; you *don't* need to press a special key or issue a command. Thus, you might want to use Auto-Correct rather than AutoText for text that you insert frequently. Also, you can have the AutoCorrect facility perform certain general text replacements; for example, you can have it automatically capitalize the first letter of a sentence if you fail to do so.

The following are the steps for enabling AutoCorrect text replacements, and for defining one or more AutoCorrect entries:

1 If the text you want to save in the AutoCorrect entry has already been entered in a document, select it. (This step is optional because you can type the text later.)

2 Choose AutoCorrect from the Tools menu to open the Auto-Correct dialog box, and then click the AutoCorrect tab if this tab isn't already displayed.

3 Make sure the Replace Text As You Type option is turned on to activate the AutoCorrect entries.

II

Microsoft Word

4 Type a name for the AutoCorrect entry you want to define in the Replace text box.

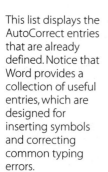

NOTE

Make sure that the name you choose for an AutoCorrect entry is *not* a word that you might need to type into a document; for example, if you assigned the name *a*, each time you tried to enter *a* into a document, Word would insert the associated AutoCorrect entry.

5 If you selected text prior to opening the AutoCorrect dialog box, that text will already be contained in the With text box. If you didn't select text, type the text for the entry into the With box.

6 Click the Add button to define the new entry and add it to the list. Figure 5-6 shows the AutoCorrect dialog box after you have defined a new entry.

FIGURE 5-6.
The AutoCorrect dialog box after adding a new entry named *g*.

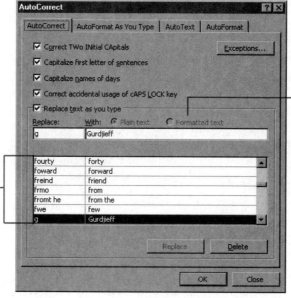

If you selected text, you can select the Formatted Text option to have Word save the text's formatting as part of the entry.

This list displays the AutoCorrect entries that are already defined. Notice that Word provides a collection of useful entries, which are designed for inserting symbols and correcting common typing errors.

To define an additional entry, repeat steps 4 through 6. When you are finished adding AutoCorrect entries, click Close to register your changes and exit the dialog box.

⭐ TIP

Two Ways to Create Symbols Quickly

As mentioned previously in the chapter (in "Inserting Special Characters," page 127), you can open the AutoCorrect dialog box from within the Symbol dialog box, which allows you to quickly create an AutoCorrect entry containing a specific symbol.

You can also define AutoCorrect entries while you are using the Word spelling checker (described in "Checking Your Spelling," page 265). These entries will automatically correct spelling errors, as well as insert symbols you often use.

After you have performed these steps, Word will immediately replace the name of an AutoCorrect entry with the entry text, whenever you type the name followed by a space, tab, return (that is, pressing the Enter key), or punctuation character. For example, if you had defined the entry shown in Figure 5-6, typing *g* followed by a space would cause Word to erase the *g* and insert *Gurdjieff.* Remember that you must type the entry name as a separate word; that is, the word must immediately follow a space, tab, return, or punctuation character, or be typed at the beginning of a line.

Notice also that you can have Word perform several kinds of general text replacements by turning on one or more of the four options at the top of the AutoCorrect dialog box. For example, if you select the first option (Correct TWo INitial CApitals), whenever you type a word beginning with two capital letters (and the rest of the characters are lowercase), Word will automatically correct the error by converting the second letter to lowercase. If you turn on the second option (Capitalize First Letter Of Sentences), Word will automatically capitalize the first letter of a sentence if you fail to do so.

To add or delete exceptions to the Capitalize First Letter Of Sentences and Correct TWo INitial CApitals options, click the Exceptions button in the AutoCorrect dialog box. Word will display the dialog box shown on the following page.

II

Microsoft Word

On this tab, you add or delete exceptions to the Capitalize First Letter Of Sentence option.

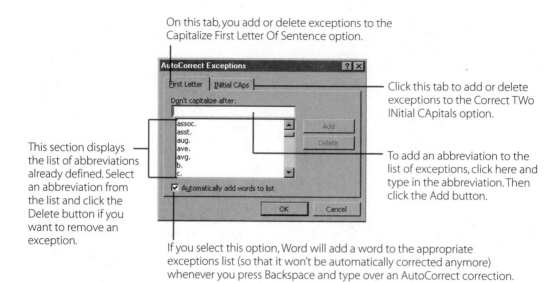

Click this tab to add or delete exceptions to the Correct TWo INitial CApitals option.

This section displays the list of abbreviations already defined. Select an abbreviation from the list and click the Delete button if you want to remove an exception.

To add an abbreviation to the list of exceptions, click here and type in the abbreviation. Then click the Add button.

If you select this option, Word will add a word to the appropriate exceptions list (so that it won't be automatically corrected anymore) whenever you press Backspace and type over an AutoCorrect correction.

Moving the Insertion Point

After you've created a document, the first step in editing it is to move the insertion point to the position where you want to make the change. Word gives you numerous ways to move quickly through your documents, to suit your fancy. This section describes some of the basic ways to move the insertion point.

 SEE ALSO

For advanced methods to navigate through a document, see "Other Ways to Navigate Through a Document," page 156.

The easiest way to move the insertion point to a document position that is currently visible in the window is to simply click on the position, using the left (primary) mouse button:

Clicking the left mouse button will place the insertion point here.

Move the I-beam mouse pointer to the desired position of the insertion point and click.

You can use the keys or key combinations in Table 5-1 to move the insertion point to *any* position in a document:

TABLE 5-1.
Shortcut Key Combinations for Moving the Insertion Point

Use This Key or Key Combination	To Move
←	To previous character
→	To next character
↑	One line up
↓	One line down
Ctrl+←	Backward through the document one word at a time
Ctrl+→	Forward through the document one word at a time
Ctrl+↑	Backward through the document one paragraph at a time
Ctrl+↓	Forward through the document one paragraph at a time
Home	To beginning of line
End	To end of line
Ctrl+Home	To beginning of document
Ctrl+End	To end of document
Page Up	One window up (that is, move up a distance equal to the height of the window)
Page Down	One window down

Microsoft Word

⭐ **TIP**

You can use the scroll bars (usually the vertical one) to temporarily view another part of your document. To quickly return to your original position, simply press an arrow key. Word will automatically scroll back to the position of the insertion point (which is *not* moved when you use a scroll bar).

FIGURE 5-7.
The effects of clicking on various scroll bar positions to scroll through a document (drag rather than click, where indicated). In this figure, the label *scroll one window* means scrolling a distance equal to the current size of the document window, in the direction you choose.

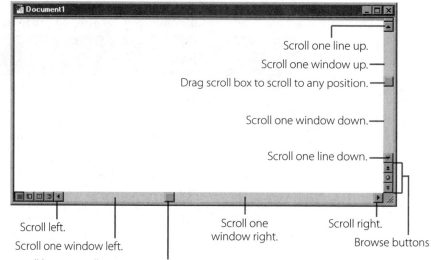

Scroll one line up.

Scroll one window up.

Drag scroll box to scroll to any position.

Scroll one window down.

Scroll one line down.

Scroll left.

Scroll one window left.

Scroll one window right.

Scroll right.

Browse buttons

Drag scroll box to scroll to any position.

You can also use the horizontal and vertical scroll bars to bring text into view in a document window, as shown in Figure 5-7. If either scroll bar is not currently displayed, you can make it visible by choosing Options from the Tools menu, clicking the View tab, and turning on the Horizontal Scroll Bar or the Vertical Scroll Bar option. Note that when you view text using a scroll bar, the insertion point is *not* moved; in fact, after scrolling, the insertion point might not even be visible in the window. To move the insertion point, scroll and then click the position where you want the insertion point to appear.

? **SEE ALSO**

For information about searching for text, see "Finding and Replacing Text," page 151.

Editing Text

Once you have moved the insertion point to the position in your document where you want to make a change, the next step is to apply a Word editing command. Word gives you an assortment of editing commands for deleting, replacing, copying, moving, or capitalizing text.

To begin, you can delete a limited number of characters by simply positioning the insertion point and pressing one of the following keys or key combinations:

Press These Keys	To Delete
Del	The character after the insertion point
Ctrl+Del	Through the end of the word containing (or following) the insertion point
Backspace	The character before the insertion point
Ctrl+Backspace	Through the beginning of the word containing (or preceding) the insertion point

You can hold down any of these keys or key combinations to delete several characters or words. Remember that you can choose Undo from the Edit menu, press Ctrl+Z, or click the Undo button to restore text that you have deleted by mistake. If you held down the Backspace key to delete a group of characters, the Undo command will restore all of them. If you used any of the other deleting keys or key combinations, Undo will restore only the most recently deleted character or word. (You can then repeat the Undo command to restore additional characters or words.)

Selecting Text

Most of the Word editing techniques—as well as the formatting techniques that will be discussed in the next chapter—require that you first *select* or *highlight* a block of text (which is known as a *selection*) and then *issue a command* that affects that block of text. Selecting text lets you quickly modify blocks of text—even entire documents.

This text is selected. In Word, you *first* select text and *then* act on the selected text.

For example, you could first select a block of text and then press the Delete key. Notice that having a selection changes the usual effect of the Delete command—it erases an entire block of characters rather than erasing a single space or character. Selecting text removes the normal insertion point; that is, at a given time a document has either a selection or an insertion point, never both. You can select text using either the keyboard or the mouse.

II

Microsoft Word

Selecting with the Keyboard

The basic method for selecting text with the keyboard is to simply hold down the Shift key and then press any of the keys or key combinations for moving the insertion point that were discussed in the section "Moving the Insertion Point," page 138. With the Shift key pressed, the keyboard command will select text rather than merely move the insertion point. For example, you can hold down Shift and an arrow key to extend the selection character-by-character or line-by-line in the direction you want.

Undoing and Redoing Editing and Formatting Actions

You can reverse the effect of your most recent editing or formatting action by pressing Ctrl+Z or by choosing Undo from the Edit menu. Clicking the Undo button on the Standard toolbar

has the same effect. If you repeat the Undo command, Word will undo your *next* most recent action. Consider, for example, that you type a word, then format a paragraph, and then delete a character. If you subsequently issue the Undo command three times, Word will first replace the character, then restore the paragraph to its original format, and then erase the word.

Also, as a shortcut for undoing multiple actions, you can click the down arrow next to the Undo button, drag the pointer down to highlight all the actions you want to undo, and then release the button:

1 Click here to display list of actions.

2 Select action(s) to undo.

(The actions are listed in order from the most recent to the least recent, and you can undo them only in this order.)

As you learned in the section "Using the Repeat Command," page 129, you can issue the Repeat command (by pressing Ctrl+Y or F4 or by choosing Repeat from the Edit menu) to perform again your most recent editing or formatting operation. If, however, your most recent operation was to undo an action using

---

Undoing and Redoing Editing and Formatting Actions *continued*

any of the methods just described, the Repeat command will *redo* the action (and in this case, the command on the Edit menu will be labeled Redo rather than Repeat). For example, if you delete a word and then press Ctrl+Z, the word will be restored; if you then press Ctrl+Y, the word will again be removed.

You can also redo an action by clicking the Redo button on the Standard toolbar:

As with the Undo button, you can click the adjoining down arrow and select the exact actions you want to redo. (Note that unlike the Ctrl+Y and F4 shortcut keys and the Repeat [Redo] Edit menu command, the Redo button can be used *only* to redo an action; it cannot be used to repeat an action.)

Table 5-2 summarizes the key combinations for selecting text. Keep in mind that these are not wholly unfamiliar commands; they simply combine the Shift key with the insertion point-moving keys or key combinations you already saw in Table 5-1, page 139.

TABLE 5-2.   Shortcut Keys for Extending a Selection

Press This Key or Key Combination	To Extend the Selection
Shift+←	Through the previous character
Shift+→	Through the next character
Shift+↑	One line up
Shift+↓	One line down
Shift+Ctrl+←	Through the beginning of the current word (or previous word if already at the beginning of a word)
Shift+Ctrl+→	Through the beginning of the next word
Shift+Ctrl+↑	Through the beginning of the current paragraph (or previous paragraph if already at the beginning of a paragraph)
Shift+Ctrl+↓	Through the end of the current paragraph

(continued)

II

Microsoft Word

TABLE 5-2. *continued*

Press This Key or Key Combination	To Extend the Selection
Shift+Home	Through the beginning of the line
Shift+End	Through the end of the line
Shift+Ctrl+Home	Through the beginning of the document
Shift+Ctrl+End	Through the end of the document
Shift+Page Up	One window up (that is, extend up a distance equal to the height of the window)
Shift+Page Down	One window down

An alternative way to select text using the keyboard is to press the F8 key or double-click the EXT indicator in the status bar to activate the *Extend mode*. (When the Extend mode is active, the EXT indicator is displayed in darker characters.) While working in the Extend mode, you can make selections by pressing any of the keys or key combinations from Table 5-2 *without the Shift key*. For example, you can select all characters through the end of the line by pressing F8 and then End. To cancel the Extend mode, either press the Escape key or double-click the EXT status bar indicator. (This will not remove the selection, but merely end the Extend mode.) Also, the Extend mode will be canceled *automatically* if you perform any editing or formatting action on the selected text.

 TIP

Use the F8 Key for Selection Shortcuts

You can press F8 repeatedly to select increasingly larger portions of your document. The first press activates the Extend mode, the second press selects the current word, the third press selects the current sentence, the fourth press selects the current paragraph, and the fifth press selects the entire document.

Also, you can quickly extend the selection through the next occurrence of a letter by pressing F8 and then typing the letter.

Finally, you can select the entire document by pressing Ctrl+A or choosing Select All from the Edit menu.

To *cancel* a selection—and display the insertion point—simply click at any position in the document or press an arrow key. (Remember, if you are in Extend mode, you first have to press Escape or double-click the EXT indicator on the status bar.)

Selecting with the Mouse

The basic technique for selecting with the mouse is simply to move the pointer to the beginning of the desired selection, press the left button, and then drag over the text or graphics that you want to select. If you reach a window border while dragging, Word automatically scrolls the document so that you can keep extending the selection.

> If the When Selecting, Automatically Select Entire Word option is turned on, dragging will select text word-by-word rather than character-by-character. That is, as the selection is extended, entire words will be added to the selection rather than individual characters. If you prefer to select text character-by-character, turn off this option. You can find this option on the Edit tab of the Options dialog box, opened by choosing Options from the Tools menu.

You can also select any amount of text as follows:

1 Click the position where you want to start the selection.

2 Hold down the Shift key while clicking on the position where you want to end the selection.

Table 5-3 lists some mouse shortcuts you can use to select various amounts of text:

TABLE 5-3. Mouse Shortcuts for Selecting Text

To Select	Do This
A word	Double-click the word.
A sentence	Hold down the Ctrl key while clicking within the sentence.
A line	Click in the selection bar next to the line.
Several lines	Drag down or up in the selection bar.

(continued)

II

Microsoft Word

TABLE 5-3. *continued*

To Select	Do This
A paragraph	Double-click in the selection bar next to the paragraph, *or* triple-click within the paragraph.
Several paragraphs	Double-click in the selection bar and then drag down or up.
The entire document	Triple-click in the selection bar or hold down the Ctrl key while clicking in the selection bar.

The *selection bar* is the area within the document window to the immediate left of the text. It's easy to tell when the mouse pointer is within the selection bar because the pointer changes to an arrow pointing up and to the right:

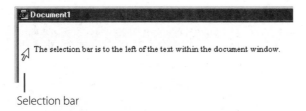

Selection bar

Finally, you can select a column of text by holding down the Alt key and dragging over the area you want to select:

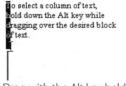

Drag with the Alt key held
down to select a column of text.

Pressing the Delete key with the selection shown above would erase the first character of each line.

To cancel the selection, either click at any position in the document or press an arrow key.

Editing the Selection

Once you have selected a block of text, you are ready to apply an editing or formatting command. This section describes the basic editing commands that you can apply to selections. As you begin using these techniques, keep in mind that you can reverse your editing action by issuing the Undo command, as described previously, even if the amount of text deleted or altered is large.

First, if the Typing Replaces Selection option is active, you can replace the selection by simply typing the new text. When you type the first letter, the entire selection is automatically deleted, and the new text you type is inserted in its place. (If Typing Replaces Selection is not active, the selected text is left in place, the selection is canceled, and the new text is inserted in front of the former selection.) To turn Typing Replaces Selection on or off, choose Options from the Tools menu and click the Edit tab, and then select or deselect the option.

To erase the selected text, simply press the Backspace key or the Delete key, or choose Clear from the Edit menu.

To change the case of the letters in the selection (that is, to lowercase, UPPERCASE, Sentence case, or Title Case), you can choose Change Case from the Format menu and click the desired capitalization option in the Change Case dialog box. (See Figure 5-8.) Alternatively, you can press Shift+F3—repeatedly if necessary—to switch among various capitalization styles.

FIGURE 5-8.
The Change Case dialog box.

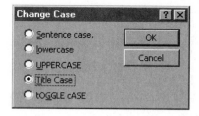

Moving and Copying Text

You can use the mouse to quickly move or copy text, as follows:

1   Select the text.

2 Place the mouse pointer over the selection (the pointer will change from an I-beam to an arrow), and hold down the left mouse button:

Other text. This text will be moved or copied. Other text.

SEE ALSO

For information about moving blocks of text in Outline view, see "Using Outline View to Organize Your Documents," page 358.

3 To move the text, simply drag it to its new location. To copy the text, hold down the Ctrl key while dragging with the mouse. The target location can be within the same document or within a different Word document. (To move or copy text to a different document, both document windows must be visible.)

To use this method, the Drag-And-Drop Text Editing option must be enabled. You'll find the option by choosing Options from the Tools menu and clicking the Edit tab.

⭐ **TIP**

> **Use Shortcut Keys to Move a Paragraph Up or Down**
> You can quickly select and move an entire paragraph with a single key combination. First, place the insertion point anywhere within the paragraph. Then, to move the paragraph up (that is, before the previous paragraph), press Shift+Alt+Up arrow. To move it down (that is, after the next paragraph), press Shift+Alt+Down arrow.

You can also move or copy text using the *Clipboard*, which is a Windows facility that temporarily stores text or graphics. The following is the procedure:

1 Select the text.

2 To move the text, choose Cut from the Edit menu or press Ctrl+X. This will *cut* the text—that is, remove it from the document and place it in the Clipboard.

To copy the text, choose Copy from the Edit menu or press Ctrl+C. This will *copy* the text—that is, leave the text in the document and place a copy of the text in the Clipboard.

3 Place the insertion point at the position where you want to insert the text that has been cut or copied to the Clipboard. The target location can be within the original document or within a different document.

4 Choose Paste from the Edit menu or press Ctrl+V. This will *paste* the text—that is, insert it into the document.

Cut
Copy
Paste

Word provides two additional ways to cut, copy, or paste text that also use the Clipboard. One method is to simply click the appropriate buttons on the Standard toolbar.

Another method to cut or copy a block of selected text is to click on the selection with the *right* mouse button and then choose Cut or Copy from the shortcut menu that is displayed:

Likewise, to paste the text, you can click on the target location with the *right* mouse button, and then choose Paste from the shortcut menu. To remove the shortcut menu without choosing a command, press the Escape key or click anywhere within the document.

One advantage of using the Clipboard is that when you paste, the text is not removed from the Clipboard. Therefore, you can paste repeatedly to insert several copies of the text. However, the text in the Clipboard will be lost if you perform another cut or copy operation in Word or in another program (the Clipboard is shared by all Windows-based programs). You can preserve the text currently in the Clipboard while moving or copying another block of text by using one of the techniques that don't use the Clipboard, such as dragging with the mouse (described above) or using the Spike (described below). Also, you can make a permanent copy of text that you want to insert repeatedly, by using the AutoText or AutoCorrect feature.

Another advantage of using the Clipboard is that you can use it to move or copy text or graphics between separate Windows-based programs. These techniques are discussed in Chapter 39, "Sharing Data Among Office Applications."

II

Microsoft Word

Setting Clipboard Options

Word provides two options that affect moving and copying text with the Clipboard. To set these options, choose Options from the Tools menu and click the Edit tab.

First, if the Use The INS Key For Paste option is enabled, you can paste by pressing the Insert key rather than pressing Ctrl+V or using one of the other methods described earlier.

Second, if the Use Smart Cut And Paste option is enabled, Word will remove extraneous spaces that remain after you cut text. For example, if you cut only the word *expression* from the following text,

(a parenthetical expression)

Word would automatically remove the space following *parenthetical*.

Using the Spike

The *Spike* is actually a special-purpose AutoText entry that is assigned the name "Spike." (It derives from the old days when newspaper editors would cut out blocks of lines from typed copy and impale them on a metal spike on their desk for possible later use.) You can use the Spike commands to remove several blocks of text from a document, and then insert all these blocks together at a single document location. The following is the usual procedure:

1 Select a block of text.

2 Press Ctrl+F3 to remove the block from the document and store it in the Spike.

3 Repeat steps 1 and 2 for each additional block of text you would like to add to the Spike.

4 Place the insertion point at the document position where you want to insert the text and press Shift+Ctrl+F3. All the blocks of text will appear in the document, and the Spike will be emptied. The blocks will be inserted in the order in which they were stored in the Spike.

In the first three steps of the preceding list, Word adds text to the Spike AutoText entry, and in step 4, Word inserts all the entry text into the document and deletes the entry. You can insert the text without deleting the entry by typing *Spike* and then pressing F3 (or by using any of the other AutoText insertion techniques discussed in "Using the AutoText Feature," page 129).

Finding and Replacing Text

You can quickly search for text, formats, or special items such as paragraph marks and graphics, using the Find command. The following is the basic procedure for using this command to conduct a search in Word:

1 If you want to limit the search to within a specific block of text, select the text.

2 Choose Find from the Edit menu or press Ctrl+F to open the Find tab of the Find And Replace dialog box. (See Figure 5-9.)

3 If you want to quickly perform a search using the options you set the previous time you used the Find command, proceed to step 4. If, however, you want to set one or more search options, click the More button to display the options—if they aren't already displayed—and select the ones you want. (See Figure 5-10 on the following page.) The search options are summarized in Table 5-4 on the following page. (If you want Word to search only within the block of text you selected in step 1, you must select Down or Up in the box next to Search. If the All option is selected, Word will search the entire document.)

FIGURE 5-9.
The Find tab of the Find And Replace dialog box, without displaying search options.

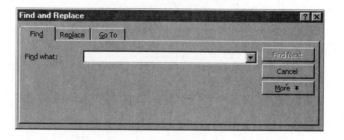

FIGURE 5-10.
The Find tab of the Find And Replace dialog box, displaying all options.

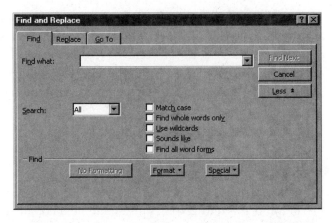

TABLE 5-4. **Search Options on the Find Tab of the Find And Replace Dialog Box**

Find Dialog Box Option	Effect
All (item in Search list)	Searches entire document (from insertion point to end of document, then from beginning of document down to insertion point), including headers, footers, annotations, and footnotes.
Down (item in Search list)	Searches from insertion point (or start of selection) to end of document (or selection), excluding headers, footers, annotations, and footnotes.
Up (item in Search list)	Searches from insertion point (or end of selection) to beginning of document (or selection), excluding headers, footers, annotations, and footnotes.
Match Case	Searches only for text that matches case of each letter in search text.
Find Whole Words Only	Excludes matching text that is part of another word (for example, if searching for *cat*, doesn't find *catatonic*).
Use Wildcards	Allows search text to include general symbols for matching text; for example, *, which matches a string of characters. To include these symbols in the Find What text box, click the Special button and select from the pop-up menu. (For more information, see the "wildcards search and replacing" topic in the Word online Help Index.)
Sounds Like	Searches for all text that sounds like the search text. For example, if the search text is *there*, finds *their* as well as *there*.
Find All Word Forms	Finds all forms of the search text. For example, if search text is *go*, finds *go*, *goes*, *gone*, and *went*. (This option will be available only if you installed the Find All Word Forms component of the Office Tools when you ran Setup.)

4 If you want to search for text (that is, specific words or phrases), enter that text into the Find What box. (You can click the down arrow to select previous search text.) To include a nonprinting character or other special feature in your search text (for example, a paragraph mark or a graphic), click the Special button and choose the appropriate item. (If the Special button or other button mentioned in these instructions isn't visible, click the More button to reveal it.)

5 If you want to search for a particular format or combination of formats, click the Format button, choose a formatting type, and specify the format in the dialog box that is displayed.

You can enter search text into the Find What text box *and* choose formatting. In this case, Word will search for text that matches your search text and has the specified formatting. To remove your formatting specifications, click the No Formatting button. (See the additional discussion on formatting following this list.)

6 Click the Find Next button to find each occurrence of the search text or formatting. Word will highlight the text it finds. You can edit your document while the Find And Replace dialog box is open; simply click the document to edit and then click anywhere in the Find And Replace dialog box to continue searching. (If the Find And Replace dialog box is covering the text, click on the title bar of the dialog box and drag it out of the way.)

7 To close the Find And Replace dialog box, click the Cancel button. After the dialog box is closed, you can continue to search for the *same* text or formatting using the keyboard. Each time you press Shift+F4, Word will search for the next occurrence of the text or formatting, moving in the direction you specified in the Find And Replace dialog box. Each time you press Ctrl+Page Down, Word will search for the next occurrence moving *down* in the document, and each time you press Ctrl+Page Up, Word will search for the next occurrence moving *up* in the document. You can also have Word search for the next occurrence moving either down or up in the document using the browse buttons at the bottom of the vertical scroll bar; these buttons are described later in the chapter (in the section "Using the Browse Buttons," page 159).

II

Microsoft Word

To choose formatting features (in step 5), you can also use the Formatting toolbar or press the appropriate formatting key combinations (such as Ctrl+B for the bold character format) when the insertion point is in the Find What text box. When searching for a particular format, you can search either for text that *has* the format, or for text that does *not* have the format. For example, you can select Bold (to search for text that is bold and meets other criteria) or Not Bold (to search for text that is not bold and meets other criteria), or you can turn off both bold options (to search for text that meets other criteria whether or not it is bold). The formatting that you have chosen is displayed below the Find What box. For more information on choosing formatting, see Chapter 6.

You can find *and* replace text or formatting using the Replace command. Like the Find command, Replace allows you to search for text, formatting, or a combination of text and formatting. You can replace the text that is found, change its formatting, or both replace the text and change its formatting. The following are the basic steps:

1 If you want to replace only within a specific block of text, select the text.

2 Choose Replace from the Edit menu or press Ctrl+H to open the Replace tab of the Find And Replace dialog box.

3 If you want to quickly perform a replace operation using the options you set the previous time you used the Replace command, proceed to step 4. If, however, you want to set one or more search options, click the More button to display the options—if they aren't already displayed—and select the ones you want. (See Figure 5-11.) These options are the same as those available in the Find dialog box and are summarized in Table 5-4, page 152. (If you want Word to search only within the block of text you selected in step 1, you must select Down or Up in the box next to Search. If the All option is selected, Word will search the entire document.)

4 If you want to search for particular text, type it in the Find What box. (You can click the down arrow to select previous search text.) To include a nonprinting character or other special feature in your search text (for example, a paragraph mark or a graphic), click the Special button and choose the appropriate item.

FIGURE 5-11.

The Replace tab of the Find And Replace dialog box, displaying all options.

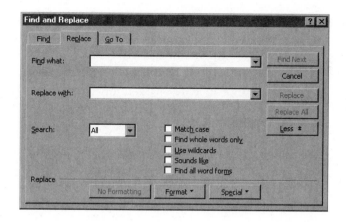

5 If you want to search for a particular format or combination of formats, make sure that the insertion point is within the Find What box. Then, click the Format button, choose a formatting type, and click options for the format you want in the dialog box that is displayed. You can also specify formatting using the Formatting toolbar or formatting key combinations.

6 If you want to replace the text that is found, type the replacement text in the Replace With box. To include a special character in the replacement text (such as a paragraph mark), click the Special button. Word will display only those special characters that are appropriate for replacement text.

7 If you want to change the formatting of the text that is found, make sure that the insertion point is within the Replace With box and choose the formatting you want, as described previously. Word will display the replacement format you have chosen below the Replace With box. Note that if you leave the Replace With box empty and do not choose replacement formatting, each block of text that is found will be deleted.

8 Either click the Replace All button to replace all occurrences of the text or formatting, without confirmation, or click the Find Next button to view and verify the first replacement.

SEE ALSO
For information on choosing formatting, see Chapter 6, "Formatting a Word Document."

9 If you clicked Find Next, Word will highlight the first matching text. You can now click Replace to replace the text or formatting and find the next occurrence, or click Find Next to leave the text unaltered and go on to the next occurrence. You can repeat this step until all text has been replaced, or you can click Close to close the dialog box and stop the process. (The Cancel button is labeled Close after the first replacement.) Recall that you can leave the Find And Replace dialog box displayed while you manually edit the document. (You may have to move the Find And Replace dialog box out of the way by dragging its title bar.)

Other Ways to Navigate Through a Document

You've already learned how to move the insertion point within a document using simple keys or shortcut keys as well as the horizontal and vertical scroll bars (in the section "Moving the Insertion Point," page 138). In the following sections, you'll learn some additional ways to move through a document. These techniques are especially useful for larger documents.

Marking and Retrieving Text with Bookmarks

You can use Word's bookmarks to mark and then quickly return to specific positions in a document.

To mark a position in a document, you need to define a bookmark using the following method:

1 Place the insertion point at the position you want to mark or select a block of text to mark.

2 Choose Bookmark from the Insert menu, or press Ctrl+Shift+F5, to open the Bookmark dialog box.

3 Type an identifying name into the Bookmark Name box and click the Add button. See Figure 5-12.

FIGURE 5-12.

Defining a bookmark named *start* in the Bookmark dialog box.

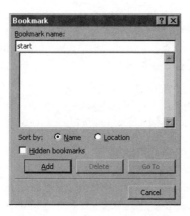

You can use this technique to mark any number of positions in a document. Note that you can make bookmarks visible by choosing Options from the Tools menu, clicking the View tab, and turning on the Bookmarks option (in the Show area); Word will then display a I symbol at the location of each bookmark or, if you marked a block of text, Word will place bracket markers around the bookmark.

> **NOTE**
>
> Bookmarks can be used for a variety of other purposes, some of which will be discussed later in the book—for example, defining cross-references and creating index entries that refer to a range of pages (creating indexes is discussed in Chapter 12, "Writing Long Documents").

> **SEE ALSO**
>
> For instructions on writing macros for quickly marking and returning to a document location, see "Recording and Running Macros," page 400.

To quickly move the insertion point to a position marked with a bookmark, open the Bookmark dialog box (choose Bookmark from the Insert menu or press Ctrl+Shift+F5), select the name that you assigned when you defined the bookmark (in step 3 above), and click the Go To button. Word will immediately move the insertion point to the marked position. You can also use the Go To command, discussed in the next section, to move to a particular bookmark.

> **TIP**
>
> If you select a block of text prior to defining a bookmark, the bookmark will be assigned to the entire selection. In this case, when you go to the bookmark, Word will select the text.

Microsoft Word

Using the Go To Command

You can use the Go To command to move the insertion point (or selection highlight) to a position marked by a bookmark or to one of a variety of other locations in a document. To issue the Go To command, choose Go To from the Edit menu, press Ctrl+G or F5, or double-click the left half of the status bar. Word will open the Go To tab of the Find And Replace dialog box (shown in Figure 5-13).

To go to one of the other types of targets, select the appropriate item in the Go To What list, and then enter the number or name for the particular target into the text box, which will be labeled appropriately—for example, Enter Page Number or Enter Bookmark Name. (For certain types of targets, such as bookmarks or comments, you can select the name of the target from a list.) For example, to go to a specific page in your document, select Page in the Go To What list and then type the page number in the Enter Page Number box. Likewise, to go to a particular document line, select Line and type the line number in the Enter Line Number box. (Note that for the Go To command, line numbering begins at 1 with the first line in the document and is incremented throughout the rest of the document. In contrast, the line number displayed on the status bar refers to the number of the line within the current page).

FIGURE 5-13.
Using the Go To command to move the insertion point to the *start* bookmark.

2 Type the name of the bookmark here or select the bookmark name from the list.

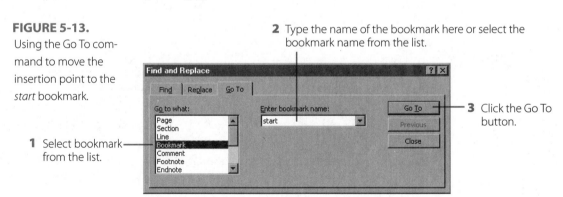

1 Select bookmark from the list.

3 Click the Go To button.

For some types of Go To targets—such as Page (if you don't enter a specific page number), Comment, or Footnote—buttons labeled Next and Previous are displayed in the dialog box. You can use these buttons to browse through the different instances of the target item. For example, if you select Comment in the Go To What list, clicking Next will take you to the *next* comment in the document (comments are explained in Chapter 11, "Working with Word in Workgroups").

Finally, you can enter a + or - followed by a number into the text box to move forward or back by a certain number of items. For example, if you have selected Page in the Go To What list, you can enter +4 into the Enter Page Number box to move forward by four pages.

You can leave the Find And Replace dialog box open while you work in your document. After you close it, you can press the Shift+F4 key to return to the last target you specified on the Go To tab (or to the *next* instance of a target if you were searching for an item that can have multiple occurrences, such as a footnote). Unfortunately, however, the Shift+F4 key is also used to repeat the last Find operation (as described in "Finding and Replacing Text," page 151). Therefore, if you perform a Find, you can no longer use Shift+F4 to return to your last Go To target. (Likewise, if you use the Go To command, you can no longer press Shift+F4 to repeat your last Find.) Note that you can also use the browse buttons, as discussed in the next section, to return to your previous Go To target (or to find additional instances of a multiple target).

NOTE

Another way to move through a document is to press Shift+F5, the Go Back key. Each time you press Shift+F5, Word moves the insertion point back to the location where you most recently added or edited text. You can move to three prior positions, at most; if you press the key a fourth time, the insertion point will cycle back to its original position.

Using the Browse Buttons

Word provides a set of browse buttons at the bottom of the vertical scroll bar (they are a new feature of Office 97). (See Figures 5-14 and 5-15 on the following page.) These convenient buttons allow you to quickly locate various types of objects within your documents. For example, if you select the Comment browse object, clicking the Next button will take you to the next comment found in the document and clicking Previous will take you to the previous one (comments are described in Chapter 11, "Working with Word in Workgroups").

FIGURE 5-14.
How to use the browse buttons.

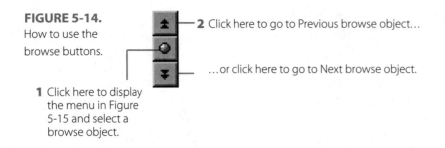

2 Click here to go to Previous browse object...

...or click here to go to Next browse object.

1 Click here to display the menu in Figure 5-15 and select a browse object.

FIGURE 5-15.
The different browse objects that you can select. This menu is displayed when you click the middle browse button (Select Browse Object).

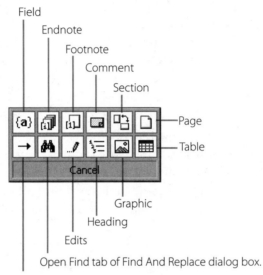

Field
Endnote
Footnote
Comment
Section
Page
Table
Graphic
Heading
Edits
Open Find tab of Find And Replace dialog box.
Open Go To tab of Find And Replace dialog box.

 NOTE

If you select the Edits browse object, clicking the Previous button has the same effect as pressing the Go Back key (Shift+F5) that was described in the prior note. Clicking the Next button moves you through your most recent edits in the opposite order.

Should you use the browse buttons rather than the Go To command? On the negative side, the browse buttons don't provide some of the targets offered by the Go To command (such as Line and Bookmark). Also, you can't specify a particular item number (for example, you can't go directly to page 25). On the plus side, the browse buttons are quicker to use. Also, if you have previously used the Find command or the Go To command, you can click the Next or Previous browse button to instantly go to the next or previous Find or Go To target.

Inserting and Navigating with Hyperlinks

A final navigation tool discussed in this chapter is the *hyperlink*, which is also a new feature provided with Office 97. A hyperlink connects a block of text in a Word document with another location; this location can reside in the same Word document, in another Word document, in a document or file created by another program, or even on the Internet. When you click a block of text that has been assigned a hyperlink, Word takes you immediately to the associated location.

To create a hyperlink, do the following:

1 Select the text to which you want to assign the hyperlink, or simply place the insertion point at the position in your document where you want Word to insert hyperlink text for you.

Insert
Hyperlink

2 Open the Insert Hyperlink dialog box (see Figure 5-16 on the following page) by choosing Hyperlink from the Insert menu, pressing Ctrl+K, or clicking the Insert Hyperlink button on the Standard toolbar.

3 In the Link To File Or URL box, enter the name of the target document (that is, the file you want to open when you click the hyperlink) or the address of a target site on the Internet (for example, *http://www.microsoft.com* to open Microsoft's home page on the World Wide Web). For help in locating a file, click the Browse button to the right of the Link To File Or URL box.

If the Use Relative Path For Hyperlink option is turned on, you can enter a file path that is relative to the current document (for example, *Book\Chapter 5.*) If this option is not turned on, you'll have to enter the full file path (for example, *C:\My Documents\Book\Chapter 5.*)

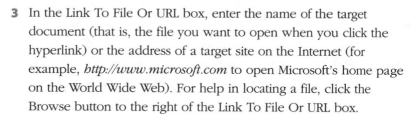

FIGURE 5-16.

Assigning a hyperlink to a block of Word text through the Insert Hyperlink dialog box.

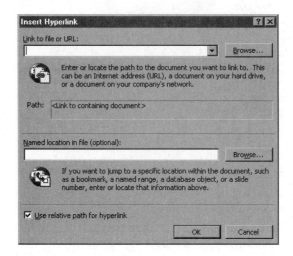

4 If you want the hyperlink to take you to a specific location within the target document, click the Browse button to the right of the Named Location In File (Optional) box and select the desired location from the choices listed. For example, if the target is a Word document, you select the name of the bookmark assigned to the location (you must create this bookmark before you define the hyperlink), and if the target document is an Excel workbook, you select a specific worksheet and possibly a named range within that worksheet.

5 Click OK.

If you selected text in step 1, Word will convert it to hyperlink text; if your didn't select text, Word will insert hyperlink text that consists of the file path or Internet address (that is, the URL) that you entered into the Link To File Or URL box in step 3. The hyperlink text is assigned the Hyperlink built-in character style, which initially creates blue, underlined text (if you want to change the appearance of your hyperlink text, you can modify this style). As you move the mouse pointer over the hyperlink text, it turns into a hand and Word displays the target document path or address in a box. To go to the target location associated with the hyperlink, simply click the underlined text:

This text has been assigned a hyperlink. To open the
document associated with this hyperlink, click here.

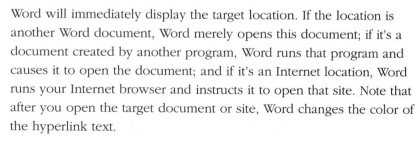

For information on identifying tobacco ash, see my <u>monograph</u> on the topic.

? SEE ALSO

For information on
using the Document
Map to rapidly move
through a document,
see "Browsing Through
Outline Headings,"
page 366.

Word will immediately display the target location. If the location is
another Word document, Word merely opens this document; if it's a
document created by another program, Word runs that program and
causes it to open the document; and if it's an Internet location, Word
runs your Internet browser and instructs it to open that site. Note that
after you open the target document or site, Word changes the color of
the hyperlink text.

When you first access a hyperlink, Word also automatically displays the
Web toolbar, which was described in Chapter 2 (you can display this
toolbar at any time by pointing to Toolbars on the View menu and choosing Web from the submenu that pops up, or by clicking the Web Toolbar
button on the Standard toolbar). Once you have used a hyperlink to
move to a different location one or more times, you can use the Web
toolbar to quickly move through the series of locations you have visited:

Web
Toolbar

Click here to move Back through series of hyperlink locations.

Click here to move Forward through series of hyperlink locations.

II

Microsoft Word

Formatting a Word Document

I n this chapter, you'll learn the basic techniques for *formatting* a document—that is, for adjusting the document's appearance. You'll learn how to format individual characters as well as how to format entire paragraphs of text.

This chapter presents formatting techniques, beginning with the most automated techniques and then moving on to methods that give you greater levels of formatting control. For many of the documents you create, you might be able to save time by using the more automated methods. For other documents, you might need to use techniques described later in the chapter to modify automatically applied formats or to achieve more exacting formatting results.

The next two chapters—Chapter 7, "Customizing Styles and Templates," and Chapter 8, "Arranging Text in Columns and Lists"—will provide additional information on formatting paragraphs.

In Word, you can also adjust the appearance of one or more entire pages. The appearance of a page is generally known as its *setup* rather than its format; this topic will be covered primarily in Chapter 10, "Designing Pages."

TIP

> As you learn the techniques presented in this chapter, keep in mind that you can reverse the effect of any formatting command by issuing the Undo command, using any of the methods discussed in the sidebar "Undoing and Redoing Editing and Formatting Actions," page 142.

Formatting Documents Automatically

After you have finished entering text into your document, you can use the AutoFormat command to enhance the appearance of the entire document. The AutoFormat command will apply a consistent and attractive set of formatting features to the text throughout the document. You can also have the AutoFormat command automatically make certain replacements in your document text—for example, it can replace straight quotes (" ") with curly quotes (" "), for a professionally typeset appearance. After using AutoFormat, you can quickly adjust the overall look of your document by using the Word Style Gallery.

TIP

Adjust AutoFormatting with Manual Formatting Techniques
Even if you're going to use the AutoFormat command, you might want to manually apply character formatting (such as bold or italic) to emphasize individual words or phrases as you enter text into your document. Also, after using Auto-Format, you might need to manually adjust some of the document's formatting. In either case, you can use the manual formatting techniques given later in the chapter.

AutoFormat formats your document by analyzing each paragraph and assigning it an appropriate paragraph *style*, which is a set of formatting features identified with a unique name. For instance, if the document begins with a paragraph consisting of a single line of text (which starts with a capital letter and has no ending period), AutoFormat assigns it the Heading 1 paragraph style, which contains formatting features that are appropriate for a document heading. These features typically include a relatively large font, bold characters, and additional space above and below the paragraph. Likewise, if a paragraph is a simple block of text comprising several lines, AutoFormat assigns it the Body Text style, which contains formatting features appropriate for normal paragraphs of text. These features typically include an average-size font, regular characters, and a small amount of extra space following the paragraph.

> **NOTE**
>
> The actual formatting features belonging to a particular style, such as Body Text, depend on the template that was used to create the document. Also, as you'll learn in Chapter 7, "Customizing Styles and Templates," the formatting features of a style can be modified.

Before using AutoFormat for the first time, you should specify how you want the command to work. To do this, choose AutoCorrect from the Tools menu, click the AutoFormat tab, and turn on the particular options you want. (See Figure 6-1.) The AutoFormat options are given in Table 6-1 on the following page.

FIGURE 6-1.
Setting AutoFormat options on the AutoFormat tab of the AutoCorrect dialog box.

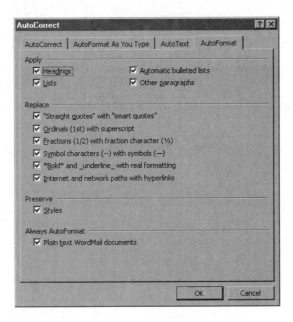

II

Microsoft Word

TABLE 6-1. AutoFormat Options

AutoFormat Option	Effect If Option Is Selected
Apply	
Headings	Document headings are assigned appropriate styles (Heading 1 through Heading 9, depending on the heading importance).
Lists	Simple or numbered lists are assigned appropriate list styles (List through List 5, depending on the level of indentation).
Automatic Bulleted Lists	Bulleted lists are assigned appropriate bulleted list styles (List Bullet through List Bullet 5, depending on the level of indentation). These styles automatically add bullet symbols such as • . (Existing bullet characters, such as *, are first removed.)
Other Paragraphs	Document paragraphs *other than* headings and lists are given appropriate styles (such as Body Text, Inside Address, or Salutation).
Replace	
"Straight Quotes" With "Smart Quotes"	Pairs of straight quotes (" " or ' ') are replaced with pairs of curly quotes (" " or ' '). Also replaces single straight quote (') with curly apostrophe (').
Ordinals (1st) With Superscript	Plain ordinal expressions (such as 1st, 2nd, and 3rd) are replaced with superscripted expressions (such as 1st, 2nd, and 3rd).
Fractions (1/2) With Fraction Character ($\frac{1}{2}$)	The fractional expressions 1/4, 1/2, and 3/4 are replaced with the fraction symbols $\frac{1}{4}$, $\frac{1}{2}$, and $\frac{3}{4}$.
Symbol Characters (--) With Symbols (—)	The symbol expressions (C), (R), (TM), and -- are replaced with the actual symbols ©, ®, ™, and —.
Bold And _Underline_ With Real Formatting	Characters enclosed in asterisks are formatted as bold and characters enclosed in underscore characters are formatted as underlined. For example, *help* would be converted to **help**. This option is useful for converting text-only e-mail messages (which typically emphasize words by surrounding them with * or _ characters) into formatted document text.
Internet And Network Paths With Hyperlinks	Internet and network paths are converted into actual hyperlinks that can be used to navigate to the sites. See the discussion on hyperlinks in the section "Inserting and Navigating with Hyperlinks," page 161.
Preserve	
Styles	Only paragraphs with the Normal or Body Text style are assigned new styles. Paragraphs with other styles are left unaltered.

TABLE 6-1. *continued*

AutoFormat Option	Effect If Option Is Selected
Always AutoFormat	
Plain Text WordMail Documents	Automatically applies AutoFormat to plain-text WordMail messages when you open them (for more information, look up "WordMail" in the Word online Help).

If you want to automatically format only a portion of your document, select that portion *before* you issue the AutoFormat command. To format the entire document, simply place the insertion point anywhere within the document.

To automatically format your document, perform the following steps:

1 Choose AutoFormat from the Format menu to open the AutoFormat dialog box.

4A If you want Word to quickly format the entire document or selection without giving you the opportunity to accept or reject each change, select this option.

4B If you want to review and possibly modify each formatting change before accepting it, select this option.

2 Select the item from this list (General Document, Letter, or Email) that best describes the document to help AutoFormat apply appropriate formatting.

3 Click the Options button if you want to change any of the AutoFormat options before proceeding with the formatting. (See Table 6-1.)

5 Click OK to start the formatting.

6 If you selected AutoFormat And Review Each Change, after the formatting is complete Word displays a different dialog box that is also labeled AutoFormat. Note that while this dialog box is displayed, you can scroll through the document to examine the changes.

II

Microsoft Word

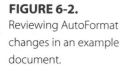

If you want to close the dialog box without reviewing the changes, click the Accept All button to retain all changes or click Reject All to cancel all changes.

Click the Review Changes button to review each of the formatting changes that Word made.

Click the Style Gallery button to change the overall formatting scheme, as described in the section "Using the Style Gallery," page 174.

7 If you clicked the Review Changes button, Word will mark the changes it made to the document and it will display the Review AutoFormat Changes dialog box. Figure 6-2 shows an example document in which one of the formatting changes has been selected.

Word labels the changes with *revision markings*, which will be described in Chapter 11, "Working with Word in Workgroups." Note that while the Review AutoFormat Changes dialog box is displayed, you can manually scroll through the document and make any editing or formatting changes you want.

FIGURE 6-2.
Reviewing AutoFormat changes in an example document.

Click the Hide Marks button to hide the revision markings.

You can undo your previous change by clicking Undo.

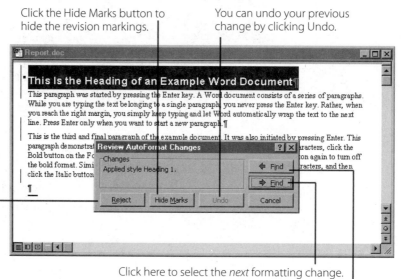

Click the Reject button to cancel the selected change. If you *don't* click Reject, the change is accepted.

Click here to select the *next* formatting change.

Click here to select the *previous* change.

8 When you have finished reviewing changes and making modifications, click the Cancel button to close the Review AutoFormat Changes dialog box. You'll return to the AutoFormat dialog box.

9 In the AutoFormat dialog box, click the Accept All button to accept all AutoFormat changes—except those that you rejected— plus any manual changes that you made. Alternatively, if you click Reject All, all AutoFormat changes and all manual changes you made will be canceled, and the document will be restored to its state immediately before you issued the AutoFormat command.

Using the AutoFormat As You Type Feature

You can also have Word automatically make certain formatting changes *as you type* your documents. To do this, choose AutoCorrect from the Tools menu and click the AutoFormat As You Type tab. Then, check the options for the formatting changes you want Word to make. (See Figure 6-3.) Table 6-2 on the following page describes the effect of each of the AutoFormat As You Type options.

FIGURE 6-3.
Setting AutoFormat As You Type options.

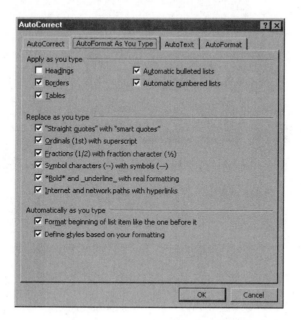

Microsoft Word

NOTE

When you first install Word, the AutoFormat As You Type options might already be selected. To disable automatic formatting as you type, you must individually turn off all the AutoFormat As You Type options.

TABLE 6-2. The AutoFormat As You Type Options and Their Effects

AutoFormat As You Type Option	Effect If Option Is Selected
Apply As You Type	
Headings	If you type a line of text at the beginning of the document or following a blank line and then press Enter twice, Word will assign it the Heading 1 style. If the line starts after a blank line and with a single tab or a $\frac{1}{2}$-inch indent, Word will assign it the Heading 2 style; if the line starts after a blank line and with two tabs or a 1-inch indent, Word will assign it Heading 3; and so on.
Borders	If you type a line consisting of three hyphens (---), underscores (___), equal signs (===), asterisks (***), tildes (~~~), or number signs (###), Word will replace the line with a horizontal border—a thin border for hyphens, a thick border for underscores, a double border for equal signs, a dotted line for asterisks, a wavy line for tildes, or a decorative line for number signs.
Tables	If you type a plus sign followed by a series of hyphens followed by another plus sign, and so on (for example +---+----+---+), Word will automatically insert a table. Each + sign indicates a column border, and the number of hyphens between + signs indicates the width of each column. For information on tables, see "Using Tables," page 228.
Automatic Bulleted Lists	If you begin a paragraph with a bullet, asterisk, hyphen, or related character, followed by a space or tab, Word will format the paragraph—and each paragraph you subsequently type—as an automatically bulleted list (described in Chapter 8, "Arranging Text in Columns and Lists"). To restore normal paragraph formatting, press Enter twice after a list item.
Automatic Numbered Lists	If you begin a paragraph with a number or letter followed by a period, hyphen, closing parenthesis, or related character, Word will format the paragraph—and each paragraph you subsequently type—as an automatically numbered list (described in Chapter 8, "Arranging Text in Columns and Lists"). To restore normal paragraph formatting, press Enter twice after a list item.

(continued)

TABLE 6-2. *continued*

AutoFormat As You Type Option	Effect If Option Is Selected
Replace As You Type	
"Straight Quotes" With "Smart Quotes"	Pairs of straight quotes (" " or ' ') are replaced with pairs of curly quotes (" " or ' '). A single straight quote (') is replaced with a curly apostrophe (').
Ordinals (1st) With Superscript	Plain ordinal expressions (such as 1st, 2nd, and 3rd) are replaced with superscripted expressions (such as 1st, 2nd, and 3rd).
Fractions (1/2) With Fraction Character ($\frac{1}{2}$)	The fraction expressions 1/4, 1/2, and 3/4 are replaced with the fraction symbols $\frac{1}{4}$, $\frac{1}{2}$, and $\frac{3}{4}$.
Symbol Characters (--) With Symbols (—)	Two hyphens immediately preceded and followed by text are replaced with an em dash (—). Also, if you type a space followed by a single hyphen followed by one or no space, the hyphen will be replaced with a en dash (–).
Bold And _Underline_ With Real Formatting	Characters enclosed in asterisks are formatted as bold and characters enclosed in underscore characters are formatted as underlined. For example, *help* would be converted to **help**. This option is useful for converting text-only e-mail messages (which typically emphasize words by surrounding them with * or _ characters) into formatted document text.
Internet And Network Paths With Hyperlinks	Internet and network paths are converted into actual hyperlinks that can be used to navigate to the sites. See the discussion on hyperlinks in "Inserting and Navigating with Hyperlinks," page 161.
Automatically As You Type	
Format Beginning Of List Item Like The One Before It	When you insert a new item in a list, Word automatically applies the same character formatting (such as bold) that was applied to the beginning of the previous list item. For information on lists, see "Creating Bulleted and Numbered Lists," page 246.
Define Styles Based On Your Formatting	Word will automatically create new styles based on the paragraph formatting you manually apply to paragraphs, so that you can quickly reuse the formatting by applying the new styles to other paragraphs.

II

Microsoft Word

When the AutoFormat feature makes a formatting modification as you type your document, and if the Office Assistant is visible, a description of the modification will appear in the Office Assistant balloon. You can accept the modification, reverse it, or have the Office Assistant show you how to turn off the AutoFormat option.

SEE ALSO
For information about bulleted and numbered lists, see "Creating Bulleted and Numbered Lists," page 246.

Note that the Office Assistant does *not* display information on text replacements (the options listed in Table 6-2 under the "Replace As You Type" and "Automatically As You Type" headings, such as replacing straight quotes with smart quotes). To reverse a text replacement that is made automatically as you type your document, simply issue the Undo command.

Using the Style Gallery

After you have automatically formatted your document, you can quickly modify the overall appearance of the document by using the Style Gallery. You can open the Style Gallery by clicking the Style Gallery button in the AutoFormat dialog box while you're performing step 6 of the procedure for reviewing automatic formatting changes given earlier in the section "Formatting Documents Automatically." Alternatively, you can choose Style Gallery from the Format menu. Whichever method you use, Word will open the Style Gallery dialog box, shown in Figure 6-4.

FIGURE 6-4.
Using the Style Gallery dialog box.

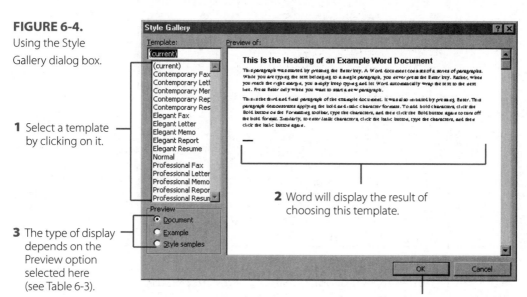

1 Select a template by clicking on it.

2 Word will display the result of choosing this template.

3 The type of display depends on the Preview option selected here (see Table 6-3).

4 When you have selected the template you want, click the OK button. Word will then reformat your entire document, using the styles from this template.

TABLE 6-3. Preview Options

Preview Option	Resulting Display
Document	Word will display a reduced image of your document, as it would appear if formatted with the selected template.
Example	Word will show an example document formatted with the selected template. An example might not be available for a particular template.
Style Samples	Word will display the name and appearance of each style provided by the selected template. Samples might not be available for a particular template.

How the Style Gallery Works

When you choose to automatically format your document, each paragraph is assigned one of Word's standard styles. For instance, a heading might be assigned the Heading 1 style, a paragraph of body text might be assigned the Body Text style, and a paragraph within a list might be assigned the List style. The actual formatting features provided by a given style, however, depend on the template you used to create your document (and on whether you have altered the style). When you choose a template in the Style Gallery, Word copies each of the styles from the template into your document, replacing the original document styles. For example, the template's Heading 1 style would replace your document's original Heading 1 style, and the appearance of every paragraph that is assigned Heading 1 would be modified.

Note that before you use the Style Gallery, you should have used the Auto-Format command or manually applied styles so that the paragraphs in your document are assigned standard Word styles. Otherwise, using the Style Gallery will have little effect. (The process of applying styles manually is discussed in the next section.)

? SEE ALSO

For instructions on choosing a template for creating a new document, see "Creating and Printing a Document from Start to Finish," page 113. For information on modifying, creating, and copying styles, see Chapter 7, "Customizing Styles and Templates."

II

Microsoft Word

Applying Styles

You'll now learn how to manually apply styles to the text in your document. You might need to use the techniques given here to modify the formatting applied by the AutoFormat command or to format a document yourself rather than using AutoFormat at all. (In this case, you might apply styles *as* you're entering the document text.) Word provides two types of styles: *paragraph* styles (such as those applied by AutoFormat) and *character* styles (for emphasizing individual characters).

Applying styles has several advantages over directly assigning character and paragraph formatting. First, applying a style can save you time because it allows you to assign an entire group of formatting features with a single command. Also, using styles promotes consistent formatting—all text that is assigned a given style will look the same. Finally, as you'll learn in Chapter 7, "Customizing Styles and Templates," you can easily change the format of all text throughout a document that has a given style by merely adjusting the style itself. For example, you could make all top-level headings bold by assigning the bold format to the Heading 1 style rather than individually reformatting all these headings in the document.

When you create a new document, it obtains, in effect, a private copy of the styles that are stored in the template that was used to create it. You saw previously how to use the Style Gallery to replace these styles with the styles stored in a different template. In the following sections, you'll learn how to apply the document's styles to paragraphs or blocks of characters within the document. You can use these techniques to apply both *predefined* styles (that is, those supplied with the Word program) and styles that you define yourself. In the next chapter, you'll learn how to modify the predefined styles and how to define new styles.

Applying Paragraph Styles

A *paragraph style* stores a complete set of paragraph and character formatting features. When you apply the style to a paragraph, all these features are assigned to the paragraph text. Table 6-4 on the following page summarizes all the formatting features that are stored in a paragraph style, divided into six categories (these categories correspond to the commands that are used to choose the formatting features, as described later in the book).

If you haven't used AutoFormat or applied styles to your document, paragraphs will usually have the Normal style. (Paragraphs in documents based on certain templates, however, might be initially assigned

? **SEE ALSO**
For information on finding and replacing styles, see "Finding and Replacing Text," page 151.

a different style, such as Body Text). The Normal style has a set of formats suitable for the bulk of the text in a typical document. In the Normal template supplied with Word, the formatting features of the Normal style include the Times New Roman font, a font size of 10 points, single line spacing, and flush-left paragraph alignment (these features can be changed).

TABLE 6-4. Formatting Features Stored in a Paragraph Style

Category	Chief Formatting Features
Font	The font name (for example, Times New Roman), as well as the character size, style (Bold or Italic), underlining, effects (such as strikethrough or superscript), color, intercharacter spacing, and animation.
Language	The dictionaries (for example, English, French, or German) that the Word proofing tools (such as the spelling and grammar checkers) use to correct the text. The proofing tools are discussed in Chapter 9, "Using Word's Proofing Tools."
Paragraph	Indentation, space before or after a paragraph, line spacing, alignment (left, right, centered, or justified), and page break control.
Tabs	Position and type of tab stops in effect within a paragraph.
Borders And Shading	Borders around a paragraph and background shading.
Bullets And Numbering	Automatic display of bullet or number for a paragraph in a list.

To apply a different style to one or more paragraphs, perform the following two steps:

1 To apply a style to a single paragraph, simply place the insertion point anywhere within the paragraph. To apply a style to several paragraphs, select at least a portion of all the paragraphs. If you have not yet started entering text for a new paragraph, just place the insertion point before the paragraph mark of the new paragraph. You can do this whether or not the paragraph mark is visible.

Microsoft Word

II

2 Choose Style from the Format menu, and select the style you want in the Style dialog box, as shown in Figure 6-5.

Select a style by clicking on it. Style names prefaced with ¶ are paragraph styles. (Styles prefaced with **a** are character styles, which will be discussed in the next section.

FIGURE 6-5.
Choosing a style in the Style dialog box. The name of each style suggests its purpose. The description and previews help you find an appropriate style.

Choose All Styles here to list all available styles.

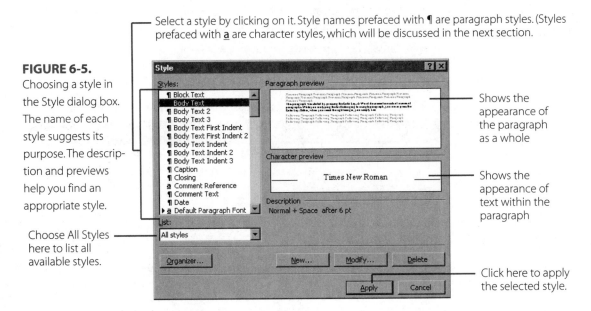

Shows the appearance of the paragraph as a whole

Shows the appearance of text within the paragraph

Click here to apply the selected style.

> NOTE

Some of the predefined styles are used for standard Word features. For example, Word automatically assigns comment text (discussed in Chapter 11) the Comment Text style, and page headers the Header style. You can, however, assign these styles to any paragraphs in your document.

Rather than opening the Style dialog box, if you know the name of the style you want, you can quickly apply it by selecting it from the Style list on the Formatting toolbar or by typing the style name into the box at the top of the list:

To list *all* available styles, press Shift while you click the down arrow. Also, Word provides the shortcut keys shown in Table 6-5 for applying several of the paragraph styles:

TABLE 6-5. Shortcut Keys for Styles

Style	Shortcut Key
Normal	Ctrl+Shift+N
List Bullet	Ctrl+Shift+L
Heading 1	Alt+Ctrl+1
Heading 2	Alt+Ctrl+2
Heading 3	Alt+Ctrl+3

 TIP

Speed Your Work by Using Predefined Styles

Use the predefined styles Heading 1 through Heading 9 for the headers in your document! Not only do these styles save time and ensure consistency while providing appropriate formatting for various levels of headings; using them will also let you view the organization of your document in Outline view, to quickly navigate through your document with the Document Map, and to easily generate tables of contents.

Additionally, when you drag the scroll box on the vertical scroll bar, Word will display the text of each heading to make it simpler to find the desired location in your document. (Headings, outlines, the Document Map, and tables of contents will be fully discussed in Chapter 12, "Writing Long Documents.")

Also, if you use the Body Text style rather than Normal for the body text in your document, you'll be able to easily modify the formatting of the body text without altering other text in your document. (This topic will be fully discussed in Chapter 7, "Customizing Styles and Templates.")

? SEE ALSO

For details on defining your own shortcut keys for quickly applying styles, see the section "Modifying Styles," page 200.

When you press Enter at the end of a paragraph, the new paragraph that is inserted generally has the same style as the previous paragraph. Some styles, however, are defined so that the new paragraph has a different style. For example, if you press Enter while in a paragraph with the Heading 1 style, the new paragraph will typically have the Normal style.

Applying Character Styles

You can use a *character style* to quickly apply a set of character formatting features to emphasize one or more characters within a paragraph. Character styles differ from paragraph styles in the following ways:

- A character style can store only character formatting, that is, only the first two categories of features in Table 6-4 on page 177 (Font and Language).

- You assign a character style to one or more individual characters rather than to an entire paragraph.

- A character style does not need to fully specify the character format. For example, a particular character style might specify only the bold and italic features. If you assigned this style to a block of text, Word would simply apply the bold and italic features to the text, and preserve all the other character formatting features that are specified by the paragraph style, such as the character font, size, and effects.

Word provides few predefined character styles. Therefore, the techniques given here will not be truly useful until you learn how to define your own character styles in Chapter 7, "Customizing Styles and Templates."

To apply a character style to a group of characters:

1 Select the text, or to apply the style to the text you're about to type, place the insertion point at the position where you want to insert the text. To apply a character style to a single word, simply place the insertion point anywhere within the word, without selecting it.

2 Choose Style from the Format menu, and in the Style dialog box (see Figure 6-5 on page 178) select a character style from the list. The names of character styles are prefaced with **a**. Notice that Word displays sample text formatted with the selected style. Click the Apply button when you have selected the style you want.

   Alternatively, if you know the name of the character style you want, you can simply select it in the Style list on the Formatting toolbar. To list all available styles, press Shift while you click the down arrow.

SEE ALSO

For instructions on defining your own character styles, see "Creating New Styles," page 209.

3 If you did not select characters in step 1, begin typing. The character style will be applied to all characters you type until you move the insertion point or press Ctrl+Spacebar or Ctrl+Shift+Z.

To remove a character style, select the text and either press Ctrl+Spacebar or Ctrl+Shift+Z or apply the Default Paragraph Font character style. Choosing this special-purpose character "style" removes any character style or manually applied character formatting previously applied to the text.

Applying Character Formatting Directly

Directly applying individual character formatting features gives you the finest level of control over the character formatting in your document.

SEE ALSO

For information about finding and replacing character formatting, see "Finding and Replacing Text," page 151.

The paragraph style specifies the *predominant* character formatting of the paragraph text. Frequently, you'll apply character formatting to one or more characters *within* the paragraph to emphasize them. For example, you might italicize a word or convert a character to superscript. The character formatting that you directly apply overrides the character formatting that is specified by the paragraph style or by any character style assigned to the text.

The character formatting features that you can apply are shown in Table 6-6 on the following page. (Notice that these features comprise the first two formatting categories given in Table 6-4, Font, page 177.)

TIP

> **Include Character Formatting in Paragraph Styles**
>
> Don't directly apply character formatting to entire paragraphs or groups of paragraphs. Rather, assign paragraph styles that include the predominant character formatting that you want, and use direct character formatting only to emphasize smaller blocks of text within paragraphs. This approach will make it easier to modify the predominant character formatting and will tend to make your character formatting more consistent throughout the document.

II

Microsoft Word

TABLE 6-6. Directly Applied Character Formatting Features

Character Formatting Option	Description
Font	
Font	The general type of the characters: Times New Roman, Courier New, and so on.
Font Style	The basic look of the characters: Regular, Italic, Bold, or Bold Italic.
Size	Height of characters, measured in points (1 point = 1/72").
Underline	Character underlining: Single, Words Only (which skips spaces), Double, Dotted, Thick, Dash, Dot Dash, Dot Dot Dash, and Wave.
Color	The color of characters on a color monitor or color printer: Auto, Black, Blue, Cyan, and so on. (The "Auto" color choice, which is often black, is the Window font color selected through the Appearance tab of the Display Properties dialog box.)
Effects	Character enhancements: Strikethrough, Double Strikethrough, Superscript, Subscript, Shadow, Outline, Emboss, Engrave, Small Caps, All Caps, and Hidden.
Character Spacing	
Scale	Amount by which characters are increased or decreased in width (expressed as a percent of normal character width).
Spacing	Amount added to or subtracted from intercharacter spacing to produce expanded or condensed text.
Position	Amount by which characters are raised or lowered (unlike the Subscript or Superscript effects, character size is not reduced).
Kerning For Fonts	Moving certain character pairs (for example A and W) closer together.
Animation	
Animation	Animated text effects that move or flash for documents that will be read online. The animated effects do not print.
Language	
Language	Language of dictionaries used by the proofing tools to correct the text (discussed in "Marking the Language," page 264).

The following are the general steps for directly applying character formatting:

1 Select the text, or to apply the formatting to the text you're about to type, place the insertion point at the position where you want your new text to appear.

To apply character formatting to a word, you can simply place the insertion point anywhere within the word rather than selecting the word.

2 Open the Font dialog box by choosing Font from the Format menu and select the formatting features you want. Alternatively, you can apply certain character formatting features by pressing a shortcut key or by using the Formatting toolbar. These three different methods are discussed individually in the following three chapter sections.

3 If you did not select characters in step 1, begin typing. The character formatting will be applied to all characters you type until you move the insertion point or press Ctrl+Spacebar or Ctrl+Shift+Z. (A newly typed character normally acquires the character formatting of the previous character. If, however, the character is typed at the beginning of a new paragraph, it acquires the formatting of the *following* character.)

NOTE

One of the character formatting features you can apply is the language. This feature tells the Word proofing tools (such as the spelling and grammar checkers) which dictionaries to use to correct the text. You can use the procedure in the preceding list to set the language; in step 2, however, point to language on the Tools menu, choose Set Language from the submenu (rather than opening the Font dialog box), and select the language you want the proofing tools to use. See Chapter 9, "Using Word's Proofing Tools," for a complete discussion on selecting the language and using the Word proofing tools.

To *remove* directly applied character formatting and restore the character formatting specified by the paragraph's style, select the text and press Ctrl+Spacebar or Ctrl+Shift+Z.

II

Microsoft Word

To find out what formatting and style (or styles) have been applied to text in your document, choose What's This? from the Help menu, or press Shift+F1, and then click anywhere within the text of interest.

Using the Font Dialog Box

The Font dialog box allows you to apply any of the character formatting features shown in Table 6-6 on page 182, except the Language feature. To open the Font dialog box, choose Font from the Format menu or click on the selected text with the right mouse button and choose Font from the shortcut menu that appears. The Font tab of the Font dialog box is shown in Figure 6-6, the Character Spacing tab is shown in Figure 6-7 on the following page, and the Animation tab is shown in Figure 6-8 on the following page. Selecting the formatting features you want is easy because the Preview area of the Font dialog box shows a text example formatted with the selected features.

FIGURE 6-6.
The Font tab of the Font dialog box.

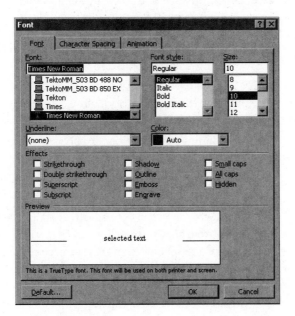

When the Font dialog box is first displayed, it shows the current formatting of the selected text. If a particular formatting feature varies within the selected text (for example, part of the text is bold and part is not bold), the box indicating the feature will be left blank. (Or if the feature is selected by means of clicking a check box, the check box will contain a dim check mark.) If you specify a formatting option, it will be applied to *all* the text in the selection.

FIGURE 6-7.
The Character Spacing tab of the Font dialog box.

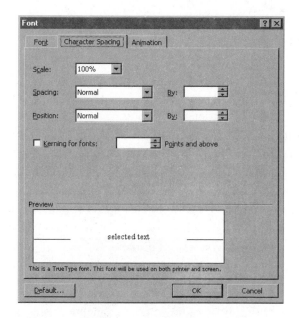

FIGURE 6-8.
The Animation tab of the Font dialog box.

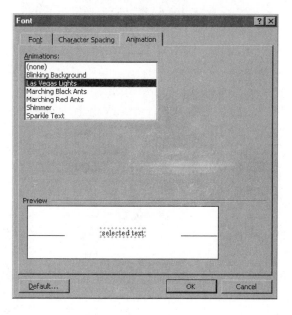

The Font list contains the names of all the fonts that are installed on your system. Notice that Word marks the different types of fonts:

Printer font

TrueType font

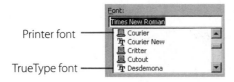

Printer fonts are provided by your current default Windows printer; if you change the default Windows printer, the printer fonts in the list might also change. A given printer font might be available in only a limited number of sizes. TrueType fonts are installed in Windows. These fonts are *scalable*—that is, you can make them any size—and they produce high-quality characters on almost any screen or printer. A TrueType font is a good choice if you want to be able to display the characters in a range of sizes or if you want to be able to print your document on a variety of printers.

Clicking the Superscript or Subscript box raises or lowers the text by a standard amount and reduces the character size. To simply raise or lower the text by any amount, without changing its size, use the Character Spacing tab and select either Raised or Lowered in the Position list (see Figure 6-6 on page 184) and then enter in the By box the exact amount that the text should be moved, in points (1 point equals $\frac{1}{72}$ inch).

If you click the Hidden effect, you can make the text invisible on the screen or on a printed copy of the document. To control the visibility of hidden text, choose Options from the Tools menu. Hidden text will be visible on the screen only if the Hidden Text option is enabled on the View tab, and it will be visible on a printed copy of the document only if the Hidden Text option is enabled on the Print tab.

Note that the Small Caps and All Caps effects change only the way the text is displayed and printed; they don't change the actual characters stored in the document. Therefore, if you remove the effect, the original capitalization of the text will reappear.

When you specify a value in the Scale box (on the Character Spacing tab) other than 100%, you change the actual width of each character. In contrast, when you select Expanded or Condensed in the Spacing list, you affect the spaces *between* the characters, but leave the widths of the characters themselves unchanged:

enlarged Scale

E x p a n d e d   t e x t

If you click the Kerning For Fonts option on the Character Spacing tab, Word will reduce the spacing between certain character pairs (such as A and W) to give the text a more compact appearance (in contrast, selecting the Condensed option in the Spacing list reduces the spacing between *all* characters in the selected text). Word will perform kerning

Entering Measurements into Dialog Boxes

Some of the boxes in Word dialog boxes require you to enter measurements (for example, the By boxes following the Spacing and Position lists in the Font dialog box). Word displays the current value as a number followed by an abbreviation for the units. If you enter a new value, you should generally use the same units.

For example, consider a box in which Word displays the value 3 pt, meaning 3 points. If you typed either *5* or *5 pt* into this box, the value would be changed to 5 points. You can use another unit of measurement, provided that you specify the units. For example, you could enter *.05 in* into this box, and the value would be changed to .05 inches. The next time you opened the dialog box, Word would display this value in points—that is, 3.6 pt. (In some cases, Word will adjust the measurement to match its internal rules. For example, text can be raised or lowered only in half-point increments; therefore, in the By box following the Position list, Word would change .05 in to 3.5 pt.)

Note that you can change the standard units that Word uses for many of the values entered into dialog boxes. To do this, choose Options from the Tools menu, click the General tab, and select the units you want in the Measurement Units list.

The following table will help you work with the different units of measurement that Word recognizes:

Units	Abbre- viation	Points	Picas	Lines	Centi- meters	Inches
Points	pt	1	1/12	1/12	.035	1/72
Picas	pi	12	1	1	.42	1/6
Lines	li	121	1	1	.42	1/6
Centimeters	cm	28.35	2.38	2.38	1	.39
Inches	in *or* "	72	6	6	2.54	1

SEE ALSO

For information on embedding TrueType fonts in a document so that the document can be edited by other users, see "Sharing Fonts," page 354.

only on characters that have a size equal to or greater than the size you enter into the Points And Above box. Also, the selected font must be a TrueType (or Adobe Type 1) font.

The Animation tab allows you to select from a list of animated text effects that move or flash (such as Marching Red Ants or Las Vegas Lights). These effects are useful for documents that will be viewed on-line; they do not appear in a printed copy. To turn off an animated effect, select (None) from the list.

Finally, you can click the Default button to change the *default* character formatting so that it conforms to the styles that you have selected on the Font, Character Spacing, and Animation tabs of the Font dialog box. Clicking Default (and responding Yes when prompted) assigns the selected features to the Normal style of the document and to the Normal style of the template that was used to create the document. (As you'll learn in Chapter 7, "Customizing Styles and Templates," modifying Normal affects many other styles, which are based on Normal.) As a result, whenever you create a new document using this template, the document text will display the new formatting features. (Clicking Default will not, however, affect other documents that have already been created using the template.)

Using Shortcut Keys to Apply Character Formatting

You can also use the shortcut keys in Table 6-7 to apply many of the character formatting features to the selected text.

The keys that *toggle* work as follows: If the first character of the selection does *not* have the formatting feature, pressing the key applies the format; if the first character of the selection already *has* the formatting feature, pressing the key removes the feature. For example, if you select text in which the first character is nonbold and press Ctrl+B, all the text will become bold; if you press Ctrl+B again, all the text will become nonbold.

TABLE 6-7. Character Formatting Shortcut Keys

Character Formatting Option	Shortcut Key	Toggles?
Bold	Ctrl+B	Yes
Italic	Ctrl+I	Yes
Underline	Ctrl+U	Yes
Double Underline	Ctrl+Shift+D	Yes
Words Only Underline	Ctrl+Shift+W	Yes
Subscript (P_1)	Ctrl+=	Yes
Superscript (1st)	Ctrl+Shift+=	Yes
Hidden	Ctrl+Shift+H	No
SMALL CAPS	Ctrl+Shift+K	Yes
ALL CAPS	Ctrl+Shift+A	Yes
Increase font size to next size on Font Size list	Ctrl+>	No
Decrease font size to next size on Font Size list	Ctrl+<	No
Increase font size by exactly 1 point	Ctrl+]	No
Decrease font size by exactly 1 point	Ctrl+[	No
Assign Symbol font	Ctrl+Shift+Q	No

Using the Formatting Toolbar to Apply Character Formatting

A final way to apply several of the character formats is to use the Formatting toolbar:

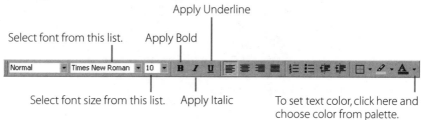

Apply Underline

Select font from this list. Apply Bold

Select font size from this list. Apply Italic

To set text color, click here and choose color from palette.

Like the corresponding keystrokes, the Bold, Italic, and Underline buttons toggle the formatting feature. When the feature is currently assigned to *all* characters in the selection, the button will appear pressed.

To make it easier to find fonts, Word lists the recently applied fonts at the top of the Font list. Below these fonts (and separated by a double line) Word lists *all* available fonts, in alphabetical order.

Applying Paragraph Formatting Directly

? SEE ALSO

The Tabs, Borders And Shading, and Bullets And Numbering categories are explained in Chapter 8, "Arranging Text in Columns and Lists."

Paragraph formatting features affect the appearance of entire paragraphs. Paragraph formatting comprises the last four formatting categories listed in Table 6-4 on page 177—that is, Paragraph, Tabs, Borders And Shading, and Bullets And Numbering. In this section, you'll learn how to directly apply formatting features belonging to the Paragraph category of paragraph formatting—that is, those features that you can apply by using the Paragraph dialog box.

Generally, you should format your paragraphs by applying an appropriate style. (If you don't have a style suitable for the purposes of your document, you can modify an existing style or define a new one, as explained in Chapter 7, "Customizing Styles and Templates.") However, you might want to directly apply paragraph formatting to make an occasional adjustment to the appearance of a paragraph; for example, you might want to highlight a paragraph by centering it or underlining all its text or increasing its left indent. (If you make the same adjustment often, you should probably define a new style.) Directly applied paragraph formatting overrides that specified by the paragraph's style. Note that even if you seldom apply paragraph formatting directly, you'll need to understand the techniques and concepts given here when you begin defining your own paragraph styles.

In this chapter you'll learn how to apply the paragraph formatting features described in Table 6-8.

TABLE 6-8.   Paragraph Formatting Features Covered in This Chapter

Paragraph Formatting Option	Description
Indents And Spacing	
Alignment	Justification of paragraph text: Left (text aligned with left indent), Right (aligned with right indent), Centered (centered between left and right indents), Justified (aligned with both indents).
Indentation	Horizontal position of paragraph text relative to document margins.
Spacing Before	Additional space inserted above paragraph.
Spacing After	Additional space inserted below paragraph.
Line Spacing	Height of each line of text in paragraph—for example, single or double spacing, or an exact line height.
Line And Page Breaks	
Widow/Orphan Control	Prevents printing last line of paragraph by itself at top of new page (a *widow*), or printing first line by itself at bottom of page (an *orphan*).
Keep Lines Together	All lines in paragraph will be printed on same page—that is, Word will not insert a page break within the paragraph.
Keep With Next	Prevents Word from inserting a page break between the selected paragraph and the next paragraph.
Page Break Before	Paragraph printed at top of a new page.
Suppress Line Numbers	If you apply line numbering to document, paragraph is excluded from numbering. (See Chapter 10, "Designing Pages.")
Don't Hyphenate	If you hyphenate document, this paragraph is excluded from hyphenation. (See Chapter 9, "Using Word's Proofing Tools.")

The following are the two basic steps for directly applying paragraph formatting:

1   To format a single paragraph, place the insertion point anywhere within the paragraph, or select all or part of the paragraph. To format several adjoining paragraphs, select at least a portion of each of the paragraphs.

2 Open the Paragraph dialog box by choosing Paragraph from the Format menu and select the desired formatting features. Alternatively, you can apply certain paragraph formatting features by pressing a shortcut key combination or by using the Formatting toolbar or the ruler. These three different methods are discussed individually in the following three sections.

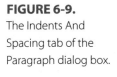

SEE ALSO

For information on finding and replacing paragraph formatting, see "Finding and Replacing Text," page 151. For information on applying other paragraph formatting features (tabs, borders, shading, and bulleted and numbered lists), see Chapter 8, "Arranging Text in Columns and Lists."

To remove directly applied paragraph formatting and restore the paragraph formatting that is specified by the paragraph's style, select the paragraph or paragraphs as in step 1 and then press Ctrl+Q. (Alternatively, you can reapply the paragraph's style using one of the methods for applying styles described previously in the chapter.)

Using the Paragraph Dialog Box

You can apply any of the formatting features described in Table 6-8 on the preceding page using the Paragraph dialog box. To open this dialog box, choose Paragraph from the Format menu, or click within the selected text with the right mouse button and then choose Paragraph from the shortcut menu that appears. Figure 6-9 shows the Indents And Spacing tab of the Paragraph dialog box, and Figure 6-10 shows the Line And Page Breaks tab. As with the Font dialog box, choosing formatting features in the Paragraph dialog box is easy because Word displays a text example formatted with the selected features.

FIGURE 6-9.

The Indents And Spacing tab of the Paragraph dialog box.

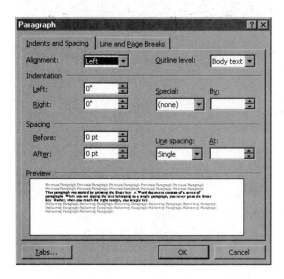

The Outline Level paragraph formatting feature (set through the Indents And Spacing tab of the Paragraph dialog box) is discussed in "Using Outline View to Organize Your Documents," page 358.

FIGURE 6-10.
The Line And Page Breaks tab of the Paragraph dialog box.

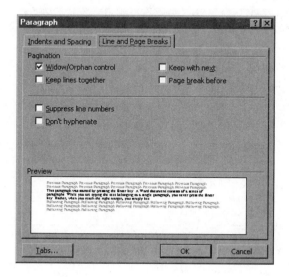

SEE ALSO
For instructions on setting the document margins and a description of the difference between margins and indents, see "Adjusting the Page Setup," page 300.

The *left paragraph indent* is the distance that the left edge of the paragraph text is moved *in* from the left margin (a positive indent) or *out* into the left margin (a negative indent). Likewise, the *right paragraph indent* is the distance the right edge of the text is moved *in* from the right margin (a positive indent) or *out* into the right margin (a negative indent). The *margins* are the distances between the text and the edges of the page (assuming that the indents are 0). You set the margins when you adjust the page setup, as described in Chapter 10, "Designing Pages." The easiest way to learn how to use the various indentation settings is to change the values and observe the effects on the preview text.

If you select the First Line item in the Special box, the first line of the paragraph will be moved to the right of the other paragraph lines (by the amount you enter into the following By box). If you select the Hanging option in the Special box, all lines *except* the first will be to the right of the first line (by the amount you enter into the following By box).

The *line spacing* is the total height of each line of text in a paragraph. The options you can select in the Line Spacing list box have the effects shown in Table 6-9.

TABLE 6-9.   Line Spacing Options

Line Spacing Option	Effect
Single	Each line will be made just high enough to accommodate the characters in the line. (If a particular line contains an unusually tall character, that line will be made higher than the others.)
1.5 Lines	Multiplies the Single line spacing by 1.5.
Double	Multiplies the Single line spacing by 2.
At Least	Sets the minimum height of a line. If a character in a line is taller than this value, the height of that line will be increased.
Exactly	Sets the exact height of each line. This option makes all lines evenly spaced. However, if a character in a line is taller than the line height, it will be cut off.
Multiple	Multiplies the Single line spacing by the number you enter into the At box.

Using Shortcut Keys to Apply Paragraph Formatting

You can use the shortcut keys in Table 6-10 to quickly apply many of the paragraph formatting features to the selected paragraph or paragraphs.

 TIP

Use the Tab and Backspace Keys to Adjust Left Indents

If you turn on the Tabs And Backspace Set Left Indent option (choose Options from the Tools menu and click the Edit tab), you can use the Tab and Backspace keys to adjust the left indent of a paragraph. To set the left indent of the first line only, place the insertion point at the beginning of the first line; to set the left indent of all lines in the paragraph, place the insertion point at the beginning of any line except the first. Then, press Tab to increase the left indent to the next tab stop, or press Backspace (or Shift+Tab) to decrease the left indent by one tab stop.

Note that you can't use this technique to create a negative left indent; nor can you use it to indent a new paragraph that does not yet contain text.

TABLE 6-10. Shortcut Keys for Paragraph Formatting

Paragraph Formatting Action	Shortcut Key	Comment
Increase left paragraph indent	Ctrl+M	Indent is moved to the next tab stop. (See Chapter 8, "Arranging Text in Columns and Lists," for information on tab stops.)
Decrease left paragraph indent	Ctrl+Shift+M	Indent is moved to previous tab stop; cannot be used to create a negative left indent.
Increase hanging indent	Ctrl+T	All paragraph lines are indented except the first line. Each time you press the key combination, the indent is moved to the next tab stop.
Decrease hanging indent	Ctrl+Shift+T	Hanging indent is moved to the previous tab stop.
Add or remove 12 points of extra space above paragraph	Ctrl+0 (zero)	Toggles feature on or off.
Create single spacing	Ctrl+1	Same as Single option in the Paragraph dialog box.
Create 1.5 spacing	Ctrl+5	Same as 1.5 Lines option in the Paragraph dialog box.
Create double spacing	Ctrl+2	Same as Double option in the Paragraph dialog box.
Left-align paragraph	Ctrl+L	Text aligned with left indent.
Right-align paragraph	Ctrl+R	Text aligned with right indent.
Center paragraph	Ctrl+E	Text centered between left indent of the first line and right indent.
Justify paragraph	Ctrl+J	Text aligned with left and right indents (Word adjusts character spacing).

Microsoft Word

Using the Formatting Toolbar and Ruler to Apply Paragraph Formatting

You can also use the Formatting toolbar and the ruler to apply paragraph formatting. (If the ruler is not displayed, choose Ruler from the View menu or you can display it temporarily by placing the mouse pointer over the gray band at the top of the document window.)

To temporarily display the ruler, hold the mouse pointer over this gray bar.

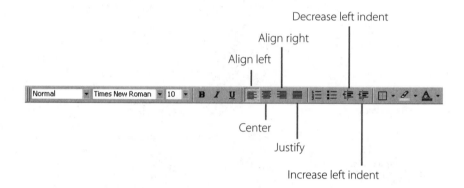

You can click the following buttons on the Formatting toolbar to apply paragraph formats:

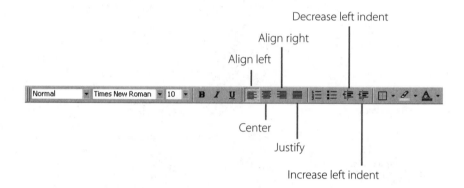

You can use the ruler to set paragraph indents, as follows:

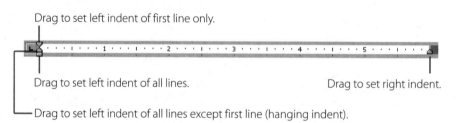

Drag to set left indent of first line only.

Drag to set left indent of all lines.   Drag to set right indent.

Drag to set left indent of all lines except first line (hanging indent).

Copying Formatting

If you have formatted a block of text in a document and want to apply the same formatting to one or more additional blocks of text, you can save time by copying the formatting.

One way to copy formatting is to use the Format Painter tool on the Standard toolbar, as follows:

1 Select the text that has the formatting that you want to copy. If you want to copy the paragraph formatting, select the entire paragraph or simply place the insertion point anywhere within the paragraph without selecting text.

Format Painter

2 Click the Format Painter button on the Standard toolbar. A small paintbrush will appear next to the standard I-beam mouse pointer.

3 Move the I-beam pointer to the text you want to format, and drag the highlight over the text. When you release the mouse button, the formatting will be copied to the text. If you want to apply the paragraph formatting that you copied in step 1, either select the entire paragraph or simply place the insertion point anywhere within the paragraph without selecting text.

 TIP

Paint Several Blocks of Text
If you want to copy the formatting to several blocks of text, you can save time by double-clicking the Format Painter button in step 2. Then, perform step 3 on every block of text that you want to format. When you're done, either click the Format Painter button again or press the Escape key.

You can also copy formatting using the keyboard, as follows:

1 Select the text that has the formatting you want to copy (if you want to copy the paragraph formatting, select the entire paragraph or simply place the insertion point anywhere within the paragraph without selecting text), and press Ctrl+Shift+C.

2 Select the text you want to format and press Ctrl+Shift+V. If you want to apply the paragraph formatting that you copied in step 1, either select the entire paragraph or simply place the insertion point anywhere within the paragraph without selecting text and press Ctrl+Shift+V.

II

Microsoft Word

⭐ **TIP**

Use the Clipboard to Copy or Move Text Without Formatting

Normally, when you copy or move text, the text formatting is copied or moved with it (the character formatting, plus the paragraph formatting if the paragraph mark is included). To copy or move text without including its formatting, use the Clipboard technique given in "Moving and Copying Text," page 147. However, rather than issuing the Paste command at the target location, choose Paste Special from the Edit menu, select the Paste option button, select the Unformatted Text item in the As list, and click OK. (See Figure 6-11.) When the text is inserted, it will acquire the format of the preceding text—just as if you had typed it!

Finally, you can copy paragraph formatting by using the standard text-copying methods (given in Chapter 5, "Entering and Editing Text in a Word Document") to copy the paragraph mark following the paragraph that has the desired format. (Click the Show/Hide ¶ button if the paragraph mark is not showing.) Conceptually, a paragraph mark stores the paragraph's style as well as any directly applied paragraph formatting features. Therefore, when you insert a copy of a paragraph mark at a new document location, the preceding text acquires the same paragraph style and formatting as the paragraph from which you copied the paragraph mark.

FIGURE 6-11.
Inserting unformatted text using the Paste Special command on the Edit menu.

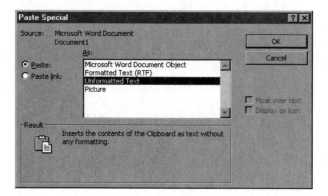

CHAPTER 7

Customizing Styles and Templates

In the previous chapter, you saw how to quickly format characters or paragraphs by applying the styles available in your document. In this chapter, you'll greatly extend the usefulness of styles by learning how to modify styles, create new styles, and copy styles between documents and templates. You'll also learn how to customize Word templates, which store styles as well as other important document items, such as standard text, AutoText entries, and macros.

Modifying Styles

Each time you open a new document, it obtains a copy of the styles that are stored in the template used by Word to create the document. The particular styles that are provided, as well as the formatting features stored in each of these styles, vary according to the template you select. All templates have a basic set of general-purpose styles known as *built-in* styles—for example, Normal, Body Text, and Heading 1 through Heading 9. Some templates provide additional predefined styles for special purposes. For instance, the Professional Report template provides the Company Name, Title Cover, and Subtitle Cover styles for formatting elements on the report's title page. Also, a template or document can contain styles that you define yourself, using the techniques that will be given later in the chapter.

You can modify any of the styles in your document. When you modify a style, all text in your document that is assigned the style acquires the style's new format. This is an important advantage of using styles rather than directly formatting text. Because each document has its own private set of styles, modifying a style affects only the document itself; it does not affect the template or other documents based on the template. (As you'll see later, however, you can easily copy styles between documents and templates.)

When you modify or create a style, keep in mind that one style can be based on another style. In the Normal template supplied with Word, the Normal style is the base style for most other paragraph styles. For example, Body Text is defined as "Normal plus 6 points of space following the paragraph." This definition means that Body Text has all the formatting features stored in Normal except the amount of space after the paragraph—Normal has 0 points of space after the paragraph while Body Text has 6 points of space. Any formatting features specifically assigned to a style *supersede* the formatting of the base style.

TIP

> **Use Built-In Styles to Change the Appearance of Standard Document Elements**
>
> As mentioned in Chapter 6, Word assigns certain built-in styles to standard elements of your document. For example, it assigns the Comment Text style to *comment* text, the Footer style to page footers, and the Page Number style to page numbers. You can therefore change the appearance of one of these standard elements by changing the corresponding style. For example, if you change the Header style, you'll modify the appearance of the headers on all pages of your document. (Assigning headers, footers, and page numbers is discussed in Chapter 10, "Designing Pages." Comments are discussed in Chapter 11, "Working with Word in Workgroups.")

If you change a style such as Normal, all styles based on it instantly change. For example, if you assigned the Courier New font and "10 points of space following the paragraph" to the Normal style, Body Text would acquire the Courier New font. Body Text would not, however, acquire "10 points of space following the paragraph" because it contains an explicit "space following" value (that is, it does not derive this formatting feature from Normal).

Basing one style on another promotes formatting consistency. For example, if you assign a new font to the Normal style, all related styles automatically acquire the new font, and you avoid having dissimilar fonts throughout your document.

SEE ALSO

For information on applying styles, see "Formatting Documents Automatically," page 166, and "Applying Styles," page 175.

In Chapter 6, "Formatting a Word Document," you learned one way to modify the Normal style: When you click the Default button in the Font dialog box, you change the character formatting stored in Normal to the features selected in the dialog box. The Normal style is also modified when you click the Default button in the Language dialog box, which is discussed in Chapter 9, "Using Word's Proofing Tools." In the next two sections, you'll learn the two basic ways to modify any feature of any style: by using example text and by using the Style dialog box.

II

Microsoft Word

⭐ **TIP**

Modifying Styles by Example

The easiest way to modify a style is to use example text. You can use this method to modify any style except Normal, and the Formatting toolbar must be displayed. The steps are as follows:

1   Select text in your document that is assigned the paragraph or character style you want to modify. (If necessary, apply the style to text somewhere in your document.) The style name will appear in the Style list on the Formatting toolbar. (If you select text that has been assigned a character style, the name of the character style rather than the name of the paragraph style will appear in the Style list, and you'll be able to use this method to modify only the character style.)

2   Apply the new formatting directly to the text. You can use any of the methods for directly formatting text that were described in Chapter 6, "Formatting a Word Document." The best way to modify a character formatting feature of a paragraph style is to directly apply the feature to *all* text in the paragraph.

3   Click in the Style list on the Formatting toolbar or press Ctrl+Shift+S to highlight the style name, and then press Enter:

Press Enter to modify the Body Text style to conform to the formatting assigned to the selected paragraph.

4 Word will display the Modify Style dialog box, which is shown in Figure 7-1.

FIGURE 7-1.
The Modify Style dialog box.

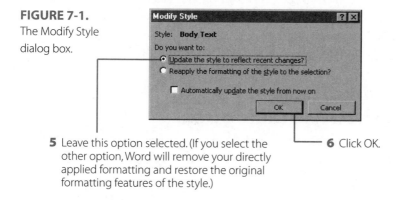

5 Leave this option selected. (If you select the other option, Word will remove your directly applied formatting and restore the original formatting features of the style.)

6 Click OK.

> **NOTE**
>
> For a paragraph style, if you turn on the Automatically Update The Style From Now On option in the Modify Style dialog box, or if you have turned on the Automatically Update option when modifying the style using the Style dialog box (as described in the next section), Word will *automatically* modify the style whenever you directly apply formatting to a paragraph that has been assigned the style. (Word will also instantly apply the new formatting features to all other paragraphs in the document that have this style).
>
> In other words, you'll be able to modify a style by performing only steps 1 and 2 in the above procedure. The Automatically Update feature thus ensures that all text throughout the document that has a particular style will have a consistent format. You'll need to use the Modify Style dialog box (the one shown in Figure 7-3 on page 205) to turn this option off.

SEE ALSO
For information on directly formatting text, see "Applying Character Formatting Directly," page 181, and "Applying Paragraph Formatting Directly," page 190.

You can also use the Style list on the Formatting toolbar to define one or more aliases for a style. A style *alias* is an alternative name for the style. To define one or more aliases, type them after the style name in the Style list, separating each name with a comma, and then press Enter:

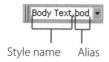

Style name   Alias

Microsoft Word

To apply a style, you can type either its name or any of its aliases into the Style list and press Enter. You can also apply the style by clicking the down arrow next to the Style list box and selecting the style name from the drop-down list. Any aliases will be included after the style name separated by commas. You will not see separate list items for each alias.

Modifying Styles Using the Style Dialog Box

Modifying a style using the Style dialog box is not as quick as modifying the style by example, but it provides the following additional options:

- You can rename the style.

- You can change the style on which the modified style is based.

- You can change the style that Word automatically assigns to a paragraph that follows a paragraph assigned the modified style.

- You can define a shortcut key for quickly applying the style.

- You can copy the modified style to the document's template.

- You can delete the style.

The following is the procedure for modifying a style using the Style dialog box:

1 Choose Style from the Format menu to open the Style dialog box, which is shown in Figure 7-2.

2 Select the name of the style you want to modify in the Styles list. If you can't find the style, choose the All Styles option in the List drop-down list.

3 Click the Modify button. Word will display the Modify Style dialog box, which is shown in Figure 7-3.

4 You can change the name of the style, provided that it is not a built-in style, by typing a new name into the Name box. Each style must have a unique name, and style names are case-sensitive—for example, *List* and *list* are considered different styles.

FIGURE 7-2.
The Style dialog box.

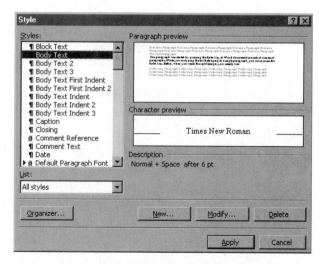

FIGURE 7-3.
The Modify Style
dialog box.

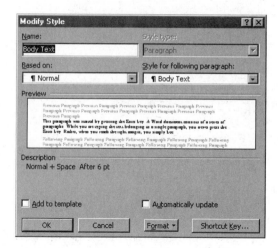

Also, for any type of style, you can define one or more aliases by typing them after the style name in the Name box, separating the names with commas.

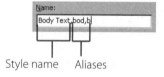

Style name   Aliases

5 You can change the base style by selecting a style name from the Based On list.

II

Microsoft Word

Alternatively, if you choose the (No Style) option, the paragraph style will *not* be based on another style, and it will contain its own complete set of paragraph and character formatting features. (The Normal style can't be based on another style.) The result of basing one style on another was discussed previously in the chapter.

You can base a character style on another character style. Alternatively, if you choose the Default Paragraph Font or (Underlying Properties) option, the character style will be based directly on the paragraph style of the text to which it is applied. Consider, for example, a character style that is based on Default Paragraph Font and includes the Bold and Italic character formats. If you assigned this style to a block of text, Word would apply the Bold and Italic features to the text, remove any directly applied character formatting, and preserve the character formatting features that are specified by the paragraph style.

NOTE

If you apply a character style to text that has already been assigned a paragraph style and there are conflicts between the character formatting assigned in the two styles, the character formatting instructions in the character style will override those in the paragraph style. Also, if both styles apply the same character attribute (such as bold or italic), applying one on top of the other will toggle *off* the character attribute.

6 You can change the style for the *following* paragraph by choosing a style name in the Style For Following Paragraph list. For example, if you were modifying the Heading 1 style, you might choose Body Text in the Style For Following Paragraph list.

As a result, if you pressed Enter while typing a paragraph with the Heading 1 style, Word would assign the Body Text style to the newly inserted paragraph. (For most styles, you typically choose the *same* style in the Style For Following Paragraph list so that the style doesn't change when you press Enter.) This feature applies to paragraph styles only.

7 Turn on the Add To Template option if you want to modify the copy of the style within the template that was used to create the document. If you leave this option turned off, modifying the style will affect only the copy of the style within the current document.

The Automatically Update option in the Modify Style dialog box was discussed previously in the chapter, in "Modifying Styles by Example," page 202.

8 To change the formatting features stored in the style, click the Format button and, from the menu that pops up,

choose the category of the feature or features you want to change. When you choose a category, Word will display a dialog box that allows you to modify the individual formatting features. Each of these dialog boxes is the same as the dialog box that is displayed when you directly format text in a document. Table 7-1 lists each category and indicates the place in the book where the dialog box is discussed. When you have made the changes you want in each of the dialog boxes, click OK to return to the Modify Style dialog box. Note that for a character format, you can choose only the Font, Border, or Language category.

TABLE 7-1. Categories of Formatting You Can Assign to a Style

Style Format Category	Look Here for Discussion of Its Dialog Box
Font	"Applying Character Formatting Directly," page 181
Paragraph	"Applying Paragraph Formatting Directly," page 190
Tabs	"Using Tabs," page 224
Border	"Using Borders and Shading," page 253
Language	"Marking the Language," page 264
Frame	"Using Text Boxes to Position Text on the Page," page 309
Numbering	"Creating Bulleted and Numbered Lists," page 246

II

Microsoft Word

❓ SEE ALSO

See "Defining Shortcut Keys," page 414, for details on defining custom shortcut keys. Also, recall from Chapter 6 that Word has already defined shortcut keys for several styles. (These are listed in Table 6-5 on page 179.)

9 When you have finished making all the changes to the style, click OK in the Modify Style dialog box to return to the Style dialog box and to store your changes.

10 In the Style dialog box, click Apply to return to the document and apply the newly modified style to the selection, or click Close to return to the document without applying the style.

Assigning a Style to a Shortcut Key

If you want to assign a style to a shortcut key so that you can quickly apply the style by pressing a key combination, open the Style dialog box, select the style you want to use, and click the Modify button. In the Modify Style dialog box click the Shortcut Key button. Word will display the Customize Keyboard dialog box, which is shown in Figure 7-4.

FIGURE 7-4.

Defining a shortcut key for applying a style in the Customize Keyboard dialog box.

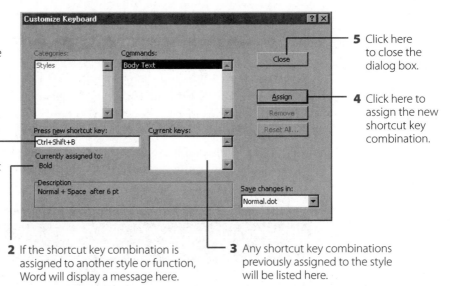

1 With the insertion point here, press the desired shortcut key combination.

5 Click here to close the dialog box.

4 Click here to assign the new shortcut key combination.

2 If the shortcut key combination is assigned to another style or function, Word will display a message here.

3 Any shortcut key combinations previously assigned to the style will be listed here.

Deleting a Style

To delete a style, open the Style dialog box (by choosing Style from the Format menu), select the style to delete, and click the Delete button. When you delete a style, Word removes it from any text to which it has been applied. (For a paragraph style, Word then formats the paragraph with the Normal style.)

To quickly delete a group of styles, use the Organizer, explained in "Modifying Templates," page 218.

See the comments on deleting built-in styles in the following sidebar.

> ### Built-In Styles
>
> Some of the predefined styles that Word provides are known as *built-in* styles. A built-in style is one that is always available to any template or document. To see all the built-in styles (not just those currently assigned to text in the document), choose the All Styles item in the List drop-down list in the lower left corner of the Style dialog box; or, if you're using the Style list on the Formatting toolbar, press Shift while you click the down arrow. You can't rename a built-in style, although you can assign it an alias.
>
> If you select a built-in style other than Normal or Heading 1 through Heading 9 in the Style dialog box, you can click the Delete button to "erase" the style from the current document, provided that the style has been assigned to text in the document or that it has been modified. Word, however, does not actually delete the style; rather, it does the following:
>
> - Word removes the style from any text to which it has been applied. (If the style is a paragraph style, it then assigns the Normal style to each paragraph.)
>
> - If the style has been modified, Word restores it to its original state. Clicking Delete is thus a convenient way to remove any modifications you have made to a built-in style.
>
> After you click Delete, the built-in style will still be listed in the Style dialog box when the All Styles option is selected.

? SEE ALSO
For information on defining shortcut keys, toolbar buttons, and menu commands to apply styles, see "Customizing Toolbars, Menus, and Shortcut Keys," page 407. For information on copying styles between documents and templates, see "Copying Styles," page 213.

Creating New Styles

If you find yourself frequently applying the same set of formatting features to characters or paragraphs, it's probably time to define a new style. Doing so will save you time and help improve the consistency of your formatting. For example, if you often format figure labels by applying a 14-point Arial font, centered alignment, and extra space above the paragraph, you could define a paragraph style—perhaps named Label—that has all these features. Likewise, if you frequently emphasize words by applying a larger font size and the red color, you could define a character style—say, named Big Red—that has both these features.

Just as when you modify a style, you can create a new style either by example or by using the Style dialog box.

Creating Paragraph Styles by Example

The easiest way to create a paragraph style is by example. (However, you can't use this method to create a character style.) Proceed as follows:

1 Select or place the insertion point within a paragraph in a document. You can save time if you choose a paragraph that already has formatting close to the formatting you want to assign the new style.

2 Directly apply any additional character or paragraph formatting that you want to assign to the style, using the methods given in Chapter 6, "Formatting a Word Document." The best way to include character formatting features in the style is to directly apply the features to *all* text in the paragraph.

3 Type a unique name for the new style into the Style list on the Formatting toolbar and press Enter.

Name for new style

SEE ALSO
For information on directly formatting text, see "Applying Character Formatting Directly," page 181, and "Applying Paragraph Formatting Directly," page 190.

Word will add the new paragraph style to the styles stored in the document, and it will apply the style to the example paragraph. The new style will be based on the style that was originally assigned to the example paragraph, and it will store all the paragraph and character formatting features you directly applied to the example paragraph.

Creating Styles Using the Style Dialog Box

Although using the Style dialog box to define a style is slower than using the Formatting toolbar, it provides the following additional options:

- You can define a character style as well as a paragraph style.

- You can choose the style on which the new style is based.

- You can choose the style that Word automatically assigns to a paragraph that follows a paragraph assigned the new style.

■ You can define a shortcut key for quickly applying the new style.

■ You can copy the new style to the document's template.

The following is the basic procedure for defining a new style using the Style dialog box. Many of these steps are similar to the steps for modifying a style. The list emphasizes the differences in the procedures; for more detailed explanations of the techniques and concepts, be sure to first read the previous section, "Modifying Styles Using the Style Dialog Box," page 204.

1 To save time, select or place the insertion point within a paragraph that has formatting similar to the formatting you want to assign to the new style. (This step is optional.)

2 Choose Style from the Format menu to open the Style dialog box (see Figure 7-2 on page 205) and click the New button. Word displays the New Style dialog box, which is shown in Figure 7-5.

FIGURE 7-5.
Creating a style in the New Style dialog box.

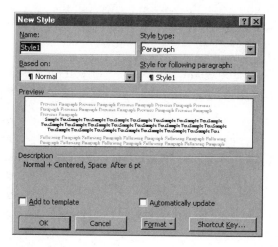

3 Word assigns the new style a tentative name, such as Style1. To assign a different name, type it into the Name box. You can include spaces in the name, and the case of the letters is significant (for example, *label*, *Label*, and *LABEL* would be considered different styles). You can also enter aliases into the Name box by separating them with commas, as described previously.

4 In the Style Type list, select either Paragraph or Character to specify the type of style you want to define.

5 Word initially sets the base style to the style assigned to the text that is currently selected in the document. To base the new style on a different style—or on no style—choose the appropriate option in the Based On list.

6 Word initially makes the style for the next paragraph the same as the new style. To have Word assign a different style to a paragraph that follows a paragraph with the new style, choose a style in the Style For Following Paragraph list. This feature applies to a paragraph style only.

7 If you want to assign a shortcut key that you can use to quickly apply the new style, click the Shortcut Key button in the New Style dialog box and follow the procedure that was explained previously, in the section "Assigning a Style to a Shortcut Key," page 208.

8 Turn on the Add To Template option if you want to copy the new style to the template that was used to create the document. If you leave this option turned off, the style will be available only within the current document.

9 Turn on the Automatically Update option to have Word automatically update the style whenever you directly apply formatting to text that is assigned the style (as explained in the note on page 203).

10 Word initially assigns the new style all the formatting features that are assigned to the current document selection. To change any of these features, click the Format button, choose the appropriate formatting category, and enter the desired settings into the dialog box that Word displays. See Table 7-1 on page 207 for a list of the categories and where to find information on each of the dialog boxes.

11 When you have finished making changes to the style, click OK in the New Style dialog box to return to the Style dialog box and save your changes as a new style.

12 In the Style dialog box, click Apply to return to the document and apply the new style to the selection, or click Close to return to the document without applying the style.

? SEE ALSO

For a more complete explanation on using the Style dialog box, see "Modifying Styles Using the Style Dialog Box," page 204.

Copying Styles

As you have seen, when you create a new document, it acquires a copy of all the styles that are stored in the template that was used to create it. Each document and each template has its own private set of styles. Therefore, adding or modifying a style in a document does not normally affect the template, and adding or modifying a style in a template does not normally affect documents that were already created using the template. You can, however, use several Word options and commands to copy styles between documents and templates (or even between two documents). Copying styles allows you to take advantage of any style that is contained in any document or template.

The following two sections describe various ways to copy styles from templates to documents and from documents to templates.

Copying Styles from a Template to a Document

To take advantage of a style that is stored in a template, you must copy it into a document. Styles can be copied from a template to a document in a variety of ways. First, when you create a new document, all styles currently stored in the template on which you base the document are automatically copied into the document.

SEE ALSO
For information on using the Style Gallery, see "Using the Style Gallery," page 174. For information on using the Organizer, see "Modifying Templates," page 218.

If you already have a document and want to add the styles from another template to it, there are a number of ways to accomplish this. As explained in Chapter 6, you can use the Style Gallery to copy entire sets of styles from any template into your current document, thereby quickly changing the overall look of the document. Alternatively, you can use the Organizer, as described later in the chapter. The Organizer lets you copy as many or as few styles as you want from a template to a document, and is discussed in the section on modifying templates because it is used for copying a variety of template items in addition to styles.

Microsoft Word

Finally, you can have Word automatically copy all styles from the document's template into the document each time you open the document. This option is useful if you periodically update the styles stored in the template and want a particular document always to have the latest style versions. To enable this option, make sure that the document you want to update is in the active document window and choose Templates And Add-Ins from the Tools menu to open the Templates And Add-Ins dialog box. See Figure 7-6.

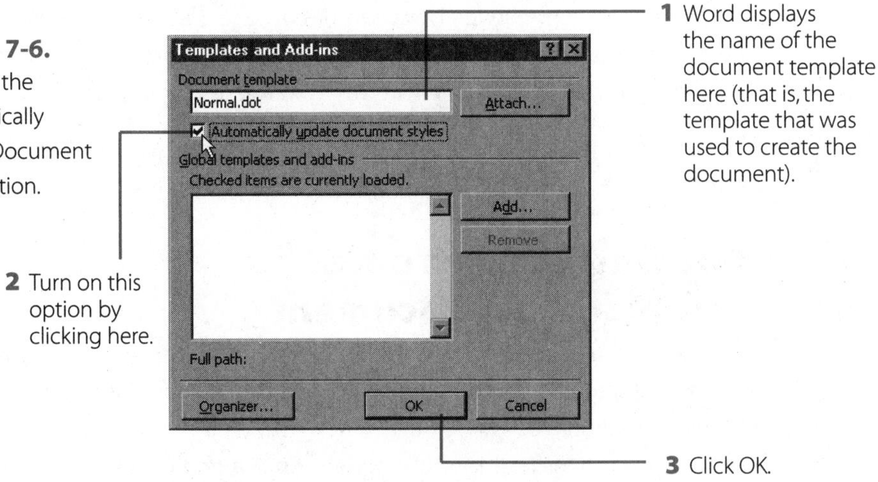

FIGURE 7-6.
Enabling the Automatically Update Document Styles option.

1 Word displays the name of the document template here (that is, the template that was used to create the document).

2 Turn on this option by clicking here.

3 Click OK.

Style Copying Rules

Whenever Word copies all styles from a template or a document to another template or document—for example, when you use the Style Gallery or choose the Automatically Update Document Styles option—it observes the following rules for each style. (Recall that a style is identified with a unique name in each document or template.)

- If a style exists only in the source template or document, Word adds the style to the target template or document.

- If a style exists only in the target template or document, Word leaves it in place, unaltered.

- If a style exists in both the source and target template or document (that is, both the source and the target have a style with the same name), Word replaces the target style with the source style.

Copying Styles from a Document to a Template

When you create or modify a style in a document, you might want to copy the style into a template so that it will be stored there and will be readily available for use in other documents. There are several different ways to do this. First, when you modify or create a style in the Modify Style or the New Style dialog box, you can turn on the Add To Template option. Word will then copy the modified or new style into the document template, as explained previously in the chapter. (If you want to store a style without changing it, you can open the Modify Style dialog box with the style selected, turn on the Add To Template option, and click OK without changing any of the formatting settings.)

SEE ALSO

For a description of the Font dialog box, see "Using the Font Dialog Box," page 184. For a description of the Language dialog box, see "Marking the Language," page 264.

Also, when you select character formatting in the Font or Language dialog box, you can click the Default button and respond Yes when prompted. Word will assign the selected formatting features to the document's Normal style, and it will copy the updated Normal style to the document template.

Finally, you can use the Organizer to copy as many or as few styles as you want from a document to a template. With the Organizer, you can even copy styles from one document to another. Using the Organizer is discussed in the section "Modifying Templates," page 218.

Modifying and Creating Document Templates

A template stores a variety of items that form the basis of a Word document. When you create a new document, some of the items, such as text and styles, are copied into the document from the template that you select. Other items, such as AutoText entries and macros, are kept in the template. The template, however, remains *attached* to the document so that the document can access these items.

II

Microsoft Word

Every Word document is based on a template. If you create a document through the New command on the File menu, the New Office Document command on the Start menu, or the New Office Document button on the Office Shortcut Bar, you can choose the template. If you create a new document by clicking the New button on the Standard toolbar, the document will be based on the Normal template.

Note that the template that the document is based on is also called the *document template* and is referred to as the *template attached to the document*. As you'll learn later in the chapter, you can change the document template after the document has been created.

Table 7-2 lists the template items that are copied into a new document. Once a new document has been created, the document and the template each has its own private copy of these items. Changing one of these items in the document will not affect the template, and changing an item in the template will not affect the document.

NOTE

Word *will* copy style changes from documents to templates or vice versa if you turn on the Add To Template option in the Modify Style dialog box or the Automatically Update Document Styles option in the Templates And Add-Ins dialog box. See "Modifying Styles Using the Style Dialog Box," page 204, and "Copying Styles from a Template to a Document," page 213.

TABLE 7-2. Template Items That Are Copied to a New Document

Template Item	Comments
Text and graphics, together with the formatting assigned to them	Includes headers, footers, footnotes, and comments
Page setup	Margins, paper size and source, page layout, and other features (explained in Chapter 10, "Designing Pages"); also, default tab stops (explained in Chapter 8, "Arranging Text in Columns and Lists")
Styles	Predefined and custom styles

Table 7-3 lists the items that are kept in the template when a new document is created. A document can access any item stored in the document template. It can also access any item stored in the Normal template (of course, if the document is based on Normal, the document template and Normal are the same). Finally, it can access any item that is stored in a template that has been explicitly loaded as a *global template*. (Loading global templates is discussed in "Changing the Template Attached to a Document and Loading Global Templates," page 221.) For example, if an AutoText entry named Close is defined in either the document template or the Normal template, you can insert it into your document using any of the methods discussed in Chapter 5, "Entering and Editing Text in a Word Document." If an AutoText entry named Close is defined in both the document template and the Normal template, Word inserts the text defined in the document template. (That is, an item defined in the document template overrides a similarly named item in the Normal template or other global templates.)

? SEE ALSO

For information on choosing a template when you create a new document, see "Creating and Printing a Document from Start to Finish," page 113.

> NOTE

Beginning with the Office 97 version of Word, when you create a macro, a custom toolbar or menu, or a shortcut key definition, you have the option of storing it within the document rather than within a template, so that the item will be private to that document.

TABLE 7-3. Template Items Kept Within the Document Template

Template Item	Comments
AutoText entries	An AutoText entry is a frequently used block of text or graphics that can be inserted into a document (as explained in "Using the AutoText Feature," page 129).
Macros	A macro is a script for automating a Word task (as discussed in "Recording and Running Macros," page 400).
Custom toolbar and menu configurations	Creating new toolbars is discussed in "Creating and Managing Custom Toolbars," page 408. Modifying toolbars and menus is discussed in "Modifying Toolbars and Menus," page 410.
Shortcut key definitions	Defining shortcut keys to run commands, apply styles, or perform other tasks is discussed in "Defining Shortcut Keys," page 414.

Microsoft Word

Modifying Templates

Word templates are modified in a variety of ways. First, templates are modified as a result of the following common Word actions:

- Creating any of the items listed in Table 7-3 on the preceding page—that is, an AutoText entry, a macro, a custom toolbar or menu, or a shortcut key. When you create any of these items, you can save it in the Normal template *or* in the document template if it's other than Normal.

- Clicking the Default button in the Font, Language, or Page Setup dialog box and responding Yes when prompted. Clicking Default saves the character formatting, language, or page setup in the document template. The character formatting and language are stored within the Normal style of the document template.

You can also explicitly affect the contents of one or more templates by using the Organizer. With the Organizer, you can delete, rename, or copy (from one template to another) styles, AutoText entries, custom toolbars, or macros. To open the Organizer dialog box, either choose Style from the Format menu or choose Templates And Add-Ins from the Tools menu, and then click the Organizer button (in the Style or Templates And Add-Ins dialog box). In the Organizer dialog box, first click the tab corresponding to the type of template item that you want to manage, and then follow the guidelines given in Figure 7-7.

You can delete, copy, or rename styles, custom toolbars, or macros stored in either a document or a template. AutoText entries, however, are stored *only* in templates.

To select a range of items in the Organizer list, press Shift and click the first and then the last item. To select several items that are not adjoining, press Ctrl and click each item.

FIGURE 7-7.
Using the Organizer to copy, delete, or rename template items.

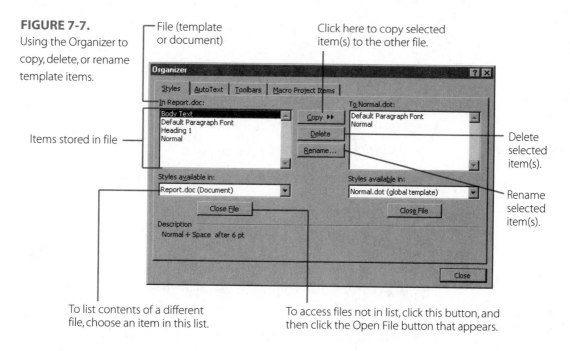

File (template or document)

Click here to copy selected item(s) to the other file.

Items stored in file

Delete selected item(s).

Rename selected item(s).

To list contents of a different file, choose an item in this list.

To access files not in list, click this button, and then click the Open File button that appears.

A final way to modify a template is to open the template file and edit it in the same way you edit a document. The following are the general steps:

1 Choose Open from the File menu, or click the Open button on the Standard toolbar.

2 In the Open dialog box, choose Document Templates in the Files Of Type list and then select the template file you want to modify. Most templates are stored within the Templates subfolder of the folder in which you have installed Office (usually \Program Files\Microsoft Office).

3 Edit and format the template using the same techniques used for documents. You can add or modify any of the template items listed in Tables 7-2 (page 216) and 7-3 (page 217). For the items listed in Table 7-3, be sure to save your changes in the template itself rather than in the Normal template.

? SEE ALSO

For information on the Page Setup dialog box, see "Adjusting the Page Setup," page 300.

II

Microsoft Word

4 Choose Save from the File menu or click the Save button to save your changes.

Creating New Templates

The procedure for creating a new template is similar to that for creating a new document. The following are the basic steps:

1 Choose New from the File menu.

2 In the New dialog box, turn on the Template option in the lower right corner,

select an existing template to use as the basis for your new template, and click OK.

3 Enter text and graphics, edit, and format the new template using the same techniques used for documents. You can add any of the items listed in Tables 7-2 and 7-3 on pages 216 and 217.

4 Choose Save from the File menu or click the Save button to save the new template.

If you want the New command to display the template you create, you must save it in the Templates folder in your Office folder (usually \Program Files\Microsoft Office), or in one of the subfolders within Templates (Memos, Publications, and so on). Alternatively, you can change the folder where the New command looks for templates by choosing Options from the Tools menu, clicking the File Locations tab, and modifying the User Templates or Workgroup Templates items. Also, you must name the template file with the DOT extension or omit the extension. (If you omit it, Word will add the DOT.) Note that extensions might not be displayed when you list files, depending on the options you have chosen in Windows 95.

TIP

> **Base a New Template on an Existing Document**
> You can get a head start in creating a new template by basing it on an existing document. To do this, open the document and immediately choose Save As from the File menu, select Document Template in the Save As Type list, enter a name for the new template in the File Name box, and click OK. (Word will save the new template in the folder listed for User Templates on the File Locations tab of the Options dialog box.) Then, make any changes you want and use the Save command to save these changes.

Changing the Template Attached to a Document and Loading Global Templates

You can change the template that is attached to a document. When you do this, all the AutoText entries, macros, custom toolbars and menus, and shortcut keys that are stored in the new template become available to the document (in place of the items stored in the previous template). To change the document template, do the following:

1 Make sure that the document you want to change is displayed in the current active document window.

2 Choose Templates And Add-Ins from the Tools menu. Word will display the Templates And Add-Ins dialog box. (See Figure 7-6 on page 214.)

3 Click the Attach button.

4 Select the desired template in the Attach Template dialog box. Make sure that Document Templates is selected in the Files Of Type list. Then click the Open button.

Also, Word allows you to load one or more templates in addition to the document template. An additional template that you have loaded is known as a *global template,* and all the AutoText entries, macros, custom toolbars and menus, and shortcut keys that are stored in these

II

Microsoft Word

templates also become available to any open document. (An item defined in the document template overrides a similarly named item in any of the global templates you load.) To load a global template, choose Templates from the File menu and do the following:

- If the template is listed within the Global Templates And Add-Ins list, simply check it.

- If the template is not in the list, click the Add button. In the Add Template dialog box, make sure that the Document Templates item is chosen in the Files Of Type list, select the template you want, and click OK. The template will be added to the Global Templates And Add-Ins list and will be checked.

 NOTE

> You can also load a Word add-in, which is a utility program that supplies enhancement features to Word. (You typically obtain such a program from a software vendor.) To do this, use the procedure for opening an additional template, except that in the Add Template dialog box you should choose the Word Add-Ins item in the Files Of Type list.

A global template or add-in will remain loaded only for the remainder of your current Word session. When you exit and restart Word, you'll need to reload it. Alternatively, you can place a copy of a template in the Startup folder within your Winword folder (which is usually found with the \Program Files\Microsoft Office folder). This template will then be loaded automatically whenever you run Word.

CHAPTER 8

Arranging Text in Columns and Lists

This chapter presents a diverse collection of techniques that allow you to arrange, sort, group, and emphasize paragraphs of text in your documents. You'll learn how to arrange text in rows and columns using simple tab characters or sophisticated Word tables. You'll learn how to arrange text in snaking newspaper-style columns. You'll learn how to create various kinds of lists, and how to sort the contents of lists as well as of Word tables. Finally, you'll learn how to arrange or emphasize paragraphs of text by adding borders and background shading.

Many of the features described in this chapter—tabs, bulleted and numbered lists, borders, and shading—are types of paragraph formatting. This chapter thus extends the discussion on basic paragraph formatting that was the focus of Chapter 6, "Formatting a Word Document."

Using Tabs

Pressing the Tab key inserts white space into your document and moves the insertion point so that the next character you type will be aligned on the next *tab stop*. The Tab key doesn't insert a series of space characters; rather, it inserts a single nonprinting character that you can delete with a single press of the Backspace or Delete key. You can make tab characters visible on the screen—as small arrows—by choosing Options from the Tools menu, clicking the View tab, and turning on the Tab Characters option. (Or you can click the Show/Hide ¶ button on the Standard toolbar to show *all* nonprinting characters.) See Figure 8-1.

FIGURE 8-1.
Tab characters
and tab stops.

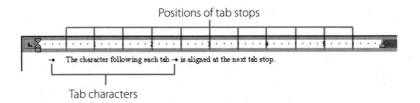

You can use tabs to arrange numbers or small blocks of text into rows and columns. In general, however, Word tables (discussed in the next section) are easier to use and a more versatile method for arranging text into rows and columns, especially if any of the individual blocks of text you're arranging won't fit on a single line.

● TIP

Use Ctrl+Tab to Insert Tabs in Outline View or in Tables
To insert a tab character within a Word table or to insert a tab when you're in Outline view, press Ctrl+Tab. You must also press Ctrl+Tab to insert a tab at the beginning of a line of text if you have selected the Tabs And Backspace Set Left Indent editing option. This option is described in "Using Shortcut Keys to Apply Paragraph Formatting," page 194.

In Word, you can adjust both the spacing and the type of the tab stops. Word has two kinds of tab stops: *default* and *custom*. Default tab stops apply to the entire document; they are not, therefore, strictly paragraph formatting. In documents created from most templates, the default tab stops are set at 0.5". This means that anywhere in the document (unless you have set custom tab stops), tab stops will be placed at half-inch intervals, starting at the left margin. The default tab stops are marked with small vertical lines at the bottom of the ruler:

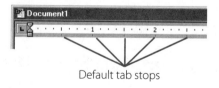

Default tab stops

You can change the default tab stops for the document in the active window, as follows:

1 Choose Tabs from the Format menu. Word will open the Tabs dialog box. (See Figure 8-2.)

2 Type a new value in the Default Tab Stops box and click OK.

FIGURE 8-2.
The Tabs dialog box.

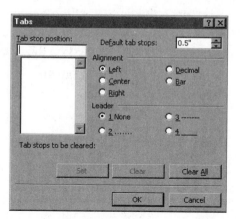

 TIP

Changing the default tab stops will affect only the active document. To change the default tab stops for all documents you create based on a particular template, open that template and perform the steps given above.

You can also define *custom* tab stops. Unlike default tab stops, custom tab stops are a paragraph formatting feature; therefore, they affect only the paragraph or paragraphs to which you have applied them. You can define custom tab stops using either the ruler or the Tabs dialog box.

Microsoft Word

> Because custom tab stop settings are a paragraph formatting feature, you can use the techniques for paragraph formatting that were discussed in the previous chapters. For example, you can find or replace tab stop formatting, copy the formatting from one paragraph to another, or assign the formatting to a paragraph style.

Defining Custom Tab Stops Using the Ruler

The easiest way to define custom tab stops is to use the horizontal ruler. (If the ruler isn't shown, choose Ruler from the View menu. You can also temporarily view the ruler by holding the mouse pointer over the gray bar at the top of the document window.) The following is the procedure:

1 Select the paragraph or paragraphs for which you want to define custom tab stops.

2 Click the button at the left end of the ruler to choose one of the four types of tab stops. Each time you click, the type changes, as indicated by the symbol displayed on the button:

Symbol	Type of Tab Stop
L	Left
⊥	Center
⌐	Right
⊥	Decimal

The different types of tab stops control the alignment of the text that you type after pressing Tab, as shown in Figure 8-3.

3 Click the position on the ruler where you want to place the tab stop. Word will mark the position of the tab stop using the symbol for the tab stop type. Notice that whenever you position a custom tab stop, Word removes all default tab stops to the left of the custom tab stop. Default tab stops to the right remain in place. The default tab stops work as left tab stops wherever they appear.

You can change the position of a custom tab stop by dragging it to a new location on the ruler, and you can remove a custom tab stop by dragging it off the ruler.

FIGURE 8-3.
The four different kinds of tab stops.

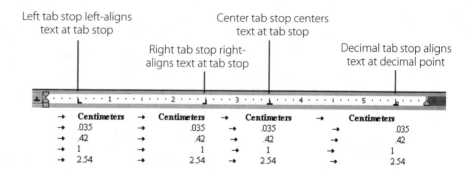

Left tab stop left-aligns text at tab stop

Center tab stop centers text at tab stop

Right tab stop right-aligns text at tab stop

Decimal tab stop aligns text at decimal point

Defining Custom Tab Stops Using the Tabs Dialog Box

You can also define custom tab stops using the Tabs dialog box, which provides the following additional features:

- You can enter precise measurements for the positions of the tab stops.

- You can fill the space preceding the tab with a *leader* character.

- You can add a vertical line that passes through a paragraph.

To use the Tabs dialog box, do the following:

1 Select the paragraph or paragraphs for which you want to define custom tab stops.

2 Open the Tabs dialog box (see Figure 8-2, page 225) by choosing Tabs from the Format menu. *Or* you can click the Tabs button within the Paragraph dialog box as described in Chapter 6, "Formatting a Word Document."

3 To define a new tab stop, enter its position (that is, its distance from the left margin) into the Tab Stop Position box.

4 Choose the type of tab stop you want by selecting one of the options in the Alignment area. The different types are shown in Figure 8-3. The Bar option adds a vertical line to the paragraph rather than defining a custom tab stop.

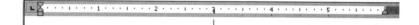

5 If you want to fill the blank space before the tab using a leader character, select option 2, 3, or 4 in the Leader area of the dialog box. For example, the following numbers are aligned with decimal tabs that have been assigned a leader character (option 2):

```
Rent ......................→.....................$843.00
Advertising................→..............$640.00
Entertainment..........→..........$8,432.00
```

6 Click the Set button. The tab will be added to the list.

7 Repeat steps 3 through 6 for each additional custom tab stop that you want to define. To remove a custom tab stop, select it in the list and click Clear (or Clear All to remove all custom tab stops and restore the default tab stops).

8 Click OK to accept your custom tab stop or stops and return to the document.

 NOTE

> If you want to set or modify tab stops for text you have already entered, you must first select *all* of the tabular text. (Generally each line of tabular text is entered as a separate paragraph.) Otherwise the new tab stops will take effect only for the single paragraph currently containing the insertion point.

Using Tables

A Word *table* is a highly versatile element for arranging text in rows and columns. Figure 8-4 shows a Word table as it appears on the screen. There are many advantages to using a table instead of tab characters. For example, if a particular text item doesn't fit on a single line, Word automatically creates a new line and increases the height of the row. (The table shown in Figure 8-4 would be difficult to create using tab stops.) Also, with tables you can easily rearrange and adjust the size of the rows and columns, and you can emphasize table items with borders and background shading.

FIGURE 8-4.
A Word table as it
appears on the screen.

Paragraph Formatting Action	Shortcut Key	Comment
Increase left paragraph indent	Ctrl+M	Indent is moved to the next tab stop. (See Chapter 8 for information on tab stops.)
Decrease left paragraph indent	Ctrl+Shift+M	Indent is moved to previous tab stop; cannot be used to create a negative left indent.
Increase hanging indent	Ctrl+T	All paragraph lines are indented except the first line. Each time you press the key combination, the indent is moved to the next tab stop.
Decrease hanging indent	Ctrl+Shift+T	Hanging indent is moved to the previous tab stop.
Add or remove 12 points of extra space above paragraph	Ctrl+0 (zero)	Toggles feature on or off.

 TIP

Use the Insert Microsoft Excel Worksheet Button for Complex Tables

In some cases, it might be better to insert an Excel worksheet rather than a Word table into your Word document (for example, if the table contains complex calculations, statistical analysis, or charts). To insert an Excel worksheet, click the Insert Microsoft Excel Worksheet button on the Standard toolbar and drag the mouse pointer to select the number of rows and columns. An Excel worksheet will be embedded in your Word document and you will have access to the Excel menu and toolbars. For more information, see the chapters in Part III, "Microsoft Excel."

Inserting a Table

To construct a table at the position of the insertion point, simply use the Insert Table button on the Standard toolbar, as shown below:

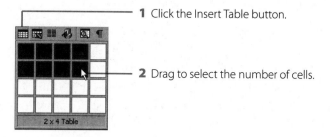

1 Click the Insert Table button.

2 Drag to select the number of cells.

The new table will consist of rows and columns of empty *cells*. The lines defining these cells are known as *gridlines*. Gridlines can be shown in a variety of different ways. The gridlines in a newly created table are marked with thin, solid *borders*. A border is a line that is visible both on the screen and on the printed copy of the document (borders can also be added to paragraphs and other objects). Later in the chapter, you'll learn how to modify or remove one or more borders from a table. If you remove a border, the gridline will be marked with a light gray line that appears on the screen but is not printed; this line will appear, however, only if the Show Gridlines option on the Table menu is turned on.

 TIP

Add New Rows to a Table by Pressing Tab

If you don't know how many rows you'll need when you insert a table, simply choose a single row. As you'll see, it's very easy to add new rows to the end of the table as you enter the table text. (You should, however, try to choose the actual number of columns, because inserting additional columns is not as easy.)

Entering Text into a Table

To add text to a cell in a table, simply click in the cell and type the text in the same way that you would type text into an ordinary paragraph. Notice that if you reach the right border of the cell, Word wraps the text down to the next line and automatically increases the height of the entire row to accommodate the new text. If you press Enter while typing in a cell, Word will insert a new paragraph *within* the cell. (Each cell contains one or more entire paragraphs.) You can edit and format text within a cell using the standard Word editing and formatting techniques given in the previous chapters.

To move the insertion point to another cell, click in the cell or use the arrow keys. To move to the next cell (in row-by-row order) and select any text it contains, press Tab. To move to the previous cell and select any text it contains, press Shift+Tab. When you're in the last cell of the table, pressing Tab adds a new row to the end of the table.

 TIP

Insert Tabs in Tables

To insert a tab character in a table cell, press Ctrl+Tab. You set the position of tab stops as described in the previous section. There is one oddity—when you set a decimal tab, the text in the cell is moved to that tab stop without your having to put a tab character in front of it.

Inserting and Deleting
Rows, Columns, and Cells

To insert or delete rows, columns, or groups of cells, you must first select the appropriate portion of the table. You can select a cell, row, or column as follows:

Units	Points	Picas	Centimeters	Inches
Points	1	1/12	.035	1/72
Picas	12	1	.42	1/6
Centimeters	28.35	2.38	1	.39
Inches	72	6	2.54	1

To select a cell, click here.

Units	Points	Picas	Centimeters	Inches
Points	1	1/12	.035	1/72
Picas	12	1	.42	1/6
Centimeters	28.35	2.38	1	.39
Inches	72	6	2.54	1

To select a row, click here.

Units	Points	Picas	Centimeters	Inches
Points	1	1/12	.035	1/72
Picas	12	1	.42	1/6
Centimeters	28.35	2.38	1	.39
Inches	72	6	2.54	1

To select a column, click here.

II

Microsoft Word

After you have selected a single cell, row, or column, you can keep the mouse button pressed and drag to select additional cells, rows, or columns. Alternatively, you can select any block of cells by placing the insertion point within a cell and then pressing an arrow key while holding down Shift. If the Num Lock feature is turned off and the insertion point is located somewhere in the table, you can select the entire table, by pressing Alt+5 (the 5 on the numeric keypad).

The following is the method for adding entire rows or columns to an existing table:

1 To insert rows at a particular position in a table, select existing rows just below that position; the number of rows you select should be the same as the number you want to add. For example:

To insert two rows above row B, select here.

To insert a single row, you can simply place the insertion point anywhere in the row.

Likewise, to insert columns, select an equal number of columns to the right of the position where you want to place the new ones.

Insert Rows   Insert Columns

2 If you're inserting rows, click the Insert Rows button on the Standard toolbar, or if you're inserting columns, click the Insert Columns button.

 NOTE

> The Standard toolbar actually has only *one* button for table insertion. When table rows, columns, or cells are selected, the button is labeled Insert Rows, Insert Columns, or Insert Cells. When the insertion point or selection is *outside* a table, the button is labeled Insert Table and it inserts a new table. With each type of selection, the image on the button changes to indicate its function.

Alternatively, you can click on the selection using the right mouse button, and choose Insert Rows, Insert Columns, or Insert Cells from the shortcut menu. The command on the shortcut menu changes depending on what part of a table is selected.

After clicking the Insert Rows button or choosing the Insert Rows command from the shortcut menu, the example table shown above (under step 1) looks like this:

Two new rows are inserted above row B.

Word marks the end of each table cell with an end-of-cell mark, and the end of each table row with an end-of-row mark. You can make these marks visible by clicking the Show/Hide ¶ button on the Standard toolbar. In step 1 above, if you want to insert rows you should include the end-of-row marks in your selection, whether or not they are visible. To insert a column at the right end of a table, select the entire "column" of end-of-row marks before clicking the Insert Columns button:

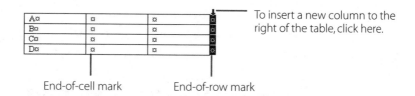

To insert a new column to the
right of the table, click here.

End-of-cell mark   End-of-row mark

As you learned earlier in this chapter, you can insert a row at the *end*
of a table by pressing Tab in the last cell.

To insert a block of one or more cells without inserting entire rows or
columns, do the following:

1 Select a block of existing cells that has the number and arrangement of the cells you want to insert.

2 Click the Insert Cells button, or click the selection with the right
mouse button and choose Insert Cells from the shortcut menu.
Word will display the Insert Cells dialog box, which you can see
in Figure 8-5.

FIGURE 8-5.

The Insert Cells
dialog box.

3 Choose Shift Cells Right to have Word move the existing cells
to the right when it inserts the new cells, or choose Shift Cells
Down to have it move the cells down. You can also choose Insert
Entire Row or Insert Entire Column to insert complete rows or columns even though you didn't select complete rows or columns.

To delete table rows, columns, or cells, simply select them and choose
Delete Rows, Delete Columns, or Delete Cells from the Table menu.
Alternatively, you can click on the selection with the right mouse button
and choose Delete Rows, Delete Columns, or Delete Cells from the shortcut menu. (The command will be labeled according to the current selection.) If you have selected a block that doesn't include complete rows or
columns, Word will display the Delete Cells dialog box, which lets you
choose the way the remaining cells are rearranged after the deletion.

To delete the *contents* of rows, columns, or cells—that is, the text or graphics contained in them—without removing the cells themselves, select the rows, columns, or cells and press the Delete key.

Adjusting the Size of Table Cells

You can adjust the width of a table column by dragging the right column gridline:

To change width of this column...   ...drag here.

Units	Points	Picas	Centimeters	Inches
Points	1	1/12	.035	1/72
Picas	12	1	.42	1/6
Centimeters	28.35	2.38	1	.39
Inches	72	6	2.54	1

To adjust the width of one or more specific cells in a column (rather than an entire column), select the cells before dragging. The cells in a single column can vary in width.

When adjusting the width of a column, you can modify the way Word changes the widths of the cells to the right of the column gridline, if there are any, by pressing additional keys while dragging:

If You Press This Key While Dragging Gridline	Effect on Cells to Right of Gridline, If Any
No key	Word changes width only of the cells to the immediate right of gridline, without changing overall table width.
Alt	Same effect on table as pressing no key, but Word displays the width of each column within the ruler.
Ctrl	Word changes width of all cells to the right proportionately, without changing overall table width.
Shift+Ctrl	Word does *not* change width of cells to the right. Instead, it changes the overall table width.

Of course, if you drag the rightmost gridline in a table, you'll always change the overall table width (and pressing Ctrl or Shift+Ctrl will have no effect). Note that if you drag the leftmost gridline in the table, you'll change the indent of the selected rows (or the entire table if no rows are selected) from the left document margin.

Changing the Text Orientation in a Table Cell

You can modify the orientation of the text in a table cell so that rather than the text reading from left to right, it reads from bottom to top or from top to bottom. You might want to do this to make information fit into a particular table, or to improve the appearance or readability of a table. To change the text orientation within a table, select one or more cells (but don't select an entire column, or an entire row including the end-of-row mark), right-click within the selection and choose Text Direction from the shortcut menu. (To change a single cell, you can simply right-click within the cell without selecting it.) Then, select the desired orientation in the Text Direction dialog box:

Click one of these three boxes to set the orientation of the text within the selected table cells.

II

Microsoft Word

You can have Word automatically adjust the width of table columns to accommodate the text that they contain. To do this, select the column or columns (to change a single column, you can simply place the insertion point anywhere within the column). Then, choose Cell Height And Width from the Table menu, select the Column tab, and click the AutoFit button.

As you have seen, Word automatically adjusts the height of a table row to accommodate the text contained in the row. You can also manually adjust the height of a row by dragging the gridline at the bottom of the row. Note that unlike columns, you can't adjust the height of selected cells within a row—you always change the height of *all* the cells in the row.

Finally, you can make two or more rows have the same height by selecting them and choosing Distribute Rows Evenly from the Table menu (or by right-clicking the rows and choosing this command from the shortcut menu). Likewise, you can make two or more columns have the same width by selecting them and choosing Distribute Columns Evenly from the Table menu or the shortcut menu.

Moving and Copying Rows, Columns, and Cells

To *move* entire rows or columns within a table, select them and then use the mouse to drag them to a new location. The rows or columns will be removed from their current location and inserted into the table at the new location. To *copy* rows or columns, press the Ctrl key while dragging. When you select rows, you must include the end-of-row marks. Otherwise, you'll merely move or copy the contents of the cells.

> To use the techniques discussed in this section, the Drag-And-Drop Text Editing option must be enabled. To locate this option, choose Options from the Tools menu and click the Edit tab.

To *move* the contents of table cells, select the cells and drag to a new location in the table. Word will delete the contents of the cells you selected (leaving empty cells behind) and it will insert these contents into the cells at the target location, overwriting the current contents of the target cells. To *copy* the contents of table cells, press the Ctrl key while dragging. (To move or copy cell *contents*, you must not select entire columns. You can select entire rows as long as you don't include the end-of-row marks.) You can copy the text from one cell to another without overwriting the contents of the second cell. To do this, select the *text* within the first cell (rather than selecting the entire cell) and then drag to the new location. The copied text will be added to the contents of the second cell.

Using the Table Menu Commands

The previous sections have focused on working with tables using the Standard toolbar, mouse, and shortcut menus. In general, these interactive methods are the quickest and most convenient. The Table menu provides alternative methods for inserting and modifying tables; it also allows you to perform some additional table operations not possible with the interactive techniques. Table 8-1 summarizes the use of these commands:

TABLE 8-1. **Table Menu Commands and Their Effects**

Command	Description
Draw Table	Allows you to "draw" a table. This command is discussed in the next section.
Insert	Inserts a new table into a document, or inserts new rows, columns, or cells into an existing table. The command is labeled Insert Table, Insert Rows, Insert Columns, or Insert Cells, according to the current selection or position of the insertion point.
Delete	Deletes the selected table rows, columns, or cells. The command is labeled Delete Rows, Delete Columns, or Delete Cells, according to the current selection.
Merge Cells	Combines adjacent cells into a single cell.
Split Cells	Divides a single cell into two or more cells.
Select Row	Selects the table row containing the insertion point.
Select Column	Selects the table column containing the insertion point.
Select Table	Selects the entire table.
Table AutoFormat	Allows you to quickly modify the overall look of a table by choosing one of a set of predefined table formats.
Distribute Rows Evenly	Makes multiple rows the same height. This command is discussed in the next section.
Distribute Columns Evenly	Makes multiple columns the same width. This command is discussed in the next section.
Cell Height And Width	Lets you adjust the height, left indent, and alignment of rows, as well as the width of columns and the spacing between them.
Headings	Marks one or more rows at the top of a table as a heading. If a page break occurs within a table, Word repeats the heading at the top of the next page.

(continued)

II

Microsoft Word

TABLE 8-1. *continued*

Command	Description
Convert Table To Text	Removes the selected table and converts the text it contains to ordinary paragraphs. If text outside a table is selected, the command is labeled Convert Text To Table and it creates a new table and inserts the selected text into the table.
Sort	Sorts the contents of rows within a table. If the selection is outside a table, the command sorts paragraphs of text.
Formula	Inserts a formula into a table cell. A formula displays the result of a mathematical computation on numbers within table cells. This command allows you to use a Word table as if it were a simple spreadsheet.
Split Table	Divides a table into two separate tables, and inserts a regular paragraph between the two tables.
Show Gridlines	When selected, this menu option causes Word to mark the gridlines around cells in all tables using light gray lines. These lines are visible only on the screen (they don't print) and only where borders have not been applied. Note that when selected, the option is labeled Hide Gridlines, and when not selected it's labeled Show Gridlines.

? SEE ALSO

For information on using the Sort command on the Table menu, see "Sorting Lists and Tables," page 250.

Drawing Tables

Beginning with the Office 97 version of Word, you can interactively draw a table in much the same way that you draw lines or rectangles in a drawing program (or using the Word Drawing toolbar discussed in Chapter 10, "Designing Pages"). To draw a table, choose Draw Table from the Table menu or click the Tables And Borders button on the Standard toolbar.

Tables And Borders

When you choose the Draw Table command or click the Tables And Borders button, Word does the following:

- It switches to Page Layout view, if you're not already in it.

- It displays the Tables And Borders toolbar, which provides tools for working with tables, borders, and shading. This toolbar is shown in Figure 8-6, which labels the buttons used for working with tables; the other buttons will be described later in the chapter (in "Using Borders and Shading," page 253).

■ It selects the Draw Table tool on the Tables And Borders toolbar, which converts the mouse pointer into a pencil.

FIGURE 8-6.
The Tables And Borders toolbar buttons that are used for working with tables.

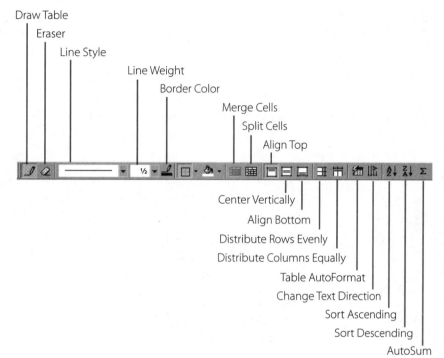

You can now create a table using the Draw Table tool, as follows:

1 Place the pencil-shaped pointer at one corner of the position in your document where you want to insert the table, press the mouse button, and drag the pointer to the opposite corner. The rectangle you draw defines the *outside* gridlines of the table, which initially consists of a single cell.

Microsoft Word

2   You can now divide the table into any number of cells by using the Draw Table tool to draw internal cell gridlines. Drag the pencil-shaped pointer to draw each cell gridline:

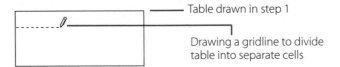

Table drawn in step 1

Drawing a gridline to divide table into separate cells

3   To *remove* a table gridline, click the Eraser button on the Tables And Borders toolbar and drag over the gridline. As you drag, the gridline will be highlighted, and when you release the mouse button, the gridline will be removed. Click the Eraser button again to turn it off when you are finished.

4   If you would like multiple table rows to be of equal height, select the rows and click the Distribute Rows Evenly button. To make multiple columns the same width, select the columns and click the Distribute Columns Evenly button. You can use the two Distribute buttons at any time—when you first draw the table or after you have entered the cell contents.

When you draw a table using the Draw Table tool, the way the gridlines are marked depends upon the current selections in the Line Style, Line Weight, and Border Color tools on the Tables And Borders toolbar. If you choose the No Border item in the Line Style list, the gridlines will be marked with light-gray lines, provided that the Show Gridlines option on the Table menu is turned on. These lines will appear on the screen but won't be printed. If you choose a border style in the Line Style list (such as a single, double, or dotted line), the gridlines will be marked with borders that appear both on the screen and on the printed copy, and the appearance of these borders will be affected by the settings in the Line Weight and Border Color tools. Note that changing a setting in the Line Style, Line Weight, or Border Color tool affects only the table gridlines that you *subsequently* draw or redraw; it won't affect table gridlines that you've already drawn. Later in the chapter (in the section "Using Borders and Shading"), you will learn how to modify or remove the borders of a table you have already drawn. Borders are discussed in a separate section because you can apply them to normal text, pictures, or frames, as well as to tables.

The Tables And Borders toolbar provides a number of buttons that allow you to quickly make modifications to an existing table (these are the 12 buttons on the right of the toolbar shown in Figure 8-6 on page 239). Note that the commands provided by these buttons—except for AutoSum—are also available either on the Table menu or on the shortcut menu that appears when you right-click in a table.

Creating Newspaper-Style Columns

Unlike the columns created with tables, newspaper-style columns are not divided into rows of side-by-side items. Rather, the text flows from the bottom of one column to the top of the next column, just like the familiar columns in newspapers and magazines. See Figure 8-7.

If you want to view newspaper-style columns on the screen, you must switch to Page Layout view or Print Preview. In Normal view, text is always displayed in a single column. You can create newspaper-style columns using either the Columns button on the Standard toolbar or the Columns dialog box.

FIGURE 8-7.
A page of a Word document, in which the text following the heading is divided into two newspaper-style columns.

Setting Up Columns Using the Columns Button

To quickly set up equal-width newspaper-style columns throughout your entire document, or for a portion of the document, do the following:

1 To create columns in a part of your document, select that part. To create columns throughout your entire document, place the insertion point anywhere in the document.

2 Click the Columns button and drag to indicate the number of columns you want (from 1 through 6):

 Drag to select the number of columns.

Word will divide the selected text, or the entire document, into the specified number of columns. The columns will be equal in width and will be separated by 0.5 inches.

(?) SEE ALSO

For more information on sections, as well as the features that can be applied to sections, see Chapter 10, "Designing Pages."

If you selected part of the document in step 1, Word will insert *section breaks* before and after your selection; that is, the selected text will be placed in a separate document section and newspaper-style columns will be applied to that section. In general, a Word document can be divided into separate sections, and each section can be assigned different page setup features, such as margins, headers, footers, and newspaper-style columns. Sections allow you to vary page setup features within a document. You can manually divide a document into sections using the Break command on the Insert menu. The steps given in this part of the chapter will work somewhat differently if you have previously divided your document into sections.

Setting Up Columns Using the Columns Dialog Box

The Columns dialog box lets you set up newspaper-style columns with the following additional features:

■ You can create columns of unequal width.

- For each column, you can specify the exact column width and the amount of space between that column and the next.

- You can force the columns to remain equal in width, even if you later adjust the column width.

- You can add vertical lines between the columns.

To set up newspaper-style columns with the Columns dialog box, do the following:

1 To create columns in a part of your document, select that part. To create columns from a specific position in the document through the end of the document, place the insertion point at that position. To create columns throughout the entire document, place the insertion point anywhere within the document.

2 Choose Columns from the Format menu to open the Columns dialog box, which is shown in Figure 8-8.

3 Choose an option in the Apply To list to tell Word the portion of your document you want to modify. If you selected text prior to opening the Columns dialog box, choose Selected Text to add columns to the selection only, or choose Whole Document to add columns to the entire document. If you didn't select text, choose Whole Document to add columns to the entire document, or choose This Point Forward to add columns from the position of the insertion point through the end of the document.

FIGURE 8-8.
The Columns dialog box.

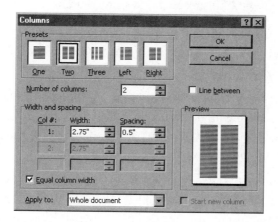

Microsoft Word

4 Choose a column arrangement.

- To use a standard column arrangement, choose one of the items in the Presets area.

- To create a custom column arrangement, choose the number of columns you want in the Number Of Columns box, and then for each column specify its width in the Width box and enter the space you want between that column and the next column in the Spacing box.

5 To force Word to keep the widths of the columns equal, turn on the Equal Column Width option. If this option is enabled, adjusting the column width—using the procedures described in the next section—will affect *all* columns simultaneously. If this option is *not* enabled, you can adjust the width of each column individually. Note that if you choose the One, Two, or Three option in the Presets area, Equal Column Width is selected automatically.

6 To add a vertical line between each column, turn on the Line Between option. To force Word to move the text following the insertion point to the start of a new column, turn on the Start New Column option (for this option to be available, you must select This Point Forward in the Apply To list box).

Adjusting Columns

Once you have applied newspaper-style columns, you can change the column width, insert breaks within columns, and adjust other features.

The easiest way to change the width of columns is to activate Page Layout view (choose Page Layout from the View menu) and drag a *column marker* on the horizontal ruler, as shown in Figure 8-9.

If you selected the Equal Column Width option in the Columns dialog box, dragging any column marker will adjust the widths of all columns simultaneously. If you didn't select this option, you can change the width of each column independently.

You can force Word to move text into the next column by inserting a *column break* anywhere within a column (see Figure 8-10). To do this, place the insertion point where you want to break the column, choose

Break from the Insert menu, and turn on the Column Break option, or simply press Ctrl+Shift+Enter.

You can also *prevent* Word from inserting a column break within a paragraph by applying the Keep Lines Together paragraph formatting feature. To locate this formatting option, choose Paragraph from the Format menu and click the Line And Page Breaks tab.

If you want to change any of the other column features, such as the number of columns, just repeat the procedure for setting up columns given in the previous sections.

FIGURE 8-9.
Adjusting the width of newspaper-style columns using the column markers on the ruler in Page Layout view.

Drag here to change width of both columns.

Drag this column marker to change left column width.

Drag this column marker to change right column width.

FIGURE 8-10.
Inserting a column break within a newspaper-style column.

Creating Bulleted and Numbered Lists

You can quickly create lists in your document by having Word add bullet characters or numbering, together with appropriate indents. Such automatic bullets and numbering are a part of the paragraph formatting. Unlike any bullet characters or numbers you might add manually, you can't select or perform normal editing on automatic bullets or numbers. Also, if you rearrange the paragraphs in a numbered list, Word renumbers the list for you. Figure 8-11 shows examples of the three kinds of lists you can create by adding bullets or numbers.

FIGURE 8-11.

Examples of bulleted, numbered, and outline-numbered lists.

Bulleted Lists
- Word inserts a bullet character at the beginning of each paragraph.
- You can't select or edit the bullet characters.
- Word indents each paragraph.

Numbered Lists
1. Word inserts a number at the beginning of each paragraph and indents the paragraph.
2. You can't select or edit the numbers.
3. If you add or delete a paragraph from the list, Word automatically updates the numbering.

Outline-Numbered Lists
1) Features
   a) Arrange body text in an outline format.
   b) Word automatically inserts the numbers or letters.
2) Techniques
   a) You convert paragraphs to an outline-numbered list using the Outline Numbered tab of the Bullets and Numbering dialog box.
   b) You adjust the level of a paragraph by clicking the Increase Indent or the Decrease Indent button on the Formatting toolbar.

You can apply bullets and numbers using the Formatting toolbar or using the Bullets And Numbering dialog box.

 NOTE

Because bullets and numbering are a paragraph formatting feature, you can use most of the techniques for paragraph formatting that were discussed in the previous chapters. For example, you can copy the formatting from one paragraph to another, or assign the formatting to a paragraph style.

Adding Bullets and Numbering Using the Formatting Toolbar

The quickest way to have Word apply bullets or numbering to a list is to use the Bullets button or the Numbering button on the Formatting toolbar, as follows:

1 Type the list. Press Enter at the end of each list item so that it's contained in a separate paragraph.

2 Select all the paragraphs in the list.

Bullets Numbering

3 Click the Bullets button to apply bullets, or click the Numbering button to apply numbering.

? SEE ALSO

For information on automatically creating bulleted and numbered lists with the AutoFormat command, see "Formatting Documents Automatically," page 166. For instructions on numbering the lines in a document, see "Adjusting the Page Setup," page 300.

If you apply numbering to a series of paragraphs and then delete or rearrange one or more of them, Word will automatically update the numbering. If you place the insertion point at the end of a bulleted or numbered paragraph and press Enter, the new paragraph will also be bulleted or numbered. If, however, you press Enter twice without typing text, the new paragraphs will *not* be bulleted or numbered; this is a convenient way to *stop* adding bullets or numbering when you reach the end of your list.

You can remove bullets or numbering by selecting one or more paragraphs and clicking the Bullets button or the Numbering button again. You can also remove the bullet or number from a single paragraph by placing the insertion point immediately following the bullet or number and pressing Backspace.

To control the starting number for a list of automatically numbered paragraphs, you'll need to use the Bullets And Numbering dialog box, described in the next section.

Number Cells in Tables

You can number the cells in a Word table by selecting the cells and clicking the Numbering button. Word will number the cells beginning with the upper-left cell and progressing through each row from left to right. If you want to number just the first cell in each row, select the first column before clicking the Numbering button.

II

Microsoft Word

Adding Bullets and Numbering Using the Bullets And Numbering Dialog Box

If you apply bullets or numbering using the Bullets And Numbering dialog box rather than the Formatting toolbar, you have the following additional options:

- You can choose any bullet character for a bulleted list.

- You can specify the starting number for a numbered list.

- You can modify the appearance and position of the bullet characters or numbering.

- You can create an outline-numbered list, which displays normal text in an attractive outline format (without using the Heading styles or Outline view).

The following is the procedure:

1   Select all the paragraphs in the list.

2   Open the Bullets And Numbering dialog box by choosing Bullets And Numbering from the Format menu, or by clicking the selection with the right mouse button and choosing Bullets And Numbering from the shortcut menu.

3   To apply *bullets*, click the Bulleted tab of the Bullets And Numbering dialog box:

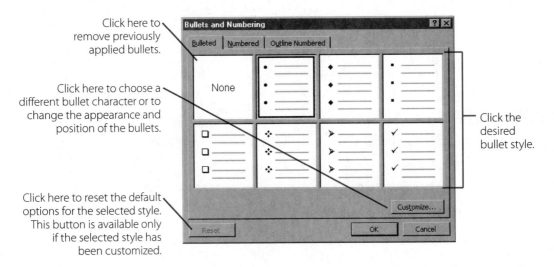

Click here to remove previously applied bullets.

Click here to choose a different bullet character or to change the appearance and position of the bullets.

Click here to reset the default options for the selected style. This button is available only if the selected style has been customized.

Click the desired bullet style.

To apply *numbering*, click the Numbered tab:

Click here to remove previously applied numbering.

Click here to start numbering the list with 1.

Click here to reset the default options for the selected style. This button is available only if the selected style has been customized.

Click here to continue the numbering sequence of the previous list.

Click the desired numbering style.

Click here to create a custom numbering style or to specify the starting number.

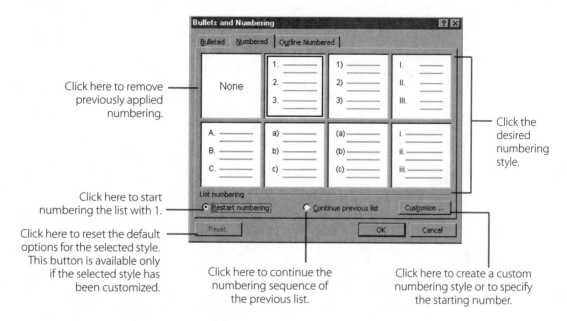

To apply *outline numbering*, click the Outline Numbered tab:

Click here to remove previously applied outline numbering.

Click here to start numbering the list with 1.

Click here to reset the default options for the selected style. This button is available only if the selected style has been customized.

Click here to continue the numbering sequence of the previous list.

Click the desired numbering style.

Click here to create a custom numbering style or to specify the starting number.

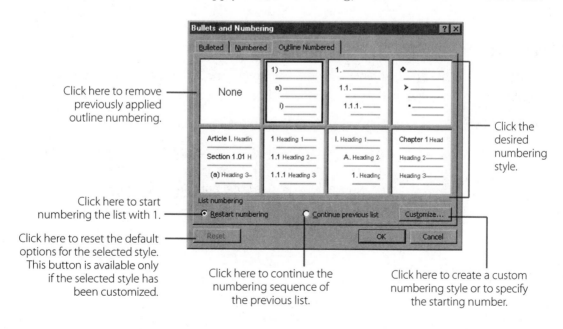

Microsoft Word

SEE ALSO

For instructions on using Outline view, see "Using Outline View to Organize Your Documents," page 358.

The outline-numbered list feature allows you to arrange text with an outline format. (See the example in Figure 8-11 on page 246.) Once you have applied this feature to a series of paragraphs using the procedure above, you can adjust the level of each paragraph as follows:

- To demote a paragraph (that is, convert it to a lower-level list item), place the insertion point in the paragraph and press Alt+Shift+Right arrow or click the Increase Indent button on the Formatting toolbar.

Increase Indent

- To promote a paragraph (that is, convert it to a higher-level list item), place the insertion point in the paragraph and press Alt+Shift+Left arrow or click the Decrease Indent button on the Formatting toolbar.

Decrease Indent

NOTE

The outline-numbered list feature is convenient for permanently formatting any amount of document text as an attractive outline. In contrast, Outline view allows you to temporarily view an entire document in outline form so that you can quickly organize the text.

Sorting Lists and Tables

You can have Word sort the items in a list consisting of a series of paragraphs. You can also have it sort rows within a table.

To sort a list of paragraphs, do the following:

1 Select all the paragraphs that make up the list. (Recall that a paragraph consists of any amount of text followed by a paragraph mark—a single word, a phone number, or a person's name.)

2 Choose Sort from the Table menu to open the Sort Text dialog box, shown here:

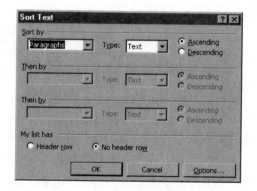

3 In the Sort By list, choose the part of the text that is to be used as the sort criterion. To sort a list, you normally choose the Paragraphs item to base the sort on all text in each paragraph. If, however, each paragraph is divided into *fields* (entries within the paragraphs separated with tabs, commas, or another character), you can base the sort on a specific field by choosing Field 1, Field 2, and so on. For instance, if you wanted to sort the following list by birthdate,

John, December 18

Sue, April 25

Pete, April 25

Joan, June 10

you would select Field 2. You can also choose a second and a third sort field in the Then By boxes, which Word will use if the previous sort fields are identical. In the example above, if you chose Field 1 in the second Then By box, Word would use the names to sort the paragraphs for Sue and Pete, who have identical birthdays—that is, it would place Pete before Sue.

4 Select an item in the Type list to indicate the way the text should be sorted. You can choose Text to sort alphabetically. If the information you're sorting on consists of numbers, you can choose Number to sort it numerically. If it consists of dates, you can choose Date to sort it chronologically.

5 Select Ascending to sort text from the beginning to the end of the alphabet, numbers from smaller to larger, and dates from earlier to later. Select Descending to sort in the opposite order.

6 Select Header Row to eliminate the first paragraph from the sort, or No Header Row to sort all selected paragraphs. When Header Row is selected, the items in the first row are used to name the fields; in this case, you can select a name from the Sort By or Then By list (rather than selecting Field 1, Field 2, and so on).

7 If you want to modify the way Word sorts text, click the Options button to open the Sort Options dialog box. (See below.) This dialog box lets you specify the character used to separate fields. (The example in step 3 uses commas.) Also, if you turn on the Case Sensitive option, a capitalized word will follow the same word in lowercase (when you sort text in ascending order). Finally, you can select a specific language in the Sorting Language list to cause Word to use the sorting rules defined by that language.

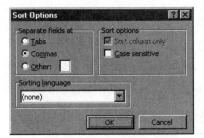

NOTE

If you sort a list of paragraphs to which you have applied automatic numbering, Word will renumber it properly.

You can also use the steps listed previously to sort rows within a Word table, with the following provisos:

■ In step 1, select the rows and columns you want to sort. To sort the entire table, you can simply place the insertion point anywhere within the table. Note that Word sorts only in the vertical direction; you can't, for example, select a single row and have Word sort the cells of that row (nor would you want to).

- In the Sort By and Then By lists, you choose the table columns that you want to use as sort criteria (assuming that you have selected more than one column in the table).

 SEE ALSO

For information on using the Undo command, see the sidebar "Undoing and Redoing Editing and Formatting Actions," page 142.

- In the Sort Options dialog box, you can turn on the Sort Column Only option to have Word sort only the selected column or columns. Otherwise, Word will sort entire rows even if you haven't selected all the columns.

After you have sorted a list of paragraphs or the contents of a table, you can, if you want, unsort it by immediately issuing the Undo command.

Using Borders and Shading

You can emphasize, organize, or set apart portions of your document by adding borders or background shading. You can add borders or shading to blocks of characters, to paragraphs, to cells within tables, or to entire tables (see Figure 8-12). You can also have Word print borders around entire pages in your document (see Figure 8-13 on the following page).

FIGURE 8-12.
Borders and shading applied to a block of characters, a paragraph, and a table.

You can apply borders and shading to blocks of characters.

You can apply borders and shading to entire paragraphs.

You can apply borders and shading to tables:

Units	Points	Picas	Centimeters	Inches
Points	1	1/12	.035	1/72
Picas	12	1	.42	1/6
Centimeters	28.35	2.38	1	.39
Inches	72	6	2.54	1

NOTE

As you have learned, if you create a table using the Insert Table menu command or button, it initially has a thin, solid border around all cells; and if you create a table using the Draw Table button on the Tables And Borders toolbar, you can assign it any style of borders (or no borders). In this section, you'll learn how to modify, remove, or add borders to a table that has already been created. Recall also that if you remove a border, Word will mark the cell gridline with a light-gray line (which appears on the screen but doesn't print), provided that the Show Gridlines option on the Table menu is turned on.

II

Microsoft Word

FIGURE 8-13.
Borders around a
document page.

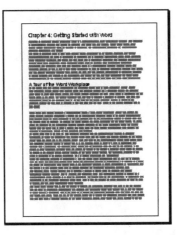

To apply borders and shading to characters, paragraphs, or tables, you can use either the Tables And Borders toolbar or the Borders And Shading dialog box. To apply borders to pages, you must use the Borders And Shading dialog box.

> **NOTE**
>
> Borders or shading applied to paragraphs (not to characters, tables, or pages) are a paragraph formatting feature. You can therefore use the techniques for paragraph formatting that were discussed in the previous chapters. For example, you can copy the formatting from one paragraph to another, or assign the formatting to a paragraph style.

Formatting Borders and Shading Using the Tables And Borders Toolbar

SEE ALSO
For information about adding horizontal borders automatically, see "Using the AutoFormat As You Type Feature," page 171.

You already learned how to use the Tables And Borders toolbar to create and modify tables (in the section "Drawing Tables," page 238). In this section, you'll learn how to use it to quickly apply (or modify) borders or shading around characters, paragraphs, cells within tables, or entire tables. Figure 8-14 shows the Tables And Borders toolbar, labeling each of the tools that you use for applying borders and shading. If the toolbar isn't visible, you can display it by pointing to Toolbars on the View menu or right-clicking on the menu bar or another toolbar and choosing Tables And Borders from the submenu that pops up.

FIGURE 8-14.
The Tables And Borders toolbar buttons that are used for applying borders and shading.

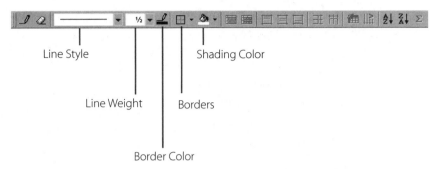

Line Style

Shading Color

Line Weight

Borders

Border Color

The first step in adding borders or shading is to make an appropriate selection. To apply borders or shading *outside* a table, do one of the following:

- To add borders or shading to a block of characters, select the characters *without* including the paragraph mark at the end of the paragraph.

- To add borders or shading to one or more entire paragraphs, select the paragraphs. To add borders or shading to a single paragraph, include the paragraph mark in your selection, or simply place the insertion point anywhere within the paragraph without selecting text.

- To add borders or shading to table cells, select one or more entire cells. To format a single cell, you can simply place the insertion point within the cell without selecting any text. To add borders or shading to text within a table cell without assigning borders or shading to the cell itself, select the text without selecting the end-of-cell mark.

To add borders to your selection, do the following:

1 Select the desired style, thickness, and color of the border or borders you want to add from the Line Style, Line Weight, and Border Color tools on the Tables And Borders toolbar. (Note that the Automatic color choice applies the current Window Font color set through the Windows Control Panel, which is usually black.)

II

Microsoft Word

2 Click the down arrow next to the Borders button and from the palette that Word displays, click the button that corresponds to the border or combination of borders that you want to apply:

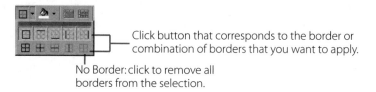

Click button that corresponds to the border or combination of borders that you want to apply.

No Border: click to remove all borders from the selection.

 NOTE

The Borders button also appears on the Formatting toolbar. On both the Formatting and the Tables And Borders toolbars, the image on the button and the button name displayed in the ScreenTip change according to which border style was most recently applied.

As you position the pointer over each button on the palette, Word displays a ScreenTip describing the border that will be applied (Top Border, Bottom Border, Left Border, and so on). When you click the button, Word will immediately apply the border or borders to the selection in your document.

You can repeat step 2 to apply more than one border. For example, to apply borders to the left and right of a paragraph, you could first click the Left Border button, and then click the Right Border button. If you want the borders to have different properties (for example, different colors), you will have to return to step 1 before applying each border.

To remove a border, you can simply click the same button on the Borders palette that you used to apply the border, provided that the border's original style, weight, and color are still selected on the toolbar. To remove *all* borders, click the No Border button on the Borders palette.

TIP

To *modify* the properties of a border that has already been applied, first select the new properties from the Line Style, Line Weight, and Border Color tools (step 1 above); and then use the Borders tool to reapply the border (step 2 above).

To apply shading to the selected paragraph or table cells, click the down arrow next to the Shading Color button on the Tables And Borders toolbar and then select the desired shading color from the palette. To remove shading, select the None item at the top of the palette.

 TIP

Drawing a Table *Without* Borders

To draw a table without borders, select No Border from the Line Style list box before clicking the Draw Table button and drawing the new table.

Formatting Borders and Shading Using the Borders And Shading Dialog Box

The Borders And Shading dialog box is not quite as easy to use as the Tables And Borders toolbar, but it provides the following additional options:

- You can create borders with a shadow effect or a 3-D effect.

- You can specify the distance between the borders and the text.

- You can apply a shading pattern as well as a background shading color (the Tables And Borders toolbar lets you apply only a background shading color).

- You can place a border around entire document pages.

To add borders or shading to paragraphs or tables, you must first make the appropriate selection. To apply borders and shading *outside* a table, do one of the following:

- To add borders or shading to a block of characters, select the characters *without* including the paragraph mark at the end of the paragraph.

- To add borders or shading to one or more entire paragraphs, select the paragraphs. To add borders or shading to a single paragraph, include the paragraph mark in your selection or simply place the insertion point anywhere within the paragraph without selecting text.

To add borders or shading to table cells, select one or more entire cells. To add borders or shading to the entire table, simply place the insertion point anywhere within the table, without selecting any text. To add borders or shading to text in a table cell without affecting the cell itself, select the text without selecting the end-of-cell mark.

To apply one or more borders to your selection, proceed as follows:

1 Open the Borders And Shading dialog box by choosing Borders And Shading from the Format menu.

2 Click the Borders tab:

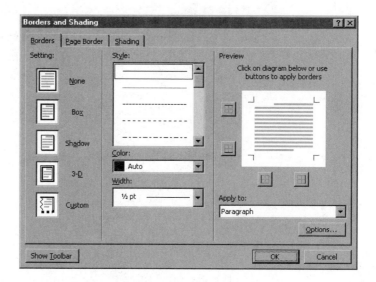

3 From the Style, Color, and Width lists, choose the properties of the border or borders that you want to apply.

4 Click one of the items in the Setting area to specify the basic look and arrangement of the border or borders. The specific choices in this area will depend on what you selected prior to opening the dialog box. Click the Custom item if you want to apply a custom combination of borders. If you want to *remove* all borders, click the None item and then click the OK button to close the dialog box (in this case, you can skip the remaining steps).

5 If you wish, you can add or remove specific borders by clicking appropriate buttons in the Preview area. If you want to modify the properties of a specific border, make the desired selections in the Style, Color, and Width lists just before clicking the button to add the border. (You can thus assign different properties to each border.)

6 If you have selected paragraphs, you can modify the clearance between the borders and the text by clicking the Options button and in the Border And Shading Options dialog box adjusting the measurements in the From Text area. If you have selected characters, a table, or table cells, you can't adjust the clearance.

7 You can choose an item in the Apply To list to modify the portion of your document that receives borders. For example, if you had selected several paragraphs, borders would normally be applied to the entire paragraphs (and the Paragraph item would be selected in the list); if you chose the Text item, however, the borders would be placed around the individual characters rather than around the entire paragraphs.

8 When the example borders shown in the Preview area have the look you want, click the OK button.

To apply shading to your selection, do the following:

1 Open the Borders And Shading dialog box and click the Shading tab:

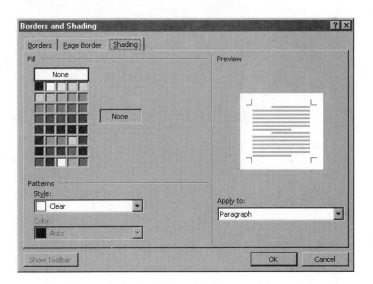

2 Select a background shading color (or select None) from the palette in the Fill area in the upper-left corner of the dialog box. (Note that this is the only shading property you can select when you apply shading using the Tables And Borders toolbar.)

3 Select a shading pattern from the Style list, or select Clear if you don't want a pattern.

4 If you selected an item other than Clear in the Style list, select the color of the shading pattern from the Color list.

5 If you wish to change the portion of your document that is to be shaded, select an item in the Apply To list as explained in step 7 above.

6 When the example shading shown in the Preview area has the look you want, click the OK button.

Adding Page Borders

To give your document a polished or decorative look, you can have Word draw borders around entire document pages. To add page borders, do the following:

1 Choose Borders And Shading from the Format menu to open the Borders And Shading dialog box, and click the Page Border tab:

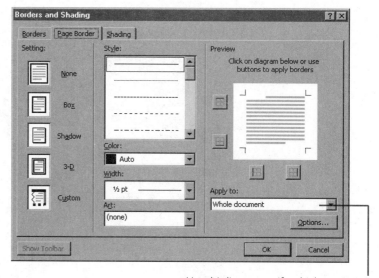

Use this list to specify which sections in your document will have borders.

2 Using the techniques described in the previous section for applying borders to characters, paragraphs, and tables, choose options until the example borders shown in the Preview area have the look you want.

3 Rather than applying a page border that consists of lines, you can create a border consisting of artwork. Word provides a large variety of different images and patterns. Simply choose the one you want from the Art list (or choose the (None) item to remove an artwork border).

4 You can click the Options button to choose several additional options that are not available for applying borders to characters, paragraphs, and tables:

Choose the reference point for the measurements entered into the text Margin boxes above.

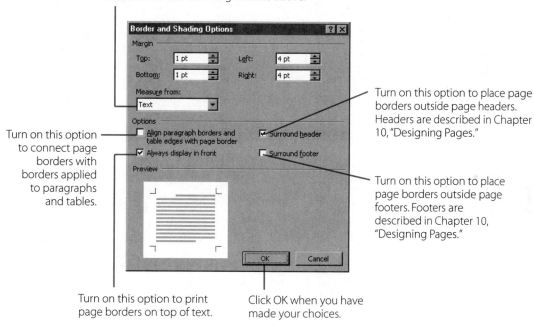

Turn on this option to connect page borders with borders applied to paragraphs and tables.

Turn on this option to place page borders outside page headers. Headers are described in Chapter 10, "Designing Pages."

Turn on this option to place page borders outside page footers. Footers are described in Chapter 10, "Designing Pages."

Turn on this option to print page borders on top of text.

Click OK when you have made your choices.

5 When the example border in the Preview area has the look you want, click the OK button.

CHAPTER 9

Using Word's Proofing Tools

Word's proofing tools will help you polish your writing and improve the appearance of your documents. You can use the proofing tools while you type (if you turn on Word's automatic spelling and grammar checking options or if you need to look up a word with the thesaurus) or after you have finished entering, editing, and formatting the text in your document, but before you preview the printed appearance of the document and make the final adjustments to the page setup that will be discussed in the next chapter.

 **TIP**

If you're missing any of the commands for running the proofing tools discussed in this chapter, you'll need to run the Office Setup program and install the proofing tools.

Marking the Language

If your document contains text in a foreign language, or text that you want to exclude from proofing, you should perform the steps discussed in this section before using the proofing tools; otherwise, you can safely skip this section.

In the version of Word sold in the United States, all text is initially marked as English (US), meaning English as written in the United States. If all or some of the text in your document is written in a different language or non-US English and you want to be able to proof this text, you should mark each block of such text. To do this, select the non-US English text, point to Language on the Tools menu, and then choose Set Language from the submenu to open the Language dialog box. (See Figure 9-1.)

FIGURE 9-1.
The Language
dialog box.

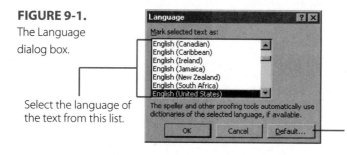

Select the language of
the text from this list.

To have Word use the selected
language as the default, click here.

SEE ALSO

For information on
character formatting,
see "Applying Char-
acter Formatting
Directly," page 181. For
information on assign-
ing character format-
ting to a style, see
"Modifying Styles,"
page 200.

Language is a type of character formatting. When you click the Default button, Word assigns the selected language format to the Normal style of the document *and* to the document's template. This affects all text based on the Normal style in the current document as well as in all new documents subsequently created using the same template.

Marking text with a particular language causes the Word proofing tools to search for the appropriate dictionary when you apply those tools to that text. The standard dictionary supplied with the version of Word sold in the United States can be used to proof text marked as any form of English (United States, British, Australian, and so on). (The term *dictionary* here refers to the set of data files used by the proofing tools. The standard dictionary includes support for nine regional variations of English.)

If you choose a language other than English, you must install the appropriate foreign language dictionary before you can proof that text. For information on obtaining foreign dictionaries, open the Word on-line Help Index topic "dictionaries (spelling)" and read the instructions on using a supplemental dictionary.

★ TIP

Use Styles to Assign Language to Text

If you frequently mark blocks of text with a particular language, you can save time by assigning the language to a style that you can apply to all blocks of text written in that language.

II

Microsoft Word

Your document might contain blocks of text that you want to exclude from proofing. For example, if you're writing a paper on *Beowulf*, you might want to exclude direct quotations that come from the poem so that the spelling checker won't flag all the archaic words and the grammar checker won't try to "improve" the writing style. To do this, use the steps given above but observe the following guidelines:

- First, select the text you want to exclude from proofing.

- In the Language dialog box, select the (No Proofing) item from the Mark Selected Text As list.

Checking Your Spelling

You can use the Word spelling checker to verify and help you correct the spelling of the text in your document. You can have Word automatically check your spelling as you type, or you can manually run the spelling checker to check text that you have already entered.

Checking Your Spelling Automatically as You Type

To have Word automatically check your spelling as you type, choose Options from the Tools menu, click the Spelling & Grammar tab (see Figure 9-2), and turn on the Check Spelling As You Type option in the Spelling section at the top of the dialog box.

FIGURE 9-2.
The Spelling & Grammar tab of the Options dialog box.

This button is labeled Recheck Document if you have previously checked the spelling or grammar.

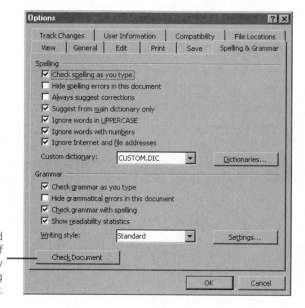

Word will then check the spelling of any text that has already been entered into your document, and it will check the spelling of each new word immediately after you type it. If the spelling checker encounters a word that it judges to be misspelled (that is, a word that it doesn't find in its dictionary), it marks the word with a wavy red underline. You can then ignore the word, correct it manually, or click on it with the right mouse button to display the following shortcut menu:

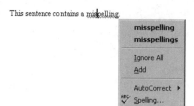

On the shortcut menu, choose one of the following options:

- Choose one of the suggested spellings at the top of the menu (if any) to correct the word.

- Choose Ignore All to have the spelling checker stop marking the word during the remainder of the current Word session (or until you click the Recheck Document button on the Spelling & Grammar tab of the Options dialog box).

- Choose Add to add the word to the custom dictionary so that Word will permanently stop marking the word as misspelled (custom dictionaries will be discussed on page 272).

- Choose AutoCorrect and choose one of the suggested spellings for the word from the submenu that pops up:

SEE ALSO

For information on using AutoCorrect, see "Using the AutoCorrect Feature," page 135.

Word will then correct the word in your document, and it will add the correction to the Replace Text As You Type list of the AutoCorrect feature. From then on, Word will automatically *correct*— not just mark—the misspelling whenever you type it, provided that you have turned on the Replace Text As You Type option. To locate this option, choose AutoCorrect from the Tools menu and click the AutoCorrect tab in the dialog box that appears.

- Choose Spelling to open the Spelling dialog box, which provides several additional options for correcting spelling and is described in the next section.

If the check-spelling-as-you-type feature has marked one or more words in your document, you can locate (and correct) these words by double-clicking the Spelling And Grammar Status icon on the Word status bar.

Spelling And Grammar Status

Each time you double-click this icon, Word moves the insertion point to the next marked word and opens the shortcut menu shown above so that you can correct the spelling.

Hide All Spelling Errors

If you turn on the Hide Spelling Errors In This Document option on the Spelling & Grammar tab of the Options dialog box (see Figure 9-2, page 266), Word will remove the wavy lines from all misspelled words in the active document, which might be distracting as you're writing your document. You can later restore the wavy lines, during your editing pass through the document, by turning this option off.

Manually Running the Spelling Checker

You might find it easier to check the spelling of a block of text—or an entire document—after you have typed it, rather than having to deal with misspellings while you write. In this case, you can either turn off the check-spelling-as-you-type feature or simply ignore the wavy underlines. Then, when you're ready to check your spelling, you can manually run the spelling checker.

After Word checks the spelling of the words in a sentence, it then checks the grammar of the sentence if the Check Grammar With Spelling option on the Spelling & Grammar tab of the Options dialog box is turned on (see Figure 9-2 on page 266). Also, after it has completed its check, it will display readability statistics if the Show Readability Statistics option on the Spelling & Grammar tab is turned on. The instructions in this section assume that both of these options are turned off. Checking grammar and displaying readability statistics are discussed later in the chapter ("Checking Your Grammar," page 276).

To check the spelling of text you've already entered, do the following:

1 If you want to check the spelling of your entire document, place the insertion point anywhere in the document. If you want to check the spelling of a portion of your document, select that portion. (You can quickly select a single word by double-clicking it.)

Spelling And Grammar

2 Begin the spelling check by choosing Spelling And Grammar from the Tools menu, pressing F7, or clicking the Spelling And Grammar button on the Standard toolbar.

3 Whenever the spelling checker encounters a word that it can't find in its dictionary, it displays the Spelling And Grammar dialog box (see Figure 9-3). Within this dialog box, the Not In Dictionary box displays a copy of the sentence containing the questionable word (which is shown in red), and the Suggestions list contains one or more possible correct spellings for the word (provided that the spelling checker can derive any, and that the Always Suggest Corrections option is selected, as discussed later).

FIGURE 9-3.

The Spelling And Grammar dialog box.

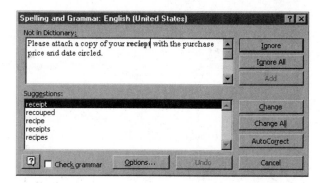

To deal with this word, you should do one or more of the following:

- To change the word and then search for the next misspelling, *either* correct the spelling of the word within the Not In Dictionary box (for your convenience, Word places the insertion point just after the word) and click the Change button, *or* simply select the correct spelling—if it's present—in the Suggestions list and click the Change button or the Change All button. Clicking Change will replace only the current occurrence of the word. Clicking Change All will replace the current occurrence of the word plus all occurrences that the spelling checker subsequently finds in the document (it won't change any occurrences that the spelling checker previously encountered and you chose to ignore). (The Change All button is not available when you correct the word manually in the Not In Dictionary box.)

Note that if you edit the word within the Not In Dictionary box you can click the Undo Edit button (which replaces the Ignore button), before you click another button, to restore the word. Note also that if you retype the word in the Not

In Dictionary box and Word still doesn't recognize the spelling, it will flag the word again.

 TIP

Find Repeated Words with the Spelling Checker

The spelling checker will also stop at any word that repeats the previous word (except for words that are commonly repeated, such as *that* and *had*). If the spelling checker encounters a repeated word, it will replace the Change button with the Delete button. You can click Ignore to leave the repeated word in the document, or click Delete to delete the second word.

- To leave the word unchanged and search for the next misspelling, click the Ignore or Ignore All button. If you click the Ignore button, the spelling checker will continue to flag other occurrences of the word that it subsequently finds. If you click the Ignore All button, the word will not be flagged again during the remainder of the spelling check or during any future spelling checks until you click the Recheck Document button on the Spelling & Grammar tab, as described in Table 9-1 in the next section.

- To leave the word unchanged and to add it to a custom dictionary so that Word will *permanently* stop flagging it, click the Add button. (Custom dictionaries are discussed in the next section.)

- To reverse your previous correction, click the Undo button.

SEE ALSO

For information about using the AutoCorrect feature, see "Using the AutoCorrect Feature," page 135.

- If the Suggestions list contains the correct spelling, you can select this spelling and click the AutoCorrect button to have Word define an AutoCorrect entry that will automatically correct the misspelling whenever you type it.

- If the Check Grammar With Spelling option is turned on, Word will check your grammar as well as your spelling. (As mentioned previously, you can also set this option through the Spelling & Grammar tab. The instructions in this section assume that this option is off.)

- To change the way Word checks your spelling, click the Options button. (Spelling options are discussed in the next section.)

> **Edit with the Spelling And Grammar Dialog Box Displayed**
> You can edit your document while the Spelling And Grammar dialog box remains displayed. To edit, click in the document. To resume the spelling check, click the Resume button in the Spelling And Grammar dialog box.

Customizing the Spelling Checker

You can tailor the way Word checks your spelling to your own preferences by clicking the Options button in the Spelling And Grammar dialog box, or by choosing Options from the Tools menu and clicking the Spelling & Grammar tab. Either way, Word will display the Spelling & Grammar tab that was shown in Figure 9-2 on page 266. Table 9-1 describes the actions you can perform on this tab that affect the spelling checker (the one you run manually). Note that these actions affect both the as-you-type spelling checker and the manual spelling checker unless otherwise noted in the table. The Check Spelling As You Type and Hide Spelling Errors In This Document options were discussed previously, and the options that affect the grammar checker will be discussed later in the chapter (in the section "Checking Your Grammar," page 276).

TABLE 9-1. Options on the Spelling & Grammar Tab

Action	Result
Turn on the Always Suggest Corrections option.	Whenever the spelling checker finds a misspelled word, the Suggestions list in the Spelling And Grammar dialog box will display, if possible, one or more replacement words. You can choose an appropriate replacement word to quickly correct your misspelling. This option does *not* affect the as-you-type spelling checker.
Turn on the Suggest From Main Dictionary Only option.	The spelling checker will suggest words only from its main dictionary and not from any custom dictionaries. Both dictionaries are used to check spelling. (Custom dictionaries are discussed in the next section.)

(continued)

II

Microsoft Word

TABLE 9-1. *continued*

Action	Result
Select a dictionary file name in the Custom Dictionary list.	The spelling checker will add words to this dictionary whenever you click the Add button in the Spelling And Grammar dialog box (or whenever you choose the Add shortcut menu command while correcting a word underlined by the check-spelling-as-you-type feature). This list contains the names of all custom dictionaries that are currently in use (that is, *opened*, as will be explained later).
Click the Dictionaries button.	Word will display the Custom Dictionaries dialog box, which allows you to create, open, remove, or edit custom dictionaries.
Turn on the Ignore Words In UPPERCASE option.	The spelling checker will not check the spelling of words that are in all capital letters. This option prevents the spelling checker from flagging acronyms.
Turn on the Ignore Words With Numbers option.	The spelling checker will not check the spelling of words that contain one or more numbers, such as R2D2.
Turn on the Ignore Internet And File Addresses option.	The spelling checker will not check the spelling of Internet addresses (such as http://www.microsoft.com) or file paths (such as C:\Book\Chapter1.doc).
Click Recheck Document.	If you have already run the spelling checker, this deletes the current list of ignored words and allows you to recheck your spelling.

Using Custom Dictionaries

Both the manually run spelling checker and the check-spelling-as-you-type feature look up words in the main spelling dictionary and in one or more custom dictionaries as well. When you install Word, it creates a single custom dictionary file named Custom.dic. Initially, this dictionary file is empty. However, every time you click the Add button in the

Spelling And Grammar dialog box, and whenever you choose the Add shortcut menu command while correcting a word underlined by the check-spelling-as-you-type feature, the current word is added to Custom.dic so that the word will no longer be flagged as a misspelling.

If using a single custom dictionary meets your needs, you don't need to do anything except occasionally add a word to it via the Add command. You might, however, want to create and use one or more special-purpose custom dictionaries. For example, if you write both computer books and science fiction, you might create one dictionary that contains the technical terms you use when writing computer books (perhaps named Computer.dic) and another dictionary that contains the invented words you use when writing science fiction (perhaps named Fiction.dic).

To create a new custom dictionary, do the following:

1 Choose Options from the Tools menu and click the Spelling & Grammar tab, or click the Options button in the Spelling And Grammar dialog box that appears during a spelling check. The Spelling & Grammar tab that will be displayed is shown in Figure 9-2 on page 266.

2 Click the Dictionaries button on the Spelling & Grammar tab to open the Custom Dictionaries dialog box:

3 Click the New button and in the Create Custom Dictionary dialog box, type a name for the dictionary in the File Name box:

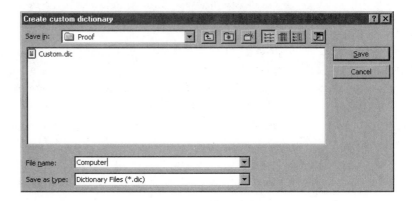

You can either include the DIC extension in the name you type, or omit the extension (in this case, Word will add the DIC extension for you). You can accept the default file location that Word initially selected or you can select a new one. When you click Save, Word will create a new, empty custom dictionary. Also, it will add this dictionary to the list in the Custom Dictionaries dialog box and it will check the box next to the dictionary name, which indicates that the dictionary has been opened (opening custom dictionaries is explained later).

4 If you want to use your new custom dictionary for checking text in a specific language, choose that language in the Language box in the Custom Dictionaries dialog box. The spelling checker will use the dictionary *only for text that has been marked for that language*. (Marking the language of text was described in the first section of the chapter.) If you select (None) in the Language list, the dictionary will be used for *all* text, regardless of its language format.

5 Click OK.

To use a custom dictionary that you have created or one that you have purchased or obtained from someone else, do the following:

1 Open the dictionary. (If you created a new dictionary using the steps above, it should already be open and you can skip this step.) To open a dictionary, click the Dictionaries button on the Spelling & Grammar tab (shown in Figure 9-2 on page 266) and click the check box next to the name of the dictionary in the Custom Dictionaries list:

Click here to open or close the custom dictionary.

A check mark will appear in the box next to the name, indicating that the dictionary is open. If the dictionary is not in the list, click the Add button and select the dictionary file. When you're done, click OK in the Custom Dictionaries dialog box and on the Spelling & Grammar tab.

The spelling checker will look up words in all custom dictionaries that have been opened. To close a dictionary, and not have Word use the words it contains, repeat this step but *remove* the check mark from the dictionary name in the Custom Dictionaries dialog box.

⭐ TIP

Remove or Edit a Dictionary

While the Custom Dictionaries dialog box is open, you can click the Remove button to remove the selected custom dictionary from the list. (This doesn't delete the dictionary file itself.) Also, if you're not currently running the manual spelling checker, you can click Edit to manually add or remove words from the selected dictionary file. Note that Word turns off the check-spelling-as-you-type feature when you edit a custom dictionary. After editing, close the dictionary and reselect this option on the Spelling & Grammar tab.

II

Microsoft Word

2 To add words to the custom dictionary, select the dictionary name in the Custom Dictionary list on the Spelling & Grammar tab (which lists all custom dictionaries that are currently open). Subsequently, whenever you click the Add button in the Spelling And Grammar dialog box or choose Add from the shortcut menu of the check-spelling-as-you-type feature, the current word will be added to the selected custom dictionary.

Checking Your Grammar

You can use the Word grammar checker to help polish your writing. The grammar checker will indicate possible errors or weaknesses in *grammar*, such as a disagreement between subject and verb or the use of a passive sentence construction. It will also flag expressions that exhibit poor writing *style*, such as clichés or misused words. You can have Word automatically check your grammar as you type, or you can manually run the grammar checker (along with the spelling checker) to check text that you've already entered. Finally, when you run the grammar checker manually, you can have it display *statistics* on the general readability of your document after it has completed its check.

Checking Your Grammar Automatically as You Type

To have Word automatically check your grammar as you type, choose Options from the Tools menu, click the Spelling & Grammar tab (see Figure 9-2 on page 266), and turn on the Check Grammar As You Type option. Word will then check the grammar of any text that has already been entered into your document, and it will begin checking the grammar of each new sentence you enter, immediately after you finish typing it. If the grammar checker encounters a sentence that violates one of its current grammar rules (later you'll see how to modify these rules), it marks the offending portions of the sentence with a wavy green underline (recall that Word marks a misspelled word with a wavy *red* underline). You can then ignore the mark, correct the sentence manually, or right-click on the underlined portion to display the following shortcut menu:

On the shortcut menu, choose one of the following options:

- Choose one of the suggested grammar corrections at the top of the menu (if any) to correct the sentence.

- Choose Ignore Sentence to have the grammar checker ignore any unchecked portion of the sentence and to remove the wavy underline or underlines from the sentence.

- Choose Grammar to open the Grammar dialog box, which is the same as the Spelling And Grammar dialog box displayed when you manually run the grammar checker. It is described in the next section.

If the check-grammar-as-you-type feature has marked one or more errors in your document, you can locate (and correct) them by double-clicking the Spelling And Grammar Status icon on the Word status bar.

Spelling And Grammar Status

Each time you double-click this icon, Word moves the insertion point to the next flagged error and opens the shortcut menu shown above so that you can correct the grammar.

If you turn on the Hide Grammatical Errors In This Document option on the Spelling & Grammar tab of the Options dialog box (see Figure 9-2 on page 266), Word will remove the wavy lines from all grammar errors in the active document. It will, however, maintain a record of the errors, and you can later restore the wavy lines by turning this option off.

Manually Running the Grammar Checker

You might prefer to check the grammar of a block or text—or an entire document—after you have typed it, rather than having to deal with possible grammatical errors while you write. In this case, you can either turn off the check-grammar-as-you-type feature or simply ignore the wavy underlines. Then, when you're ready to check your grammar, you can manually run the grammar checker.

Microsoft Word

If the grammar checker isn't currently enabled, enable it by choosing Options from the Tools menu, clicking the Spelling & Grammar tab, and turning on the Check Grammar With Spelling option. If you want to see the readability statistics, also turn on the Show Readability Statistics option.

Once it has been enabled, the grammar checker will be run whenever you perform a spelling check, as described previously ("Manually Running the Spelling Checker," page 268). The specific steps for checking your grammar are as follows:

1   If you want to check your entire document, place the insertion point anywhere in the document. If you want to check only a portion of your document, select that portion.

2   Choose Spelling And Grammar from the Tools menu, press F7, or click the Spelling And Grammar button on the Standard toolbar.

Spelling And
Grammar

3   For each sentence in the document (or selection), Word first checks the spelling of the words it contains. To handle any word that is flagged as a possible misspelling, follow the instructions that were given under step 3 of the process for checking your spelling, on page 269.

4   After checking the spelling of a sentence, Word will check the grammar. If the grammar checker finds a violation of one of its grammar or style rules, it opens the Spelling And Grammar dialog box (see Figure 9-4). At the top of this dialog box is a description of the possible grammar or style violation, together with a copy of the sentence with the offending words shown in green. Below this, the Suggestions list displays one or more blocks of replacement text (if the grammar checker can generate a replacement).

FIGURE 9-4.
The Spelling And
Grammar dialog box.

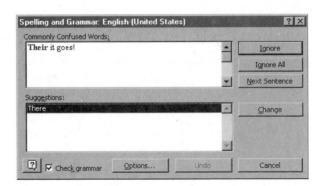

To deal with the possible error, you should do one or more of the following:

- To correct or improve your sentence, first *either* directly edit the copy of the sentence displayed at the top of the Spelling And Grammar dialog box *or* simply select a block of replacement text in the Suggestions list (if one is present). Then, click the Change button.

- To ignore the suggestions and move on to the next error, click the Ignore button. The next error might be in the same sentence.

- To ignore the suggestions and stop Word from flagging violations of the same grammar or style rule during the remainder of the grammar check, click Ignore All. The checker will then move on to the next error.

- To ignore the suggestions for the current sentence and to move on to the next sentence, click the Next Sentence button. If the current sentence has additional errors, the grammar checker will skip them.

- To reverse your previous correction, click the Undo button.

- You can turn off the Check Grammar option to stop Word from checking your grammar. Word will then check only your spelling, until you turn the option back on. (As mentioned previously, you can also set this option through the Spelling & Grammar tab.)

- To modify the way the grammar checker works, click the Options button. (Setting options is explained in the next section.)

 TIP

Edit with the Spelling And Grammar Dialog Box Displayed
You can edit your document while the Spelling And Grammar dialog box remains displayed. To edit, click in the document. To resume the grammar check, click the Resume button in the Spelling And Grammar dialog box.

II

Microsoft Word

If the Show Readability Statistics option is enabled on the Spelling & Grammar tab, Word will display the Readability Statistics dialog box after it has finished the spelling and grammar check. This dialog box shows statistics on the text that was checked, including several standard indicators of the general readability of the text. Figure 9-5 shows the statistics that Word displayed for the original draft of the chapter you're reading.

FIGURE 9-5.

The Readability Statistics dialog box displayed after running a spelling and grammar check on the preliminary draft of this chapter.

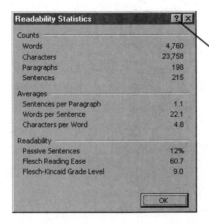

For an explanation of any of the information in this dialog box, click here and then click on the part of the dialog box displaying the information.

 TIP

You can display statistics about the number of pages, words, and so on in your document by choosing Word Count from the Tools menu, or by choosing Properties from the File menu and clicking the Statistics tab.

Customizing the Grammar Checker

You can modify the way the grammar checker works by clicking the Options button in the Spelling And Grammar dialog box, or by choosing Options from the Tools menu and clicking the Spelling & Grammar tab. Word will display the Spelling & Grammar tab, which was shown in Figure 9-2 on page 266.

If you turn on the Show Readability Statistics option, the grammar checker will display the statistics that were described in the previous section.

You can select an option in the Writing Style list to specify the general type of writing you want to check—for example, Basic Proof, Casual Communication, Technical Writing, or Fiction Writing. When Word checks your grammar, it will apply a set of rules that is most appropriate for the selected type of writing. To have Word apply a general-purpose set of rules, select the Standard item in the Writing Style list. You can also choose Formal to apply almost all the grammar and style rules, or Casual to omit more of the rules.

You can also customize *any* of the grammar styles (not just the Custom ones), to specify exactly which rules the grammar checker will apply when that style is selected. On the Spelling & Grammar tab, click the Settings button to open the Grammar Settings dialog box (see Figure 9-6).

FIGURE 9-6.
The Grammar
Settings dialog box.

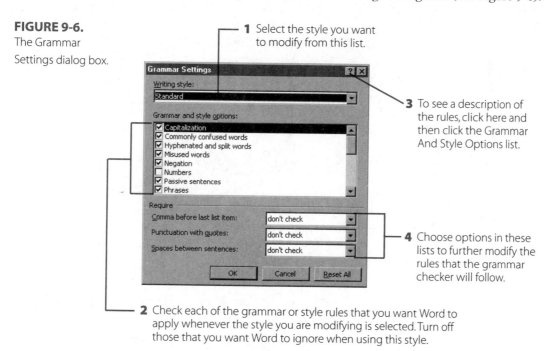

1 Select the style you want to modify from this list.

3 To see a description of the rules, click here and then click the Grammar And Style Options list.

4 Choose options in these lists to further modify the rules that the grammar checker will follow.

2 Check each of the grammar or style rules that you want Word to apply whenever the style you are modifying is selected. Turn off those that you want Word to ignore when using this style.

Microsoft Word

Finding Synonyms with the Thesaurus

You can use the Word thesaurus to look up synonyms or antonyms for a word or phrase in your document. You'll probably want to use the thesaurus as you are entering text into your document (in contrast to the other proofing tools, which you often use after you have finished entering text). The following are the basic steps for using the thesaurus:

1 Select the word or phrase. To find synonyms for a single word, you can simply place the insertion point anywhere within the word rather than selecting it:

That looks pretty good.

2 Press Shift+F7 or point to Language on the Tools menu and choose Thesaurus on the submenu that appears. Word will open the Thesaurus dialog box. Here is the Thesaurus dialog box as it would appear if the word *pretty* were selected in the document:

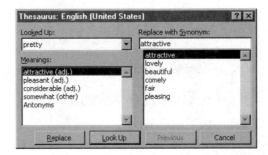

3 In the Meanings list, select the intended meaning of the word. (Note the part of speech following most words: *adj.* for adjective, *adv.* for adverb, *noun* for noun, and so on.) The thesaurus will then list synonyms for this meaning in the Replace With Synonym box.

The Meanings list will sometimes contain the item Antonyms or the item Related Words. Choosing Antonyms displays a list of antonyms for the word; for example, if the selected word is *pretty*, the thesaurus would list the words *ugly, grotesque, unpleasant*, and *completely*. (The list of antonyms might be for different meanings of the word.) Choosing the Related Words option displays a list of other word forms; for example, if the selected word is *going*, the thesaurus would list *go*.

Finally, if the thesaurus doesn't have information on the selected word, it displays an alphabetical list of words with similar spellings.

You can select one of these words and click the Look Up button to find synonyms.

4 Click the best synonym (or the best antonym or related word) in the Replace With list, and click the Replace button. Here is the Thesaurus dialog box after looking up *pretty* and then choosing the meaning *somewhat* and the synonym *rather*:

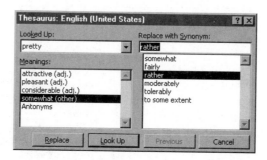

When you click Replace, Word will replace the selected word in the document with the chosen synonym, matching the capitalization (if any) of the original word:

That looks rather good.

 TIP

> **Look Up Synonyms to Find More Word Choices**
>
> After selecting a synonym in step 4, you can click the Look Up button to find synonyms for the *synonym*! (Clicking Look Up finds synonyms for the word in the Replace With Synonym box). Doing this one or more times might help you find precisely the word you want. Consider this scenario: You look up the word *pretty* and select the synonym *beautiful*, which is better than *pretty* but not perfect. You therefore click the Look Up button and find the perfect synonym, *gorgeous*.

Hyphenating Your Documents

You can improve the appearance of your document by hyphenating words at the ends of the lines. Once hyphenated, text that is not justified will be less ragged at the margin, and justified text will have more uniform spacing between the characters. You can hyphenate text in one of three ways.

- You can have Word automatically hyphenate your entire document.

- You can have Word hyphenate text but allow you to confirm the placement of each hyphen.

- You can manually insert various types of hyphen characters.

NOTE

You should hyphenate your document *after* you finish editing, formatting, and using the other proofing tools, because these operations can change the position of line breaks. Also, if you later change features of the page design that affect line breaks, such as the margins, you might need to hyphenate your document again.

Having Word Hyphenate Your Document Automatically

You can let Word automatically hyphenate the document in the active window, by pointing to Language on the Tools menu and then choosing Hyphenation to open the Hyphenation dialog box:

1 Click here to turn on automatic hyphenation.

2 If you want Word to hyphenate words in all capital letters (such as acronyms), turn on this option.

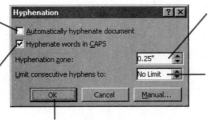

5 Click OK. Word will automatically hyphenate all text in the document.

3 To adjust the hyphenation zone (described below), enter a new value into this box.

4 To limit the number of consecutive lines that Word will hyphenate, enter a number into this box. (The default value is No Limit.) Limiting consecutive hyphenations prevents unsightly "stacking" of hyphen characters along the right margin.

⊗ CAUTION

When you turn on the Automatically Hyphenate Document option, Word will hyphenate your *entire* document even if you have selected only a portion of the document.

The *hyphenation zone* controls the number of hyphenations that Word performs. It works as follows: When Word encounters a word that extends beyond the right indent, it must decide whether it can simply wrap the word (that is, move the entire word down to the next line) or whether it should hyphenate the word. If wrapping the word would leave space at the end of the line that is narrower than the hyphenation zone (.25" wide by default), Word wraps it:

❓ SEE ALSO

For information on applying the Don't Hyphenate and other paragraph formatting features, see "Applying Paragraph Formatting Directly," page 190. For information on applying the (No Proofing) format, see "Marking the Language," page 264.

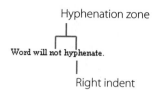

If, however, wrapping the word would leave a space wider than the hyphenation zone, Word hyphenates it:

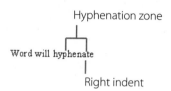

Choosing a wide hyphenation zone reduces the number of hyphenations that Word must perform, but it increases the raggedness of the margin (or makes the intercharacter spacing less uniform in justified text).

 ⭐ TIP

> You can assign a paragraph the Don't Hyphenate paragraph formatting feature to exclude it from automatic hyphenation or hyphenation with confirmation (discussed in the next section). In contrast, applying the (No Proofing) language formatting feature, mentioned near the beginning of the chapter, blocks *all* proofing (spelling, grammar, and hyphenation).

Having Word Hyphenate Your Document with Confirmation

If you want Word to hyphenate your document but allow you to confirm the placement of each hyphen, do the following:

1 If you want to hyphenate your entire document, place the insertion point anywhere in the document. If you want to hyphenate only a portion of your document, select that portion.

2 Point to Language on the Tools menu and then choose Hyphenation to open the Hyphenation dialog box.

II

Microsoft Word

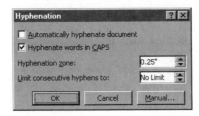

3 In the Hyphenation dialog box, set any hyphenation options you want (except Automatically Hyphenate Document). These options were explained in the previous section.

4 Click the Manual button. Word activates Page Layout view and begins looking for possible hyphenations. (When Word is finished hyphenating, it returns you to your original document view.)

5 Whenever Word encounters a word that requires hyphenation, it displays the Manual Hyphenation dialog box, which shows the word and the proposed position of the hyphen (together with all other possible hyphen positions in the word):

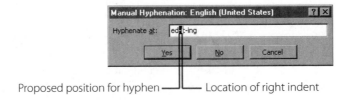

Proposed position for hyphen ————— Location of right indent

You should now do one of the following:

- To hyphenate the word at the proposed position, just click Yes.

- To hyphenate the word at a different position (say, to avoid a hyphen after only the first two letters of a long word, as in the example), move the insertion point to that position and then click Yes.

- To skip hyphenating the word, click No. (The word will be wrapped rather than hyphenated.)

Manually Inserting Hyphen Characters

When Word hyphenates a word, it inserts a special character known as an *optional hyphen*. If a word containing an optional hyphen is shifted so that it no longer falls at the end of a line, the hyphen is not printed. However, the optional hyphen remains within the word, and it will reappear and allow the word to be broken if the word shifts back to the end of a line.

You can manually insert optional hyphens, as well as several other related special characters, as shown in Table 9-2.

 TIP

If you click the Show/Hide ¶ button on the Standard toolbar, Word displays on the screen all the characters listed in Table 9-2. To display optional hyphens only, choose Options from the Tools menu, click the View tab, and turn on the Optional Hyphens option in the Nonprinting Characters area.

TABLE 9-2.   Manually Inserted Hyphens and Nonbreaking Spaces

Special Character	Shortcut Key for Inserting It	Properties
Optional hyphen	Ctrl+hyphen (hyphen key on top row of keyboard, *not* on numeric keypad)	When an optional hyphen falls at the end of a line, it is printed and the word that contains it is broken. When it falls within a line, it doesn't print.
Nonbreaking hyphen	Ctrl+Shift+hyphen (hyphen key on top row of keyboard, *not* on numeric keypad)	A nonbreaking hyphen is always printed. A word is never broken at the position of a nonbreaking hyphen. It can be used to keep a hyphenated word or expression together on a single line.
Normal hyphen	hyphen ("-" on top row of keyboard *or* on numeric keypad)	A normal hyphen is always printed. A word can be broken at the position of a normal hyphen.
Nonbreaking space	Ctrl+Shift+Spacebar	A line break can't occur at the position of a nonbreaking space. This character can be used to keep several words together on a single line (for example, a heading).

II

Microsoft Word

CHAPTER 10

Designing Pages

In the previous chapters in this part of the book, you learned how to control the appearance of individual characters and paragraphs of text in your document. In this chapter, you'll learn how to design and preview the appearance of entire pages. You'll learn how to modify the general appearance of all pages in a document or document section by adding page numbers, headers, or footers, or by adjusting the margins or other page setup features. You'll also learn how to enhance the appearance of individual pages by placing blocks of text at specific positions on the page, or by adding graphics.

This chapter concludes the presentation of the basic steps for creating and printing typical Word documents. The following chapters in this part of the book explore techniques for creating longer and more specialized kinds of documents.

Adding Page Numbers

You can use the Page Numbers dialog box to quickly add page numbering to your document. You can display numbers at the top or at the bottom of each page, and you can choose from a variety of numbering formats. Although you can't see page numbers in Normal document view, they will be shown in Page Layout view and Print Preview, and of course on the printed copy of the document. When you add page numbers using the Page Numbers dialog box, Word creates a simple header or footer consisting only of the page number. In the next section, you'll learn how to place additional information on a page by adding headers or footers, as well as how to modify or remove them.

To add page numbering to the document in the active window, do the following:

1 Choose Page Numbers from the Insert menu to open the Page Numbers dialog box:

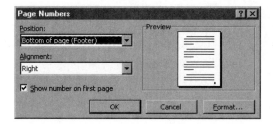

2 In the Position list, choose Top Of Page (Header) to place the page numbers at the top of each page (that is, within headers), or Bottom Of Page (Footer) to place the page numbers at the bottom of each page (that is, within footers).

3 In the Alignment list, choose the position of the page numbers within the headers or footers. Choose Left, Center, or Right to place the page numbers at the left margin, centered between the margins, or at the right margin on each page. Choose Inside to place the page numbers at the right on even-numbered pages and at the left on odd-numbered pages. Choose Outside to place the page numbers at the left on even-numbered pages and at the right on odd-numbered pages (as in this book).

4 If you want to eliminate the page number from the first page of the document (or from the first page of the current document section if you've divided your document into sections) turn off the Show Number On First Page option. If you do this, Word will omit the page number from the first page, though it will count the first page in numbering the pages. For example, if you start numbering at 1, Word won't display a number on the first page, but it will number the second page with 2.

5 If you want to modify the style of the numbering or change the starting number, click the Format button to open the Page Number Format dialog box:

Click here to add chapter numbers to the page numbering.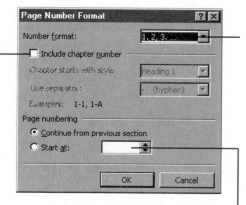

Choose the type of page numbers (Arabic numbers, letters of the alphabet, or Roman numerals) from this list.

To change the starting page number for the document or for the current document section (if you have divided your document into sections), enter a number here.

SEE ALSO

For an overview of the different document views and how to switch between them, see "Changing the Way You Display Documents," page 121.

To modify or delete page numbers, use the Header And Footer command on the View menu, as described in the next section. (Even though you can see page numbers in Page Layout view, you can't modify them unless you choose the Header And Footer command or double-click on the header or footer area.)

TIP

To change the character formatting of page numbering throughout your document, modify the Page Number character style. Word automatically assigns this style to page numbers. For information on modifying styles, see "Modifying Styles," page 200.

II

Microsoft Word

Working with Sections

As mentioned in Chapter 8, "Arranging Text in Columns and Lists," you can divide a document into separate sections, and then assign different features to each section. The following are the features that you can vary from section to section:

- The number of newspaper-style columns (discussed in "Creating Newspaper-Style Columns," page 241).

- Headers and footers, including page numbering (discussed here and and on the facing page, under "Adding Headers and Footers").

- The features set through the Page Setup dialog box, such as the margins and the paper size (discussed later under the heading "Adjusting the Page Setup," page 300).

The page numbering you create using the Page Numbers dialog box is applied to *all* document sections. You can, however, suppress the first page number (step 4 above) or change the starting page number (step 5) for a specific section; to do this, simply place the insertion point in that section before opening the Page Numbers dialog box and performing the step. In the next discussion ("Adding Headers and Footers") you'll learn how to apply completely different headers, footers, or page numbering to different document sections.

To divide your document into separate sections, place the insertion point at the position where you want to insert a section break, choose Break from the Insert menu, and select one of the options in the Section Breaks area:

If you select Next Page, the text in the new section will be started on the next page.

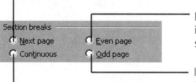

If you select Even Page, the text in the new section will be started on the next even page.

If you select Odd Page, the text in the new section will be started on the next odd page.

If you select Continuous, the text in the new section will be placed immediately following the text in the previous section.

In Normal or Outline view, Word marks a section break as follows:

This is the last line of a section.
==Section Break (Continuous)==
This is the first line of a new section.

Working with Sections *continued*

The text in parentheses will vary according to the type of break inserted. In Page Layout, Online Layout, or Master Document view, section breaks are visible only if the Show/Hide ¶ button is pressed on the Standard toolbar.

To remove a section break, simply select the mark and press the Delete key. The sections before and after the break will be merged into a single section, which will acquire the section features (page numbering, margins, and so on) of the section that followed the mark. Any section features that you assigned to the section preceding the mark will be lost. Conceptually, a section mark stores the section features of the preceding section so if you delete the section mark you delete these characteristics.

Adding Headers and Footers

You'll now learn how to create and modify running headers or footers that Word prints on each page of your document. If you've used the Page Numbers dialog box to create simple headers or footers consisting only of page numbers, you can use the techniques given here to modify, add to, or delete these headers or footers.

To create or modify headers or footers for the document in the active window, do the following:

1   Choose Header And Footer from the View menu. Word then does the following:

- It switches to Page Layout view.

- It marks the header area and the footer area of the page with dotted lines, and activates these areas so that you can work within them.

- It dims all text outside the header or footer area. (You won't be able to work on this text.)

- It displays the Header And Footer toolbar, which provides commands for working on the headers and footers.

Figure 10-1 shows the header area in the Word window after the Header And Footer command has been chosen. The footer area at the bottom of the page is similar.

FIGURE 10-1.
The header area
and the Header
And Footer toolbar.

Body text

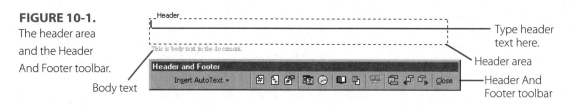

Type header
text here.

Header area

Header And
Footer toolbar

⭐ **TIP**

If you're in Page Layout view and if the header or footer already contains text, you can work on the headers or footers by simply double-clicking on this text rather than choosing the Header And Footer menu command.

2 If necessary, move the insertion point to either the header area or the footer area by pressing the Down or Up arrow key, or by clicking the Switch Between Header And Footer button on the Header And Footer toolbar (see Figure 10-2).

FIGURE 10-2.
The Header And
Footer toolbar.

Insert Page Number
Insert Number of Pages
Format Page Number
Insert Date
Insert Time

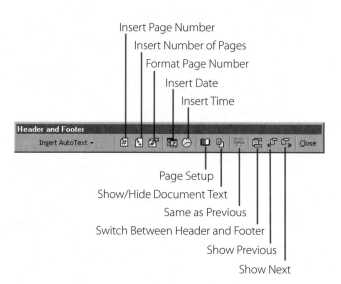

Page Setup
Show/Hide Document Text
Same as Previous
Switch Between Header and Footer
Show Previous
Show Next

NOTE

Using the arrow keys or other navigation keystrokes, you can move to the header or footer area on any page in the document. Usually, it doesn't matter which page you work on because the headers and footers are the same throughout the document. Later, however, you'll learn how to vary the headers or footers within the document (to reflect, for example, different section or chapter names in the document). In this case, you must move to the appropriate page before working on the header or footer.

3 Type the text for the header or footer into the header area or the footer area. You can enter one or more paragraphs of text into a header or footer, and you can edit and format the text in the same way that you edit and format text in the body of a document.

TIP

Use the Borders And Shading command on the Format menu to emphasize your headers or footers by adding visible borders around them. Use distinctive fonts, in bold or italic or in contrasting sizes, for a different kind of emphasis.

You can press the Tab key to align text on the two predefined tab stops; the first tab stop aligns text in the center of the header or footer and the second tab stop right-aligns text at the right edge of the header or footer. (Note that the tabs might be set differently in documents based on certain templates.) To *remove* headers or footers, simply delete all the text in the header or footer area.

TIP

While working on headers or footers, you can completely hide the body text on the page by clicking the Show/Hide Document Text button. (Normally, when you work on headers and footers, document text is shown in a dimmed font.)

You can quickly insert the page number, the total number of pages in the document, the date, or the time into your header or footer text. To do this, place the insertion point at the position where you want the information and click the Insert Page Number, Insert Number Of Pages, Insert Date, or Insert Time buttons on the Header And Footer toolbar, as shown in Figure 10-2.

II

Microsoft Word

(Note that the number of pages, the date, or the time will be updated when you print your document to reflect the *current* value.) You can also insert a variety of different kinds of information by clicking the down arrow next to the Insert AutoText button, pointing to Header or Footer, and choosing an item from the submenu. For example, you can point to Header and choose Filename to insert the name of the document; or you can choose Author, Page #, Date to insert your name, the page number, and the date. (The items on this menu are predefined AutoText entries provided with Word.)

4 When you have finished creating or modifying the headers or footers, click the Close button on the Header And Footer toolbar or choose Header And Footer from the View menu to return to the view you were using previously.

 TIP

Use Styles to Format Headers, Footers, and Page Numbers
Word logically assigns the Header paragraph style to headers, the Footer paragraph style to footers, and the Page Number character style to page numbers within headers or footers. You can therefore change the format of headers, footers, or page numbers throughout your entire document by modifying the corresponding style. You can also modify page numbering (the starting number, and so on) by clicking the Format Page Number button on the Header And Footer toolbar to open the Page Number Format dialog box that was described in the previous section.

Note that changing the Page Number style or making changes in the Page Number Format dialog box affects page numbers that you have added either by clicking the Insert Page Number button or via the Page Numbers command on the Insert menu.

Sizing and Moving Headers or Footers

The header or footer text you enter is normally confined within the header area or the footer area at the top or bottom of each page. You can change the size or position of these areas, however, or extend the header or footer text *outside* the header or footer area, using one or more of the following techniques:

■ You can move the top or bottom boundary of the header or footer area by dragging a marker on the vertical ruler:

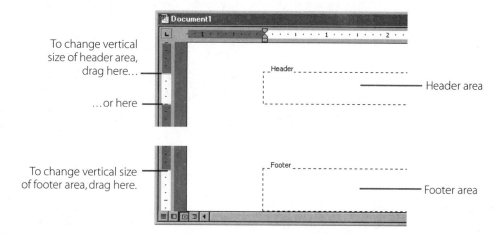

To change vertical size of header area, drag here...

...or here

Header area

To change vertical size of footer area, drag here.

Footer area

If the vertical ruler isn't currently visible, you can display it by choosing Page Layout from the View menu to switch to Page Layout view, and then choosing Options from the Tools menu, clicking the View tab, and turning on the Vertical Ruler option.

NOTE

If the text or graphics you insert into a header is higher than the current header area, Word will automatically move the bottom boundary of the header area down, so that the header won't overlap the main document text. Likewise, if the text or graphics you insert into a footer is higher than the footer area, Word will move the top boundary of the footer area up.

■ You can also adjust the vertical position of the header or footer area by changing the measurements in the Header box or Footer box on the Margins tab of the Page Setup dialog box, which will be described later in the chapter (in "Adjusting the Page Setup," page 300).

■ To move text to the left or to the right of the header or footer area, assign a negative left indent or a negative right indent to one or more paragraphs of header or footer text. To do this, you can use the horizontal ruler or Paragraph dialog box, as explained in Chapter 6, "Formatting a Word Document."

For information on the Margins tab of the Page Setup dialog box, see "Adjusting the Page Setup," page 300. For instructions on creating positive and negative indents, see "Applying Paragraph Formatting Directly," page 190.

■ You can insert some or all of the header or footer text into a Word *text box*, so that you can drag it to *any* position on the page. To do this, first choose Header And Footer from the View menu, and then insert the text box. Text boxes—and the methods for inserting them—are discussed later in the chapter ("Using Text Boxes to Position Text on the Page," page 309). Even though you can place such a text box anywhere on the page, it is still part of the header or footer and therefore you can modify it only after you choose the Header And Footer command. Note that a page number inserted by the Page Numbers dialog box is automatically placed within a frame, which is an element similar to a text box, so that you can drag it wherever you want.

Watch Your Head!

Normally, if you extend the header or footer area beyond the current top or bottom margin area, Word automatically adjusts the top or bottom margin so that the header or footer text doesn't overlap the text in the body of the document. However, if you enter a minus sign before the Top or Bottom margin setting on the Margins tab of the Page Setup dialog box (discussed later), Word will not adjust the margins; in this case, the header or footer text might overlap the text in the body of the document.

Varying Headers or Footers Within the Document

Normally, the same header or footer is printed on every page in the document. There are, however, three ways that you can vary headers and footers within your document.

First, you can create a different header and footer on the first page of the document, or on the first page of a section if you have divided your document into sections that begin on a new page. (This procedure does not work for continuous section breaks.) You might want to do this, for example, to eliminate the header from the title page of a report. The following are the steps:

1   If you have divided your document into sections, place the insertion point within the section for which you want to create a different first page header and footer.

2   Choose Header And Footer from the View menu.

3   Click the Page Setup button on the Header And Footer toolbar (see Figure 10-2 on page 294), and click the Layout tab in the Page Setup dialog box.

4   Turn on the Different First Page option and click OK.

Second, you can create different headers and footers on odd and even pages. You might do this, for example, if you're writing a book and want the book title at the top of the left page of facing pages (called the *verso* page by book designers), and the chapter title at the top of the right page (called the *recto* page). The following is the technique:

1   Choose Header And Footer from the View menu.

2   Click the Page Setup button on the Header And Footer toolbar, and click the Layout tab in the Page Setup dialog box.

3   Turn on the Different Odd And Even option and click OK.

Note that you can create a different first page header or footer for a specific section within a document. Creating different odd and even page headers or footers, however, always applies to the entire document, even if it has been divided into sections.

Finally, if you have divided your document into sections, the headers or footers in separate sections can have different contents. Initially, the headers and footers in every section (except the first) are connected to the headers and footers in the previous section, meaning that they'll be exactly the same as those in the previous section. To create different headers and footers in different sections, do the following:

1   Move the insertion point to any position within the section where you want the headers and footers to be different from the previous section.

2   Choose Header And Footer from the View menu.

3 The Same As Previous button on the Header And Footer toolbar will initially be selected (it will appear pressed). Click this button so that it is *not* selected. This will remove the connection between the current section and the previous one. You can now modify the headers or footers for the current section without changing those belonging to the previous section.

If you have varied the headers and footers using *any* of these three methods, then you must, when you choose the Header And Footer command, move to an appropriate document page to enter or modify each of the different headers or footers. For example, if you have created a different first page header, you must move to the first page to enter or modify the first page header or footer; you must then move to any other page to enter or modify the headers or footers for the other pages. When headers and footers differ within a document, each header or footer is labeled appropriately, for example "Header -Section 2-" or "First Page Footer":

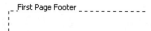

To quickly move to the header or footer on the appropriate page, you can click the Show Previous or Show Next button on the Header And Footer toolbar:

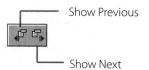

Adjusting the Page Setup

The Page Setup dialog box allows you to adjust a wide variety of features that affect the general appearance of the pages throughout your entire document or in one or more document sections. These features include the document margins, the paper size, the vertical alignment of text on the page, and line numbering. To set any of these features, follow these steps:

1 Select the portion of your document you want to modify by doing one of the following:

- If you want to modify the entire document, simply place the insertion point anywhere within the document.

- If you want to modify the document from a given position through the end of the document, place the insertion point at that position.

- If you want to modify a portion of the document, select that portion.

- If you have divided the document into sections, place the insertion point in the section you want to modify, or select several sections.

2 Choose Page Setup from the File menu to open the Page Setup dialog box, which has four tabs: Margins, Paper Size, Paper Source, and Layout.

3 In the Apply To list (which appears on all tabs), choose the part of the document you want to modify:

In general, you can modify either the entire document or one or more document sections. The specific choices that appear in the Apply To list depend on the part of your document you have selected and whether you have divided your document into sections. Note that if you choose the This Point Forward option, Word will insert a section break at the position of the insertion point, and if you choose the Selected Text option, Word will insert a section break at the beginning and at the end of the selected text. Choosing one of these options is a convenient way to divide your document into sections without having to manually insert section breaks.

4 If you want to use the features you select as the default settings, click the Default button (which appears on all tabs) and respond Yes. Word will assign the current settings on each of the four tabs to the document and to the document template so that the settings will apply to any new documents you create based on this template.

5 Select the page setup features you want. The features displayed on each of the four tabs are discussed in the following four sections. Notice that the Preview area shows the effect of the features that are currently set on *all* the tabs.

Adjusting the Margins

To set the page margins, do the following:

1 Click the Margins tab of the Page Setup dialog box. (See Figure 10-3.)

FIGURE 10-3.
The Margins tab of the Page Setup dialog box.

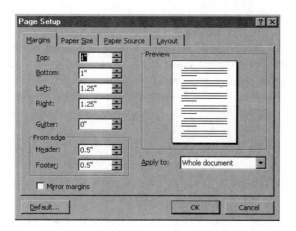

2 If you're printing on both sides of the paper and want the margins on facing pages (called a *spread* by book designers) to be symmetrical, turn on the Mirror Margins option.

3 Set the page margins in the Top, Bottom, Left, and Right boxes; the corresponding margins are shown in Figure 10-4.

If you turned on Mirror Margins, the boxes will be labeled Top, Bottom, Inside, and Outside; the corresponding margins for a two-page spread are shown in Figure 10-5.

FIGURE 10-4.

The page margins set through the Top, Bottom, Left, and Right boxes of the Page Setup dialog box, when the Mirror Margins option is *not* turned on.

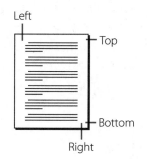

FIGURE 10-5.

The page margins set through the Top, Bottom, Inside, and Outside boxes of the Page Setup dialog box, when the Mirror Margins option is turned on.

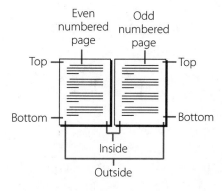

> If you're printing on both sides of the paper, you can also make the headers or footers symmetrical by turning on the Different Odd And Even option on the Layout tab of the Page Setup dialog box, and formatting your headers and footers appropriately.

4 You can add space to the inside margin on each page to make room for the binding. To do this, enter the desired amount of space into the Gutter box. If you have turned on Mirror Margins, the gutter space will be added to the right margin on even pages and to the left margin on odd pages, as shown in Figure 10-6 on the following page.

If you have not turned Mirror Margins, the gutter space will be added to the left margin on all pages (because in business or academic documents the left margin often is wider than the right margin).

5 To adjust the amount of space between the top of the page and the start of the header text, enter a new measurement into the Header box. Likewise, to adjust the space between the bottom of the page and the start of the footer text, enter a measurement into the Footer box. As you learned previously in the chapter, you can also adjust either of these measurements by choosing Header And Footer from the View menu and dragging markers on the vertical ruler.

FIGURE 10-6.

The gutter space set through the Gutter box of the Page Setup dialog box, with the Mirror Margins option turned on.

Even page   Odd page

Gutter areas

? SEE ALSO

For information on changing the size or position of headers and footers, see "Sizing and Moving Headers or Footers," page 296.

Alternatively, you can adjust a page margin using a ruler. If you have divided your document into sections, first place the insertion point in the section you want to modify, or select several sections to modify all of them. To adjust a margin, switch to Page Layout view (choose Page Layout from the View menu) or Print Preview (choose Print Preview from the File menu) and drag the appropriate marker on the horizontal or vertical ruler. (If the rulers aren't visible, choose Ruler from the View menu. If the vertical ruler isn't visible in Page Layout view, choose Options from the Tools menu, click the View tab, and turn on the Vertical Ruler option.) Figure 10-7 shows the markers for adjusting the left, right, and top margins in Page Layout view. (The marker for adjusting the bottom margin is similar to that for adjusting the top margin.)

When you're adjusting the left or right margin, make sure the pointer has become a double-headed arrow. You could otherwise inadvertently change the indent for the selected paragraph rather than the margin:

Position the pointer between the indent markers.

 **TIP**

To see the exact margin measurements, hold down the Alt key while you drag a margin marker on a ruler.

FIGURE 10-7.
Adjusting the left, right, and top margins using the rulers in Page Layout view.

Drag here to adjust left margin.

Drag here to adjust right margin.

Drag here to adjust top margin.

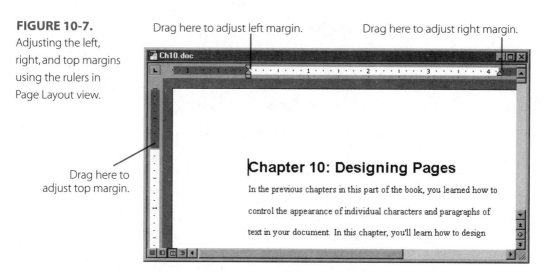

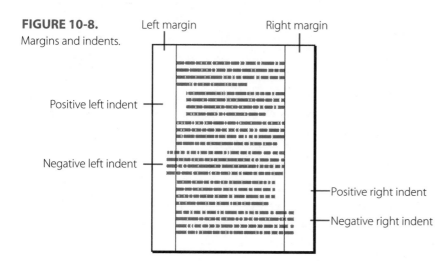

FIGURE 10-8.
Margins and indents.

Left margin

Right margin

Positive left indent

Negative left indent

Positive right indent

Negative right indent

? SEE ALSO
For instructions on setting paragraph indents, see "Applying Paragraph Formatting Directly," page 190.

Don't confuse the left and right *margins* with the left and right *indents*. A margin is the normal distance between the text and the edge of the paper, and it applies to an entire document or section. An indent is an *adjustment* to this distance that applies to one or more individual paragraphs. (It's a paragraph formatting feature.) If the left or right indent measurement is 0, the paragraph text is aligned with the left or right margin. If the indent measurement is positive, the paragraph text is moved *in* from the margin, and if it's negative the text is moved *out* from the margin. See Figure 10-8.

II

Microsoft Word

Adjusting the Paper Size and Orientation

Word normally assumes that you're printing on $8\frac{1}{2}$-inch by 11-inch paper. If you're using a different paper size, you must change the paper size setting. You can also change the orientation of the text on the page. To alter either of these settings, do the following:

1 Click the Paper Size tab of the Page Setup dialog box (see Figure 10-9).

2 To specify the size of the paper, choose one of the standard paper sizes in the Paper Size list. (The contents of this list depend on your current default printer.) If you can't find the correct size in the list, type the correct size into the Width and Height boxes.

3 In the Orientation box of the dialog box, choose Portrait (the usual setting) to print the lines of text at right angles to the direction of the paper feed, or choose Landscape to print the lines of text in the direction of the paper feed:

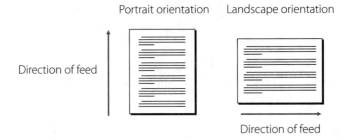

If, for example, your document contains a wide table, you might place the table in its own section and assign the Landscape orientation to that section, leaving the other document sections in Portrait orientation. Word would then print the table sideways so that it would fit on the paper.

When you switch paper orientations, Word automatically swaps the current settings of the top and bottom margins for the settings of the left and right margins so that the text occupies the same portion of the page.

FIGURE 10-9.
The Paper Size tab of the Page Setup dialog box.

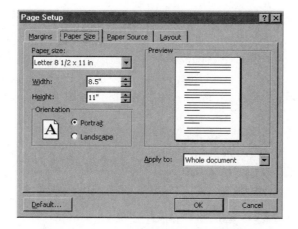

Adjusting the Paper Source

If your printer has more than one paper bin, manual feed slot, or other paper source, you can print the first page of the document (or of the section) on paper from one source and print all remaining pages on paper from a different source. You could use this feature, for example, to print the first page of a letter on letterhead stock and the remaining pages on blank stock.

To set the paper source, click the Paper Source tab of the Page Setup dialog box (see Figure 10-10).

FIGURE 10-10.
The Paper Source tab of the Page Setup dialog box. (The contents of these lists depend on your current default printer.)

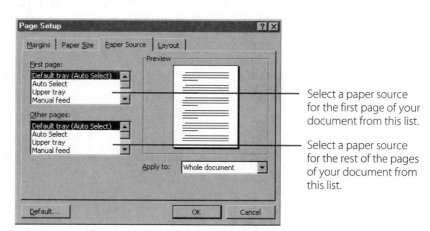

Select a paper source for the first page of your document from this list.

Select a paper source for the rest of the pages of your document from this list.

Microsoft Word

Adjusting the Page Layout

Finally, you can adjust a variety of page setup features by clicking the Layout tab of the Page Setup dialog box. (See Figure 10-11.) To control the location of the text at the beginning of the selected document section or sections, choose an item in the Section Start list.

FIGURE 10-11.
The Layout tab of the Page Setup dialog box.

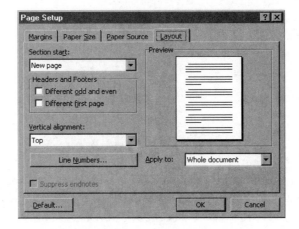

SEE ALSO
For information on the Headers and Footers options, see "Varying Headers or Footers Within the Document," page 298.

You can choose an option in the Vertical Alignment list to affect the way Word arranges paragraphs—in the vertical direction—on pages that are not completely filled with text. Figure 10-12 shows the effect of the different options. You might, for example, choose the Center option for the title page of a report (though this alignment would probably not look attractive for a final, short page).

FIGURE 10-12.
The Vertical Alignment options.

Top   Center   Justified

NOTE

To see the effect of whatever Vertical Alignment option you've chosen, you must be in Page Layout view or Print Preview.

? SEE ALSO

For a description of the Paragraph dialog box, see "Applying Paragraph Formatting Directly," page 190.

You can have Word print line numbers in the left margin within one or more document sections by clicking the Line Numbers button. In the Line Numbers dialog box (see Figure 10-13), turn on the Add Line Numbering option and select the line numbering features you want. Line numbers are displayed only in Page Layout view and Print Preview and on the printed copy of the document; lawyers and publishers often use line numbering to facilitate discussion of specific lines among several people. Note that you can block line numbering for a specific paragraph by applying the Suppress Line Numbers paragraph formatting feature, which you'll find on the Line And Page Breaks tab of the Paragraph dialog box.

FIGURE 10-13.

The Line Numbers dialog box.

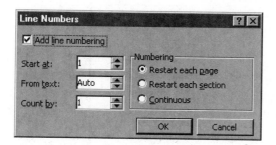

★ TIP

You can change the character formatting of line numbers throughout your document by modifying the Line Number character style, using the techniques given in Chapter 7, "Customizing Styles and Templates."

Using Text Boxes to Position Text on the Page

The text in the body of a document is contained in a stream of characters that flows from line to line and from page to page. Generally, you neither know nor care where a particular block of text will fall on a page. In this section, however, you'll learn how to place material at a specific position on the page, outside the normal stream of characters. You can use these techniques to position margin notes, figures, tables, sidebars, and other elements that need to be set apart from the body text, and to control how text flows around these elements.

To place a block of text at a specific position on the page, you insert it into a Word element known as a *text box*, which you can then move to the desired position. Because a text box is not part of the normal flow of characters in the document, it is said to *float* over the text. Figure 10-14 shows a margin note that was created by inserting text into a text box, and Figure 10-15 shows a Word table that was inserted into a text box.

FIGURE 10-14.

A margin note created by inserting text into a text box.

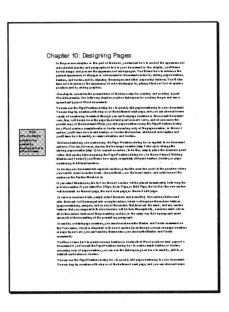

FIGURE 10-15.

A Word table placed in a text box so that it can be positioned apart from the body text.

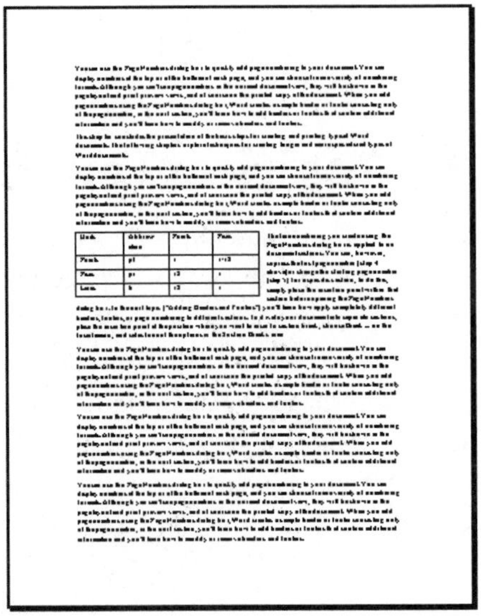

To place a text box around existing text in your document, do the following:

1 Select the text you want to include in the text box. You can include one or more characters or paragraphs, or a Word table.

2 Choose Text Box from the Insert menu.

Word will then create a new text box, and it will move the selected text into the text box. You'll now probably need to adjust the size, position, and format of the text box, as will be described later.

> You must be in Page Layout or Online Layout view or Print Preview to be able to see or work with a text box. If you're not in one of these views when you insert a text box, Word will automatically switch you to Page Layout view.

You can also create an empty text box and then insert text into it, as follows:

1 Without selecting text, choose Text Box from the Insert menu. The insertion point can be anywhere within the document.

2 Drag the crosshairs pointer to indicate the size and position you want for the text box:

Or, simply click in the document to insert a default-sized text box.

3 You can now insert text into the text box. Make sure the insertion point is in the text box, and then enter, edit, and format text just as you would for a normal paragraph. A text box can contain one or more paragraphs.

As you type text in a text box, Word will wrap the text when you reach the right text box edge. Word won't, however, automatically increase the height of the box when you reach the bottom; you'll have to manually increase the height of the box to make the text at the bottom visible. (Or, as you'll see later, you can link the text box to another text box so that excess text automatically flows into the second text box.)

To change the height or width of a text box, do the following:

1 Click anywhere on the text box to select it. When a text box is selected, Word displays a thick band around it, which contains eight sizing handles:

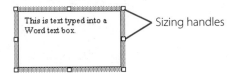

Sizing handles

2 Drag any of the sizing handles to resize the text box as you want. To maintain the original proportions of the text box as you change its size, press Shift while dragging one of the corner sizing handles. To resize the text box symmetrically about its center, hold down the Ctrl key while dragging any sizing handle.

You can move a text box as follows:

1 Place the pointer over one of the edges of the text box (but not over a sizing handle if the text box is selected). Cross-arrows will be displayed at the top of the mouse pointer:

2 Drag the text box to the position you want on the page. If you want to copy the text box rather than move it, hold down Ctrl while you drag.

If you move a text box onto an area of the page occupied by text, you'll notice one of the following two types of behavior:

■ If you selected existing text in the document before inserting the text box (that is, you used the first method that was given for creating a text box), the document text will move away from the text box; that is, the document text will *wrap* around the text box. Figure 10-15 on page 310 shows text wrapping around a text box.

- If you *didn't* select text before inserting the text box (that is, you used the second method for creating a text box), the text box will simply overlap the document text; that is, the document text *won't* wrap around the text box.

If your text box doesn't interact with the document text the way you want, don't worry. You can turn text wrapping on or off, change the style of wrapping, and modify *many* other features of the text box by formatting it using the following procedure:

1 Click anywhere on the text box to select it.

2 Choose Text Box from the Format menu to open the Format Text Box dialog box.

3 Select options on the various tabs of the Format Text Box dialog box, as shown here:

Modify the margins between the text and the edges of the text box.

These options aren't available for a text box (only for a picture, which is described later).

Turn text wrapping on or off, and set the style of wrapping.

Change position of text box on page.

Modify the text box size or rotate the text box.

Select a background fill color and set the color, style, and thickness of the lines around the text box.

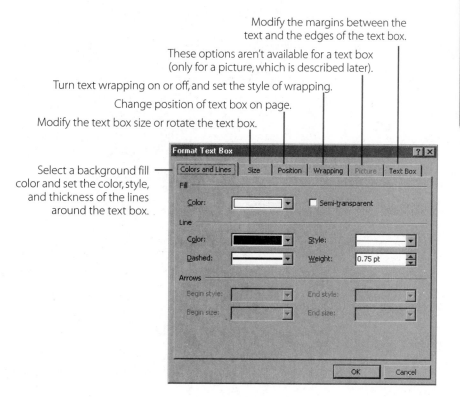

When a text box is selected, Word normally automatically displays the Text Box toolbar (if it isn't displayed when a text box is selected, point to Toolbars on the View menu and choose Text Box from the submenu). You can use this toolbar to *link* text boxes and to change the direction of the text within the selected text box:

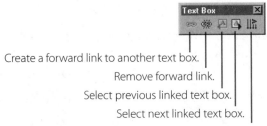

Create a forward link to another text box.

Remove forward link.

Select previous linked text box.

Select next linked text box.

Change text direction (toggles between left-to-right, top-to-bottom, and bottom-to-top orientations.)

When two text boxes are linked, text will automatically flow from one text box to another; that is, any text that doesn't fit in the first text box will be moved to the next linked text box (just like document text flows from one page to the next).

To remove a text box, plus the text it contains, select it by clicking *on one of its edges* and then press the Delete key. (If you select the text box by clicking inside of an edge, the insertion point will be placed within the text and pressing Delete will delete only a single character.) If you want to move text from a text box into the main part of the document, be sure to copy the text from the text box and paste it into the document *before* you delete the box.

Adding Graphics

Graphics are another important element you can add to a page. To add graphics, either you can import a picture from a file or from another program, or you can create a drawing object using Word's built-in drawing tools.

Importing Pictures

You can import graphics into a document either by inserting the contents of an entire graphics file, or by copying a block of graphics from another program and pasting it into the Word document. After a graphic has been imported into a Word document using one of these techniques, it is known as a *picture*.

 TIP

> **Install the Graphics Filters**
>
> If you install the Graphics Filters component of Office, you'll be able to import graphics created by a wide variety of other programs. If you haven't already installed this component, you can do so by running the Office Setup program.

To obtain a picture from a graphics file, do the following:

1 Place the insertion point at the approximate position where you want to insert the picture into your document.

2 Point to Picture on the Insert menu and choose From File from the submenu. This will open the Insert Picture dialog box, which is similar to the Open dialog box for opening documents.

3 In the Insert Picture dialog box, locate and select the graphics file you want to import. If you installed the Graphics Filters component of Office, you can import graphics files in a wide variety of different formats (for example, BMP, WMF, GIF, and JPG files). Also, if you installed the Clip Gallery component of Office (which is part of the Office Tools component), you can select from a large number of graphics files provided by Office.

4 Select any options you want in the Insert Picture dialog box.

If you want to make the document file smaller, you can turn on the Link To File option and turn off the Save With Document option. Word will then store only a link to the original graphics file rather than storing the actual graphics data. In this case, however, the original graphics file must always be available on the disk when you open the document. See Chapter 39, "Sharing Data Among Office Applications," for more information on linking data.

Also, turn on the Float Over Text option if you want to be able to move the picture anywhere on the page and to have text wrap around the picture. Turn off this option if you want the picture to

II

Microsoft Word

be inserted into the stream of text like a normal character. (Note that you can later change the "Float" property of a picture through the Position tab of the Format Picture dialog box, described later.)

> NOTE

You can also add graphics to your document by inserting clip art using the Microsoft Clip Gallery program (provided that you've installed this component of Office). To run the Clip Gallery, point to Picture on the Insert menu and choose Clip Art from the submenu. Details are given in "Using the Clip Gallery," page 1018.

You can also insert a picture by copying graphics from another program (such as the Paint program that comes with Windows), as follows:

1 Select the graphics in the other program and choose the Copy command from that program's Edit menu.

2 Place the insertion point at the approximate position in the Word document where you want to insert the picture.

3 Choose Paste from the Word Edit menu or press Ctrl+V.

See Chapter 39, "Sharing Data Among Office Applications," for detailed information on copying data from one program to another.

Once you've inserted a picture, you can move it to the exact position where you want it. If you imported the picture from a graphics file and turned on the Float Over Text option, or if you copied the picture from another program, you can move the picture to any position on the page using the following method (which is similar to the method for moving a text box, described previously):

1 Place the pointer over the picture (but not over a sizing handle if the picture is selected). Cross-arrows will be displayed at the top of the mouse pointer:

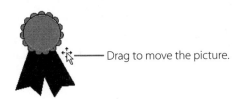

Drag to move the picture.

2 Drag the picture to the position you want on the page.

If you move the picture over a portion of the page occupied by text, you'll notice that the text wraps around the picture (it's placed above and below the picture). Later, you'll learn how to modify the text wrapping style for the picture or to eliminate wrapping, using either the Picture toolbar or the Format Picture dialog box.

If you imported the picture from a graphics file and *turned off* the Float Over Text option, the picture will become an integral part of the body text of the document and will be treated as if it were a single text character. It will therefore move automatically as the text moves on the page. To move it to a different position within the text, use the Cut and Copy commands or any of the other methods for moving ordinary text that were given in Chapter 5.

You can change the size of a picture the same way you resize a text box. That is, click on the picture to select it and then drag one of the eight sizing handles:

Drag one of the eight sizing handles to change the size of the picture.

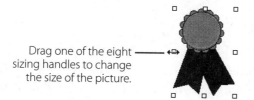

To maintain the original proportions of the picture, press Shift while you drag a corner sizing handle. To change the size of the picture without moving the position of its center, press Ctrl while you drag any handle. Note that using either of these methods to resize a picture *scales*—that is, compresses or expands—the graphics contained in the picture. You can also *crop* a picture, which changes the size or proportions of the picture itself without changing the size or proportions of the graphics it contains. Cropping results in either cutting off some of the image or adding additional white space around it. The illustration on the following page shows the difference.

Microsoft Word

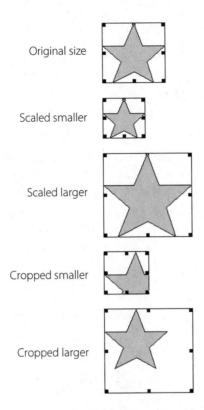

Original size

Scaled smaller

Scaled larger

Cropped smaller

Cropped larger

To crop a picture, you can use either the Picture toolbar or the Format Picture dialog box. These two features are described next.

When you select a picture by clicking on it, the Picture toolbar normally appears automatically (if it doesn't appear when a picture is selected, point to Toolbars on the View menu and choose Picture from the submenu). You can use the Picture toolbar to modify the picture in a variety of ways, as shown on the facing page.

You can make an even greater variety of changes to a picture by using the Format Picture dialog box, which is quite similar to the Format Text Box dialog box described previously, with a few differences in available options. To use the Format Picture dialog box, do the following:

1 Click anywhere on the picture to select it.

Insert Picture: insert new picture from file.

Image Control: use original colors (Automatic) or convert picture to black-and-white, grayscale, and so on.

More Contrast: increase intensity of colors in picture.

Less Contrast: decrease intensity of colors.

More Brightness: add white to colors in picture.

Less Brightness: remove white from colors.

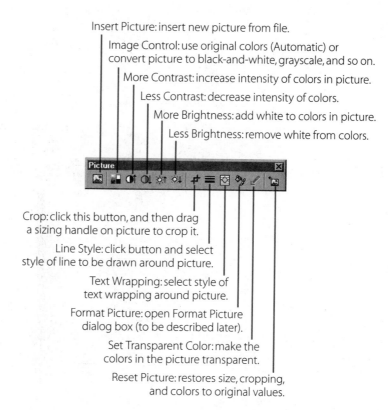

Crop: click this button, and then drag a sizing handle on picture to crop it.

Line Style: click button and select style of line to be drawn around picture.

Text Wrapping: select style of text wrapping around picture.

Format Picture: open Format Picture dialog box (to be described later).

Set Transparent Color: make the colors in the picture transparent.

Reset Picture: restores size, cropping, and colors to original values.

2 Click the Format Picture button on the Picture toolbar, or choose Picture from the Format menu (in some cases this command might be labeled Object rather than Picture).

3 Select options on the various tabs of the Format Picture dialog box, as shown on the following page.

You can also edit the contents of a picture by double-clicking it. The type of editing you can perform depends on the format and origin of the picture. The following are among the ways that Word allows you to edit a picture:

■ If the picture is compatible with a Word drawing, Word will open a separate window and allow you to alter each of the picture's component drawing objects. (Drawing objects are discussed in the next section.)

II

Microsoft Word

These options aren't available for a picture.

Crop picture; convert picture colors; set color contrast and brightness.

Turn text wrapping on or off, and set the style of wrapping.

Change position of picture on page; turn floating on or off.

Change size of picture, scaling the graphics it contains.

Select a background fill color; and set the color, style, and thickness of the lines around the text box.

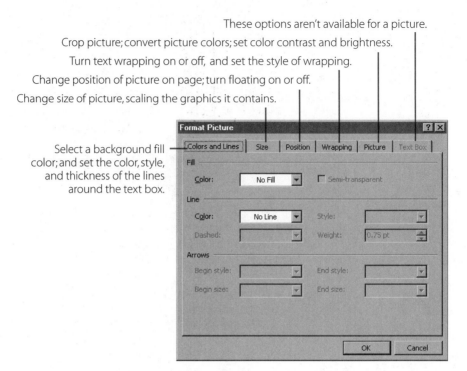

- If the picture isn't compatible with a Word drawing, you might not be able to fully edit the original picture, but only to change its size and add drawing objects to it.

- If you copied the picture from another program, Word might be able to activate the original program so that you can use that program's own tools and commands to edit the picture. For information about this method of editing a picture, see "Linking Data," page 1003 and "Embedding Data," page 1010.

To *delete* a picture, simply click on it to select it and then press Delete.

Finally, note that you can perform several of the operations discussed in this section by right-clicking a picture and choosing a command from the shortcut menu.

Creating Drawings in Word

A final way to add graphics to a document is to use Word's built-in drawing tools to draw them yourself. Each component of a drawing you create in this manner is termed a *drawing object*. You've already seen one type of drawing object, the text box. In this section, you'll learn how to create and modify many additional types of drawing objects, such as lines, cubes, free-form shapes, and special text effects.

As already explained for text boxes, all drawing objects *float* over text, meaning that they aren't part of the normal stream of characters in the document but rather can be positioned anywhere on the page. Also, when a drawing object is placed on a portion of a page occupied by text, either you can have the text flow around the drawing object or you can have the text and the object overlap (in this case, the text and drawing object are said to be in different *layers*, and you can control whether the text or the drawing object is on top).

The first step in creating or modify drawing objects is to display the Drawing toolbar by pointing to Toolbars on the View menu and choosing Drawing from the submenu, or by simply clicking the Drawing button on the Standard toolbar.

Drawing

To view or work with drawing objects, you must be in Page Layout or Online Layout view or Print Preview. If you aren't already in one of those views when you display the Drawing toolbar, Word will automatically switch the view to Page Layout view. The following is the Drawing toolbar:

The different groups of buttons on this toolbar will be explained in the following sections.

Inserting Drawing Objects

You can use the middle group of buttons on the Drawing toolbar to insert various types of drawing objects:

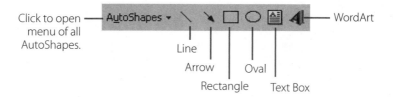

There are three main categories of drawing objects that you can insert: AutoShapes, WordArt, and text boxes.

An AutoShape is a predefined or free-form figure, such as a line, oval, cube, flowchart symbol, banner, free-form "scribble," and so on. You can insert a line, arrow, rectangle, or oval AutoShape object by simply clicking one of the buttons on the Drawing toolbar labeled on the preceding page. To insert one of the other types of AutoShapes, click the AutoShapes button, choose a category from the menu, and then click the button for the specific figure you want. For example, you would insert a crescent moon AutoShape figure as follows:

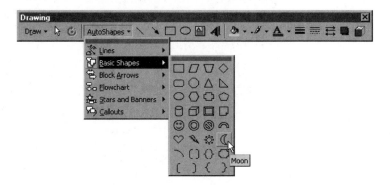

After clicking the button for the AutoShape, simply click at the position on the document page where you want to display the figure, and Word will insert a standard-sized AutoShape object (you can later change the size, shape, or position). If you want to give the object a specific initial size and shape, press the mouse button and drag to create the figure:

Another Way to Insert AutoShapes

If you wish, you can insert AutoShapes using the compact AutoShapes toolbar rather than the general-purpose Drawing toolbar. To display the AutoShapes toolbar, point to Picture on the Insert menu and choose AutoShapes from the submenu.

A WordArt drawing object allows you to insert text that's formatted in unusual ways—for example, curved, slanted, or three-dimensional text. The following is the method for adding WordArt:

1 Click the WordArt button on the Drawing toolbar, or point to Picture on the Insert menu and choose WordArt from the submenu. The WordArt Gallery dialog box will then be displayed:

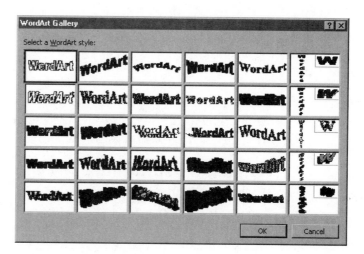

2 Select the style of WordArt you want by double-clicking one of the boxes in the WordArt Gallery dialog box (or click the box and then click OK). Word will now open the Edit WordArt Text dialog box:

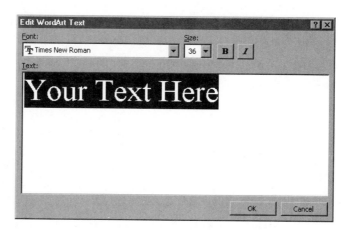

3 In the Edit WordArt Text dialog box, enter the text, and select the font, character size, and—if you wish—the bold or italic format. Click OK when you're done.

Word will then insert into your document a drawing object that contains the specially formatted text, as in the following example:

Example WordArt Object

Finally, you can enter a text box drawing object either by clicking the Text Box button on the Drawing toolbar, or by choosing Text Box from the Insert menu. Text boxes were discussed previously in the chapter (in "Using Text Boxes to Position Text on the Page," page 309).

Working with Drawing Objects

As when you work with document text, the general procedure for working with a drawing object is to first select the object, and then perform an action on it. To select a drawing object, first click the Select Objects button on the Drawing toolbar, and then click on the object you want to select. To select several objects so that you can perform some action on them simultaneously, simply drag a selection rectangle around all of them, as in this example:

Select
Objects

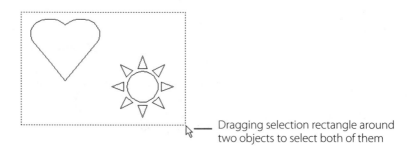

Dragging selection rectangle around two objects to select both of them

Alternatively, you can select several objects by pressing Shift while you click each one; this method allows you to select several objects in a rectangular area without selecting *all* the objects in this area. To restore the normal I-beam mouse pointer so that you can work with text, click the Select Objects button again. Note that if you're selecting only a single object, and it's not displayed behind text, you can simply click on it without first clicking the Select Objects button.

> If you've selected several objects, you can combine them into a single object so that you can work with them as a unit. To do this, click the Draw button on the Drawing toolbar to open the Draw drop-down menu, and then choose the Group command. You can later break apart the group into its constituent objects by selecting the group and choosing the Ungroup command from this same menu (you can then choose Regroup if you change your mind!).

To delete the selected object or objects, press the Delete key.

Resizing and Moving Drawing Objects

When you select an object, Word displays rectangular sizing handles around it. You can change the overall dimensions of the object by dragging one of these sizing handles. For some AutoShape objects, Word also displays a special, diamond-shaped sizing handle that's colored yellow; dragging this handle lets you change some aspect of the object's shape, such as the angle of the sides of a trapezoid:

Drag a rectangular sizing handle to change the overall dimensions of the trapezoid.

Drag the diamond-shaped sizing handle to modify the shape of the trapezoid (that is, the angle of the vertical sides).

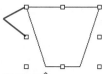

(The effect of dragging the diamond-shaped sizing handle varies widely among different types of AutoShape objects.) To maintain the original proportions of the object as you change its size, press Shift while dragging one of the corner sizing handles. To resize the object symmetrically about its center, hold down the Ctrl key while dragging a rectangular sizing handle.

To move a drawing object, place the pointer over the object, and when the pointer displays cross-arrows, drag the object to its new location on the page:

To copy rather than move the object, hold down the Ctrl key while you drag. Alternatively, when an object's selected, you can use the keyboard to move it by pressing the appropriate arrow key (Up, Down, Left, or Right). Notice that as you move a drawing object over an area of the page that contains text, the object *overlaps* the text. You can use the Format dialog box, discussed near the end of this section, to cause the text to *wrap* around the object as well as to pick a wrapping style.

Control What's on Top

If a drawing object overlaps text (that is, text wrapping is turned off), you can display the object either in front of or behind the text. Also, you can control the overlapping order of different drawing objects that intersect on the page. To make these changes, select the object, click the Draw button on the Drawing toolbar, point to Order on the menu that's displayed, and choose the appropriate command from the submenu.

You can also use commands on the Draw drop-down menu (click the Draw button on the Drawing toolbar to open it) to move, align, rotate, or flip the selected object or objects:

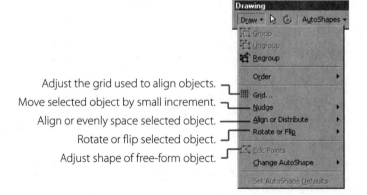

Adjust the grid used to align objects. — Grid...
Move selected object by small increment. — Nudge
Align or evenly space selected object. — Align or Distribute
Rotate or flip selected object. — Rotate or Flip
Adjust shape of free-form object. — Edit Points

Free
Rotate

Another way to rotate the selected drawing object is to click the Free Rotate button on the Drawing toolbar, and then drag one of the rotation handles that's displayed to rotate the drawing object by any amount.

Changing the Colors and Styles of Drawing Objects

You can use the following group of buttons on the Drawing toolbar to change the selected object's fill color or pattern, line color and style, and font color; or to add shadow or three-dimensional effects to the object:

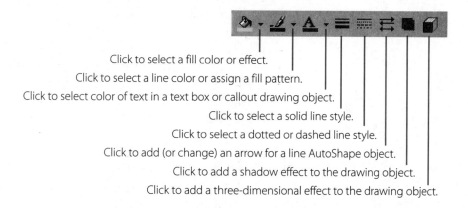

Click to select a fill color or effect.
Click to select a line color or assign a fill pattern.
Click to select color of text in a text box or callout drawing object.
Click to select a solid line style.
Click to select a dotted or dashed line style.
Click to add (or change) an arrow for a line AutoShape object.
Click to add a shadow effect to the drawing object.
Click to add a three-dimensional effect to the drawing object.

As an example, the following figure shows a rectangle AutoShape object as it appeared when it was first inserted—and then as it appears after adding a fill color and a three-dimensional effect:

You can experiment freely with these features. If you don't like the result of applying a particular feature or effect, simply issue the Undo command to remove it (for information on Undo, see the sidebar "Undoing and Redoing Editing and Formatting Actions," page 142). If you *do* like the result of a particular combination of effects, you can make them the default effects that will automatically be applied to all objects that you subsequently draw. To do this, select the object that has the combination of effects you want and then choose Set Auto-Shape Defaults from the Draw drop-down menu (click Draw on the Drawing toolbar to open this menu).

Microsoft Word

Special-Purpose Drawing Toolbars

Word provides several special-purpose toolbars to help you work with specific types of drawing objects and drawing effects. First, when you select a WordArt object, the WordArt toolbar normally appears automatically; and when you select a Text Box or Callout AutoShape object, the Text Box toolbar normally appears automatically. If either of these toolbars doesn't appear, you can display it by selecting the object and then pointing to Toolbars on the View menu and choosing the appropriate command from the submenu. The WordArt toolbar lets you insert a new WordArt object, or change the text, style, format, text alignment, and other features of the object. The Text Box toolbar assists you primarily in linking text boxes, and was explained in the section, "Using Text Boxes to Position Text on the Page," page 309.

Also, you can use the Shadow Settings toolbar to add a shadow effect to a drawing object, or to modify a shadow effect in a great variety of ways. To display this special-purpose toolbar, click the Shadow button on the Drawing toolbar, and then click the Shadow Settings button on the palette that pops up.

Finally, you can use the 3-D Settings toolbar to add a three-dimensional effect to a drawing object or to customize this effect. To display the toolbar, click the 3-D button on the Drawing toolbar and then click the 3-D Settings button on the palette.

 TIP

Convert an AutoShape to the One You Want

If you've spent some time inserting, sizing, and formatting an AutoShape drawing object and then realize that you'd rather be working with a different type of object, you don't need to delete the object and start over. Rather, you can simply convert it to the AutoShape object you want. To do this, select the object, click the Draw button on the Drawing toolbar, point to Change AutoShape on the drop-down menu, and then choose the new type of AutoShape object you want from the submenu.

Using the Format Dialog Box

Finally, you can extensively modify a drawing object by using the Format dialog box. This dialog box is labeled Format AutoShape, Format WordArt, or Format Text Box depending on the type of the drawing object that you're modifying. You open this dialog box by selecting the drawing object and then choosing AutoShape, WordArt, or Text Box from the Format menu. You've already seen a description of the Format

Text Box dialog box (page 313). Here's the Format AutoShape dialog box, which has the same features as the Format WordArt dialog box:

Turn text wrapping on or off for the object, and set the wrapping style.

Change the position of the object on the page.

Modify the object size or rotate the object.

Select a background fill color; and set the color, style, and thickness of the lines around the text box.

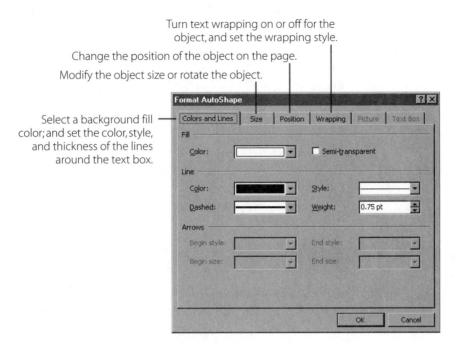

Microsoft Word

⭐ **TIP**

Use the Shortcut Menu when Drawing Objects

You can perform several of the operations discussed in this section by clicking on a drawing object with the right mouse button and choosing the command that accomplishes what you want from the shortcut menu that pops up. The commands provided on this menu depend on the type of the drawing object and the features that have been applied to it. Note that if you right-click a closed AutoShape figure such as an oval or star, the shortcut menu provides an interesting command that isn't available elsewhere: Add Text. This command lets you add text to the AutoShape object, so that it functions just like a text box (but with an interesting shape), as in the following example:

Previewing and Printing Documents

When you have finally finished entering text and graphics into your document, as well as editing, formatting, proofing, and adjusting the page design, you're ready to print the document. Before doing so, however, you might want to preview the printed appearance of the document on the screen and possibly make a few last-minute adjustments.

As you have already learned, Word provides two document views that display the document exactly as it will be printed: Page Layout and Print Preview. These two views have many features in common; in general, however, Page Layout view is best for editing the document and working with text boxes and graphics, while Print Preview is best for viewing the overall appearance of the document pages immediately before printing.

Online Documents and Online Layout View

You might be able to skip the entire process of print previewing, printing, distributing, and updating document hard copies by creating a document that can be read directly online. For example, you might create a manual in Word, which you store on your network server and which other employees open and read directly in Word. You could also post a Word document to a Web site, which users could download and read directly in Word (or in a Word document viewer program). In fact, if a user has installed Word and is using the Microsoft Internet Explorer 3.0 or later Web browser, a Word document on a Web site can be downloaded, viewed, and edited directly within the browser. (Internet Explorer 3.0 lets you view and edit Office documents directly within its own window, much like the Binder program discussed in Chapter 40.)

Word now provides a view that is designed specifically for creating and reading online documents: Online Layout. To switch to this view, choose Online Layout from the View menu or click the Online Layout View button at the left end of the horizontal scroll bar. This view has the following advantages for working with online documents (that is, documents that you don't intend to print):

- Unlike Normal view, Online Layout view displays all text, text boxes, pictures, and drawing objects.

Online Documents and Online Layout View *continued*

- Unlike Page Layout view, Online Layout view doesn't break up the document into pages or display headers and footers.

- Small fonts are enlarged to make them easier to read (to control this feature switch to Online Layout view, choose Options from the Tools menu, click the View tab, and enter a font size into the Enlarge Fonts Less Than box).

- The document can be viewed with an attractive background color or pattern (similar to the background displayed on many Web pages).

When you are designing a document that is intended to be read in Page Layout view rather than printed, you can enhance its appearance and readability by using one or more of the following techniques:

- You can assign the document a background color or pattern by pointing to Background on the Format menu and on the submenu that is displayed, choosing a color to assign a background color, or choosing Fill Effects to assign a background pattern. The background will be displayed only when the document is viewed in Online Layout view.

- To make it easier to browse through the document online, you can add hyperlinks that refer to other positions in the document, other documents, or even Internet sites. See the section "Inserting and Navigating with Hyperlinks," page 161.

- Displaying the Document Map can also make it easier to navigate through an online document. The Document Map is discussed in the section "Browsing Through Outline Headings," page 366.

- You can enhance text that is viewed online by assigning it animation formatting, which was discussed in the section "Using the Font Dialog Box," page 184.

Microsoft Word

Print
Preview

To switch to Print Preview, choose Print Preview from the File menu or click the Print Preview button on the Standard toolbar. The Print Preview screen appears as shown in Figure 10-16 on the following page. To edit your document while in Print Preview, deselect the Magnifier button on the toolbar. Click the Close button to close Print Preview and return to the view you were working in earlier.

FIGURE 10-16.
Print Preview shows
how your document
will appear when
printed.

Print

Magnifier

One Page

Multiple Pages

Zoom

View Ruler

Shrink to Fit

Full Screen

Context-Sensitive Help

Print Preview toolbar

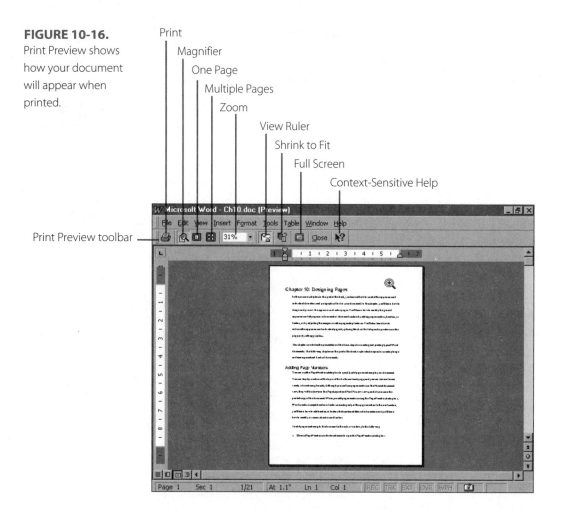

Pagination

Before printing your document, you might want to view and adjust the positions
of the page breaks. You should do this after editing, formatting, and proofing
your document because these actions can change the positions of page breaks.

In Page Layout view or Print Preview, you can readily see the positions of
page breaks because each page is displayed exactly as it will print. In Normal
view, Word marks the position of each page break with a dotted horizontal line
if you have turned on the Background Repagination option. (To turn on this
option, choose Options from the Tools menu and click the General tab.)

Pagination *continued*

As you saw in Chapter 6, "Formatting a Word Document," the following paragraph formatting features can affect the positions of page breaks: Widow/Orphan Control, Keep Lines Together, Keep With Next, and Page Break Before. See Table 6-8 on page 191 for an explanation of each of these features.

Also, the positions of page breaks can be affected by the current setting of the print options that tell Word what to include in the printed copy of the document. These options are contained in the Include With Document area of the Print tab of the Options dialog box, shown in Figure 10-17 on the following page. To open this tab, choose Options from the Tools menu and click the Print tab, or click the Options button in the Print dialog box (to be described shortly).

A page break that Word automatically generates when the text reaches the bottom of a page is known as a *soft page break*. You can also force a page break at any position in a document by inserting a *hard page break*. The position of a hard page break is fixed, and it always causes a page break regardless of its location on the page. To insert a hard page break at the insertion point, press Ctrl+Enter, or choose the Break command from the Insert menu and select the Page Break option. In Normal view, Word marks the position of a hard page break with a horizontal dotted line labeled Page Break. (In contrast, the horizontal line marking the position of a soft page break is not labeled.)

....   Soft page break mark

....................................Page Break....................................   Hard page break mark

In Page Layout view, the text following a hard page break is forced to a new page, but the mark itself appears only if the Show/Hide ¶ button on the Standard toolbar is pressed.

To *remove* a hard page break, just select the mark and press Delete.

? **SEE ALSO**

For basic information about previewing and printing documents, see "Printing Documents," page 57.

When you're ready to print a copy of your document, choose Print from the File menu or press Ctrl+P. Word will display the Print dialog box, which is shown in Figure 10-18 on the following page. Before clicking the OK button to start printing, you can choose the printer, change printer settings, and select printing options.

Alternatively, you can quickly print your document using the current default printer and the default print settings by simply clicking the Print button on the Standard toolbar or on the Print Preview toolbar (which is displayed when you switch to Print Preview).

Print

FIGURE 10-17.
The Print tab of the
Options dialog box.

FIGURE 10-18.
The Print dialog box.

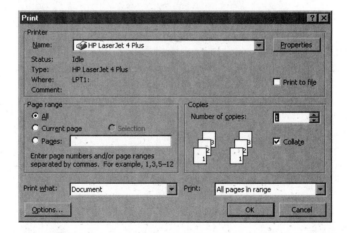

Print Other Document Elements

Rather than printing the document itself, you can print various document elements by choosing an item other than Document in the Print What list of the Print dialog box. You can print the document properties (that is, the information displayed and set through the Properties command on the File menu), the comments in the document, a description of the document styles, the contents of the document's AutoText entries, or a list of the document's current shortcut key assignments.

CHAPTER 11

Working with Word in Workgroups

This chapter presents Word features and techniques that can facilitate your work with other people in the production of a document. You might, for example, work with other authors, editors, reviewers, proofreaders, or indexers. The members of your workgroup might work on a single copy of a document, which is shared on a network or is routed from one person to another using Microsoft Exchange on a network or a floppy disk. Alternatively, you might distribute a separate document copy to each member using a network, electronic mail, or floppy disks. This chapter focuses on the Word-specific techniques for *preparing* and *working with* shared documents. The mechanics of sharing documents using networks, electronic mail, and Microsoft Exchange are discussed in "Sharing Documents in a Workgroup," page 92).

Adding Comments to Your Documents

You can add comments to a Word document without modifying the main document text. Comments are edited and viewed within a separate pane at the bottom of the document window and don't appear on the printed document copy (although you can print them separately). Comments are useful for adding notes, explanations, suggestions, and other types of information to specific parts of your document. You might add comments to save information for your own use, or to communicate with other members of your workgroup. Figure 11-1 shows a document with several comments.

FIGURE 11-1.
Viewing comments in a Word document.

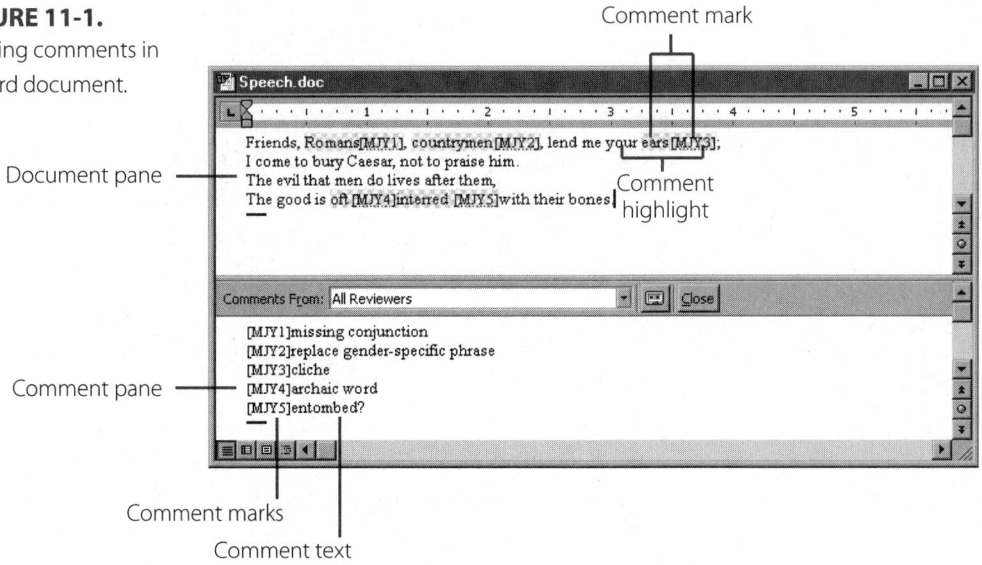

Comment mark

Document pane

Comment highlight

Comment pane

Comment marks

Comment text

To make it easier to use comments, display the Reviewing toolbar (choose Toolbars from the View menu and choose the Reviewing option from the submenu that pops up). The five buttons at the left end of the toolbar can be used for working with comments (see Figure 11-2).

To insert a comment into a document, do the following:

1 Select the text to which you want to attach the comment. To attach a comment to a single word, you can simply place the insertion point anywhere within the word.

FIGURE 11-2.
The buttons on the
Reviewing toolbar
for working
with comments.

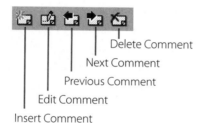

Delete Comment

Next Comment

Previous Comment

Edit Comment

Insert Comment

2 Choose the Comment command from the Insert menu or click the Insert Comment button on the Reviewing toolbar. Word then does the following:

- It permanently highlights selected text in your document. The comment will be attached to this text.

- It places a comment mark at the end of the selected text.

- It opens a separate pane in which you enter and later view the comment text.

- It inserts a matching comment mark in the comment pane and places the insertion point following the mark.

3 Type the text for the comment following the mark in the comment pane. You can use the basic Word editing and formatting techniques on comments in the same way you would for any other Word text.

If you want, you can leave the comment pane open while you resume editing the document. To move the insertion point from one pane to the other, press F6 or click in the pane in which you want to work. If you want more room on the screen for your main document, you can close the comment pane by clicking on the Close button at the top of the pane, or by clicking on the Edit Comment button on the Reviewing toolbar.

Notice that the comment mark consists of your initial or initials, followed by the number of the comment. The initials included in comment marks let you distinguish the comments added by different members of your workgroup. Note that the comment marks in the document pane are formatted as hidden text; accordingly, they're not visible on the screen unless the comment pane is open, the Show/Hide ¶ button on the Standard toolbar is pressed, or the Hidden Text viewing option is turned on (to locate this option, choose Options from the Tools menu and click the View tab).

To view the text of the comment that is attached to a particular block of text in your document, you can simply place the mouse pointer anywhere over the highlighted text (whether comment marks are visible or not). Word will display the name of the comment author as well as the comment text. (Note, however, that the ScreenTips option must be turned on. You set this option by choosing Options from the Tools menu and opening the View tab.)

Michael Young:
archaic word

The good is oft interred with their bones.

> **NOTE**
>
> You can change the initials that Word adds to the comments you insert, as well as the author name that is displayed when you place the pointer over a comment. To do this, choose Options from the Tools menu, click the User Information tab, and enter new initials into the Initials box or a new name into the Name box.

You can browse through the comments in a document by clicking the Previous Comment or the Next Comment button on the Reviewing toolbar.

You can also view comment text within the comment pane. If the comment pane isn't open, either choose Comments from the View menu or click the Edit Comment button on the Reviewing toolbar. Initially, Word displays the comments made by *all* authors. If you want to view only the comments entered by a specific individual, choose the author's name (rather than All Reviewers) in the Comments From list at the top of the comment pane. Then scroll through the comment pane—if necessary—to view the comment text. (The name used for each author is the name that was contained in the Name box on the User Information tab of the Options dialog box at the time the comment was entered.)

If you double-click a comment mark in the document, Word will open the comment pane and display the corresponding comment text.

Notice that if you scroll the comment pane, Word automatically scrolls the document pane to reveal the corresponding comment mark. Likewise, if you scroll the document pane, Word scrolls the comment pane.

 TIP

Go to Comment Marks with Any of Several Shortcuts

To locate comment marks in the document, you can use the Find command, the Go To command, or the browse buttons, which were described in Chapter 5, "Entering and Editing Text in a Word Document." When using the Find command, enter ^a into the Find What box. When using the Go To command or browse buttons, select the Comment target.

You can remove a comment by selecting the comment mark in the document and pressing Delete, or by placing the insertion point anywhere within the highlighted text in the document and clicking the Delete Comment button on the Reviewing toolbar. Word will remove both the comment mark and the associated comment text.

 TIP

Remove Your Comments Quickly with Replace

Perhaps your comments are personal and you want to remove *all* of them from the copy of a document that you turn over to a co-worker. A quick way to do this is to choose Replace from the Edit menu, and in the Replace tab enter ^a into the Find What box, leave the Replace With box empty, and click the Replace All button. (See Chapter 5, "Entering and Editing Text in a Word Document," for more information on the Replace command.)

If you have the necessary sound equipment installed on your computer (a sound card and a microphone), you can also add or listen to *voice comments*.

To add a voice comment, click the Insert Sound Object button and use a microphone to record your message.

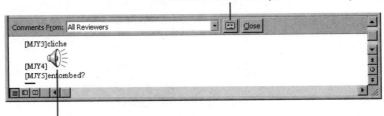

Word will insert this sound symbol into the comment text in the comment pane. To listen to a voice comment (which requires a sound card), double-click the sound symbol in the comment text.

Printing Comments

You can print the document comments alone, or you can print the comments together with the document.

To print only the comments, choose Print from the File menu and select Comments in the Print What list in the Print dialog box.

To include the comments whenever you print the document, choose Options from the Tools menu, click the Print tab, and turn on the Comments option (in the Include With Document area). Notice that when you turn on this option, Word automatically turns on the Hidden Text option so that the comment marks (which are formatted as hidden text) will be printed. Whenever you subsequently print the document, the comment text will be printed after the document text, starting on a new page.

? SEE ALSO

For a description of hidden text, see "Using the Font Dialog Box," page 184.

Tracking Document Revisions

You can use the Word revision feature to track and mark all changes you make to a document, so that you or another author or editor can later review these changes and either accept or reverse them. For each change that is tracked, Word stores the exact modification that was made, as well as the name of the author, the date, and the time of the change; and it displays all this information when you review the revisions. (The name used to indicate the author of a revision is the name that was contained in the Name box on the User Information tab of the Options dialog box at the time the revision was made.)

To start tracking revisions to a document, point to Track Changes on the Tools menu and choose Highlight Changes from the submenu that pops up. Then turn on Track Changes While Editing in the Highlight Changes dialog box and click OK. Alternatively, you can simply press Ctrl+Shift+E, or double-click the TRK indicator on the Word status bar:

You can also start tracking revisions by clicking the Track Changes button on the Reviewing toolbar, which is shown in Figure 11-3. (To display this toolbar, choose Toolbars from the View menu and choose the Reviewing option from the submenu that pops up.)

FIGURE 11-3.
The buttons on the Reviewing toolbar used for revision tracking.

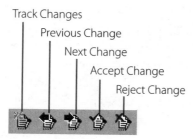

When revision tracking is enabled, the TRK indicator on the Word status bar is displayed in dark type.

To *stop* tracking revisions, just repeat any of these procedures (each procedure toggles revision tracking on or off). When you turn off revision tracking, Word retains a record of all revisions that have already been tracked, but it doesn't track changes that you subsequently make.

When revision tracking is turned on, Word stores information on each change you make to the document, so that any change can later be reviewed, accepted, or reversed. You can also have Word visibly *mark* each revision that has been tracked. If visible revision marks aren't already enabled, you can turn them on by pointing to Track Changes

II

Microsoft Word

on the Tools menu and choosing Highlight Changes from the submenu that pops up. Then, in the Highlight Changes dialog box, turn on Highlight Changes On Screen to show revision marks on the screen, and turn on Highlight Changes In Printed Document to include them when the document is printed:

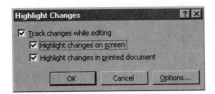

Figure 11-4 shows a document with several revision marks. Notice how Word marks inserted text and deleted text. Notice also that it places a vertical line in the margin to flag any line that contains a revision. Additionally, when you move the mouse pointer over a revision mark in the window, Word displays the author, date, time, and the type of the revision (for example, Inserted or Deleted):

Later in the chapter (in the section "Customizing Revision Marking," page 344), you'll learn how to modify the way Word marks revisions.

You can hide revision marking on screen or in the printed document by turning off the appropriate option in the Highlight Changes dialog box described above. Word, however, will retain a record of all revisions that have been tracked, and you can make them visible again by turning the option back on. (The only way to remove a revision that has been tracked is to accept or reject it, as described in the next section.)

FIGURE 11-4.
A Word document containing revision marks.

Mark indicating revised line

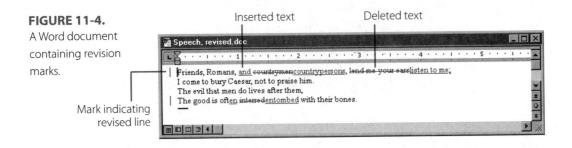

Reviewing Revisions

You can review all revisions that have been tracked in your document, and either accept or reject any of them. If you accept a revision, the indicated change is made permanent; if you reject a revision, the text is restored to its original state. In either case, Word discards its record of the revision and removes the revision mark. To review the revisions, point to Track Changes on the Tools menu and choose Accept Or Reject Changes from the submenu that pops up. Word will open the Accept Or Reject Changes dialog box (see Figure 11-5). You can accept or reject all revisions in the document or review each revision separately, as shown in that figure.

FIGURE 11-5.
The Accept Or Reject Changes dialog box.

Click the Find Previous button to select the previous revision in the document.

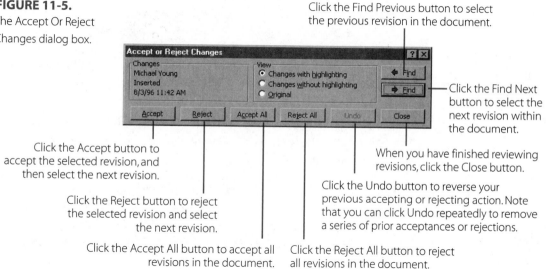

Click the Find Next button to select the next revision within the document.

Click the Accept button to accept the selected revision, and then select the next revision.

Click the Reject button to reject the selected revision and select the next revision.

Click the Accept All button to accept all revisions in the document.

When you have finished reviewing revisions, click the Close button.

Click the Undo button to reverse your previous accepting or rejecting action. Note that you can click Undo repeatedly to remove a series of prior acceptances or rejections.

Click the Reject All button to reject all revisions in the document.

TIP

Choose the Way You View Revision Marks

You can select an option in the View area of the Accept Or Reject Changes dialog box to temporarily change the way Word displays your revisions. The Changes With Highlighting option displays revision marks in the document (as shown in Figure 11-4); the Changes Without Highlighting option hides revision marks but displays all changes made to the document; and the Original option hides the marks and shows all document text as it was before you changed it. Note that merely selecting one of these options does *not* make a permanent change to the document, but only affects the way revisions are displayed while the Accept Or Reject Changes dialog box is open.

Notice that to help you identify the origin of each revision, the Accept Or Reject Changes dialog box displays the name of the author, whether the change was a deletion or an insertion, the date, and the time of the selected revision. Also, if several authors have made changes to the document, Word normally marks each author's revisions using a different color. (As you'll see in the next section, however, you can have Word use a single color for all revisions.)

⭐ **TIP**

Use Toolbar Buttons to Review Your Revisions
You can browse through the revisions that have been tracked in your document, whether or not revision marks are visible, using the Next Change and Previous Change buttons on the Reviewing toolbar (see Figure 11-3, page 341). Clicking the Next Change button selects the next block of revised text in the document, and clicking Previous Change selects the previous block of revised text. You can also accept or reject the selected revision, whether or not revision markings are visible, using the Accept Change or Reject Change button on the Reviewing toolbar.

Customizing Revision Marking

You can modify the style as well as the color of the revision marks that Word uses, as follows:

1 Choose Options from the Tools menu and click the Track Changes tab, or click the Options button in the Highlight Changes dialog box that was described previously (in the section "Tracking Document Revisions," page 340). The Track Changes tab is shown in Figure 11-6.

2 For each kind of revision that Word tracks (inserted text, deleted text, changed formatting, and changed lines), choose the type of mark that Word will use by selecting an item in the corresponding Mark list.

3 For each kind of revision, choose the color that Word assigns to the revised text by selecting an item in the corresponding Color

list. For any kind of revision mark except the one used to indicate changed lines, you can choose By Author to have Word use a different color for the revisions of each author, or you can choose a single color that Word will use for all revisions. The Auto item refers to your normal window text color (set through the Windows Control Panel), which is usually black.

FIGURE 11-6.

The Track Changes tab of the Options dialog box.

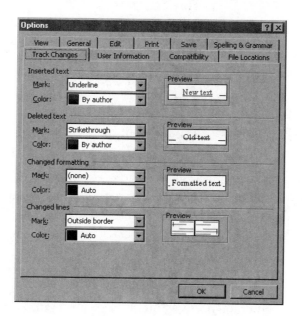

Working with Different Document Versions

In the previous sections you learned how to use Word's revision feature to keep track of the changes you make to a document, and to communicate changes or proposed changes to other members of your workgroup. Word provides two additional features that can help you keep track of the changes you or members of your workgroup have made to a document: the Compare Documents command, which helps you find the differences between two different versions of a document, and the Share Document command, which allows you to easily save and retrieve separate document versions.

Comparing Document Versions

If you have saved a previous version of a document in a separate file, you can compare the previous version to the current version and, if you wish, you can restore parts of the current version to the way they are in the previous version. The procedure is as follows:

1 Open the current document version.

2 Point to Track Changes on the Tools menu and choose Compare Documents from the submenu that pops up. Word will display the Select File To Compare With Current Document dialog box, which is similar to the standard Open dialog box that is displayed when you open a document.

3 Select the name of the previous document version and click the Open button.

Word will add revision marks to the current document version to show how it differs from the previous version. These marks will be the same as those that would be created if you opened the previous document version, turned on revision tracking and visible revision marks, and edited the document so that it matched the current version. You can review, accept, or reject these revisions using the techniques that were explained earlier in this chapter. Note that rejecting a revision restores that part of the document to the way it is in the previous version.

Maintaining Separate Document Versions

You can use Word's Version command to store several separate versions of a document, all within a single document file. Say, for example, that you've just finished writing Chapter 1 for your latest novel in a document called Chapter1. You now want to revise the chapter, but before doing so you want to save the current version so that you can refer back to it if necessary. Previously, you would have had to save the current version in a separate file (perhaps by making a copy of the file, or by using the Save As command). With Word 97, however, you can save the current document version right within the Chapter1 file.

To do this, choose Versions from the File menu and in the Versions dialog box, click the Save Now button; Word then prompts you to add a descriptive comment for the version. You can then proceed to revise your chapter and save your work when you are done. The original document version will be stored within the Chapter1 file, along with the revised version. However, when you open the document you won't see the original version unless you again choose the Versions command from the File menu and use the Versions dialog box to open the original version in a separate window, as shown here:

Save the current document contents as a separate version whenever you close the document.

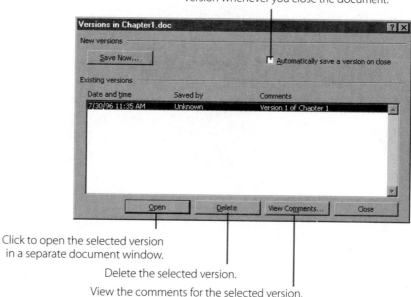

Click to open the selected version in a separate document window.

Delete the selected version.

View the comments for the selected version.

You can use this same technique to store additional document versions within the same document file.

Using Other Workgroup Techniques

In the following sections, you'll learn several additional Word techniques that are useful when working in workgroups.

Protecting Documents

You might want to distribute a document—or copies of a document—to other members of your workgroup so that they can review, edit, or make additions to the document. Before you do so, however, you can *protect* the document to limit the kinds of changes reviewers can make, thereby ensuring the document's integrity. To protect a document, do the following:

1 Make sure the document you want to protect is displayed in the active document window.

2 Choose Protect Document from the Tools menu to open the Protect Document dialog box:

3 Choose one of the three types of protection in the Protect Document For area of the dialog box:

- Select the Comments option to allow comments to be added to the document, but to prevent changes from being made to the actual document text.

- Select the Tracked Changes option to permanently turn on revision tracking for the document. With this option, revision tracking can't be turned off, nor can revisions be accepted or rejected. (After you remove the document protection, you'll be able to review, accept, or reject any of the changes made by reviewers.) Note that this option also permits comments to be added to the document.

- If you have divided your document into sections, you can select the Forms option to disallow all changes within one or more specific document sections. Click the Sections button to select the particular section or sections you want to protect. Note that this option permits changes within *form fields* as well as within unprotected sections. (Form fields are not covered in this book. For more information, look up the topic "form fields" on the Index tab of Word online Help.)

4 To prevent reviewers from removing the protection, type a password into the Password box. (Word will display only * characters as you type.) You'll be asked to retype the password after you click OK.

Note that the protection you choose will apply to you as well as to other users.

If you have routed a single copy of the document among the members of your workgroup, when you receive the document back, you'll probably want to remove the protection. You can do so by choosing the Unprotect Document command from the Tools menu (which replaces the Protect Document command when the document is protected). If you entered a password when you protected the document, Word will prompt you for it.

? SEE ALSO

For instructions on merging revisions, see "Merging Revisions," page 352.

If you have distributed a separate copy of the document to each member of the workgroup, when these documents are returned to you, you can merge the revisions they contain into the original document.

File-Sharing Protection

You can also protect a document against unauthorized changes by selecting file-sharing options, as follows:

1 Make sure the document you want to protect is displayed in the active document window.

II

Microsoft Word

2 Choose Options from the Tools menu and click the Save tab, or click the Options button in the Save As dialog box. The Save tab is shown in Figure 11-7.

FIGURE 11-7.
The Save tab of the
Options dialog box.

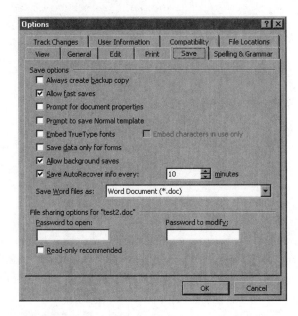

3 Set one or more of the options in the File Sharing group at the bottom of the Save tab, as follows:

- To prevent unauthorized users from *opening* the document, type a password into the Password To Open box. Word will ask you to retype the password when you click OK. No user will be able to open the document without typing this password.

- To prevent unauthorized users from *changing* the document, type a password into the Password To Modify box. Word will ask you to retype the password when you click OK. Any user will be able to open the document in read-only mode, which doesn't allow changes to the document to be saved. Only users who know the password, however, will be able to open the document in the normal read-write mode, which allows saving changes.

- If you don't assign a password, you can have Word *suggest* opening the document in read-only mode by turning on the Read-Only Recommended option. Whenever any user opens the document, Word will display a message suggesting that the document be opened in read-only mode. The user, however, can choose whether to open the document in read-only or in normal read-write mode.

You can turn off file-sharing protection (assuming that the document is open in the normal read-write mode) by opening the Save tab again and then deleting the password or turning off the Read-Only Recommended option.

Note that you can open any document in the read-only mode—even one that's not protected—by choosing Open from the File menu, clicking the Commands And Settings button at the far right of the toolbar in the Open dialog box, and choosing the Open Read Only command from the menu that pops up:

Commands
And Settings

When a document is opened in read-only mode, you can freely make changes to its contents. You can't, however, save the modified document under the same name (that is, you can't overwrite the original document version with the changed version), although you can save a *copy* of the modified document under a different name by choosing the Save As command from the File menu.

Merging Revisions

If you've distributed a separate copy of a document to each member of a workgroup, when you receive these copies back, you can merge into the original document all the revisions that have been tracked within the document copies. After doing this, the original document will contain all the changes made by the other members of your workgroup; you can then review, accept, or reject each change, as described previously (in the section "Reviewing Revisions," page 343).

The following is the procedure for merging revisions:

1 Open the original document (the one you want to *receive* the merged revisions).

2 Choose Merge Documents from the Tools menu to open the Select File To Merge Into Current Document dialog box, which is similar to the standard Open dialog box.

3 In the Select File To Merge Into Current Document dialog box, select the name of a document that contains revisions you want to merge into the original document and click the Open button. Word will then copy all the revisions contained in the selected document into the original document that you opened in step 1.

4 Repeat step 3 for any additional documents that contain revisions you want to merge into the original document.

TIP

Protect Your Document Before Distributing Multiple Copies

To successfully merge revisions from a copy of a document into the original document, the copy must not contain any untracked revisions. To ensure that revision tracking is turned on when the copy is edited, before you distribute the copy you might open it and enable the Tracked Changes option in the Protect Document dialog box, as discussed previously (at the beginning of the section "Protecting Documents," page 348).

Highlighting Text

You can use the Word Highlight tool to permanently mark blocks of text in a document, similar to the way that you would use a yellow marker pen to highlight text on a printed page. The text you mark is highlighted both on the screen and on the printed copy of the document.

To highlight a block of text, do the following:

1 Select the text you want to highlight.

Highlight

2 To highlight using the color currently shown on the Highlight button, simply click the Highlight button on the Formatting toolbar or on the Reviewing toolbar. To highlight with a different color, click the down arrow at the right of this button and then click the color you want on the palette that Word displays:

You can quickly highlight several blocks of text as follows:

1 Without selecting text beforehand, click the Highlight button or click a color on the palette, as described previously.

2 With the mouse, drag over each block of text that you want to highlight.

3 When you have finished highlighting text, click the Highlight button again or press the Escape key to return to normal editing mode.

You can remove highlighting by doing the following:

1 Select the text from which you want to remove the highlighting.

2 Click the down arrow at the right of the Highlight button.

Microsoft Word

3 Click the None item on the color palette:

Click None to remove highlighting.

 TIP

Hide Highlighting

You can temporarily hide all highlighting on the screen by choosing Options from the Tools menu, clicking the View tab, and turning off the Highlight option in the Show area. You can make highlighting reappear by turning on this same option. Also, highlighting will automatically become visible if you add new highlighting to a document.

You can quickly remove highlighting from several blocks of text using the same technique described for highlighting several blocks. In step 1, simply click the None item on the palette.

 **TIP**

If you print a document containing highlighting on a monochrome printer, the highlight color will be converted to a shade of gray. For best results on a monochrome printer, choose a light highlighting color (such as yellow).

Sharing Fonts

One problem that you might encounter when you work in a workgroup is that a co-worker might not be able to view or print a particular font that you have assigned to text in a document. To avoid this problem, you should make sure that your document uses only True-Type fonts. A TrueType font can be viewed or printed with almost any computer running Windows 95 on which the font is installed. The common TrueType fonts (such as Times New Roman, Arial, and Courier New) are installed on virtually every computer that runs Windows 95.

 SEE ALSO

For a description of TrueType fonts, see "Using the Font Dialog Box," page 184.

If, however, you use one or more TrueType fonts that might not be installed on a co-worker's computer, you can embed TrueType fonts in your document so that they can be viewed and printed even on a machine that doesn't have them installed. (Doing so, however, will increase the size of the document.)

To embed TrueType fonts, do the following:

1 Make sure that the document in which you want to embed fonts is contained in the active document window.

2 Choose Options from the Tools menu and click the Save tab.

3 Turn on the Embed TrueType Fonts option. To reduce the size of the document, you can also turn on the Embed Characters In Use Only option, which causes Word to save font information only for those characters that actually appear in the document.

II

Microsoft Word

CHAPTER 12

Writing Long Documents

I n this chapter, you'll learn how to organize, footnote, index, or add tables of contents to your Word documents. Although these techniques are especially useful for developing long or complex documents, such as books, manuals, and academic papers, they can be used for writing any type of document.

Using Outline View to Organize Your Documents

Outline view can be a great help while you're planning or organizing a document, and even while you're entering the bulk of the document text. The following are among the important features and advantages of Outline view:

- The outline headings in the document—and the text that follows them—are indented by various amounts, so that you can immediately see the hierarchical structure of your document.

- You can control the level of detail that is visible in the outline. For example, you can hide all body text and view only the headings.

- You can quickly move an individual paragraph, or an entire heading together with all text and subheadings that follow it.

- You can usually see more text on the screen in Outline view than in other views, because all text is single spaced, regardless of the paragraph formatting.

 NOTE

In Outline view, paragraph formatting is not displayed and you can't open the Paragraph dialog box to apply paragraph formatting. (You can control whether or not *character* formatting is displayed.) Therefore, to modify the formatting of your paragraphs, you should switch out of Outline view.

Activating Outline View

Outline View

To activate Outline view, choose Outline from the View menu, or click the Outline View button on the horizontal scroll bar. Word will display the document as an outline, and it will show the Outlining toolbar, as illustrated in Figure 12-1. In Outline view, the term *heading* refers to any paragraph that has been assigned one of the built-in heading styles: Heading 1 through Heading 9. A heading assigned the Heading 1 style is at the highest level and is not indented. A heading assigned Heading 2 is at a lower level and is indented a small amount when displayed in Outline view, a heading assigned Heading 3 is at an even lower level and is indented more, and so on. The term *body text* refers to all paragraphs visible in Outline view that have *not* been assigned a heading style.

FIGURE 12-1.

A Word document in Outline view.

Outlining toolbar

Level 1 heading (Heading 1)

Body text

Level 2 heading (Heading 2)

Level 3 heading (Heading 3)

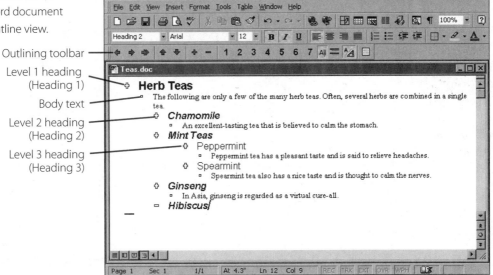

 NOTE

Switching to Outline view doesn't change your document. It merely displays the document in a different way and allows you to work with it differently.

In Outline view, Word displays one of the following symbols in front of each paragraph:

Symbol	Type of Paragraph
✚	Heading with subtext
▭	Heading without subtext
▫	Body text

The term *subtext* refers to either subheadings or body text that immediately follows a heading.

If you have already assigned the Heading 1 through Heading 9 styles to your document headings (as recommended in Chapter 6, "Formatting a Word Document"), Word will indent the headings appropriately

SEE ALSO

For a general description of styles, see "Applying Styles," page 175. For information about modifying styles, see "Modifying Styles," page 200.

in Outline view and the document will look like an outline, as shown in Figure 12-1 on the preceding page. If, however, you haven't already assigned the built-in heading styles to your heading paragraphs, the document will consist of a simple list of body text paragraphs, as shown in Figure 12-2, and it won't look much like an outline. Don't worry—by using the buttons on the Outlining toolbar, you can quickly apply heading styles and convert the document into outline form.

FIGURE 12-2.
A document in Outline view with headings that haven't been assigned the built-in heading styles.

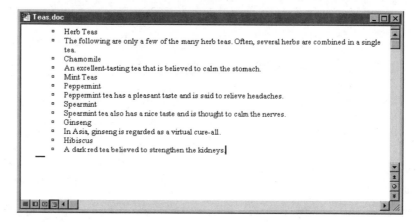

> **NOTE**
>
> Because each level of heading is assigned a different style, it generally has different formatting. Higher level headings are typically formatted with larger, bold fonts to convey their relative importance; lower level headings are typically formatted with smaller, nonbold fonts. To quickly change the appearance of a particular level of heading throughout your document, you can modify the corresponding heading style.

Changing Heading Levels

You can use the first three buttons on the Outlining toolbar

Demote to Body Text

Demote

Promote

to change the level of a heading, to convert a paragraph of body text to a heading, or to convert a heading to a paragraph of body text.

In general, you can perform outlining operations on more than one paragraph (headings or body text) by selecting several paragraphs prior to carrying out the command. For simplicity, however, the discussions on outlining use the singular terms *heading* or *paragraph*.

To select a heading together with all its subtext, simply click on the symbol in front of the heading:

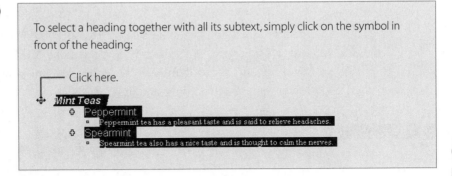

To change the level of a heading, do the following:

1 Place the insertion point in the heading you want to change (or select several headings).

2 To promote the heading to the next higher level, click the Promote button (which points left, to suggest its result of moving the heading further out in the margin for prominence). To demote the heading to the next lower level, click the Demote button.

Alternatively, you can press the Alt+Shift+Left arrow key combination or Shift+Tab to promote the heading, and you can press the Alt+Shift+Right arrow key combination or Tab to demote it.

To enter a tab character while you're in Outline view, press Ctrl+Tab.

You can also change the level of a heading as well as any subheadings that follow it by dragging the heading symbol to the left to promote it, or to the right to demote it:

This marker indicates the new level for the first heading in the selection.

II

Microsoft Word

When Word changes the level of a heading, it assigns it a new heading style. For example, if you demote a top-level heading, Word changes the style from Heading 1 to Heading 2.

? SEE ALSO

For information on applying built-in styles, see "Applying Styles," page 175.

You can convert a paragraph of body text to an outline heading by either promoting it or demoting it, using the methods just described. You can select more than one paragraph of body text, but don't include a heading in the selection. If you promote a paragraph of body text, it's converted into a heading at the same level as the preceding heading, and if you demote it, it's converted into a heading one level lower than the preceding heading.

TIP

Use Shortcuts to Quickly Convert Headings and Text

You can also change the level of a heading, convert body text to a heading, or convert a heading to body text, by directly assigning the paragraph the appropriate style (Heading 1 through Heading 9 for a heading, or a style such as Normal for body text). Recall from Chapter 6, "Formatting a Word Document," that you can quickly apply the Heading 1, Heading 2, or Heading 3 style by pressing Alt+Ctrl+1, Alt+Ctrl+2, or Alt+Ctrl+3, and you can apply the Normal paragraph style by pressing Ctrl+Shift+N.

To convert a heading to body text, place the insertion point within the heading (or select several headings) and click the Demote To Body Text button, or, if Num Lock is off, press Alt+Shift+5 (5 on the numeric keypad). Word will assign the paragraph the Normal style.

You can also convert *any* paragraph to an outline heading when not in Outline view (whether or not the paragraph has been assigned one of the Heading styles) by selecting the paragraph, choosing Paragraph from the Format menu, clicking the Indents And Spacing tab, and choosing the desired heading level (Level 1 through Level 9) in the Outline Level list. (You can choose the Body Text item in this list to convert an outline heading to outline body text.) In general, however, it's much better to create outline headings by assigning the Heading 1 through Heading 9 built-in styles, for several reasons.

First, in Outline view you can quickly and easily assign a Heading style using the Outlining toolbar or the keystrokes that were described. Also, assigning a Heading style will apply appropriate formatting for a heading (such as a larger font, bold type, and so on). Finally, using the Heading styles will make it easier to maintain consistent formatting of your headings and to quickly modify this formatting throughout the document.

Moving Blocks of Text

You can quickly move one or more paragraphs using these two buttons on the Outlining toolbar:

Move Up

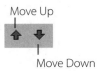

Move Down

The paragraphs can be either headings or body text. The following is the procedure:

1 Place the insertion point within the paragraph you want to move (or select several paragraphs).

2 Click the Move Up button to move the paragraph above the previous paragraph, or click the Move Down button to move the paragraph below the following paragraph.

   Alternatively, you can press the Alt+Shift+Up arrow key combination to move the paragraph up, or press the Alt+Shift+Down arrow key combination to move the paragraph down.

3 Repeat step 2 as necessary to move the paragraph to the desired final position.

You can also quickly move a paragraph by dragging the paragraph's symbol up or down in the document:

This marker indicates the new position for the text being moved.

⊕ Peppermint
   ▫ Peppermint tea has a pleasant taste and is said to relieve headaches.
✦ Spearmint
   ▫ Spearmint tea also has a nice taste and is thought to calm the nerves.

This method always moves a single heading together with all its subtext, because the heading and subtext are selected when you begin dragging the symbol.

Collapsing and Expanding Text

You can use the following buttons on the Outlining toolbar to change the level of detail that is visible in the outline:

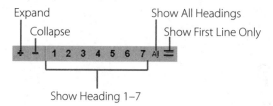

To hide the subtext—subheadings or body text—that follows a heading, perform these steps:

1 Place the insertion point within the heading (or select several headings).

2 Click the Collapse button, or press the hyphen (-) key on the numeric keypad. Word will hide the lowest level of subtext that is currently visible.

   For example, if a level 1 heading is followed by level 2 headings, level 3 headings, and body text, the first time you click the Collapse button, the body text will be hidden (body text is considered to be at the lowest level). The next time you click Collapse, the level 3 headings will be hidden, and the third time you click Collapse, the level 2 headings will be hidden.

3 Repeat step 2 as necessary to hide the desired amount of subtext.

To redisplay collapsed subtext, use this same procedure but in step 2 click the Expand button, or press the plus (+) key on the numeric keypad.

You can also fully collapse a heading (that is, hide *all* its subtext) by double-clicking its symbol:

Double-click here to hide all subtext.

◇ *Mint Teas*
  ◇ Peppermint
    ▫ Peppermint tea has a pleasant taste and is said to relieve headaches.
  ◇ Spearmint
    ▫ Spearmint tea also has a nice taste and is thought to calm the nerves.

To fully expand the heading, double-click again. Notice that when a heading contains collapsed subtext, Word marks it with wavy underlining:

Double-click here to show all subtext.

◇ *Mint Teas*

This marker indicates hidden subtext.

You can also change the levels of headings that are displayed throughout the entire document. To display only level 1 headings, click the Show Heading 1 button or press Alt+Shift+1. To display level 1 and level 2 headings, click the Show Heading 2 button or press Alt+Shift+2. In the same way, you can click the Show Heading 3 through Show Heading 7 buttons (or press the Alt+Shift+3 through Alt+Shift+7 key combinations) to include increasingly lower levels of headings. Note that all these buttons and key combinations hide body text.

To display all headings, including body text, click the Show All Headings button or press Alt+Shift+A or the asterisk (*) on the numeric keypad, so that the Show All Headings button on the Outlining toolbar appears pressed.

To display all headings *without* body text, click Show All Headings or press the asterisk key again, so that the button is not pressed (this will hide body text but leave all headings visible).

Finally, you can display only the first line of all paragraphs of body text (together with their headings) by clicking the Show First Line Only button or by pressing the Alt+Shift+L key combination, so that the Show First Line Only button is pressed. To show all lines of body text, click the Show First Line Only button or press Alt+Shift+L again to turn that option off. Word indicates the presence of hidden body text by displaying an ellipsis (. . .) at the end of the first line of each body text paragraph.

II

Microsoft Word

The following are the last two buttons on the Outlining toolbar:

Master Document View

Show Formatting

? SEE ALSO

For information about character formatting, see "Applying Character Formatting Directly," page 181.

To hide character formatting that you have applied, click the Show Formatting button or press the slash (/) key on the numeric keypad so that the button is *not* pressed. Word will display all characters with the Normal character formatting (that is, the character formatting specified by the Normal style). This doesn't remove the applied character formatting, but merely suppresses its display. To restore the display of all character formatting exactly as you have applied it (the font, character size, font style, and so on), click the button or press the key again, so that the button is pressed.

Finally, clicking the Master Document View button so that it's pressed activates Master Document view. Clicking this button again, so that it's *not* pressed, switches back to Outline view. Master Document view allows you to divide a long Word document into separate subdocuments, all of which belong to a single *master document*. For information on creating and using master documents, look up the topic "master documents" in the Word online Help Index.

Browsing Through Outline Headings

In Office 97, Word provides two new features that let you quickly scroll to a particular outline heading in a document. These features furnish additional reasons for incorporating outline headings in your documents.

First, when you drag the scroll box on the vertical scroll bar, Word displays the page number of the current position as well as the preceding outline heading as shown on the facing page.

To locate a particular outline heading, simply drag the scroll box until you see the heading displayed and then release the mouse button. Note that you don't need to be in Outline view to use this feature.

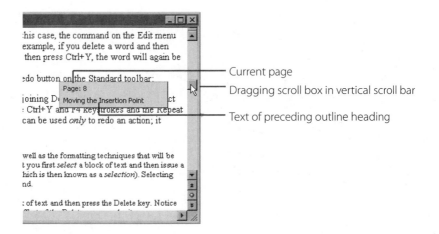

Current page

Dragging scroll box in vertical scroll bar

Text of preceding outline heading

A second feature that makes it easy to scroll to a particular outline heading is the Document Map, which is displayed in a separate pane in the document window (see Figure 12-3). To display the Document Map, choose the Document Map command from the View menu or click the Document Map button on the Standard toolbar.

Document
Map

FIGURE 12-3.

The Document Map for displaying and scrolling to outline headings in a document.

Document Map
scroll bar

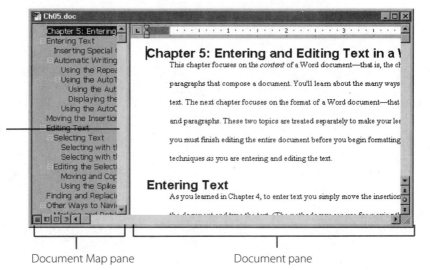

Document Map pane

Document pane

The Document Map lets you see all your outline headings, even if you're not in Outline view. Notice that when you place the mouse pointer over a heading, Word highlights the heading and displays the full heading text:

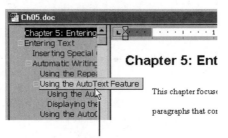

Click to scroll document to the highlighted heading.

To have Word scroll your document to a particular heading, simply click that heading within the Document Map. (If not all headings fit in the Document Map, you can use the vertical scroll bar within the Document Map pane to see additional headings.)

Notice also that if a heading is followed by one or more subheadings, Word displays a square symbol to the left of the heading in the Document Map. You can hide the subheadings in the Document Map by clicking the box:

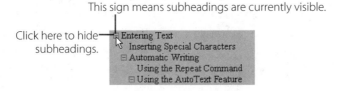

This sign means subheadings are currently visible.

Click here to hide subheadings.

You can show the subheadings by clicking the box again:

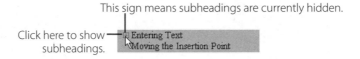

This sign means subheadings are currently hidden.

Click here to show subheadings.

If you're in Outline view, hiding or showing headings in the Document Map also hides or shows them in the document pane. In Normal, On-line Layout, and Page Layout views, hiding or showing headings in the Document Map doesn't affect the document pane.

? SEE ALSO

To review printing, see "Printing Documents," page 57, and "Previewing and Printing Documents," page 330.

Printing an Outline

When you're in Outline view and print your document, Word prints only the headings and body text that are currently visible. To print the whole document, you can click the All button on the Outlining toolbar or switch out of Outline view before printing.

 TIP

> **A Better-Looking Printed Outline**
>
> The appearance of a document printed in Outline view is often disappointing. Paragraph formatting doesn't show, lines are always single spaced, and you can't add extra space between paragraphs. Also, the symbols that visually separate paragraphs of body text don't print. To print an attractively formatted outline, consider switching out of Outline view and formatting the text in the document as a outline-numbered list, as explained in Chapter 8.

Adding Footnotes and Endnotes

Word makes it easy to add footnotes or endnotes to your document. The text for a *footnote* is placed at the bottom of the page that contains the reference mark (or you can choose to place a footnote beneath the text that contains the reference mark). The text for an *endnote* is placed at the end of the document (or you can choose to place an endnote at the end of the section that contains the reference mark). Figure 12-4 shows a footnote.

FIGURE 12-4.

A footnote in a Word document.

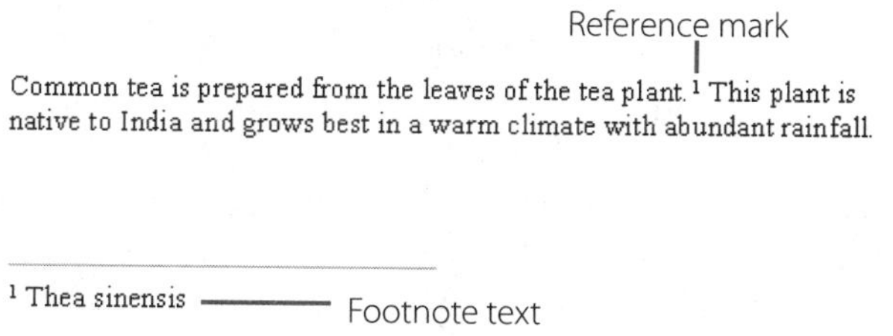

Reference mark

Common tea is prepared from the leaves of the tea plant.[1] This plant is native to India and grows best in a warm climate with abundant rainfall.

---
[1] Thea sinensis ——— Footnote text

To add a footnote or endnote to your document, do the following:

1 Place the insertion point where you want to insert the footnote or endnote reference mark.

2 Choose Footnote from the Insert menu to open the Footnote And Endnote dialog box:

3 Select the Footnote option to create a footnote, or Endnote to create an endnote.

4 In the Numbering area, choose the type of reference mark you want to insert, as follows:

- To use an automatically generated number, letter, or other symbol for the reference mark, choose AutoNumber. By default, Word will number footnotes using *1, 2, 3,* and so on; and it will number endnotes using *i, ii, iii,* and so on (which can be difficult for many readers to comprehend after about *xv,* or 15).

- To use a custom reference mark, choose Custom Mark and type a character, such as * (asterisk), in the Custom Mark box. Rather than typing a custom mark, you can click the Symbol button to select a symbol, such as •, †, ‡, or §. Clicking Symbol opens the Symbol dialog box, which is similar to the Symbol dialog box opened by choosing Symbol from the Insert menu (as described in "Inserting Special Characters," page 127).

5 To modify the type of numbering inserted by the AutoNumber option, or to set other footnote and endnote options, click the Options button to open the Note Options dialog box. (See Figure 12-5 on the following page.)

FIGURE 12-5.

The All Footnotes (A) and All Endnotes (B) tabs of the Note Options dialog box.

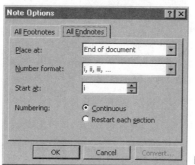

A

B

6   Click the OK button in the Footnote And Endnote dialog box. Word will insert the reference mark into the body text. Also, in Normal or Outline view, it will open a separate footnote pane and position the insertion point in this pane, as you see here:

Document pane ———

Footnote pane ———

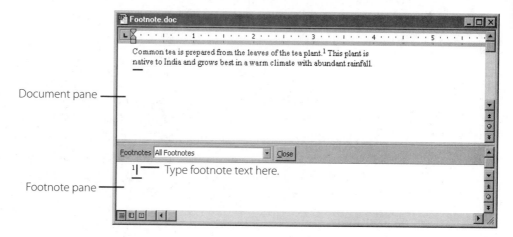

In Page Layout view or Print Preview, Word will place the insertion point at the actual position of the footnote or endnote on the page.

7 Type the footnote or endnote text.

8 In Normal or Outline view, you can close the footnote pane by clicking the Close button at the top of the pane. In Page Layout view or Print Preview, click on the document pane to move the insertion point back to the document text.

> To quickly add a footnote or endnote using AutoNumber and all other default options, place the insertion point where you want the reference mark and press Alt+Ctrl+F for a footnote or Alt+Ctrl+E for an endnote.

If you later want to view or edit your footnote or endnote text, choose Footnotes from the View menu or simply double-click a footnote or endnote reference mark. In Normal or Outline view, Word will open the footnote pane. If you have both footnotes and endnotes, choose the kind of notes you want to view from the list at the top of the footnote pane. In Page Layout view or Print Preview, Word will move the insertion point to the footnote or endnote area of the page. You can also view the text of your footnote or endnote by holding the mouse pointer over the reference mark:

SEE ALSO
For techniques on moving or copying text, see "Moving and Copying Text," page 147.

Thea sinenis

Common tea is prepared from the leaves of the tea plant.[1] This plant is native to India and grows best in a warm climate with abundant rainfall.

To move or copy a footnote or endnote, simply move or copy the reference mark to a new document location, using any of the editing methods explained in Chapter 5, "Entering and Editing Text in a Word Document." If you chose the AutoNumber option, Word will automatically renumber your reference marks if necessary. If you copy the reference mark, Word will make a copy of the footnote or endnote text.

TIP

> To change the format of footnote or endnote reference marks or text through-out your document, you can modify the built-in character styles Footnote Reference and Endnote Reference or the built-in paragraph styles Footnote Text or Endnote Text.

To delete a footnote or endnote, simply select the reference mark and press the Delete key. Word will delete both the reference mark and all the footnote or endnote text.

Creating Indexes and Tables of Contents

You can have Word generate an index or a table of contents for your document. A good index and an accurate table of contents help the intended reader and add greatly to the usefulness of a long document, whether it be a business proposal, a paper summarizing academic findings, or a nonfiction book on a variety of topics.

NOTE

> If you have inserted captions using the Caption command on the Insert menu, you can have Word generate a table of figures. Also, you can have it generate a table of authorities for a legal brief. These sorts of tables are not as common as indexes and tables of contents and are not discussed in this book. For information, look up the following topics in the Word online Help Index: "captions," "tables of figures," and "tables of authorities."

Creating an Index

Preparing an index in Word is a two-step process: First, you mark a series of index entries, and then you compile and insert the index based on these entries.

A typical index entry consists of the name of a topic followed by the number of the page on which the topic is discussed:

oolong tea, 1

II

Microsoft Word

When you *mark* an index entry, you specify the topic name and you mark the location of the topic in the document so that Word can determine the page number when you compile the index. To mark an index entry, do the following:

1 If all or part of the word or phrase that you want to appear in the index entry (such as *oolong tea* in the example above) is contained in the document text to be indexed, select this word or phrase.

Select the text that you want to appear in the index entry.

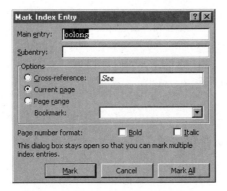

There are three basic types of tea: green, black, and oolong. The leaves for black and oolong teas are first fermented, and are then dried and heated. The leaves for green tea are dried and heated without fermentation.

Otherwise, simply place the insertion point at the beginning of the document text that you want to index.

2 Choose Index And Tables from the Insert menu and click the Mark Entry button on the Index tab of the Index And Tables dialog box or press the Alt+Shift+X key combination to open the Mark Index Entry dialog box:

3 If you selected text in step 1, this text will appear in the Main Entry box; otherwise, the box will be empty. If necessary, edit the contents of this box so that it contains the exact text you want to appear in the index:

4 If you want to create an index subentry, enter the subentry text in the Subentry box. For example, typing the following into the Main Entry and Subentry boxes

Main entry:	tea
Subentry:	types of

would create the following index entry and subentry:

tea
    types of, 1

5 Make sure the Current Page option is selected so that the index entry will display the number of the page that contains the indexed topic.

 NOTE

Rather than selecting the Current Page option, you can select the Cross-Reference option or the Page Range option. If you select Cross-Reference, the index entry will display the cross-reference that you type into the box, for example, "*See* herb teas," rather than a page number. If you select Page Range, the index entry will display the range of pages that are marked with the bookmark that you select in the Bookmark list. (Bookmarks are discussed in "Marking and Retrieving Text with Bookmarks," page 156)

6 To modify the format of the page number in the index entry, select Bold, Italic, or both.

7 Click the Mark button.

 TIP

If you want to mark as index entries *all* occurrences of text in your document that exactly match the contents of the Main Entry box, click the Mark All button rather than the Mark button.

8 If you want to mark additional index entries, you can leave the Mark Index Entry dialog box open while you move the insertion

II

Microsoft Word

point to additional locations in your document. When you have finished marking entries, click Close to remove the dialog box.

> Word marks an index entry by inserting a block of instructions known as a *field* into the document. The field contains the XE code (for *index entry*) and it is formatted in hidden text. If you can't see it, you can make it appear by clicking the Show/Hide ¶ button on the Standard toolbar.

When you have marked all the index entries, the next step is to compile and insert the index itself. Do this as follows:

1 Place the insertion point at the position in your document where you want to insert the index.

2 Choose Index And Tables from the Insert menu to open the Index And Tables dialog box, and click the Index tab:

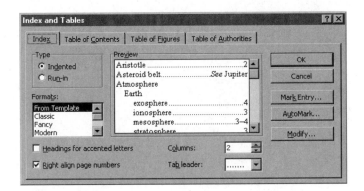

3 If you want to modify the appearance of the index, choose options in the dialog box until the model index in the Preview area has the look you want for your index. You can set the type, format, alignment, number of columns, and tab leader character for the index.

⭐ **TIP**

Customize Your Index Entries

To create custom formatting for your index entries, choose the From Template item in the Formats list. Then, click the Modify button to open the Style dialog box, which lets you modify the built-in styles that Word assigns to index entries. (It assigns Index 1 to main entries, and Index 2 through Index 9 to subentries.) This dialog box is similar to the Style dialog box that is opened when you choose Style from the Format menu, except that it lets you modify only the index entry styles. You can also use the methods given in "Modifying Styles," page 200, to change the formatting of index headings (that is, the A, B, C, and so on that precede each index section) by modifying the Index Heading built-in style.

❓ **SEE ALSO**

For instructions on using the Style dialog box to modify styles, see "Modifying Styles Using the Style Dialog Box," page 204.

4 Click the OK button. Word will compile an index and insert it into the document. Word will also add section breaks before and after the index so that it's contained in its own document section.

Word creates the index and marks its location by inserting an INDEX field into the document. If you see the field code rather than the actual index, you can make the index appear by placing the insertion point within the field code and pressing Shift+F9. The field code will look something like this:

```
{ INDEX \c "2" }
```

Creating a Table of Contents

You can also add a table of contents to your document, which lists all your document headings and the page numbers on which they occur, as well as any part or chapter headings that you have used. The following is the easiest way to create a table of contents:

1 Make sure that every heading you want included in the table of contents has been assigned one of the built-in heading styles, Heading 1 through Heading 9. You can assign these styles using Outline view or the methods for applying styles given in "Applying Styles," page 175.

2 Place the insertion point at the position in your document where you want to insert the table of contents.

II

Microsoft Word

3 Choose Index And Tables from the Insert menu and click the Table Of Contents tab:

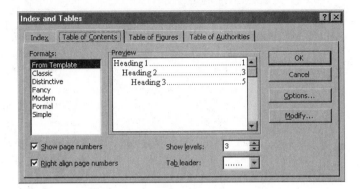

4 If you want to modify the appearance of the table of contents, choose options on the Table Of Contents tab until the model table of contents in the Preview area has the look you want for your table of contents. You can choose the table format, alignment of numbers, number of levels, and tab leader character. You can also add or remove page numbers.

5 Click the OK button.

Word creates a table of contents and marks its location by inserting a TOC field. If you see the field code rather than the table of contents, you can make the table of contents appear by placing the insertion point within the field code and pressing Shift+F9. The field code will look something like this:

{ TOC \o "1-3" }

Customize Your Table of Contents

To create custom formatting for your table of contents, choose the From Template item in the Formats list. Then, click the Modify button to open the Style dialog box, which lets you modify the built-in styles that Word assigns to table of contents entries (TOC 1 through TOC 9). This dialog box is similar to the Style dialog box that is opened when you choose Style from the Format menu, except that it lets you modify only the table of contents styles.

CHAPTER 13

Using Word to Automate Mailing

In this chapter, you'll learn two ways that you can use Word to automate mailing. First, you'll learn how to quickly print a single envelope or mailing label. Second, you'll learn how to use Word's mail merge commands to print form letters, as well as sets of envelopes or labels.

Printing Individual Envelopes and Labels

? SEE ALSO

For information on using the mail merge facility to print groups of envelopes or labels, see "Printing Sets of Envelopes," page 393 and "Printing Sets of Mailing Labels," page 396.

You can print an individual envelope or label using the Envelopes And Labels command on the Tools menu. This command is especially useful for mailing a letter that you have just finished typing. You can also use the Word mail merge facility, described later in the chapter, to print envelopes or labels for an entire group of delivery addresses.

Printing Individual Envelopes

To print a single envelope, this is what you do:

1 If you have already typed the delivery address into a document (for example, in the heading of a letter), open that document. (This step is optional because you can type the address later.)

2 Choose Envelopes And Labels from the Tools menu and click the Envelopes tab in the Envelopes And Labels dialog box:

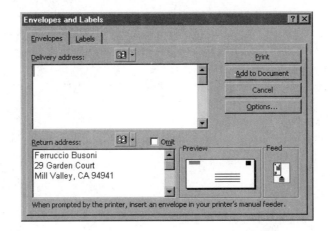

3 Type the delivery address into the Delivery Address box. If Word finds an address in the document, this address will already be contained in the Delivery Address box. In this case, you can simply edit the text, if necessary.

4 If you want to print a return address, type it into the Return Address box.

   If you have specified a personal mailing address in Word, this address will automatically appear in the Return Address box. In this case, you can edit the text, if necessary. (To specify a personal mailing address, choose Options from the Tools menu, click the User Information tab, and enter the address into the Mailing Address box.) Note that if you enter or edit text in the Return Address box of the Envelopes tab, Word will ask if you want to save the new address as your "default return address." If you click Yes, Word saves the text as your personal mailing address.

If you don't want to print a return address (perhaps you're using preprinted envelopes), you can either delete any text in the Return Address box or simply turn on the Omit option above the box.

TIP

Create Envelopes Using Your Address Book

If you have entered addresses into an address book or an Outlook 97 or Schedule+ 95 contact list, you can click the Insert Address button at the top of the Delivery Address box or at the top of the Return Address box (see below) to select an address from an address book rather than typing one.

Click to quickly select an address from address book.

Click to open Select Name dialog box.

5 If you need to change any of the envelope printing options, click the Options button on the Envelopes tab to open the Envelope Options dialog box. (See Figure 13-1 on the following page.)

6 To complete the envelope, do either of the following:

- To print the envelope immediately, place an envelope in your printer and click the Print button. You should insert the envelope into the printer with the orientation that is shown in the Feed area in the lower right corner of the Envelopes And Labels dialog box. (The orientation is selected on the Printing Options tab of the Envelope Options dialog box, as shown in Figure 13-1. You can quickly open this tab by clicking in the Feed area.)

II

Microsoft Word

FIGURE 13-1.
The Envelope
Options (A) and
Printing Options (B)
tabs of the Envelope
Options dialog box.

Specify the envelope size here.

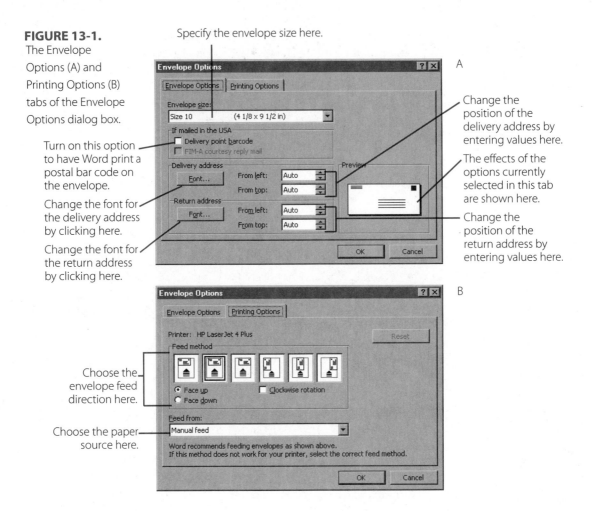

Turn on this option
to have Word print a
postal bar code on
the envelope.

Change the font for
the delivery address
by clicking here.

Change the font for
the return address
by clicking here.

Change the
position of the
delivery address by
entering values here.

The effects of the
options currently
selected in this tab
are shown here.

Change the
position of the
return address by
entering values here.

Choose the
envelope feed
direction here.

Choose the paper
source here.

? SEE ALSO

For information on
setting the margins,
paper size, and other
page setup features for
a document section,
see "Adjusting the
Page Setup," page 300.

• To add the text for the envelope to the document in the active window, click the Add To Document button (if you have already added envelope information to the document, this button will be labeled Change Document, and it will replace the former envelope with the new one). Word will insert the envelope text into a separate section at the beginning of the document, and it will assign to this section the correct margins, paper size, printing orientation, and paper source for printing the envelope. If necessary, you can edit the envelope text or add text or graphics to it. Thereafter, whenever you print the document, the envelope will automatically be printed with it. You could use this technique to include the text for both a letter and its envelope within a single document, so that both can be printed with only one print command.

Printing Individual Labels

You can print a single label, or you can print the same text on every label on a full sheet of labels, by doing the following:

1 If you have already typed the label text into a document (for example, an address in a letter heading), open that document. (This step is optional because you can type the text later.)

2 Choose Envelopes And Labels from the Tools menu and click the Labels tab in the Envelopes And Labels dialog box:

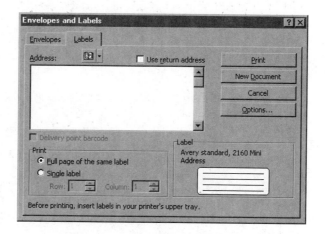

3 Type the label text into the Address box. If Word finds an address in the document, this text will already be contained in the Address box. In this case, you can simply edit the text, if necessary.

Alternatively, you can turn on the Use Return Address option to have Word copy into the Address box your personal mailing address (the address set through the User Information tab of the Options dialog box, as described in the previous section). You could do this to print return address labels for yourself.

II

Microsoft Word

Also, if you have entered names into an address book, you can use the Insert Address button at the top of the Address box to select an address. For more information, see the tip given under step 4 in the previous section.

4 To tell Word how many labels to print, do either of the following:

- To print a full page of labels—with the same text on each label—choose the Full Page Of The Same Label option. You might select this option, for example, to prepare a full sheet of return address labels.

- To print a single label, choose Single Label and enter the row and column position on the label sheet of the label you want to print.

5 If you need to change any of the label printing options, click the Options button to open the Label Options dialog box. (See Figure 13-2.)

FIGURE 13-2.
The Label Options dialog box.

Select the tray or feeder containing the label sheet here.

Choose a label brand from this list.

Specify the type of printer by selecting one of these options.

Select the specific label type from this list.

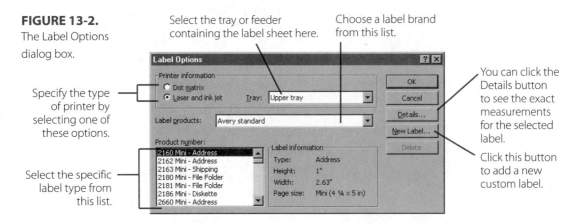

You can click the Details button to see the exact measurements for the selected label.

Click this button to add a new custom label.

If your label sheet doesn't match any of the standard labels, you can specify *custom* label measurements by selecting the closest standard label, clicking the New Label button, and modifying the measurements in the New Custom dialog box (see Figure 13-3). You must give your custom label a name, and you can later delete the custom label by selecting its name in the Product Number list of the Label Options dialog box and clicking the Delete button.

FIGURE 13-3.
The dialog box for creating custom label measurements.

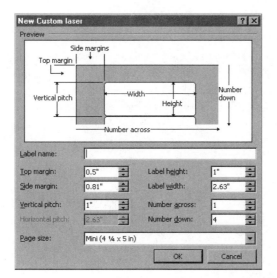

When you click OK in the Label Options dialog box, you'll return to the Envelopes And Labels dialog box.

TIP

Insert Postal Bar Codes for Faster Delivery
If you have selected a sufficiently large label and if the label text contains a valid postal code, you can turn on the Delivery Point Barcode option on the Labels tab of the Envelopes And Labels dialog box to have Word print a postal bar code at the top of the label. The bar code is a machine-readable representation of the postal code and including it might expedite mail delivery.

6 To finish the label, do either of the following:

- To print the label immediately, insert a label sheet into your printer and click the Print button.

- If you're printing a full page of labels (that is, if you chose the Full Page Of The Same Label option), you can click the New Document button to have Word store the label text in a new document. You can then print the labels by printing this document, and you can save the document so that you can print the same labels again in the future.

Have Word Write Your Letters!

You can have Word automatically insert into a document all the basic elements of a letter, and format them according to your specifications. To do this, choose the Letter Wizard command from the Tools menu to open the Letter Wizard dialog box. Then, on the tabs of this dialog box choose the options you want and supply the required information on the letter sender and recipient.

Using Mail Merge for Large Mailings

You'll now learn how to use Word's mail merge feature to print form letters, as well as sets of envelopes or mailing labels.

Printing Form Letters

When you print a set of form letters, some text is the same on all the letters (for example, the letterhead, the body of the letter, and the closing), while some text varies from letter to letter (the recipient's name and address, and the name in the salutation). To print form letters, you create two documents: a *main* document and a *data source* document. The main document contains the text that is the *same* on all letters, as well as instructions for inserting the variable text. The data source document stores the variable text. You then merge these two documents to generate the form letters, as shown in Figure 13-4.

The following are the steps for printing form letters:

1 Open the main document. Either you can create a new document (choose New from the File menu), or you can open a letter that you have already written (choose Open from the File menu).

If you create a new main document, you can get a head start in writing an attractive letter by basing it on one of the letter templates supplied with Word. Choose New from the File menu and click the Letters & Faxes tab in the New dialog box to view the available templates.

2 Choose Mail Merge from the Tools menu to open the Mail Merge Helper dialog box (see Figure 13-5).

FIGURE 13-4.
The mail merge process: merging the data source document with the main document to generate form letters.

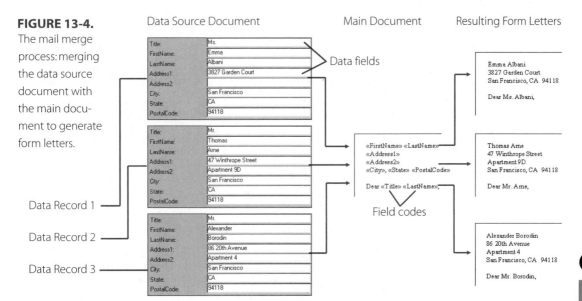

Data Source Document

Main Document

Resulting Form Letters

Data fields

Field codes

Data Record 1

Data Record 2

Data Record 3

FIGURE 13-5.
The Mail Merge Helper dialog box.

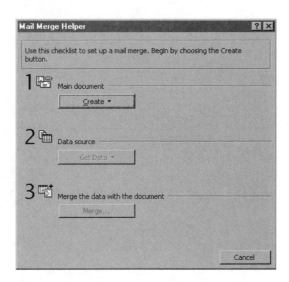

3 Click the Create button and from the menu that appears, choose Form Letters:

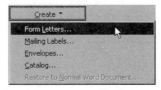

In the message box that Word next displays, click the Active Window button to use the document you opened in step 1 as the main document. (If you were to click the New Main Document button instead, Word would create another new document, based on the Normal template, to use as the main document.)

Before you enter text into the main document, you need to create the data source document to hold the text that will vary in each document. You'll come back to the main document later.

4 To create the data source document, click the Get Data button and from the menu that appears choose Create Data Source:

Word will open the Create Data Source dialog box, which allows you to assign a name to each data field of variable data:

To add a new data field, type name in box and click Add Field Name button.

Click to delete selected field.

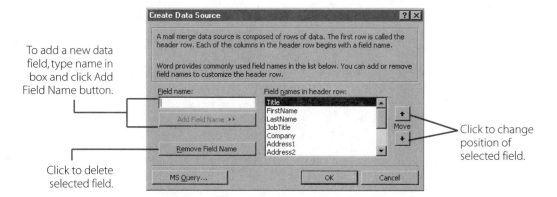

Click to change position of selected field.

The text in the data source document is divided into *data records*. Each data record contains all the variable text to be used for one form letter (for example, the letter to Emma Albani). Each data record is divided into *data fields*; a data field contains a single item of information (for example, the addressee's last name or the street address). (See Figure 13-4 on page 387.) You must assign a name to each data field so that you can reference it in the main document. Initially, the Create Data Source box contains a set of names for the typical data fields you might use in a letter—for example, FirstName for the addressee's first name, Address1 for the first line of the address, and so on. Be sure not to put a space between the two words of a field name (such as JobTitle); capitalization isn't important (the name could be jobtitle or JOBTITLE).

⭐ TIP

Rather than creating a new data source document, you can click the Get Data button and choose Open Data Source to open a data source document that you created previously. Also, if you have created a personal, Schedule+, or Outlook address book, you can choose Use Address Book to use the data that it stores.

5 Use the Create Data Source dialog box to remove any data fields you don't need, and to add any new data fields that you need. You can also use the Move buttons to change the order of the data fields. The data field order affects the order in which the fields are displayed in the Data Form dialog box (described later); it doesn't affect the order in which they appear on the printed letter.

6 When you're done defining the data field names, click OK in the Create Data Source dialog box, enter a filename for the data source document into the Save As dialog box, and click the Save button. Word will then display the following message box:

7 Click the Edit Data Source button so that you can add the variable text to the data source document. (Clicking Edit Main Document would let you add text and merge information to the main document; you won't do this until later.)

Word will open the Data Form dialog box:

Data Form		? X
Title:		OK
FirstName:		Add New
LastName:		Delete
JobTitle:		
Company:		Restore
Address1:		Find...
Address2:		
City:		View Source
State:		

Record: |◄ ◄ 1 ► ►|

Notice that this dialog box displays a box for each data field that you defined in step 5.

8 Enter text into the data fields for the first data record. When you're done with the first data record, click the Add New button to define the second data record. Repeat this process to define all the data records, one for each person or company to whom you want to write a letter. When you have entered text into the last data record, click the OK button rather than clicking Add New. Word will return you to the main document that you opened in step 1.

 NOTE

> If you click the View Source button in the Data Form dialog box, Word will open the data source document, which will contain the data that you have entered using the Data Form dialog box. Notice that the data source document stores the data in a Word table. The first row of the table, called the *header row*, contains the names of the data fields, and each of the following rows contains the text for a single data record, one data field per cell. If you want, you can add or modify the text directly in this table. (Word displays the Database toolbar, which can help you work with the data source document.) But in general, it's easier to use the Data Form dialog box to enter, modify, or delete data records.

9 Enter the letter text into the main document.

When the main document is active, Word displays the Mail Merge toolbar:

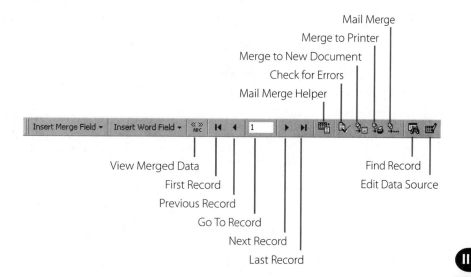

To add a data field from the data source document, click the Insert Merge Field button on this toolbar and choose the name of the data field from the menu that drops down. For example, to add the addressee's first name, click Insert Merge Field and choose FirstName. Word will insert a code for this data field, known as a *merge field*. You can recognize a merge field by the chevrons («, ») that surround it:

«FirstName»

When you print the merge letters, the merge field on each letter will be replaced with the text from the data field in the corresponding merge record of the data source document. Note that the text will be formatted with the character formatting features that are assigned to the merge field. Therefore, to modify the formatting of the merged text, simply select the merge field in the main document, and assign the desired character formatting features (such as bold or italic). Figure 13-6 on the following page shows the beginning of a letter containing merge fields as well as ordinary text.

II

Microsoft Word

FIGURE 13-6.
The beginning of
a main document.

«FirstName» «LastName»
«Address1»
«Address2»
«City», «State» «PostalCode»

Dear «Title» «LastName»,

 TIP

> **Preview Your Form Letters and Check Data Record Text**
> You can preview each form letter by clicking the View Merged Data button on the Mail Merge toolbar. Word will replace each merge code with the text from the first data record, just as it will do when it prints the first form letter. To view the text from other data records, click the Next Record and Previous Record buttons. To view the merge codes again, click View Merged Data once more.

10 To generate the form letters, click the Mail Merge button on the Mail Merge toolbar to open the Merge dialog box. (See Figure 13-7.) Choose the options you want and then click the Merge button.

If you chose Printer in the Merge To list of the Merge dialog box, Word will immediately print the merged letters (one letter for each record that you defined in step 8). If you chose New Document in the Merge To list, Word will insert all the form letters into a single new document. You can then view or edit the form letters within this document, and you can print the form letters by printing the document. You can use the Merge dialog box to select specific records to merge, either by entering a range of records or by clicking the Query Options button and defining query or sort options. For more information about query options, look up the topic "queries, mail merge" in the Word online Help Index.

If you want to merge all data records without changing any of the merge options, you can simply click either the Merge To New Document button or the Merge To Printer button on the Mail Merge toolbar.

CAUTION

When you close the main mail merge document, Word will ask if you want to save the data source document. Be sure to click the Yes button to save your data.

SEE ALSO

For information on choosing a template for a new document, see "Creating and Printing a Document from Start to Finish," page 113. For a description of Word tables, see "Using Tables," page 228.

FIGURE 13-7.

The Merge dialog box.

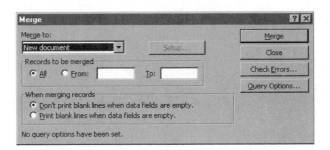

> **NOTE**

You can also *e-mail* or *fax* the merged letters to the different recipients by choosing the Electronic Mail option or the Electronic Fax option in the Merge To list, and then clicking the Setup button to provide address and subject information. (To do this, you must have set up e-mail or fax capabilities in Exchange or Outlook, as explained in Chapter 41.)

Printing Sets of Envelopes

You can also use Word's mail merge facility to print a set of envelopes. For example, if you have used mail merge to print form letters, you can also use it to print the envelopes for mailing the letters.

The following are the steps:

1 Open a new document and choose Mail Merge from the Tools menu to display the Mail Merge Helper dialog box (shown in Figure 13-5 on page 387).

2 Click the Create button and choose Envelopes from the menu that appears.

3 In the message box, click the Active Window button to use the document you opened in step 1 as the main document for the envelopes.

4 In the Mail Merge Helper dialog box, click the Get Data button, and then do one of the following:

 • To use a data source document that you have already created (for example, when you created form letters), choose Open Data Source, select the name of the document in the Open Data Source dialog box, and click the Open button.

In the message box, click the Set Up Main Document button. Word will then open the Envelope Options dialog box.

- To create a new data source document, choose Create Data Source. In the Create Data Source dialog box, define names for the required data fields and click OK. In the Save As dialog box, enter a name for the data source document, click the Save button, and in the message box that Word displays, click the Edit Data Source button. Enter all the data records into the Data Form dialog box, and click OK. For more information on this procedure, see steps 4 through 8 in the previous section, "Printing Form Letters." Word will return you to the main document you opened in step 1. You should now click the Mail Merge Helper button on the Mail Merge toolbar, and in the Mail Merge Helper dialog box, click the Setup button in the Main Document area. Word will then open the Envelope Options dialog box.

Mail Merge
Helper

- If you have created a personal, Outlook, or Schedule+ address book, you can choose Use Address Book to use the addresses that it contains as your data source. In the Use Address Book dialog box choose the particular address book you want to use and click OK. Then, in the message box, click the Set Up Main Document button to have Word open the Envelope Options dialog box.

5 In the Envelope Options dialog box (see Figure 13-1 on page 382), make any required adjustments to the envelope or printing options. When you click OK, Word will display the Envelope Address dialog box.

6 Enter the delivery address into the Sample Envelope Address box in the Envelope Address dialog box. To insert a merge field, click the Insert Merge Field button and choose the name of the merge field from the menu that appears. (For more information on merge fields, see step 9 in the section "Printing Form Letters," earlier in the chapter.) In addition to the merge fields, you'll probably need to add spaces, commas, or other characters. Figure 13-8 shows a completed address. When you're done, click OK; Word will return you to the Mail Merge Helper dialog box.

FIGURE 13-8.
The Envelope Address
dialog box, after the
merge fields and text
for an address have
been entered.

TIP

You can have Word print a postal bar code above the address by clicking the
Insert Postal Bar Code button in the Envelope Address dialog box, and specifying
the data fields that contain the postal code and the street address.

7 In the Mail Merge Helper dialog box, click the Edit button in the
Main Document area and choose the name of the document created in step 1 on the menu that appears. Word will now display
the main document containing the merge fields for your envelope. Notice that Word inserts the merge fields as you arranged
them in the Envelope Address dialog box. Also, it inserts your personal mailing address in the return address position (that is, the
address that is set through the Mailing Address box on the User
Information tab of the Options dialog box), and it modifies the
page setup (the margins, paper size, paper source, and so on) for
printing envelopes.

8 If necessary, edit the return or delivery address in the main document. For example, if you're using preprinted envelopes, you'll
need to delete the return address. You can use the Mail Merge
toolbar as described previously. (See step 9 in "Printing Form Letters," page 390.) On the following page you see a completed
main document for an envelope.

II

Microsoft Word

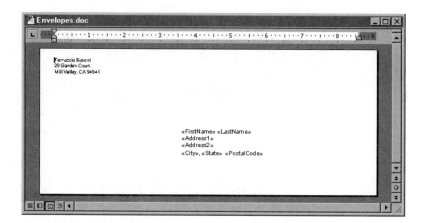

Mail
Merge

9 To generate the envelopes, click the Mail Merge button on the Mail Merge toolbar to open the Merge dialog box. (See Figure 13-7 on page 393.) Choose the options you want and then click the Merge button. If you want to merge all data records without changing any of the merge options, you can simply click either the Merge To New Document button or the Merge To Printer button on the Mail Merge toolbar.

Printing Sets of Mailing Labels

The procedure for printing sets of labels using Word's mail merge feature is similar to the procedure for printing sets of envelopes. You can print mailing labels (perhaps to mail a set of form letters you have printed), or you can print other types of labels, such as name tags or disk labels.

> Although you can also use the Envelopes And Labels command (discussed earlier in the chapter in the section "Printing Individual Labels," page 383) to print entire sheets of labels, all labels will be the same. In contrast, when you use the Mail Merge command, each label can be different.

The following are the steps:

1 Open a new document and choose Mail Merge from the Tools menu to display the Mail Merge Helper dialog box. (See Figure 13-5 on page 387.)

2 Click the Create button and choose Mailing Labels from the menu that appears.

3 In the message box, click the Active Window button to use the document that you opened in step 1 as the main document for the labels.

4 In the Mail Merge Helper dialog box, click the Get Data button, and then do either of the following:

- To use a data source document that you have already created (for example, when you created form letters), choose Open Data Source, select the name of the document in the Open Data Source dialog box, and click the Open button. In the message box, click the Set Up Main Document button; Word will then open the Label Options dialog box.

- To create a new data source document, choose Create Data Source. In the Create Data Source dialog box, define names for the required data fields and click OK. In the Save As dialog box, enter a name for the data source document, click the Save button, and in the message box that Word displays, click the Edit Data Source button. Enter all the data records into the Data Form dialog box, and click OK. For more information on this procedure, see steps 4 through 8 in "Printing Form Letters," earlier in the chapter. Word will return you to the main document you opened in step 1. You should now click the Mail Merge Helper button on the Mail Merge toolbar, and in the Mail Merge Helper dialog box, click the Setup button in the Main Document area. Word will then open the Label Options dialog box.

Mail Merge
Helper

- If you have created a personal, Outlook, or Schedule+ address book, you can choose Use Address Book to use the addresses that it contains as your data source. In the Use Address Book dialog box choose the particular address book you want to use and click OK. Then, in the message box, click the Set Up Main Document button to have Word open the Label Options dialog box.

II

Microsoft Word

5 In the Label Options dialog box (see Figure 13-2 on page 384), make any required adjustments to the way that Word prints the labels as described in step 5 of "Printing Individual Labels," page 383. When you click OK, Word will display the Create Labels dialog box.

6 Enter the delivery address or other label text into the Sample Label box in the Create Labels dialog box. To insert a merge field, click the Insert Merge Field button and choose the name of the merge field from the menu that appears. (For more information on merge fields, see step 9 in the section "Printing Form Letters," earlier in the chapter.) In addition to the merge fields, you'll probably need to add spaces, commas, or other characters. When you're done, click OK. Word will return you to the Mail Merge Helper dialog box.

 TIP

You can have Word print a postal bar code at the top of the label by clicking the Insert Postal Bar Code button in the Create Labels dialog box, and specifying the data fields that contain the postal code and the street address.

7 In the Mail Merge Helper dialog box, generate the labels by clicking the Merge button (in the Merge The Data With The Document area) to open the Merge dialog box. (See Figure 13-7 on page 393.) Choose the options you want and then click the Merge button.

Automating and Customizing Word

This chapter focuses on the most powerful ways to enhance the Word workplace. First, you can automate simple or complex Word tasks by creating macros. A macro stores a series of Word actions and allows you to perform these actions by issuing a single command. By recording macros, you can save time and make Word easier to use. When you create a macro, you essentially add a new command to Word. Also, you can extensively customize the Word toolbars, menus, and shortcut keys. When you modify one of these elements, you enhance the way you *issue* Word commands. For information on several other ways you can modify the Word workplace, see "Changing the Way You Display Documents," page 121.

Recording and Running Macros

You might find yourself frequently performing a Word task that requires a series of steps. For example, you might often need to save the current position of the insertion point so that you can later return to it. Doing so, however, requires that you choose the Bookmark command from the Insert menu, type a bookmark name, and click the Add button. You can make such a task much easier by *recording a macro*. When you record a macro you store a series of Word commands. You can later perform all these commands by simply running the macro. You can run a macro through the Macros dialog box, or, if you make the proper assignment, you can run it by choosing a menu command, clicking a toolbar button, or pressing a shortcut key.

Recording Macros

To record a macro, follow this procedure:

1 Point to Macro on the Tools menu and then choose Record New Macro from the submenu that pops up, *or* simply double-click the REC indicator on the Word status bar:

To record a macro, double-click here.

Word will open the Record Macro dialog box, which is shown in Figure 14-1.

2 You can now perform one or more of the following optional steps:

- Type a name for the macro into the Macro Name box. Word initially assigns it a default name such as Macro1. You might want to enter a descriptive name that indicates the purpose of the macro. (Doing so will make it easier to identify the macro if you need to modify it or perform one of the other operations described in the following sections.)

FIGURE 14-1.
The Record Macro dialog box.

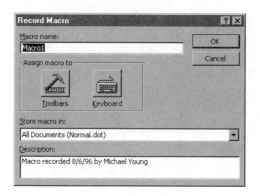

- Type a description for the macro into the Description box. The default description indicates merely the author of the macro and the date it was recorded. You might want to provide a more detailed description. (The description is displayed when the macro is selected in the Macros dialog box, described in the next section; an accurate description will help ensure that you select the correct macro.)

- To assign the macro to a toolbar button or a menu command, click the Toolbars button. To assign the macro to a shortcut key, click the Keyboard button. In either case, follow the instructions in the dialog box that Word displays; for more information, see the section "Customizing Toolbars, Menus, and Shortcut Keys," page 407. Assigning the macro to one of these elements makes it considerably easier to run the macro. If you don't assign the macro to one of these elements, don't worry; you can still run it through the Macros dialog box, as discussed in the section "Running Macros," page 404.

- By default, the new macro will be stored in the Normal template so that it will be available when you're working on *any* document. If the template attached to the current document isn't Normal, you can select the name of the document template in the Store Macro In list; doing so will make the macro available only when you work on a document based on this same template. Or, you can select the name of the current document in the Store Macro In list to make the macro available only when you work on that particular document.

3 Click the OK button to begin recording the macro. While a macro is being recorded, Word does the following:

- It displays a cassette symbol next to the mouse pointer.

- It highlights the REC indicator in the status bar.

- It displays the Stop Recording toolbar:

Stop Recording ———————— Pause Recording

4 Perform all the actions that you want to record in the macro. Because the macro recorder doesn't record mouse movements within a document window, it won't let you use the mouse to select text or move the insertion point. You'll need to use other editing methods. (Editing methods are discussed in Chapter 5, "Entering and Editing Text in a Word Document.")

If you want to temporarily stop recording your actions before the macro is finished, click the Pause Recording button on the Stop Recording toolbar. To resume recording, click this button again.

5 When you're finished recording commands, click the Stop Recording button on the Stop Recording toolbar or double-click the REC indicator. The Stop Recording toolbar will be removed and your macro will be saved.

Managing Macros

You can change a macro description, delete a macro, or change the contents of a macro by doing the following:

1 Point to Macro on the Tools menu and then choose Macros from the submenu that pops up, or simply press Alt+F8. Word will open the Macros dialog box (see Figure 14-2).

SEE ALSO
For general information on templates see "Modifying and Creating Document Templates," page 215. For a description of editing methods, see "Editing Text," page 140.

FIGURE 14-2.

The Macros dialog box.

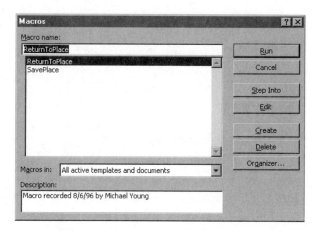

2 Select the macro in the Macro Name list.

If the macro doesn't appear in the Macro Name list, select the All Active Templates And Documents item in the Macros In list. Word will then list *all* macros available to the current document.

3 Perform one or more of the following actions:

- To modify the macro description, change the text in the Description box.

- To delete the macro, click the Delete button.

- You can change the macro itself by clicking the Edit button. Word will open the Visual Basic Editor, which will display a description of the macro in the Visual Basic for Applications (VBA) programming language.

  Using the Visual Basic Editor, you can modify macros that you have recorded, or you can write complex macros that perform tasks that can't be recorded. For information on editing or creating macros using Visual Basic for Applications, use the Help menu in the Visual Basic Editor. Note that you can also open the Visual Basic Editor by pointing to Macro on the Tools menu and choosing Visual Basic Editor from the submenu, or by simply pressing Alt+F11.

II

Microsoft Word

TIP

You can click the Organizer button in the Macros dialog box to open the Organizer dialog box, which allows you to delete, rename, and copy groups of macros known as *macro project items* or *modules*. For more information on the Organizer, see "Modifying Templates," page 218.

Running Macros

If you have assigned the macro to a toolbar, a menu, or a shortcut key, you can quickly run the macro by clicking the toolbar button, choosing the menu command, or pressing the shortcut key combination. There are two ways you can assign a macro to one of these elements. First, when you record the macro, you can make an assignment by clicking the Toolbars or Keyboard button in the Record Macro dialog box, as mentioned previously in the chapter. Second, you can make an assignment after the macro has been recorded by choosing Customize from the Tools menu. Both approaches are based on the techniques that will be given in "Customizing Toolbars, Menus, and Shortcut Keys," later in the chapter.

You can run *any* macro—even if you haven't assigned it to a toolbar, menu, or shortcut key—by doing the following:

1 Point to Macro on the Tools menu and then choose Macros from the submenu that pops up to open the Macros dialog box (see Figure 14-2 on the preceding page).

2 In the Macros In list, choose either the All Active Templates And Documents item or the name of the specific template or document that stores the macro.

3 Select the macro in the Macro Name list. The selected macro's description, if any, will appear in the Description box.

4 Click the Run button.

TIP

You can also use the Macros dialog box to run any built-in Word command. To do this, choose the Word Commands item in the Macros In list, select the command in the Macro Name list, and click Run.

Macro Examples

This section provides several examples of macros to give you a general idea of the types of Word tasks that you can easily automate.

The first example consists of a pair of macros. One macro, named SavePlace, lets you save the current position of the insertion point (or the current selection) by pressing Ctrl+Shift+S. The second macro, named ReturnToPlace, lets you later return the insertion point to the saved position (or restore the saved selection) by pressing Ctrl+Shift+R.

You can define the SavePlace macro this way:

1 Begin recording the macro by double-clicking the REC indicator on the status bar and typing the macro name *SavePlace* into the Record Macro dialog box (see Figure 14-1 on page 401).

2 To define the shortcut key combination, click the Keyboard button to open the Customize Keyboard dialog box. Make sure that the insertion point is in the Press New Shortcut Key box and press the Ctrl+Shift+S key combination. Click Assign and then click Close. This returns you to your document, ready to record your macro.

3 Choose Bookmark from the Insert menu.

4 Type the bookmark name *MarkedLocation* into the Bookmark Name box and click the Add button.

5 Stop recording the macro by clicking the Stop Recording button on the Stop Recording toolbar.

You can define the ReturnToPlace macro as follows:

1 Begin recording the macro by double-clicking the REC indicator on the status bar and typing the macro name *ReturnToPlace*.

2 Define the shortcut key by clicking the Keyboard button, and in the Customize Keyboard dialog box pressing the Ctrl+Shift+R key combination, clicking Assign, and then clicking Close.

3 Choose Bookmark from the Insert menu.

II

Microsoft Word

❓ SEE ALSO

For information about bookmarks, see "Marking and Retrieving Text with Bookmarks," page 156.

4   Select the bookmark name MarkedLocation in the Bookmark Name box, click the Go To button, and click the Close button.

5   Stop recording the macro by clicking the Stop Recording button on the Stop Recording toolbar.

You can now test these macros as follows: Place the insertion point anywhere in a document (or select a block of text) and then press Ctrl+Shift+S. Word will mark your position (or selection). Then, move the insertion point anywhere else within the same document, and perform any editing or formatting actions you wish. When you're ready to go back to your original location in the document, press Ctrl+Shift+R; Word will immediately move the insertion point back to its original position (or restore the original selection).

The following are several additional examples of macros that you might record:

- Record a pair of macros to turn the Wrap To Window option on or off. You might want to turn this option on while you're editing in Normal view so that the window contains the maximum amount of text, but then quickly turn it off to view the actual positions of line breaks on the printed copy. To create the first macro, start recording and then choose Options from the Tools menu, click the View tab, and turn on the Wrap To Window option. To record the second macro, perform these same steps but turn off the option.

- Record a pair of macros to switch between the blue window background and the white window background. You might want to enable the blue background to prevent eyestrain, but then switch to the white background to view items that are hard to see with a blue background (for example, dark lines drawn with Word's Drawing toolbar). To create the first macro, start recording, choose Options from the Tools menu, click the General tab, and turn on the Blue Background, White Text option. To record the second macro, perform these same steps but turn off the option.

- Write a macro to prepare a document for printing. Such a macro would be useful if you like to write and edit a document with one set of formatting features, such as single line-spacing and a large monospaced font (such as 14-point Courier), but want to print the document using a different set of formatting features, such as double line-spacing and a small proportional font (such as 9-point Times New Roman). In recording the macro, perform all actions that are necessary for printing the document, such as assigning different formatting features to the document's styles. Run the macro just before printing.

Customizing Toolbars, Menus, and Shortcut Keys

You can extensively modify the Word interface to suit your working style. You can create new, custom toolbars; you can modify existing toolbars and menus; you can define new shortcut keys for quickly executing Word commands or running macros; and you can set a variety of options that affect the Word interface. This section discusses several general principles that apply to *all* ways of customizing the Word interface. The following sections then present the specific techniques for making each type of modification.

⊗ CAUTION

Making extensive modifications to the Word toolbars, menus, or shortcut keys might make it difficult to learn tasks from this book or from the Word manuals and online Help, because these sources refer to the standard configurations. You might therefore wait until you're familiar with the Word skills involved before making extensive customizations.

When you create a toolbar, modify a toolbar or menu, or define a shortcut key, you can choose where to save your modification by selecting an item in the Save In, Save Changes In, or Make Toolbar Available To list, which will be displayed at the bottom of dialog box in which you make the modification. In most cases, you must choose an item in this list *before* you make the modification in the dialog box (choosing a new item in the list *won't* affect modifications that you've already made). If you choose the Normal item, the modification will be stored in the Normal.dot template and will be in effect while you work on *any* document. This choice is best for designing a general-purpose toolbar or menu or for defining a shortcut key that you'll use frequently.

? SEE ALSO

For information on templates, see "Modifying and Creating Document Templates," page 215.

Alternatively, you can choose the name of the document template (assuming that the document is based on a template other than Normal.dot). In this case, the modification will be in effect only while you work on a document based on the same template. This choice is best when you make changes that are useful for a specific type of document. For example, if you want to create a menu with commands useful for writing faxes, you could save your modifications in the template that you use for creating faxes.

II

Microsoft Word

Finally, you can choose the name of the document itself. In this case, the modification will be in effect only when you work on that particular document. This choice is best for highly specific modifications.

Display or
Hide Office
Assistant

Note that while you're making a modification, you can get help from the Office Assistant (described in Chapter 1, "A Quick Tour of Microsoft Office"). If the Office Assistant isn't visible, click the Office Assistant button at the bottom of the Customize dialog box.

Creating and Managing Custom Toolbars

You can create new, custom toolbars, which you can display in addition to the toolbars that are supplied with Word. To create a custom toolbar, proceed as follows:

1 Choose Customize from the Tools menu and click the Toolbars tab:

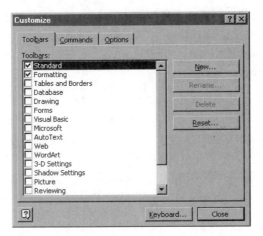

2 Click the New button to open the New Toolbar dialog box:

3 Type a name for your toolbar into the Toolbar Name box.

4 Choose an item in the Make Toolbar Available To box. If you choose Normal.dot, the toolbar can be displayed when you work on any document; if you choose the name of the document template, it can be displayed only when you work on a document based on this same template; and if you choose the name of the current document, it can be displayed only when you work on this document. These choices were explained in greater detail in the previous section.

5 Click OK. Word will display your new toolbar (which initially won't contain any buttons), and will return you to the Toolbars tab.

6 Add buttons to your toolbar using the Commands tab of the Customize dialog box, as explained in the next section.

On the Toolbars tab of the Customize dialog box, you can also show, hide, rename, delete, or reset a toolbar, as follows:

- To show a toolbar that isn't currently visible (a custom toolbar or one supplied with Word), check the box to the left of the toolbar name in the Toolbars list. To hide the toolbar, clear the box. (To show or hide a toolbar, you can also choose Toolbars from the View menu or click any toolbar with the right mouse button, as explained in Chapter 5, "Entering and Editing Text in a Word Document.")

- You can also rename or delete a *custom* toolbar (not one supplied with Word) by selecting the toolbar in the Toolbars list and clicking the Rename or Delete button.

? SEE ALSO

For instructions on using the Organizer to copy, delete, or rename a custom toolbar, see "Modifying Templates," page 218.

- You can remove any modifications that you have made to one of the toolbars supplied with Word (*not* a custom toolbar) by selecting the toolbar in the Toolbars list and clicking the Reset button. In the dialog box that Word displays, choose the template or document for which you want to reset the toolbar (the choices were explained in the previous section) and click OK. The methods for making modifications to toolbars will be discussed in the next section.

II

Microsoft Word

Modifying Toolbars and Menus

Word lets you extensively modify both menus and toolbars (custom toolbars as well as those provided with Word). You can add, remove, or rearrange toolbar buttons, menus, or items on menus. You can also change the text or the icon that is associated with a toolbar button or menu item, and you can even change the name of a menu. Finally, you can specify whether a toolbar button or menu item contains text only, an icon only (for a button), or both text and an icon.

To make any of these modifications, the first step is to choose Customize from the Tools menu to open the Customize dialog box. If you want to modify a toolbar that isn't currently visible, you must first display it by clicking the Toolbars tab in the Customize dialog box and checking the box next to the toolbar name. Then, click the Commands tab:

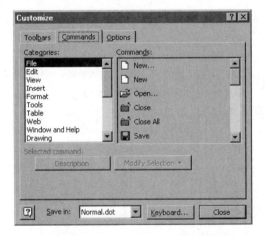

Before you make any of the modifications described in this section, choose the appropriate item in the Save In list at the bottom of the dialog box. If you choose Normal.dot, the modifications will be in effect when you work on *any* document; if you choose the name of the document template, they will be in effect only when you work on a document based on this same template; and if you choose the name of the current document, they will be in effect only when you work on this document. These choices were explained in greater detail at the beginning of the section "Customizing Toolbars, Menus, and Shortcut Keys," page 407.

To add a toolbar button or a menu item, do the following:

1 In the Categories list, choose the category of the Word command or feature that you want to assign to the toolbar button or menu item that you're adding. Choose the Macros, Fonts, AutoText, or Styles category if you want to assign a macro, a text font, an AutoText entry, or a style. Choose Built In Menus to assign a sub-menu (you can select any of the standard Word menus, such as File or Edit). Choose any of the other items in the Categories list to assign a built-in Word command.

NOTE

> Every toolbar button or menu item is assigned a Word command, a macro, a font, an AutoText entry, a style, or a submenu. Clicking the button or choosing the menu item will execute the command, run the macro, apply the font, insert the AutoText entry, assign the style, or open the submenu.

2 In the Commands list, find the specific Word command or feature (macro, font, AutoText entry, style, or menu) that you want to assign to the new button or menu item, and use the mouse to drag it directly to the position on the toolbar or menu where you want to insert the button or menu item. Note that when you drag a command or other feature to a menu, Word automatically opens the menu when the mouse pointer moves over the menu name on the menu bar.

While the Customize dialog box is displayed, you can *move* a toolbar button or menu item to a new position (on any toolbar or menu) by simply dragging it to the new location. To make a *copy*, press the Ctrl key while you drag. To *remove* a toolbar button or menu item, drag it off the toolbar or menu. You can use these same techniques to move, copy, or remove an entire menu by dragging the menu name that appears on the Word menu bar.

 TIP

> To add a *new* menu to the menu bar, select New Menu in the Categories list on the Commands tab of the Customize dialog box. Then select New Menu in the Commands list and drag the item to the location where you want the new menu. Then, modify the text and add items to the new menu as desired.

II

Microsoft Word

While the Customize dialog box is open, you can also modify a specific toolbar button, menu item, or menu by clicking the button, the menu item, or the menu name (Word will draw a selection border around the item you click), and then clicking the Modify Selection button on the Commands tab. Choose the appropriate command from the menu that Word opens:

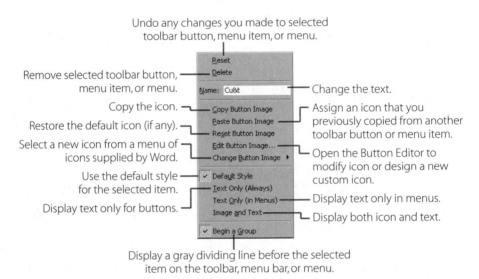

Undo any changes you made to selected toolbar button, menu item, or menu.

Remove selected toolbar button, menu item, or menu.

Change the text.

Copy the icon.

Restore the default icon (if any).

Assign an icon that you previously copied from another toolbar button or menu item.

Select a new icon from a menu of icons supplied by Word.

Open the Button Editor to modify icon or design a new custom icon.

Use the default style for the selected item.

Display text only in menus.

Display text only for buttons.

Display both icon and text.

Display a gray dividing line before the selected item on the toolbar, menu bar, or menu.

This menu will be referred to as the Modify Selection menu throughout the remainder of this discussion. Note that you can select an object *and* open the menu by simply clicking a toolbar button, a menu item, or a menu name using the right mouse button.

If you selected a menu name (for example, File or Edit) prior to opening the Modify Selection menu, the command you choose will affect the entire menu. However, only the first three commands will be available; that is, you can only reset the menu, delete the menu, or change the menu name.

If you selected a toolbar button, you can choose one of the four options at the bottom of the Modify Selection menu to specify whether the button shows the default style, an icon only, text only, or both an icon and text. If you selected a menu item, you can choose Text Only

(In Menus) to display only text on the menu item, or Image And Text to display both text and an icon.

You can change the text component of a toolbar button, a menu item, or a menu name by typing the new text into the Name box on the Modify Selection menu. For a toolbar button, this text will be displayed on the button if you choose the Text Only (Always) or the Image And Text option, *and* it will be displayed in a ScreenTip box whenever you place the mouse pointer over the button (provided that ScreenTips are enabled, as explained near the end of the chapter). For a menu item, this text will always appear on the menu. For a menu, the text will be displayed on the Word menu bar.

If you insert an ampersand (&) into the text, Word will underline the character that follows the ampersand. You can open a menu or execute a button command by pressing the Alt key together with the character that is underlined within the menu name or button text. Once a menu has been opened, you can choose a command from this menu by simply pressing a character that is underlined within a menu item, without pressing Alt. (Be sure that the same underlined character does not occur more than once on the same menu, or on a toolbar button or the menu bar.)

Open

Most of the Word commands and other features you can add to a toolbar or menu have a default icon. For example, the Open command in the File category has a default icon that depicts an opened file folder.

If you don't like the default icon for the selected object (or there is no icon), there are three ways to replace it (or to add an icon). First, you can click Change Button Image on the Modify Selection menu and choose an icon from the palette of images that Word displays:

Second, you can modify the icon or draw a new one by choosing the Edit Button Image command and designing the image you want in the Button Editor dialog box. Finally, if you have spotted an attractive icon on another toolbar button or menu item, you can *copy* that icon to your button or menu item, as follows:

1 With the right mouse button, click the button or menu item that has the icon you want to copy.

2 Choose Copy Button Image from the menu.

3 With the right mouse button, click the button or menu item you want to modify.

4 Choose Paste Button Image from the menu.

You can restore the default icon for the selected button or menu item by choosing the Reset Button Image command from the Modify Selection menu.

If you choose the Reset command with a toolbar button or menu item selected, any change that you've made to the button or item will be removed. If you choose Reset with an entire menu selected, the menu will be restored to its default configuration. That is, any item you have added to the menu will be removed, any item you have removed will be replaced, and any item you have modified will be restored to its default state.

You can also reset the entire Word menu bar by clicking the Toolbars tab of the Customize dialog box, selecting the Menu Bar item in the list, and clicking the Reset button. This will remove any menus you have added and replace any menus that you have removed. It won't, however, reset individual menus to their default configurations; you must reset each menu separately using the method in the previous paragraph.

⚙ SEE ALSO
For a general discussion on arranging and working with toolbars in Office programs, see "Using Toolbars," page 52.

Finally, to restore a Word toolbar to its default configuration, select the name of the toolbar on the Toolbars tab and click Reset. Note that you can't use this method for a custom toolbar.

Defining Shortcut Keys

You can assign a Word command, a macro, a font, an AutoText entry, a style, or a symbol to a shortcut key. Pressing the shortcut key will quickly choose the command, run the macro, apply the font, insert the AutoText entry, assign the style, or insert the symbol.

To assign one of these items to a shortcut key, do the following:

1 Choose Customize from the Tools menu and click the Keyboard button at the bottom of the Customize dialog box (you can be on any tab of the Customize dialog box). Word will open the Customize Keyboard dialog box:

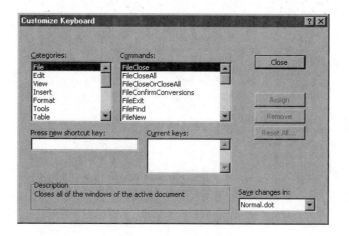

2 Choose an item in the Save Changes In list. If you choose Normal.dot, the shortcut key will be available when you work on *any* document; if you choose the name of the document template, it will be available only when you work on a document based on this same template; and if you choose the name of the current document, it will be available only when you work on this document. These choices were explained in greater detail at the beginning of the section "Customizing Toolbars, Menus, and Shortcut Keys," page 407.

3 Select a category in the Categories list. Notice that in addition to the categories available for adding toolbar buttons or menu items, you can select the Common Symbols category to assign a symbol to a key combination, so that you can quickly insert a symbol that doesn't appear on the keyboard.

4 In the list to the right of the Categories list, select the specific command that you want to assign to the shortcut key. (This list

? SEE ALSO

For information on
using the Symbol dia-
log box, see "Inserting
Special Characters,"
page 127.

will be named Commands, Macros, Fonts, AutoText, Styles, or
Common Symbols, according to the current selection in the Categories list. To simplify the remainder of the discussion, the term
command will be used to refer to a Word command, macro, font,
AutoText entry, style, or symbol that you select in the list.)

If you have chosen the Common Symbols category but don't
see the character you want in the Common Symbols list, select
Insert from the Categories list and Symbol from the Commands
list, click the Symbol button that Word displays, and choose the
character you want in the Symbol dialog box.

★ TIP

> If you have selected the Styles category but don't see the style you want in the
> Styles list, you can assign *any* style to a shortcut key by clicking the Shortcut Key
> button in the Modify Style dialog box, as explained in "Assigning a Style to a
> Shortcut Key," page 208.

If the selected command has already been assigned to one or
more shortcut keys, these keys will be shown in the Current Keys
list. Note that you can assign a command to several shortcut keys;
each shortcut key will provide an alternative way to carry out the
command.

5 Click in the Press New Shortcut Key box and press the key combination to which you want to assign the selected command. Word
will then display a message below the box indicating whether
a command has already been assigned to that shortcut key. If a
command has already been assigned, your shortcut key will
replace the former one.

6 Click the Assign button. The key combination will then be added
to the Current Keys list.

You can remove a specific shortcut key assignment by selecting the
key combination in the Current Keys list and clicking the Remove button. You can remove *all* shortcut key assignments for *all* commands by
clicking the Reset All button. (Note that this will remove the assignments only from the template or document currently selected in the
Save Changes In list.)

Setting Other Interface Options

You can set several additional options that affect toolbars and menus by clicking the Options tab of the Customize dialog box:

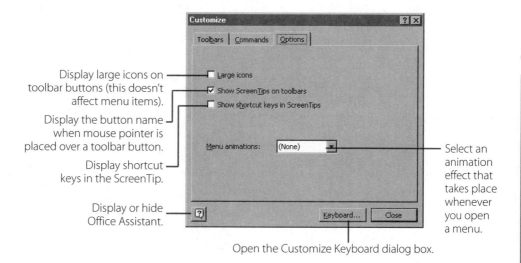

Display large icons on toolbar buttons (this doesn't affect menu items).

Display the button name when mouse pointer is placed over a toolbar button.

Display shortcut keys in the ScreenTip.

Display or hide Office Assistant.

Select an animation effect that takes place whenever you open a menu.

Open the Customize Keyboard dialog box.

Note that the *button name* that is displayed if you turn on the Show ScreenTips On Toolbars option and then place the mouse pointer over a toolbar button is the same as the text entered into the Name box on the Modify Selection menu. This was described previously in the section "Modifying Toolbars and Menus."

Note also that the options you choose on the Options tab will be in effect when you work on *any* document in *any* Office 97 application.

PART III

Microsoft Excel

CHAPTER 15

Building a Worksheet

Microsoft Excel 97 is a general-purpose electronic spreadsheet used to organize, calculate, and analyze business data. The tasks you can perform with Excel range from preparing a simple invoice for your house-painting services or planning a budget for a family vacation to creating elaborate 3-D charts or managing a complex accounting ledger for a medium-sized business. This section of the book introduces you to Excel and teaches you how to accomplish a variety of useful tasks with the newest version of Microsoft's flagship spreadsheet application. You'll receive training and support for virtually all your Excel needs, from creating a simple worksheet to recording macros or forecasting expenses and income. Along the way, you'll learn how to use the newest features of Excel, and how to customize Excel to work the way you do. We'll also share our favorite Excel productivity tips with you, including several that come directly from the Excel development team.

This introductory chapter gives you a quick tour of the Excel workplace and shows you how to build a simple worksheet from start to finish. A *worksheet* is an Excel document containing rows and columns of information that can be formatted, sorted, analyzed, and charted. Building a worksheet involves starting Excel, entering information, editing and rearranging the data in cells, adding formulas, saving your data, and printing. If you want to get fancy, you can even add hyperlinks to your worksheet to access supporting files on your hard disk or the Internet.

Starting Excel

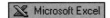

Excel is started or *launched* like most programs in the Office application suite. To start Excel, click the Start button on the taskbar, point to the Programs folder, and then click the Microsoft Excel program icon.

When Excel first starts, it displays a new, empty workbook (which will be defined shortly) in the application workplace. Figure 15-1 shows the default opening Excel screen, featuring a standard menu bar, toolbars, formula bar, status bar, and blank workbook. The application window has been maximized to display all the elements of the Excel user interface. If your application window does not appear maximized when you start it, you can click the Maximize button on the Excel title bar to give you more space to work with. The worksheet has also been maximized by clicking its own Maximize button, to show as much of the worksheet as possible.

SEE ALSO

To learn how to configure your Office applications so that they start in maximized windows automatically, see Chapter 1, "A Quick Tour of Microsoft Office."

The *menu bar* gives you access to the complete range of commands and settings in the Excel application. For example, to save a file in Excel you would choose the Save command from the File menu. The *toolbars* provide access to the most common Excel commands and procedures. During installation, Excel is configured to display the Standard toolbar and the Formatting toolbar below the menu bar. To use one of the toolbars, simply click the button containing a picture of the task you want to complete. For example, to save a file using the toolbar, you would click the button on the Standard toolbar with the picture of a disk on it. (You'll see many of these command buttons on Excel menus.)

Like most Office applications, the Excel application window also contains *sizing buttons* you can use to minimize, maximize, restore, and close windows, plus a *status bar* that shows the state of various keyboard keys, including Num Lock. (Note that Excel 97 no longer displays entries for

FIGURE 15-1.

The Microsoft Excel user interface with important elements labeled.

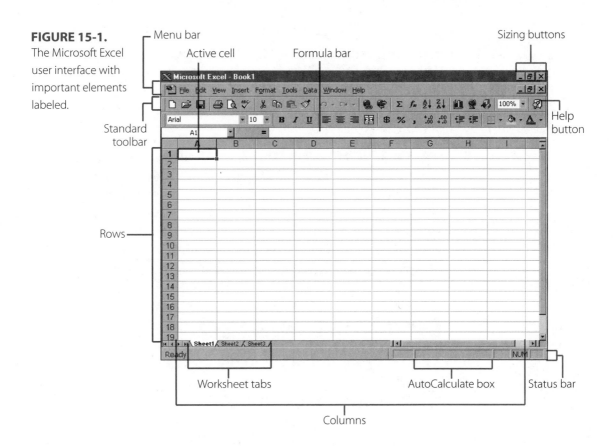

Menu bar

Active cell

Formula bar

Sizing buttons

Standard toolbar

Help button

Rows

Worksheet tabs

AutoCalculate box

Status bar

Columns

? SEE ALSO

For more information about using menus, dialog boxes, toolbars, and application windows, see Chapter 2, "Learning the Basics: Windows, Toolbars, and Printing." For more details about starting and configuring the Office Assistant, see Chapter 1 "A Quick Tour of Microsoft Office."

Caps Lock or Scroll Lock on the status bar.) A special feature of the Excel status bar is the *AutoCalculate box*, which displays the result of the selected function (SUM by default) using the highlighted cells in the active worksheet. To get additional help with the Excel interface or any Excel command, click the Microsoft Excel Help button on the right side of the Standard toolbar. If the animated Office Assistant is not already running, this button will start it.

Excel's application workplace is designed to hold one or more worksheet collections, called *workbooks*. When you first open Excel, the default workbook (Book1) appears on the screen with the first worksheet displayed (Sheet1). A worksheet is divided into a grid of rows and columns, as shown in Figure 15-1. (An Excel 97 worksheet can

III

Microsoft Excel

For information about managing the worksheets in a workbook and opening additional workbooks, see Chapter 17, "Organizing Information with Workbooks."

contain up to 65,536 rows and 256 columns.) A letter is assigned to each column of the worksheet, and a number is assigned to each row. At the intersection of the rows and columns are worksheet *cells*, which are referenced individually by their *cell names*. For example, the cell at the intersection of column A and row 1 is known as cell A1. Cell names are also called *cell addresses*.

At the bottom of the workbook window are tabs that give you instant access to the remaining worksheets in the workbook. A workbook can contain one or more worksheets, and can also hold chart sheets containing graphic pictures of your worksheet data. Special macros called Visual Basic modules can also be stored in the workbook, but they are not listed among the worksheets. (You'll learn how to create Visual Basic macros, to boost your productivity, in Chapter 23.) Workbooks help you organize your projects and keep related items in one place, and Excel lets you name your worksheets, add new worksheets, or delete blank or obsolete worksheets. Finally, each workbook window contains scroll bars you can use to move from one worksheet to the next, or from place to place in the active worksheet.

Navigating a Worksheet

On a typical Excel worksheet, information is stored in dozens or even hundreds of cells. To place information in cells that can be used in calculations and that is both visually pleasing and instantly comprehensible, you need to organize your cells carefully. Accordingly, you need to be comfortable with several methods for moving around in or *navigating* a worksheet.

To move the active cell from one location to another, you can press the arrow keys (the Up, Down, Left, and Right arrow keys) or click the cell you want to activate with the mouse. This is called *selecting* or *highlighting* a cell. (You can see the name of the selected cell by looking in the Name box.) When you first move the mouse pointer onto the worksheet, it changes its shape to the *cell pointer*, as shown in Figure 15-2. You can use the cell pointer to select individual cells or ranges of cells, as you'll learn later in the chapter.

FIGURE 15-2.

Use the cell pointer to select a cell on the worksheet, or use the scroll bars to move to cells not currently visible.

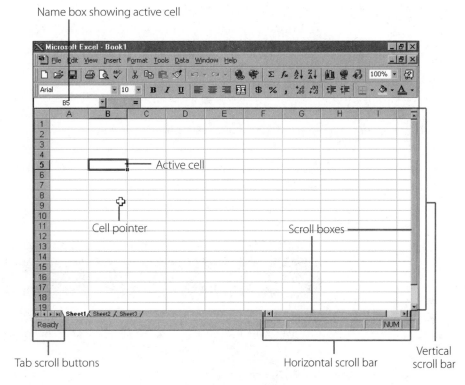

Name box showing active cell

Active cell

Cell pointer

Scroll boxes

Tab scroll buttons

Horizontal scroll bar

Vertical scroll bar

To view part of a worksheet that isn't currently visible in the workbook window, you can click the vertical or horizontal scroll bars with the mouse. Each time you click a scroll arrow at the top or bottom of the vertical scroll bar, the active worksheet scrolls vertically one row. Each time you click a scroll arrow at the left or right end of the horizontal scroll bar, the active worksheet scrolls horizontally one column. Note that when you scroll with the scroll bars you change only your view of the worksheet—scrolling moves the screen but does not change the active cell. Your relative position in the worksheet is identified by the scroll boxes in each scroll bar. (These boxes change size as your worksheet changes size, representing the relative portion of the entire worksheet that is currently visible.)

To move among the worksheets in your workbook, you can click on the worksheet tabs or use the tab scroll buttons to move among many worksheet tabs.

III

Microsoft Excel

To scroll down one page, click the scroll bar below the scroll box. You can also drag the scroll box to move greater distances. As you drag the scroll box, Excel displays the new top row (or leftmost column) in a pop-up window to help you find your place.

Using the Keyboard

Several key combinations let you move quickly throughout your worksheet. Unlike scroll bar movements, these key combinations also highlight a new, active cell. Table 15-1 lists the most useful keyboard navigation keys in a worksheet:

TABLE 15-1.   Useful Worksheet Navigation Keys

Use This Key or Key Combination	To Move
↑, ↓, ←, →	To the next cell in the direction pressed
Ctrl+↑, Ctrl+↓, Ctrl+←, Ctrl+→	To the next cell containing data (the next non-blank cell) in the direction pressed
Enter	One cell down
Tab	One cell to the right
Shift+Enter	One cell up
Shift+Tab	One cell left
Home	To column A of current row
Page Up	Up one screen
Page Down	Down one screen
Alt+Page Up	One screen to the left
Alt+Page Down	One screen to the right
Ctrl+Home	To cell A1
Ctrl+End	To the cell in the last row and last column that contains data
Ctrl+Backspace	To reposition the visible portion of the worksheet to display the active cell or selected ranges that have scrolled out of view

Jumping to a Specific Cell with the Go To Command

To highlight a specific cell in the active worksheet by name, you can choose the Go To command from the Edit menu or press F5. When you choose the Go To command, Excel displays the Go To dialog box, as shown in Figure 15-3. You can jump to a specific cell by typing the name of the cell in the Reference text box and clicking OK. (You can also double-click the name of the cell if it appears in the list box.)

If you would like to highlight a range of cells based on a special attribute, such as all the cells containing formulas or comments, click the Special button and specify the cell contents you're interested in. You can also move to a specific cell by clicking the Name box located to the left of the formula bar, typing the cell name, and pressing Enter.

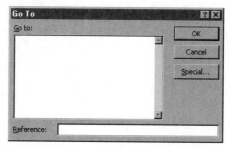

FIGURE 15-3.
The Go To dialog box lets you jump instantly to a certain cell.

Entering Information

Excel lets you enter the following types of information into a worksheet cell:

- Numeric values, like the numbers 15,000, $29.95, and 33%

- Text values, like the words *Total*, *1st Quarter*, and *1820 Warren Avenue*

- Dates and times, like Feb-97, 11/19/63, or 1:00 PM

- Comments to yourself or others, like *This region leads in sales* or an appropriate recorded sound or voice message

- Formulas, like =B5*1.081 or =SUM(B3:B7)

- Hyperlinks to Internet sites or other documents

Each type of information has its own formatting characteristics, meaning that Excel stores and displays each entry type differently. The following sections show you how to enter these values into a worksheet step by step.

Entering Numeric Values

To enter a number in a cell, select the cell you want with the mouse or keyboard, type the number, and press Enter. As you type, the number appears simultaneously in the active cell and in the *formula bar* above the worksheet. The formula bar serves as an editing scratch pad; if you make a mistake entering a long cell entry, you can click the formula bar and use the insertion pointer to locate the mistake in the entry and correct it, without having to retype the entry (and in so doing possibly making a new error). You can also double-click the active cell and then move the insertion pointer within the cell to edit your entry. To the left of the formula bar is a Cancel button, which you can click to discard an unwanted entry on the formula bar (if you haven't already accepted the entry by pressing Enter), and an Enter button, which you can click to accept or "lock in" a revised entry. See Figure 15-4.

⊗ CAUTION

When you use a slash to create a fraction in a numeric entry, be sure to include a leading zero (0) if the fractional value is less than 1. If you don't, Excel interprets your fraction as a date. For example, Excel interprets the fraction 3/4 as the date March 4 unless you enter the fraction as 0 3/4. You'll learn more about date and time formatting in Chapter 16.

A numeric value can be an integer (such as 32), a decimal number (such as 499.95), an integer fraction (such as 10 3/4), or a number in scientific notation (such as 4.09E+13). You can use several mathematical symbols in numbers, including plus (+), minus (-), percent (%), fraction (/), and exponent (E), as well as the dollar sign ($). If you enter a number that is too large to fit into a cell, Excel will automatically widen the cell to fit the number or adjust its display of the number by using scientific notation or showing fewer decimal places. If Excel displays the number in scientific notation or places ######## in the cell, you'll need to manually increase the column width to see the number in its entirety. Excel always stores the actual number you typed internally, no matter how it is displayed in

FIGURE 15-4.

New values appear both on the formula bar and in the cell when you enter them.

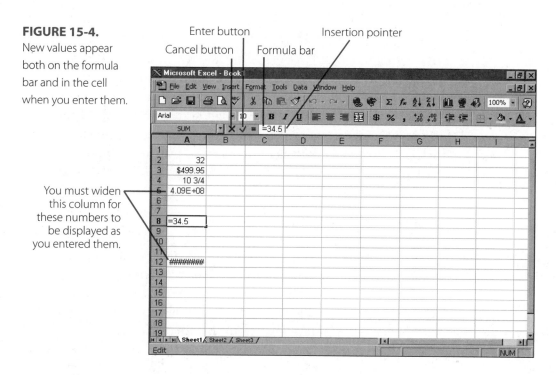

Enter button

Cancel button

Formula bar

Insertion pointer

You must widen this column for these numbers to be displayed as you entered them.

the cell, and you can view this *underlying value* on the formula bar whenever the cell is active. By default (the preset arrangement), numeric values are aligned to the right edge of a cell.

Follow these steps to enter numeric values:

1 Select the cell you want to store the number in. (You can click the cell with the mouse or use the keyboard to achieve this.)

2 Type the numeric value. (Notice how the number appears both in the cell and on the formula bar.)

3 Press Enter or select a new cell to enter the number.

 TIP

Use Arrow Keys to Move from Cell to Cell

If you plan to enter additional numbers, you can use the arrow keys to enter a number and move to a new cell in one step. For instance, if you type a number and press the Down arrow key, the cell pointer moves down one line. The Left, Up, and Right arrow keys move the pointer one cell left, up, or right.

III

Microsoft Excel

Entering Text Values

To enter a text value into a cell, select the cell, type your text, and press Enter. A text value or *label* can be any combination of alphanumeric characters, including uppercase and lowercase letters, numbers, and symbols. Excel automatically recognizes text values and aligns them to the left margin of each cell. If no information appears in adjacent cells, Excel allows longer text entries to overlap the cells on the right. If the adjacent cells do contain information, the display of the text is cut off, or truncated; however, just as with a truncated value, Excel correctly stores the full text internally, and you can see it in the formula bar when the cell is active.

SEE ALSO

For details about changing column widths to make room for more information in cells, see "Changing Column Widths and Row Heights," page 481.

If you want Excel to store a value such as a numeric address, date, or part number as a text value, simply precede the value with a single quotation mark. For example, if you enter '55 in a cell, the number 55 will appear left-aligned in the cell without a quotation mark, and a quotation mark will appear in the formula bar to identify the number as a text value. Figure 15-5 shows an example of a cell with overlapping text, a few cells with truncated text, and several numeric text entries (that is, numbers stored internally as text).

FIGURE 15-5.
Text values are left-aligned and can overlap adjacent cells if they don't contain information.

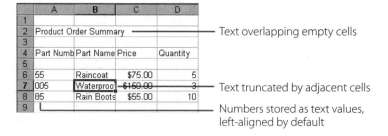

Text overlapping empty cells

Text truncated by adjacent cells

Numbers stored as text values, left-aligned by default

Follow these steps to enter text values:

1 Select the cell you want to store the text in. (You can click the cell with the mouse or use the keyboard to achieve this.)

2 Type the text value. (If you're entering a number, date, or time that should be stored as text, enter a single quotation mark before the value.)

3 Press Enter, or select a new cell to enter the text value.

TIP

> **Speed Your Work with AutoComplete**
>
> If Excel recognizes the pattern you're typing when you enter a sequence of characters, it will attempt to complete the pattern using a feature called *AutoComplete*. AutoComplete can be a major time-saver for you if you manage lists in Excel or find that you are entering the same values or functions over and over again. If you activate the AutoComplete feature while entering data, review the insertion and, if it makes sense to you, press Enter and move on.

Entering Dates and Times

If you want to store a date or a time in a worksheet cell, you should use one of Excel's predefined date and time formats to enter the value so that it can be formatted with the Cells command or used later in a formula. Excel stores dates and times internally as *serial numbers* (a value determined by counting the number of days, starting with 1, which is January 1, 1900, at midnight) that can be displayed in different time and date formats and even used in chronological calculations. (For example, you can compute the number of days between two holidays by subtracting the first date from the second date.) Serial numbers don't appear in worksheet cells, but they do free you from being locked into a particular date or time format after you enter it. As you'll learn in the next chapter, Excel lets you change the format of times and dates with a few simple commands.

 SEE ALSO

For information about changing the format of date and time values, see "Changing Number Formats," page 468.

 TIP

> To enter the current date in the active cell, press Ctrl+; (the semicolon key). Excel will use the format *m/d/yy* for the date.

Table 15-2 on the following page shows you some of the time and date formats supported by Excel. See Figure 15-6 on the following page for an example of each.

Follow these steps to enter dates or times:

1 Select the cell you want to store the date or time in. (You can click the cell with the mouse or use the keyboard.)

Microsoft Excel

2 Type the date or time in one of the accepted formats. (See Table 15-2.) If you want to enter the current date, hold down Ctrl and press semicolon (;).

3 Press Enter or select a new cell to enter the value.

TABLE 15-2. **Date and Time Formats Supported by Excel**

Format	Pattern	Example
Date	*m/d/yy*	10/1/97
Date	*d-mmm-yy*	1-Oct-97
Date	*d-mmm*	1-Oct
Date	*mmm-yy*	Oct-97
Time	*h:mm AM/PM*	10:15 PM
Time	*h:mm:ss AM/PM*	10:15:30 PM
Time	*h:mm*	22:15
Time	*h:mm:ss*	22:15:30
Time	*mm:ss.0*	15:30.3
Combined	*m/d/yy h:mm*	10/1/97 22:15

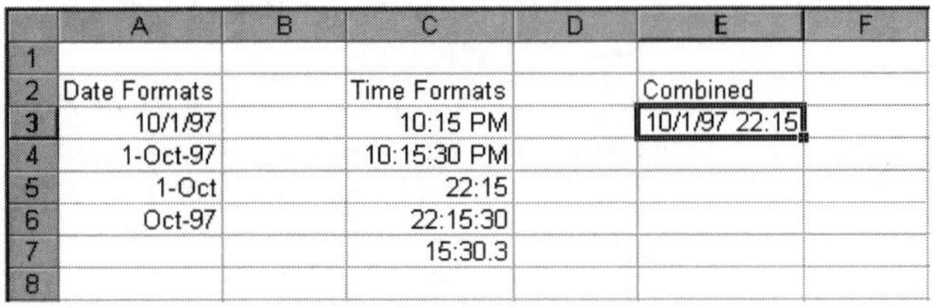

FIGURE 15-6.
Time and date values can be displayed in a variety of formats.

	A	B	C	D	E	F
1						
2	Date Formats		Time Formats		Combined	
3	10/1/97		10:15 PM		10/1/97 22:15	
4	1-Oct-97		10:15:30 PM			
5	1-Oct		22:15			
6	Oct-97		22:15:30			
7			15:30.3			
8						

Entering Comments

If you plan to share your Excel worksheets with other users, you might want to annotate a few important cells with *comments* to provide instructions or highlight critical information. You can add a pop-up comment to a cell by highlighting the cell and choosing the Comment command from the Insert menu. The Comment command displays a scratch pad with a blinking cursor and your name in it, so you can type a short note in the cell. (See Figure 15-7.) When you're finished typing the comment, click another cell to "lock in" the note.

FIGURE 15-7.
The Comment command lets you add a descriptive note to a cell.

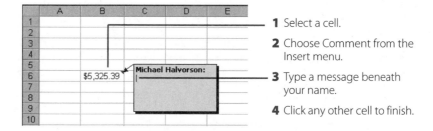

1 Select a cell.

2 Choose Comment from the Insert menu.

3 Type a message beneath your name.

4 Click any other cell to finish.

> To change the name that appears when you enter a comment, choose Options from the Tools menu, click the General tab, and change the name in the User Name text box.

Active comments are identified by tiny red dots in the upper right corner of a cell. To display a comment in a worksheet, hold the mouse pointer over the annotated cell until a pop-up comment box appears, as shown in Figure 15-8. Remember that because comments are cell annotations, they exist in *addition* to the other entries in cells—they don't *replace* them. To delete an existing comment, select the cell containing the comment in the worksheet, click the Edit menu, point the mouse pointer to the Clear submenu, and click the Comments command.

FIGURE 15-8.
Comments are identified by tiny red dots in a cell.

Comments pop up when the cell pointer moves over the cell.

III

Microsoft Excel

Managing Your Comments

You can view all the comments in your workbook by enabling the Comments command on the View menu. The Comments command is a toggle that is either off or on; when it is enabled, all the comments in your workbook appear in pop-up windows; when it is disabled, comments only appear when you hold the mouse over the cells in which they reside. The Comments command also activates the Reviewing toolbar, shown in Figure 15-9, which contains a number of useful command buttons. To edit an existing comment, click the Edit Comment button on the toolbar, or right-click the cell containing the comment that needs editing and choose the Edit Comment command from the shortcut menu.

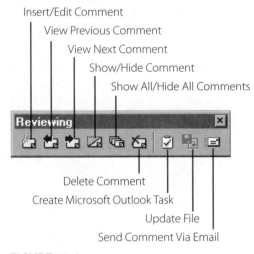

FIGURE 15-9.
The Reviewing toolbar helps you manage the comments in your workbook.

Entering Formulas

? SEE ALSO
For detailed information about formula syntax, see "Building a Formula," page 556. For detailed information about Excel's collection of built-in functions, see "Using Built-In Functions," page 562.

To compute a calculation in a worksheet, you could find your pocket calculator and work the problem. Better yet: enter a formula in an Excel cell, and have that formula available instantly, from any cell in your worksheet, for future calculations and modification. A *formula* is an equation that calculates a new value from existing values. For example, a simple formula could calculate the total cost of an item by adding its price, sales tax, and shipping costs. Formulas can contain numbers, mathematical operators, cell references, and built-in equations called *functions*. One of Excel's great strengths is its vast collection of powerful and easy-to-use functions. Entering a formula in a cell is the key to unlocking this potent ally.

All formulas in Excel begin with an equal sign (=). The equal sign signals the beginning of a mathematical operation, and tells Excel to store the equation that follows as a formula. For example, the following formula calculates the sum of three numbers:

=10+20+30

Excel stores your formulas internally (you can see them on the formula bar), but it displays the result of each calculation in the cell in which you placed the formula. You can use the standard mathematical operators in a formula—plus (+), minus (-), multiplication (*), division (/), and exponentiation (^) as well as a few specialty operators described in Chapter 19. Figure 15-10 lists the steps to follow to enter a simple formula in a worksheet cell.

FIGURE 15-10.
Entering a formula in a cell.

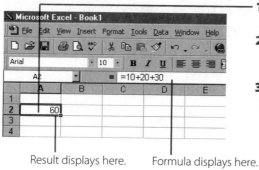

Result displays here.   Formula displays here.

1 Select a cell for entering a formula.

2 Type an equal sign (=) and the equation you want to calculate.

3 Press the Enter key or highlight a new cell to complete the formula and display the result.

If your formula results in the message *Error In Formula*, you used an invalid operator or typed the formula incorrectly. Fix the formula in the formula bar, or edit it in the cell by selecting the cell and pressing F2.

NOTE

If you don't begin formulas with an equal sign (=), Excel will interpret the equation as a text value, and the formula will not be calculated. If you make this common mistake, press F2 to edit the cell, press the Home key to move the insertion pointer to the beginning of the formula, type an equal sign (=), and then press Enter.

III

Microsoft Excel

Using Cell References in Formulas

(?) SEE ALSO

You can also include groups of cells in formulas. See "Selecting Cells and Ranges," page 445.

Formulas can also contain worksheet *cell references*—cell names such as A1 or B5—so that you can include the contents of cells in formulas and combine them in any way you choose. Cell references can be used along with numbers, mathematical operators, and built-in functions. To specify cell references in formulas, you can type in their names, or highlight them individually with the mouse, or highlight them individually with the keyboard. (See procedures below.) For example, to add the contents of cell B5 to the contents of cell C5, you would create the following formula:

=B5+C5

Figure 15-11 shows the results of such a calculation.

FIGURE 15-11.

To use the contents of cells in a formula, include cell references in the equation (here, B5 and C5).

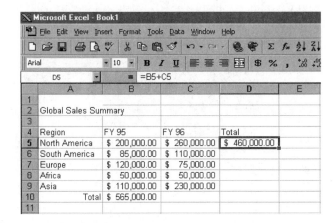

Creating Cell References by Typing

Follow these steps to create a formula that includes cell references you type by hand:

1 Select the cell you want to place the formula in.

2 Type an equal sign (=), and then type the formula you want to create. When it comes time to enter the cell references in your formula, type each cell name in column-first/row-next format. For example, to add cell B5 to cell C5, type =*B5+C5*.

3 Press Enter to store the formula. Excel calculates the result and displays it in the cell.

Creating Cell References by Using the Mouse

Follow these steps to create a formula that includes cell references you highlight with the mouse:

1 Select the cell you want to place the formula in.

2 Type an equal sign (=) to start the formula. Click the first cell you want to place in the formula, and then type a mathematical operator. For example, click cell B5 and then press the plus (+) key to add B5+ to the formula bar. When you click the cell, a flashing border surrounds the cell, and its name appears on the formula bar. The border disappears when you type the operator.

3 Click the second cell you want to place in the formula. If the cell you want is not currently visible, use the scroll bars to locate it. If you want to include additional mathematical operators and cell names, you can add them now.

4 Press the Enter key to store the formula. Excel calculates the result and displays it in the cell.

Creating Cell References by Using Arrow Keys

Follow these steps to create a formula that includes cell references you highlight with the arrow keys (Right, Down, Up, Left) on the keyboard:

1 Select the cell you want to place the formula in.

2 Type an equal sign (=) to start the formula. Use the arrow keys to highlight the first cell you want to add to the formula, and then type a mathematical operator. For example, highlight cell B5 and then press the plus (+) key to add B5+ to the formula bar. As you move the cursor around the worksheet, a flashing border surrounds the currently highlighted cell and its name appears in the formula bar.

3 Highlight the second cell you want to place in the formula. If the cell you want is not currently visible, use arrow keys to locate it. (If you want to include additional mathematical operators and cell names, you can add them now.)

4 Press the Enter key to store the formula. Excel calculates the result and displays it in the cell.

❓ SEE ALSO

For more information about saving workbooks, see "Saving a File," page 80. For information about saving summary information in workbooks, see "Working with Property Sheets," page 88.

Saving the Workbook

After you enter information into a new workbook, it's a good idea to save the data to disk, before you make some phone calls and get distracted, or go to lunch. This way, you can protect the information and use it again later. Each workbook is stored in its own file on disk, and is assigned a filename that is unique to the folder it is stored in. To assign a new filename to a workbook, use the Save As command on the File menu. To save edits you have made to an existing workbook file, use the Save command on the File menu.

Using the Save As Command

Figure 15-12 shows you the steps to follow to save your workbook to disk. From the File menu, choose the Save As command. The Save As dialog box appears, prompting you for a filename, as shown in Figure 15-12.

FIGURE 15-12.
Saving your workbook to disk under a new filename.

2 Click the down arrow to display your Desktop;

Click the Up One Level button to move to a higher-level folder;

Click the Look In Favorites button to open that folder; or

Click the Create New Folder button and type a folder name.

1 Select the file folder in any of the following ways.

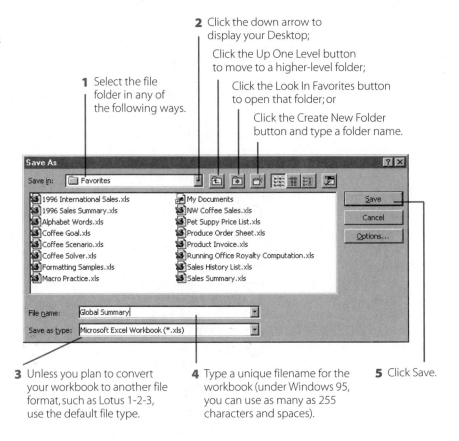

3 Unless you plan to convert your workbook to another file format, such as Lotus 1-2-3, use the default file type.

4 Type a unique filename for the workbook (under Windows 95, you can use as many as 255 characters and spaces).

5 Click Save.

Save Your Favorite Files in a Special Folder

We recommend that you place the files you use most often in the Favorites folder, a special location on your hard disk set aside for especially useful files. (If you like, you can also create subfolders in this folder.) To open the Favorites folder in the Save As dialog box, click the Look In Favorites button.

Using the Save Command

To save revisions you have made to a workbook that already has a filename, choose the Save command from the File menu. That's all there is to it—choosing Save updates your file on disk automatically. We recommend that you use the Save command every 10 minutes or so to avoid losing data. If you decide you want to create a new version of the file while preserving the original, use the Save As command and specify a new filename.

Save

Quick Saves

You can also save your file by clicking the Save button on the Standard Excel toolbar or by pressing Ctrl+S on your keyboard.

Inserting Hyperlinks

Excel 97 includes a new feature that allows you to add *hyperlinks* to cells in your workbook, connecting them to other electronic documents on your hard disk, the Internet, or an attached computer network. Hyperlinks in Excel give you a handy way to combine a series of related workbooks or let you provide your users with "on demand" access to supporting documents or Internet materials on the World Wide Web (the Web). You create a hyperlink with the Hyperlink command on the Insert menu, and the command prompts you for the name of the supporting file and underlines the text in the worksheet cell that was selected when you ran the command. (The underlined word appears in a special color, and looks similar to linked topics that appear in the Office online Help.) After a hyperlink has been

III

Microsoft Excel

established to another document, you can activate it simply by clicking the underlined word in your worksheet.

Note that you can specify any supporting document for your hyperlink—provided that you have the Windows 95 application necessary to open the document on your computer. For example, if you have Microsoft Office Professional Edition installed, you can insert a hyperlink in your worksheet to any Word, Excel, PowerPoint, Access, or Outlook document, and Excel will automatically open that document when you click the underlined "hyperlink" cell in your workbook. Similarly, if you have Microsoft Internet Explorer or another Windows 95 Internet browser, you can create a hyperlink to any resource on the Internet for which you have a proper address.

Creating a Hyperlink in Your Worksheet

The following steps show you how to add a hyperlink to your worksheet that opens a document on your hard disk, the Internet, or a network to which you're attached:

1 In your worksheet, select the cell you want to associate the hyperlink with. You can create a hyperlink in an empty cell, or in a cell containing information, artwork, or a formula.

 TIP

Place descriptive text in each cell that contains a hyperlink. That way, other users will be able to see what document the hyperlink refers to before they activate it.

Insert
Hyperlink

2 From the Insert menu, choose the Hyperlink command or click the Insert Hyperlink button on the Standard toolbar. If you haven't recently saved your worksheet, Excel will prompt you to do so now. Then the Insert Hyperlink dialog box appears, prompting you for the name of the file that will open when the hyperlink is activated. If you wish, you can specify a particular location in the file that should appear on the screen; if not, the document simply opens at the beginning.

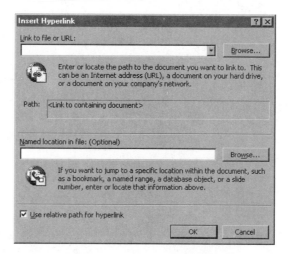

3 Click the Browse button in the Insert Hyperlink dialog box. (You could also type the complete pathname of the file you wanted to open, but browsing is usually easier.) The Link To File dialog box appears, as shown in the following screen:

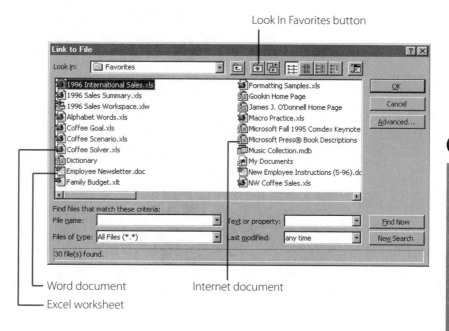

Look In Favorites button

Word document

Excel worksheet

Internet document

4 Select the folder containing the file you want to open, and then double-click the hyperlink filename in the File list box. You can click the Look In Favorites button to see a list of your favorite Office documents, or (if you're using Microsoft Internet Explorer) you can view your most recent Internet connections by opening the /Program Files/Plus!/Microsoft Internet/History folder. An Internet shortcut icon appears next to documents on the Internet.

5 Click OK to add the hyperlink to your worksheet. When the Insert Hyperlink dialog box closes, the text in the highlighted cell appears in underlined type, and the Web toolbar opens.

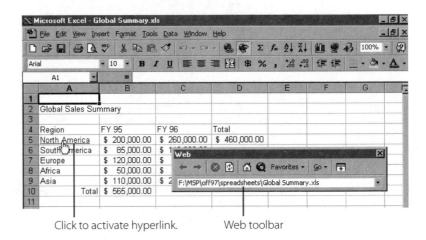

Click to activate hyperlink.   Web toolbar

Activating a Hyperlink

To activate a hyperlink in a worksheet, simply click the underlined cell containing the hyperlink and Excel will automatically start any necessary applications and load the linked document. (If the document is an Excel workbook, Excel simply opens the workbook in a new window.) If the hyperlink requires an Internet or other network connection, you may be prompted for a member ID (also called username) and password when you activate the hyperlink, as shown in Figure 15-13. (In most cases, you'll need an Internet browser, a modem, and an open phone line to establish a connection to the Internet.)

FIGURE 15-13.

A hyperlink that requires an Internet connection will prompt you for a member ID and password.

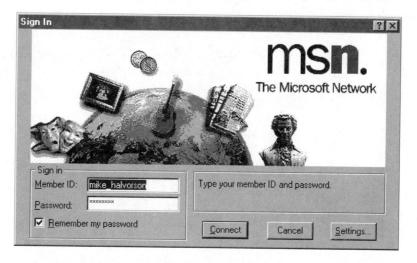

The Web Toolbar

After you activate a hyperlink in Excel, a special Web toolbar appears on the screen, which lets you switch back and forth between open hyperlinks, establish additional Internet connections, or run special network-related commands. You don't have to use the Web toolbar when switching between hyperlinks (you can also use the Excel Window menu), but in many cases you'll benefit from doing so. To close the Web toolbar, click the Close button on the toolbar's title bar.

Go back to last open hyperlink.
Go forward to next open hyperlink.
Stop current jump.
Refresh current page.
Open Start page.
Search the Web.

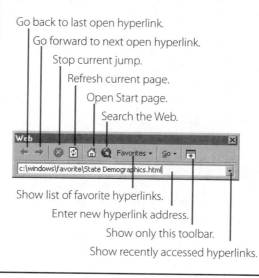

Show list of favorite hyperlinks.
Enter new hyperlink address.
Show only this toolbar.
Show recently accessed hyperlinks.

III

Microsoft Excel

Hyperlink
pointer

If you're not sure whether an underlined word represents a hyperlink, simply place the mouse pointer directly over the cell and see if the mouse pointer changes shape. The mouse pointer over a cell containing a hyperlink resembles a hand with a pointing finger.

After a hyperlink has been activated, you can jump back and forth between the home document and any supporting hyperlinks by clicking the Back and Forward buttons, respectively, on the Web toolbar. If the hyperlink launched a separate Windows application to load the document—say, the hyperlink started Microsoft Word—you can also use the Windows 95 taskbar to move back and forth quickly between the applications. When you're finished viewing a hyperlinked Excel workbook, close it by choosing the Close command from the Excel File menu. When you're finished using documents associated with other applications, simply close the application (if you're using the Internet, this will end your connection).

? SEE ALSO

For more information about using Internet documents and the Web toolbar, see "Accessing the Internet," page 97.

Removing a Hyperlink

To remove a hyperlink from a worksheet cell, follow these steps:

⊗ CAUTION

Don't click the cell containing the hyperlink or you'll activate it.

1   Click a cell near the hyperlink you want to remove, and then use the arrow keys to highlight the cell containing the unwanted hyperlink.

2   From the Edit menu, choose the Clear command and choose All from the submenu. If your hyperlink cell contains no other data, you can also press the Delete key to quickly remove the link. If you regret your decision, reverse the command by immediately choosing the Undo Clear command from the Edit menu.

Editing the Worksheet

If you make a mistake while building a worksheet, you're not expected to live with it. Excel features a variety of traditional and innovative electronic editing techniques, so that you can fix your typos, reorganize your data, make certain subtotals and totals stand out, and create room for more information. In this section, you'll learn the following editing techniques:

For information about tracking and approving edits in a multiuser environment, see "Accepting or Rejecting Revisions," page 517.

- How to select cells and ranges

- How to clear cells and delete cells

- How to copy data from one cell to another

- How to move cells by using drag and drop

- How to add new rows and columns to the worksheet

- How to undo and repeat commands

Selecting Cells and Ranges

Several Excel commands work with individual cells or groups of cells called *ranges*. Selecting a cell means making it the active cell, so that its name appears in the Name box to the left of the formula bar. To select an individual cell or a range of cells, you can use either the mouse or the keyboard.

SEE ALSO

To make cell ranges easier to work with, you can assign a name to a cell range and then use the name in place of the cell reference. See "Using Range Names in Functions," page 572.

Excel requires a particular notation when you type out cell ranges. For example, A1:E1 represents a single row of five cells along the top edge of the worksheet, and E5:E8 represents a single column of four cells oriented vertically in the worksheet. Each cell range starts with a "beginning" cell name, followed by a colon and the "ending" cell name. You'll use cell ranges in many of the formulas and functions you create in Excel worksheets. In this illustration, a rectangular block of 45 cells named A1:E9 has been selected:

III

Microsoft Excel

Selecting a Range with the Mouse

The following steps show you how to select a range of cells with the mouse:

1 Position the cell pointer over the first cell you want to select.

2 Hold down the mouse button, and then drag the mouse over the remaining cells in the selection. Release the mouse button.

3 If you want to select additional, noncontiguous cell ranges (that is, ranges of cells that don't touch), hold down the Ctrl key and then repeat steps 1 and 2 until all the ranges have been selected. When you're finished, release the Ctrl key. Figure 15-14 shows a multiple-range selection.

FIGURE 15-14.
Multiple selected ranges are shown in reversed color.

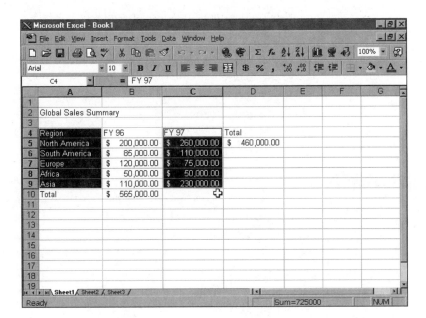

 NOTE

In Figure 15-14, two ranges of cells are selected (A4:A9 and C4:C9). Only one of the cells, however, is the active cell—C4—denoted by the bar around the cell. Most commands will affect all the selected cells, including the active cell. Entering new information and a few special commands will affect only the active cell and will not change anything in the other cells.

Selecting a Range with the Keyboard

The following steps show you how to select a range of cells with the keyboard:

1 Use the arrow keys to move to the first cell you want to select.

2 Hold down the Shift key, and then press the appropriate arrow key to select the remaining cells in the range. Release the Shift key.

3 To select additional, noncontiguous cell ranges, press Shift+F8. The Add indicator appears on the status bar, indicating that you can add a range to the selection. Repeat steps 1 and 2 to add the range.

Clearing Cells and Deleting Cells

Now that you know how to select ranges of cells, you can put your new skill to work and build a worksheet that is of value to you. First, if you want to clear the contents from a group of cells, simply select the cells and press the Delete key. Excel removes the content but keeps the cell formatting so that you can enter new values in the same format. (For example, if you clear cells formatted for dollar values, the next time you place a number in one of these cells it will automatically be formatted for dollars.) To see the complete range of clear options, choose the Clear command from the Edit menu, and Excel will display a submenu with commands for clearing the formatting, the contents, the comments, or all three items together.

 TIP

You can also clear the contents of a cell by clicking the cell with the right mouse button, and then choosing the Clear Contents command from the shortcut menu.

If you'd rather delete a single cell from the worksheet, moving the rows below it up, or shifting columns over to the left, choose the Delete command rather than the Clear command. In many applications, the terms *delete* and *clear* have the same meaning, but in Excel there is a distinct difference between the two commands. Clearing a cell is like using an eraser to remove the contents or the format from a cell, but deleting a cell is like cutting it out with a tiny pocket knife, and then moving the remaining cells up or over to fill the gap.

The following steps show you how to use the Delete command to delete cell ranges, entire rows, or entire columns from a worksheet:

1 Place the cursor in the cell, row, or column you want to delete from the worksheet. If you want to delete a range of cells, select the range.

III

Microsoft Excel

2 From the Edit menu, choose the Delete command. The dialog box shown in Figure 15-15 appears.

3 Click the option button that corresponds to the way you want remaining cells moved after the deletion. For example, in Figure 15-15 where B3 is the selected cell, to delete cell B3 and move cells over to fill the gap, click Shift Cells Left. To delete cell B3

Selecting Rows and Columns with the Mouse

If you want to quickly select part or all of your worksheet, you can click one of several "hot points" on your screen. To select an entire column with a single mouse click, click the column letter at the top of the column. To select an entire row, click the row number on the left edge of the row. You can also select multiple columns or rows by selecting a row or column head and dragging across the heads of the rows or columns you want to select. Best of all, if you need to select the entire worksheet, you can click the Select All box in the upper left corner of the worksheet. Here you see a worksheet with three columns selected.

Three columns are selected.

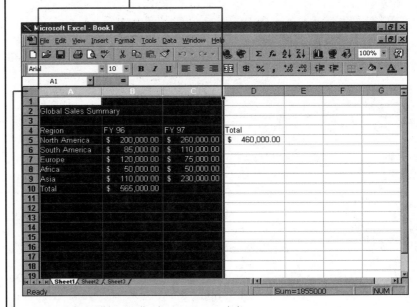

Select All box will select entire worksheet.

and move cells up to fill the gap, click Shift Cells Up. You can also click Entire Row or Entire Column to remove all the selected rows or columns. In Figure 15-15 you could, for example, remove row 3 or column B.

4   Click OK to delete the selected cells and move other cells to fill the gap.

FIGURE 15-15.
The Delete command lets you remove a cell, row, or column from the worksheet and fill the gap with adjacent cells.

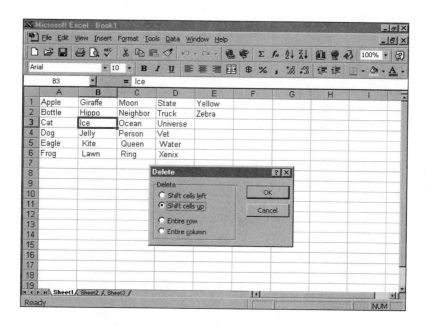

Undoing Commands

If you make a mistake when deleting a range of cells or executing another Excel command, you can undo your mistake by immediately choosing the Undo command from the Edit menu. For example, if you deleted a range of cells in error, choosing Undo will return the cells to the worksheet as if you had never deleted them.

Undo

You can also click the Undo button on the Standard toolbar, or press Ctrl+Z, to undo a command.

In Excel 97, the Undo button on the Standard toolbar now has multiple levels of undo (like Microsoft Word). This lets you "go back in time" to fix editing mistakes you made 3, 4, or 10 commands back. This is an extremely useful feature, because now and then you'll probably think better of a modification you made that took several steps to accomplish. By clicking the small arrow attached to the Undo button, you can scroll through a list of the edits you've made and pick the one you want to reverse. (See Figure 15-16.) Excel will then undo each command, from your most recent action back to and including the one you just picked.

FIGURE 15-16.
Undoing the third action, Delete, also undoes the more recent actions above it.

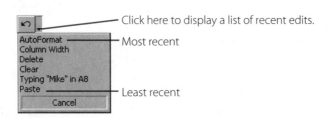

Undo has a few limitations. For example, you can't undo the actions of adding a new worksheet to your workbook or deleting an existing worksheet. You also can't undo the actions of saving revisions to a file or customizing the Excel interface. If Undo is not available for a particular command, the Undo command on the Edit menu will be dimmed and will read Can't Undo.

> Excel is smart about tracking your actions during a given work session. It doesn't create an Undo command when you use the scroll bars, press keyboard navigation keys, run online Help, or look for cell data with the Go To or Find commands. However, your ability to undo ends when you close your workbook or exit from Excel.

Redoing Commands

What happens if you decide to, well, undo an Undo command? For example, what do you do if you delete a range of cells, restore them with Undo, and then, on reflection, decide to remove them after all? One option is to select the cells again and choose the Delete command. But Excel makes it even easier to be fickle. After you use the Undo command, Excel changes the name of the Undo command to Redo on the Edit menu, so that you can run your last command again. This gives you the opportunity to switch back and forth between two different editing commands, to see which result you like best. Excel also adds the commands you have reversed to the Redo button on the

Redo

Standard toolbar, letting you redo several commands at once. (This makes the Redo button the functional opposite of the Undo button, allowing you to restore and remove edits you have made.)

Repeating Commands

Below the Undo command on the Edit menu is the Repeat command, which lets you repeat the command you just executed, but at a different place in the worksheet. For example, if you just used the Cells command on the Format menu to place a border around cell B3, you can use the Repeat command to add the same border to a new cell by simply highlighting the new cell and clicking Repeat on the Edit menu. To make it even faster, press the shortcut key combination Ctrl+Y.

Follow these steps to use the Repeat command:

1 Execute a command you plan to repeat. (The best commands are those that require several steps to complete.) For example, to place a border around a cell, select the cell, choose the Cells command from the Format menu, click the Border tab, click the Outline box, and then click OK.

2 Select the next cell you want to modify with the same command.

3 From the Edit menu, choose the Repeat command.

 CAUTION

In Excel 97 the Repeat button has been moved from the Standard toolbar to the Edit menu, where you can see its new button design. Taking its place on the Standard toolbar is the new Redo button. Redo and Repeat are different animals (albeit from the same savanna), so be sure not to confuse them.

Repeat

 TIP

> **Think "Repeat" or "Threepeat"**
>
> The Repeat command is a speed feature, designed to help you work faster in Excel. But most people forget to use it, because they don't anticipate repetitive actions. Think about how you work, and you might discover several clever uses for the Repeat command. (We use Repeat most often for formatting labels and changing number formats.)

Using Cut and Paste to Move Data

At times you'll want to move cell entries from one place to another on your worksheet. To accomplish this task, you can use the Cut and the Paste commands on the Edit menu. When you cut a range of cells with the Cut command, Excel places a dotted-line marquee around the cells to indicate which cells will be moved, and then places the cell contents

III

Microsoft Excel

(including comments and formatting) into a temporary storage location known as the Windows Clipboard. When you select a new location for the data and choose the Paste command, the cells and their formatting are pasted from the Clipboard into their new location and the original cells are replaced. (If you're pasting a range of cells, the cells are inserted in a block, with the location you selected being the upper left corner of the paste area.) To cancel the move after the marquee appears, press the Escape key.

NOTE

If you cut and paste more than one cell, they must be in a block. Excel doesn't allow you to move noncontiguous blocks of cells. Also, by contrast with other Windows applications, you can only paste one time after you cut. To paste multiple times, use the Copy command.

Figure 15-17 shows a group of cells after the Cut command has been selected (notice the marquee), while Figure 15-18 shows the same worksheet after the Paste command. Note that you can also copy over cells containing data with the Paste command, so *use some caution* when moving information. As alternatives to the Cut and Paste commands on the Edit menu, you can use the Cut and Paste buttons on the Standard toolbar or the standard Windows key combinations Ctrl+X and Ctrl+V.

FIGURE 15-17.
The Cut command marks the selected cells with a marquee.

Marquee   Text selected for cut   New starting location for cells

FIGURE 15-18.
The Paste command copies data from the Clipboard into the active cell.

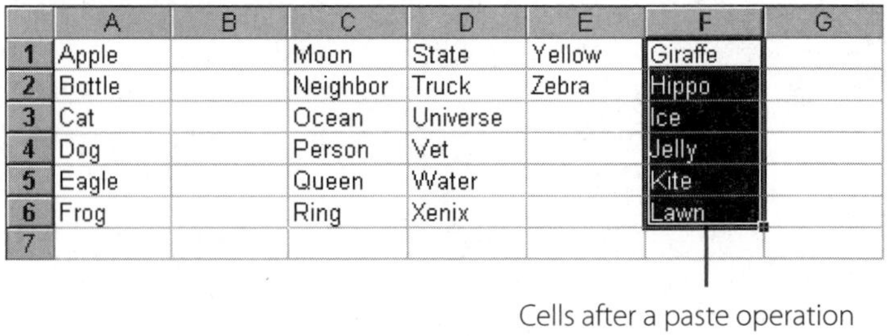

Cells after a paste operation

The following steps show you how to move a range of cells with the Cut and Paste commands:

1   Select the group of cells you want to move.

Cut

2   From the Edit menu, choose the Cut command. (You can also click the Cut button on the toolbar or press the Ctrl+X key combination.)

3   Click the cell to which you want to move the data. (If you're moving a group of cells, highlight the cell in the upper left corner of the area you're copying to.)

Paste

4   From the Edit menu, choose the Paste command. (Or click the Paste button on the toolbar or press the Ctrl+V key combination.)

Using Copy and Paste to Duplicate Data

If you just want to duplicate a range of cells in the worksheet, not move them, you can use the Copy command on the Edit menu. The Copy command places a copy of the cells you have selected in the Clipboard, and you can transfer these cells any number of times to your worksheet with the Paste command. The Copy command indicates the cells you're duplicating with the dotted-line marquee, so that you can see what you're copying as you do it. As with the Cut command, you're limited to copying contiguous (touching) blocks of cells with the Copy command.

To speed up your copy operations, you can use the Copy button on the Standard toolbar, or the key combination Ctrl+C.

The following steps show you how to copy a range of cells with the Copy and Paste commands:

1   Select the group of cells you want to copy.

Copy

2   From the Edit menu, choose the Copy command. (You can also click the Copy button on the toolbar or press Ctrl+C.)

3   Click the cell to which you want to copy the data. (If you're duplicating a group of cells, highlight the cell in the upper left corner of the area you're copying to.)

4 From the Edit menu, choose the Paste command. (Or click the Paste button on the toolbar or press Ctrl+V.)

Moving Cells by Using Drag and Drop

The fastest way to move a group of worksheet cells is by using a mouse movement called *drag and drop*. By means of the drag and drop technique, you can edit a worksheet in an efficient and visibly uncomplicated way—by dragging a group of cells from one location to another. To enable drag and drop, you need to select cells (usually with the mouse), release the mouse button, and then move the cell pointer toward an outside edge of the selected cells until the cell pointer changes into the arrow pointer. When the pointer changes shape, you can hold down the left mouse button and drag the selection to a new location. As you move the cells, Excel displays both an outline of the range (identified by the label "New location (drop)" in Figure 15-19) and the current range address so that you can align the cells properly in your worksheet.

New location (drop)

FIGURE 15-19.
The quickest way to move cells in the worksheet is with the drag and drop mouse technique.

Selected cells (drag)

⚠ **WARNING**

If when you use drag and drop you happen to drop cells onto existing data, Excel will warn you that you're about to overwrite the contents of your copy destination. Click OK if you want to overwrite the old cells, or click Cancel if you want to choose a new place for the data.

The following steps show you how to move a range of cells with the drag and drop mouse technique:

1 Select the group of cells you want to move, and then release the mouse button.

2 Move the cell pointer toward the edge of the selected cells, until the cell pointer changes into an arrow pointer.

3 Hold down the left mouse button and drag the selected cells to their new location. As you move the selection, an outline of the range appears, helping you position the contents.

4 Release the left mouse button to complete the move.

> To copy cells by using drag and drop, hold down the Ctrl key while you drag the selected cells. When you drag with the Ctrl key down, a plus (+) sign is added to the arrow pointer to let you know you're copying data.

Adding Rows and Columns to the Worksheet

Now and then you'll want to add new rows or columns to your worksheet to create space. You might decide to add cells because your existing data is too crowded, or perhaps you're creating a report that has changed in scope and requires a new layout to communicate effectively. You add new rows and columns to your worksheet with the Rows and Columns commands on the Insert menu. When you add rows or columns to your worksheet, the existing data shifts down to accommodate new rows or shifts to the right to allow for new columns.

The following steps show you how to add a row to your worksheet:

1 Select the row *below* the place you want to enter a new, blank row. (Select the row by clicking the row number.)

2 From the Insert menu, choose the Rows command.

The following steps show you how to add a column to your worksheet:

1 Select the column to the *right* of the place you want to enter a new column. (Select the column by clicking the column letter.)

2 From the Insert menu, choose the Columns command.

Inserting Individual Cells

Excel lets you add individual cells to the rows or columns of your worksheet with the Cells command on the Insert menu. Before you use the Cells command, you should select the worksheet cell below or to the right of the new cell you want. For example, if you want to add a new cell to column B between cells B3 and B4, highlight cell B4 before choosing the Cells command. When you choose Cells, the Insert dialog box appears.

Use the Insert dialog box to tell Excel to shift the cells to the right or down. If you're adding a cell to a column, click Shift Cells Down. If you're adding a cell to a row, click Shift Cells Right. You can also insert entire rows and columns as you did above with the Insert Rows and Insert Columns commands.

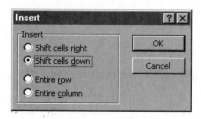

Entering a Series of Labels, Numbers, and Dates

Excel streamlines the task of entering worksheet data by allowing you to fill a range of cells with one repeating value or a sequence of values, called a *series*. This capability saves you time when you're entering groups of labels, numbers, or dates in a report. For example, you can replicate the same price for many products in a report, or create part numbers that increment predictably. To enter a series of values into a range of cells, you use the Fill command on the Insert menu or a mouse technique called AutoFill. The following sections show you how you can enter data automatically using these commands.

? SEE ALSO
For information about replicating formulas in a worksheet, see "Replicating a Formula," page 557.

Using AutoFill to Create a Series

The easiest method for entering repeating or incrementing data is to use Excel's AutoFill feature. The AutoFill feature is activated when you drag a tiny black square called the *fill handle* over new cells. The fill handle is located in the lower right corner of the active cell or a selected range of cells, as shown in Figure 15-20. When you position the cell pointer over the fill handle, the cell pointer changes to a plus sign, indicating the AutoFill feature has been enabled. To create a series of labels, numbers, or dates, you simply drag the pointer over the cells you want to fill with information, and then release the mouse button. (Notice that Excel shows the next value in the series in a pop-up box.) Like magic, you have a list of new values!

FIGURE 15-20.
Follow these steps to quickly AutoFill a series of cells.

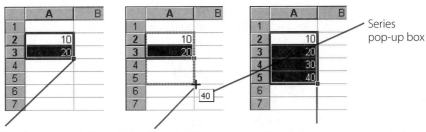

Series pop-up box

1 Click the fill handle.   **2** Drag down the AutoFill pointer (cross).   **3** Release the mouse button.

The AutoFill feature obeys a clear set of rules when it replicates data in cells, as shown in Table 15-3. When you drag the fill handle down or to the right, AutoFill creates values that increase based on the pattern in the range of cells you first select. When you drag the fill handle up or to the left, AutoFill creates values that decrease based on the pattern. If AutoFill doesn't recognize the pattern, it simply duplicates the selected cells.

TABLE 15-3. AutoFill Insertion Patterns

Pattern Type	Series	Example
Label (Text)	No pattern, text is duplicated	Units, Units, Units
Number	Values increased based on pattern	10, 20, 30
Text with number	Series created by changing number based on pattern	Unit 1, Unit 2, Unit 3
Day	Series created to match day format	Mon, Tues, Wed
Month	Series created to match month format	Jan, Feb, Mar
Year	Series created to match year format	1997, 1998, 1999
Time	Series created to match time interval	1:30 PM, 2:00 PM, 2:30 PM

⭐ **TIP**

To suppress the AutoFill feature (and just duplicate the selected cells), hold down the Ctrl key while you drag the fill handle.

The following steps show you how to create a series of values in a worksheet with the AutoFill feature:

1 Select the first cell in the series, and if it does not already contain a value, type one in. (Use Table 15-3 on the preceding page for pattern guidelines.) If the series is based on multiple values, enter values in at least two additional cells to establish a pattern.

2 Select all the cells containing values in the series. If you're starting with a single cell, skip this step.

3 Position the cell pointer over the fill handle so that it becomes a small black cross.

4 Drag the fill handle over the worksheet cells you want filled with the series, and then release the mouse button. (Note the series pop-up box that appears as you drag.)

Using the Fill Commands

The mouse-driven AutoFill feature is designed to handle most of the data copying and replication in a worksheet, but you can also use a collection of Fill commands on the Edit menu to accomplish simple copying tasks. You'll find these commands useful if you want to copy one cell into many adjacent cells, or if you want to fine-tune how the patterns in an AutoFill series are created.

Filling Up, Down, Right, and Left

When you choose the Fill command from the Edit menu, a submenu appears with several replication commands, including Up, Down, Right, and Left. These commands let you copy information from one cell to a group of selected, adjacent cells. Figure 15-21 shows how the Fill Down command is used to copy the contents of cell A2 to cells A3 through A5. Note that cell comments are *not* copied when the Fill commands are used (because comments are not considered essential to the calculation process).

FIGURE 15-21.
Select the range
you want to fill and
choose Up, Down,
Right, or Left from
the Fill submenu.

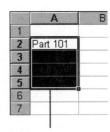

1 Select the fill range.   **2** Choose the Down command from the Fill submenu.

The following steps show you how to fill a range with the Fill command:

1 Place the cell pointer on the cell you want to replicate, and then drag the mouse over the cells you want to fill.

2 Choose the Fill command from the Edit menu and then choose the command from the Fill submenu corresponding to the direction you want to copy.

The Excel key combination for the Down command is Ctrl+D. The key combination for the Right command is Ctrl+R.

The Fill Series Dialog Box

If you want to specify a custom series, such as a number that increments in fractional portions or a maximum value for the series, select your fill range and choose the Series command from the Fill submenu of the Edit menu. The dialog box shown in Figure 15-22 appears. This dialog box lets you specify the value type and date type—characteristics that are usually set automatically when you use the AutoFill feature.

FIGURE 15-22.
The Series dialog
box lets you create
custom fill sequences.

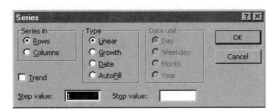

What makes the Series dialog box handy is the Step Value and Stop Value text boxes, which let you control how the specified series increments and specify its final value. For example, if you want to increment a numeric series by 1.5, type *1.5* in the Step Value text box. Similarly, if you want to set 10 as the highest number in the series, type *10* in the Stop Value text box. Figure 15-23 shows the results you get when you start with the number 1 and use both these values in the Series dialog box. Notice that although cells A8, A9, and A10 were selected in the fill range (just as a guess), they were left empty because the stop value in the Series dialog box had been reached.

FIGURE 15-23.
The Series command lets you increment by an amount you specify and stop when a limit you set has been reached.

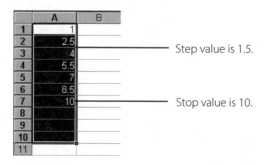

Step value is 1.5.

Stop value is 10.

Exiting Excel

Building your worksheet may take you just a few minutes, or several laborious hours, but when you're finished entering the data, you should end your Excel session by following several standard steps:

1 Save your workbook to disk with a clear, easy-to-remember filename. Use the Save As command on the File menu if you're creating a new file, or the Save command on the File menu to save an existing file.

 TIP

Don't wait until you're finished creating your document to save it to disk. Try to save your work every 10 minutes or so to avoid losing data in a power outage or system crash.

2 Give the spelling of labels and text in your worksheet a once-over with the Spelling command on the Tools menu. (The Spelling checker ignores numeric values.)

3 Print your worksheet with the Print command on the File menu. If you'd like to adjust the margins, headers, or footers in your worksheet before you print, choose the Page Setup command on the File menu. You can also use the Print Preview command on the File menu to see how your worksheet will look before it is printed, as well as the Page Break Preview command on the View menu to adjust your page breaks.

4 When you're finished working, exit Excel with the Exit command on the File menu. If you're prompted to save changes in your workbook, click Yes to retain them. (If you click No, your changes will be permanently discarded.)

SEE ALSO

For more information about saving and printing files, see Chapter 3, "Managing Documents: From Your Hard Disk to the Internet."

5 After you exit Excel, consider making a backup copy of your workbook file on a floppy disk using Windows Explorer or another utility. (You might back up important files once a day or once a week, depending on their value and the loss in time and money you'd suffer if they were damaged.) Keeping a separate backup copy of your files on a floppy disk can be an important time-saver if your hard disk ever fails; you might even sleep better at night, knowing you have a backup.

CHAPTER 16

Formatting a Worksheet

After you enter information in worksheet cells, you can format the data to highlight important facts and make the worksheet easier to read. In this chapter, you'll learn how to format worksheet cells, change column widths and row heights, add and remove page breaks, use formatting styles, work with predesigned worksheet templates, and add preexisting and original artwork. You'll be surprised at how quickly you can improve the appearance of your Excel worksheets with the powerful techniques discussed in this chapter.

Formatting Cells

Effective worksheet formatting is crucial when you present important business information. Formatting the contents of a cell doesn't change how the data is stored internally; rather it changes how the information looks on your screen and how it appears in print. In this section, you'll learn the following techniques for formatting the data in cells:

? SEE ALSO

For information about creating conditional formatting based on the values stored in worksheet cells, see "Creating Conditional Formatting," page 486.

- How to change the vertical and horizontal alignment of data in a cell

- How to change number formats

- How to change the font, text color, and background color

- How to add decorative borders and patterns to cells

- How to apply combinations of formatting effects with the AutoFormat command

Changing Alignment

The gateway to Excel's formatting commands is the Cells command on the Format menu. When you select a range of cells in the worksheet and choose the Cells command, the Format Cells dialog box appears, as shown in Figure 16-1. The Format Cells dialog box contains six tabs of formatting options you can use to adjust the appearance of information in worksheet cells. You use the Alignment tab, shown in Figure 16-1, to change the alignment and orientation of information in worksheet cells. You can also use the Formatting toolbar to set the most popular alignment options.

★ TIP

You can display the Format Cells dialog box quickly by selecting the range of cells you want to format with the right mouse button, and then choosing the Format Cells command from the shortcut menu.

Adjusting the Horizontal Alignment

To adjust the horizontal (side-to-side) alignment of data in a range of cells, select the range you want to align, choose the Format Cells command, select the Alignment tab, and choose one of the seven

FIGURE 16-1.

Alignment tab of the Format Cells dialog box.

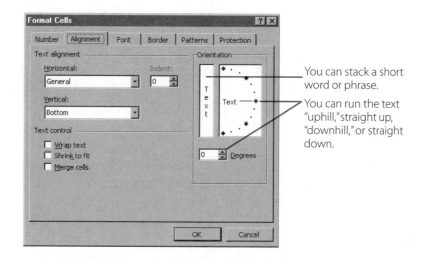

You can stack a short word or phrase.

You can run the text "uphill," straight up, "downhill," or straight down.

alignment options in the Horizontal drop-down list box. General alignment (the default) aligns text to the left edge of the cell and numbers to the right edge. This basic alignment will be suitable for most of your cells entries. Left, Center, and Right align text to the left, center, and right edges of the cell, respectively, and you can also use toolbar buttons for these common formatting options. (See Figure 16-2.) The Fill option repeats the data in a cell to fill all the cells selected in the row (although the data is still stored only in the first cell) for interesting formatting effects. The Wrap Text option wraps text into multiple lines in a cell. When text hits the margin in a cell with wrap text alignment, it continues on a new line below. In addition, the Justify option aligns text evenly between the cell borders when longer cell entries wrap within a cell. To enable this command, you must also turn on the Wrap Text check box on the Alignment tab.

The final option in the Horizontal drop-down list box is Center Across Selection, which centers the data in the first cell across a range of selected columns. For example, to center the contents of cell A1 across columns A, B, C, and D, select cells A1 through D1, choose the Cells

FIGURE 16-2.

Use the Formatting toolbar to set the more common cell formats.

Align data to center of selected cells.

Align data to left edge of selected cells.

Center text across the selected range of columns.

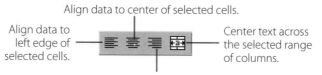

Align data to right edge of selected cells.

III

Microsoft Excel

command from the Format menu, select the Alignment tab, and click the Center Across Selection option in the Horizontal list box. Alternatively, you can select cells A1 through D1, and then click the Center Across Selection button on the toolbar. (See Table 16-1 on page 469.) By the way, Center Across Selection will not display text over occupied cells, so for the command to function properly, cells B1 through D1 must be empty. When you choose the command, Excel aligns the data to the center of the selection, but the information is still stored internally in the leftmost cell. By using these seven horizontal alignment options, you can create virtually any tabular formatting effect. Figure 16-3 shows the result of several types of horizontal alignment formatting.

FIGURE 16-3.
The Horizontal alignment options can create a variety of useful formatting effects.

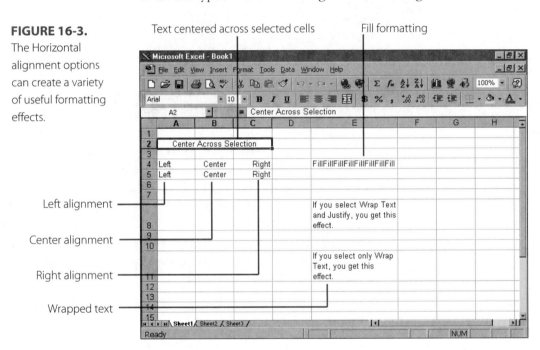

Adjusting the Vertical Alignment

The Alignment tab also lets you adjust the vertical (top to bottom) alignment in cells. The default vertical alignment is Bottom, meaning the cell contents are aligned to the bottom of the cell. However, if you change the row height to add additional white space to cells (you'll learn how to do this later in the chapter), you might enhance the appearance of your worksheet by selecting the Top or Center option in the Vertical drop-down list box. If you have multiple lines of text in a cell, you can also use the Justified alignment option, which aligns text evenly between the top and bottom edges of the cell.

Adjusting the Text Orientation

A powerful formatting option on the Alignment tab is the Orientation setting, which changes the text orientation in the selected cells from the default horizontal orientation to an exact angle (measured in degrees) on a 180 degree semicircle. This new feature lets you create a ledger with any of the attractive column labels shown in Figure 16-4. (See step-by-step instructions on the following page.) One nonintuitive option in this new Orientation setting is the button you use to "stack" letters vertically in worksheet cells, the effect we demonstrate in cell B3 in Figure 16-4. To create this neat effect, click the vertical bar on the Alignment tab containing the word "Text" (see Figure 16-1, page 465). When this bar is highlighted, Excel will create the stacked-letter effect shown in cell B3 and the text orientation will be set to zero (0) degrees. This is a useful and visually interesting effect for column labels, especially if the text is five or fewer characters long.

FIGURE 16-4.
The new Orientation option on the Alignment tab lets you specify an exact angle for your text—just like using a protractor in art class!

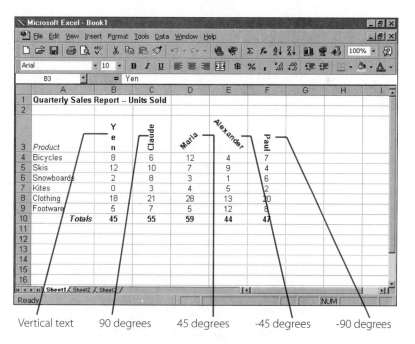

Vertical text   90 degrees   45 degrees   -45 degrees   -90 degrees

To change the text angle for the labels in a group of cells, follow these steps:

1 Select the cells you want to reorient.

2 From the Format menu, choose the Cells command and then click the Alignment tab.

3 In the Orientation box, click the angle you want to use for the text on the alignment compass. Excel will show you a preview of the orientation you select.

TIP

You can specify an exact text angle with the Degrees scroll box from -90 degrees to +90 degrees.

4 Click OK on the Alignment tab to reorient the selected cells.

Changing Number Formats

Excel lets you change the appearance of your numeric entries with several formatting options on the Number tab of the Format Cells dialog box, shown in Figure 16-5. To change the number format for a range of cells, select the cells, choose the Cells command from the Format menu, click the Number tab, choose a category in the Category list box, and then, if necessary, pick the format you want to use. To help you make your selection, Excel displays formatting examples when there is more than one option to choose from. You can also specify the

FIGURE 16-5.
The Number tab of the Format Cells dialog box lets you change the format of your numeric entries.

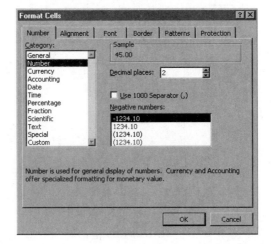

number of decimal places in most of the formats, and in certain cases, the presence of the currency symbol ($) for dollar amounts and of the comma separator (,) for numbers over 1,000.

Table 16-1 describes the purpose of each numeric format category on the Number tab, and shows an example of each.

TABLE 16-1.   The Numeric Formats on the Number Tab

Category	Purpose	Examples
General	The default number format, right-aligned, with no special formatting codes.	15.75 5425
Number	A flexible numeric format that can be enhanced with commas, variable decimal places, and (for negative numbers) colors and parentheses.	3.14159 (1,575.32)
Currency	A general monetary format that can be enhanced with dollar signs, variable decimal places, and (for negative numbers) colors and parentheses.	$75.35 ($1,234.10)
Accounting	A special currency format designed to align columns of monetary values along the decimal point. (The dollar sign appears along the left side of the cell.)	$ 75.00 $ 500.75
Date	A general-purpose date format that displays calendar dates in several standard styles.	1/15/97 Jan-15-97
Time	A general-purpose time format that displays chronological values in several standard styles.	3:30 PM 15:30:58
Percentage	A format that multiplies the value in the selected cell by 100 and displays the result with a percentage symbol (%).	175% 15.125%
Fraction	A format that expresses numbers as fractional values. (You specify the number of digits and denominator.)	1/8 2/16
Scientific	An exponential notation for numbers with a large number of digits.	1.25E-08 4.58E+12
Text	A format that treats numbers like text. (It aligns them on the left edge of the cell and displays them exactly as they are entered.)	500.35 12345.0
Special	A collection of useful formats that follow an alphanumeric pattern, including Zip Code, Phone Number, and Social Security Number.	98109-1234 535-65-2342
Custom	A list of all standard formats (such as formats for foreign currency) and any custom numeric formats you create. (See next section.)	INV-0075 £150.50

In addition to the options on the Number tab, you can use the Formatting toolbar buttons shown in Figure 16-6 to quickly format the numeric entries in selected cells.

FIGURE 16-6.

The buttons controlling numeric formatting on Excel's Formatting toolbar.

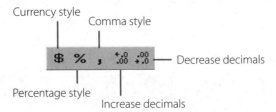

Currency style

Comma style

Decrease decimals

Percentage style

Increase decimals

Changing Excel's Default Currency Symbol

To change the currency symbol used in Excel and other Windows-based applications, open the Control Panel folder and double-click the Regional Settings icon, and then select the country you want to use in the drop-down list box in the Regional Settings tab. For example, if you want Excel to display the British pound sign (£) as its default currency symbol, choose English (British) in the drop-down list box and click OK. Windows 95 will reconfigure your Windows-based applications so that the pound sign (£) is used rather than the dollar sign ($) in all your documents.

If you want to change only particular currency symbols on a worksheet, enter them individually in cells or customize a number format to display them as needed. If standard alphabetical letters or other symbols normally represented on your keyboard are used for the symbol, simply type them in the appropriate format. For example, the currency symbol for German Marks is DM, and the symbol follows the monetary value, such as 550.57 DM. If a special ANSI code is required for the symbol, turn on Num Lock, hold down the Alt key, and type the appropriate four-digit currency code. The following table lists some of the most popular currency symbols and their ANSI codes:

Country	Denomination	Symbol	ANSI Code
United Kingdom	Pound	£	Alt+0163
Japan	Yen	¥	Alt+0165
United States	Cent	¢	Alt+0162

Creating a Custom Number Format

If you routinely enter numeric values in a format that isn't recognized by Excel, you should consider creating a custom number format that you can use to organize nonstandard numeric entries in a consistent and visually appealing manner. For example, you may want to create a custom number format for part numbers or invoice numbers that includes both letters and numbers, or a monetary format that features international currency symbols. To create this type of custom format, choose the Cells command from the Format menu, choose the Number tab, select Custom from the Category list box, and then either:

- Modify an existing format by selecting it in the list box and then editing it in the Type box, or

- enter a new one in the Type box using characters and one or more of Excel's special formatting symbols.

Figure 16-7 shows the Custom option on the Number tab after creating a currency format with the British pound (£) symbol. (The £ symbol is entered by holding down the Alt key and typing *0163* on the numeric keypad with Num Lock on.)

FIGURE 16-7.

To create a custom number format, select the Custom option and modify an existing format or create a new one.

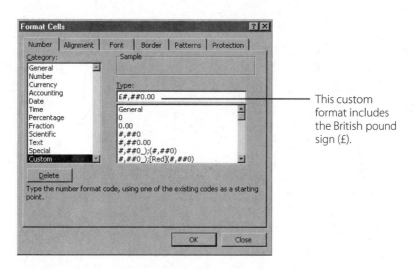

This custom format includes the British pound sign (£).

To help you organize your custom number format, Excel lets you enter placeholders for digits, special symbols, and other useful characters with the formatting symbols shown in Table 16-2 on the following page. You can also enter characters (such as currency symbols, or useful abbreviations such as *Part* or *INV*) to be included in the format. For example, to create a custom part number format that translates the cell value 25 to the formatted part number *Part AA-025*, enter the code

Part AA-000 in the Type text box. To use the custom format later, click the Number tab, click the Custom Category, and then double-click the custom format in the list box. You can also delete custom formats by highlighting the format and clicking the Delete button. (Excel will not let you delete the default formats.)

TABLE 16-2. **Useful Formatting Characters for Building Custom Number Formats**

Character	Purpose	Example	Number Entered	Result
#	Creates a placeholder for significant digits, rounding to fit if necessary.	##.###	50.0048 2.30	50.005 2.3
0	Rounds numbers to fit like the # character, but fills any empty positions with zeros to align numbers and to fill all specified positions	00.00	50.1 5	50.10 05.00
?	Also rounds numbers to fit, but fills any empty positions with spaces rather than extra zeros (if necessary) to align numbers and fill positions.	??.??	5.6 .70 73.27	5.6 .70 73.27
"text"	Adds the characters specified to the value in the cell.	"ID "##	75 2	ID 75 ID 2
comma (,)	Separates thousands in numbers.	#,###	5600	5,600
$,-,+,:,/,(,), space	Standard formatting characters. Each appears as specified in the custom numeric format.	$#.000	500.5	$500.500
%	Multiplies value by 100 and adds percentage symbol.	##%	.25	25%

 TIP

Get Quick Help with Formats

For more information about Excel's formatting characters, start Excel's Help, select Contents And Index, select the Index tab, type *formatting numbers*, and double-click the "custom number formats" subentry. Then select "Custom number, date, and time format codes" and click Display.

Changing Text Font and Text Color

To emphasize headings and distinguish different kinds of information in your worksheet, you can use the Font tab of the Format Cells dialog box, shown in Figure 16-8. The Font tab lets you change the font, style, size, and color of the data in selected cells. It also controls whether data is underlined and lets you create special formatting effects such as strikethrough, superscript, and subscript. The fonts displayed on the Font tab depend on the type of printer you are connected to and the fonts installed on your system. Fonts preceded by a TrueType symbol are TrueType fonts designed to appear in print exactly as they do on the screen. You might also see fonts on the Font tab with tiny printer icons in front of them; these are scalable fonts, which will look sharp when printed but may not display accurately on the screen (the size will probably be right but the character shapes may not exactly match). You can see both typeface symbols in Figure 16-8.

FIGURE 16-8.
You can change the font and text color for selected cells with the Font tab of the Format Cells dialog box.

Scalable fonts ⎯⎯
TrueType ⎯⎯
scalable fonts

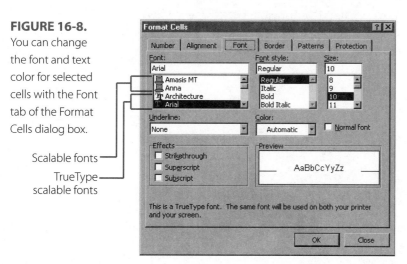

In addition to selecting formatting options on the Font tab, you can also use Excel's Formatting toolbar to change several font and text color options. Figure 16-9 on the following page shows the buttons you can use to increase your formatting speed.

FIGURE 16-9.

Selected text cells can be formatted with these Formatting toolbar buttons.

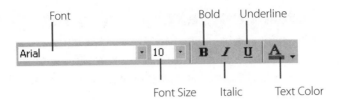

To change the font and text color formatting in one or more cells, follow these steps:

1 Select the cells you want to format. (To format individual characters in a cell, see the sidebar below.)

2 From the Format menu, choose the Cells command, and then click the Font tab.

3 Use the list boxes and check boxes on the Font tab to adjust the font characteristics you want to change. Use the Preview window to verify that the appearance is what you want.

> If you wish to return to the default font setting, turn on the Normal Font check box on the Font tab.

4 When you're finished, click OK. Figure 16-10 shows a sample worksheet with a few useful formatting effects.

Formatting Individual Characters in a Cell

You can also format individual characters in a cell if the entry contains text. This useful feature lets you emphasize important words in a long entry or create dramatic effects in headings. For example, you can format one word with italic in a cell containing many words or change the first letter of a heading to a larger point size. To format individual characters in a cell, double-click the cell and select the characters you want to change. Then choose the Format Cells command and change the attributes you want, or click the appropriate buttons on the Formatting toolbar. When you press Enter, the formatting will take effect.

FIGURE 16-10.

Formatting entries in a worksheet serves to highlight important information.

Individual character formatting

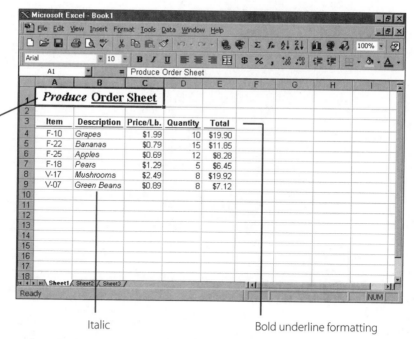

Italic

Bold underline formatting

Adding Borders to Cells

Another useful technique for highlighting specific information in a worksheet is adding borders to important cells with the Border tab of the Format Cells dialog box, shown in Figure 16-11 on the following page. The Border tab lets you place a solid or dashed line along one or more cell edges, allowing you to create a summary line or boxed effect, or even an interesting combination of squares and rectangles. In Excel 97, you can also create diagonal lines in worksheet cells, so that your spreadsheets can contain triangles, "X" patterns, or other intriguing shapes. You specify borders for the cells you have selected by first clicking one of the 14 line styles in the Style box (the "None" style removes existing borders). Then click the lines you want on the "preview" diagram in the Border box, or click the buttons along the left and bottom of the Border box for the same result. As a shortcut, you can also use one of the three border styles in the Presets box: None (to remove an existing border), Outline (to place a border around the outside edge of the selected cells), or Inside (to draw lines along the

FIGURE 16-11.
The Border tab lets
you underline or box
selected cells.

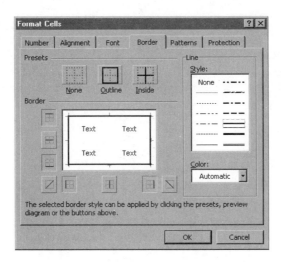

inside edges of selected cells). You can also change the color of the border by opening the Color list box.

Figure 16-12 shows an example of the Outline button at work. In the example, we selected cells A3:E9 in the worksheet, chose the Format

FIGURE 16-12.
The Outline button
quickly adds a
box around the
selected text.

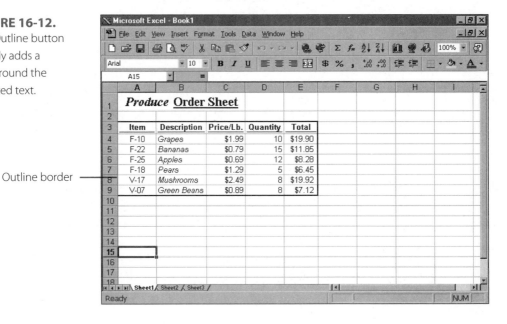

Outline border

> ### Making Borders Faster: Using the Borders Toolbar Button
>
> A useful shortcut for the Border tab is the Borders button on Excel's Formatting toolbar. In this case, using the Formatting toolbar is really much faster than using the Format Cells dialog box, and the toolbar also gives you single-step access to some formatting designs that require multiple steps using the Format Cells dialog box. To use the Borders button, select the range of cells you want to highlight, click the Borders button, and then pick from the 12 border options that appear on the Borders toolbar, as shown in the illustration below. The 12 options are actually border formatting shortcuts, and a few of them feature a combination of aesthetically pleasing styles. For example, the bottom left style—useful for creating worksheet tables—places a light border on the top of the cell and a heavier border on the bottom of the cell. Learning to use these border styles will save considerable time as you format your worksheets.
>
>

Cells command and the Border tab, clicked a heavy border style and the color black, and then clicked the Outline button. The resulting border appears only around the perimeter of the range we selected. If we wanted to have each of the cells outlined as well as the outer perimeter, we could have selected both the Outline button and the Inside button. Or, to provide a line that runs continuously under the table headings in Figure 16-12, we would select the headings and then select just the bottom border line in the weight we want.

Adding Shading to Cells

The Patterns tab of the Format Cells dialog box (see Figure 16-13 on the following page) lets you add a background color and optional colored pattern to one or more cells in your worksheet, to create effects that complement the borders produced by the Border tab. By default, the color you select has no pattern added to it, so you see a solid color

FIGURE 16-13.
The Patterns tab lets you add color background shading to your cells.

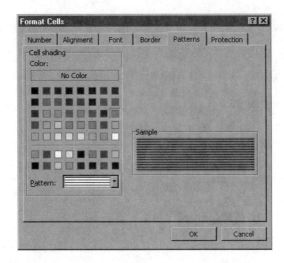

in your cells. However, you can also add a background pattern and change its color from the default black to any of the colors displayed in the Pattern drop-down list. To add color and shading to cells, simply select the cells you want to format, choose the Cells command from the Format menu, click the Patterns tab, pick a Cell shading color, and then pick a shading pattern in a second color from the Pattern drop-down list box.

Color can make a striking addition to your worksheet, and is ideal—if used in moderation—for documents created to be viewed electronically, such as status reports, departmental ledgers, sales projections, and the like. If you don't have a color printer, your color shading effects will be converted to gray tones when you print. (Not to worry, Excel usually does a good job at this.) To see what this conversion is like, you can view your worksheet with the Print Preview command on the File menu. Figure 16-14 shows a sample worksheet with color and pattern shading.

Fill Color

You can also use the Color button on the Formatting toolbar to change the background color (but not the pattern) used in worksheet cells. To remove the existing color in worksheet cells, click the No Color option.

FIGURE 16-14.
Color and pattern shading look nice, even if you don't have a color printer.

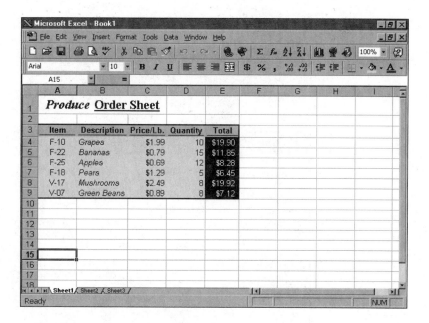

Copying Formatting with the Format Painter Button

Format Painter

Occasionally you'll need to copy the formats from one cell to another cell without copying the data in the cell. For example, you might want to copy the cell formats you used to create a 14-point, bold, Times New Roman heading with a thick border to a second heading you're creating later in the worksheet. Excel lets you accomplish this task with the Format Painter button on the Standard toolbar. To copy formatting with the Format Painter button, follow these steps:

1 Select the cell you want to copy formats from.

2 Click the Format Painter button on the toolbar. A marquee will appear around the selected cell and a paintbrush will be added to the mouse pointer.

3 Select the range of cells you want formatted with the new format.

If you decide you don't like the format you copied, remember that you can choose the Undo command from the Edit menu to remove it. To remove the selection marquee, press Escape.

III

Microsoft Excel

TIP

If you want to copy formats to cells or ranges that are not contiguous, double-click the Format Painter button and then select the cells you want to format one by one. When you've finished, click the Format Painter button again.

Advanced Pattern and Border Formatting

Excel's flexible Patterns and Border tabs allow you to create some innovative shading effects if you have a talent for layout and design. The following illustration shows how Excel's Patterns and Border tabs were used to create a Log Cabin–style wall quilt. This doll quilt pattern (commercially produced by Sweet Peas, Inc. of Redmond, Washington) is based on a symmetric series of rectangular shapes and shading blocks. If you plan to work extensively with shading, we recommend that you use lighter shading tones in cells that contain important information, so that the text is not obscured by dots. Lighter colors also seem to work better than darker colors, especially if black is used for the text color. Have fun!

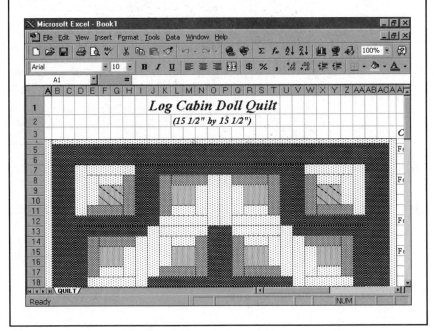

Changing Column Widths and Row Heights

Excel gives you room for about eight digits in a worksheet cell if you use the default 10-point Arial font. In previous versions of Excel, you had to manually adjust the width of a cell whenever you entered a number that exceeded this basic limit. (Excel placed pound characters—########—in the cell to let you know there wasn't enough room to display the number.) In Excel 97, worksheet cells are automatically resized whenever a number doesn't fit. Note that if you intentionally reduce a cell so that a number won't fit, Excel will then display the overflow characters. Most of the time this is a good thing—unless you have a specific reason for keeping a column the default width. Fortunately, it's easy to fiddle with your column widths and row heights if you want to format them in a special way. You can resize rows and columns by dragging with the mouse (the fastest method), or by using commands on the Format menu. We'll cover both techniques in this section.

> **NOTE**

Different columns can be different widths in a worksheet, but each cell in a particular column must be the same width. Likewise, different rows in the worksheet can have different heights, but each cell in a particular row must be the same height.

Adjusting the Height or Width Manually

You can widen a column by dragging the right column edge with the mouse, or by specifying a larger width, using the Width command on the Column submenu of the Format menu. In addition, you can change the height of a row by dragging the lower edge of the row, or by specifying a new height, using the Height command on the Row submenu of the Format menu. Each method is described in the following sections.

> **SEE ALSO**
> For an automatic means of fitting spaces to dates, see "Using the AutoFit Command," page 484.

Changing Column Width with the Mouse

Figure 16-15 on the following page shows how to change column width using the mouse.

III

Microsoft Excel

FIGURE 16-15.
Follow these steps to change the column width using the mouse.

1 Position the mouse pointer on the right edge of the column heading until it changes into a sizing pointer, with arrows on the right and left edges.

2 Drag the sizing pointer to the right or left to change the column width.

3 A dotted line indicates the new column width.

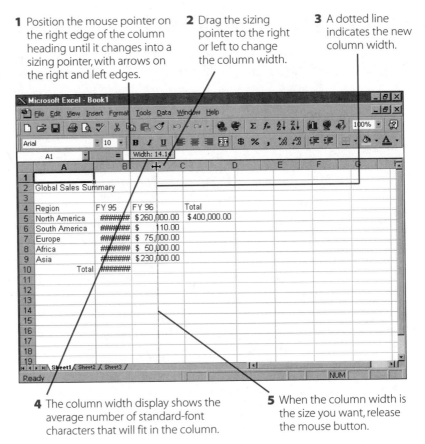

4 The column width display shows the average number of standard-font characters that will fit in the column.

5 When the column width is the size you want, release the mouse button.

To change the width of multiple columns with the mouse, select the columns you want to resize, and then drag and adjust one of the columns—when you release the mouse, each of the columns will be the width of the one you changed.

Changing Column Width Using the Column Width Command

The Width command on the Column submenu is useful if you want to type an exact width for the column you're resizing. The number you specify is the average number of characters that will fit in the cell using the default font (defined as part of the Normal style). To change the column width using the Width command, follow these steps:

1 Select a cell in the column you want to resize. To resize multiple columns, select a cell in each of the columns you want to adjust.

2 From the Format menu, choose the Column command, and then choose the Width command from the submenu. The Column Width dialog box appears.

3 Type the new size you want in the Column Width text box.

4 Click OK to resize the column.

 TIP

Set Your Preferred Column Widths, Instantly

To set the default or "standard" width of columns in your worksheet, choose the Standard Width command from the Column submenu. This command adjusts the width of every column in the worksheet that has not already been resized, or every column you select. To select all the columns of the worksheet, even those you've previously changed, first click the Select All button above row 1 and to the left of column A. This is a good way to customize the cells in your worksheet if you always want them to be a certain shape.

Changing Row Height with the Mouse

Excel automatically adjusts the row height to fit the font and text orientation you're using, but now and then you'll want to increase the row height to add white space to your worksheet or decrease the row height to save room. To change row height with the mouse, follow the steps shown in Figure 16-16 on the following page.

To change the height of multiple rows with the mouse, first select the rows you want to resize, and then drag and adjust one of the rows—when you release the mouse button, each of the rows will be height of the one you adjusted.

Changing Row Height Using the Row Height Command

The Height command on the Row submenu is useful if you want to type an exact height for the row you're resizing. The row height is measured in points and the standard height is based on the size of the default font. To change the row height with the Height command, follow these steps:

1 Highlight a cell in the row you want to resize. If you want to resize multiple rows, select a cell in each of the rows you want to adjust.

FIGURE 16-16.
You can quickly change the row height using the mouse.

4 The row size is displayed in points, and a dotted line indicates the bottom of the new row.

2 Position the mouse pointer on the lower edge of the row heading until it changes into a sizing pointer, with arrows on the top and bottom edges.

3 Drag the sizing pointer down or up to change the row height.

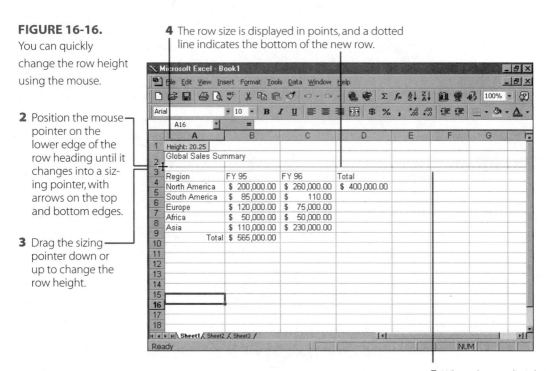

5 When the row height is the size you want, release the mouse button.

6 From the Format menu, choose the Row command, and then choose the Height command from the submenu. The Row Height dialog box appears.

7 Type the new size in points that you want the row or rows to be.

8 Click OK to resize the selected rows.

Using the AutoFit Command

If you want Excel to automatically size your rows or columns for you, use the AutoFit commands on the Column and Row submenus. When you select a column and choose the AutoFit Selection command from the Column submenu, Excel resizes the column to fit the largest entry in the column. This saves you the trouble of manually calculating point sizes or scanning every entry in a column as you drag the mouse. If you select a group of cells in a column, Excel adjusts the width based on the widest cell value in the selection, not the entire column.

Excel automatically resizes rows when you modify the font, so the row AutoFit command is less dramatic. When you select a row and choose the AutoFit command from the Row submenu, Excel simply returns the row to the default height for the largest font being used in the row. The AutoFit command won't compress a row—therefore, you can't read the information in it—but it will remove any extra white space in it.

Hide Rows or Columns for Security or Ease in Working

If you want to hide a row or column in your worksheet, either to shield the data from unauthorized glances or to keep it out of your way while you work, select the row or column you want to hide and choose the Hide command from the Row or Column submenu. When you choose this command, the entire row or column, including the row number or column letter, will seem to disappear from the worksheet (though it hasn't actually been deleted).

To restore the hidden row or column, select the rows or columns on both sides of the hidden entry, and choose the Unhide command from the Row or Column submenu. The hidden row or column will appear as you last saw it.

Applying a Combination of Effects with AutoFormat

If you're formatting a block or table of cells, you can apply several formatting effects in one fell swoop by using the AutoFormat command on the Format menu. The AutoFormat command displays a dialog box that features several predesigned table styles in the Table Format list box. Figure 16-17 shows one of the table formats that creates a three-dimensional effect. To see how the formats look, simply click on a

FIGURE 16-17.
The 3D Effects 2 style is only one of many AutoFormats requiring just a single click to format your worksheet.

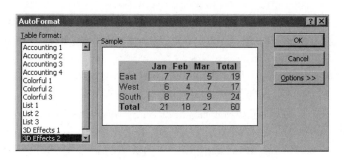

table style and examine the results in the Sample window. When you find the style you want, click OK to format the block of cells you selected as a table. You might try several styles on your own data, to get the true visual effect and determine which one offers the most impact.

By default, the AutoFormat command sets the Number, Border, Font, Patterns, Alignment, and Width/Height options automatically to match the table style you select. You can limit the options used in the Auto-Format by clicking the Options button in the dialog box and turning off the formats you don't want. For example, if you like a particular table but don't want the border that is included, turn off the Border check box (by clicking on it) and click OK to apply other characteristics of the format.

Creating Conditional Formatting

Another new feature of Excel 97 is the ability to add *conditional formatting* to your worksheet, formatting that automatically adjusts depending on the contents of worksheet cells. In plain English, this means that you can highlight important trends in your data—such as the rise in a stock price, or a sudden spurt in your college expenses—based on conditions you set in advance with the Conditional Formatting dialog box. Using this feature, an out-of-the-ordinary number will "jump out" at anyone who routinely uses the worksheet.

The following example shows how to add conditional formatting to a sample worksheet that tracks stock prices. If a stock in the Gain/Loss column rises by more than 20 percent, the conditional formatting will display numbers in bold type on a light-blue diagonal background. If a stock in the falls by more than 20 percent, the number will be displayed in bold type on a solid red background. (Our worksheet is shown in Figure 16-18.)

Here is how you would create such a conditional format.

1 Create a worksheet containing one or more cells of numeric information. (The worksheet can be an invoice, a financial document, a sales report, or any other document with useful numeric data.)

FIGURE 16-18.

Conditional formatting highlights noteworthy numbers automatically, according to your specifications.

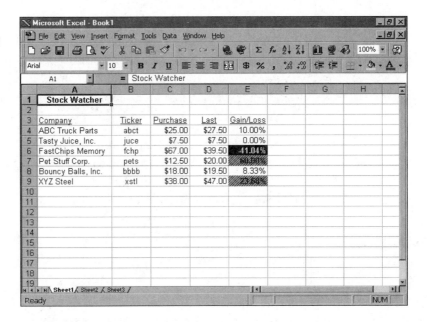

2 Select the cell range to which you want to apply the conditional formatting. (Note that each cell can maintain its own, unique conditional formatting, so that you can set up several different conditions.)

3 From the Format menu, choose the Conditional Formatting command. The Conditional Formatting dialog box appears with several drop-down list boxes.

4 In the first list box, indicate if you want Excel to use the current formula or the current value from the cells that you have selected. (In most cases, you'll want to use the cell value.)

5 In the second list box, indicate the comparison operator you would like to use in the conditional formatting. For our example, we selected greater than (>), because we're looking for stock returns greater than 20 percent.

6 In the third list box, type the number you want to use in the comparison. We typed *20%* or *0.2*, because we want to isolate gains over 20 percent.

III

Microsoft Excel

7 Now click the Format button and specify the formatting you'll use for the cells if the conditional statement you specified in steps 4 through 6 becomes true. A modified Format Cells dialog box appears with three formatting tabs. We selected Bold on the Font tab, plus a diagonal light-blue stripe on the Patterns tab, and then clicked OK.

8 We clicked the Add button in the Conditional Formatting dialog box to add another condition to the scenario. (We also want to highlight losses of more than 20 percent.) The dialog box expands to accept an additional condition.

> **NOTE**

> The Add button lets you add up to three conditions. The Delete button removes conditions you no longer want.

9 We specified less than (<) as the operator in the second drop-down list box, and then typed *-20%* or *-0.2* in the third list box.

10 We clicked the Format button for Condition 2 and selected bold yellow type on a solid black background. Our screen looks like this:

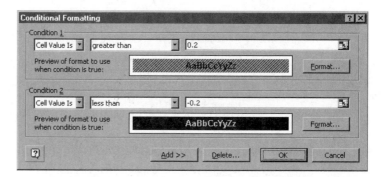

11 Click OK to close the dialog box and see the conditional formatting applied to the selected text. If any numbers fall into the ranges you specified, the formatting you specified will be carried out. Figure 16-18 on the preceding page shows two gains and one loss highlighted by the conditional formatting we entered for this example. Our efforts certainly paid off, especially if we now act on the knowledge of our profits or losses!

Using Styles

If you routinely use the same formatting options for cells in your worksheets, you might want to consider creating a formatting *style* (a collection of formatting choices) that you can save with your workbook and use whenever you format information with the same attributes. After you create a new formatting style, or modify an existing one, you can use that style in any worksheet in your workbook, *or* you can copy the style to other open workbooks. In this section you'll learn the following techniques:

- How to create your own styles

- How to apply existing styles

- How to copy or *merge* styles from other workbooks

Creating Your Own Styles

Styles are created with the Style command on the Format menu. When you choose the Style command, the Style dialog box appears, as shown in Figure 16-19.

FIGURE 16-19.
You can manage the formatting styles in your worksheet with the Style dialog box.

Check boxes indicate which formatting options are set by the current style.

Style Name drop-down list box containing currently defined styles

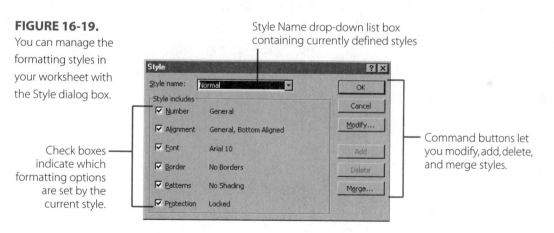

Command buttons let you modify, add, delete, and merge styles.

If the cell you selected before choosing the Style command has not yet been formatted with a style, the Normal style will be displayed in the Style Name box. Excel predefines several styles in addition to the Normal style, including comma, currency, and percent styles. If you want to modify one of these styles throughout the workbook, you select the style in the Style Name drop-down list box, click the Modify button, update the style with the tabs in the Format Cells dialog box, and click OK to return to the Style dialog box. When you click OK in the Style dialog box, the updated style will be changed throughout your workbook.

The easiest way to create a new style is by selecting a cell with formatting you want to save, choosing the Style command, and giving the style a new name. This way of creating a style is called "by example," because you use your own worksheet formatting to define the style.

> **NOTE**

You can also create styles from scratch by using the Add button in the Style dialog box.

The following steps show you how to create a new style by example. The style we created is the vertically oriented column heading for Claude, shown in cell C3 in Figure 16-20. The heading is bold, dark blue, center-aligned, and rotated up 90 degrees in the cell. We call it Vertical Head.

FIGURE 16-20.

To create a new style "by example," you first select a cell in your worksheet with the style you want to save.

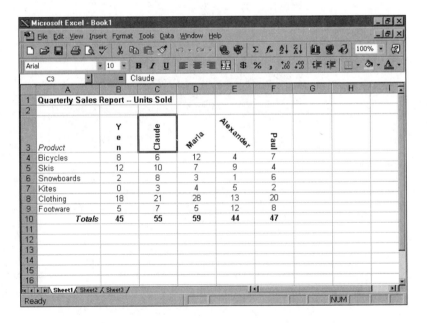

To create the Vertical Head style "by example," we followed these steps:

1 Format the cell you want to create your style from. For example, you could use the Alignment tab of the Format Cells dialog box to center the text horizontally and change the orientation, and then use the Font tab to change the font style to bold and dark blue.

2 Select the cell you just formatted.

3 Choose the Style command from the Format menu.

4 Type *Vertical Head* (or another name of your choice) in the Style Name text

6 Click OK to add the new style to your workbook.

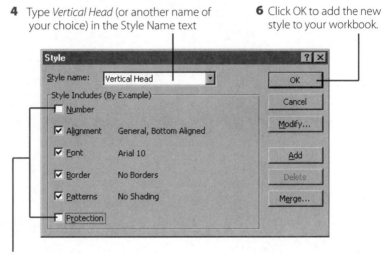

5 Turn off (remove the check marks from) the Number and Protection check boxes, because these options aren't relevant to the style you're creating.

When a style option is turned off (no check mark in its check box), it means that anytime you apply the associated style, the selected cells will keep their existing formatting for these categories

 TIP

To delete a custom style you no longer want, select the style in the Style Name drop-down list box and click the Delete button.

III

Microsoft Excel

Applying Existing Styles

To apply an existing style in your workbook, either a predefined style or one that you have created, select the cell or range of cells you want to format with the style, and then follow these steps:

1 From the Format menu, choose the Style command to open the Style dialog box.

2 Click the Style Name drop-down list box to display the styles available in your workbook.

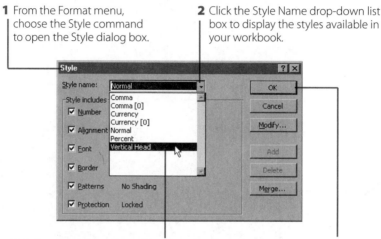

3 Select the style you want. We want the Vertical Head style created above.

4 Click OK. Excel formats the selected cells with the specified style.

Merging Styles from Other Workbooks

When you create a new style, you can use it only in the workbook where you create it—the new style is saved in the current workbook and will not appear in other workbooks. (This way, you won't mix up styles for your stock portfolio with those for your college expense budget.) However, you can copy or merge styles from other workbooks into the current workbook by using the Merge button in the Style dialog box. Merging is a powerful tool, and you should use it with some caution. If the workbook you merge styles into has matching style names, the new styles will override your existing styles (without warning) and be applied throughout your workbook.

Merging styles is a useful way to give your workbooks a consistent look. Excel templates (discussed in the next section) can also be used to format documents in a standard manner.

To merge styles from other Excel workbooks, follow these steps:

1 Open the source workbook (the workbook you want to copy styles from) and the destination workbook (the workbook you want to copy the styles to).

2 From the Window menu, click the destination workbook (its name should appear near the bottom of the menu) to make it the active window.

3 From the Format menu, choose the Style command.

4 Click the Merge button to display the Merge Styles dialog box shown below:

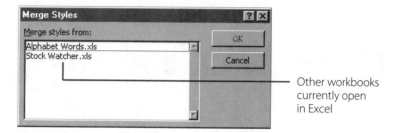

Other workbooks currently open in Excel

5 Select the name of the workbook you want to copy styles from (the source workbook), and then click OK.

Excel copies all the styles from the source workbook to the destination workbook. If the source workbook contains formatting styles with the same names as in the destination workbook, a warning message will appear asking whether you want to merge the styles anyway. If you click Yes, the styles will be merged and the source styles will be applied throughout the workbook.

WARNING

The Undo command does *not* reverse the effects of the Merge Styles dialog box. Be sure you want to copy over *all* the styles from the source workbook before you click the Merge button. (Remember that you can delete unwanted styles before the merge, by using the Delete button in the Style dialog box.)

III

Microsoft Excel

Creating Templates

Using formatting styles is a good way to organize existing data in a standard format. If you're routinely creating similar documents from scratch, however—such as monthly reports, purchase orders, or product invoices—consider creating an Excel template. A *template* is a file that serves as a model for worksheets you create in your workbooks. You can use the many preformatted templates that are included with the Microsoft Office software, or you can create your own templates that you can use whenever you want to create data in a particular format. In this section, you'll learn:

- How to open and modify an existing template file

- How to create a new template file

SEE ALSO
You can use Office templates and wizards to create many standard documents automatically. For more information, see "Creating Files with a Document Template," page 21.

New

> **TIP**
>
> **Use an Existing Template**
> If you just want to use an *existing* Excel template to create a new worksheet (rather than *modify* a template to create a new *type* of worksheet), choose the New command from the File menu or click the New button on the Standard toolbar. Select a template from an appropriate tab, and then click OK.

Opening and Modifying an Existing Template File

To open an existing template file—either a template included with Office or one you created on your own—choose the Open command from the Excel File menu, specify Templates (*.xlt) in the Files Of Type list box, and double-click the template file icon in the files list box. You can also click the Open A Document button on the Microsoft Office Shortcut Bar to display the Open dialog box. Unless you intend to make changes to the original template, your first step after opening a template should be to save the workbook under a new filename to protect the original template.

To open an existing template, follow these steps:

Open

1 From the File menu, choose the Open command or click the Open button on the Standard toolbar. The Open dialog box appears:

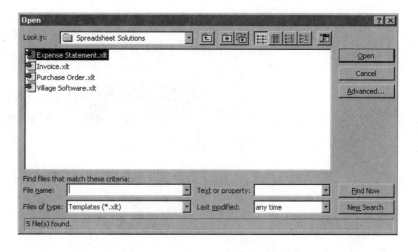

2 Select Templates (*.xlt) in the Files Of Type drop-down list box.

3 Select the folder containing the template you want to open. Office creates a Templates folder in the folder in which you installed Office. The Templates folder contains several folders of its own; you'll find several useful Excel templates in the Spreadsheet Solutions folder, as shown above.

 TIP

For a description of each of the templates included in Microsoft Excel, search for "Templates, built-in templates" in the Excel online Help.

4 Double-click the template file you want to open. The template appears in a window, such as the one shown on the next page.

If the template was included with the Office software, it typically includes several worksheet tabs, operating instructions, and a small template toolbar, which gives you access to template Help and other useful features.

5 From the File menu, choose the Save As command. When the Save As dialog box appears, give the template a new filename. You may want to save it with the Excel templates in the Spreadsheet Solutions folder, or you can select another folder. Then click Save. Now you're ready to make changes to your new template.

III

Microsoft Excel

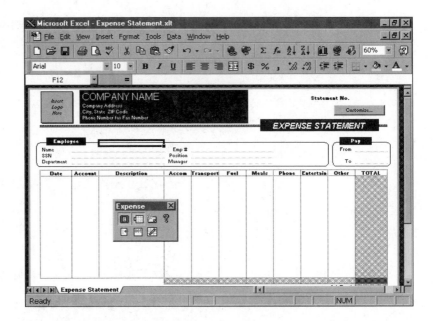

Creating a New Template File

To make a new template file using one of your own workbooks as a model, complete the following steps. When you're finished, you'll have a template you can use each time you want to create a worksheet with the formatting you've included.

1 Open the workbook you want to save as a template file. The illustration on the facing page shows an invoice worksheet that is being saved as a template.

2 From the File menu, choose the Save As command. The Save As dialog box appears.

3 Select Template (*.xlt) in the Save As Type drop-down list box.

4 Enter a name for the template in the File Name text box, specify a folder location for the template by using the Save In list box, and then click Save.

5 Close the workbook you saved as a template. The next time you want to use the template as a worksheet model, choose the New command from the File menu, locate the template, and double-click on it.

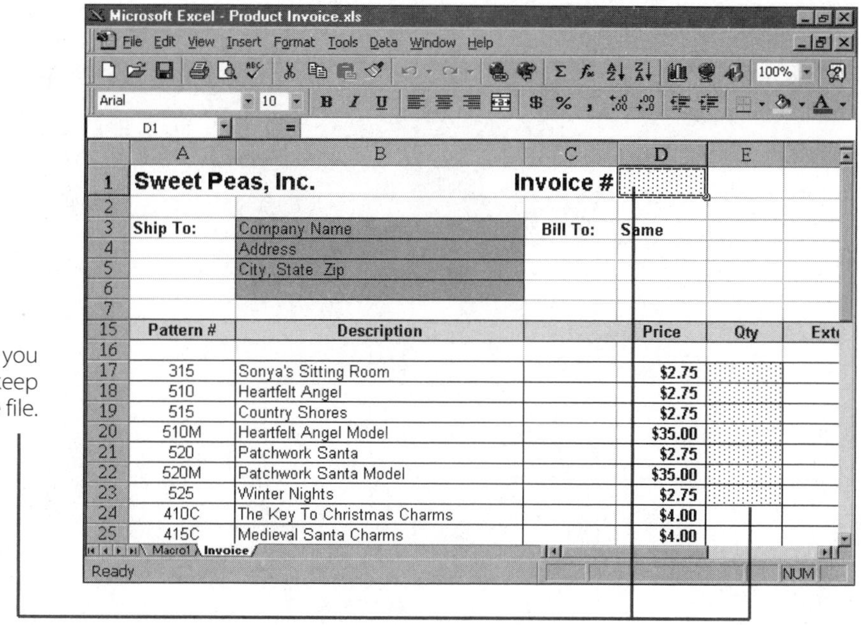

Remove data you don't want to keep in the template file.

Changing Page Breaks

After you format your worksheet, you might want to adjust where the page breaks fall, particularly for longer worksheets. A *page break* is a formatting code that tells your printer to stop printing information on one page and start printing on the next page. Excel adds a page break to your worksheet automatically when a page is full, and identifies the division with a light dashed line. (Excel adds both vertical and horizontal page breaks.) If you don't want to see these breaks as you work, choose the Options command from the Tools menu, click the View tab, and then turn off the Page Breaks Window option.

You can set your own page breaks manually in the worksheet. For example, you might choose to place a page break above a table to keep all the table entries on the same page. To set a manual page break in the worksheet, follow the steps shown in Figure 16-21 on the following page.

The highlighted cell will become the upper left corner of the new page, and the manual page break will appear as a bold dashed line.

III

Microsoft Excel

FIGURE 16-21.
In Normal view, Excel indicates page breaks with bold, dashed lines.

2 Choose the Page Break command from the Insert menu.

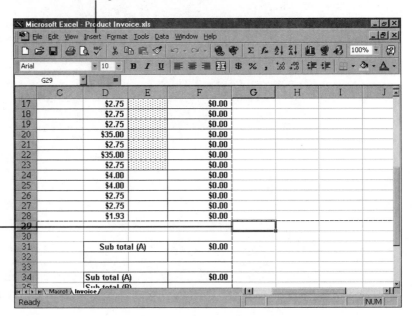

1 Select the cell below and to the right of where you want to insert the page break.

 **TIP**

Remove a Manual Page Break
To remove both the bottom and right edges of a page break, click the cell below and to the right of the page break and choose Remove Page Break from the Insert menu. You can also remove just the bottom of the page break or just the right side of the page break by clicking any cell directly below or directly to the right of the page break.

Using Page Break Preview

Excel 97 also provides a special worksheet view called Page Break Preview that quickly identifies the page breaks in your worksheet and lets you easily manipulate them. Page Break Preview shows you a miniature version of your worksheet (a little like the Print Preview command on the File menu), but marks page breaks with a thick bold line and highlights page numbers with giant labels so that you can quickly find your place. (See Figure 16-22.) To turn on the page break preview, choose the Page Break Preview command from the View menu; to turn it off, choose the Normal command from the View menu.

FIGURE 16-22.
To change a page break, simply drag a break line to a new location.

Page break line

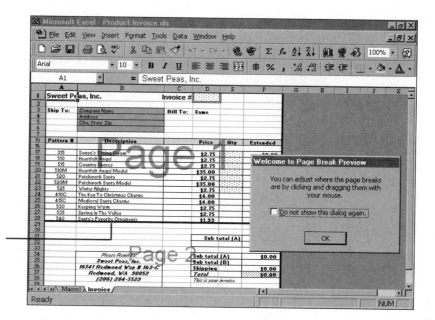

To view and modify page breaks in Page Break Preview, follow these steps:

1 From the View menu, choose the Page Break Preview command. Excel starts Page Break Preview mode, as shown in Figure 16-22.

2 If you see a dialog box with a welcome message, read the instructions about modifying page breaks, and then click OK. (You can suppress this dialog box by clicking Do Not Show This Dialog Again.)

3 Examine the page breaks in your worksheet by using the vertical and horizontal scroll bars. Individual pages will be marked with large labels, and page breaks will be marked with bold lines.

⭐ **TIP**

Page Break Preview is an active editing mode, so you can add information to worksheet cells, select ranges, issue commands, or edit individual entries while you preview your page breaks. However, you'll probably find it easier to read the contents of worksheet cells in Normal view.

III

Microsoft Excel

4 To change a page break marked with a bold line, drag the break line with the mouse to a new location in the worksheet. When you release the mouse button, Excel will repaginate the worksheet and display the new page break. (If you think better of the change, you can reinstate the old page break, by simply clicking the Undo button on the Standard toolbar.)

5 When you're finished working in Page Break Preview, choose the Normal command from the View menu.

Adding Artwork

Nothing improves the presentation of a report like tastefully applied artwork. After you've worked your magic with formatting commands, you may want to add some pictures to enhance the appeal of the worksheet you've created. Excel features a special Picture submenu on the Insert menu that lets you add artwork to worksheets. The submenu commands let you insert artwork from files (such as bitmaps or metafiles), add electronic images from the Microsoft Clip Gallery, create your own drawings with the Draw toolbar, add textual effects with Word-Art, or insert images from a scanner. These commands are similar to the tools available on Word's Picture submenu (under the Insert menu), so if you want to learn more about them, read the section "Adding Graphics," page 314.

If you're interested in geographic maps, you may also want to read about Excel's unique Map command, which lets you add a thematic map to your worksheet, complete with customized geographic regions, labels, and numeric information from your worksheet. For more information, see "Creating Special Effects," page 596.

CHAPTER 17

Organizing Information with Workbooks

I f worksheets are the basic building blocks used to store information in Excel, workbooks are the organizational tools you can use to manage data effectively. By default, each Excel workbook contains three worksheets. In this chapter, you'll learn how to switch between worksheets, name worksheets, add worksheets to a workbook, delete unwanted worksheets from a workbook, and rearrange worksheets. You'll also learn how to work with more than one workbook at once, how to link information between worksheets and workbooks, how to create and manage shared workbooks on a network, and how to protect worksheets and workbooks with password protection. When you're finished, you'll have all the tools you need to manage workbooks effectively.

Managing Worksheets

Workbooks help you organize the reports, ledgers, tables, and forms you use every day. In the first electronic spreadsheets, users typically created a new file for each worksheet they built. This approach worked fine for casual spreadsheet users, but experienced business users, who often worked with literally hundreds of worksheets, were soon swamped with files and folders. (If this sounds like you now, you'll like this section!) Excel now provides the ability to create default workbooks containing up to 255 worksheets. To smooth out the file management problem, all the worksheets in a workbook are now stored in one file. Although you're not actually required to place more than one worksheet in a workbook, this organizational feature gives you the option of collecting similar worksheets in one place. For example, you could store all the worksheets related to product development costs (Research, Manufacturing, Marketing, Packaging, and so on) into one workbook entitled 1997 Development Costs.

In the first part of this chapter, you'll learn the basic skills needed to manage worksheets in workbooks. You'll learn how to:

- Switch between worksheets in a workbook

- Give names to your worksheets

- Delete worksheets from a workbook

- Add worksheets to a workbook

- Change the order of worksheets in a workbook

Switching Between Worksheets

By default, each new Excel workbook contains three identical worksheets, named Sheet1, Sheet2, and Sheet3. (This is a reduction from 16 worksheets, the default in Excel version 7.) Each worksheet is identified by a *worksheet tab* at the bottom of the worksheet window, as shown in Figure 17-1. To switch between worksheets, you simply click the worksheet tab you want to display, and it appears as the active worksheet in the workplace. To the left of the worksheet tabs are the *tab scroll buttons* which you can use to display worksheet tabs not

FIGURE 17-1.
Switching between
worksheets.

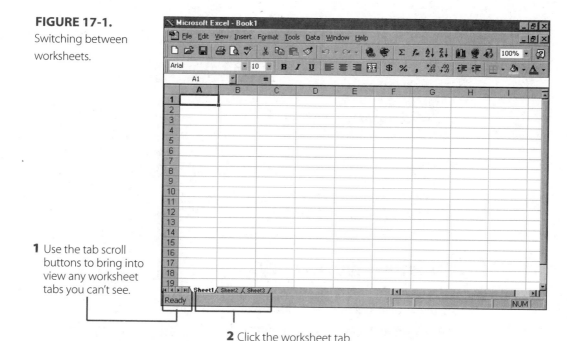

1 Use the tab scroll
buttons to bring into
view any worksheet
tabs you can't see.

2 Click the worksheet tab.

currently visible. The outside navigation arrows display the first and
last tabs in the workbook, respectively, and the inside arrows display
hidden tabs to the left and right, respectively.

To switch between worksheets in a workbook, follow the steps in
Figure 17-1.

Naming Worksheets

The default names for worksheets—Sheet1, Sheet2, and so on—are just
placeholders for more useful and intuitive names that you devise. You
can name or rename a worksheet at any time by double-clicking the
worksheet tab to select the title, and then typing a new name in the tab.
Figure 17-2 on the following page shows the two-step process. (To cancel your edit, press the Escape key.) You can use up to 31 characters in
your worksheet names (including spaces), but remember that the more
characters you use for the name, the less room you leave for other worksheet tabs. It's a good idea to strike a balance between meaningful and
brief names.

III

Microsoft Excel

FIGURE 17-2.
Renaming a
worksheet tab.

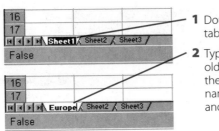

1 Double-click the worksheet tab you want to rename.

2 Type the new name over the old name, paste a name from the Clipboard, or edit the old name using the text pointer, and then press Enter.

You can also use a menu command to rename the worksheet that is currently visible: Choose Sheet from the Format menu, choose Rename from the submenu, and then type the new worksheet name and press Enter.

Deleting Worksheets

While each empty worksheet in a workbook only takes up about 500 bytes of disk space, if you don't plan to use all the worksheets in a workbook, you can delete the unused worksheets to save space. (You can always add new worksheets later.) To delete a worksheet, you display it in the workplace window, and then choose the Delete Sheet command from the Edit menu.

⊘ WARNING

Once you delete a worksheet—even if it contains several rows and columns of data—the worksheet will be permanently erased and you won't be able to undo the command.

To delete a worksheet, follow these steps:

1 Display the worksheet you want to delete in the workplace window by selecting its tab.

2 To select multiple sheets, hold down Ctrl and click additional tabs, or hold down Shift to select a tab and all the tabs in between.

3 From the Edit menu, choose the Delete Sheet command. Excel displays the following dialog box to confirm the deletion:

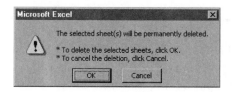

4 Click OK to permanently delete the worksheet.

Inserting Worksheets

Excel lets you add a new, empty worksheet to your workbook at any time with the Worksheet command on the Insert menu. When you insert a new worksheet, Excel places it before the active worksheet and numbers it consecutively; that is, the eleventh worksheet will be given the name Sheet11. Figure 17-3 shows how a new sheet will be inserted if your workbook contains three worksheets and if West is the active worksheet. After you insert a new worksheet, you can change its name, as described in "Naming Worksheets," page 503.

FIGURE 17-3.
Excel inserts a new worksheet before the active worksheet in the workbook.

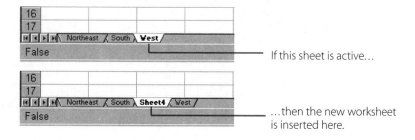

If this sheet is active…

…then the new worksheet is inserted here.

To add a new worksheet to your workbook, follow these steps:

1 Click the worksheet tab that you want shifted to the right to make room for a new worksheet.

2 From the Insert menu, choose Worksheet. A new worksheet appears in the workbook, and it becomes the active worksheet.

If you right-click a worksheet tab, a shortcut menu appears with commands that let you insert, delete, rename, move, or copy the active worksheet. You can use this technique to speed up many of your workbook management tasks.

III

Microsoft Excel

Changing the Default Number of Worksheets

By default, Excel 97 displays three worksheets in a workbook. However, you can adjust this number by choosing the Options command from the Tools menu and specifying a new number on the General tab. On the General tab (shown below), specify the number of worksheets you want in the Sheets In New Workbook text box, either by typing a new number in the text box or by using the text box scroll arrows to increase or decrease the current value. You can specify any number from 1 through 255. This feature is very useful, especially if you find you're usually adding extra worksheets to your workbooks.

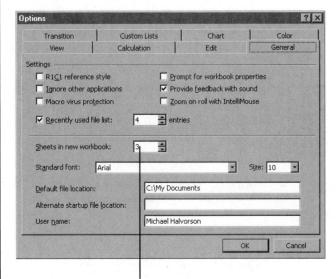

Set the default number of worksheets for new workbooks here.

Moving Worksheets

If you don't like the placement of the worksheets you've created, you can easily move them within the workbook by using a simple drag and drop technique. To relocate a worksheet, simply click the worksheet tab you want to move and then drag it between two other worksheet tabs. (A tiny arrow appears to help you place the worksheet.) Figure 17-4 shows how the two-step process works.

FIGURE 17-4.
To move a worksheet, drag the worksheet tab to a new location.

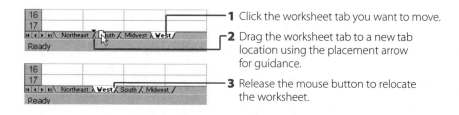

1 Click the worksheet tab you want to move.

2 Drag the worksheet tab to a new tab location using the placement arrow for guidance.

3 Release the mouse button to relocate the worksheet.

 TIP

Make a Duplicate Worksheet with the Ctrl Key

You can duplicate a worksheet in a workbook by holding down the Ctrl key while you drag a tab from one location to another. This procedure creates an extra copy of the worksheet in the workbook, with identical rows and columns. The name will be copied also, with a "(2)" added to show that it's the second worksheet with that name.

Linking Information Between Worksheets

SEE ALSO

To learn how to link worksheets together in different workbooks, see "Linking Information Between Workbooks," page 512.

When you create a workbook containing several worksheets, you'll often want to reference the data in one worksheet when you build a formula in another worksheet. Setting up a connection between worksheets is called creating a *link* in Excel terminology. For example, if your workbook contains a separate worksheet for each sales region in the country, you could create a Summary worksheet that included sales data from each of the supporting worksheets. Linked worksheets also provide an additional advantage: When you make changes to the source worksheet, Excel automatically updates the related information in the linked worksheet.

The following procedure shows you how to create formulas that link worksheets together. The workbook used as an example contains five worksheet tabs, named Summary, Northwest, South, Midwest, and West. The four regional worksheets contain quarterly sales data for each of a company's sales representatives active in the region. (The sales reps are listed individually by name.) The Summary worksheet

III

Microsoft Excel

presents an overview of the sales activity throughout the year and uses several SUM formulas to calculate the quarterly totals from each of the linked worksheets. You might want to use this worksheet structure in your own workbooks.

To create formulas that calculate totals from linked worksheets and place them on a single summary worksheet, follow these steps. Our example uses regional sales data.

1 Create your regional worksheets in a workbook, or use your own data containing a similar pattern of detail-level worksheets that you want to be summed in a summary worksheet. The following screen shows the sample worksheet named Northeast, containing quarterly sales figures for the six sales reps active in the Northeast sales region.

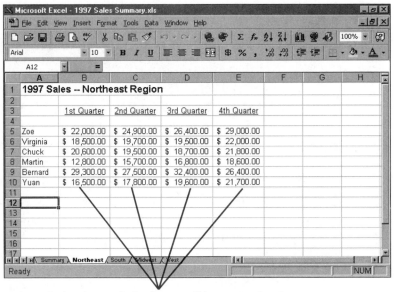

Each column of sales figures will be summed and displayed in the Summary worksheet.

2 Add a Summary worksheet to your workbook to display the totals from the other worksheets. You need to do this in two steps. Add the worksheet using the Worksheet command on the Insert menu. Then change the name of the worksheet to *Summary* or another appropriate name.

3 Add formulas that compute totals with the SUM function to the Summary worksheet. Begin each formula by typing =SUM(

4 To specify a range for the SUM function, click the worksheet tab you want to include in the formula, and then select the range of cells you want to use within the link. For example, to add the six sales figures from the 1st Quarter column in the Northeast worksheet, click the Northeast worksheet tab, and then select cells B5 through B10. The customized formula appears in the formula bar, with the worksheet name and cell range separated by an exclamation mark (Northeast!B5:B10).

5 Press the Enter key to complete the formula. Excel will add a closing parenthesis to complete the function. Excel calculates the result and displays it in cell B4 of the Summary worksheet, as shown in the following illustration. The completed formula also appears in the formula bar.

Formula for cell B4

Sum of 1st Quarter Sales from the Northeast worksheet

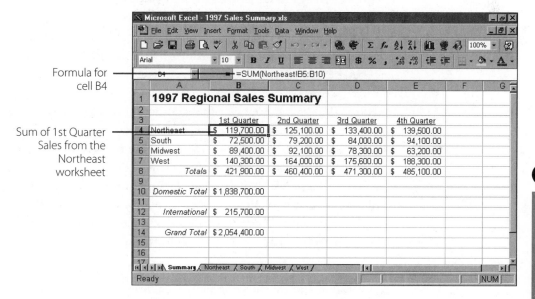

6 Repeat steps 2 through 5 to add linking formulas for the remaining summation cells.

Using More Than One Workbook

As you complete daily tasks with Excel, you'll often find it necessary to open additional workbooks to review sales figures, prepare an invoice, copy data, or complete other work. Excel lets you load as many workbooks into memory as your system can handle. Each workbook appears in its own window, and you can switch between workbook windows by choosing the workbook's filename from the Window menu. (Excel lists files on the Window menu in the order you open them.) The following section shows you how to:

- Switch between workbook windows

- Link information between open workbooks

- Use multiuser workbooks in a network setting

Switching Between Workbooks

You can open additional workbooks in Excel by choosing Open from the File menu, and then locating the workbook you want to open in the Open dialog box and double-clicking on it. When multiple workbooks are loaded, you can view them one at a time in maximized windows (the default) or side by side in the workplace. To view workbook windows side by side, use the Arrange command on the Window menu. The Arrange dialog box includes four useful window orientation options that display different parts of the workbook: These options are Tiled, Horizontal, Vertical, and Cascade. Figure 17-5 shows how two open workbooks are arranged if you select the Vertical option button and click OK. To switch between these open workbooks, simply click the workbook you want to work with. (The active workbook's title bar will be displayed using your system's Active Title Bar color settings.)

You can also switch between open workbook windows by using a key combination and by choosing filenames from the Window menu.

To switch between windows using the keyboard, follow these steps:

1 Load the workbooks you want to work with by using the Open command.

2 Cycle among workbooks by pressing Ctrl+F6. (To cycle through the workbooks in the opposite direction, press Ctrl+Shift+F6.)

FIGURE 17-5.
The Arrange command lets you view more than one workbook at once.

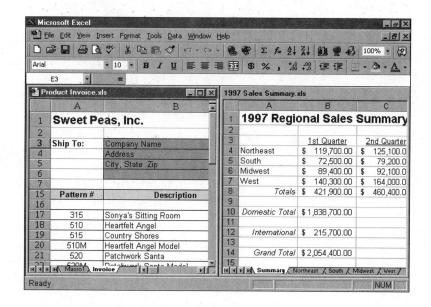

To switch between workbooks with the Window menu, follow these steps:

1 Load the workbooks you want to work with by using the Open command.

2 From the Window menu, choose the workbook you want to display in the active window. The following illustration shows what the Window menu looks like with four workbooks loaded. The active workbook (1997 Sales Summary) is identified by a check mark next to its filename.

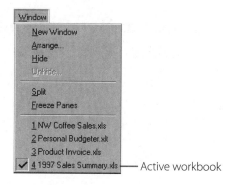

Active workbook

III

Microsoft Excel

Saving a Workspace File

If you often use the same collection of workbooks in Excel, consider creating a *workspace file* to save information about which workbooks are open and how they appear on the screen. The next time you want to use the workbooks, simply open the workspace file, and everything will be arranged as it was when you last saved the workspace. The workspace file doesn't include changes you make to your worksheets—you need to save these separately with the Save or Save As command—but it *does* keep track of your open windows and worksheets, so that you can pick up right where you left off.

To save the arrangement of open workbooks in a workspace file, follow these steps:

1   Open and organize your workbooks as you would like them saved in the workspace file. (Creating a workspace file is a little like taking a picture, so get everything positioned just where you want it.)

2   From the File menu, choose Save Workspace. The Save Workspace dialog box appears.

3   Type a name for the workspace file in the File Name text box, and specify a folder location if necessary.

4   Click OK to save the workspace file. (You might also be prompted to save one or more of the open workbooks.)

When you're ready to open the workspace file later, simply load it with the Open command on the File menu, as you would any file. Your workbooks and worksheets will appear just as you left them, including any cell selections you had made.

Linking Information Between Workbooks

Earlier in this chapter, you learned how to build formulas that reference other worksheets in the workbook. You can also build formulas that reference worksheets in other workbooks. Before you create the linked formula, however, each of the workbooks you plan to use must be open. The following example adds the total revenue from a workbook named 1997 International Sales to the domestic total calculated in the 1997 Regional Sales workbook.

If you want to create formulas that reference other workbooks, follow these steps:

1 Open the workbooks you plan to reference in your formulas. The following screen shows a sample workbook named 1997 International Sales, which computes the total revenue received by a company from areas outside the United States:

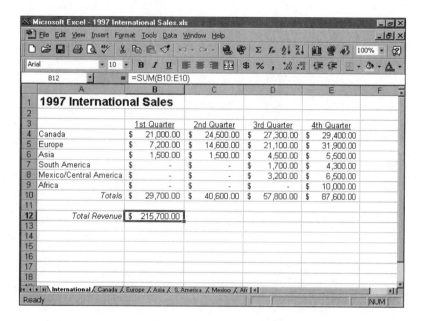

2 Add a formula to your worksheet that references cells in other workbooks. For example, to copy a grand total from the International worksheet in the 1997 International Sales workbook, start in the cell where you want the copy, type an equal sign (=), click the Window menu, click the 1997 International Sales workbook, click the International worksheet tab, click the cell with the total you want to incorporate (B12 in this example), and press Enter. The linking formula appears in the formula bar, with the workbook filename enclosed in square brackets, an exclamation mark following the worksheet name, and dollar signs ($) preceding the linked cell's column letter and row number. Your screen will look similar to the one on the following page.

III

Microsoft Excel

Formula showing the linked workbook, worksheet, and cell address

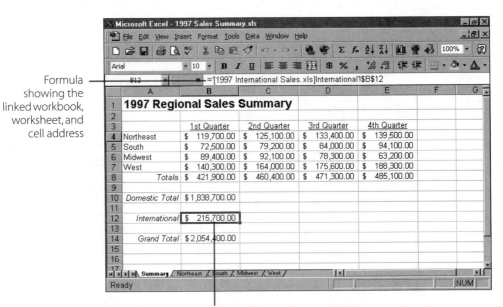

Cell containing data from a different workbook

 TIP

Consolidate Worksheets with Identical Formats

If you want to link together several worksheets that share a common organizational format, you can also use the Consolidate command on the Data menu to assemble workbook information automatically. When you consolidate worksheets, you can use one or more *statistical functions* on the cell ranges you select to get useful information about your data. The statistical functions available include Sum, Count, Average, Max, Min, and StdDev. (You'll learn more about using statistical functions in Chapter 19, "Crunching Numbers with Formulas and Functions.") For a useful tutorial on applying the Consolidate command, search for *consolidating data* in the Excel online Help, pick a scenario you're interested in, and follow the instructions.

Managing Shared Workbooks

If you have access to a shared folder on the Internet or an attached network, you can create shared workbooks that can be opened and used by several people simultaneously. This powerful feature lets you distribute the responsibility for creating group tasks, such as revolving product inventories, incoming customer orders, or corporate mailing

SEE ALSO

If your workbook contains information arranged under uniform headings, you can set it up as an Excel *database*. See Chapter 21, "Managing Information in Lists."

lists. (In previous versions of Excel, shared workbooks were called multiuser workbooks or shared lists.) Workbooks have a few limitations on the changes you can make to them while they are being shared. These are detailed in the online Help under "shared workbooks, limitations." But you can insert and delete rows and columns, modify worksheet cells, and sort entries based on one or more criteria. The following steps show you how to create and maintain a shared workbook.

 NOTE

To use a shared workbook, you need access to a shared folder on the Internet or a computer network. If you or your colleagues don't have access to a shared folder, ask your network system administrator how to get one or how to create one on your own computer.

Creating a Shared Workbook

To create a shared workbook that can be used by several users simultaneously, follow these steps:

SEE ALSO

To learn how to add comments to worksheet cells, see "Entering Comments," page 432.

1 Build the workbook you want to share as you would normally. Because the worksheets in your workbook will be used by several users, take extra care to format the contents clearly and concisely. You might also want to add cell comments with operation instructions and tips.

2 From the Tools menu, choose Share Workbook. When the Share Workbook dialog box appears, click the Editing tab. You'll see the dialog box shown on the following page.

3 Turn on the Allow Editing check box to define the workbook as a shared workbook, and then click OK. A dialog box appears asking you if it's all right to save your workbook (a requirement if the workbook is to be shared).

4 Click OK to save the workbook. After you save the workbook, the word Shared appears in the title bar between brackets, indicating you're now editing a multiuser or shared workbook. As long as the Allow Changes check box is turned on in the Editing tab, you won't be able to save formulas in the workbook or modify any cell formatting.

III

Microsoft Excel

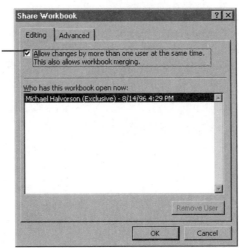

Turn on this check box to share the worksheet.

5 Use Windows Explorer to copy the shared workbook to a shared folder on your network, and then notify your associates the file is available for use. From this moment on, each time a user saves changes to the shared workbook, their changes will be copied to the shared list and any changes made by other users will be uploaded into their system as well. Excel handles and distributes the revisions automatically!

Monitoring a Shared Workbook

Once a shared workbook is active, you can monitor it with the Share Workbook command to find out who is using it. To see a list of the users working on the file, follow these steps:

1 From the Tools menu, choose the Share Workbook command. The Share Workbook dialog box appears.

2 On the Editing tab, a list of the users working on the file appears, as shown in Figure 17-6. The time displayed next to each user is the moment that user started editing the workbook.

3 If you want to prohibit a user from working on the shared work-book, highlight the user's name and click the Remove button. The user will be excluded from the editing session, and won't be able to modify the shared copy of the file.

FIGURE 17-6.

To see who is working on a shared workbook with you, use the Editing tab of the Share Workbook dialog box.

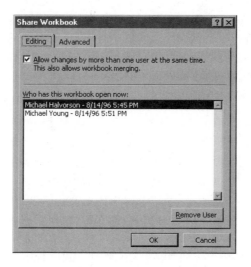

To "turn off" the shared workbook feature and disable multiuser editing in a workbook, choose Share Workbook from the Tools menu, click the Editing tab, and turn off the Allow Changes check box.

> ⚠ **WARNING**
>
> Don't turn off the Share Worksheet feature until each of your users has finished editing the workbook and has saved their changes, or you'll lock them out of the file. Closing a shared workbook discards any revision information in the file and prohibits users from saving their changes to the multiuser copy of the workbook, even if you reopen sharing.

Accepting or Rejecting Revisions

If users enter data or change data in different cells, each change will be accepted automatically and updated in everyone's workbook as each user saves their workbook. The changes to the workbook coming from other users will be highlighted after each save. Moving the cell pointer over each highlight will pop up a window showing who made the change.

An interesting problem arises, however, when two or more users change the same cells in different ways. Should Excel accept one person's entry for the shared workbook, or the other's? Excel gives you two options for resolving the conflict.

In the first method, the most recently saved workbook's values replace the values that were entered into the cells on an earlier save. Choose this approach when you feel confident that later changes are always more accurate than earlier changes, such as when entering order numbers or tracking inventory quantities.

The second method enables the user saving the shared workbook to review the conflicting cells and decide whose changes take precedence. The user saving the workbook can accept all their own changes, accept all of another's changes, or decide cell by cell. Choose this method if you want to review the accuracy of changes before accepting them, or if you want to give one person's changes precedence over those of another. These choices and other multiuser options are provided on the Advanced tab of the Share Workbook dialog box, shown in Figure 17-7. To customize how your shared workbook deals with conflicts in a multiuser environment, use these settings.

FIGURE 17-7.
Customizing how workbooks are shared using the Advanced tab.

Select how you want to resolve conflicting edits.

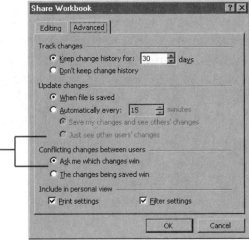

When you're ready to examine the list of editing activities in a shared workbook, choose Track Changes from the Tools menu, and choose either Highlight Changes or Accept Or Reject Changes from the submenu. (Note that the Track Changes submenu is available only when a shared workbook is active and when Shared appears in the Excel title

FIGURE 17-8.

To have Excel automatically highlight new edits in a shared workbook, use the Highlight Changes command on the Track Changes submenu.

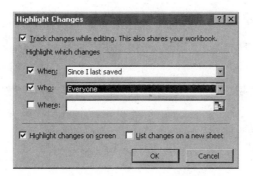

bar.) The Highlight Changes command displays a dialog box asking you to specify the editing changes you want Excel to highlight in the workbook, as shown in Figure 17-8. You can highlight changes that were made at a particular time, by a particular user, or in a particular worksheet range. When you click OK, Excel highlights each modified cell in the workbook that matches your search criteria with a blue outline and a small triangle in the upper left corner of each affected cell. To see how a highlighted cell was changed, place the cursor over the cell and Excel will display a comment box containing the user name, date, time, and substance of the edit.

If you want to step through the list of revisions in the workbook and either accept or reject them, use the Accept Or Reject Changes command on the Track Changes submenu. When you choose this command, Excel saves the workbook, and then displays a dialog box asking for your search criteria. As with the Highlight Changes command, you specify the time, person, and location of the edits you're looking for with the drop-down list boxes in the dialog box. When you click OK, Excel displays the changes one at a time in a dialog box similar to the one shown in Figure 17-9 on the following page. (If more than one user wants to modify a cell, Excel identifies each user and the edits they're requesting.) To accept an edit and store it in the shared workbook, click the Accept button. To reject the change, click the Reject button. Some cells might have more than one edit, in which case you must click on the edit you want to accept. After you accept or reject an edit, Excel removes the revision highlighting from that cell.

III

Microsoft Excel

FIGURE 17-9.

Excel tracks each edit in a shared workbook and lets you accept or reject it. If a change made by another user is inappropriate, you can discard it.

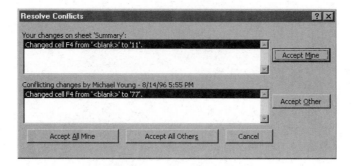

Merging Workbooks

Another method for consolidating changes in a shared workbook is to merge two copies of the workbook together, using the Merge Workbooks command on the Tools menu. Merging workbooks is a useful technique when two users are working with slightly different copies of the same file and one user wants to incorporate all the changes the other user has made. Merging workbooks is a one-step process—you simply choose the Merge Workbooks command and the file you want to merge with the active workbook, and Excel compares the two workbooks and copies any differences to the active file. Unlike the Accept Or Reject Changes command, however, the Merge Workbooks command doesn't give you a chance to compare or sort out the differences between the different copies. Its sole purpose is to update one copy of a workbook with another.

To merge two copies of a shared workbook, follow these steps:

1 Before you make any edits, use the Share Workbook command on the Tools menu to identify the original file as a shared workbook. (The Merge Workbooks command works only on copies of the same file that have been marked as shared.)

2 Use the Save As command on the File menu to create a second copy of the shared workbook. Give this copy of the file a unique name, and then deliver it to the user who will be making the edits via a network, the Internet, or a removable disk.

3 When you're ready to consolidate the changes made to the file, open your original copy of the shared workbook in Excel, and then choose Merge Workbooks from the Tools menu to access the updated copy. Click OK to save the file to disk when prompted, and then choose the copy of the workbook in the Select Files To Merge dialog box.

> **NOTE**
>
> The file you specify for merging must be a copy of the original file with a unique filename. It must also be marked as shared.

4 Click OK to merge the files. After a moment, Excel updates the original file with changes from the merge file. (If there are no changes, Excel will notify you in a dialog box.) That's all there is to it!

> **WARNING**
>
> Remember, the Merge Workbooks command doesn't give you a chance to accept or reject changes, so use it only if you want all revisions merged into your original file.

Protecting Worksheets and Workbooks

> **SEE ALSO**
> You can even require a password from users when they open a workbook. See "Requiring a Password for File Access," page 524.

In Chapter 16, you learned how to hide rows and columns in your worksheet from unauthorized glances. (Turn to the tip on page 485 if you'd like a refresher course.) Excel also lets you protect complete worksheets or an entire workbook from tampering, with a feature called *password protection*. When you guard worksheets or workbooks in this way, users can open the file, but they can't change the parts you have protected. If you want to share your workbooks with others, while protecting them from modification, this is the feature for you.

Protecting Worksheets

To protect a worksheet in the workbook from modification, follow these steps:

1 Click the worksheet tab corresponding to the worksheet you want to protect.

III

Microsoft Excel

2 From the Tools menu, choose Protection, and then choose Protect Sheet from the submenu. The Protect Sheet dialog box appears, as shown:

The Protect Sheet dialog box contains a Password text box, and three protection check boxes that are enabled by default. When the Contents check box is the only one turned on, all the cells in the worksheet are protected, but any objects (such as clip art images) and worksheet scenarios will remain unprotected. To safeguard these items, be sure the Objects and Scenarios check boxes are also turned on.

3 Type a short password in the Password text box and click OK. Note that Excel distinguishes uppercase letters from lowercase letters, so remember any variations you make in your password's capitalization. If you forget this password in the future, you won't be able to unprotect the worksheet.

 TIP

Use a Password (If Any) with Care

A password isn't required to protect worksheets. If you're afraid you'll forget the password, set worksheet protection without entering a password and you'll preserve the worksheet from accidental entries and mistakes. (However, a renegade user could easily turn off worksheet protection and then modify your document.)

4 When Excel asks you to verify your password, type it in again and then jot it down for future reference. (Try not to put it in an obvious place, however.) If anyone attempts to modify this protected worksheet in the future, Excel will display the following dialog box:

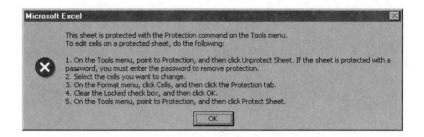

5 To remove worksheet protection at a later time, choose Protection from the Tools menu, and choose the Unprotect Sheet command from the submenu. If you didn't originally use a password, that's all there is to it! If you did, the following dialog box will appear and you must enter the worksheet password:

Lock Specific Cells or Fields

If you want to let users modify some cells in your worksheet but not others, select the cells and clear the Locked option on the Protection tab of the Format Cells dialog box. This technique is useful if you have a field for comments or an area in the worksheet that is typically used for data entry. You must do this *before* you use the Protect Sheet command on the Protection submenu, or else the Format Cells command will be unavailable to you. If this happens, turn off Protection, unlock the desired cells or fields, and then turn Protection back on.

Protecting Workbook Structure

To protect the structure of an entire workbook from modification (that is, guard the names and the order of the worksheets), follow these steps:

1 From the Tools menu, choose Protection, and then choose Protect Workbook from the submenu. The Protect Workbook dialog box appears, as shown in Figure 17-10 on the following page. The Protect Workbook dialog box contains a Password text box and three protection check boxes. When the Structure check box

III

Microsoft Excel

FIGURE 17-10.
The Protect Workbook dialog box.

is turned on, users can't insert, delete, hide, rename, copy, or move worksheets in the workbook, although they *can* modify data in the worksheets if worksheet protection is not set. When the Windows check box is turned on, users can't resize the windows displaying the workbook. Finally, turning on the Sharing With Revision History check box prohibits users in a multiuser environment from modifying the revision history of a shared workbook.

2 Type a password in the Password text box and click OK. Note any variations you make in your password's capitalization, and take steps not to forget the name. You can also click OK without typing a name, to set workbook protection without a password.

3 Retype the password when Excel asks for it. From this point on, no user will be able to modify the worksheet's structure without first unprotecting the workbook with the Unprotect Workbook command on the Protection submenu.

Requiring a Password for File Access

If you're using Excel to track confidential information, you might want to limit access to your file by requiring a password before it opens. This control goes further than protecting the content and structure of the workbook: it prevents anyone lacking an entry key from viewing your document at all.

> ⚠ **WARNING**
>
> Take care when using password protection. If you forget your password, you'll have no way to open the protected file.

To save a file with password protection, follow these steps:

1 Create your workbook as you normally would. You don't need to hide or protect confidential parts of the file—your password protection will limit access to every component automatically.

2 From the File menu, choose the Save As command to display the Save As dialog box. If you haven't already specified a filename, type one now in the File Name text box.

3 Click the Options button in the dialog box. The Save Options dialog box appears, as shown in Figure 17-11. It contains two password protection text boxes: Password To Open, which prohibits users from opening the file unless they know the specified password, and Password To Modify, which prohibits users from saving changes to the file without knowing the password.

If you want to recommend, but not require, the file to be opened as a read-only document, turn on the Read-Only Recommended check box.

4 Type a password in the Password To Open text box and click OK, to limit access to your workbook. When Excel asks for it, reenter the password to verify that you spelled it as intended.

5 The next time you or another user try to open the file, Excel will prompt for the password in a dialog box. To remove password protection in the future, choose the Save As command, click the Options button, and remove the password from the Password To Open text box.

FIGURE 17-11.
To protect your file from unauthorized access, type a password in the Save Options dialog box.

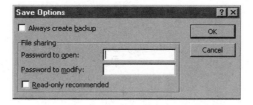

III

Microsoft Excel

Customizing Excel to Work the Way You Do

A short time ago, one of the editors of this book moved into a new office. Our first visit to her new digs was a shock; in place of the familiar, delightfully idiosyncratic workspace stood an empty desk, a computer wrapped in packing tape, several boxes of books and supplies, and four white walls bathed in pale, phosphorescent light. However, after several hours of patient adjustment and tinkering, her simple 10'×10' room again reflected her personality and interests. Books and treasures lined the walls, a soft lamp replaced cold overhead lighting, and the computer displayed a familiar electronic photograph. In a way, this routine relocation reminded us of one of the many things we really like about Office applications: They're eminently adaptable to your preferences and work style. In this chapter, you'll learn several useful techniques for customizing Excel and making it work the way *you* want it to. You'll learn how to magnify the worksheet and save your favorite views, customize toolbars, set your most typical printing options, and configure a time-saving feature called AutoCorrect. You'll also learn how to control recalculation and adjust other "hidden" settings by using the Options dialog box. When you're finished, you'll have all the techniques you need to create your own, personalized Excel interface.

Adjusting Views

In Chapter 16, you learned how to increase the point size in worksheet cells to make numbers and headings more readable. You can also change the magnification of the worksheet to zoom in on information you want to see, or back up to view it from a distance. In this section, you'll learn how to use the Zoom command to vary the magnification in your workbook, and you'll discover how to save different views with the Custom Views command.

Using the Zoom Command

The Zoom command on the View menu changes the magnification of the selected worksheets. This feature allows you to enlarge the worksheet temporarily to examine a group of cells, or shrink the worksheet so that you can judge its overall appearance. (It doesn't change any of your data or formatting.) When you choose the Zoom command, the Zoom dialog box appears, as shown in Figure 18-1. The default worksheet magnification is 100%, or Normal view. To enlarge the worksheet to twice its normal size, select the 200% option button. To shrink the worksheet, select the 75%, 50%, or 25% option button. Perhaps the most useful option button is Fit Selection, which adjusts the magnification to display exactly the cells you select before choosing the Zoom command. Finally, the Custom option button lets you specify an exact magnification percentage, from 10% reduction to 400% enlargement.

FIGURE 18-1.
The Zoom dialog box lets you enlarge or shrink the selected worksheets without changing cell formatting.

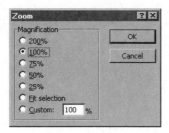

After you select a magnification percentage and click OK, your worksheet is resized and displayed in the workplace window. Figure 18-2 shows an example of the Fit Selection option button at work. Before we chose the Zoom command, we selected cells A1 through C8 in the Summary worksheet—the only cells we wanted to appear in the workplace window. The enlarged worksheet can be edited just like a normal-sized worksheet (with the enlargement giving your eyes a break), and if you save it to disk, the zoomed view will appear when you reopen the workbook.

FIGURE 18-2.
The Fit Selection option button zooms the worksheet to show only the selected cells.

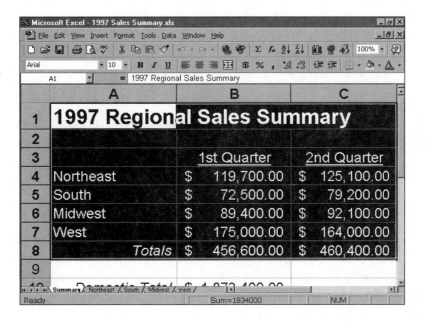

The Zoom Control on Excel's Standard toolbar also gives you access to many of the magnification options in the Zoom dialog box. To use the Zoom Control, follow these steps:

1   If you plan to magnify your worksheet based on a selection, highlight a range of cells in the worksheet. If you want to magnify several worksheets in the workbook, hold down Shift and click the worksheet tabs you want resized.

2   Click the Zoom Control on the Standard toolbar. Your toolbar will look similar to the one on the following page.

III

Microsoft Excel

3 Select the magnification option you want. Excel responds by resizing the selected worksheets.

Not all the worksheets in a workbook need to be viewed with the same magnification. Occasionally, you might want to vary how your worksheets appear within the workbook.

Saving Views with the Custom Views Command

If you find you like rotating between two or three different views when you work in your workbook, you can save your views to disk and switch between them freely with the Custom Views command on the View menu. Custom Views is a replacement for the View Manager add-in available in previous versions of Excel. When you save a view you give it a name, and Excel records the display options, window settings, printing options, and current selection in your worksheet. You can quickly switch back and forth between these views.

To save a view with the Custom Views command, follow these steps:

1 Set the view and display settings you want to save as a custom view. For example, set the magnification of the worksheet, select a cell to make it the current selection each time you use the view, or resize the workplace window.

2 From the View menu, choose the Custom Views command. The Custom Views dialog box opens, and any custom views you have previously defined appear in the list box.

3 Click the Add button. You'll get the Add View dialog box:

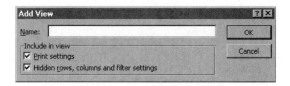

4   Type a descriptive name for your worksheet view, such as *Top Sales Rep*, and then click OK. Excel saves your custom view with the current worksheet. To display this named view later, click the worksheet tab containing the custom view, and choose Custom Views from the View menu. The Custom Views dialog box appears:

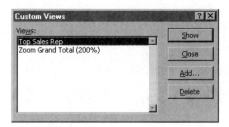

5   Double-click the view you want to show. The dialog box closes and the worksheet adjusts to your custom settings.

Each worksheet in a workbook contains different named views. Before you use the Custom Views command to display a particular view, be sure to select the worksheet the view is stored in. To delete a custom view, highlight the view in the Custom Views dialog box and click Delete.

Customizing Toolbars

Excel gives you complete control over the toolbars displayed in your workplace. You can change the location of the toolbars, add or remove toolbars, or customize the buttons displayed on them. This section describes how you customize toolbars by adding, removing, rearranging, and editing their buttons.

III

Microsoft Excel

? SEE ALSO

For more information about running commands with toolbar buttons, moving toolbars around the screen, and adding new toolbars to the workplace, see "Using Toolbars," page 52.

The doorway to customizing toolbars is the Customize command on the Toolbars submenu of the View menu. When you choose the Customize command, the dialog box shown in Figure 18-3 opens. By default, Excel displays the menu bar and the Standard and Formatting toolbars, but almost two dozen specialty toolbars are also available. You can use any combination of these toolbars in your daily work, although we recommend limiting the number to five or fewer to avoid cluttering up your screen. To add a toolbar to the Excel workplace, simply click the Toolbars tab, place a check mark in the box next to the toolbar you want to display, and then click Close. To remove a toolbar, remove the check mark and click Close.

FIGURE 18-3.
The Customize dialog box gives you access to Excel's predesigned toolbars.

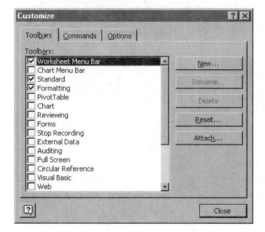

Adding Buttons to a Toolbar

You can add buttons to a toolbar from the Commands tab of the Customize dialog box. This tab contains the Categories list box, which displays the types of commands you can use. When you select a category in the list box, the associated command buttons appear in the Commands list box to the right. (For example, the File category contains 15 command buttons in the list box.) Many of the buttons featured in the functional categories are not included in the default toolbars, so take a few minutes to review your options and pick your favorites. To learn what a button does, simply click it, and then click the Description button near the bottom of the dialog box.

To add a button to a toolbar, follow these steps:

1 Display the toolbar you want to modify.

2 From the View menu, choose Toolbars, choose the Customize command from the submenu, and then click the Commands tab.

3 Click the group in the Categories list box containing the button you want to select. For example, to add the Strikethrough button (a button that formats text by drawing a line through it), click the Format category.

X CAUTION

Adding buttons to a full toolbar may cause some to be hidden from view. See the next page to learn how to remove infrequently used buttons.

4 Drag the button you want to insert from the dialog box to the target toolbar, as shown in Figure 18-4. (As you drag, the mouse pointer changes to a toolbar pointer.) Place the button exactly where you want it in the toolbar, and then release the mouse button. Excel will shift existing buttons to the right to make room. To create a new toolbar, drag the button outside the dialog box and drop it within an area of the workspace that doesn't already contain a toolbar.

FIGURE 18-4.

Adding a button to a toolbar.

Drag the selected button to its new location.

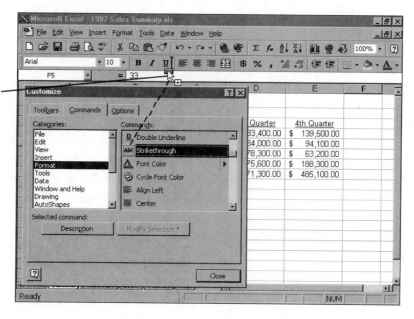

Microsoft Excel

5 Repeat steps 3 and 4 to add additional toolbar buttons if necessary. When you're finished, click Close.

Removing Toolbar Buttons

If you've added buttons to your toolbars and notice a gray, double-arrowhead (>>) at the right edge of a toolbar, it indicates that not all the toolbar's buttons are currently visible. In this case, you will probably want to remove your least-used buttons until the remaining buttons are all visible. To remove one or more buttons, follow these steps:

1 Choose Toolbars from the View menu, and then choose Customize from the submenu. Opening the Customize dialog box enables you to remove buttons from the toolbars and also causes any toolbars with hidden buttons to automatically resize themselves to show all their buttons.

2 Pick a toolbar button you want to remove. Choose one you don't use very often, one that you won't miss. (You might also want to make sure you know how to run the equivalent command using the menus.)

3 Click and drag the toolbar button (on the toolbar, *not* from the dialog box) away from the toolbar until an "X" appears in the mouse pointer, as shown in Figure 18-5. You can now release the mouse button and the toolbar button will be removed from your toolbar. The remaining buttons will shift to the left.

4 Continue to remove as many buttons as you wish. When each toolbar fits on one line, you will no longer have any hidden buttons. (Sometimes you can squeeze an extra button onto a toolbar if you have a Zoom, Font, or other text box that Excel can automatically resize to accommodate an extra button or two.) When you're finished, or if you want to check whether Excel will be able to fit all your buttons onto the screen, Click the Close button in the Customize dialog box.

⭐ TIP

Restore Buttons or Toolbars
When you remove a toolbar button, you don't actually delete it from your system. You can always insert it again by selecting the category it came from on the Commands tab, and then dragging it back to a toolbar. You can also restore an entire toolbar with its default buttons by clicking Reset on the Toolbars tab of the Customize dialog box.

FIGURE 18-5.
Removing a button
from a toolbar.

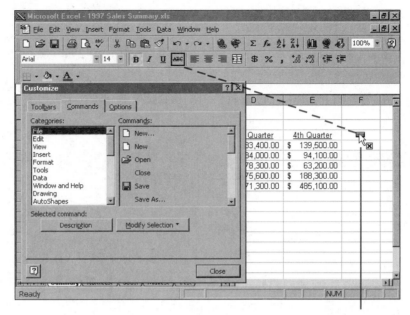

Drag and drop the button away from the toolbars.

Rearranging Toolbar Buttons

You can also change the order of toolbar buttons, or copy buttons
from one toolbar to another, while the Customize dialog box is open.
Like the simple process of adding and removing toolbar buttons, the
process of rearranging toolbar buttons is a matter of dragging the buttons from one location to the next.

To rearrange toolbar buttons, follow these steps:

1 Display the toolbar you want to rearrange. If you want to move
buttons from one toolbar to another, display both toolbars.

 NOTE

> If the toolbars you need aren't visible, choose Toolbars from the View menu and
> select the missing toolbars.

2 From the View menu, choose Toolbars and then choose the
Customize command on the submenu to open the Customize
dialog box.

III

Microsoft Excel

3 Drag toolbar buttons from one location to the next, using the gray bar that appears above the mouse pointer as your guide for placement. When you release the mouse button, the button you're dragging is relocated.

4 When you're finished, click the Close button in the Customize dialog box.

 TIP

Copy a Toolbar Button Quickly
To copy, rather than just move, a button from one toolbar to another, hold down the Ctrl key while dragging the button. When you release the mouse button, the toolbar button will appear on both toolbars.

Editing the Picture in Toolbar Buttons

SEE ALSO
Custom toolbar buttons are also useful when you want to create macros that automate repetitive tasks in Excel. For more information about creating macros and adding macro buttons to the toolbar, see Chapter 23, "Increasing Productivity with Macros."

Toolbar buttons are displayed as *bitmap* images composed of rows and columns of dots. If you're not content with the picture displayed in a toolbar button, you can edit it in Excel's Button Editor dialog box. You can rearrange the dots or *pixels* in an existing toolbar button, or even create a completely new image. The following example shows you how to change the background lettering in Excel's Spelling button from ABC to XYZ. The change is subtle, but if your friends notice, they're sure to ask how you did it!

To edit the picture in a toolbar button, follow these steps:

1 From the View menu, choose Toolbars, and then choose Customize from the submenu.

2 On the toolbar, right-click the toolbar button you want to edit. A menu appears with a list of commands. (In our example, we edited the Spelling button on Excel's Standard toolbar.)

3 Click Edit Button Image. The Button Editor dialog box opens (shown above step 4).

Your toolbar button now appears as a bitmap image divided into rows and columns of dots. To the right of the bitmap is a color palette with 16 color options.

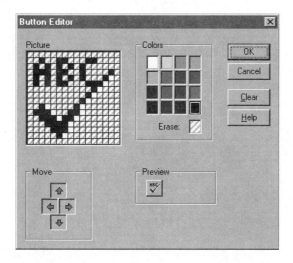

4 To change the color of a dot, simply highlight the color you want to use in the color palette, and then click the dots on the toolbar button you want to change. (The area you can draw in is slightly smaller than the button itself. That's to allow for the button's border.) Notice how your changes are reflected in the Preview window in the lower right corner of the dialog box.

5 If you want to erase a few dots, click the Erase box in the palette before clicking. You'll find it takes a little time to create artwork with these crude squares, but you can actually create some impressive effects if you keep at it. The following screen shows how we modified the Spelling button:

New pattern ——

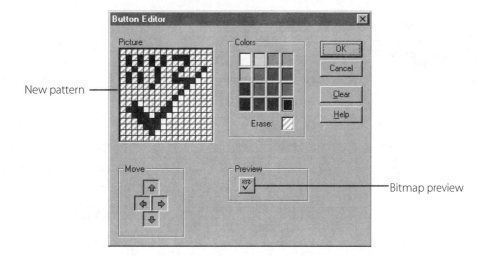

——Bitmap preview

III

Microsoft Excel

6 When you're finished editing the button, click OK to close the Button Editor dialog box, and then click Close to close the Customize dialog box and add the button to the toolbar. The results are shown below.

 The default Spelling button (ABC)

 Our customized Spelling button (XYZ)

> **What to Do If You Don't Like Your New Button**
> Should you decide you don't like your new design, open the Customize dialog box again, and right-click on the button you want to restore. This time choose Reset Button Image from the shortcut menu to return to the original design, or choose Change Button Image to choose from a menu of alternate button images. Then close the Customize dialog box.

Setting Printing Options

Few changes to a workbook are as noticeable as the options you select before printing. With the Page Setup command on the File menu, you can control the orientation of your page, the width of your margins, the text placed in headers and footers, and the presence of extras like gridlines and cell notes. The Page Setup dialog box contains four tabs that control how printing options are printed. We'll cover each tab in this section.

> In Excel 97, you can also display the Page Setup dialog box by choosing the Header And Footer command from the View menu.

Controlling Page Orientation

To customize your printing options, choose Page Setup from the File menu. Its Page tab, shown in Figure 18-6, lets you control orientation and other options related to the physical page you'll be printing on.

Orientation governs the direction your worksheet appears on the printed page. Portrait, the default, is a vertical orientation designed for worksheets that are longer than they are wide. If, as is often the case, your worksheet is too wide to fit on one page in this orientation, choose the Landscape option to orient your document horizontally.

The Scaling options let you reduce or enlarge your worksheet so that it fits in the specified number of pages. The percentage you type in the Adjust To text box is similar to the percentage you specify when creating custom views with the Custom Views command (discussed in "Saving Views with the Custom Views Command," page 530), except in this case it affects the printed page, *not* the view on your screen.

The Paper Size and Print Quality options let you specify a custom paper size and printing resolution. These options are drawn from the settings of your selected Windows-based printer. To set the unique features of your printer, click the Options button in the Page Setup dialog box and make your changes on the dialog box tabs.

FIGURE 18-6.
The Page tab lets you adjust page orientation and other paper options.

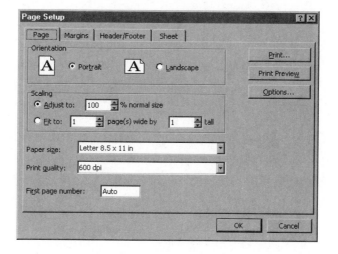

Adjusting the Margins

The Margins tab of the Page Setup dialog box allows you to adjust the margins in your workbook. (See Figure 18-7 on the following page.) Typical margin settings are 1 inch for the top and bottom, and 0.75 inch for the left and right. As you change the margins, Excel shows you in the Preview window which margin in your document is

FIGURE 18-7.

The Margins tab gives you control over the placement of your worksheet relative to the edges of the paper you print it on.

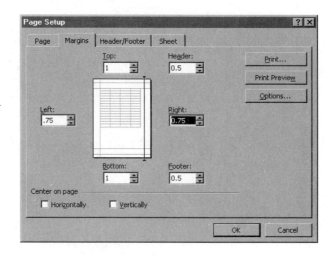

affected. Customizing the margin settings is especially useful if you're printing on letterhead paper or other sheets that contain graphics or text you don't want to overprint.

If you want to center your worksheet between the margin settings, turn on the Horizontally check box at the bottom of the Margins tab to center the printout from left to right or the Vertically check box to center the printout from top to bottom.

Adding Headers and Footers

The Header/Footer tab of the Page Setup dialog box (see Figure 18-8) lets you add a header or a footer to your worksheet when it prints. Headers and footers typically contain reference information about a document, such as the worksheet name, the time or date, or the current page number. Excel permits you to pick headers and footers from a predefined list on the Header/Footer tab, or you can create your own custom entries by clicking the Custom Header or Custom Footer buttons.

The following steps show you how to choose predefined headers and footers from the Page Setup dialog box:

1 From the File menu, choose Page Setup. (You can also choose Header And Footer from the View menu.) When the Page Setup dialog box opens, click the Header/Footer tab.

FIGURE 18-8.
The Header/Footer tab lets you choose a header or footer from a predefined list or create your own version.

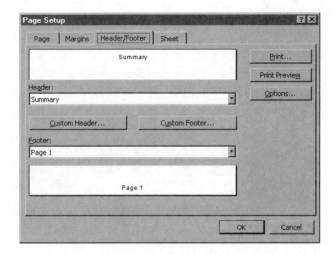

2 By default, the header contains the name of the current worksheet. To pick a new header, click the Header drop-down list box and choose one of the 18 formats listed. The first format—(None)—removes the header. Note that commas between items separate the header components, which will be aligned to the left, center, and right margins. When you select a format (and release the mouse button), the header is shown in the header preview window above the closed list box.

Pick your favorite header from the list.

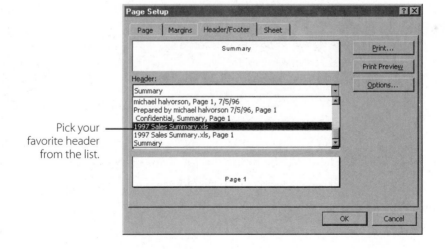

III

Microsoft Excel

3 To pick a new footer, click the Footer list box and choose one of the 18 formats listed. Again, the (None) option removes the footer from the document. Commas in the footer show how the footer will be organized on the page, while the footer preview window below shows how it will look. After you set headers and footers, your screen should resemble the following:

Header preview ——

Footer preview ——

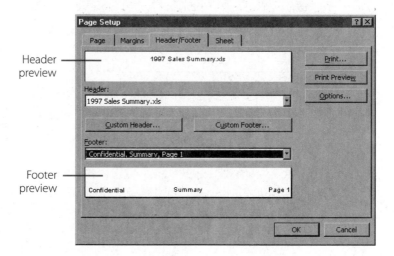

4 When you're finished, click OK. When you print, the specified headers and footers will appear on each page of your document.

Delete Headers and Footers Quickly

To remove all headers and footers from a document, select the (None) option in both the Header and Footer drop-down list boxes.

If you don't like the predefined headers and footers, you can create your own by clicking the Custom Header and Custom Footer buttons on the Header/Footer tab. The following steps show you how:

1 From the File menu, choose Page Setup. When the Page Setup dialog box opens, click the Header/Footer tab.

2 To create a custom header, click the Custom Header button. The following dialog box appears:

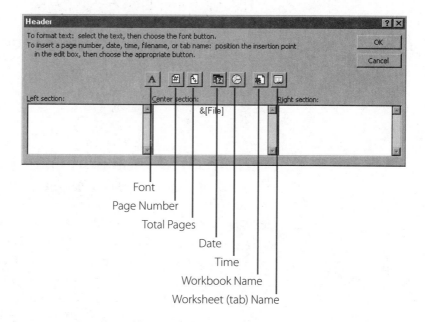

The Header dialog box lets you specify your header in three sections: left, center, and right.

3 Click in one of the sections, and then type the text you want. You can supplement the text you type by clicking any of seven special buttons to enter codes in your document. For example, if you click the button on the right side of the group (the Worksheet Name icon), the code &[Tab] is placed in the header. This is Excel's special formatting code for inserting the name of the current worksheet of your workbook at this location in the header.

4 To change the formatting of the text, select the portion you want to format and click the Font button.

5 When you're finished with the header, click OK to view the customized header in the Preview window. If you don't like the results, repeat the above steps and make further changes.

III

Microsoft Excel

6 If you want to create a custom footer, click the Custom Footer button and follow steps 3 through 5 as you did for creating a custom header.

7 When your header and footer are the way you want them, click OK.

 **TIP**

To create multiline headers or footers, press Enter at the end of each line in the section portion of the Header or the Footer dialog box.

Adding Gridlines and Other Options

The Sheet tab of the Page Setup dialog box (see Figure 18-9) lets you include visual or interpretive aids such as gridlines, comments, and repeating row and column headings in your printout. To print gridlines with your worksheet, simply turn on the Gridlines check box in the Print category. Gridlines are the dividing lines you normally see on your screen that run down each column and across each row, identifying the cells in the worksheet. Cell comments are special notes you create with the Comments command on the Insert menu. You can specify how they're printed by choosing a selection in the Comments list box. The default (None) is *not* to print any comments the worksheet might contain.

FIGURE 18-9.
The Sheet tab lets you include extras such as gridlines and cell comments in your printout.

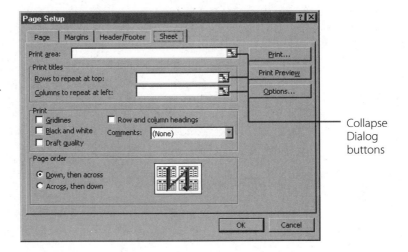

Collapse Dialog buttons

⭐ **TIP**

To remove gridlines from your screen, choose the Options command from the Tools menu, click the View tab, and turn off the Gridlines check box.

Two other useful features on the Sheet tab are the Print Area and Print Titles text boxes. Both these features let you select ranges for printing. In the Print Area text box you specify the worksheet range that will be printed, and in the two Print Titles text boxes you can choose to repeat either row or column headings (or both) on multipage printouts. To use the Print Area feature, follow these steps:

1 From the File menu, choose Page Setup.

2 When the Page Setup dialog box opens, click the Sheet tab.

3 Click the Collapse Dialog button at the right edge of the Print Area text box. The dialog box will temporarily shrink to enable you to see your worksheet. If it still obscures your view, drag its title bar and move it out of the way.

⭐ **TIP**

To delete a print area, open the Sheet tab and delete the cell range in the Print Area text box. (This will not change your original data, only the way it prints.)

4 Select the cells you want to print in the worksheet.

As you select the cells, a marquee appears around the range, a pop-up box shows the number of rows and columns you're selecting, and a description of the cells appears in the Print Area text box, as shown on the following page.

5 When you have selected the cells you want, click again on the Collapse Dialog button.

6 After making any other changes, click the Print button and then click OK in the Print dialog box to print the cells you selected.

III

Microsoft Excel

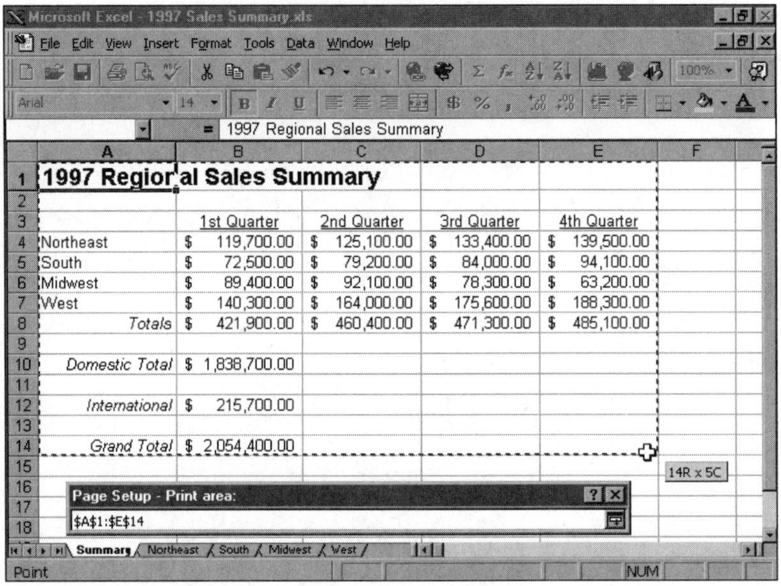

X Microsoft Excel - 1997 Sales Summary.xls						

File Edit View Insert Format Tools Data Window Help

Arial ▾ 14 ▾ **B** _I_ U ≡ ≡ ≡ ▦ $ % , ‰ �ₒ‰ ⌐⌐ ▦ ▾ ♦ ▾ **A** ▾

= 1997 Regional Sales Summary

	A	B	C	D	E	F
1	**1997 Regional Sales Summary**					
2						
3		1st Quarter	2nd Quarter	3rd Quarter	4th Quarter	
4	Northeast	$ 119,700.00	$ 125,100.00	$ 133,400.00	$ 139,500.00	
5	South	$ 72,500.00	$ 79,200.00	$ 84,000.00	$ 94,100.00	
6	Midwest	$ 89,400.00	$ 92,100.00	$ 78,300.00	$ 63,200.00	
7	West	$ 140,300.00	$ 164,000.00	$ 175,600.00	$ 188,300.00	
8	Totals	$ 421,900.00	$ 460,400.00	$ 471,300.00	$ 485,100.00	
9						
10	Domestic Total	$ 1,838,700.00				
11						
12	International	$ 215,700.00				
13						
14	Grand Total	$ 2,054,400.00				
15						

14R x 5C

Page Setup - Print area:	? X
$A$1:$E$14	

|◄ ◄ ► ►| \ **Summary** / Northeast / South / Midwest / West /

Point   NUM

TIP

To delete a print area or choose a different one (without changing your data), open the Sheet tab and delete the cell range in the Print Area text box. Leave it blank or draw a new range on your worksheet.

To repeat row or column headings (or both) on each printed page of a long (or wide) worksheet, follow these steps:

1 From the File menu, choose Page Setup.

2 When the Page Setup dialog box opens, click the Sheet tab.

3 Click one of the Collapse Dialog buttons under the Print Titles heading to select repeating rows or repeating columns.

4 Select the rows or columns you wish to repeat on each page. You can click any cells in the rows or columns you want to repeat, or you can select the row or column headings. Excel will highlight the entire rows or columns you select with a marquee, as shown in the following screen.

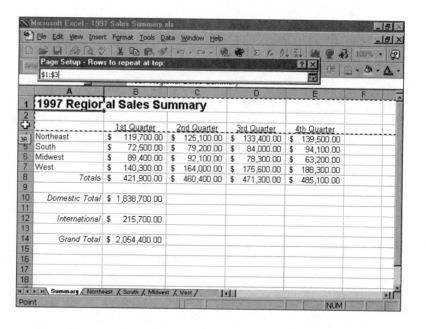

5 Click the Collapse Dialog button again to complete your selection.

6 You can repeat steps 3–5 if you want to repeat both rows and columns on your printed worksheet. When you are finished, select OK to close the Page Setup dialog box, or continue on and print your worksheet by clicking the Print button and then the OK button in the Print dialog box.

7 After making any other changes, select OK to close the Page Setup dialog box, or click the Print button and then click OK in the Print dialog box to print the worksheet.

 TIP

You can verify how your print options will look by clicking the Print Preview button in the Page Setup dialog box or choosing Print Preview from the File menu. This gives you a chance to decide whether to make cosmetic adjustments and to ensure that you have chosen the portion of the worksheet you want.

III

Microsoft Excel

Setting AutoCorrect Options

Just like Microsoft Word, Excel contains an AutoCorrect feature that automatically fixes mistakes you make in text entries as you enter them in worksheet cells. For example, if you type the word *abscence* (a common misspelling that AutoCorrect recognizes) in a cell and press Spacebar or Enter, Excel automatically changes the word to *absence*, correcting the mistake. You can customize the AutoCorrect feature by adding words you commonly mistype to the Replace list or turning on or off the five AutoCorrect options. You display the AutoCorrect dialog box, shown in Figure 18-10, by choosing AutoCorrect from the Tools menu.

If you don't want Excel to change the capitalization of words that begin with two capital letters, turn off the Correct TWo INitial CApitals check box. Removing the check mark will stop Excel from changing labels like *USmail* to *Usmail*. (Excel will never change a word that starts with three or more capital letters.) Likewise, you can stop Excel from capitalizing days of the week by removing the check mark from the Capitalize Names Of Days check box. When you disable this AutoCorrect feature, *monday* will remain *monday*.

FIGURE 18-10.
The AutoCorrect dialog box lets you control how spelling and capitalization mistakes are fixed in your worksheet.

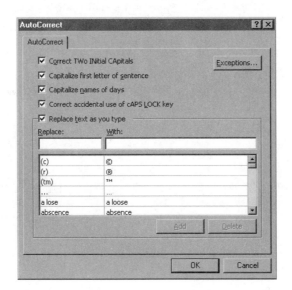

The word correction feature of AutoCorrect is controlled by the Replace Text As You Type check box. To turn off word replacement, remove the check mark from this box by clicking on it. (Note, however, that capitalization correction is still enabled unless you remove the check marks from the two capitalization check boxes.) When the Replace Text As You Type option is active, Excel will use the pairs listed in the Replace and With lists to fix your typing mistakes. You can also use this feature to add abbreviations that you want expanded, saving you time and ensuring accuracy. For example, you can direct Excel to convert the letters *po* into the words *Post Office Box,* or to change *sd* to *San Diego.* To add a correction pair, type the word or phrase you want Excel to replace in the Replace text box, type the correct word or expanded phrase in the With text box, and then click the Add button. To remove a correction pair, highlight the pair and click the Delete button.

Create Exceptions for Special Words You Use

In Excel 97, you can stop the AutoCorrect feature from fixing words that you want to have two initial capitals (like *USmail*) or from assuming that a new sentence is beginning after certain abbreviated words (like *three hrs. per day*). To create a list of special words you *don't* want Excel to fix, click the Exceptions button in the AutoCorrect dialog box, and then indicate your spelling preferences in the First Letter and INitial CAps tabs.

Customizing Excel with the Options Dialog Box

To change the way Excel looks and works, experiment with the customization choices in the Options dialog box, shown in Figure 18-11 on the following page. As with Word, you display the Options dialog box by choosing Options from the Tools menu. The Options dialog box contains tabs that control virtually every aspect of the Excel interface. Although some tabs customize features that you might not be familiar with, such as the settings that help you make a transition from other spreadsheet programs, you can often learn a lot about how Excel

FIGURE 18-11.
The Options dialog box lets you customize many of Excel's commands and features. The General tab controls basic options like the standard font.

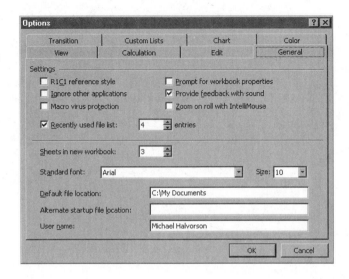

works by just browsing through the tabs in this dialog box. In this section, you'll experiment with the following features:

- Formula calculation settings, like manual recalculation and update remote references

- Worksheet appearance options, like scroll bars and colors

- Adjustable editing options, like drag and drop and default decimal places

Controlling Calculation

When you enter a formula, Excel automatically computes the result or *recalculates*. Most of the time, you'll want Excel to recalculate automatically when you modify cells that are included in formulas—it makes sense to keep your numbers up to date. But occasionally you'll want to configure Excel so that it recalculates only when you want it to. For example, you might want to refer to the previous result of a calculation while you enter new values in a worksheet. Or, you might want to disable recalculation temporarily if you're entering several complex formulas in a worksheet, since lengthy calculations can take some time to finish.

To customize formula calculation in your worksheet, choose the Options command from the Tools menu, and then click the Calculation tab of the Options dialog box. You'll see the dialog box shown in Figure 18-12. To select manual calculation, click the Manual option button in the Calculation area, and then click OK. From this point on, Excel will only recalculate formulas when you enter or edit them, when you press F9 to calculate manually, or when you open the Calculation tab again and click the Calc Now (F9) button. If you're disabling automatic recalculation, you might also want to disable automatic updating from other applications linked to your worksheet. To remove this option, turn off the Update Remote References check box in the Workbook Options portion of the Calculation tab, and Excel won't update links that rely on other programs for data.

FIGURE 18-12.

To control recalculation in a worksheet, click the Calculation tab.

Click here for manual calculation.

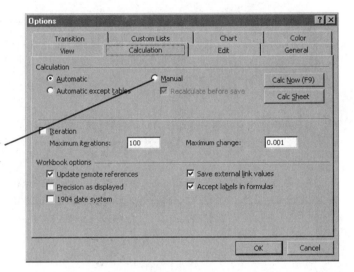

<table>
<tr><td colspan="4">Options</td><td>? ×</td></tr>
<tr><td>Transition</td><td>Custom Lists</td><td>Chart</td><td>Color</td></tr>
<tr><td>View</td><td>Calculation</td><td>Edit</td><td>General</td></tr>
</table>

Calculation
- ⦿ Automatic
- ○ Automatic except tables
- ○ Manual
  - ☑ Recalculate before save

Calc Now (F9)
Calc Sheet

☐ Iteration
Maximum iterations: 100   Maximum change: 0.001

Workbook options
- ☑ Update remote references
- ☐ Precision as displayed
- ☐ 1904 date system
- ☑ Save external link values
- ☑ Accept labels in formulas

OK   Cancel

⚠ WARNING

> Remember to select the Automatic option in the Calculation box and to turn on the Update Remote References check box when you're finished entering data. Otherwise, your workbook might display out-of-date information and present incorrect results.

Customizing Worksheet Appearance

You've already learned how to add toolbars to your workplace and change the layout of workbook windows. With the View tab in the Options dialog box, you can make further adjustments to your worksheet's appearance. The View tab includes option buttons and check

III

Microsoft Excel

boxes that enable and disable several visual features, as shown in Figure 18-13. You can remove the formula bar and status bar from the screen, giving you more real estate for your worksheet, by turning off the Formula Bar and Status Bar check boxes. If you don't like the red box that signifies a comment has been placed in a cell, you can choose None in the Comments category, instead of the Comment Indicator Only or Comments & Indicator options. The red boxes will disappear, but the comments will remain.

FIGURE 18-13.
The View tab controls how your worksheet appears on the screen.

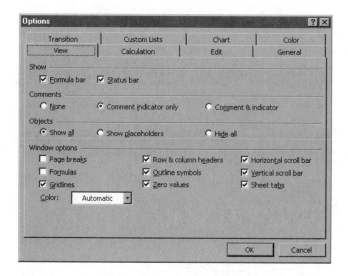

You might also find it useful to examine the selections in the Window Options category of the View tab. You can use these options to choose whether to view automatic page breaks, gridlines (or alter their color), scroll bars, and other visual features of your worksheet. When you're finished customizing your worksheet's appearance, click OK to close the Options dialog box.

Customizing Editing Options

If you want to change how Excel responds to your editing instructions, you can modify several special settings, including the way drag and drop works, the way Excel updates linked worksheets, and the action of the AutoComplete feature. Figure 18-14 shows the Options dialog box's Edit tab, which controls these customization features and more.

FIGURE 18-14.

You can personalize Excel's editing behavior by enabling or disabling options on the Edit tab.

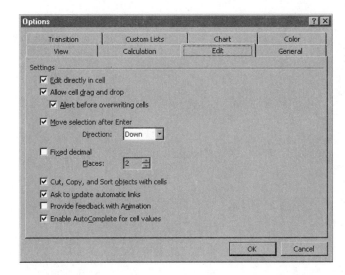

To disable direct cell editing—the feature that lets you move the insertion pointer into cells when you double-click a cell—turn off the Edit Directly In Cell option. You might want to cancel this feature if you often accidentally double-click cells when selecting ranges. When this feature is turned off, you must edit the cell's contents in the formula bar.

A related option is Allow Cell Drag And Drop, which enables the drag and drop method for copying and moving cells. If you tend to accidentally drag cells, you can disable the feature by turning off the check box. (We recommend that you *never* remove the Alert Before Overwriting Cells safety feature.)

You might consider disabling the AutoComplete feature if you grow weary of Excel automatically entering data for you based on your last entry. While this capability is extremely useful, it can also be tiresome if Excel doesn't guess your intentions correctly. To stop AutoComplete, turn off the Enable AutoComplete For Cell Values check box. When you're finished selecting your editing choices, click OK to close the Options dialog box.

III

Microsoft Excel

CHAPTER 19

Crunching Numbers with Formulas and Functions

A *formula* is an equation that calculates a new value from existing values. In Chapter 15 you learned how to build simple formulas with numbers and cell references, and in Chapter 17 you expanded your skills by creating formulas that linked to cells from other worksheets and workbooks. In this chapter, you'll discover how to build more sophisticated formulas. You'll learn how to use arithmetic operators and parentheses to control how your formulas are evaluated, you'll explore techniques for replicating formulas, and you'll practice using range names to make your formulas more readable and easier to modify. In addition, you'll learn how to use Excel's impressive collection of built-in functions for specialized tasks such as totaling columns, computing averages, and calculating the monthly payments for an auto loan. With well-organized formulas and functions, you can evaluate business data in new ways, spot important trends, and plan your financial future.

Building a Formula

Figure 19-1 shows two basic Excel formulas. The first calculates a value by multiplying two numbers, and the second calculates a sum by adding three cell references. These formulas have several characteristics in common. First, each begins with an equal sign (=). The equal sign tells Excel that the following characters are part of a formula that should be calculated and the result displayed in a cell. (If you omit the equal sign, Excel treats the formula as plain text and doesn't compute the result.) Second, each formula uses one or more arithmetic operators to combine numbers or cell references. An arithmetic operator is not required when a function is used in a formula, but in all other cases, operators are necessary to tell Excel what to do with the values in an equation. If your formula contains more than one arithmetic operator, you can include parentheses to clarify how the formula is evaluated.

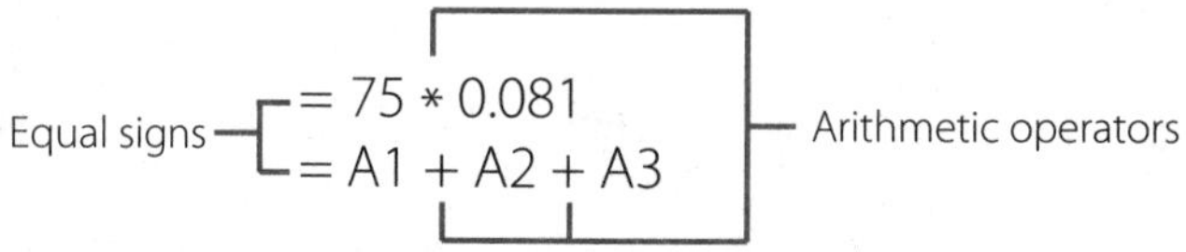

FIGURE 19-1.

The anatomy of two simple Excel formulas.

Equal signs —⌐ = 75 * 0.081
          └ = A1 + A2 + A3   — Arithmetic operators

The examples in this chapter feature an order-form worksheet that catalogs the merchandise sold in a small pet shop. It's the type of worksheet that pet-shop employees might use to take orders over the phone or that customers might use to purchase mail-order items. As you work through this chapter, you'll see how Excel formulas and functions are used to add information to the order-form worksheet. You can create the worksheet and follow the examples exactly if you want to, or you can customize the worksheet for your own purposes.

Multiplying Numbers

Formulas that multiply the numbers in two cells are the most basic and the easiest to enter. The following example shows you how to multiply a price cell and a quantity cell to create a subtotal.

  1 Create a product order form, price list, or other worksheet containing well-organized Price, Quantity, and Subtotal columns. The order-form worksheet we'll use looks like this:

| Microsoft Excel - Pet Suppy Price List.xls | | | | | | | |

Pet Supply Price List

	A	B	C	D	E	F	G
1	Pet Supply Price List						
2							
3	Item	Name	Price	Quantity	Subtotal		
4	#101	Cat Collar	$ 7.95	10			
5	#102	Dog Collar	$ 8.95	10			
6	#201	OK-Brand Dog Food	$ 14.95	12			
7	#202	Healthy Pup Dog Food	$ 27.95	6			
8	#505	Dog Dish	$ 19.95	5			
9	#601	Assorted Pet Toys	$ 6.95	20			
10			Totals				
11							

2 In the Subtotal column, click the cell that will contain the multiplication formula (E4 in our example).

3 Type the equal sign (=) to begin the formula. An equal sign appears on the formula bar and in the highlighted cell. From this point on, any numbers, cell references, arithmetic operators, or functions that you type will be included in the formula.

4 In the Price column, click the cell containing the first number to be multiplied (C4 in this example). A dotted-line marquee appears around the highlighted cell and the cell reference appears in the formula bar.

5 Type * to add the multiplication operator to the formula.

6 In the Quantity column, click the cell containing the second number to be multiplied (D4 in this example). The complete formula now appears in the highlighted cell and on the formula bar. Your screen should look similar to the one shown on the following page.

7 Press Enter to end the formula. Excel calculates the result (79.5 in this example) and displays it in the cell containing the formula. Later you'll add currency formatting to the cell.

Replicating a Formula

Excel makes it easy to copy, or *replicate*, a formula into neighboring cells, using the Fill submenu of the Edit menu. The slick thing about the Fill submenu is that its commands automatically adjust the cell references in your formula to match the rows and columns you're copying to. For

SEE ALSO

To learn more about entering simple formulas, referencing cells, and using the formula bar, see "Entering Formulas," page 434.

III

Microsoft Excel

The formula bar records your formula as you build it.

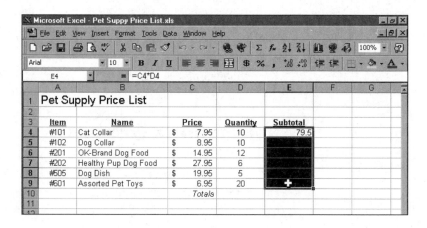

SEE ALSO

For more information about the commands on the Fill submenu, see "Using the Fill Commands," page 458.

example, if you replicate a formula down a column with the Down command, Excel automatically adjusts the row numbers so that the formula includes new references in each cell. (Excel automatically adjusts cell references when you delete cells too.) The following example shows you how to use the replication feature in the order-form worksheet.

To replicate a formula, follow these steps:

1 Highlight the cell with the formula and the empty cells you want to fill as one selection. (The Fill command replicates formulas in only one direction; commands on the Fill submenu copy to neighboring, or contiguous, cells only, so be sure that the formula cell is at the top, bottom, left, or right end of the empty cell range.) Our screen looks like this:

2 From the Edit menu, choose Fill and then choose Down from the submenu if your formula is at the top of the selected range, or choose Right, Left, or Up as appropriate. Your formula is replicated through the selected cells, as shown here:

	A	B	C	D	E	F	G
1	Pet Supply Price List						
2							
3	Item	Name	Price	Quantity	Subtotal		
4	#101	Cat Collar	$ 7.95	10	79.5		
5	#102	Dog Collar	$ 8.95	10	89.5		
6	#201	OK-Brand Dog Food	$ 14.95	12	179.4		
7	#202	Healthy Pup Dog Food	$ 27.95	6	167.7		
8	#505	Dog Dish	$ 19.95	5	99.75		
9	#601	Assorted Pet Toys	$ 6.95	20	139		
10				Totals			
11							

TIP

You can also replicate a formula by using the AutoFill mouse technique. Simply select the cell you want to replicate, click on the tiny box in the lower right corner of the cell, and drag it over the cells you want to fill.

Using Arithmetic Operators

As you learned in the previous example, Excel lets you build your formulas by using one or more arithmetic operators to combine numbers and cell references in an equation. Table 19-1 on page 561 shows a complete list of the arithmetic operators you can use in a formula. When you enter more than one arithmetic operator, Excel follows standard algebraic rules to determine which calculations to accomplish first in the formula. These rules—called Excel's *order of evaluation*—dictate that exponential calculations are performed first, multiplication and division calculations second, and addition and subtraction last. If there is more than one calculation in the same category, Excel

SEE ALSO
To control how Excel calculates formulas, see "Controlling Calculation," page 550.

III

Microsoft Excel

evaluates them from left to right. For example, when evaluating the formula =6-5+3*4, Excel computes the answer using these steps:

=6-5+**3**∗**4**

=**6-5**+12

=**1+12**

=13

Editing Formulas

Excel lets you edit formulas in the same way that you edit any other cell entry. Simply double-click the cell, locate the mistake with the arrow keys, make your correction, and press Enter. You can also insert new cell references while editing a formula by positioning the cursor in the formula bar and highlighting new cells with the mouse. This handy feature lets you specify replacement cells in your formula if you selected the wrong cells the first time. The following screen shows what a formula in cell E9 looks like when you edit it in a cell. Note that Excel places color outlines around the other cells involved in the formula to make it easy to see their relationships. If you prefer, you can also highlight a cell and click the formula bar to edit the cell's contents there.

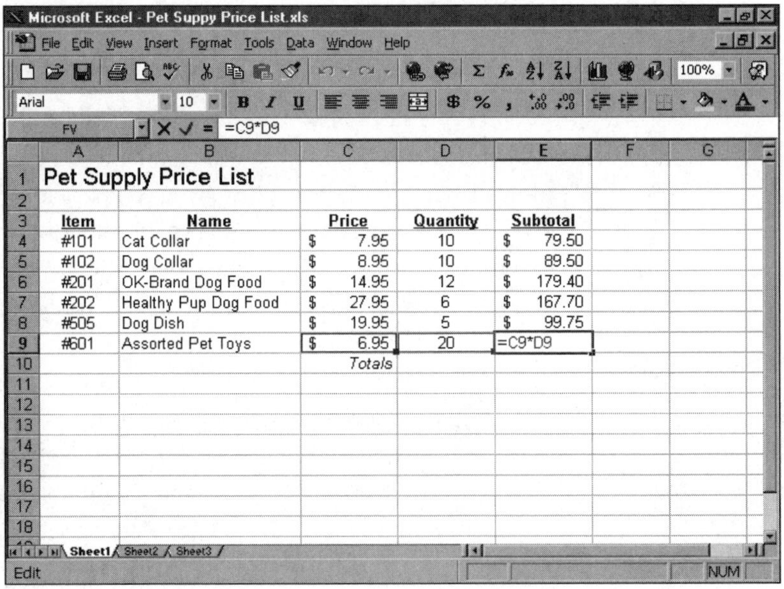

TABLE 19-1. Excel's Arithmetic Operators, in Order of Evaluation

Operator	Description	Example	Result
()	Parentheses	(3+6)*3	27
^	Exponential	10^2	100
*	Multiplication	7*5	35
-	Subtraction	12-8	4
+	Addition	5+5	10
-	Subtraction	12-8	4

Parentheses and Order of Evaluation

To change Excel's order of evaluation, you can include one or more pairs of parentheses in a formula. This lets you control how Excel uses operators in a formula, and can also make your equation easier to read and revise later. For example, consider how parentheses create a difference in evaluation between these two formulas:

=10+2*0.25

=(10+2)*0.25

The first formula produces a result of 10.5, while the second formula produces a result of 3. By modifying Excel's order of evaluation in the second formula you create an entirely different answer.

Parentheses can also make a formula easier to read, and you can add any number of parentheses as long as you use them in matching pairs. For example, though the following formulas both produce the answer 15, the first formula is a bit easier to decipher.

=((5*4)/2)+(10/2)

=5*4/2+10/2

  NOTE

If you specify an uneven number of parentheses in a formula, or a pair of parentheses that don't match, Excel displays the message *Parentheses do not match* or *Error in Formula* and highlights the location of the mistake. You can correct the mistake on the formula bar.

III

Microsoft Excel

Using Built-In Functions

? SEE ALSO

For more information on the PMT function, see "Determining Loan Payments with PMT," page 567.

To accomplish more sophisticated numerical and text processing operations in your worksheets, Excel lets you add built-in calculations called functions to your formulas. A *function* is a predefined equation that operates on one or more values and returns a single value. Excel includes a collection of over 250 functions in several useful categories, as shown in Table 19-2. For example, you can use the PMT function from the Financial category to calculate the periodic payment for a loan based on the interest rate charged, the number of payments desired, and the principal amount.

Each function must be entered with a particular *syntax*, or structure, so that Excel can process the results correctly. For example, the PMT function has a function syntax that looks like this:

PMT(**rate,nper,pv**,fv,type)

TABLE 19-2. Categories of Excel Functions

Category	Used For	Number of Functions
Financial	Loan payments, appreciation, and depreciation	52
Date & Time	Calculations involving dates and times	20
Math & Trig	Mathematical and trigonometric calculations like those found on a scientific calculator	58
Statistical	Average, sum, variance, and standard-deviation calculations	80
Lookup & Reference	Calculations involving tables of data	16
Database	Working with lists and external databases	13
Text	Comparing, converting, and reformatting text in cells	23
Logical	Calculations that produce the result TRUE or FALSE	6
Information	Determining if an error has occurred in a calculation	17

The abbreviated words shown between the parentheses are called *arguments*. In this function, *rate* is the interest rate, *nper* is the number of payments you'll make, and *pv* is the principal amount. To use this function correctly, you must specify a value for each required argument, and you must separate each argument with a comma. The arguments shown in bold are required, and the others are optional. In the online Help, the required functions are also in bold.) For example, to use the PMT function to calculate the loan payment on a $1,000 loan at 19% annual interest over 36 months, you could type the following formula:

=PMT(19%/12,36,1000)

When Excel evaluates this function, it places the answer ($36.66) in the cell containing the function. (The answer is negative, indicated by the parentheses, because it is money you must pay out.) Note that the first argument (the interest rate) was divided by 12 in this example to create a monthly rate for the formula. This demonstrates an important point—you can use other calculations, including other functions, as the arguments for a function. Although it takes a little time to master how these arguments are structured, you'll find that functions produce results that can otherwise take hours to calculate by hand.

The Versatile SUM Function

Perhaps the most useful function in Excel's collection is the SUM function, which automatically totals the range of cells you select. Because SUM is used so often, the AutoSum button appears on the Standard toolbar to make adding numbers faster. In the following example, we'll use the AutoSum button to sum the Subtotal column in the order-form worksheet.

Σ

AutoSum

To total a column of numbers with the SUM function, follow these steps:

1 Click the cell in which you want to place the SUM function. (If you're totaling a column of numbers, select the cell directly below the last number in the column.)

2 Click the AutoSum button. Excel places the SUM function in the formula bar and (if possible) automatically selects a range of neighboring cells as an argument for the function. If you selected a cell directly below a column of numbers, your screen will look similar to the one in Figure 19-2 on the following page.

III

Microsoft Excel

FIGURE 19-2.

The AutoSum button inserts the SUM function and automatically suggests the cells to use for the argument.

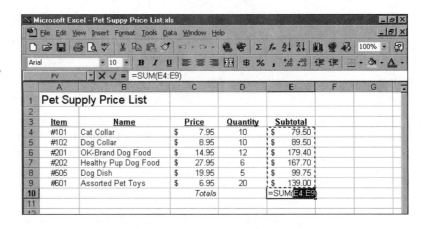

3 If Excel selected the range you want to total, press Enter to complete the function and compute the sum. If Excel didn't guess the range correctly, select a new range now by dragging the mouse over the range and pressing Enter. (You can specify any block of cells in any open workbook to be an argument to the SUM function.) To cancel the AutoSum command, press the Escape key.

 TIP

Use SUM to Add Nonadjacent Ranges

You can use the SUM function to add multiple noncontiguous ranges by separating the cell ranges with commas. For example, =SUM(A3:A8,B3:B8) adds six cells in column A to six cells in column B and displays the total. You might find it easier to use the mouse and select cells by clicking each cell or range of cells while pressing the Ctrl key.

The Insert Function Command

With so many functions to choose from, it might seem daunting to experiment with unfamiliar features on your own. Excel makes it easier by providing a special command named Function on the Insert menu, to help you learn about functions and enter them into formulas. The Paste Function dialog box, shown in Figure 19-3, lets you browse through the nine function categories and pick just the calculation you want. You can also use the Office Assistant to help you learn how each function works and what arguments it requires. (The more than 250 functions are carefully documented in the online Help.) When you double-click a function in

Help

the Function Name list box, Excel displays a second dialog box prompting you for the required arguments. Give it a try now with a useful statistical function called AVERAGE.

To use AVERAGE to calculate the average of a list of numbers, follow these steps:

1 Click the cell in which you want to place the results of the AVERAGE function. (In the pet-shop example, this is B12. The label "Avg. Price:" has been added in A12.)

2 From the Insert menu, choose the Function command. The Paste Function dialog box appears, as shown in Figure 19-3. The nine functional categories appear in the Function Category list box along with the choice for All functions and those Most Recently Used, and the functions in each category are listed alphabetically in the Function Name list box.

FIGURE 19-3.
Clicking the Help button in the Paste Function dialog box toggles the Office Assistant off and on to guide you through the process of picking and using a function.

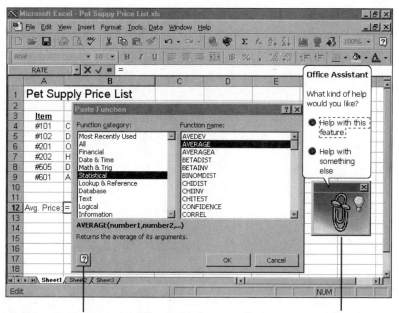

Click the Help button to toggle the Office Assistant on or off.   Office Assistant

III

Microsoft Excel

★ TIP

f_x

You can save time opening the Paste Function dialog box by clicking the Paste Function button on the Standard toolbar.

Paste
Function

3 Click the Statistical category. The mathematical functions in the Statistical category appear in the Function Name list box.

4 Click the AVERAGE function, and then click OK. A second dialog box appears, asking you for the arguments in the function. In the AVERAGE function, you can specify either individual values to compute the average or a cell range. This time, you'll specify a cell range.

5 Click the Collapse Dialog button (small red arrow at the right edge of the Number 1 text box shown below) and the dialog box will shrink to show only the text box you're about to fill.

6 Select the cells you want to average. In our example, we selected the numbers in the Price column (cells C4 through C9) to determine the average price of pet supplies in the store.

7 Release the mouse button and press Enter. The dialog box returns to its normal size and the cell range you selected appears in the dialog box and in the AVERAGE function on the formula bar. Our screen looks like this:

Paste Function

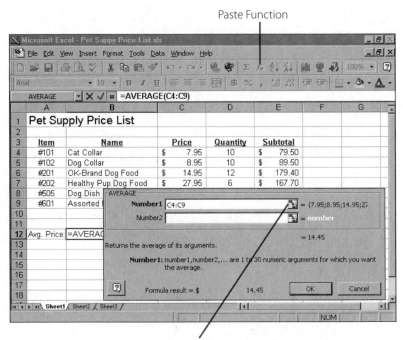

Shrink the dialog box so that it doesn't obscure the cells you're selecting.

8 Click OK to complete the formula and calculate the result. The average ($14.45) appears in the cell containing the AVERAGE formula.

> You can include one function as an argument in *another* function if the result is compatible. For example, the formula =SUM(5,SQRT(9)) adds together the number 5 and the square root of 9, and then displays the result (8).

Analyzing Finances with Functions

Although Excel includes too many functions to discuss exhaustively in this book, we thought you might enjoy seeing a few more examples of functions and formulas to prompt your own exploration. We've decided to highlight three of Excel's most useful financial functions: PMT, FV, and RATE. Using these functions, you can precisely calculate loan payments, the future value of an investment, or the rate of return produced by an investment.

Determining Loan Payments with PMT

The PMT function returns the periodic payment required to amortize a loan over a set number of periods. In plain English, this means that you can estimate what your car payments will be if you take out an auto loan or what your mortgage payments will be if you buy a house. Try using the PMT function now to determine what the monthly payments will be for a $10,000 auto loan at 9% interest over a 3-year period.

To use the PMT function, follow these steps:

1 Click the worksheet cell in which you want to display the monthly payment.

2 Choose the Function command from the Insert menu or click the Paste Function button on the Standard toolbar. The Paste Function dialog box appears.

3 Click the Financial category, and then double-click PMT in the Function Name list box. The arguments dialog box appears, with a description of the PMT function and five text boxes ready for the function's arguments. You'll enter numeric values for Rate

III

Microsoft Excel

(the interest rate), Nper (the number of payments), and Pv (the present value, or loan principal).

4 Type *9%/12* and press Tab, type *36* and press Tab, and type *10000*. The dialog box should look like this:

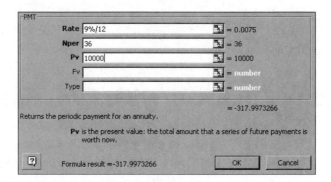

The result of the calculation is displayed near the bottom of the dialog box using the number format for the cell. In this case, the cell is set to display the General number format and the result is shown as -317.9973266.

> To calculate monthly payments, be sure to type the annual interest with a percent sign and divide it by 12 to create a monthly interest rate. Likewise, be sure to specify the number of payments in months (36), not years (3).

5 Click OK to complete the function and display the result. Your monthly loan payment, less any applicable loan fees, appears in the cell you highlighted. The result, formatted as currency, is -$318.00. The amount appears as a negative value because it represents money that you must pay out.

Computing Future Value with FV

Although monthly loan payments are often a fact of life, Excel can help you with more than just debt planning. If you enjoy squirreling away money for the future, you can use the FV function to determine the future value of an investment. This is one of the tools that financial planners use when they help you to determine the future value of an annuity, IRA, or SEP account. The following example shows you how to compute the future value of an IRA in which you deposit $2,000 per year for 30 years at a 10 percent annual interest rate—a possible scenario if you invested $2,000 per year between the ages of 35 and 65.

To use the FV function to calculate the value of your investment at retirement, follow these steps:

1 Click the worksheet cell in which you want to display the investment total. In our worksheet, the cell is already assigned the Currency format.

2 Open the Paste Function dialog box.

3 Click the Financial category, and then double-click FV in the Function Name list box. A dialog box appears, with a description of the FV function and five text boxes for the function's arguments. (The arguments are related to those of the PMT function, but now a Pmt field is added so that you can enter the amount you're contributing each period.)

4 Type *10%* in the Rate text box and press Tab, type *30* in the Nper text box and press Tab, type *-2000* in the Pmt text box and press Tab twice, and then type *1* in the Type text box. (Note that Rate and Nper must be based on the same units of time. In the previous example months were the basis, here years are the basis for the calculation.) Your screen should look like the following:

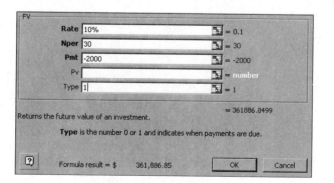

5 Click OK to display the result. In our example, the 30-year IRA has a future value of $361,886.85. Not bad for a total investment of $60,000.

> **NOTE**

By placing a 1 in the Type text box, you direct Excel to start calculating each year's interest at the beginning of the year—a sensible move if you place one lump sum in your IRA at the same time each year. If you omit this argument, Excel will calculate each year's interest at the end of the year, and the total future value will be smaller—about $33,000 less in this example.

Evaluating Rate of Return with RATE

You'll often want to evaluate how a current investment is doing or how a new business proposition looks. For example, suppose that a contractor friend suggests you loan him $10,000 for a laundromat/brew pub project, and agrees to pay you $3,200 per year for four years as a minimum return on your investment. So what's the projected rate of return for this investment opportunity? You can figure it out quickly using the RATE function, which lets you determine the rate of return for any investment that generates a series of periodic payments or a single lump-sum payment.

To use the RATE function to determine the rate of return for an investment, follow these steps:

1 Click the worksheet cell in which you want to display the rate of return. In this example, the cell is already formatted for Percent.

2 Open the Paste Function dialog box.

3 Click the Financial category, scroll down in the Function Name list box, and then double-click RATE. A dialog box appears, with a description of the RATE function and six text boxes for the function's arguments. (Scroll down to see the sixth text box, Guess.) The arguments are similar to the ones you've used in previous financial functions, but they appear in a slightly different order.

4 Type *4* in the Nper text box and press Tab, type *3200* in the Pmt text box and press Tab, and type *-10000* in the Pv text box. Your screen should look like this:

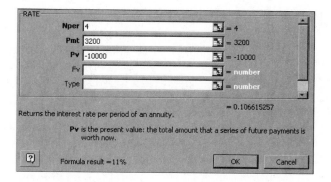

5 Click OK to display the result. In this example, your investment of $10,000 today will return 11% annually if your friend regularly pays you $3,200 per year for the next four years. With this information in hand, you can decide if the projected rate of return is enough for you, or if you'd rather try something less risky—or renegotiate the deal.

In short, Excel functions can't guarantee to you financial success, but used correctly, they can help you make decisions based on the best data available.

Function Error Values

The Paste Function dialog box makes entering functions relatively straightforward. If you *do* make a mistake when typing a function, you might receive a code called an *error value* in one or more cells. Error values begin with a # symbol and usually end with an exclamation point. For example, the error value #NUM! means that the function arguments you supplied aren't sufficient to calculate the function—one of the arguments might be too big or too small. If you see an error value in a cell, simply click the cell and fix your mistake on the formula bar, or delete the formula and enter it again. (If you're building a function, use the function's online Help to double-check your arguments.) The following table shows the most common Excel error values and their meanings:

Error Value	Description
#DIV/0!	You're dividing by zero in this formula. Verify that no cell references refer to blank cells.
#NA	No value is available. You might have omitted a function argument.

Function Error Values	*continued*

Error Value	Description
#NAME?	You're using a range name in this formula that hasn't been defined in the workbook. (See the next section, "Using Range Names in Functions.")
#NULL!	You attempted to use the intersection of two areas that don't intersect (are not contiguous). You might have an extra space character in one of your range arguments.
#NUM!	One of your function arguments might be out of range or otherwise invalid, or an iterative function you're using might not have computed long enough to reach a solution. (Entering a rough answer in the *Guess* argument might reduce the number of iterations Excel needs.)
#REF!	Your formula includes range references that have been deleted.
#VALUE!	Your formula is using a text entry as an argument.
######	The result of this calculation is too wide to fit in the cell. Increase the column width.

Using Range Names in Functions

To make your functions more readable and easier to type, you can name a range of cells in your worksheet and then use the range name in place of cell references throughout your workbook. For example, you could give the cells E4 through E9 the name Subtotal, and then use the SUM function to add the five cells by entering the following formula:

=SUM(Subtotal)

After you assign a name to a cell range, you can use the name in any formula in your workbook.

Creating Range Names

Excel gives you two techniques for naming ranges in a workbook: You can use the Create command on the Name submenu, or you can click the Name box and type a range name. Range names must begin with a letter and can't include spaces. We recommend that you limit your names to 15 characters or fewer so that they fit easily into the Name box and so that you can type them quickly in formulas.

To create a range name automatically with the Create command, follow these steps:

1 Select the range you want to name, and include a row or column heading in the selection to define the name. For example, the following selection includes the text label *Subtotal* for the range name:

D	E	F
Quantity	**Subtotal**	
10	$ 79.50	
10	$ 89.50	
12	$ 179.40	
6	$ 167.70	
5	$ 99.75	
20	$ 139.00	

2 From the Insert menu, choose Name and then choose Create from the submenu. The Create Names dialog box appears, prompting you for the location of the range name within your selection:

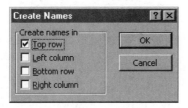

3 Click OK to accept Excel's default selection if you included a row or column label in your range; otherwise, click the option to tell Excel where to find the labels. (In this example, Excel has detected the text label Subtotal at the top of your selection.) The dialog box closes, and the name of the selected range now appears in the formula bar. You can use this name in computations on any worksheet in the workbook.

You don't need to use a bordering cell's contents as your range name. Figure 19-4 on the following page shows a flexible and fast way to create a name for any range of cells you choose.

III

Microsoft Excel

FIGURE 19-4.
Creating a named
range manually.

1 Select the cells you want to name.

2 Click the Name box.

3 Type an unused
range name and
press Enter.

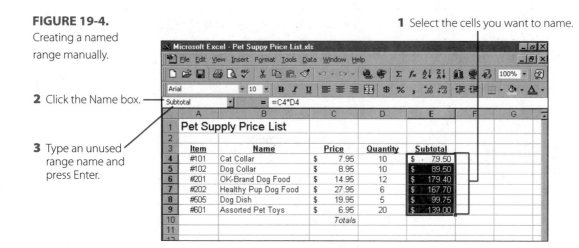

Defining Range Names

You can create a range name a third way, by choosing Define from the Name submenu of the Insert menu. When the Define Name dialog box shown below appears, follow these steps:

1 Enter a name for the new range you are going to define in the Names In Workbook text box.

2 Click the Collapse Dialog button in the Refers To text box to shrink the dialog box. Select the cells for the new range and press Enter. Alternatively, you can type the cell addresses directly into the Refers To box.

3 Click Add and the new range name is added to the list of range names.

4 Click Close to remove the dialog box.

The Define Name dialog box also enables you to modify and delete ranges, as discussed in the remainder of this chapter.

Using Range Names in Functions

You can use range names as arguments in functions wherever multiple-cell range references are permitted. For example, you could use the Subtotal range name in the SUM or AVERAGE functions because they accept ranges as arguments, but you couldn't use Subtotal in the PMT function because each of the PMT arguments must be a single number.

To insert a range name into a formula or function, follow these steps:

1 Create the formula or function as you normally would. For example, to determine the average of the cells in the Subtotal range, begin your formula as follows:

> =AVERAGE(

2 When it's time to specify a range of cells as an argument, type the named range in the formula:

> =AVERAGE(Subtotal)

3 When you've finished entering the formula, press Enter.

Forgot the Range Name?

If you can't remember the names you've given the ranges in your workbook, you can choose one from a list by using the Paste Name dialog box. To insert range names in this manner, type your formula, and when it's time to insert a range name, choose Name from the Insert menu, choose the Paste command from the submenu, and then double-click the range name that you want to include.

Modifying Ranges

Named ranges make your formulas easy to revise because when you modify the range, Excel automatically updates all your formulas. The Define command on the Name submenu lets you modify a range using the Refers To text box. You can add cells to a range or remove cells from a range, either by typing in the Refers To text box or by highlighting a new range in the worksheet.

III

Microsoft Excel

To modify the cells included in a named range, follow these steps:

1 From the Insert menu, choose Name and then choose the Define command from the submenu. The Define Name dialog box includes a list of the named ranges in your workbook and a Refers To text box listing the cells in the named range.

2 Click the named range that you want to modify.

3 Change the cell references in the Refers To text box, or select a new range of cells directly on the worksheet. Just click the Collapse Dialog button in the Refers To box to shrink the dialog box. Then select the cells and press Enter.

4 Click OK to save your changes.

Deleting Range Names

When you no longer need a range name, you can delete it from your workbook using the Define Name dialog box. Follow these steps to delete a range name:

1 From the Insert menu, choose Name and then choose the Define command. The Define Name dialog box appears.

2 Click the range name that you want to delete from the workbook.

WARNING

If you delete a range name that is currently being used by a formula, the error value #NAME? will appear in the cell containing the formula. To fix the problem, you'll need to replace the range name in the formula with an actual cell reference or with a valid range name. Note that you can't undo a range name deletion.

3 Click the Delete button. The range name is permanently removed from the workbook.

4 Click OK to close the Define Name dialog box.

Range names are an important component of well-documented formulas. When you can use range names well, you'll enjoy using formulas and functions much more.

CHAPTER 20

Creating Worksheet Charts

When you have worksheet data that you need to present to others, it often makes sense to display some of the facts and figures as a chart. Charts are graphical representations of categories of information designed to transform rows and columns of data into meaningful images. Charts can help you to identify numerical trends that can be difficult to spot in worksheets, and they can add color and flair to an important presentation. In this chapter, you'll learn how to create an Excel chart from worksheet data, format your chart's appearance, add special effects, and print your chart. If it's your job to plan for the future or to analyze the past, you'll find Excel's charting tools both useful and addictive.

Planning a Chart

Before you can create a chart, you need to do some general planning. An Excel chart is created from the data in an existing Excel worksheet, so before you build a chart, you need to create a worksheet that contains the necessary facts and figures. Excel can create a chart from data that is distributed throughout a worksheet, but you'll make the process easier if you organize your numbers so that they can be combined and selected easily. For example, Figure 20-1 shows a sales worksheet with rows and columns of data that can easily be converted into several types of charts.

You also need to plan for the type of chart that you'll be creating. Excel provides 14 chart types that you can use to present worksheet data, with several variations for each chart type. The basic chart types are shown in Table 20-1 along with the typical uses for each. For example, you can use a pie chart to describe the relationship of parts to a whole, or a bar chart to compare different categories of data with each other. If you're gathering information for an annual sales report, you might want to try out both of these chart types.

FIGURE 20-1.
Creating charts is easier with neatly organized rows and columns of data.

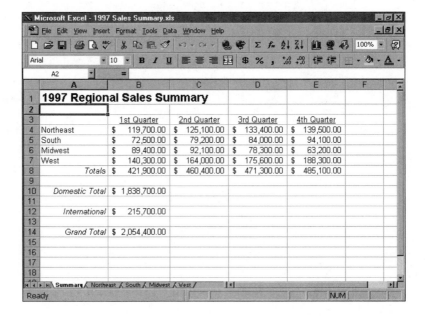

TABLE 20-1. Chart Types in Excel and Typical Uses for Each

Chart Symbol	Chart Type	Typical Use
	Column	Compares categories of data with each other vertically
	Bar	Compares categories of data with each other horizontally
	Line	Shows trends by category over a period of time
	Pie	Describes the relationship of the parts to the whole in a single group
	XY (Scatter)	Depicts the relationship between two kinds of related data
	Area	Emphasizes the relative importance of values over a period of time
	Doughnut	A more flexible pie chart with a hole in the middle; used to compare the parts to the whole in one or more data categories
	Radar	Shows changes in data or data frequency relative to a center point
	Surface	3-D chart useful for tracking changes in two variables as a third variable (such as time) changes.
	Bubble	Similar to a scatter chart; highlights clusters of values
	Stock	A combination column chart and line chart especially designed to track stock prices
	Cylinder	A variable bar or column chart with a unique cylinder shape
	Cone	A bar or column chart that emphasizes the peaks in data
	Pyramid	Similar to the cone chart; emphasizes peaks in bars or columns

III

Microsoft Excel

Measure Twice, Chart Once

Charting requires some up-front planning to get the best results. Just as a carpenter measures a length of wood twice before cutting it, you're well advised to take your time and think about your goals for a chart before creating it. As you plan your charts, ask yourself the following questions:

- What worksheet data would you like to highlight in a chart? Can you build your worksheet so that you can copy data directly to the chart?

- How will you present your chart? Would you like to store it as a separate sheet in your workbook, in an existing worksheet, or as part of a Word document or PowerPoint presentation?

- What chart type do you plan to use? Do you want to show one category of data (such as first-quarter sales by geographic region), or several (such as the four most recent quarters of sales by geographic region)?

Creating a Chart

When you have a well-organized worksheet in place, you're ready to create a chart. In the following examples, we'll use the 1997 Sales Summary workbook shown in Figure 20-1 on page 578 to create first a pie chart and then a column chart. Because a good deal of charting involves experimenting with different chart types, feel free to follow your own impulses as you complete the instructions.

To create a pie chart in a new sheet in the workbook, follow these steps:

1 Prepare a worksheet with rows and columns of information that you can use in the chart. Add row and column labels if you want them included in the chart.

 TIP

If you select labels along with the data for your chart *before* you create the chart, Excel will add the labels automatically.

2 Select the cell range containing the data to be plotted. In this example, we'll be creating a pie chart, so we want to select one category of values (one row or column). In Excel terminology, a category is called a *data series*. The following screen shows how you would select numbers in the 1st Quarter column for a pie chart, including text that you want to use as chart labels:

	A	B	C
1	1997 Regional Sales Summary		
2			
3		1st Quarter	2nd Quarter
4	Northeast	$ 119,700.00	$ 125,100.00
5	South	$ 72,500.00	$ 79,200.00
6	Midwest	$ 89,400.00	$ 92,100.00
7	West	$ 140,300.00	$ 164,000.00
8	Totals	$ 421,900.00	$ 460,400.00
9			

Chart Wizard

3 Now create the chart. From the Insert menu, choose the Chart command, or click the Chart Wizard button on the Standard toolbar. The Chart Wizard starts and you'll see the following dialog box, asking you to select a chart type:

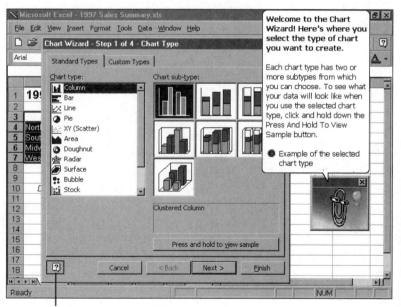

Click here to close the Office Assistant.

4 If the Office Assistant appears, click the Help button to close it so that you'll have a better view of the worksheet.

Microsoft Excel

5 Click the Pie chart type in the Chart Type list box, and then click the Exploded 3-D Pie in the Chart Sub-Type box (the names of the sub-types appear as you click each one).

6 Click Next to display the dialog box prompting you for the worksheet cells to include in the chart. The cells you selected in step 2 appear in the Data Range text box (cells A3 through E7).

If your worksheet was well organized, and if you selected the proper data, your chart should now contain the correct information (though the labels might be too small to see). If your chart doesn't look right, use the option buttons and list boxes in this dialog box to change the cells used for the data series, labels, and chart title.

7 Click Next to display the Chart Wizard dialog box that controls the chart's titles, legend, and data labels. Your pie chart appears in a sample window with the default settings, as shown in the following screen:

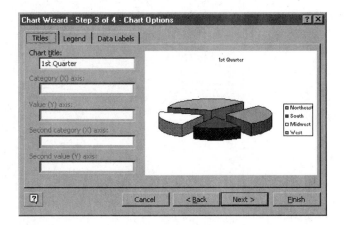

8 Starting from the Titles tab, change the chart title to *1997 Regional Sales Summary*, and then click Next. The Chart Wizard displays a dialog box asking you for the location of your new chart. You can either create a new workbook tab for the chart, or place it as an object in one of your existing worksheets.

9 Click the As New Sheet button, type *Summary Chart* in the highlighted text box, and then click the Finish button. Excel completes the pie chart and displays it in a new sheet named Summary Chart in the workbook. Excel adjusts the Zoom Control in the Standard toolbar so that the entire chart is visible.

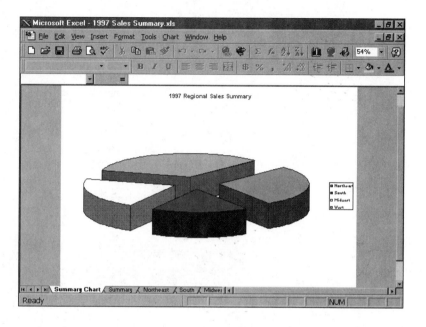

10 Choose the Save command from the File menu to save your new chart to disk as part of your open workbook. You can now display the pie chart at any time by clicking the Summary Chart tab.

TIP

To get a better look at the title, labels, and data in your new chart, click the Zoom Control on the Standard toolbar and select a higher viewing percentage. You'll find that 75% or 100% usually works well for reading the text in your chart and for formatting labels.

Creating an Embedded Chart

Excel also lets you create an in-place, or *embedded,* chart in an existing worksheet. This technique lets you closely associate graphical

III

Microsoft Excel

images with the data in your worksheet. For example, you could create an area chart depicting bagel production in a bakery worksheet containing inventory and sales data. In the following example, we'll show how to add a column sales chart to a sales-summary worksheet.

To create an embedded chart in a worksheet, follow these steps:

1 Prepare a worksheet with rows and columns of data that you can chart. As you create the worksheet, set aside some room for a rectangular column chart.

2 Select the cell range containing the data that you want to plot. In our example, we'll be creating a chart with groups of columns representing sales regions, so if you want to follow our example, you'll need to select several columns of data. Our selected columns and labels look like this:

	A	B	C	D	E	F
1	1997 Regional Sales Summary					
2						
3		1st Quarter	2nd Quarter	3rd Quarter	4th Quarter	
4	Northeast	$ 119,700.00	$ 125,100.00	$ 133,400.00	$ 139,500.00	
5	South	$ 72,500.00	$ 79,200.00	$ 84,000.00	$ 94,100.00	
6	Midwest	$ 89,400.00	$ 92,100.00	$ 78,300.00	$ 63,200.00	
7	West	$ 140,300.00	$ 164,000.00	$ 175,600.00	$ 188,300.00	
8	Totals	$ 421,900.00	$ 460,400.00	$ 471,300.00	$ 485,100.00	
9						

3 Click the Chart Wizard button on the Standard toolbar. (Creating an embedded chart is exactly like creating a stand-alone chart, except for specifying the chart location in step 10.)

4 Specify the chart type you want to use in the Chart Type dialog box, and click Next. (In this example, we'll use the default column chart type.)

5 The Chart Source Data dialog box reflects the data range selected in step 2. Click Next, unless you first want to adjust any of the settings for your data.

6 Customize your chart with the options presented in the Chart Options dialog box or accept Excel's settings. You'll notice that you have a different set of options for the column type of chart than you did for the pie chart. When you're finished, click the Next button to display the Chart Location dialog box:

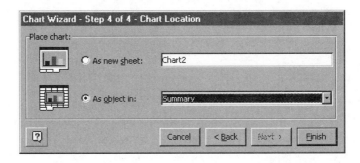

7 Click the As Object In option button, then specify the worksheet you want to place the new chart in by using the adjacent drop-down list box. (We're placing our chart in the Summary worksheet.)

8 Click the Finish button to complete the chart.

9 The Chart Wizard builds the chart to your specifications and places it in the middle of the worksheet, as shown in the follow-ing illustration. (Note that the chart is currently selected with eight selection handles.)

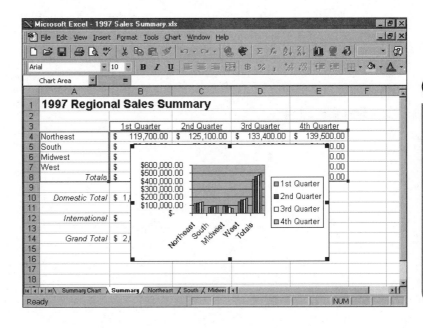

Working with Embedded Charts

When you embed an Excel chart in a worksheet, you create an object that can be resized, formatted, moved, and deleted like clip art or any other object. You can use the following editing techniques with embedded charts:

- To *resize* an embedded chart, move the mouse pointer to the edge of the chart and drag one of the selection handles.

- To *format* an embedded chart, double-click the chart, and the Format Chart Area dialog box appears. Add borders to the chart from the Patterns tab, or choose other commands from the Font or Properties tabs. (See "Formatting a Chart" below.)

- To *move* an embedded chart from one location to another in the worksheet, simply click within the object and drag it to a new location. To move the chart to a new worksheet, click the chart, and then choose the Location command from the Chart menu. To move the chart to another workbook or Microsoft Office application, click the chart, choose the Cut command from the Edit menu, open or switch to the destination document, and then choose the Paste command from the Edit menu.

- To *delete* an embedded chart, select the chart and press the Delete key.

---

10 Drag the chart to the desired location in the worksheet, and resize it to display the amount of detail you want. (Drag the chart by one of its edges, so that you don't inadvertently rearrange the chart components.)

Excel creates embedded charts in a small size to make them easy to move and format. However, your chart will usually look better if you enlarge it.

When you're finished, click outside the chart to remove the selection handles and "lock" it in place on your worksheet. (Click on the chart to reactivate the selection handles in the future.) Our chart looks like the following:

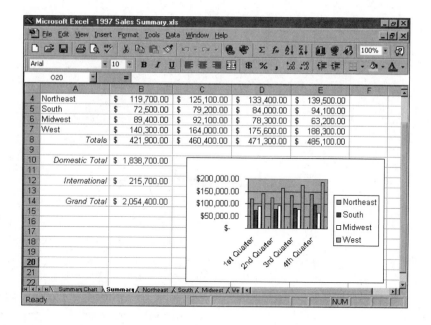

Formatting a Chart

If you're content with using Excel's default formatting for your chart, you're all finished—simply tidy up your chart and print it. If you're like most people, however, you probably can't resist adding a label here or changing the point size there. In this section, you'll learn how to format charts by changing the chart type, editing titles and gridlines, adjusting the legend, adding text, and controlling character formatting. What you learn will apply both to embedded charts and to stand-alone chart sheets in the workbook.

The Chart Menu

When you created the pie chart in the first example in this chapter, you might not have noticed that the Data menu was replaced by a Chart menu on the menu bar, and that several commands on the remaining menus changed. Excel's Chart menu features commands that are specifically designed for charting, as shown in Figure 20-2 on the following page. Whenever a chart is active, you'll see these commands.

III

Microsoft Excel

FIGURE 20-2.
Excel's Chart menu contains commands specifically designed for charting.

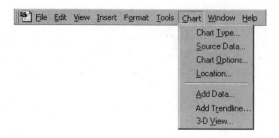

The Charting Toolbar

The Chart toolbar shown in Figure 20-3 contains several buttons designed to help you to format your chart, as well as the Chart Objects list box, which you can use to select different components of your chart for editing (such as the chart title, legend, and plot areas). Many of the buttons on the Chart toolbar correspond to commands on the Chart menu, as you'll see in the following sections. Open the Chart toolbar by choosing it from the Toolbars submenu of the View menu.

FIGURE 20-3.
The Chart toolbar appears when a chart is active in the workbook. To remove it, click the Close button.

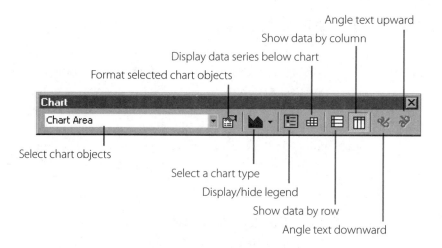

Changing the Chart Type

After you create a chart, you're not locked into one particular chart type. If your data supports it, you can reformat your chart in any of Excel's 14 chart types. (For example, you can change your pie chart into a column chart.) To switch between chart types, click the Chart Type button on the Chart toolbar or choose the Chart Type command from the Chart menu.

To change the pie chart you created earlier into a column chart by using the Chart toolbar, follow these steps:

1 If the chart is embedded, click on it to select it and open the Chart toolbar. If the chart appears on its own worksheet, simply display the worksheet.

2 Click the arrow on the Chart Type button on the Chart toolbar to display pictures of the various chart types.

3 Select the 3-D Perspective Column Chart button (when you rest the mouse over each chart type, its name will appear).

Your chart will change shape to match the selected chart type. The following screen shows how your pie chart will look when changed into a 3-D column chart.

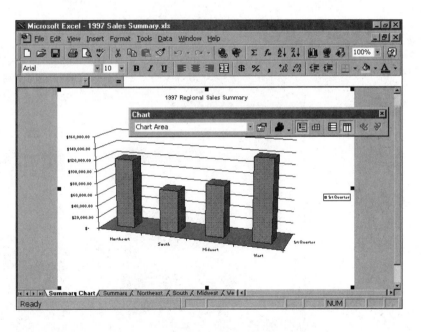

TIP

Choose Additional Chart Sub-Types
For a wider selection of chart types (for example, to change from 3-D view to 2-D view), select the chart and choose the Chart Type command from the Chart menu. Here you can pick from over 70 choices in the Chart Sub-Type list boxes for each chart type.

Changing Titles and Labels

You can edit the text in your chart's titles and labels as well as modify the font, alignment, and background pattern. If you select a data label, you can change its numeric formatting.

To edit title or label text, follow these steps:

1 Display the chart that you want to modify. If the chart is embedded in a worksheet, click the chart to activate it and to display Excel's charting menus.

⊗ CAUTION
Check that you've selected the part of the chart you want to edit by making sure the selection handles indicate the specific object and not the entire chart.

2 Use the Zoom Control to zoom in on the title or label so that you can read it, if necessary. The best view for editing text is usually 100%.

3 Click the title or label in the chart. Selection handles will surround the text, as shown in Figure 20-4.

FIGURE 20-4.
Before you can edit or format a chart title, you must select it.

Selected chart title

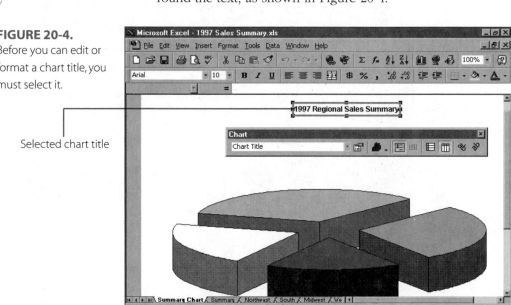

4 Click again to insert the text pointer at the spot you wish to edit. You can insert new text and use the Backspace and Delete keys to delete unwanted text.

TIP

You can check the spelling of the text in a chart by selecting the text object and choosing the Spelling command from the Tools menu.

5 When you've completed your edits, press the Escape key once to remove the text insertion marker, and then press Escape a second time to remove the selection handles.

Changing Character Formatting

To make font, alignment, and pattern changes to a title or label, follow these steps:

1 Click the chart title or a label. Selection handles will appear around the text.

2 From the Format menu, choose Selected Chart Title (for a title) or Selected Data Labels (for a label). Only one of the commands will be available. You'll see a dialog box similar to the one shown in Figure 20-5.

FIGURE 20-5.
You can format chart titles and labels in the same way as regular worksheet text.

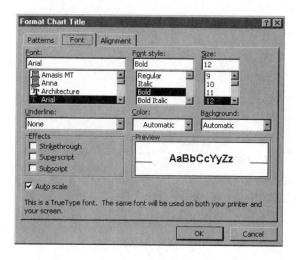

 NOTE

If you're formatting a label, the dialog box will also have a Number tab. We'll discuss this tab in the next example.

III

Microsoft Excel

SEE ALSO
To learn more about formatting text, read Chapter 16, "Formatting a Worksheet."

3 Use the Patterns, Font, and Alignment tabs to modify the borders or colors, adjust the character formatting in the text, or adjust the text orientation. For example, if you plan to print your chart, you might want to increase the point size of the text using the Font tab.

4 When you've finished formatting the text, click OK.

Adjusting Numeric Formatting in Labels

If you selected a label in your chart, your Format Data Labels dialog box includes a Number tab, as shown in Figure 20-6. The following steps show you how to use the Number tab to adjust the numeric formatting in labels:

1 Click one or more labels that contain numeric data such as percentages or dollar amounts. (To select more than one label, hold down the Shift key while clicking.) You can also select numeric values associated with the gridlines or the *axis* of the chart.

TIP

To add or change data labels, use the Chart Options command on the Chart menu.

2 From the Format menu, choose the Selected Data Labels command. (If you selected an axis, choose the Selected Axis command.)

FIGURE 20-6.
The Number tab lets you change the number formatting in chart labels.

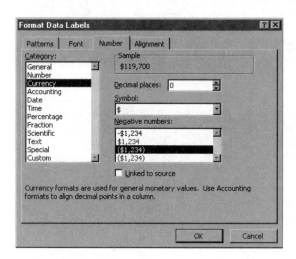

3 Click the Number tab of the Format dialog box. Your screen will look like the one shown in Figure 20-6. (If you're formatting an axis, the dialog box will also have a Scale tab, which you can use to adjust the numbers and tick marks along the *x*-axis and *y*-axis.)

4 Click the numeric category that you want to use, and specify a new number of decimal places if necessary. For example, if your labels are in the Currency format, you might want to set the decimal places to zero to remove cents and to make more room on your chart.

5 When you've finished formatting, click OK.

Adjusting Gridlines

If you're creating a column, bar, line, XY (scatter), area, radar, surface, bubble, stock, cylinder, cone, or pyramid chart, you can include gridlines that extend horizontally from the *x*-axis or vertically from the *y*-axis. Gridlines help you to associate numbers with the pictures in your chart, and they're especially useful if you need to make exact comparisons between categories of data.

To add gridlines to your chart, follow these steps:

1 Display the chart. If your chart is embedded in a worksheet, click the chart to activate Excel's charting menus.

2 From the Chart menu, choose the Chart Options command to display the Chart Options dialog box, and then click the Gridlines tab. (See Figure 20-7.)

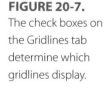

FIGURE 20-7.
The check boxes on the Gridlines tab determine which gridlines display.

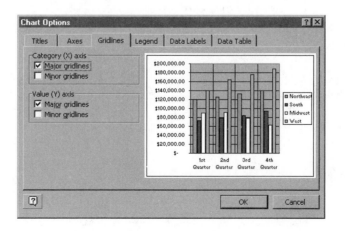

3 To add gridlines to both axes, turn on both Major Gridlines check boxes. If you want to create a denser pattern of gridlines, turn on the Minor Gridlines check boxes also.

4 Click OK to add the gridlines. To remove the gridlines, simply remove all the check marks from the Gridlines check boxes and click OK.

You can also remove gridlines by clicking the gridlines on your chart and pressing Delete.

Modifying the Chart Legend

A chart *legend* describes what each color or pattern represents in a chart so that you can compare the values in a category. Excel lets you change the font, colors, and location of an existing chart legend with a special dialog box full of formatting tabs. You can add a legend to a chart when you first build the chart with the Chart Wizard (step 3), or later by clicking the Legend button on the Chart toolbar. Because the Legend button is an on/off toggle, you can add or remove a chart legend quickly, to see whether you like it.

To modify a chart legend's font, colors, or location, follow these steps:

1 Display the chart and click the legend, which then will be surrounded by selection handles.

2 From the Format menu, choose the Selected Legend command to display the Format Legend dialog box, as shown in Figure 20-8. The dialog box contains three tabs, which let you control the border, colors, and patterns used for the legend box; the font used for the legend text; and the location of the legend in relation to the chart.

3 Use the Patterns, Font, and Placement tabs to customize the legend. When you've finished, click OK.

To quickly format the text in a chart legend, you can also use the Font, Font Size, Bold, Italic, and Underline buttons on the toolbar.

FIGURE 20-8.
To customize the chart's legend, use the Selected Legend command.

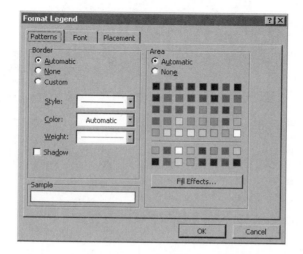

Changing the Viewing Angle in 3-D Charts

Excel offers you three-dimensional chart types in the Area, Bar, Column, Line, Pie, Radar, Surface, Cylinder, Cone, and Pyramid categories. Three-dimensional charts have much in common with two-dimensional charts, but they add a feeling of depth that contributes realism and visual interest to your data. You can change the orientation, or *viewing angle,* of a 3-D chart by selecting the chart and choosing the 3-D View command from the Chart menu. To tilt the chart up or back, click the large up or down buttons in the 3-D View dialog box above the Elevation text box. To rotate the chart left or right, click the clockwise or counterclockwise buttons beneath the chart preview window. In Excel 97, you can also change the perspective or "line of sight" angle by clicking the up or down buttons above the Perspective text box after you type a value.

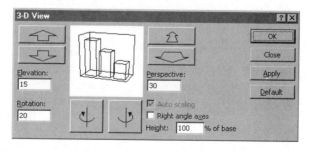

Creating Special Effects

Excel lets you add special effects to your charts to increase the visual appeal of your presentations and to highlight important trends. In this section, you'll learn the following techniques:

■ How to use arrows and callout text to emphasize key facts

■ How to add pictures to the background of a chart

■ How to use regional maps as charts

Adding Text and Arrows

? SEE ALSO

The Drawing toolbar contains several tools to further embellish your charts and work-sheets. For more information, see "Adding Graphics," page 314.

Have you ever been lost in a shopping mall, unable to determine your location or find the store you're looking for? When this happens, it's comforting to find the mall map, with its familiar *You Are Here* arrow and message that identify your current location and help you get your bearings. As you design your charts, you can use Excel's charting commands to add similar pointers to your own pictures. If you have important features that you want to highlight, this could be the perfect tool.

★ TIP

> Text and arrows are independent of each other and float freely over the chart where you place them. You can use them individually or together in your charts.

To highlight a chart feature with an arrow, follow these steps:

1 Display the chart that you want to embellish with an arrow. If the chart is embedded in a worksheet, click the chart to activate Excel's charting menus.

Drawing

2 Click the Drawing button on Excel's Standard toolbar or the Chart toolbar. Excel then displays its multipurpose Drawing toolbar, as shown in the following illustration:

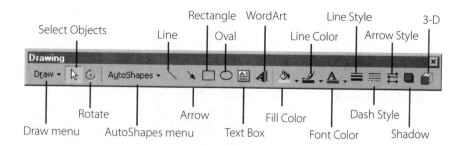

3 Click the Arrow button on the Drawing toolbar. The mouse pointer changes to drawing crosshairs.

4 Draw the line that will be your arrow from the tail to the head of the arrow. When you release the mouse button a default-style arrow appears.

5 Customize the arrow by adjusting the weight of the line with the Line Style button, selecting a dashed line style using the Dash Style button, or adjusting the tail and head of the arrow with the Arrow Style button.

6 Click the Close button on the Drawing toolbar to remove it from the screen.

To add text to the arrow, follow these steps:

1 Click the Text Box button on the Drawing toolbar.

2 Click and drag your mouse to draw a rectangle to hold your label text. When it is approximately the right size, release the mouse button.

3 Type the label text, and then click near the border of the text box to select it.

4 Use the Formatting toolbar to set the font, size, and style of the text. Use the Drawing toolbar to change the color of the text (use the Font Color button), to set the background color of the text

III

Microsoft Excel

box (use the Fill Color button), to add an outline to the text box (use the Line Style button), and to set the color of the outline (use the Line Color button).

You can reposition free-floating text boxes and arrows in your chart by selecting them and dragging with the mouse. To delete a text box or arrow, select the object and press Delete.

5 Resize the text box using the selection handles and place the text box where you want by dragging the border. Then click outside the chart area to remove the selection handles. Our chart now appears like this:

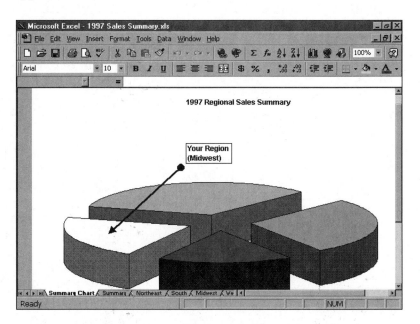

Adding Background Pictures

If the chart you're creating will take center stage in a report or presentation, you might want to embellish it further by adding electronic artwork to the background. When you add background artwork, Excel places the image that you specify behind your chart. If you specify a small pattern rather than a complete image, Excel automatically tiles the pattern to fill the entire chart.

TIP

Excel can place pictures, fill colors, textures, and gradient designs in three areas of your worksheet in any combination: behind your worksheet cells, behind the chart area, or behind the inner, plot area of the chart.

To add a bitmap, metafile, or other electronic image to the background of your chart, follow these steps:

1 Display the chart sheet to which you want to add background artwork. If the chart is an embedded chart, click it. To place a background in the outer chart area, click near the outer edge of the chart. The words *Chart Area* will pop up.

2 Choose Selected Chart Area from the Format menu, and click the Fill Effects button on the Patterns tab.

3 Click the Picture tab of the Fill Effects dialog box. Click Select Picture and locate the folder containing the artwork you want to use. You'll find several useful images in the Clipart folder in your MSOffice folder and in the Windows folder.

TIP

Try to use simple, light-colored background images in your charts so that the artwork doesn't overpower the text you're using for labels and titles. Light-gray clip art often works best.

4 To select a picture file, double-click it. You will be returned to the Fill Effects screen where you can see a preview of the picture. If you're not satisfied with it, click the Select Picture button again and try another art file. We chose the Windows 95 cloud graphic from the Windows folder, as shown on the following page.

III

Microsoft Excel

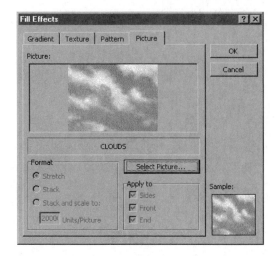

5 After you select your picture, click OK twice to add your artwork to the chart. The dialog boxes close and the background picture fills the entire chart area:

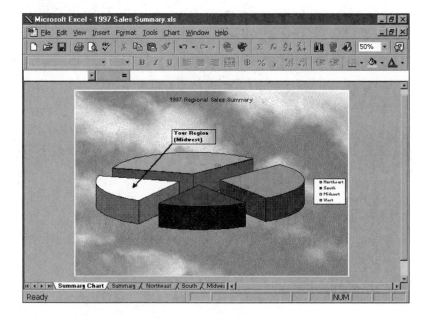

There is an additional inner area of every chart known as the Plot Area, the area where the chart itself resides. If you click in this area, the words *Plot Area* will pop up, and, if you wish, you can repeat the preceding steps to select a different picture, fill color, texture, or gradient pattern for just this inner area. By default the Plot Area is unfilled, or transparent; this is why the cloud picture we chose for the outer Chart Area displayed through the entire chart. As you can see, the effects you can achieve are nearly limitless.

Using Regional Maps as Charts

If your worksheet data has an intrinsic regional focus, you can use Excel's Data Map utility to add a geographic map to your worksheet and populate it with useful information from your worksheet or an Access database. Using regional maps to display worksheet data is not really charting, though it fits neatly into this section because you'll be using numbers and pictures to highlight worksheet data. As you work through this example, you'll build a regional map that displays coffee sales for a three-state region in an accurate and compelling format.

To create a regional map that displays worksheet information, follow these steps:

1 Create a worksheet containing geographic names in one column and numbers in a second column. If you use geographic names such as states, provinces, and countries in the first column, the Data Map utility will be able to incorporate them automatically.

You can also incorporate data from other unopened workbooks or an Access database into your data map, so don't reenter the data if you have it in another place.

2 Select the two columns of data for the map, as shown in the illustration on the following page.

III

Microsoft Excel

	A	B	C	D
1	**Pacific Northwest Coffee Sales**			
2				
3	**State**	**Sales**		
4	Washington	$ 75,000		
5	Oregon	$ 60,000		
6	Idaho	$ 28,000		
7				
8				

Map

3 Click the Map button on Excel's Standard toolbar, and then use the drawing crosshairs to draw a rectangle for the map on your worksheet. The Data Map utility runs and replaces Excel's menu bar and toolbars with its own tools. You'll see a map frame and, unless there is only one map available for the regions in your list, a dialog box similar to the following:

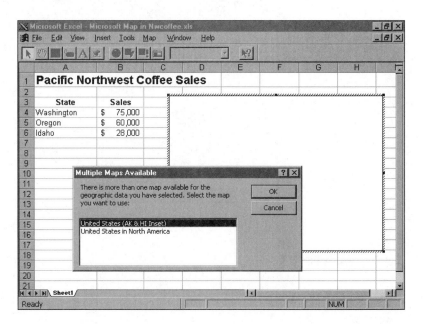

 TIP

If Excel displays a message indicating that the Data Map utility isn't available, you'll need to install it from your Setup disks before you can use it. The Data Map utility is an optional Office accessory and map library that requires almost 6 MB of disk space.

4 Click the regional map that you want to display in your map frame, and click OK. (Your choice should match the data in your worksheet.) The Data Map utility displays a basic map in the map frame, with special shading for the regions you selected. A Data Map Control dialog box also appears to help you customize the map.

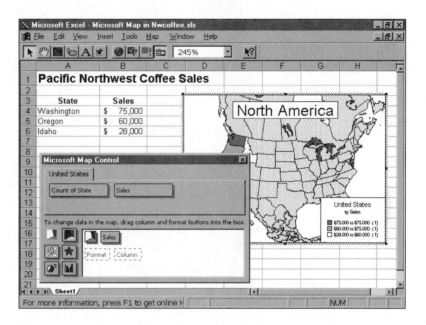

5 Click the Close button on the title bar of the Data Map Control dialog box—the dialog box contains advanced tools that you won't use in this example. (For more information about the Map Controls, read "Microsoft Map Help Topics" in the Help menu of the Microsoft Map program.)

Center Map

6 Click the Center Map button on the Data Map toolbar, and then click the center of the region that you want to display up-close. In this example, we'll click in the middle of the combined three-state area to keep it centered during zooms.

Grabber

7 Enlarge the map to show just the relevant area by entering a percentage in the Zoom Percentage Of Map text box on the Data Map toolbar. In our example, we used 850%. Use the Grabber button to adjust the map within its frame, without changing the zoom level. Our screen is shown on the following page.

III

Microsoft Excel

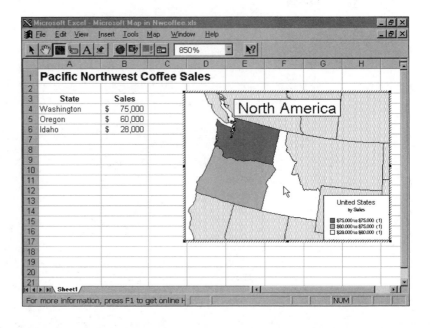

Map
Labels

8 Click the Map Labels button. In the Map Labels dialog box that appears, click the Values From option, select the column containing the data to be placed on the map from the drop-down list, and then click OK.

9 For each region on the map, click where the number is to be placed. In this example, click on Washington, Oregon, and Idaho.

 TIP

You can add geographical features to your map by choosing Features from the Map menu and then choosing the features you want to add.

10 Click the North America label, and press Delete to remove the title, or double-click it to edit the text. You can also click on the legend and press Delete to remove it or else select it and use the mouse to drag it to a new location.

11 When you've finished customizing the map, click anywhere in the worksheet to restore Excel's menus and toolbars. Your completed data map will look similar to the following:

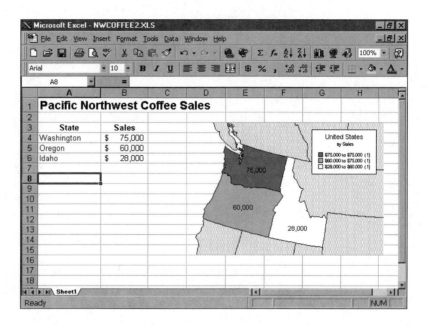

> **NOTE**
>
> To revise your data map in the future, simply double-click the map and use the Data Map menus and toolbar to format the map. To delete the map, select the map object in the worksheet and press Delete.

Printing a Chart

When you've finished creating attractive charts and maps, you'll most certainly want to print them. Printing charts is not much different from printing worksheets, but you have a few extra options available. If you're using a black-and-white printer, you'll want to examine your chart in Print Preview to verify that its colors have been properly converted to grayscale shading. Finally, if you're printing an embedded chart, you have the option of printing the chart with or without the worksheet data around it.

To double-check chart colors in Print Preview, follow these steps:

Print Preview

1 Display the chart that you want to print, and then click the Print Preview button on the Standard toolbar.

III

Microsoft Excel

2   Verify the chart shading—you should be able to distinguish one shade of gray from another. (If you're using a color printer, of course, you'll see everything in color.)

3   Click Close to exit Print Preview.

4   If you're not happy with the shading, click twice on the chart piece that you want to change to select it, and then double-click on it and specify a new color or pattern in the Patterns tab of the Format Data Point dialog box. Excel gives you complete control over the colors and shading patterns used in your charts and legends, so that you can adjust them if necessary.

To print a chart, follow these steps:

1   Display the chart that you want to print, either as a stand-alone chart sheet or as an embedded chart in the worksheet.

2   If you want to print an embedded chart only, and not the surrounding worksheet data as well, click the chart first.

3   From the File menu, choose the Print command to open the Print dialog box.

4   Specify the print options that you want, and then click OK to send your chart to the printer.

Print Your Chart as "What You Get Is What You See"

By default, Excel prints a chart on an entire page. If you want your printed chart to be the same size as the chart in your worksheet, choose the Page Setup command from the File menu, click the Chart tab, and then select the Custom option before printing. This option tells Excel to render the chart on paper exactly as it appears in your worksheet.

Managing Information in Lists

I f you routinely track large amounts of information in your business—customer mailing lists, phone lists, product inventories, sales transactions, and so on—you can use Excel's extensive list-management capabilities to make your job easier. A list is a table of data stored in a worksheet, organized into columns of fields and rows of records. A list is essentially a *database*, but because lists are stored in Excel workbooks and not in formatted files created by database programs such as Access or FoxPro, Microsoft has chosen to use the word *list* as the preferred term.

In this chapter, you'll learn how to create a list in a workbook, sort the list based on one or more fields, locate important records with filters, organize entries with subtotals, and create summary information with pivot tables. The lists that you create will be compatible with Access, and, if you're not already familiar with Access, the techniques that you learn here will give you a head start on learning several Access commands and terms.

Using a List of Cells as a Database

A list is simply a collection of rows with columns of consistently formatted data, adhering to somewhat stricter rules than an ordinary worksheet. To build a list that works with all of Excel's list-management commands, you need to follow a few basic guidelines. Figure 21-1 shows a simple sales-history list with five columns, or *fields,* and a dozen sales transaction *records.* When you create a list, it should contain a fixed number of columns or categories of information, but with a variable number of rows, reflecting records that can be added, deleted, or rearranged to keep your list up to date. Each column should contain the same type of information, and there should be no blank rows or columns in the list area. If your list is the only information on the worksheet, Excel will have an easier time recognizing the data as a list.

To create a list in Excel, follow these steps:

1 Open a new workbook or a new sheet in an existing workbook. Using a new worksheet that will contain only your list works best, so that Excel can select your data automatically when you use list-management commands.

FIGURE 21-1.
A list of information in an Excel worksheet, complete with column headings.

Each column is a field containing the same type of information.

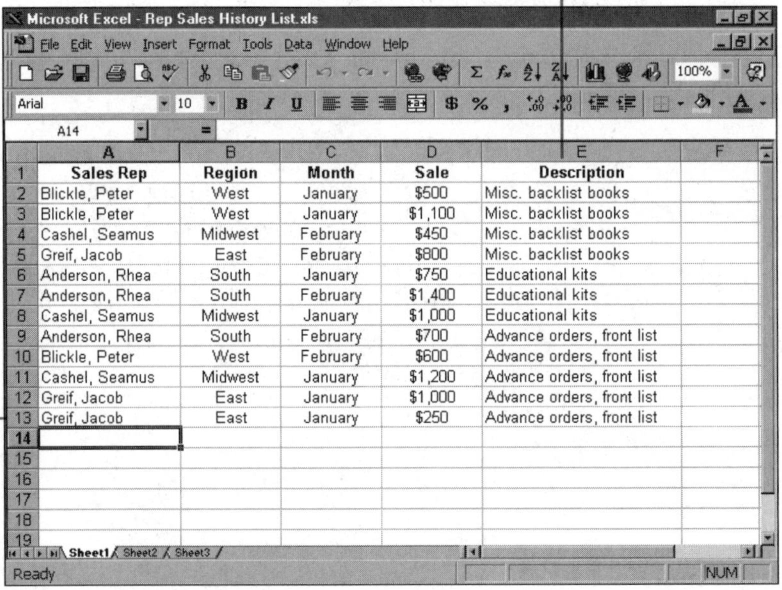

	A	B	C	D	E
1	Sales Rep	Region	Month	Sale	Description
2	Blickle, Peter	West	January	$500	Misc. backlist books
3	Blickle, Peter	West	January	$1,100	Misc. backlist books
4	Cashel, Seamus	Midwest	February	$450	Misc. backlist books
5	Greif, Jacob	East	February	$800	Misc. backlist books
6	Anderson, Rhea	South	January	$750	Educational kits
7	Anderson, Rhea	South	February	$1,400	Educational kits
8	Cashel, Seamus	Midwest	January	$1,000	Educational kits
9	Anderson, Rhea	South	February	$700	Advance orders, front list
10	Blickle, Peter	West	February	$600	Advance orders, front list
11	Cashel, Seamus	Midwest	January	$1,200	Advance orders, front list
12	Greif, Jacob	East	January	$1,000	Advance orders, front list
13	Greif, Jacob	East	January	$250	Advance orders, front list

Each row is a record.

2 Create a column heading for each field in the list, adjust the alignment of the headings, and format them in bold type.

3 Format the cells below the column headings for the data that you plan to use. This can include number formats (such as currency or date), alignment, or any other formats.

4 Finally, add new records (your data) below the column headings, taking care to be consistent in your usage of words and titles so that related records can be organized in groups later. Enter as many rows as you need, making sure that there are no empty rows in your list, not even between the column headings and the first record. See Figure 21-1 for a sample list of information.

 TIP

Let AutoComplete Finish Typing Your Words

Excel's AutoComplete feature will help you to insert repetitive list entries by recognizing the words you type and finishing them for you. To enable this time-saving feature, choose the Options command from the Tools menu, click the Edit tab, and turn on the Enable AutoComplete For Cell Values check box. It's important that repeated names and other data (such as *January*, *Midwest Region*, and so on) be entered identically from record to record, to enable Excel to recognize the data for grouping, sorting, and calculating.

? SEE ALSO

For information about sharing a list with other users over a network, see "Managing Shared Workbooks," page 514.

5 When you've finished, save your workbook. If your list grows to include many records, consider keeping a separate backup copy in a safe place as an extra precaution.

Using a Form for Data Entry

To make it easy to manage the data in your list, Excel lets you add, delete, and search for records with the Form command on the Data menu. When you choose the Form command, a customized dialog box appears, showing the fields in your list and several list-management command buttons. (See Figure 21-2 on the following page.) By default, the first record in the list appears, but you can scroll to other records by clicking the vertical scroll bar. Excel adds new records to the end of the list; to display a blank record, you can scroll to the bottom of the list or click the New button. Although you'll often add records by typing them directly in the worksheet, the Form command is a useful alternative (for, say, a less-experienced colleague you've asked to help enter data), and in some cases you'll find that it works faster.

FIGURE 21-2.

The Form command gives you another way to enter data into the rows and columns of a list.

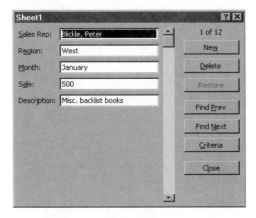

Validating Data as You Enter It

If several people are using your Excel list, you might wish to control the type of information they're allowed to enter into worksheet cells to minimize typing mistakes. For example, you might want to require that only January or February dates can be entered into the "Month" column, or that only dollar values in a particular range (say, $0–$5,000) can be entered into the "Sale" column. With Excel you can enforce input requirements such as these by using a formatting option called *data validation*. When you use data validation, you protect part or all of your worksheet from erroneous input that might cause formulas or list-management tools to produce incorrect results.

To enforce data validation on a particular range of worksheet cells, follow these steps:

1 Select the cells in the column you want to protect with data validation. This should include cells already containing data as well as the blank cells below, where you'll be adding new records.

2 From the Data menu, choose the Validation command. The Data Validation dialog box opens. Select the Settings tab.

3 In the Validation Criteria area, specify the input format you want to require for the selected cells in the Allow drop-down list box. Your options are Any Value (used to remove existing data validation), Whole Number, Decimal, List, Date, Time, Text Length, and Custom (a format you specify with your own formula). When you select a value in the Allow drop-down list box, additional text fields appear below that let you specify extra input conditions or *restrictions*, such as the smallest number and the largest number Excel will accept.

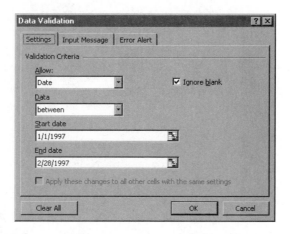

4 Select the Input Message tab and turn on Show Input Message When Cell Is Selected to specify a message that will appear when the cell is selected.

5 In the Input Message text box, type the words you want displayed in the pop-up box that appears when a user highlights a cell containing the data validation formatting. (This box is optional, but using it will help your users "discover" the requirements you've established *before* they make a mistake.)

III

Microsoft Excel

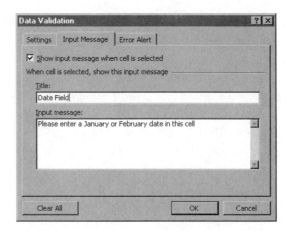

6 Select the Error Alert tab and turn on Show Error Alert After Invalid Data Is Entered to specify the type of error message you want Excel to display if a user enters inappropriate information into a cell. From the Style drop-down list box, select Stop (to block the input), Warning (to caution the user but allow the input), or Information (to display a note but allow the input).

7 In the Error Message text box, type the words you want displayed in the error message dialog box that appears if the user enters invalid data. For example, a useful phrase might be "This worksheet tracks January and February sales only."

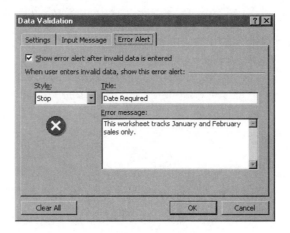

8 Click OK to complete the Data Validation dialog box. If you specified the options shown in step 7, you'll see a gentle error message similar to the following if you enter the wrong type of data in a cell with active data validation:

Sorting Rows and Columns

Once your records are organized into a list, you can use several commands on the Data menu to rearrange and analyze the data. The Sort command lets you arrange the records in a different order based on the values in one or more columns. You can sort records in ascending or descending order or in a custom order, such as days of the week or months of the year.

To sort a list based on one column, follow these steps:

1 Click a cell in the list that you want to sort.

2 From the Data menu, choose the Sort command. Excel selects all the records in your list and displays the following dialog box:

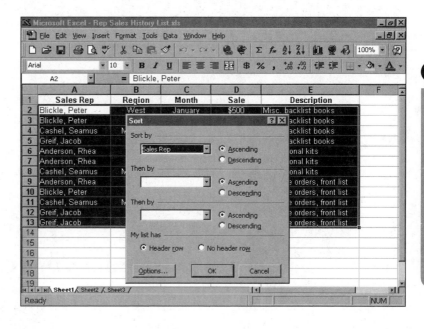

3 The Sort By drop-down list box contains the heading for either the first column or the column you last used to sort your data. You can select a different column in the drop-down list box to use for the sort.

4 Click one of the sort order option buttons to specify ascending order (A to Z, lowest to highest, earliest date to most recent) or descending order (Z to A, highest to lowest, most recent date to earliest).

5 Click OK to run the sort. If you sorted the first column in ascending order, your screen will look similar to this:

	A	B	C	D	E	F
1	**Sales Rep**	**Region**	**Month**	**Sale**	**Description**	
2	Anderson, Rhea	South	January	$750	Educational kits	
3	Anderson, Rhea	South	February	$1,400	Educational kits	
4	Anderson, Rhea	South	February	$700	Advance orders, front list	
5	Blickle, Peter	West	January	$500	Misc. backlist books	
6	Blickle, Peter	West	January	$1,100	Misc. backlist books	
7	Blickle, Peter	West	February	$600	Advance orders, front list	
8	Cashel, Seamus	Midwest	February	$450	Misc. backlist books	
9	Cashel, Seamus	Midwest	January	$1,000	Educational kits	
10	Cashel, Seamus	Midwest	January	$1,200	Advance orders, front list	
11	Greif, Jacob	East	February	$800	Misc. backlist books	
12	Greif, Jacob	East	January	$1,000	Advance orders, front list	
13	Greif, Jacob	East	January	$250	Advance orders, front list	

⭐ **TIP**

Sort Ascending

Sort Descending

Click a Cell, Sort a List

To quickly sort a list based on a single column, click a column head or a cell in the column, and then click either the Sort Ascending or Sort Descending button on the Standard toolbar. Excel rearranges the list in the order that you selected.

Sorting on More Than One Column

If you have "ties" in your sort—that is, if some of the records in your list have identical entries in the column you're sorting with—you can specify additional sorting criteria to further organize your list. To sort a list based on two or three columns, follow these steps:

1 Click a cell in the list that you want to sort.

2 From the Data menu, choose the Sort command. Excel selects the records in your list and displays the Sort dialog box.

3 Select the primary field for the sort in the Sort By drop-down list box. Specify ascending or descending order for that column.

4 Click the first Then By drop-down list box and pick a *second* column for the sort, to resolve any ties in the first sort. Specify ascending or descending order for the second sort as well.

5 Click the second Then By drop-down list box and pick a *third* column for the sort, again to resolve any ties remaining after the first two sorts. Once more, specify ascending or descending order. (Your sorts needn't be in the same direction.) A Sort dialog box with three levels of sorting is shown here:

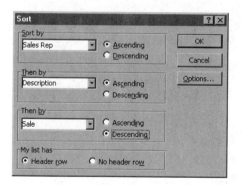

6 Click OK to run the sort. The following screen shows how a sort would look based on the options shown above. Note that the columns you specify in the Then By sections are used only to resolve ties in the list—not to control the entire sort. (For this reason, numbers in the Sale column are only in descending order when both the Sales Rep and the Description fields are identical.)

III

Microsoft Excel

Microsoft Excel - Rep Sales History List.xls

	A	B	C	D	E	F
1	**Sales Rep**	**Region**	**Month**	**Sale**	**Description**	
2	Anderson, Rhea	South	February	$700	Advance orders, front list	
3	Anderson, Rhea	South	February	$1,400	Educational kits	
4	Anderson, Rhea	South	January	$750	Educational kits	
5	Blickle, Peter	West	February	$600	Advance orders, front list	
6	Blickle, Peter	West	January	$1,100	Misc. backlist books	
7	Blickle, Peter	West	January	$500	Misc. backlist books	
8	Cashel, Seamus	Midwest	January	$1,200	Advance orders, front list	
9	Cashel, Seamus	Midwest	January	$1,000	Educational kits	
10	Cashel, Seamus	Midwest	February	$450	Misc. backlist books	
11	Greif, Jacob	East	January	$1,000	Advance orders, front list	
12	Greif, Jacob	East	January	$250	Advance orders, front list	
13	Greif, Jacob	East	February	$800	Misc. backlist books	
14						
15						
16						
17						
18						
19						

> To restore a list to its original order after a sort, choose the Undo Sort command from the Edit menu immediately after running the sort, or open the Undo button's list to reverse an earlier sort action.

Creating Your Own Custom Sort Order

Excel lets you create custom sort orders so that you can rearrange lists that don't follow predictable alphanumeric or chronologic patterns. For example, you can create a custom sort order for the regions of the country (West, Midwest, East, South), to tell Excel to sort the regions in the way *you* want rather than by strict alphabetic rules. When you define a custom sort order, it appears in the Sort Options dialog box and is available to all the workbooks in your system.

To create a custom sort order, follow these steps:

1 From the Tools menu, choose Options, and then click the Custom Lists tab.

2 Click the line NEW LIST under Custom Lists, and the text pointer will appear in the List Entries list box. This is where you'll type the items in your custom list. (In this example, you'll create the custom order West, Midwest, South, East.)

3   Type *West, Midwest, South, East,* and then click the Add button. You can either separate each value with a comma or type it on a separate line. The new custom order appears in the Custom Lists list box, as shown in Figure 21-3. You can now use this sorting order to sort your columns, as described in "Sorting with a Custom Sort Order" next.

FIGURE 21-3.

The Custom Lists tab lets you add, delete, and edit Excel's collection of custom sorting orders.

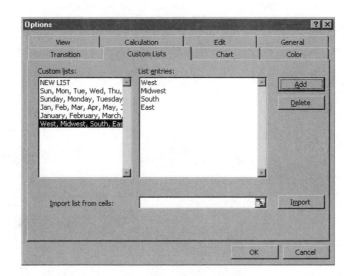

4   Click OK to close the Options dialog box.

You can also use the Custom Lists tab to edit and delete custom lists in your system. For example, you could rearrange the days-of-the-week sorting order so that Monday appears as the first day of the week and Sunday appears as the last.

Sorting with a Custom Sort Order

When you want to sort based on an order that isn't alphabetical or numerical—the days of the week, for example, or the months of the year that have been entered as text rather than dates—you can click the Options button in the Sort dialog box and specify a custom sort order to use for the comparison. To use a custom sort order, follow the steps on the next page.

III

Microsoft Excel

1 Click any cell in your list.

2 From the Data menu, choose the Sort command. Excel selects the records in your list and displays the Sort dialog box.

3 Select the primary field for the sort in the Sort By list box. Specify ascending or descending order. (The direction you specify will also apply to the custom sort.) In our example we're selecting the Region field, ascending order.

4 Click the Options button to display the Sort Options dialog box.

5 Click the First Key Sort Order drop-down list box, and click the custom order that you want to use. Your screen should like this:

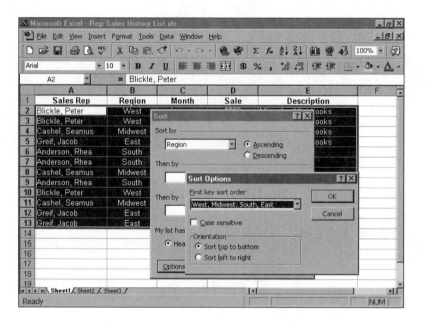

> **NOTE**
>
> You can also specify custom sort orders for the second and third sort options if you want to, in which case the title of the sort order drop-down list box will change to match the key that you're defining.

6 Click OK in each dialog box to run the sort. Your list will appear sorted with the custom criteria you specified.

Using AutoFilter to Find Records

When you want to hide all the rows in your list except those that meet certain criteria, you can use the AutoFilter command on the Filter submenu of the Data menu. The AutoFilter command places a drop-down list box at the top of each column in your list. To display a particular group of records, select the criteria that you want in one or more of the drop-down list boxes. For example, to display the sales history for all employees with $1,000 orders in January, you could select January in the Month column drop-down list box and $1,000 in the Sale drop-down list box.

To use the AutoFilter command to find records, follow these steps:

1 Click any cell in the list.

2 From the Data menu, choose Filter and then choose AutoFilter from the submenu.

3 Each column head now displays a down arrow. Click on the down arrow next to the heading that you want to use for the filter. A list box with filter options appears, similar to the one shown in the screen at the top of the following page.

4 If a column in your list contains one or more blank cells, you'll also see (Blanks) and (NonBlanks) options at the bottom of the list. The (Blanks) option displays only the records containing an empty cell (blank fields) in the filter column, so that you can locate any missing items quickly. The (NonBlanks) option displays the opposite—all records that have an entry in the filter column. Click the value that you want to use for the filter.

Excel hides the entries that don't match the criterion you specified, and highlights the active filter arrow. The illustration at the bottom of the following page shows the results of using the January criterion in the Month column.

You can use more than one filter arrow to display only the records that you want—an extremely useful feature if your list is many records long. To continue working with AutoFilter but also redisplay all your records, choose the Show All command from the Filter submenu of the

Display all records in list.

Show records with ten largest
numbers in a numerical field.

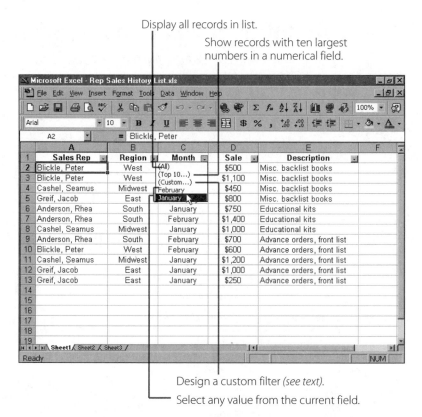

Design a custom filter *(see text)*.

Select any value from the current field.

Data menu, and Excel will display all your records again. To remove the AutoFilter drop-down list boxes, turn off the AutoFilter command on the Filter submenu.

Creating a Custom AutoFilter

When you want to display a numeric range of data, or customize a column filter in other ways, choose Custom from the AutoFilter drop-down list box to display the Custom AutoFilter dialog box. The dialog box contains two relational list boxes and two value list boxes that you can use to build a custom range for the filter. For example, you could display all sales greater than $1,000 or, as shown in Figure 21-4, all sales between $500 and $800. The list boxes are easy to deal with because the most useful values and relationships are already listed in them—all you have to do is point and click. You can further fine-tune your criteria with the And and Or option buttons as well as the ? and * wildcard characters.

FIGURE 21-4.
The Custom AutoFilter dialog box lets you build your own filter.

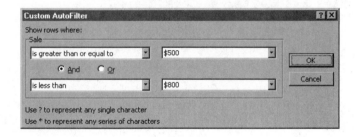

To create a custom AutoFilter, follow these steps:

1 Click any cell in the list.

2 If AutoFilter isn't already turned on, choose the Filter command from the Data menu and then choose AutoFilter from the submenu. A drop-down list box appears at the top of each column in the list.

3 Click the arrow next to the heading that you want to use for the customized filter, and select (Custom…) from the list of choices. The Custom AutoFilter dialog box opens.

4 Click the first operator list box and specify the relationship (equals, is greater than, is less than, and so on) that you want to use for the filter, and then click the first value list box and specify

the boundary that you want to set. (For example, you could specify all values greater than or equal to $500 with "is greater than or equal to $500".)

5 If you want to specify a second range, click And to indicate that the records must meet both criteria *or* click Or to indicate that the records can match either criterion. Then specify a relationship in the second operator list box, and a range boundary in the second value list box. Figure 21-4 on the preceding page shows a Custom AutoFilter dialog box with two range criteria specified.

6 Click OK to apply the custom AutoFilter. The records selected by the filter are displayed in your worksheet.

Using the Subtotals Command to Organize a List

The Subtotals command on the Data menu helps you to organize a list by displaying records in groups with subtotals, averages, or other summary information. The Subtotals command can also display a grand total at the top or bottom of your list, letting you quickly add up columns of numbers. As a bonus, Subtotals displays your list in Outline view so that you can expand or shrink each section in the list simply by clicking.

To add subtotals to a list, follow these steps:

1 Arrange the list so that the records for each group are located together. An easy way to do this is to sort on the field on which you're basing your groups. For example, you could sort based on employee, region, or store.

2 From the Data menu, choose the Subtotals command. The Subtotal dialog box opens.

3 In the At Each Change In list box, choose a group whose subtotal you want to define. This should be the same column that you sorted the list with—each time this value changes, Excel will insert a row and compute a subtotal for the numeric fields in this group of records.

4 In the Use Function list box, choose a function to use in the sub-total. SUM is the most popular, but other options are available, as described in Table 21-1 on the following page.

5 In the Add Subtotal To list box, choose the column or columns to use in the subtotal calculation. You can subtotal more than one column by checking multiple boxes, but be sure to remove any check marks that you don't want. The following screen shows the settings for a typical Subtotals command:

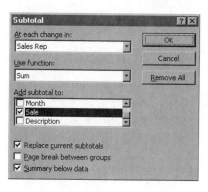

6 Click OK to add the subtotals to the list. You'll see the following screen, complete with subtotals, outlining, and a grand total:

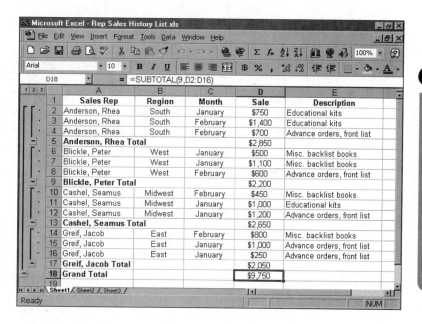

TABLE 21-1. Summary Functions in the Subtotal Dialog Box

Function	Description
SUM	Add up the numbers in the subtotal group
COUNT	Count the number of nonblank cells in the group
AVERAGE	Calculate the average of the numbers in the group
MAX	Display the largest number in the group
MIN	Display the smallest number in the group
PRODUCT	Multiply together all the numbers in the group
COUNT NUMS	Count the number of cells containing numeric values in the group
STDDEV	Estimate the standard deviation based on a sample
STDDEVP	Calculate the standard deviation for an entire population
VAR	Estimate the variance in the group based on a sample
VARP	Calculate the variance for an entire population

 TIP

You can choose the Subtotals command as often as necessary to modify your groupings or calculations. When you've finished using the Subtotals command, click Remove All in the Subtotal dialog box.

Using Your List as an Access Database

If you have the Professional Edition of Microsoft Office 97, you also have Access, Microsoft's relational database management system.

If you've been working with lists in Excel for a while, you might be wondering if your lists are compatible with Access, and when, if ever, you should move up to a more sophisticated database. What are the real differences between these two products? The short answer is that Excel is perfectly suited to list management as long as your databases don't become too large and you don't need to track unusual data or run especially advanced commands. However, Excel has the following limitations when dealing with databases:

Using Your List as an Access Database *continued*

- Worksheets are limited to 65,536 rows, meaning that you can't have more than 65,536 records (names in your mailing list, sales transactions, and the like).

- Fields can contain a maximum of 256 characters, limiting you to shorter descriptions or notes in your lists.

- Excel can't store pictures, sounds, and other types of special data in fields.

- Excel lacks advanced data protection or sophisticated backup features.

- You can't create custom data entry forms without using Access.

If you'd like to move your list into Access in the future, however, be assured the transition will be relatively painless. To convert your Excel list into an Access database, you use the Access program's Import command on the Get External Data submenu of the File menu. The Import command launches a wizard that helps you locate and save your Excel file as a table in Access.

After you import and save the table, you'll find many familiar data management and formatting commands on the Access menus. The following illustration shows what the list used in this chapter looks like when saved as an Access database. You can learn more about specific Access commands in Part V of this book.

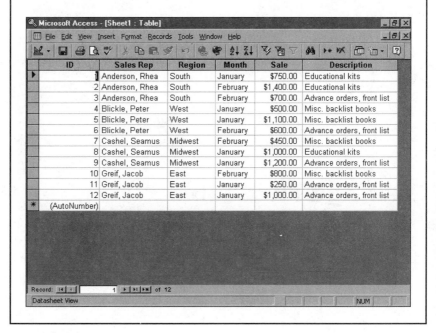

Microsoft Excel

Working in Outline View

Similar to the way Outline view functions in Word, outlines created in Excel using the Subtotals command let you examine different parts of a list by clicking buttons in the left margin, as shown in Figure 21-5.

FIGURE 21-5.

The Subtotals command creates an outline view of your list.

Show the Grand Total and subtotals.   Show all the data.

Show only the Grand Total.

Collapse a single group.

Expand a single group.

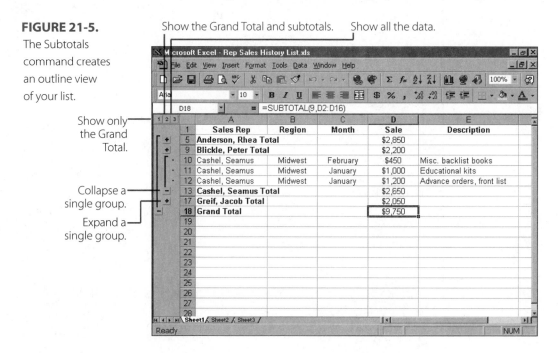

Click the numbers at the top of the left margin to choose how many levels of data you want to see. Click the plus or minus button to expand or collapse specific subgroups of data.

Creating a Pivot Table

The most sophisticated data-management feature in Excel is the Pivot-Table command, which creates a customizable table that you can use to organize the fields in your list into new and useful combinations. When spreadsheet programs for microcomputers were first developed, you couldn't easily exchange rows and columns (doing so can be useful in viewing your data from another angle) without going through contortions. Eventually the pivot table was developed, named for its ability to "pivot" rows into columns and columns into rows. Excel's pivot table feature does that, and much more.

You create a pivot table in Excel with the PivotTable Wizard, which prompts you for information and helps you to define your calculations and format the table. After the pivot table is complete, you can customize it further by rearranging fields and applying new data formats. We'll cover each technique in this section.

Using the PivotTable Wizard

The best way to learn about a pivot table is to create one. The PivotTable Wizard gives you complete control over the position of row and column headings in your table. To create a pivot table, follow these steps:

1 Click a cell in the list that you want to view with a pivot table.

2 From the Data menu, choose the PivotTable Report command. The PivotTable Wizard starts, and prompts you for the source of data for the table, as shown here:

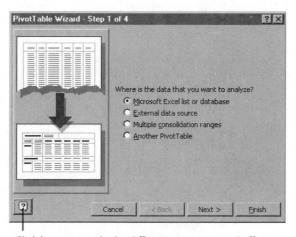

Click here to toggle the Office Assistant on and off.

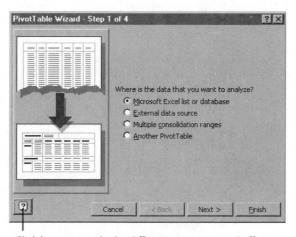 **NOTE**

If the Office Assistant is enabled, you'll have an opportunity now to learn more about pivot tables and the various options you have when creating a database report. Feel free to seek guidance from the Office Assistant as you use the Pivot-Table Wizard. When you no longer need it, click the Excel Help button in the lower left-hand corner of the PivotTable Wizard dialog box to close the Office Assistant.

III

Microsoft Excel

3 Verify that the first option, Microsoft Excel List Or Database, is selected, and click Next. In this example, you'll be creating a pivot table from a list in your worksheet. However, you can also create pivot tables from external data (such as records received through Microsoft Query), multiple consolidation ranges, or another pivot table. After you select a data source, Excel prompts you for a data range.

4 If you had a list open on screen when you started the wizard, Excel might have already selected it for you. If not, select data from an Excel list now with the mouse (be sure to include the column headings). Don't worry about the dialog box getting in the way—Excel will minimize it when you start selecting cells, giving you a full-window look at your data. Our example screen looks like this:

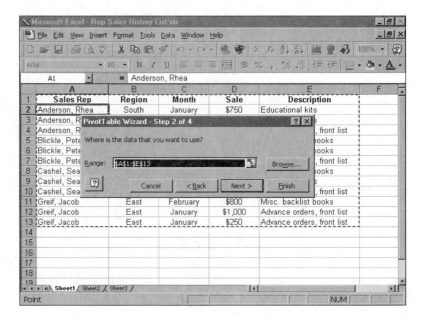

5 Click Next to display the dialog box that you'll use to organize the fields in your pivot table. You'll see a table that looks a bit like a worksheet, with areas for rows, columns, and data. The fields in your list appear as movable buttons on the right side of the dialog box.

6 Define the initial layout of your pivot table by dragging fields from the right side of the dialog box into the Row, Column, Data, and Page areas. Fields placed in the Row area will become rows in your pivot table, fields placed in the Column area will become columns, and fields placed in the Data area will be added together with the SUM function. You can rearrange, or pivot, these values later, so don't worry too much about the final placement of fields now. (The Page area is reserved for fields that you want to take a closer look at.) We selected and arranged three fields in the following way:

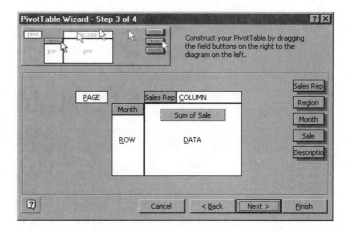

7 Click Next to display the final screen of the PivotTable Wizard. By default, Excel creates pivot tables in new worksheets, though you can also specify an existing worksheet and even an exact location within a worksheet. Click Finish to accept the default setting and complete your pivot table. Ours appears on the next page.

Evaluating a Pivot Table

It might take you a moment to recognize the data in your pivot table, because it presents an entirely new view of your list. It's almost as if you had created new row and column headings, typed all the data again, and used the Subtotals command to summarize the results! However, you didn't have to rearrange your worksheet manually—the PivotTable Wizard did it for you. Best of all, you can easily transpose one or more fields and use new functions to highlight other trends in your list.

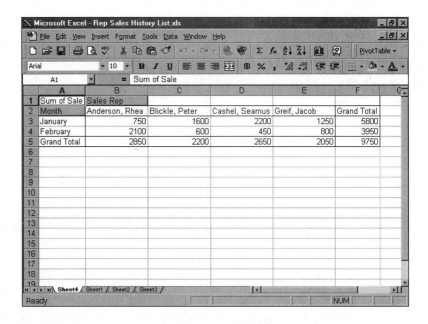

Viewing External Data with Microsoft Query

When you created your pivot table, you had the option of using external data as the source of your information. One method of extracting external data for your pivot table is using Query, a program shipped with Microsoft Office 97 that you can use to connect to external data sources through a software driver called *ODBC* (Open Database Connectivity). Microsoft Query acts as a link between Excel and database files with diverse data formats, such as Access, FoxPro, SQL Server, dBASE, Paradox, and Btrieve. Query uses ODBC to translate complex data-filtering questions, or *queries*, into a language called SQL (structured query language). As a result, you can use Query to extract information about compatible database files in very sophisticated ways. For example, your query might be, "How many sales reps do we have who sell more than $20,000 in products per year and who work in the South or the Midwest?"

When you want to work with external database files, you should consider using Query as a stand-alone tool or as a utility to import your data into Excel. Start Query within Excel by clicking the Data menu and making a selection from the Get External Data submenu. To use Query for accessing data in constructing a PivotTable, select External Data Source in step 1 of the PivotTable Wizard, and then click Get Data in step 2. For more information, search for "Query (Microsoft)" in the Excel Help Index. You can also access a series of helpful Cue Cards from within the Query Help menu. (Query is an add-in program, so you'll have to install it using the Office Setup program before it can be accessed.)

To help you work with the pivot table, Excel displays the PivotTable toolbar. It may appear next to the Standard toolbar, only partially showing. You can drag the vertical bars at the left edge of the toolbar to move the entire toolbar onto the screen, as shown in Figure 21-6. You might find this tool useful when evaluating and customizing your list. Take a moment to examine the buttons and commands on the PivotTable toolbar, and then read the summary data in your new pivot table, especially the Grand Total row and column.

FIGURE 21-6.
The PivotTable toolbar features several unique commands and buttons specifically designed for manipulating pivot tables.

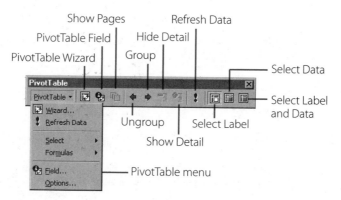

Rearranging Fields in a Pivot Table

To rearrange, or pivot, the data in your pivot table, simply click the PivotTable Wizard button or Wizard command on the PivotTable toolbar and move the fields around in the table. You can also change the function used to calculate in the Data area by double-clicking the field and choosing a new formula. As you edit or rearrange the data in the pivot table, note that your changes don't affect the data in your list (which is on its own worksheet)—your original rows and columns remain the same.

> **NOTE**
>
> Any changes that you make to your list after creating a pivot table won't be reflected in the pivot table until you choose the Refresh Data command from the Data menu or click the Refresh Data button on the PivotTable toolbar.

III

Microsoft Excel

To rearrange fields in a pivot table, follow these steps:

1 Click the PivotTable Wizard button or Wizard command on the PivotTable toolbar. (You can also choose the PivotTable Report command from the Data menu.) The third screen of the PivotTable Wizard appears, prompting you for a new field arrangement.

2 Drag the fields to new positions in the Row, Column, Data, and Page areas. Remember that you can place more than one field in an area. The following screen shows a combination of fields that will display sales representatives in rows, regions in columns, and sales summaries in the Data area. We moved the Month field to the Page area so that we could view each month separately.

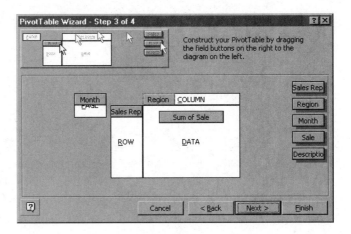

When you add a field to the Page area, a drop-down list box appears in your pivot table, giving you access to each of the values in the field.

3 Click Next to display the fourth screen of the PivotTable Wizard, and adjust any options that you want to change.

Accept the default location in the PivotTable Starting Cell text box to keep your pivot table in the same place. If you clear the text box, Excel will move your pivot table to a new worksheet.

4 Click Finish to display your new pivot table. The following screen shows the new result. To view different months in this table, you would click the down arrow for the drop-down list in cell B2, and select a new month.

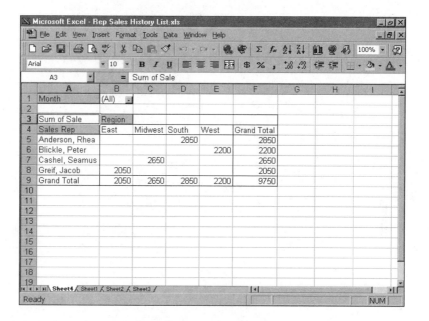

Changing the Function in a Pivot Table

By default, the PivotTable Wizard uses the SUM function to add up values in the Data area of your pivot table, but you can easily change the function to calculate another value. For example, you could use the AVERAGE function to calculate the average sales in a month, or the COUNT function to total up the number of sales orders written by a particular employee. The list of functions available is identical to the set employed by the Subtotals command, described in Table 21-1 (page 624).

To change the function used in a pivot table, follow these steps:

1 Click the PivotTable Wizard button on the PivotTable toolbar. The third screen of the PivotTable Wizard appears, displaying the fields in your table.

2 In the Data area, double-click the field that you want to summarize with a new function. (You can double-click any field to adjust its characteristics, though only fields in the Data area can

display summary information.) You'll see the PivotTable Field dialog box, as shown in Figure 21-7.

FIGURE 21-7.
The PivotTable Field dialog box lets you switch to a different function in the pivot table.

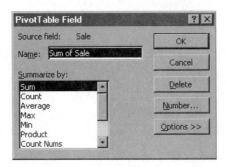

3   In the Summarize By list box, select the new function that you want to use. (For example, select the MAX function to display the largest sales in the field.)

4   Click OK to close the PivotTable Field dialog box, and then click Finish to see the results of the new function.

 TIP

> You can also use the PivotTable Field button on the PivotTable toolbar to change the function used to summarize a field in your pivot table. The PivotTable Field dialog box displays different options, depending on the type of entry selected.

Adjusting the Formatting in a Pivot Table

When you modify a pivot table with the PivotTable Wizard, Excel automatically reformats the table to match the data in your list and to calculate the result of the function that you're using. You should avoid making manual changes to the table formatting, because the AutoFormat table feature will overwrite them each time you rearrange the pivot table. However, you can make lasting changes to the numeric formatting in the Data area by following these steps:

1   Click any numeric data cell in the pivot table (not a row or column heading).

2   Click the PivotTable Field button on the PivotTable toolbar. The PivotTable Field dialog box opens.

3 Click the Number button. The familiar Format Cells dialog box appears, as shown in Figure 21-8. This dialog box lets you adjust the formatting of the numbers in the Data area. Select a type of numeric format in the Category list box, and then select a formatting style. For example, to add currency formatting to numbers, click the Currency category, specify the number of decimal places you want, and specify a style for negative numbers.

FIGURE 21-8.
Use the Number button in the PivotTable Field dialog box to display a list of numeric formatting options for data in your pivot table.

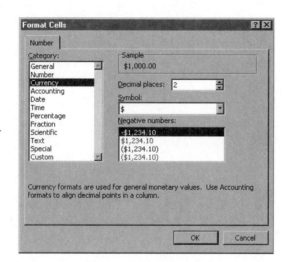

4 Click OK to close the Format Cells dialog box, and then click OK to close the PivotTable Field dialog box. Excel will change the numeric formatting in the table, and these changes will persist each time you modify the pivot table.

Use AutoFormat for Fast Style Makeovers
To change the heading and line style, highlight a cell in the pivot table and choose the AutoFormat command from the Format menu. Excel will display a list of table styles for you to choose from. Select the style you want, and then click OK to reformat and recalculate the pivot table.

III

Microsoft Excel

CHAPTER 22

Analyzing Business Data

Running a successful business requires many important skills. One of your best management tools is the capacity to build "what-if?" models to help you plan for the future. How many $1.75 coffees do you need to sell to gross $30,000? What will happen to your bottom line if you lower the price of caffè latte but increase advertising expenses? Fortunately, Excel provides several useful planning tools to help you map out a robust future. In this chapter, you'll learn how to use the Goal Seek command to find an unknown value that produces a desired result, the Solver add-in to calculate an optimum solution based on several variables and constraints, and the Scenario Manager to create and evaluate a collection of what-if scenarios containing multiple input values.

Forecasting with the Goal Seek Command

Excel's most basic forecasting command is Goal Seek, located on the Tools menu. The Goal Seek command determines the unknown value that produces a desired end result, such as the number of $14 compact discs a company must sell to reach its goal of $1,000,000 in CD sales. Goal Seek is simple because it's streamlined—it can adjust only one variable to complete its iterative calculation. If you need to consider additional variables in your forecasting, such as the effects of advertising or quantity discounts on pricing, use the Solver command.

 SEE ALSO
To learn how to use the Solver command to forecast with multiple changing variables, see the next section, "Using the Solver to Set Quantity and Pricing."

To use the Goal Seek command, set up your worksheet with the following:

- a formula that calculates your goal

- an empty cell for the missing number that will get you there

- any other values required in the formula

The empty cell should be referenced in your formula and serves as the variable that Excel changes.

> **NOTE**
>
> When you run the Goal Seek command on the Tools menu, the cell containing the formula is called the Set Cell, for it "sets" the terms that produce a result.

When the Goal Seek command starts to run, it repeatedly tries new values in the variable cell to find a solution to the problem you've set. This process is called *iteration*, and it continues until Excel has run the problem 100 times or has found an answer within 0.001 of the target value you specified. (You can adjust these iteration settings by choosing the Options command from the Tools menu and adjusting the Iteration options on the Calculations tab.) By calculating so quickly, the Goal Seek command can save you significant time and effort over the "brute force" method of trying one number after another in the formula.

To forecast with the Goal Seek command, follow these steps:

1 Create a worksheet with a formula, an empty "variable" cell, and any data that you need to use in your calculation. For example, Figure 22-1 shows how you might set up a worksheet to determine the number of cups of coffee priced at $1.75 that you would have to sell to gross $30,000.

FIGURE 22-1.
The Goal Seek command requires a formula and a blank variable cell.

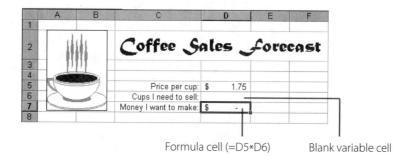

Formula cell (=D5*D6)   Blank variable cell

2 In your worksheet, select the cell containing the formula. (In the Goal Seek dialog box, this is called the Set Cell.)

3 From the Tools menu, choose the Goal Seek command. The Goal Seek dialog box opens, as shown in the following screen. The cell name you selected appears in the Set Cell text box and a marquee appears around the cell in your worksheet. Click the cell again in the worksheet to confirm it.

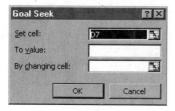

4 Type the goal that you want to reach in the To Value text box. For example, to reach $30,000 in sales, type *30000* in the To Value text box.

III

Microsoft Excel

5 Place the cursor in the By Changing Cell text box, move the Goal Seek dialog box out of the way, if necessary, and then click the cell that is to contain your answer (the variable cell). This is the value that the Goal Seek command will calculate using the formula in the Set Cell and your goal. The cell will be indicated with a selection marquee (cell D6 in this example), as shown in the following screen:

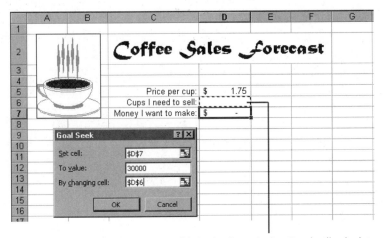

Variable in the formula that Excel will calculate

6 Click OK to find a solution for your sales goal. The Goal Seek Status dialog box will display a message when the iteration is complete, and the result of your forecast will appear in the worksheet, as shown in Figure 22-2. This forecast shows that you need to sell 17,143 coffees at $1.75 per cup to reach your sales goal of $30,000.

7 Click OK to close the Goal Seek dialog box.

 **TIP**

In a time-consuming calculation, such as a computation that involves several financial functions, you can click the Pause button in the Goal Seek Status dialog box to stop the iteration, or the Step button to view one iteration at a time.

FIGURE 22-2.
The Goal Seek command displays its result in the empty variable cell that you specified in your worksheet.

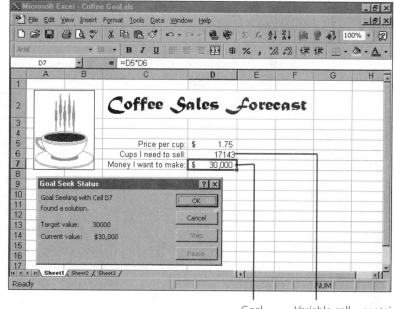

Goal

Variable cell—contains the solution that achieves the goal

Using the Solver to Set Quantity and Pricing

When your forecasting problem contains more than one variable, you need to use the Solver add-in utility to analyze the scenario. Veterans of business school will happily remember multivariable case studies as part of their finance and operations management training. While a full explanation of multivariable problem solving and optimization is beyond the scope of this book, you don't need a business-school background to use the Solver command to get help in deciding how much of a product to produce, or how to price goods and services. We'll show you the basics in this section by illustrating how a small coffee shop determines what coffee beverages it should sell, and what its potential revenue will be.

In our example, we're running a coffee shop that currently sells three coffee beverages: regular fresh-brewed coffee, premium caffè latte, and premium caffè mocha. We currently price the coffee drinks at $1.25,

III

Microsoft Excel

$2.00, and $2.25, respectively, but we're unsure what our revenue potential is and what emphasis we should give to each of the beverages. (Although the premium coffees bring in more money, their ingredients are more expensive and they're more time-consuming to make than regular coffee.) We can make some basic calculations by hand, but we want to structure our sales data in a worksheet so that we can add to it periodically and analyze it with the Solver command.

> **NOTE**
>
> The Solver is an add-in utility, so you should verify that it's installed on your system before you get started. If the Solver command isn't on your Tools menu, choose the Add-Ins command from the Tools menu and turn on the Solver Add-In option in the Add-Ins dialog box. If Solver isn't in the list, you'll need to install it by running the Office Setup program again and selecting it from the list of Excel add-ins.

Setting Up the Problem

The first step in using the Solver command is to build a worksheet that is Solver-friendly. This involves creating a *target cell* to be the goal of your problem—for example, a formula that calculates total revenue that you want to maximize—and assigning one or more *variable cells* that the Solver can change to reach your goal. Your worksheet can also contain other values and formulas that use the target cell and the variable cells. In fact, each of your variable cells must be *precedents* of the target cell for the Solver to do its job. (In other words, the formula in the target cell must depend on the variable cells for part of its calculation.) If you don't set it up this way, you'll get the error message *The Set Target Cell values do not converge* when you run the Solver.

Figure 22-3 shows a simple worksheet that can be used to estimate the weekly revenue for our example coffee shop and to determine how many cups of coffee will need to be sold. Cell G4 is the target cell that calculates the total revenue generated by the three coffee drinks. The three lines that converge on cell G4 were drawn by the Trace Precedents command on the Auditing submenu of the Tools menu. They

FIGURE 22-3.

Before you use the Solver command, you need to build a worksheet with a target cell and one or more variable cells. The Auditing submenu can help you visualize the relationship between cells.

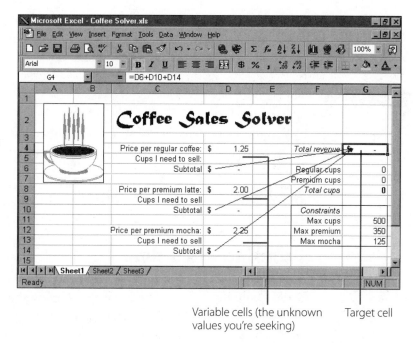

Variable cells (the unknown values you're seeking)   Target cell

show how the formula in cell G4 depends on three other calculations for its result. (The Auditing submenu contains commands that help track the links between formulas in a worksheet.) The three variable cells in the worksheet are cells D5, D9, and D13—these are the values we want the Solver to determine when it finds an optimum solution to maximizing our weekly revenue.

In the bottom right corner of our screen is a list of constraints we plan to use in our forecasting. A *constraint* is a limiting rule or guiding principle that dictates how the business is run. For example, because of storage facilities and merchandising constraints, we're currently able to produce only 500 cups of coffee (both regular and premium) per week. In addition, our supply of chocolate restricts the production of caffè mochas to 125 per week and a milk supply limitation restricts the total production of premium coffee drinks to 350 per week. These constraints will structure the problem, and we'll enter them in a special dialog box when we run the Solver command. Your worksheet must contain cells that calculate the values used as constraints (in this

III

Microsoft Excel

example, G6 through G8). The limiting values for the constraints are listed in cells G11 through G13. Although listing the constraints isn't necessary, it makes the worksheet easier to follow.

Name Key Cells

If your Solver problem contains several variables and constraints, you'll find it easiest to enter data if you name key cells and ranges in your worksheet with the Define command on the Name submenu of the Insert menu. Using cell names also makes it easy to read your Solver constraints later. For more information about naming, see "Using Range Names in Functions," page 572.

Running the Solver

After you've defined your forecasting problem in the worksheet, you're ready to run the Solver add-in. The steps below show you how to use the Solver to determine the maximum weekly revenue for your coffee shop when using the following constraints:

- No more than 500 total cups of coffee (both regular and premium)

- No more than 350 cups of premium coffee (both caffè latte and caffè mocha)

- No more than 125 caffè mochas

In addition to the maximum revenue, the Solver will tell you the optimum distribution of coffees in the three coffee groups. Complete these steps:

1 Click the target cell—the one containing the formula that is based on the variable cells you want the Solver to determine—in your worksheet. In Figure 22-3 on the preceding page, the target cell is G4.

2 From the Tools menu, choose Solver. The Solver Parameters dialog box opens, as shown in the following screen. Because you clicked the target cell in step 1, the Set Target Cell text box contains the correct reference. The correct Equal To option button

(Max) is also selected, because you want to find the maximum value for the cell.

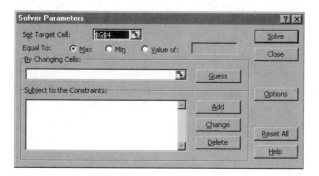

3 Highlight the By Changing Cells text box. Drag the dialog box to the right so that you can see the variable cells in your worksheet. Select each of the variable cells. If the cells adjoin one another, simply select the group by dragging across the cells. If the cells are noncontiguous, hold down the Ctrl key and click each cell. This will place a comma between each cell entry in the text box. In the following screen, the three blank cells reserved for the number of coffee drinks in each category have been selected:

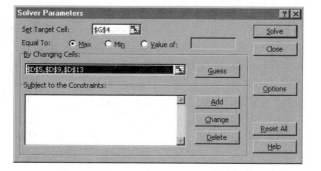

TIP

If you click the Guess button, the Solver will try to "guess" at the variable cells in your forecasting problem. The Solver creates the guess by looking at the cells referenced in the target cell formula. Don't rely on this guess—it will often be incorrect!

4 Constraints aren't required in all Solver problems, but this problem has three. Click the Add button to add the first constraint with the Add Constraint dialog box. You'll see the following screen:

5 The first constraint is that you can sell only 500 cups of coffee in one week. To enter this constraint, click cell G8 (the cell containing the total cups formula), click <= in the operator drop-down list box, and type *Max_cups* in the Constraint text box (using the underline character to link the words). (*Max_cups* is the name of cell G11 in our example.)

NOTE

> You have the option of typing a value, clicking a cell, or entering a cell name in the Constraint text box. We entered a defined cell name because it makes the constraint easier to read and modify later.

6 Click the Add button to enter the first constraint and begin the second constraint—you can sell only 350 premium coffees in one week. In the Add Constraint dialog box, click cell G7 (the cell containing the premium cups formula), click <= in the operator drop-down list box, and type *Max_premium* (the name of cell G12) in the Constraint text box.

7 Click the Add button to enter the second constraint and begin the third constraint—you can sell only 125 caffè mochas in one week. Click cell D13 (the variable cell containing the number of mocha cups), click <= in the operator drop-down list box, and type *Max_mocha* (the name of cell G13) in the Constraint text box.

8 Click OK to add all three constraints to the Solver Parameters dialog box. Your screen should look like this:

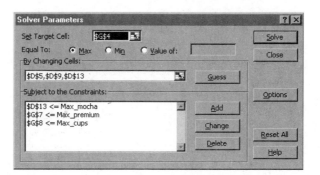

 TIP

To modify one of the constraints displayed in the Solver Parameters dialog box, select the constraint and click Change. To customize the iteration and calculation parameters in the Solver utility, click Options and make your adjustments.

9 Your forecasting problem is ready to go, so click Solve to calculate the result. After a few moments, the Solver displays a dialog box describing how the optimization analysis went. If the Solver ran into a problem, you'll see an error message, and you can click the Help button to learn more about the difficulty. If the Solver finds a solution, you'll see the following dialog box:

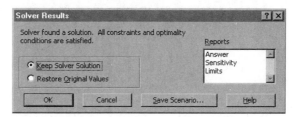

10 To display the new solution in your worksheet, select the Keep Solver Solution option button and click OK. The Solver places an optimum value in the target cell and fills the variable cells with the best solutions that match the constraints you specified, as shown in Figure 22-4 on the following page.

III

Microsoft Excel

FIGURE 22-4.
When the Solver finishes, it displays the values that produce the optimum result in the target cell.

Coffee Sales Solver

Price per regular coffee:	$ 1.25	Total revenue	$ **918.75**
Cups I need to sell:	150		
Subtotal	$ 187.50	Regular cups	150
		Premium cups	350
Price per premium latte:	$ 2.00	Total cups	**500**
Cups I need to sell	225		
Subtotal	$ 450.00	Constraints	
		Max cups	500
Price per premium mocha:	$ 2.25	Max premium	350
Cups I need to sell	125	Max mocha	125
Subtotal	$ 281.25		

These values produce the optimum revenue.

Optimum revenue

In this example, you've learned that if you're limited to selling 500 cups of coffee per week, you can expect a maximum of $918.75 in revenue, and your optimum drink distribution is 150 cups of regular coffee, 225 cups of caffè latte, and 125 cups of caffè mocha. Although this financial model doesn't consider several realistic business variables, such as the costs associated with running a shop and the benefits received through volume purchases, it does help you to forecast much more easily and quickly than with pencil and paper.

Editing Your Solver Forecast

Perhaps the best feature of a Solver forecast is that it can easily be edited to evaluate new goals and contingencies. For example, if you decide that you want to earn exactly $700 per week from coffee drinks, you can use the Solver to tell you what the optimum combination of drinks would be. Setting a target value in the Solver is a little like using the Goal Seek command to determine an unknown variable, though you can use more than one variable.

To edit your Solver forecast to find the variables to reach a specific goal, follow these steps:

1 From the Tools menu, choose the Solver command. The Solver Parameters dialog box appears, still displaying the variables and constraints of your last Solver problem. You'll adjust these to compute a new forecasting goal.

2 Click the Value option button and type *700* in the Value Of text box. The Value option button sets the target cell to a particular goal so that you can determine the variable mix you need to reach your milestone. (In this example, the variable cells represent cups of coffee.) Your dialog box should look like this:

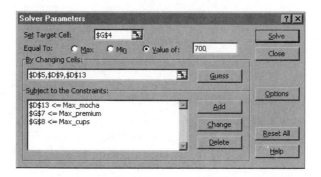

3 Click Solve to find a solution to your forecasting problem. When the Solver has finished, click OK to display the new solution in your worksheet. Figure 22-5 shows the solution the Solver generates if the variable cells are empty before you run the problem. (You can earn $700 by selling approximately 125 mochas, 151 lattes, and 94 regular coffees. The Solver calculates an exact answer, but because you can't sell partial cups of coffee, the variable cells are formatted to show integer—whole-number—values. Your actual revenue would be $700.75 and the subtotals would be slightly higher.)

FIGURE 22-5.
When you specify a target goal, the Solver computes an optimum product mix that meets your constraints.

Coffee Sales Solver

Price per regular coffee:	$ 1.25		*Total revenue*	$ 700.00
Cups I need to sell:	94			
Subtotal	$ 117.63		Regular cups	94
			Premium cups	276
Price per premium latte:	$ 2.00		*Total cups*	370
Cups I need to sell	151			
Subtotal	$ 301.12		*Constraints*	
			Max cups	500
Price per premium mocha:	$ 2.25		Max premium	350
Cups I need to sell	125		Max mocha	125
Subtotal	$ 281.25			

III

Microsoft Excel

What If There Is More Than One Solution to the Problem?

In the previous example, the Solver determined that you could sell 125 mochas, 151 lattes, and 94 regular coffees to reach your sales goal of $700. But you can also reach the $700 mark with a different product mix—for example, you could sell approximately 125 mochas and 210 lattes to reach $700. (With this mix, your revenue would actually be $701.25.) So how *did* the Solver decide what the optimum product mix would be? Since you chose not to limit its options with constraints, the Solver simply started with the numbers in the variable cells and incremented them until it found an acceptable solution. For this reason, you can get different results from a nonlinear problem with multiple solutions if you use different starting values.

You can take advantage of the way the Solver reaches its results if there's a particular product mix that you'd like to use. Enter the values that you think might be acceptable in the variable cells *before* you run the Solver, and Excel will use those as starting values when it computes the solution. If you prefer to find a true optimal solution, you'll need to add extra constraints to the Solver Parameters dialog box before you run the forecast. For example, you might specify that a certain minimum must be met in each category, or that you'd like to minimize the number of products sold to reach your goal. You can have two constraints for each variable cell (an upper bounds and a lower bounds) to structure the computation and reach an optimal solution to your problem.

Evaluating What-If Questions with the Scenario Manager

The Goal Seek and Solver commands are extremely useful, though if you run several forecasts you can quickly forget what your original values were. More important, you have no real way to compare the results of the Goal Seek and Solver commands. Each time you change the data, the previous solution is lost. To address this limitation, the

Scenario Manager helps you to keep track of multiple what-if models. Using the Scenarios command on the Tools menu, you can create new forecasting scenarios, view existing scenarios, run scenario management commands, and display consolidated scenario reports. We'll show you each technique in this section.

Creating a Scenario

A *scenario* is a named what-if model that includes variable cells linked together by one or more formulas. Before you create a scenario, you must design your worksheet so that it contains at least one formula that's dependent on cells that can be fed different values. For example, you might want to compare a best-case and a worst-case scenario for sales in a coffee shop based on the number of cups of coffee sold in a week. Figure 22-6 shows a worksheet with three variable cells and several formulas that can serve as the basis for several scenarios. (If you worked through the Solver examples, you'll recognize the coffee theme.) In the following example, we'll use this worksheet to show how to create a Best Case and a Worst Case sales scenario.

FIGURE 22-6.

Before you create a scenario, you'll need to build a worksheet with one or more formulas dependent on variable cells.

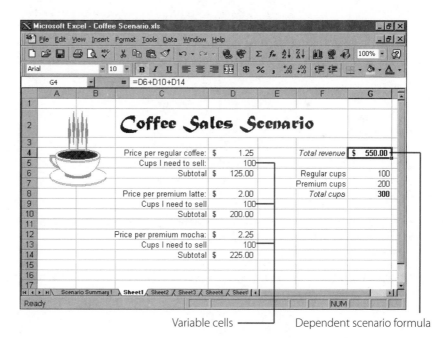

Variable cells ———   Dependent scenario formula

To create a scenario, follow these steps:

1 From the Tools menu, choose the Scenarios command. The Scenario Manager dialog box appears:

2 Click the Add button to create your first scenario. You'll see the Add Scenario dialog box.

3 Type *Best Case* (or another suitable name) in the Scenario Name text box, and press the Tab key.

4 In the Changing Cells text box, specify the variable cells that you want to modify in your scenario. You can type cell names, highlight a cell range, or hold down the Ctrl key and click individual cells to add them to the text box. (If you hold down the Ctrl key, Excel automatically places commas between the cells that you click.) To follow our example, hold down the Ctrl key and click cells D5, D9, and D13. Your screen should look like the one shown on the following page.

You might want to use cell names when you define your variable cells. That way, you'll have an easier time identifying your variables when you create your scenarios and when you type in arguments later.

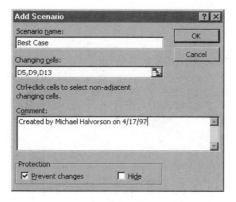

5 Click OK to add your scenario to the Scenario Manager. You'll see the Scenario Values dialog box, asking you for your model's variables. The default values are the numbers that were already in the cells.

6 Type *150*, press Tab, type *225*, press Tab, and type *125*. These are the values that will produce the revenue in your best-case scenario based on the constraints described in the section "Setting Up the Problem, page 642." Your screen will look like this:

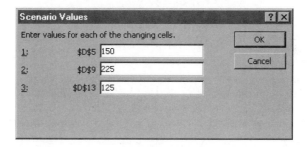

7 Click Add to create a second scenario. Type *Worst Case,* and click OK to display the Scenario Values dialog box.

8 Type *50*, *40*, and *30* in the variable cells, and then click OK. (These values represent our guess at the worst case.) The Scenario Manager dialog box appears, with the Best Case and Worst Case scenarios listed. Now you're ready to view the results of your forecasting models.

III

Microsoft Excel

9 Click Close to close the Scenario Manager dialog box.

You can save Solver problems as scenarios for future trials by clicking the Save Scenario button in the Solver Results dialog box when the Solver computes a new forecast. The Solver will prompt you for a name, which you can use later to view the scenario in the Scenario Manager.

Viewing a Scenario

Excel keeps track of each of your worksheet scenarios. You can view them with the Scenarios command on the Tools menu whenever your worksheet is open. Before you view a scenario, however, it's a good idea to save your workbook so that you can restore the original values in your worksheet if you want to.

To view a scenario, follow these steps:

1 From the Tools menu, choose the Scenarios command. You'll see a dialog box similar to the following:

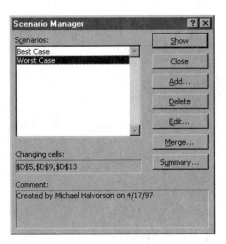

2 In the Scenarios list box, select the scenario that you want to view.

3 Click the Show button. Excel substitutes the variables in your worksheet with the values in the scenario and displays the results in your worksheet, as shown in Figure 22-7. (You might need to move the Scenario Manager dialog box to view the results.)

FIGURE 22-7.

The Show button lets you compare the results of different what-if scenarios in your worksheet.

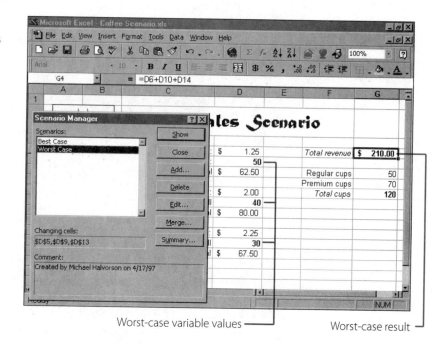

Worst-case variable values ——

Worst-case result ——

4 Select additional scenarios and click the Show button to compare and contrast the what-if models in your worksheet. When you've finished, click the Close button. The last active scenario remains in your worksheet.

Creating Scenario Reports

Although you can easily compare different scenarios by switching between them with the Show button in the Scenario Manager dialog box, you might occasionally want to view a report with consolidated information about the scenarios in your worksheet. You can accomplish this quickly by using the Summary button in the Scenario Manager dialog box. The summary report that you create will be formatted automatically and copied to a new worksheet in your workbook.

To create a scenario report, follow these steps:

1 From the Tools menu, choose the Scenarios command. The Scenario Manager dialog box opens.

2 Click the Summary button. The Scenario Summary dialog box opens, prompting you for a result cell to total in the report and a report type. A scenario summary report is a formatted table

III

Microsoft Excel

SEE ALSO

For more information about viewing pivot table summary reports, see "Rearranging Fields in a Pivot Table," page 631.

displayed in its own worksheet. A pivot table is a special summary table that can be rearranged, or "pivoted," using its rows and columns:

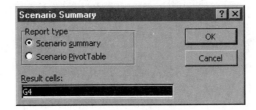

3 Select the result cell that you want to total (cell G4 in this example), select the report option button that you want to use (accept the Scenario Summary default if you're not sure), and then click OK. After a few moments, a new Scenario Summary tab will appear in your workbook, as shown in Figure 22-8. The outlining buttons in the left and top margins of your report will help you to shrink or expand the rows and columns in your scenario summary if you find it necessary to hide or expand values.

 TIP

Each time you click the Summary button in the Scenario Manager dialog box, Excel creates a new summary worksheet in your workbook. To delete unwanted summary reports in the future, click the unwanted scenario's summary tab in the workbook, and then choose the Delete Sheet command from the Edit menu.

Managing Your Scenarios

Once you've defined a scenario with the Add button, luckily you're not stuck with that scenario forever. You can edit and delete scenarios with the Edit and Delete buttons in the Scenario Manager dialog box. The Edit button lets you change the name of the scenario, remove existing variable cells, add new variable cells, or even choose a completely new group of variables. To remove a particular scenario permanently, simply highlight it in the Scenario Manager dialog box and click the Delete button. Finally, you can copy scenarios from other open workbooks into your current worksheet by clicking the Merge button in the Scenario Manager dialog box and specifying a source workbook and worksheet in the Merge Scenarios dialog box.

FIGURE 22-8.
The Summary button creates a scenario summary report in a new worksheet in your workbook.

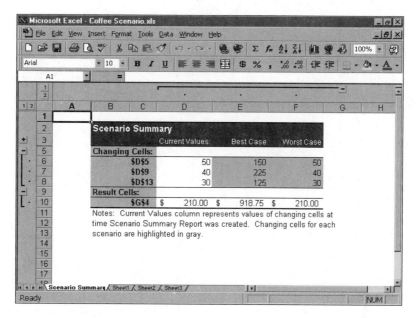

CHAPTER 23

Increasing Productivity with Macros

If you're like most Excel users, much of the work that you do in worksheets can be repetitive. For example, you might always enter a series of headings in financial reports, or routinely increase the width of the first few columns (ordinarily, the most significant ones) in your workbook. If these actions take up much of your time, consider recording your commands as a macro, and then running the macro whenever you need to do the work. A *macro* is a named set of instructions that tells Excel to perform an action for you. In this chapter, you'll learn what macros look like and how you can use them to increase your productivity. You'll also learn how to record, run, and edit macros, as well as assign them to buttons on a toolbar.

Carpe Datum:
Knowing When to Build a Macro

Excel's macro recording capabilities are impressive, but before you "seize the data," you should make sure that Excel doesn't already provide a built-in solution for your repetitive task. For example, if you routinely boldface your column headings and increase their point size, you could record a macro that will automatically format the headings for you. But it would actually be *faster* for you to use the Style command on the Format menu to apply a heading style that accomplishes the same formatting effect. In other words, don't use a macro unless the commands that you want to record are involved enough to require one.

This word to the wise doesn't mean that you shouldn't use macros to automate your worksheets. Actually, we're arguing just the opposite. But before you get started, it makes sense to take the time to become familiar with the majority of Excel's features so that you know when Excel offers a built-in solution and when to use macros to their greatest effect. Excel's Visual Basic macro language is sophisticated enough for many advanced tasks, such as communicating with other Windows-based applications or controlling an entire inventory management system. However, the most useful macros are often the ones that automate just four or five simple Excel commands. And though you can create macros from scratch with Visual Basic, the best way to learn about macros is by recording and editing them.

Recording a Macro

Let's start with a simple example. Excel's default cell width is about eight characters wide, but this space is often inadequate for the first few columns, where users typically enter longer strings for customer names, businesses, or geographic regions. In the following example, we'll record a macro that changes the first column in a worksheet to a width of 25 characters, and increases the width of each of the next three columns to 15 characters. We'll use the Record New Macro command on the Macro submenu of the Tools menu to record the macro, and then we'll name the macro in the Record Macro dialog box.

To create a macro that automatically adjusts the column width for you, follow these steps:

1 Display the worksheet in which you want to record the macro. Your macro will be stored in a separate module in the active workbook, and you'll be able to run the macro in any worksheet as long as the workbook is open.

2 From the Tools menu, choose Macro and then choose the Record New Macro command. You'll see the following dialog box:

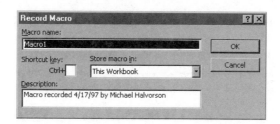

3 Type *Widen4Columns,* or another name if you prefer, in the Macro Name text box, and click OK. This is the name you'll use to run and edit the macro later (macro names can't contain spaces or punctuation marks). Excel closes the Record Macro dialog box, displays a Macro toolbar containing a Stop button, and starts recording the macro. From this point on, any cell that you highlight or any command that you execute in Excel will be "taped" by the macro recorder. (When you've finished recording, you'll click the Stop button to end your macro.)

4 Now you'll create your macro. Select the first column by clicking the column A heading; from the Format menu, choose Column and then choose Width from the submenu. You'll see the following dialog box, prompting you for a new column width:

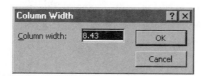

5 Type *25* in the Column Width text box, and click OK to expand column A to 25 characters.

Microsoft Excel

6 Select columns B, C, and D by dragging over each of the column headings, and then choose the Width command again. Type *15* in the Column Width text box, and click OK.

7 Finally, click cell A1 to leave the cursor in a tidy starting place. As your last step in a macro recording, you should always arrange the screen so that you can start working again with the least amount of effort. The resulting screen is shown in Figure 23-1.

FIGURE 23-1.
The Widen4Columns macro has stored the steps to automatically widen the first four columns of your worksheet.

Macro toolbar

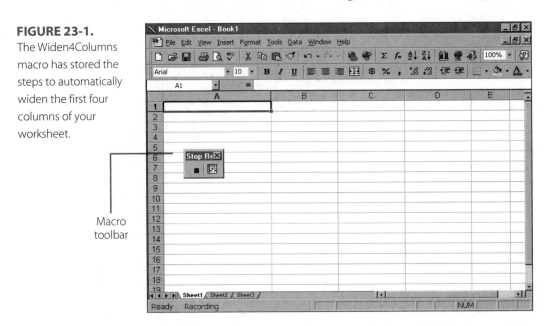

8 Click the Stop button on the Macro toolbar to end your macro recording. The macro recorder stops, and Excel stores the macro in a special location in your workbook called a *module*. (Unlike previous versions of Microsoft Excel, Excel 97 doesn't store your macro on an individual worksheet.)

9 Use the Save command on the File menu to save your workbook to disk with your macro. (In this example, we'll use the filename Macro Practice.xls.) After all, since you've gone to the trouble of creating the macro, you don't want to lose it.

Running a Macro

To give you flexibility in automating your work, Excel provides you with three ways to run your macros. You can:

- Double-click the macro name in the Macro dialog box.

- Press a macro shortcut key (if one has been assigned).

- Click a custom macro button on a toolbar (if you've created a button for the macro).

We describe the first two automation options in this section, and the last one later in the chapter. We'll use the Widen4Columns macro that we created in the preceding section.

Starting a Macro with the Macro Dialog Box

To run the Widen4Columns macro with the Macro dialog box, follow these steps:

1 Display the worksheet in which you want to run the macro. If you formatted Sheet1 in your workbook when you created the Widen4Columns macro, click the Sheet2 tab in your workbook now to practice in an empty worksheet.

2 From the Tools menu, choose Macro and then choose Macros from the submenu. The Macro dialog box opens, as shown in Figure 23-2 on the following page. It lists all the macros in your current workbook, plus any macros available in other open workbooks or in your personal macro workbook. (You'll learn more about the personal macro workbook later.)

3 Select the macro you want to run in the Macro list box and click Run. In the blink of an eye, Excel runs the macro and completes the column formatting you requested. To run the macro again in another worksheet, open the worksheet and repeat steps 2 and 3.

III

Microsoft Excel

FIGURE 23-2.
The Macro dialog
box lists the macros
available in your
workbook.

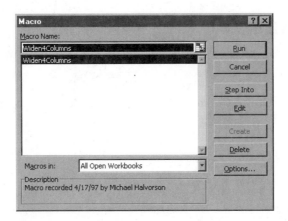

 TIP

What's Done Is Done
Excel won't let you reverse the effects of a macro with the Undo command, so
be sure that you have the correct worksheet open before you modify it. As a safeguard, you might save your workbook *before* you run a new or unfamiliar macro.
Then, if you don't like the changes made by the macro, you can close the workbook (without saving it) and the changes will be discarded.

Assigning a Shortcut Key to a Macro

You can assign a shortcut key to your macro so that it operates just like
any key combination that runs an Excel command. As an example, to
assign your Widen4Columns macro the Ctrl+Shift+W shortcut key (W
for "widen"), follow these steps:

1   From the Tools menu, choose Macro and then choose Macros
    from the submenu. You'll see the Macro dialog box.

2   Select the Widen4Columns macro in the list box, and then click
    the Options button to display a list of customization options for
    your macro. The Macro Options dialog box opens, as shown in
    Figure 23-3.

3   Hold down the Shift key and type the letter *W*. The title of the
    shortcut key expands to Ctrl+Shift+W, which is the key combina-
    tion that you'll press to run the macro.

FIGURE 23-3.

The Macro Options dialog box lets you assign a shortcut key to your macro.

 NOTE

If you type a lowercase letter in the Ctrl+ box, Excel will add Ctrl to the key you specify. If you type an uppercase letter, Excel will add Ctrl+Shift to the key you specify. Because several Excel commands already use Ctrl plus a letter for shortcut keys (for example, Ctrl+W closes the current workbook window), we recommend that you always add Shift to the letter you're using, to avoid conflicts.

4 Click OK to assign the shortcut key, and then close the Macro dialog box.

5 Now try using the shortcut key. Click the Sheet3 tab in your workbook to open a new, unformatted worksheet, and press Ctrl+Shift+W. Excel runs the Widen4Columns macro, which immediately increases the width of your first four columns.

Editing a Macro

By default, Excel stores the macros in your workbook in a Visual Basic code module called *Module1*. You can display this module periodically to examine the Visual Basic commands in your macros, add documentation to explain what a macro does, or modify a macro to change its behavior or increase its efficiency. In this section, we'll review the content of the Widen4Columns macro, add a descriptive comment, and edit one of the column width settings.

To edit the Widen4Columns macro in your workbook, follow these steps:

1 From the Tools menu, choose Macro and then choose Macros from the submenu. The Macro dialog box opens.

2 Click the Edit button to open the Widen4Columns macro in the Visual Basic Editor, a special programming tool you can use to create and edit your macros. (When you create macros in Microsoft Word, Microsoft PowerPoint, Microsoft Access, or Microsoft Visual Basic, you'll also use this code editor.) Your screen should look like Figure 23-4.

3 Excel macros are stored in individual *subroutines* in the code module, with Sub and End Sub statements that mark the beginning and the end of the macro. By default, descriptive comments in the macro appear in green type, special Visual Basic keywords appear in blue type, and all other macro commands and values appear in black type.

4 Move the cursor below the line containing the words "Macro recorded," press the Right arrow key to move the cursor after the single-quotation mark, and type the descriptive comment *Purpose: To enlarge columns A through D*. Then press the Down arrow key. The text appears in green type when you press the Down arrow key, identifying the line you typed as a comment. (See Figure 23-5.) Descriptive comment lines are for documentation purposes only; they're created by starting a line with a single quotation mark, which excludes them from being used by the macro.

FIGURE 23-4.
Excel macros are stored in the industry-standard Visual Basic language and can be modified using the Visual Basic Editor.

Descriptive comments

Visual Basic statements

End Sub concludes the macro.

Sub statement starts the macro.   Name of the macro

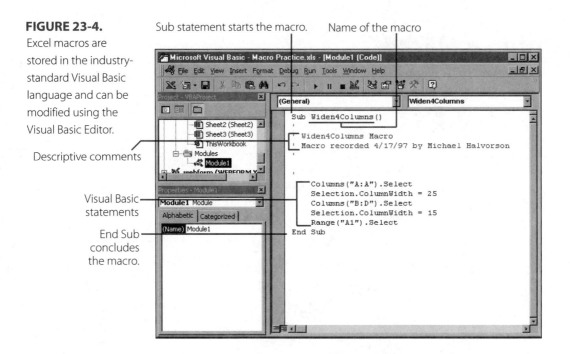

FIGURE 23-5.
Use the insertion point to move around in your macro and to position the cursor for additions or corrections.

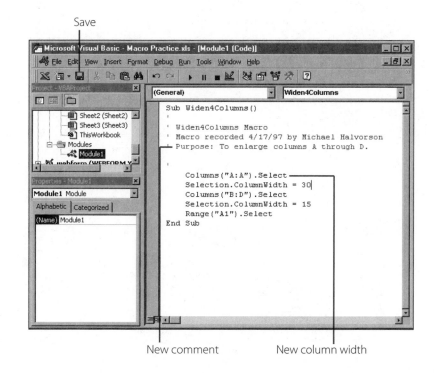

Save

New comment   New column width

5 Move the cursor to the number 25 in the Visual Basic statement

```
Selection.ColumnWidth = 25
```

This line sets the width of column A to 25 characters when you run the macro. Now we'll edit this statement to use a different column width.

6 Change the column width value from 25 to 30. Excel updates your macro with the new column size, as shown in Figure 23-5. The next time you run the macro, it will change the width of column A in the active worksheet to 30 characters, not to 25 characters.

7 Click the Save button on the Visual Basic toolbar to save your macro changes in the workbook. You're finished editing the macro.

8 From the File menu, choose the Close And Return To Microsoft Excel command. The Visual Basic Editor closes and the Excel workplace reappears. Test your revised macro by running it again on Sheet3 or another worksheet. (You can add additional worksheets to your workbook by choosing the Worksheet command from the Insert menu.) The macro should perform exactly as you expect it

III

Microsoft Excel

to. If Excel displays an error message or you get unexpected results, open the macro again in the Visual Basic Editor and double-check your work against the example shown in Figure 23-5 on the preceding page.

NOTE

To delete a macro from your workbook, choose Macro from the Tools menu, choose Run from the submenu, select the unwanted macro in the Macro dialog box, and click the Delete button.

TIP

Read More About Macros

To learn more about Visual Basic macros, use the commands on the Help menu in the Visual Basic Editor. If you still want to know more about Visual Basic, we recommend Michael Halvorson's book *Visual Basic 5 for Windows 95 Step by Step* (Microsoft Press, 1996), which describes how to write programs and macros using the Visual Basic programming language.

Using the Personal Macro Workbook

Now that you've had some practice using macros, let's create one final example that uses the Page Setup command to adjust the headers and footers in your worksheet before printing. You'll record this macro using the techniques you learned earlier in this chapter, though this time you'll store the macro in your personal macro workbook so that you can use it in all your Excel projects. You'll also learn how to create a special button for the macro on the Standard toolbar.

NOTE

The personal macro workbook is a special hidden workbook that's always open while Excel is running. It's typically used only for macros, but you can put regular worksheets in the personal macro workbook if you want to. The personal macro workbook is stored in the XLStart folder and is loaded automatically when you start Excel. Since you don't need to see it to record macros or run them, it remains hidden from view unless you open it with the Unhide command on the Window menu. (The personal macro workbook doesn't exist until you store a macro in it.)

Excel's standard worksheet header contains the name of the worksheet, while the standard worksheet footer displays the current page number. We'll record a macro that removes the header and creates a custom footer containing the word *Confidential*, today's date, and the current page number. Whenever you want to use these page setup options in a worksheet, simply run the macro.

To create a macro in the personal macro workbook to customize your worksheet headers and footers for printing, follow these steps:

1 Because this macro will be available to all your workbooks, you can open any worksheet to begin to record the macro.

2 From the Tools menu, choose Macro and then choose Record New Macro from the submenu. The Record Macro dialog box opens.

3 Type *CustomFooter* or another name of your choice (with no spaces or punctuation) in the Macro Name text box. This will be the name of your macro.

4 Click the Store Macro In list box, and then select the Personal Macro Workbook option. This option directs Excel to place your new macro in the personal macro workbook so that you can access it from any open workbook. Your dialog box should look like this:

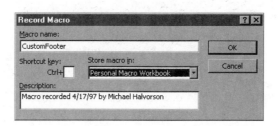

5 Click OK to start recording the macro. Excel closes the dialog box, displays the Macro toolbar, and starts recording the macro. The commands you issue now will be captured by the macro recorder and stored in your personal macro workbook.

6 From the File menu, choose the Page Setup command, and then click the Header/Footer tab. You'll see the dialog box on the following page, showing the current header and footer.

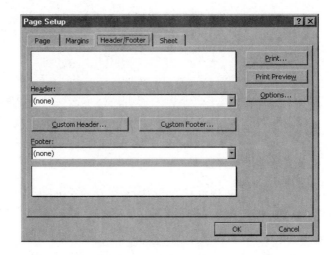

7 Click the Header drop-down list box, scroll to the top of the list, and click (None). Excel removes the current worksheet header.

8 Click the Footer drop-down list box, scroll to the top of the list, and then click the footer entry labeled *Confidential, mm/dd/yy, Page 1*, where *mm/dd/yy* appears with today's date. This is the custom footer that your macro will add to your worksheet. If you prefer a different preset option, select it instead.

9 Click OK to accept the remaining Page Setup options, and click the Stop button to stop recording your macro and to save it in your personal macro workbook.

Now follow these steps to test your new CustomFooter macro:

1 Display the worksheet in which you want to run the macro. *Do not* use the worksheet that you used to record the macro, since it already contains a custom footer. You might want to close the current workbook and open another to see that the macro is in fact not stored in the workbook where it was created, such as the Macro Practice worksheet you created earlier in this chapter.

2 From the Tools menu, choose Macro and then choose Macros from the submenu. The Macro dialog box opens, as shown in Figure 23-6. It lists all the macros in your current workbook, plus any macros available in other open workbooks and in your personal macro workbook. (Because the CustomFooter macro is in your personal macro workbook, it features the filename PERSONAL.XLS in front of it.)

FIGURE 23-6.
Macros stored in your personal macro workbook begin with the filename PERSONAL.XLS.

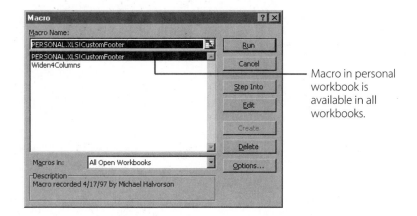

Macro in personal workbook is available in all workbooks.

3 Double-click the CustomFooter macro in the Macro dialog box. Your worksheet flickers briefly as Excel runs the commands in the macro.

> **NOTE**

Because you opened the Page Setup dialog box as you were recording, Excel reapplies each of the settings that you specified in the dialog box, including the individual header and footer items. If you'd rather not include the peripheral settings such as margin sizes and page orientation in your macro, remove the Visual Basic commands that execute them from the CustomFooter macro in your personal macro workbook.

4 When the macro stops, add one or two entries to the worksheet, if necessary, and click the Print Preview button on the Standard toolbar. (Excel won't preview the worksheet unless you have data in it.) You'll see a preview image of the first page of your worksheet.

> **CAUTION**
> You can't save this macro using the Save command on the File menu. Instead, when you exit Excel, you'll be prompted to click OK to permanently save your additions to the personal macro workbook.

5 Click the footer with the zoom pointer to examine it closely. Your footer should look similar to the one shown in Figure 23-7 on the following page.

6 When you've finished, click Close to quit Print Preview, and save your worksheet if you want to. Your new CustomFooter macro is now ready for use in all your workbooks.

III

Microsoft Excel

FIGURE 23-7.
The CustomFooter macro places a stylized footer in your worksheet.

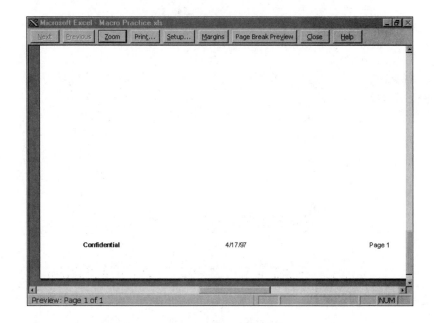

Adding a Macro to a Toolbar

If you've read through each of the chapters in this Excel section, you deserve one last special effect to make your macros even more accessible and entertaining. In addition to running your macros with shortcut keys and the Run command, you can also run macros by creating special macro buttons and adding them to one of your toolbars. To use this technique, record your macro first and give it a name. (If you want your macro button to be on the toolbar at all times, place your macro in the personal macro workbook.) After your macro is finished, use the Customize command on the Toolbars submenu of the View menu to assign the macro to a button.

To add a macro to a toolbar, follow these steps:

1 Record your macro and assign it a name. If you created the CustomFooter macro in the preceding section, you can use it for this example.

2 From the View menu, choose Toolbars and then choose Customize from the submenu. The Customize dialog box opens.

3 Click the Commands tab in the dialog box. A list of command categories appears on the left side of the dialog box, and a list of

? SEE ALSO

For more information about customizing Excel toolbars, including adding, removing, copying, and arranging toolbar buttons, see "Customizing Toolbars," page 531.

subordinate command buttons appears on the right. When a category in the left list is highlighted, related command buttons appear in the right list.

4 Scroll down the list of categories and click Macros. In the Commands list you'll see a custom button as shown in the following screen. We'll use the yellow "Smile" button for the CustomFooter macro.

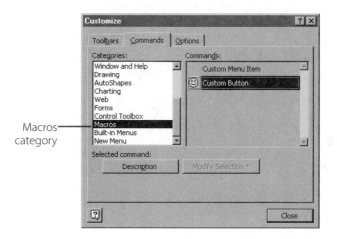

Macros category

5 Click on the "Smile" custom button and drag it to one of your toolbars. As you position it over the toolbar a vertical bar will appear to guide you in dropping it exactly where you want it to appear.

6 After you release the mouse button, the other buttons on the toolbar will shift to the right. If they no longer fit on your screen, you can remove your least-used button from the toolbar by selecting it and dragging it away from the toolbar.

NOTE

You can restore a toolbar button by opening the Customize dialog box, clicking the category that contains the missing button, and then dragging the button back onto the toolbar. Or, you can restore all the toolbar's original default settings by selecting the Toolbars tab from the Customize dialog box, selecting the toolbar, and then clicking the Reset button.

III

Microsoft Excel

? SEE ALSO

You can further cus-
tomize your new
macro button at any
time by editing the
button's bitmap (for
example, if you prefer
your smiling button to
frown instead). For
more information
about modifying
toolbar button
images, see "Editing
the Picture in Toolbar
Buttons," page 536.

7 With your new "Smile" button selected on the toolbar, click the Modify Selection button in the Customize dialog box.

8 From the submenu that appears, choose Change Button Image.

9 A collection of custom buttons now appears, from which you can choose the one you like best. If you want to further customize the button, choose Edit Button Image from the Modify Selection submenu of the Customize dialog box.

10 When you're done, close the Customize dialog box.

11 Click the new button, and the Assign Macro dialog box will appear, as shown in Figure 23-8.

12 Choose the macro for the button and click OK. The dialog box closes and Excel enables the new macro button.

13 Verify that the button works by displaying a new worksheet and clicking the button. If you assigned the CustomFooter macro to the button, go to Print Preview and verify that the header and footer were set correctly. Congratulations on your progress!

New custom macro button

FIGURE 23-8.

The Assign Macro dialog box lets you attach a macro to a custom toolbar button; it appears when you first click the new button.

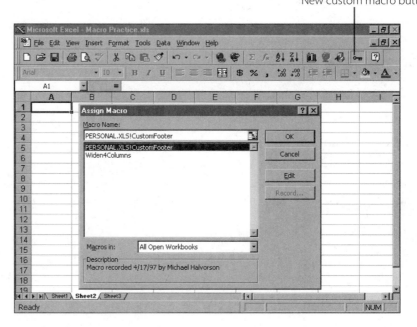

PART IV

Microsoft PowerPoint

CHAPTER 24

Getting Started with PowerPoint

You're a basement chemist who needs financial backing for a formula that makes even eggs grow hair. You're a teacher who wants students to understand how government works. You're a consultant who needs to help a client cut expenses and reorganize her business. Or perhaps you're an office manager who must show your staff how to use the new features in Office 97.

In these and hundreds of other situations, your objective is simple: clear, attention-getting, persuasive communication. The ways to this goal are many, ranging from white boards to white papers, from slides to slick charts, from memos to printed dissertations. And, of course, there's PowerPoint, the audiovisual "room" in your Office suite. When you need to teach, persuade, or explain, PowerPoint can add punch to your presentation. With it, you can create and display sets of slides that combine text with drawn objects, clip art, photos, sound, video, and even animated special effects. You can then turn your work into 35mm slides, transparencies, or printed handouts that you can present electronically or (new in PowerPoint 97 for Windows) interactively over the Internet. Furthermore, because PowerPoint is part of a package deal, you can easily blend Word outlines, Excel worksheets, and Drawing artwork into your own, original PowerPoint text and graphics.

Thus, with PowerPoint, you can create company information slides like this:

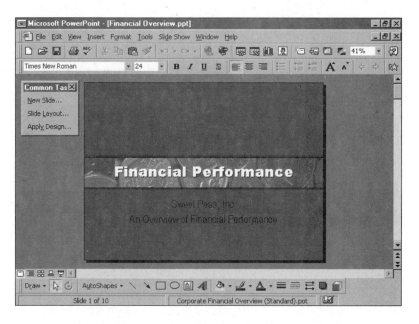

Or an Internet home page like this:

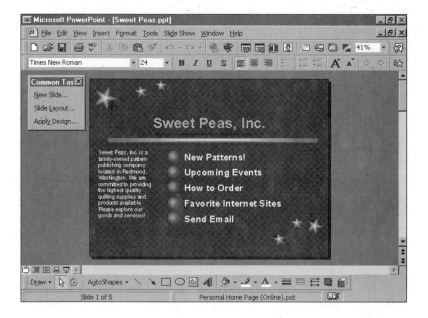

IV

Microsoft PowerPoint

The PowerPoint Window

As you already know, just as it does with the other applications in the Office 97 suite, Windows lets you start PowerPoint in any of several ways. The easiest way is to use the Start button. Click the Start button, point to Programs, and select Microsoft PowerPoint from the Programs list.

The PowerPoint window is shown in Figure 24-1. By default, PowerPoint starts by displaying a dialog box with your options for creating a new presentation. (You'll learn more about these options later in the chapter.) But for now, take a look at the significant user interface components that PowerPoint shares with the other programs in the Office 97 software suite.

- A *menu bar*, the hallmark of virtually every Windows-based application, provides access to the most important commands in the PowerPoint program. To choose a command from a PowerPoint menu, click the menu you want, point to the desired submenu (if applicable), and then click the command you want to run.

FIGURE 24-1.

Important parts of the PowerPoint window.

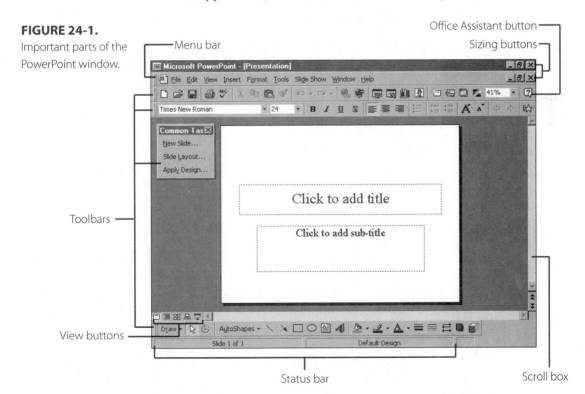

Office Assistant button

Menu bar

Sizing buttons

Toolbars

View buttons

Status bar

Scroll box

■ The *toolbars*, as usual, provide quick, one-click access to often-used commands. Because the PowerPoint window includes several toolbars, you might want to "walk" through the tools, resting the mouse pointer for a second on any that are new to you. Resting the mouse pointer on a tool, you'll recall, displays a Screen-Tip that briefly describes the function of the tool. The Drawing toolbar at the bottom of the screen, new in Office 97, replaces the old PowerPoint commands and tools used for drawing. Common Tasks is a "floating" toolbar, containing often-used commands such as New Slide and Slide Layout.

■ Like most Office applications, the PowerPoint application window also contains *sizing buttons* you can use to minimize, maximize, restore, and close windows, plus a *status bar* at the bottom of the screen that displays the number of the slide you're working on as well as the type of presentation you're creating.

■ The *scroll box* moves you from slide to slide, not up or down through the slide's text (as happens in a Word document, for example). In addition, PowerPoint displays the number and title of each slide as you drag the scroll box. You'll like this feature.

■ The two buttons with double arrowheads at the bottom of the vertical scroll bar give you another way to move through slides. Click the button with the upward-pointing arrowheads to go to the previous slide; click the button with the downward-pointing arrowheads to move to the next slide.

② SEE ALSO
For more information about using menus, dialog boxes, toolbars, and application windows, see Chapter 2, "Learning the Basics: Windows, Toolbars, and Printing." For more information about starting and configuring Office Assistant, see Chapter 1, "A Quick Tour of Microsoft Office."

■ The *View buttons* on the left end of the horizontal scroll bar, although easily overlooked, let you quickly switch to different PowerPoint views. Each view is designed to make some aspect of creating and viewing a slide show as effective as possible. Views are described in more detail in the next section.

■ The *Office Assistant button* on the right side of the Standard toolbar provides access to all the PowerPoint help documentation and the animated Office Assistant. If Office Assistant isn't already running, this button will start it.

Understanding PowerPoint Views

To use PowerPoint effectively to create and modify presentations, you need to become comfortable with PowerPoint's *views*. As the name implies, views provide you with different ways of looking at a document. They're somewhat virtual and perhaps more uniquely "computer-esque" than other aspects of Office applications because they use the power of the machine and the software to display a document in ways that paper and other "real" objects can't. PowerPoint can display your slides in any of five basic views, all of which are shown in Figure 24-2 on the following page.

- Slide view is the default view, and the one in which you work with individual slides. In Slide view, you can work not only on text and graphics, but on sound, animation, and other effects as well. You'll probably work mostly in this view.

- Outline view displays the titles and text on your slides in outline format (like the outlines you used to create in school). Outline view is valuable when you're organizing your thoughts and reordering the points you want to make.

- Slide Sorter view arranges all your slides across and down the screen as if they were laid out on your desktop or placed in one of those slide-holder sheets that you insert in an album. You use Slide Sorter view when you want to see your presentation as a whole and when you might want to rearrange the order in which your slides will be shown.

- Notes Pages view is something of a "personal" view in that it lets you include speaker's notes with each of your slides. A miniature of the slide appears at the top of each page, with room for about half a page of notes below.

- Slide Show view is the most fun. You use it when you want to preview your work and run through your presentation to see how well you did. In Slide Show view, you also see the results of transitions (how the screen changes when moving between slides) as well as any animation or sound effects you've added to the presentation.

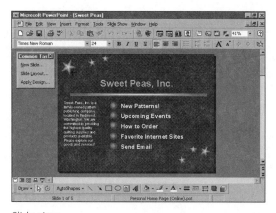

Slide view

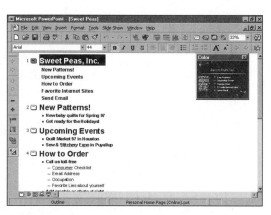

Outline view

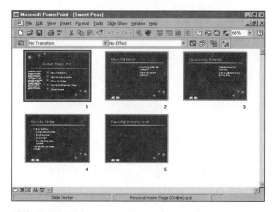

Slide Sorter view

Notes Pages view

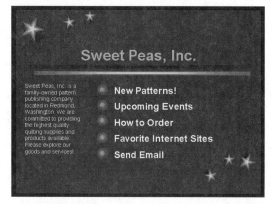

Slide Show view

FIGURE 24-2.
PowerPoint's many points of view.

Three Ways to Get Started

Once you're comfortable with the PowerPoint window and its tools and views, the burning question becomes, "How do I create a presentation?" PowerPoint, like most Office 97 applications, offers you a variety of choices. You see them listed in the dialog box shown below when you first open PowerPoint.

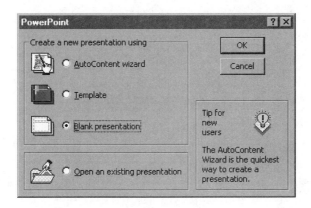

- The AutoContent Wizard, by far the easiest approach to creating a new presentation, asks for information and then creates a set of slides built around the theme you specify.

- Template, which allows you more latitude, lets you apply pre-designed "outlines," color schemes, and backgrounds to create sets of slides for standard types of presentations, such as progress reports and top-10 lists.

- Blank Presentation gives you a plain canvas on which to create a single slide; this option offers the most flexibility but, as you'd expect, also assumes that you know what you want to do and how to do it.

- The final option, Open An Existing Presentation, lets you choose a PowerPoint presentation that you've already created and saved. If you wish, you can then modify it, add some new slides, enhance its look, and save it as a new, different presentation.

Office 97 and Windows 95 both offer many ways to start programs and to create and reopen documents. You can, for instance, create or open presentations from the Office Shortcut Bar or from the New Office Document and Open Office Document commands on the Windows Start menu, or you can drag programs and documents to the Start button or create shortcuts to them on the Windows desktop. Such methods of working with programs and files are covered in Chapter 1, "A Quick Tour of Microsoft Office." Some alternatives are included here as tips, though the procedures in this part of the book concentrate on helping you work with PowerPoint the application, rather than with PowerPoint as a member of the Office 97–Windows 95 environment.

The AutoContent Wizard

Microsoft wizards provide the friendliest and simplest ways to get things done. Typically, wizards ask you to make some choices and provide some basic information, and then they use what you enter to carry out the task they're designed to do. As already mentioned, the Auto-Content Wizard walks you through the initial process of creating a presentation. To start the AutoContent Wizard when the dialog box shown on the previous page is displayed, do this:

- Click AutoContent Wizard and then click OK.

If you've been working in PowerPoint and the dialog box isn't displayed but you want to begin creating another presentation with the wizard, do this:

- Choose New from the File menu. In the New Presentation dialog box, click the Presentations tab. Click AutoContent Wizard and then click OK, or double-click the wizard icon.

However you start it, the wizard opens with an introductory screen that explains what will happen. Click the Next button to move on, and the wizard swings into action as shown on the facing page.

From this point on, the wizard is so friendly that using it is almost a no-brainer. Just remember to click Next to move to the next screen; click Back to return to an earlier screen; and click Cancel to scrap everything you've done. As you work through the wizard, PowerPoint keeps track of your progress, as shown in the bulleted list on the left

IV

Microsoft PowerPoint

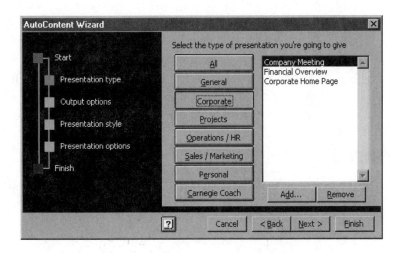

side of the dialog box. The following list summarizes the steps you go through:

- The first screen (after the starting screen), illustrated above, asks you to select the type of presentation you're going to give, by clicking on one of the eight topics displayed in the dialog box. For example, to see a list of the business presentations, click the Corporate button.

- The second screen asks you to choose the output type for the presentation you'll be making. PowerPoint comes with a number of built-in templates designed for different situations. You can choose a traditional presentation or an automated Internet or kiosk-style presentation (like the kind you see in airports or in shopping malls these days).

- The third screen asks you more about the output type for the show you'll present—that is, will you use on-screen presentations, overhead projections, or slides?—and inquires if you'll want to distribute handouts.

- The fourth screen requests information that'll be displayed on the opening, or title, slide. By default, the wizard includes the name of your presentation and your name. If you enter several items in the Additional Information text box, press the Enter key after each item to have the AutoContent Wizard display each item on a separate line. Press Enter twice to "double-space" the lines.

That's all there is to it! On the last screen, click Finish, and the Auto-Content Wizard creates a basic set of slides built around the choices you made, and ends up by displaying your presentation in Outline view. With the preliminary work done, you're now ready to add text and graphics, modify formatting to add impact to your message, and make the presentation your own, as described in the following chapters.

 TIP

PowerPoint uses the word slide to refer to each "page" of a presentation, but you can turn these slides into transparencies or printed handouts. Or you can use your computer to display them on a wall screen, on the monitors of other people on your network, or to thousands of other people over the Internet.

Using a Template

PowerPoint arrives on your desktop with two types of built-in templates. *Presentation templates* are frameworks for standard types of presentations. They have names such as Business Plan, Company Meeting, Corporate Financial Overview, Personal Home Page, and so on. As their names indicate, these templates help you to create a presentation by incorporating suggestions for key points you'll probably want to include as you cover your topic. Figure 24-3 shows some of the slides in the Business Plan template (check the status bar) to help you see what presentation templates—also just called *presentations*—are all about. Naturally, the wizard is merely a tool; it doesn't replace business professionals (lawyer, accountant, marketing pro, industry expert, and the like) whom you'd probably want to consult when preparing a business plan to take to a lender for startup capital.

In contrast to presentation templates, *design templates* (also called *presentation designs*) help you apply a consistent design and color scheme to an entire set of slides. Design templates have names such as Blue Diagonal, Contemporary, International, and Professional. Put together by professional designers, these templates combine a background color and design with a set of eight complementary colors that PowerPoint uses for elements such as titles, background, slide text, shadow effects, and so on.

FIGURE 24-3.
Presentation templates help you organize and build content.

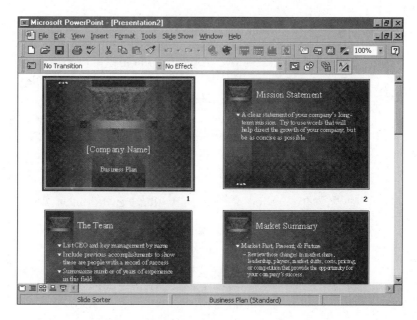

The following illustration shows a title page format based on the Portrait Notebook design template—suitably whimsical for a new tutoring program, but unsuitable for a stockholders' meeting.

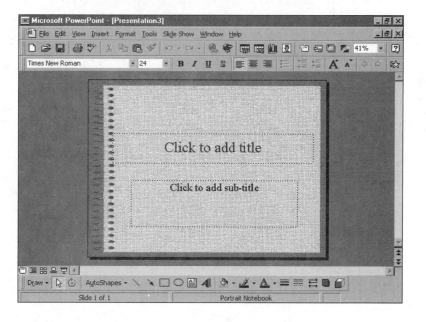

When you work with PowerPoint, it's important to understand that presentation templates and design templates are *mix-and-match* elements of a slide show. You can combine them in any way you choose. Suppose, for example, that you decide to work with the Marketing Plan presentation template. By default, PowerPoint uses a design template with a blue, green, and white color scheme for the Marketing Plan template, though you're free to choose any other design from among the many built into PowerPoint—or, when you're more experienced, from any you've created and saved for yourself.

To use templates from within PowerPoint, follow this procedure:

1 If the opening PowerPoint dialog box is displayed, choose Template and click OK. If you've been working on a different presentation, save it (if necessary) and choose New from the File menu. Either way, the New Presentation dialog box appears, as shown in Figure 24-4.

2 Click the Presentation Designs tab to select a design template, *or* click the Presentations tab to select a presentation template.

FIGURE 24-4.
The New Presentation dialog box.

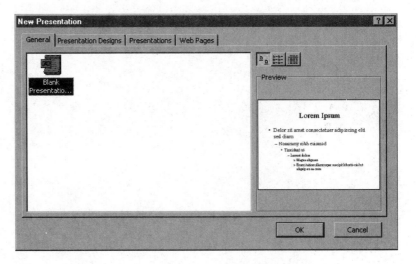

3 Click the icon for the template with the design you want or the one that most closely matches your topic. If you can't decide on a presentation template, choose Generic. Presentation templates marked *(Online)* have identical content to their *(Standard)* twins, but they include formatting that makes them suitable for use in networking settings, such as on the Internet. Notice that Power-Point shows you a preview for the template in the Preview area at the right. Note, too, that you can launch the AutoContent Wizard from the Presentations tab if you want to.

4 When you've selected the template, click OK.

- If you selected a presentation template from the Presentations tab, you'll now see the opening slide of the new presentation containing the sample text supplied by the template, and you can begin entering the text of your presentation.

- If you selected a design template from the Presentation Designs tab, choose an AutoLayout in the New Slide dialog box, as shown in Figure 24-5. A slide with the design template and *AutoLayout* you chose will appear in the Power-Point window and you can begin entering the text of your presentation.

FIGURE 24-5.
Selecting an AutoLayout in the New Slide dialog box.

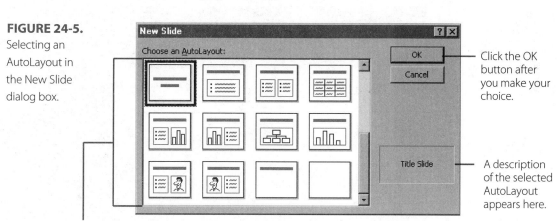

Click the OK button after you make your choice.

A description of the selected AutoLayout appears here.

Click to select the AutoLayout that includes the elements (text, tables, charts, and graphics) and arrangement that you want to appear on your slide.

Create First, Refine Later

If you don't like the design applied to the presentation template you chose, it's easy to improve it. Just create the substance of your presentation. Changing the design is very simple and is covered in Chapter 26, "Formatting Text."

Creating a Blank Presentation

When you want to opt for full creativity instead of relying on the AutoContent Wizard or a template, follow these steps:

1 If the opening PowerPoint dialog box is displayed, choose Blank Presentation and click OK. If you're already working with Power-Point, choose New from the File menu. Click to select Blank Pre-sentation on the General tab of the New Presentation dialog box, and then click OK.

2 Complete the New Slide dialog box, as shown in Figure 24-5 on the preceding page. A slide with reserved areas matching the lay-out you chose appears in the PowerPoint window, as shown in Figure 24-6.

FIGURE 24-6.

A blank slide with space for adding title, text, and a clip art graphic.

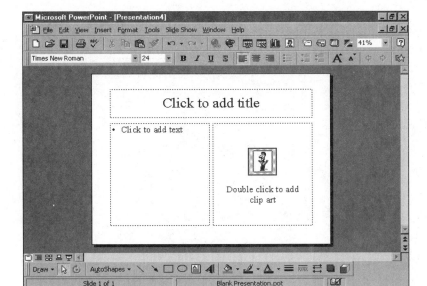

Once you've chosen the basic layout for your blank slide, you can enter, edit, and format its contents. PowerPoint uses certain fonts and font sizes by default, though you can easily change them. The sample in Figure 24-7, for example, used the default font and font size for the title and bulleted items, but the size of the text inserted inside the clip art image was reduced, and the paragraph was centered to fit inside the circle. None of this work was difficult, as you'll see in the next few chapters. First, however, take a quick look at the easy ways in which you can customize your PowerPoint environment to match your needs and preferences. The more you know about your user interface before you start, the more comfortable you'll be when you settle down to work.

FIGURE 24-7.
The same slide after adding some information.

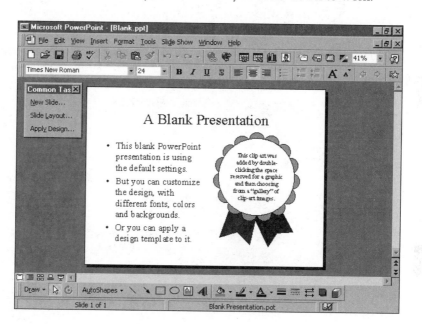

Working with Toolbars

By default, PowerPoint 97 displays the Standard, Formatting, Common Tasks, and Drawing toolbars. The Standard toolbar, as in other Office applications, contains general-purpose tools. In PowerPoint, these tools are used for creating, printing, and enhancing slides. The Formatting toolbar, as you'd expect, provides quick access to text and paragraph formatting. The Common Tasks toolbar contains the most popular PowerPoint commands, and since it appears as a "floating" palette in the PowerPoint window, you can easily drag it from one place to the next if it covers part of the slide you're working with. The Drawing toolbar, which might be new to you, helps you insert text, graphics, and special effects on slides. The Drawing toolbar appears at the bottom of the PowerPoint window above the status bar (see Figure 24-1, page 679), and is identical to the Drawing toolbar that appears in the Word and Excel applications.

PowerPoint also includes several other toolbars that you'll find useful:

- The Animation Effects toolbar—a delightful one—offers an assortment of tools for adding movement and sound to selected text and graphics on your slides. It can also be displayed by clicking the Animation Effects button on the Formatting toolbar.

- The Picture toolbar lets you adjust a number of formatting options for the selected image. For example, you can adjust the contrast, brightness, border line style, and crop marks.

- The Reviewing toolbar lets you add review comments and send electronic mail messages.

- The Visual Basic toolbar helps you create macros that automate tasks in the PowerPoint environment.

■ The Web toolbar lets you switch back and forth between open hyperlinks, establish additional Internet connections, or run special network-related commands.

■ The WordArt toolbar gives you the ability to create text entries with special formatting effects.

Try New Techniques on a Practice Slide, and Then Toss It

If you want to experiment with these toolbars— or any other PowerPoint feature, for that matter—start PowerPoint and open a throwaway slide by choosing Blank Presentation in the opening PowerPoint dialog box. Click OK, and when you're asked to choose an AutoLayout, click Blank AutoLayout (the last choice in the lower right corner), and click OK again. This will give you a blank slide to experiment with. When you're through, exit PowerPoint and click No when asked if you want to save the presentation.

Displaying Other Toolbars

It's easy to display and arrange additional toolbars. Remember, however, that each takes valuable screen space, so give yourself plenty of working room by keeping the extras to a minimum. When you're experienced with PowerPoint, you might find it helpful to create a custom toolbar with the tools you use most, and then turn off the toolbars you don't need. (When you want to display additional toolbars or turn off those that you *don't* want to display, you must be working in Slide, Outline, Slide Sorter, or Notes Pages view.)

To modify your list of open toolbars, complete the following steps:

1 Click View, and then point to the Toolbars command *or* click with the right mouse button on any open toolbar. You'll see the menu on the following page.

SEE ALSO

For more information about running commands with toolbar buttons, moving toolbars around the screen, and adding new toolbars to the workplace, see "Using Toolbars," page 52. To customize the contents of a toolbar or edit the pictures in toolbar buttons, see "Adding Buttons to a Toolbar," page 532.

2 Click the name of the toolbar you want to display or close; this adds or removes a check mark. Toolbars that have a check mark next to their names are open.

 **TIP**

Shortcuts Are a Click Away

Many times the action you want to perform can be found on the special shortcut menu that appears when you press the right (or secondary) mouse button. The menu changes with the context of your actions, so check it often for possible shortcuts to accomplish your tasks more quickly.

Customizing PowerPoint with the Options Dialog Box

To change the way PowerPoint looks and works, experiment with the customization choices in the Options dialog box, shown in Figure 24-8. You display the Options dialog box by choosing the Options command from the Tools menu.

The Options dialog box contains tabs that control virtually every aspect of the PowerPoint interface. Although some tabs customize features that you might not be familiar with, such as the settings that render and export pictures, you can often learn a lot about how PowerPoint works

FIGURE 24-8.
The Options dialog box lets you customize many of PowerPoint's commands and features. The View tab controls basic options like the appearance of the workplace, and display options in your slide show.

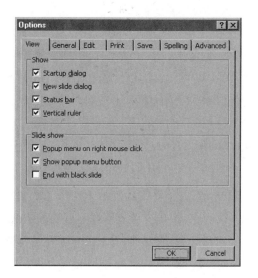

by just browsing through the tabs in the Options dialog box. When you have some spare time, we recommend that you experiment with the following features to personalize your working environment:

- The View tab, which controls the dialog boxes that appear when you start PowerPoint, and interface items like the status bar and ruler

- The General tab, which controls the size of the recently used file list on the File menu, and the username that appears in comments and e-mail messages

- The Edit tab, which controls editing features like drag and drop, and the maximum number of "undos" available

- The Save tab, which sets the default file format for PowerPoint presentations and the timing interval (in minutes) of the AutoRecover backup feature

CHAPTER 25

Entering and Editing Text

Although drawings, graphics, charts, colors, and eye-catching background designs help enormously to illustrate your points and keep your audience awake, substance and content still require words. Those words must come from you, but PowerPoint can help you add them to your slides in a number of easy and creative ways that focus attention on what you want to say.

This chapter describes ways to build the body of a presentation with elements such as titles, subtitles, and bulleted lists. You'll learn how to manage the text on a slide, expand one slide into many, and add review annotations known as comments to slides. So that you won't think of text as simply the "gray matter" on a slide, you'll also learn how to add some eye appeal with WordArt objects. Toward the end of the chapter, you'll see how to enlist PowerPoint's advice in making your slides clear and easy to read.

This chapter deals with "plain" text. PowerPoint also lets you add text, such as captions and labels, to graphics. That's done differently, however, and is covered in Chapter 27, where you meet Microsoft Draw and the Drawing toolbar.

Entering Text

The way you enter text onto a slide depends on the way you've decided to create your presentation. The basic options are as follows:

- Working with a template, including one "designed" for you by the AutoContent Wizard

- Working with a blank presentation and applying a built-in AutoLayout

- Working in Outline view

When you start a new presentation by choosing a template, text entry is literally a matter of replacing the suggested topics (the *placeholders)* that PowerPoint provides on each slide. When you start with a blank presentation and choose an AutoLayout format, text entry is much the same as if you had chosen one of PowerPoint's templates. The only difference between the two, which you can see in Figures 25-1 and 25-2, is that the template comes with a colorful presentation design and contains suggestions for content, whereas the AutoLayout offers a plain background and simply reserves portions of the slide for whatever content you want to provide.

Instead of—or in addition to—using templates and built-in layouts, you can organize your thoughts in outline form and then turn your outline into slides. If you're creating a complex presentation, or if you're a person who values structure and likes to see how the parts contribute to the whole, working with an outline is probably a good choice for you.

The following sections describe each of these options in more detail.

FIGURE 25-1.
When you use a template, PowerPoint makes suggestions about the types of information you might want to include on each slide.

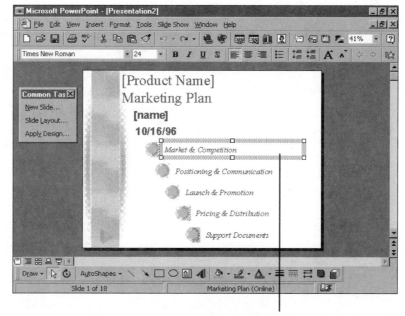

Placeholder

FIGURE 25-2.
When you start with a blank presentation and an AutoLayout, PowerPoint reserves space for text, but doesn't offer any suggestions about content.

Placeholders

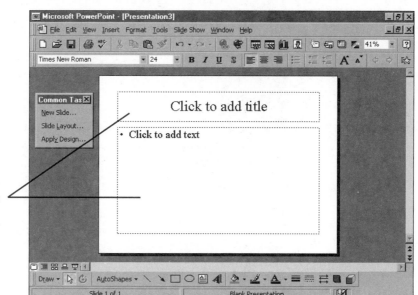

IV

Microsoft PowerPoint

Entering Text into Placeholders

Placeholders, like the ones shown in Figures 25-1 and 25-2 on the previous page, are something like templates within templates. Surrounded by a dotted or shaded line, they're preformatted with a particular font and font size, and they contain text that you replace with your own. By default, PowerPoint automatically wraps text within the placeholder as you type, so press Enter only when you want to start a new paragraph.

In both templates and AutoLayouts, you thus do the following:

1 Select the placeholder.

2 Type your own text, as shown in the following illustration.

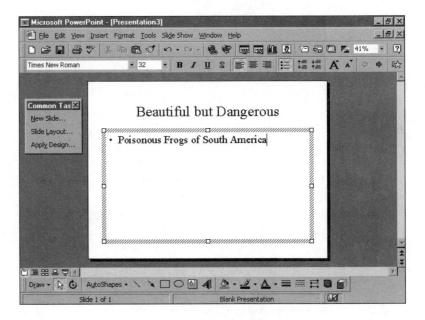

3 When you've finished entering text, click anywhere outside the placeholder to make the border disappear.

Tips for Entering Text

Text entry is simple, but keep these points in mind:

■ When you use an AutoLayout, your typing *replaces* the placeholder text.

■ When you use a template, you must select the placeholder text before typing your own text. If you don't, your typing is *inserted* into the placeholder text.

■ When you enter text that isn't found in the Office 97 dictionary or in a custom dictionary, the words are marked with a red wavy underline, indicating a potential misspelling. This as-you-type spell-check feature (new in PowerPoint 97) can be very useful, but rarely recognizes technical terms or foreign words. To add a word to your custom dictionary, click the underlined word with the right mouse button and click Add. To correct a misspelling, click the underlined word with the right mouse button and pick a correction if one is listed.

■ To insert symbols or special characters in a placeholder, choose Symbol from the Insert menu, specify the character set you want to use in the Font drop-down list box, click the symbol you want in the display window, click Insert to add the symbol, and then click Close.

■ To add a new, blank text placeholder to a slide, choose Textbox from the Insert menu, drag the mouse on the slide to create a placeholder window, and type the text you want.

Selecting Placeholder Text in a Template

When you're working with a template, there are several ways to select placeholder text that you want to replace:

■ Double-click to select a single word; triple-click to select a paragraph.

■ Position the insertion point at the beginning or the end of a line and drag across the text you want to replace.

■ On the keyboard, press Home once, and then press Shift+End to select a line or Ctrl+Shift+End to select the entire block of text in the placeholder.

Tips for Positioning Placeholders

When you're working with placeholders, here are some tips you might want to keep in mind:

- If you're having trouble fitting text onto a slide, try resizing or repositioning another placeholder before enlarging the one in which you want more text. To reposition a placeholder, click on a part of the border other than a sizing handle (the mouse pointer should be a four-headed arrow) and drag the placeholder up or down on the slide. Moving a title higher, for example, gains you extra space for a bulleted list below it.

- Because PowerPoint automatically wraps text, you can use placeholder resizing as a quick-and-dirty way to realign text. To turn a two-line paragraph into one, for instance, widen the placeholder box. To force text to fill more vertical space, make the box narrower and longer.

- Resize or realign placeholders to make room for an object, such as a graphic, that isn't provided for on your template or on your AutoLayout slide.

You can choose an *anchor point* for your text. Normally, PowerPoint adds text from the top down. By choosing a different anchor point, you can have Power-Point add text from the bottom or the middle of an object instead. This feature can help you maintain even spacing above and below text that doesn't completely fill a placeholder. To do this, select the placeholder you want to modify and choose Drawing Object from the Format menu. Select a new text anchor point in the Format AutoShape dialog box as shown here:

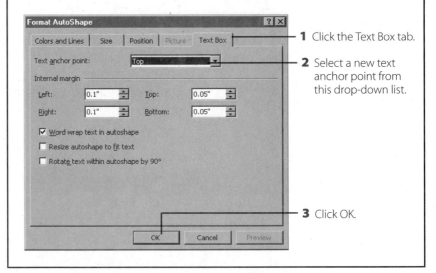

1 Click the Text Box tab.

2 Select a new text anchor point from this drop-down list.

3 Click OK.

Matching the Placeholder's Size to Your Text

When you type more text than the placeholder can hold, PowerPoint, by default, doesn't expand the placeholder vertically to contain the overflow. Although such a problem is easily corrected, you'll probably want to watch how much you type. PowerPoint will accept your text, but you might end up with a slide that looks like the one in Figure 25-3.

FIGURE 25-3.
You can do this, but your slide won't be very effective.

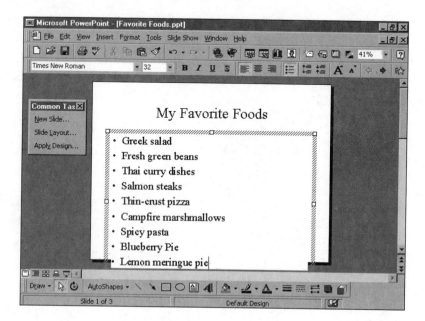

If you need to enter more text than a placeholder can hold, one easy solution is to reformat the font size, as described in the next chapter, so that the information requires less space. If you don't need such a significant change, or if one placeholder is too big and another is too small, you can also shrink or enlarge your placeholders.

With the mouse, do this:

1 Click the border of the placeholder to display its sizing handles.

2 Place the mouse pointer on one of the handles. When the pointer turns into a dark, two-headed arrow, drag the border in the direction you want to resize the box. (As with most windows in

Microsoft Office, you can also drag a corner placeholder to resize the window in two directions.) The following illustration shows a placeholder during resizing:

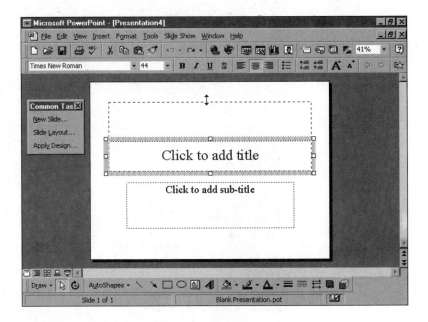

Using Outlines

Outlines in PowerPoint are exactly like the ones that you created in school. Just as in those long-ago outlines, you work with—and present to the world—a series of titles with subordinate levels and sublevels of headings, as shown in Figure 25-4.

It's easy to see from this illustration that outline indenting can help you organize your thoughts while you're creating slides, and that such indenting can also be highly effective in helping your audience understand the relative importance of the points you make.

Viewing an Outline

To work on an outline in PowerPoint, simply click the Outline View button to the left of the horizontal scroll bar.

If you've opened an existing presentation or you're using a presentation template, you see the text displayed in outline form, as shown in

FIGURE 25-4.
Subordinate outline levels in PowerPoint are indented at the left. Templates format them in different font sizes and, sometimes, with different bullet styles.

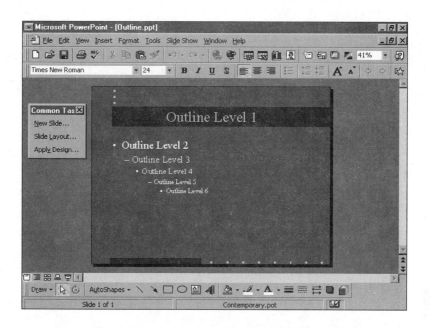

FIGURE 25-5.
In this Outline view, two slides and three different heading levels are visible.

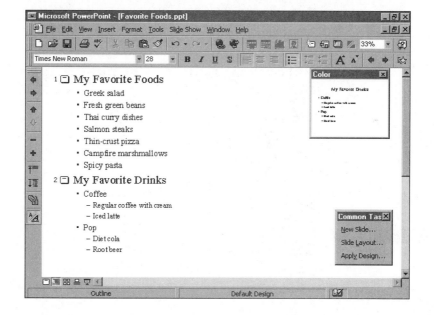

Figure 25-5. If you're working on a blank presentation, you see a slide number and a slide icon, as shown in Figure 25-6 on the following page, but, of course, no text will appear until you type some.

FIGURE 25-6.

A blank presentation in Outline view.

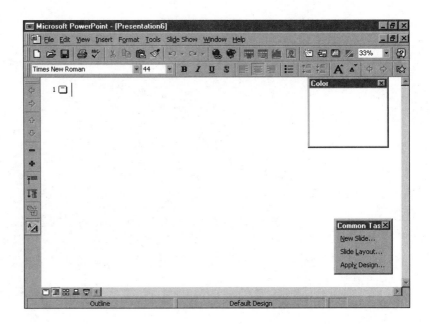

Entering an Outline from Scratch

When you've displayed a blank presentation in Outline view, generating an outline feels as if you're working on a cross between a Word document and a PowerPoint slide. Once you get the hang of it, however, it's simple. The only real trick is to remember the following:

■ Depending on the preceding outline level you typed, the key combination Ctrl+Enter *toggles* between creating a new slide and creating a bulleted item. That is, if the last text you typed was a slide title, Ctrl+Enter creates a bulleted item; if the last text you typed was a bulleted item, Ctrl+Enter creates a new slide.

Use Slide Show View for a Quick Preview

When you're working on an outline, you can always see what the actual slide will look like by clicking the Slide View button to the left of the horizontal scroll bar. To see all your slides, either click the Slide Sorter button (to see them all on screen) or press Ctrl+Home and click the Slide Show button (to see what your actual presentation will look like). If you use the Slide Show button, click to move from slide to slide, and press Escape to end the show.

■ After you've passed the title/first bullet hurdle, pressing Enter creates a new paragraph exactly like the preceding one. That is, if the last thing you typed was a bullet, press Enter to create another bullet; if the last thing you typed was a slide title, press Enter to create a new slide.

■ If you want to create an outline with several sublevels (as shown in Figure 25-4 on page 705), use the Promote and Demote buttons on the vertical Outlining toolbar:

- Click the *Promote* button to raise the importance of a paragraph one heading level—for example, to switch from outline level 3 to outline level 2.

- Click the *Demote* button to lower the importance of a paragraph one heading level—say, to switch from outline level 2 to outline level 3. You can also use the Demote button to move the top heading on one slide to the previous slide.

The Outlining toolbar is shown as a floating toolbar in Figure 25-7 on the following page. By default, this toolbar is displayed docked along the left side of your screen—though, as with all toolbars, you can drag it to another side of the screen or position it as a floating toolbar if you prefer.

Creating an outline, especially with the Enter and Ctrl+Enter key combinations, might take a little getting used to. If you stumble on your first try, the sidebar on page 709 should help you out.

Modifying an Outline

When you're comfortable with Outline view, use the following procedures to control and refine either an outline that you've created from scratch or one that you're revising using the suggestions in a template or the headings in another document:

■ To select a slide title in an outline, drag the mouse pointer over the title.

■ To select a bulleted item and all its subitems, click on the bullet (when the pointer becomes a four-headed arrow).

- To select several consecutive bulleted items, hold down the Shift key as you click. (Although Ctrl+click lets you select nonconsecutive items in other Office 97 applications, it doesn't work that way in PowerPoint.)

- To select an entire slide, click the slide icon.

- To move a paragraph, select it and either drag it to its new location or use the Move Up and Move Down buttons, shown on the Outlining toolbar in Figure 25-7.

- Use the buttons shown in Figure 25-7 to change outline levels and to control how much of the outline you see on screen.

FIGURE 25-7.
Tools on the
Outlining toolbar.

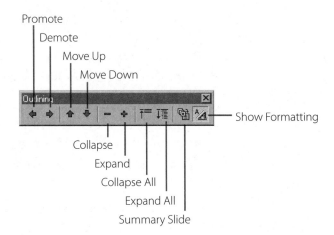

As you're working with your slides, you might find that you need to rearrange some of them. You can easily do so by dragging them to new locations in Slide Sorter view, but when you're working on an outline, drag and drop works just as well:

1 Select the slide you want to move. (Be sure to select all of it by clicking on the slide icon.)

2 Place the mouse pointer on the slide icon and drag the slide to a new location. As you drag, watch the horizontal line that shows where you're dragging the slide. To avoid dropping the slide into the body of another slide, don't release the mouse button until the "move" line is completely above or below your target.

3 To undo a move, either choose Undo Move from the Edit menu or click the Undo button.

4 When you move slides, note that PowerPoint automatically renumbers them for you. A nice touch.

Using Word to Create an Outline

To Microsoft Office, an outline is an outline, whether it's created in PowerPoint or in Word. Thus, you can easily turn a Word outline into a set of slides, and you can just as easily turn a set of slides into a Word document. The only prerequisite (on *your* part) for this to work smoothly is some familiarity with Word's heading-level styles, because heading levels in a Word document become bulleted items on PowerPoint slides, and vice versa, as shown in Figure 25-8 on the following page.

If you know Word, importing an outline is simple. If you don't know Word, the process is a little more complex. You'll just have to adjust the outline levels yourself in PowerPoint with the Promote and Demote buttons.

Creating an Outline

To generate a standard outline, beginning with a title slide, do the following:

1 Start by clicking the New button on the Standard toolbar.

2 Click OK to choose the AutoLayout default, which will begin by creating a title slide.

3 By default, PowerPoint assumes that a title slide doesn't include bulleted items. Because this slide is a little different from other slides, you can make life simple by entering the slide's title and subtitle while you're still in PowerPoint's default Slide view. Click the appropriate placeholder and type the title and subtitle that you want.

4 Now click the Outline View button to switch from Slide view to Outline view.

5 To begin creating the first of your "content" slides, position the insertion point at the end of your title or subtitle and press Ctrl+Enter.

6 Type a title for the new slide and press Ctrl+Enter. This automatically moves you to your first bulleted item. Type the text of your bullet. Press the Enter key to create another bullet; press Ctrl+Enter to create the next slide.

7 Repeat step 6 for each new slide that you create.

FIGURE 25-8.

These illustrations show how heading levels in Word match outline levels in PowerPoint.

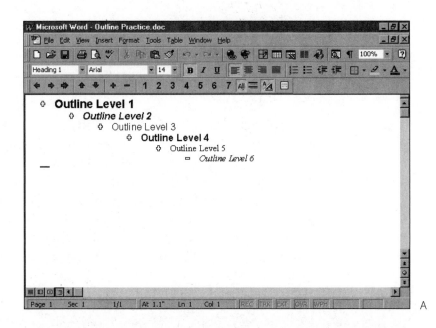

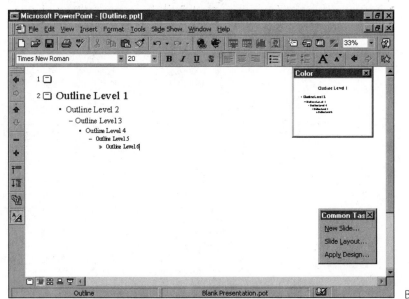

To use a Word document with heading styles as the basis for a presentation, follow this procedure:

1 Click the New button on PowerPoint's Standard toolbar.

2 Choose an AutoLayout and click OK. The default, which starts with a title slide, is a good choice because PowerPoint is so smart that it leaves the title slide for you to deal with and starts displaying the Word outline on slide 2.

3 From the Insert menu, choose the Slides From Outline command. The following dialog box appears:

Use the Look In drop-down list and the Up One Level button to find files in other folders.

4 Select the Word document you want to import.

5 Click Insert.

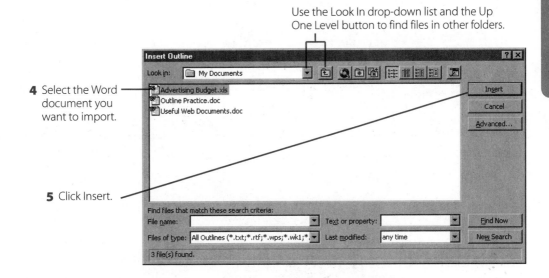

6 After PowerPoint opens the Word document and builds a presentation with the outline, use PowerPoint's Outline view and Slide view to edit the content of the presentation so that no slide has an overabundance of text. (If you used several heading levels, some of your slides might be packed with too much information to fit or to read easily.)

 TIP

Another Way to Import a Word Outline

To create a PowerPoint presentation from a Word document with heading styles, choose Open from the File menu. In the Open dialog box, select All Outlines in the Files Of Type list box. Then, double-click the name of the document you want to open. The imported Word outline will open in PowerPoint in Outline view.

> **Each Paragraph in Word Is a Slide**
> You can turn a "normal" Word document (one without heading levels) into a PowerPoint outline using these same procedures, though each paragraph in the document will become the title of a new slide. If your Word document contains five paragraphs, for example, PowerPoint will turn those paragraphs into the titles of five slides. A useful technique, if you have nothing else to start with.

? SEE ALSO

For more information on applying styles in Word, see Chapter 6, "Formatting a Word Document." For details on working on outlines in Word, see Chapter 12, "Writing Long Documents."

To reverse the procedure just described and use a PowerPoint presentation as the basis for a Word document, you have several options. You can copy the presentation as a Word outline, as a set of formatted slides, or as a combination of slides and notes.

To copy a PowerPoint presentation to Word, follow these steps:

1 Create or open the presentation in PowerPoint that you want to export to Word.

2 On the File menu, point to the Send To submenu and click Microsoft Word. The following dialog box opens, prompting you for the presentation components you want to send:

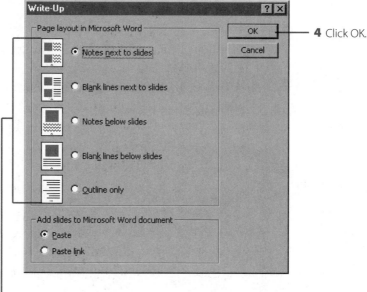

4 Click OK.

3 Select the formatting option of your choice. Select the Outline Only option if you want to send an outline of your presentation, not the clip art and other graphic objects.

IV

Microsoft PowerPoint

5   When your presentation opens in a Word window, you can edit and save it as you would any other Word document. If you used heading levels in your PowerPoint presentation, you'll see them in your Word document, and you can proceed to demote and promote the headings as you see fit in Word's Outline view.

 TIP

Create Links Between Files

If you want your new Word document to be updated automatically with any changes that occur in the PowerPoint presentation that you exported, click the Paste Link option button in the dialog box that appears when you specify how you want your presentation sent to Word. Paste Link creates an electronic pathway between the files that remains active until you break it. (As you might guess, however, this feature is *not* desirable if you want the files to have their own identity.) For more information on maintaining links, see Chapter 39, "Sharing Data Among Office Applications."

Entering Review Comments

If you plan to share your presentations with other users, you might want to annotate a few important slides with comments to provide instructions or highlight critical information. In PowerPoint 97, you can add a "yellow-sticky" note to a slide by displaying the slide in Slide view and choosing Comment from the Insert menu. The Comment command displays a yellow scratch pad with a blinking cursor and your name in it, so that you can add a short comment on the slide. (See the illustration on the following page.) To get a good look at the scratch pad while you enter your comment, we recommend that you use the Zoom list box on the Standard toolbar to change the slide magnification to 75 percent or larger.

When you finish typing a comment, resize the scratch pad so that the entire note fits within the comment window, and then click another object on your slide to "lock in" the comment. It will appear on your slide in each view as long as Comments on the View menu is selected.

Zoom list box

Reviewing toolbar ⟶

Comment box ⟶

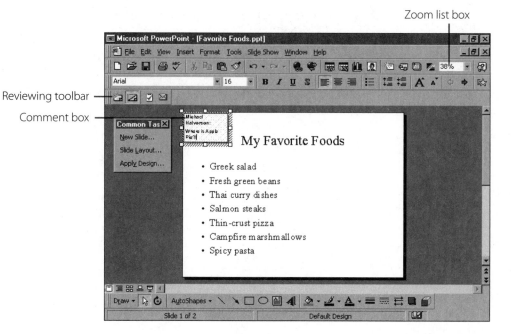

(The Comments command is a toggle, and is activated when you enter your first comment.) You can also use the Reviewing toolbar to manage your comments; it appears below the Formatting toolbar when you create your first yellow note:

Show/Hide Comments

Insert Comment

 **TIP**

Move It or Lose It

A comment is like any text box object on your slide; you can move a comment by dragging it with the mouse, or you can delete a comment by clicking its placeholder border and pressing Delete. You can also edit a comment by clicking it, and then using a combination of arrow keys and text keys to modify the text. Finally, you can change the reviewer name at the top of the comment by choosing Options from the Tools menu, clicking the General tab, and editing the Name field.

Here's what a comment looks like in Slide Show view.

Michael Halvorson:
Where is Apple Pie?!

My Favorite Foods

- Greek salad
- Fresh green beans
- Thai curry dishes
- Salmon steaks
- Thin-crust pizza
- Campfire marshmallows
- Spicy pasta

Expanding and Duplicating Slides

Other useful slide management capabilities of PowerPoint 97 are the ability to expand one slide into several slides and the ability to quickly duplicate a slide. While both techniques were possible in earlier versions of PowerPoint, in this version the procedures have been simplified.

To expand one slide into several slides, follow these steps:

1 Display in Slide view the slide you want to expand. PowerPoint expands one slide into several by breaking the slide after each internal text placeholder, bullet, or paragraph, so choose a slide with an appropriate number of divisions for the command to produce good results.

2 From the Tools menu, choose the Expand Slide command.

3 PowerPoint displays a dialog box asking if you'd like to see the new slides in Outline view or Slide view. (PowerPoint calls these new slides *agenda slides*, because this command is often used to create supporting slides from a meeting agenda list.) Immediately, PowerPoint expands the selected slide into two or more new slides, depending on the number of internal divisions. The original slide remains as slide 1 and is unchanged.

4 If you think better of the expansion and want to remove the new slides, simply choose Undo from the Edit menu.

To create an identical copy of a slide in your presentation, follow these steps:

1 Select the slide (in Outline view) or display the slide (in Slide view).

2 From the Insert menu, choose the Duplicate Slide command. PowerPoint creates a copy of the slide and places it immediately after the selected slide in the presentation.

3 If you want to move the duplicated slide to a new location, choose Slide Sorter view and drag the slide to a new place. (You'll learn more about Slide Sorter view in Chapter 29, "Perfecting Your Presentation.")

Adding Pizzazz with WordArt Objects

Lest you mistakenly think that words are better read than viewed, both Word and PowerPoint give you access to an enjoyable utility called WordArt that can add a lot of visual interest to text, as you can see in the following illustration:

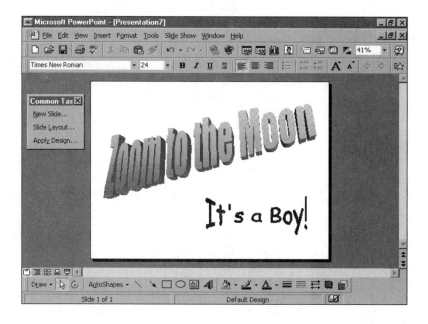

If you have a yen to add something of this sort to a slide—a special heading or logo, perhaps—it's easy. You don't even have to worry about positioning at first, because you'll be able to move and size the WordArt object later.

To create special text effects with the WordArt utility (started from the Drawing toolbar), follow these steps:

Insert
WordArt

1 Display the slide you want to modify in Slide view, and then click the Insert WordArt button on the Drawing toolbar. (If the Drawing toolbar isn't visible, open it first by using the Toolbars command on the View menu.) The following dialog box appears:

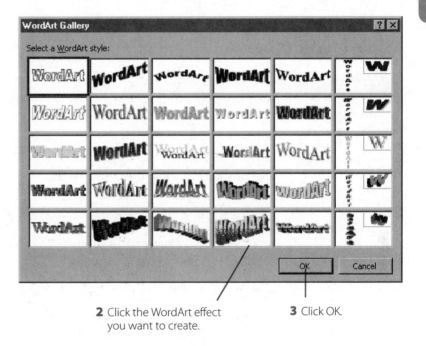

2 Click the WordArt effect you want to create.

3 Click OK.

4 Type whatever text you want in the Edit WordArt Text dialog box, and specify a different font and point size if you like.

5 Click OK to paste the WordArt on your slide. Then drag the WordArt to your preferred location and resize it with the sizing handles as desired.

WordArt is simple enough to use that you should need little more than these steps to become comfortable with it. If you need specifics, however, don't forget the Help menu, which is available at all times in PowerPoint.

What Happened to WordArt 2.0?

The WordArt icon on the Drawing toolbar is a replacement for the WordArt 2.0 program supplied with previous versions of Microsoft Office. If you installed Office 97 over a previous version of Office, you probably still have the old Word-Art utility, but you likely won't want to use it. (This one is better; trust us.)

Revising Text

Chapters 26 through 28 cover various aspects of enhancing a presentation visually, while Chapter 29 tells about checking spelling and other niceties.

Refining a document—any document—involves several tasks: editing for content and clarity, refining text and layout for effectiveness, and polishing your work by checking for spelling and other errors. The remainder of this section deals with ways to work on content.

Selecting Text to Revise

As already mentioned in this chapter and elsewhere in this book, you can select text with the mouse or the keyboard.

In addition to dragging the mouse over the text you want to select, you can use the following mouse shortcuts:

- In Outline view, click a slide icon to select the entire slide.

- In Outline view, select any bulleted item by moving the mouse pointer to the left of the item and clicking when the pointer becomes a four-headed arrow.

With the keyboard, do this:

- To move to the beginning of a line, press Home; to move to the end, press End.

- To select to the beginning or the end of a line, press Shift+End or Shift+Home.

- To select consecutive lines, hold down the Shift key as you press End or Home.

- To select one character at a time, use the Shift+Left (or Right) arrow key.

- To select one word at a time, use the Ctrl+Shift+Left (or Right) arrow key.

Making Changes

Most people do a lot of revising "on the fly" as they type. You probably do too—backspacing to erase errors and typos, and perhaps selecting text and retyping to replace it. Because PowerPoint slides don't contain as much text as Word or Excel documents, you shouldn't have any trouble revising what you've written. (Since text is so spare on a slide or transparency, any typos loom embarrassingly large—so be sure to check every word.) There are, however, a few ways you can make the job go quickly and, as you'll see, you can even ask for PowerPoint's opinion.

Making Text Revisions

The most common type of revision involves changing text, either all or in part. As you probably know, you can replace any amount of text simply by selecting it and typing something else. Your new text replaces the old text, even if you replace pages of prose with nothing more than a press of the Spacebar. Because PowerPoint, like other Windows 95 applications, is sensitive to the *right* mouse button, however, you have other easy ways to revise content:

- To insert new text, position the insertion point and simply start typing.

- To duplicate text, select it and then do one of the following:

  • Click the Copy button, position the insertion point where you want the duplicate text to appear, and click the Paste button. (Both buttons are on the Standard toolbar.)

  • Click the right mouse button on the selected text, choose Copy from the shortcut menu that pops up, place the insertion point where you want the duplicate text to appear, click the right button, and choose Paste. (This sounds like a lot of work, but it's not. Furthermore, since pop-up menus show only those actions you can "legally" apply to an object, they're very helpful when you're learning your way around a new application.)

- To move text, select it, and then use one of the following methods:

  - If you're working in Slide view, use the Cut and Paste buttons on the Standard toolbar.

  - If you're working in Outline view, select the text and drag it to its new location.

  - Click the right mouse button and use the Cut and Paste commands on the shortcut menu.

- To delete text, select it and press the Delete key or use the Clear command on the Edit menu.

- To delete an entire slide, display it (in Slide view) or select it (in Outline view) and choose Delete Slide from the Edit menu.

Searching for Terms and Replacing Them

Sometimes, instead of revising text, you want to replace specific terms—for example, change *primal scream* to *Tarzan yell*. For these jobs, you use either the Find command, which hunts for the term like a well-trained bloodhound, or the Replace command, which goes Find one better by replacing its quarry with something else.

You can use Find and Replace in any view other than Slide Show. The following describes Find, though it also applies to Replace, which is simply an expansion of Find:

1 Choose Find from the Edit menu. You'll see the following dialog box:

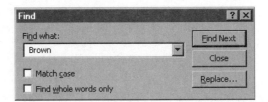

IV

2   Type all or part of the term you want to find in the Find What box. Include capitalization if you need specific instances, such as *Brown* (the name) but not *brown* (the color). If capitalization is important, turn on the Match Case check box. If you want whole words only—*brown* but not *brownie*—turn on the Find Whole Words Only check box. (Note, however, that specifying whole words means that Find will locate *Brown* or *brown*, but not *Brown's* or *browns*.)

3   Click Find Next. Find will then search through all slides and high-light the first instance of the term that it locates. Click Find Next again if the term is not the one you seek. If Find can't match the term you entered, it displays a message, telling you: *The search item was not found*.

If you want to replace one term with another, you can do so either by clicking the Replace button in the Find dialog box or by using the Replace command on the Edit menu. The Replace dialog box is identical in both cases:

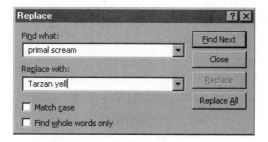

1   Enter the replacement term you want in the Replace With box, again using appropriate capitalization if necessary. (The Match Case check box applies to the text in the Find What box.) PowerPoint inserts the replacement text exactly as you type it in the Replace With box, including matching the capitalization.

2   If you want to approve each replacement, click Find Next to locate the next instance of the term in the Find What box, and then click Replace. If you want Replace to do the work for you, click Replace All. (Be sure to scan the slides afterward, however, to be sure all replacements are those you wanted.)

If you click the Replace All button and then decide you made a mistake, you can choose Undo Replace from the Edit menu to undo all replacements. If you use the Replace button, however, choosing Edit Undo Replace undoes only the *last* replacement. To undo others, use the Undo button for each replacement.

Checking for Visual Clarity

When you're satisfied with the content of your slides, PowerPoint can help you decide whether to make any adjustments to the way you've laid them out.

1   Choose Style Checker from the Tools menu, which opens the following dialog box:

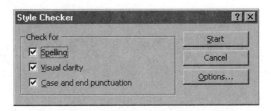

As you can see, the Style Checker is a multipurpose command that can help you with spelling and punctuation, too. Those aspects are addressed in Chapter 29, "Perfecting Your Presentation," but because checking for clarity can be more helpful when you're constructing a presentation than when you're finalizing it, the Visual Clarity option is covered here. By default, PowerPoint proposes to check all three options. To limit the check to Visual Clarity only, turn off the Spelling and Case And End Punctuation options. (PowerPoint turns them off automatically the next time you open the dialog box, so you don't have to worry about permanently turning off the spelling and punctuation options.)

2   To see what PowerPoint means by *visual clarity*, click the Options button in the Style Checker dialog box and then click the Visual Clarity tab in the Style Checker Options dialog box:

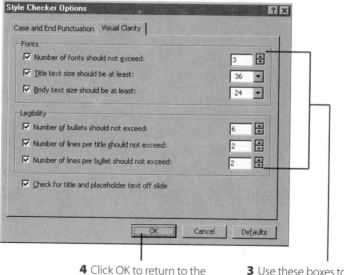

4 Click OK to return to the Style Checker dialog box.

3 Use these boxes to change settings as desired.

Notice that Visual Clarity encompasses not only fonts and font sizes, but—more important when you're constructing slides—legibility. The default settings, such as no more than six bullets per slide, contribute to a clear, well-focused presentation. When PowerPoint checks your slides, it uses these settings as guidelines and notifies you of any slides that don't match the settings.

5 To start the Visual Clarity check, click the Start button. Power-Point will check all your slides and will notify you of its findings with a dialog box like the following:

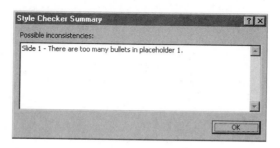

From this point on, it's up to you to decide whether and how you'll follow up on PowerPoint's advice.

Formatting Text

Formatting text means changing the appearance of text. The *look* of the words can be as important in conveying your message as the words themselves. This chapter shows you how to change the font, font size, style, and color of your text in PowerPoint. You'll see how special effects such as drop shadows and embossing can change the appearance and the *feeling* of your text. You'll learn that the way you align your text can make it easier for your audience to grasp the information that you're presenting. You can make the text easier to read by increasing the spacing between lines and adjusting the paragraph indentation.

It's easy and fun to experiment with different formatting. Your changes can be subtle or dramatic, depending on the effect that you want to create and the audience that you're targeting. Use restraint, though—for using too many design effects at once can detract from your message.

Changing the Appearance of Slide Text

If you know how to pick a new font, change alignment, and use bullets in a program like Word or Excel, then you already have the essential skills to perform these tasks in PowerPoint. If you don't want a refresher, you can skip this section and start with "Changing the Template" on page 737. If you're new to Microsoft Office, however, you'll want to read all of this section to learn how to format the text in your presentation.

Changing the Font, Font Size, Style, and Color

The font, font size, style, and color of your text are defined by settings in the current design template assigned to each text object or placeholder. For example, the Contemporary template uses Times New Roman 44-point in gray for slide titles and Times New Roman 32-point in white for slide text. (You can open the Contemporary template by choosing New from the File menu and clicking the Presentation Designs tab.) In both examples, the font style is regular (no bold or italic). With PowerPoint, you can easily change the font, font size, style, and color of the title or any other text.

Before you can change the text, you must first select it. To change all the text in a text object, click on the text object's border to select both it and all the text it contains. In general, it's best to select the entire text object to ensure that the text maintains a consistent look. There might be times, however, when you want to change just a portion of the text within a text object. For example, you might see a term that should be italicized or a word that you want to emphasize. To change the formatting for a selection, highlight by dragging the mouse over the words to be changed, and then issue your formatting command. (Chapter 25 discusses various techniques for selecting text or a placeholder.)

Figure 26-1 shows sample text formatted with the Bulleted List Auto-Layout and the Contemporary design template. All the text is initially Times New Roman with the title sized at 44 points, and the bulleted text at 32 points. In the illustration, the first two bullets (Norway and Sweden) have been selected individually with the mouse and are ready for formatting.

FIGURE 26-1.

Selecting text is the first step in formatting it. In the Contemporary template shown here, two items in the bulleted list have been selected.

Selected text

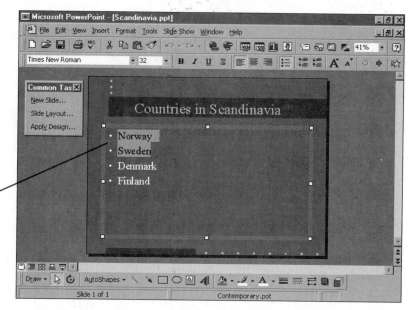

The look of your slide is achieved through the interaction of the shapes and colors that it contains. Professional designers use a combination of established graphic principles and their experience to determine how to format the text on their slides, but it's OK to simply try different looks until you find something you like. One of the first things that you might wish to change is the appearance of the text on the slide.

The way in which the text appears is controlled by settings in the Font dialog box (which is discussed in the next section), but many of the most common changes that you might want to make are controlled by buttons on the Formatting toolbar, shown in Figure 26-2 on the following page. Here's how to do a little experimenting.

■ The term *font* is used to refer to the actual design of the characters used. Your system probably contains a variety of fonts from different sources. The easiest way to discover how each font looks on your slide is by trying it.

■ To change the font, select the text and choose a font from the Font drop-down list on the Formatting toolbar. Keep trying different fonts until you find one that has the look you want.

FIGURE 26-2.
The Formatting toolbar.

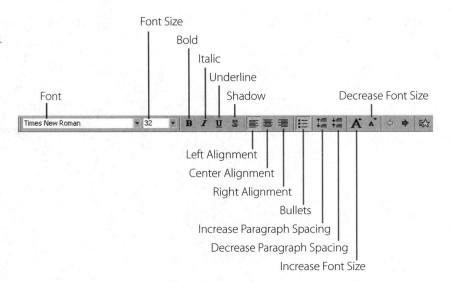

It's best to use no more than two fonts for all the text in your slide presentation. Too many fonts can spoil the effect and look too busy. If this sounds overly restrictive, remember that you can add variety by using the bold and italic styles of each font. For example, you might want to use Arial for your title and Times New Roman for text, with bold or italic here and there to emphasize certain words.

- To change the font size, select the text and choose a font size from the Font Size drop-down list box on the Formatting toolbar.

- If want to make your text larger but you're not sure what font size you need, click the Increase Font Size button on the Formatting toolbar until you get the size you want. Try increasing the title size to 54 points and the bulleted list to 36 points.

- The term *font style* refers to variations from the basic look of the font. The most common font styles, bold and italic, are often stored on your system as separate fonts. That's because the design of the characters within the font has been modified to give you the best possible appearance in these styles. Other styles, such as underline, change the formatting of the basic font. For example, when you underline text, PowerPoint draws a line under each character.

- To change the font style, select the text, and click one of the following buttons on the Formatting toolbar:

  - The Bold button makes your text bold.

  - The Italic button italicizes your text.

  - The Underline button underlines your text.

Format
Painter

- To copy text formatting from one placeholder to another, select the first placeholder, click the Format Painter button on the Standard toolbar, and click the second placeholder.

Special Effects

You can use formatting styles alone or in combination to add emphasis to text or titles. As mentioned earlier, use a little restraint, particularly with underlines, which can cut off descenders (the "tail" of a lowercase *g* or *p*, for example). For emphasis in text, it's generally better to use italics and to save the bold formatting for titles. You can also use the following special formatting effects:

Font
Color

- To change the text color, select the text, choose Font from the Format menu, and pick a new color in the Color drop-down list box. (See Figure 26-3 on the following page.) You can also click the down arrow next to the Font Color button on the Drawing toolbar and choose a color. By adding color to your text you can emphasize important words or phrases on your slide.

- Shadow effects provide another way to add emphasis and depth to your text. The Shadow option adds a shadow at the bottom and to the right of each character, making the text appear three-dimensional. To add shadow effects, select the text and click the Shadow button on the Formatting toolbar.

- To replace one font with another throughout an entire presentation, choose Replace Fonts from the Format menu, specify the font you want to replace in the Replace drop-down list box, specify the new font in the With drop-down list box, and then click Replace.

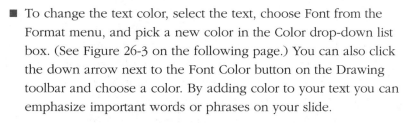

IV

Microsoft PowerPoint

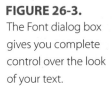**SEE ALSO**
You can also create special text formatting effects such as rotating text, changing the scale, and customizing the text background color by using the Colors And Lines command on the Format menu. Since this command also applies to formatting graphic images, we cover it in the next chapter. See "Advanced Text and Graphics Formatting," page 762.

Embossing Text with the Font Dialog Box

If you don't feel like using the Formatting toolbar, or you want to create several formatting effects at once, you can also choose the Font command from the Format menu and use the Font dialog box. (See Figure 26-3.) All the formatting changes that we discussed in the previous section can also be made by using this standard dialog box. In addition, there are a few other special effects, such as embossing and superscript, that can only be accomplished with the Font command.

If you've used Word or Excel, you'll recognize the placement of most formatting options in the Font dialog box. One obvious difference is the Superscript and Subscript check boxes, which allow you to control the amount that a character is raised or lowered with an *offset* value. Superscript reduces the font size of characters, and then elevates them above the standard line of text. The higher offset percentage you specify, the higher the characters will go. Conversely, the Subscript option reduces the font size of characters and then lowers them below the standard line of text. As you increase the Subscript offset by a negative percentage, the selected characters will drop lower and lower.

The Emboss check box creates a variation on PowerPoint's shadow text effect. When you select Emboss, PowerPoint formats the selected text with the appearance of raised letters by surrounding each character with a combination of light and dark outlines. The exact combination of colors PowerPoint uses depends on the background color of the slide. In our opinion, embossing generally works best with fonts

FIGURE 26-3.
The Font dialog box gives you complete control over the look of your text.

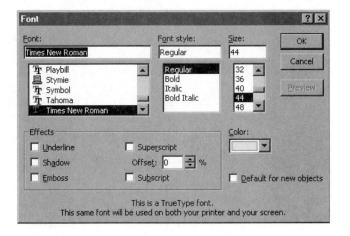

that produce thick characters or with headline-sized text (16-point or larger) that is formatted as bold.

NOTE

You can format text either to have a shadow or to appear embossed, but not both.

Changing Text Alignment

The default text-alignment settings for placeholders are included in PowerPoint's templates. For example, titles are often centered and text is usually aligned flush left. (The flush-left alignment, with its ragged-right edge, is the easiest alignment for your viewers' eyes to skim.) These alignment settings work for most slides; however, you might want to change the existing alignment or create new text that has a different alignment. You can choose among Flush Left, Centered, Flush Right, and Justified (both margins even) alignment options. Figure 26-4 shows a left-aligned title and right-aligned text.

FIGURE 26-4.
Changing alignment can help you create open spaces for artwork and other objects.

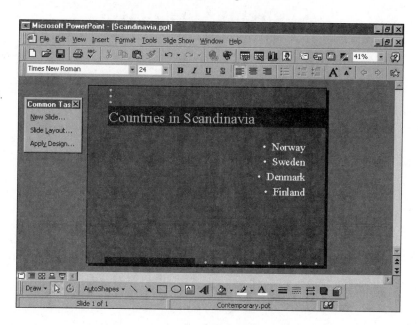

To change text alignment, follow these steps:

1 Select the text you want to align. (Either select individual lines of text with the mouse, or select entire text placeholders.)

2 Click one of the alignment buttons on the Formatting toolbar (Left, Center, or Right). If you'd like Justified alignment, a formatting option that aligns text to both left and right margins, click the Format menu, point to the Alignment submenu, and click the Justify command. (Be careful with Justify, however—it only creates useful effects when you have a lot of text on your slide.)

Use Borders for Alignment

PowerPoint uses the left and right sides of the text object to determine where it positions your text. You can move these borders to change the position of text on the slide. For example, if you wanted to align your bullets under the word *Scandinavia* in the title, you could position the mouse pointer over the left edge of the text object so that it's a two-headed arrow and then drag the border over to the letter *S*. With the left edge of the text object under the *S* and left alignment selected, the bullets would fall in a straight line below the word *Scandinavia*.

Changing Line Spacing

Just as the template defines fonts, color, and other characteristics for a presentation, it also defines line and paragraph spacing for text in a text object. PowerPoint lets you add spacing before or after selected paragraphs, and it allows you to change the amount of line spacing between the lines. For example, you might want to increase the line spacing between each item in a bulleted or numbered list.

Follow these steps to change line spacing or paragraph spacing in a text placeholder:

1 Select the text for which you want to change the line or paragraph spacing. If you're changing the spacing in a bulleted list, select the entire text object so that your choices will affect the entire list.

2 Choose Line Spacing from the Format menu to display the Line Spacing dialog box, as shown on the facing page.

If you change the Line Spacing setting (using the first pair of boxes), the space is added proportionately above and below each line within a paragraph. When your paragraphs consist of single lines of text, that's

IV

Microsoft PowerPoint

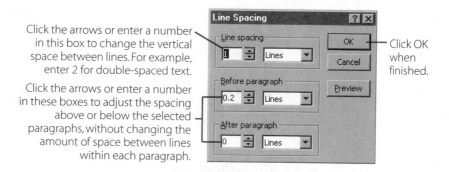

Click the arrows or enter a number in this box to change the vertical space between lines. For example, enter 2 for double-spaced text.

Click the arrows or enter a number in these boxes to adjust the spacing above or below the selected paragraphs, without changing the amount of space between lines within each paragraph.

Click OK when finished.

the same as adding the space between each entry. If, however, the text consists of paragraphs with more than one line of text, each pair of lines within each paragraph would have space added between them. There are often times when you want to add space between the paragraphs on your slide, but not to the lines within the paragraphs. You can use either the Before Paragraph or After Paragraph settings (using the second and third pairs of boxes) to add space before or after the paragraph, without changing the amount of space between the pairs of lines within the paragraph.

The following illustration shows four bulleted items in double-spaced format:

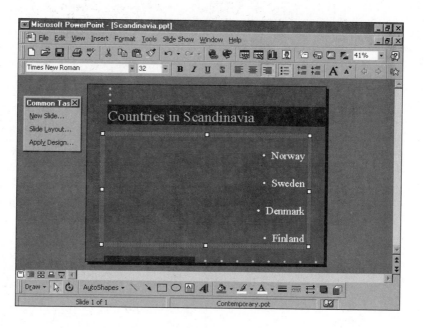

There are also two buttons on the Formatting toolbar that can be used to increase or decrease the line spacing setting by a tenth of an inch each time they're clicked.

Increase Paragraph Spacing  Decrease Paragraph Spacing

Typesetters, Welcome

When you want even more precise control of your line spacing, you can specify spacing options in printer's points (72 points per inch) rather than in lines. If you use this measurement scale, be sure to specify Points in the appropriate drop-down list box in the Line Spacing dialog box next to the spacing measurement that you're adjusting.

Working with Bullets

Bullets are useful when you need to present a list of items that aren't a series of sequential steps. When you use a bulleted-list placeholder, PowerPoint enters the bullets automatically. You can also insert a bullet in front of any paragraph that you type, including text in the text objects that you create. Simply type a paragraph (usually consisting of a single line of text) on the slide, and click the Bullets button on the Formatting toolbar. PowerPoint adds a bullet at the beginning of your text. If you change your mind and no longer want the bullet, click anywhere in the paragraph that contains the bullet, and click the Bullets button again to toggle off the bullet.

When you're feeling creative, you can turn almost any character that you want into a bullet, as well as change its color and size. For example, as shown in Figure 26-5, you can try a heart-shaped bullet from the Monotype Sorts font for the bulleted items, make it red, and then increase its size by 125 percent and use it as a decorative element.

To try a different bullet style, follow these steps:

1 Select the bulleted-list object.

2 Choose Bullet from the Format menu. Then complete the Bullet dialog box, as shown in the following illustration:

1 Choose a font here.   **3** Change the bullet size here.

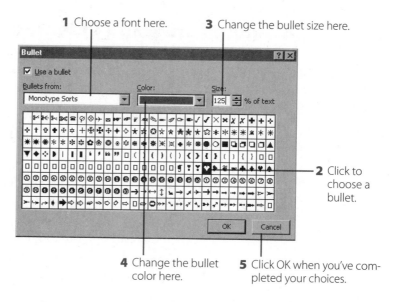

2 Click to choose a bullet.

4 Change the bullet color here.   **5** Click OK when you've completed your choices.

If you increase the size of the bullet relative to the font, it might be necessary to add some space before your text to provide enough room for the bullet. (This kerning problem is evident in Figure 26-5.) To correct this, you need to adjust the paragraph indentation as described in the next section.

FIGURE 26-5.
On this slide, the default bullets were changed to red hearts that are 125 percent of default font size.

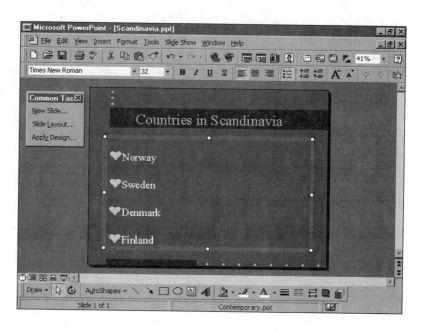

Changing Paragraph Indentations

If you adjust the size of text or bullets, you might also need to adjust the paragraph indentation set up in the template so that there's enough space between the text and bullets and so that the text aligns correctly. To do this, follow these steps:

1 Choose Ruler from the View menu to turn on the horizontal and vertical rulers.

2 Click in the text object you want to modify. The markers for the default indentation for the template will be visible on the ruler. Drag the lower triangle-shaped indent marker to change indentation for the text following the bullet and to align any additional lines in the paragraph at the same point. As you drag, you'll see a vertical dotted line, which helps you position the marker:

Drag this marker to add space between bullets and text.

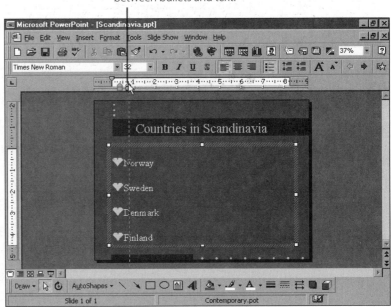

Changing the Template

A design template is a file that contains special graphical elements, colors, font sizes, font styles, slide backgrounds, and diverse special effects. PowerPoint provides dozens of professionally designed templates for you to choose from. The International template we've been using in this chapter is one of them.

When you create a new presentation, you can choose a template when you're prompted to do so. You can also choose a template and apply it to your presentation after you've already created your slides; just make sure that you have your presentation on screen when you want to change the template.

Apply
Design

To change templates, click the Apply Design button on the Standard toolbar. (The Apply Design command is also included in the Common Tasks toolbar, if you have it open.) Then complete the following dialog box:

3 Click the Apply button to attach the selected template to the current presentation.

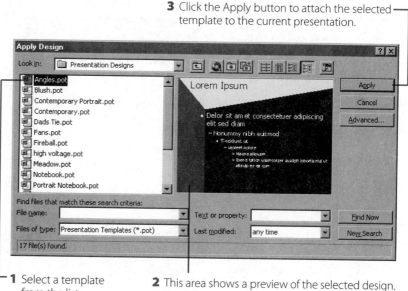

1 Select a template from the list.

2 This area shows a preview of the selected design. Try different templates until you see one you like.

In the following illustration, we changed the Contemporary template to the Professional template. (Notice that our custom heart bullets and the paragraph indentation are still the same, though. PowerPoint doesn't change the formatting elements that you entered on your own, even if they conflict with styles in the new template.)

Changing the Background Color and Shading

If you want to brighten up your presentation, or simply give it a different look and feel, you can change the background color and shading for one slide—or for *all* slides.

For overhead transparencies, use a light background; for on-screen presentations and 35mm slides, use a dark background.

To change the color scheme, click the right mouse button anywhere on the slide itself (not on a placeholder) and then from the shortcut menu choose Slide Color Scheme. (Alternatively, you can choose Slide Color Scheme from the Format menu.) With either approach, you'll see the following dialog box:

IV

Microsoft PowerPoint

1 Click the Standard tab, if necessary.

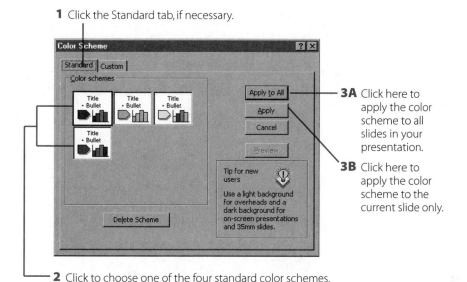

3A Click here to apply the color scheme to all slides in your presentation.

3B Click here to apply the color scheme to the current slide only.

2 Click to choose one of the four standard color schemes.

⭐ **TIP**

Create a Custom Scheme

If you have some artistic ability, or if you simply enjoy experimenting, you can customize your own color scheme. Click the Custom tab of the Color Scheme dialog box, click the presentation element you want to adjust (the current color is displayed in a box beside the element name), click the Change Color button, and pick a new color. Use this technique to customize each element in your presentation. When you're finished, click the Add As Standard Scheme button and PowerPoint will save your custom scheme on the Standard tab of the Color Scheme dialog box. Go ahead and try it—it really can be a lot of fun.

Creating a New Background

With PowerPoint's Background feature, you can create your own background design for all the slides in your presentation. You can start out by making a simple change to the background design by choosing a different color from several color choices. If you want to, you can apply a custom color. If you prefer a fancier background, you can add shading, texture, a pattern, or even a picture (say, your company's graphic logo).

If you really want to impress your audience, you can use a gradient fill, in which the color is darkest on one side of the slide and slowly becomes lighter toward the other side of the slide. For example, you can have a dark blue fill at the top of the slide, medium blue in the middle, and lighter blue toward the bottom of the slide. The direction of the gradient can be horizontal, vertical, or at any angle in between. You can use the Gradient tab (described below) to set your own gradient fill or choose from one of the predesigned gradient fills.

To create a new background design, follow these steps:

1 Choose Background from the Format menu or click the right mouse button anywhere (except in a placeholder) in the slide that you want to change and, from the shortcut menu, choose Background. With either approach you'll see the following dialog box:

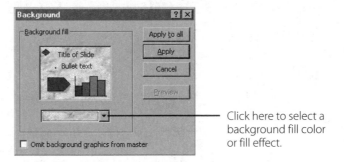

Click here to select a background fill color or fill effect.

2 From the drop-down list for the Background Fill options, choose the background fill color that you want. (If the color you want isn't listed, click the More Colors command and choose a custom color.)

3 To create a custom fill effect for your slide background, click the drop-down list box and click the Fill Effects command. You'll see the dialog box at the top of the facing page, presenting tabs that control the fill gradient, the wallpaper texture, the fill pattern, and an optional picture.

4 Pick the settings for your new background, and then click OK to close the Fill Effects dialog box.

5 Finally, click Apply To All if you want the new background added to each slide in your presentation, or click Apply if you want to modify only the current slide.

IV

Microsoft PowerPoint

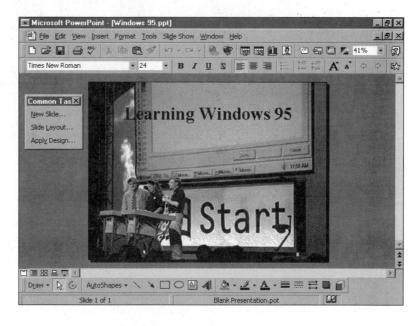

The following illustration shows a picture background we created by loading a bitmap (BMP) file with the Picture tab of the Fill Effects dialog box. The bitmap shows Jay Leno and Bill Gates demonstrating the new features of Microsoft Office and Windows 95—a background graphic that author Michael Halvorson uses for his title slide in a software training presentation.

Editing the Slide Master and the Title Master

After reviewing your presentation, you might decide that you want to change the default formatting for text on your slide. Perhaps you'd like to try a different font or a larger font size for your slide titles. You can make these changes to the Slide Master (which controls all the slides in your presentation) or the Title Master (which controls the formatting of title slides).

Formatting the Slide Master

All slides in your presentation are initially formatted based on the Slide Master, which sets the font formatting and text object positions for the slides. Whether the slide contains a bulleted list, a table, text and graphics, or an organization chart, its format is still based on the Slide Master. You can use the placeholders on the Slide Master to control the formatting and position of the title and text on any slide in your presentation.

To customize the Slide Master, complete the following steps:

1 Point to Master on the View menu, and then choose Slide Master from the submenu. The Slide Master appears as shown here:

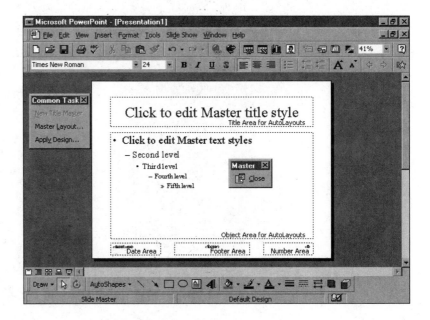

Notice that there are several distinct areas on the Slide Master. You can format the title for your slides as well as the information that appears in the Date, Footer, and Number regions. The Slide Master also shows several text entries in the main body of the slide.

Each of these entries corresponds to one level of text on the slide. As discussed in Chapter 25, all the information that you put onto a PowerPoint slide can also be viewed as an outline. Each of the different levels of entries on the Slide Master formats a different level of text in your outline. You can also change the standard bullet character used for each level, though the same text formatting is used for a level whether or not the entry displays the bullet.

2 Select the placeholder for the area that you want to change, or select the text for the outline level that you want to change.

3 Make any changes that you want using the controls on the Formatting toolbar and the commands on the Format menu, or by adjusting the indentation settings on the ruler.

4 When you're finished, click the Close button on the Master toolbar that floats above the Slide Master, to return to Slide view.

 TIP

Cast New Bullets

To change the bullet style, click in the object area, and then click the bulleted item that you want to change. Choose Bullet from the Format menu, and choose a font, bullet style, and size in the Bullet dialog box. Then click OK to confirm your choices. You'll see the new bullet style in the object area of the Slide Master.

Formatting the Title Master

Almost all presentations start with a slide that contains the title of the presentation and the subtitle, if any. This slide is called the *title slide* and might also contain information about the presentation (such as when it was created, or for what audience). In addition, title slides might be used within a presentation to separate the major sections.

You can insert a separate Title Master if you want all the title slides to be based on this rather than on the more general Slide Master. The five areas on the Title Master that can be positioned and formatted are the

Title, Subtitle, Date, Footer, and Number. To create and customize the Title Master, complete the following steps:

1 Point to Master on the View menu, and then choose Slide Master from the submenu. The Slide Master appears.

2 Choose New Title Master from the Insert menu or click the New Title Master button on the Common Tasks toolbar. The Title Master appears, as shown here:

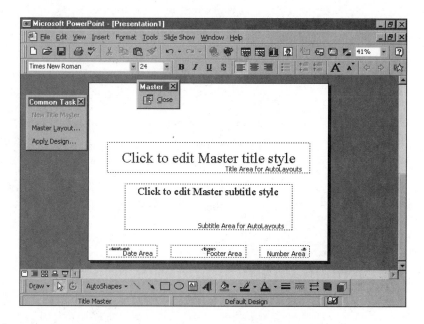

3 Select the text placeholder that you want to change.

4 If you like, apply different formatting effects by using the tools on the Formatting toolbar or the Format menu. Experiment with the font, font size, style, color, and special effects.

5 When you're finished, click the Close button on the Master toolbar that floats above the Title Master, to return to Slide view.

Any formatting changes that you make to the text objects on the Title Master are then applied to any title slides within your presentation. Only information that is still in the standard format is changed. If you've made manual changes to the formatting of a title slide (using the techniques discussed in the first section of this chapter), that formatting is maintained. You can change the position of objects on your title slides by moving the objects on the Title Master.

If you find the distinction between the Title Master and Slide Master confusing, there's an easy solution. If you hold down the Shift key while clicking on the Slide View button in the lower left of your screen (just above PowerPoint's status bar), you're taken to either the Title Slide or the Master Slide, depending on which controls the formatting of the current slide. With this approach, you're always taken to the proper place for changing the standard formatting. To return to the actual slide in your presentation, click on the Slide View button without holding the Shift key.

Inserting Graphics and Drawings

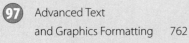
Enhancing the text in a bulleted list on a slide is not the only way to add zip to your presentation. You can use other slide layouts and add graphics to your presentation—an organization chart, a table, a chart, clip art, and even your own drawing. By peppering these graphics throughout your slide show, you can make your point quickly and effectively. Don't get carried away, though. When you use too many visual effects, you can make your presentation look over-designed and confusing. Keep it as clear and simple as possible.

PowerPoint is designed to take advantage of the work that you do in other programs. Because of this, the techniques discussed in this chapter rely on other programs included with Microsoft Office. For example, you can add tables from Microsoft Word, insert worksheets and charts from Microsoft Excel, use Microsoft Organization Chart to create an organization chart, use the Microsoft Clip Gallery as a source for clip art images, or create a drawing with the standard Drawing toolbar that is also featured in Word and Excel.

Inserting an Organization Chart

When you want your audience to see at a glance who's who in a company, you can create an organization chart that will display the hierarchy in a readable format. You could create the organization chart from scratch, using the AutoShapes button on the Drawing toolbar, but it's quicker and easier to let the Organization Chart utility do the artwork for you. The result is a good-looking chart that clearly illustrates any organization's management structure from top to bottom, as shown in Figure 27-1.

FIGURE 27-1.

A simple organization chart created with the Organization Chart utility.

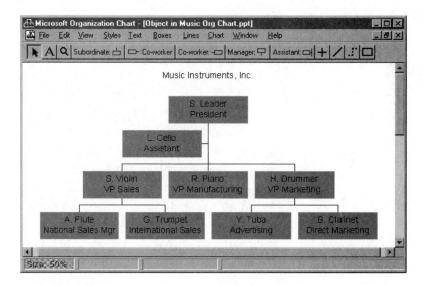

Here's how you can create an organization chart:

1 Go to where you want to insert the organization chart into your presentation. If you want to add a new slide, choose New Slide from the Insert menu. Then complete the New Slide dialog box, as shown on the facing page (top).

2 Select the title placeholder and type a title for the chart.

3 Double-click the organization chart icon in the middle of the slide. The Microsoft Organization Chart window appears, as shown on the facing page (bottom).

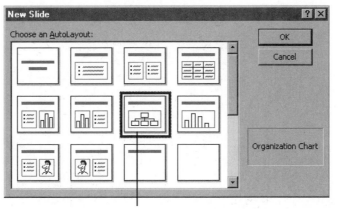

Organization Chart AutoLayout

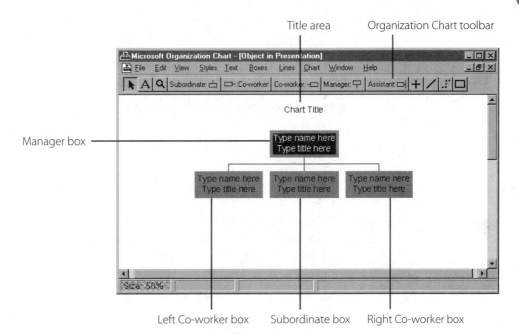

Title area

Organization Chart toolbar

Manager box

Left Co-worker box   Subordinate box   Right Co-worker box

4 In the Chart Title area, select the text and type the company name. If applicable, type a region, division, territory, or department name instead. You might want to leave this title blank and put this information in the title placeholder on the slide.

5 Click in the Manager box, and type the manager's name, title, and any comments, pressing Tab or the Enter key to move to the next item in the box. You'll notice that PowerPoint adjusts the width

IV

Microsoft PowerPoint

of the box if you enter a long name. (The comment placeholders won't show up in your organization chart if you don't add any comments.)

6 Add, delete, or rearrange other boxes and their information as necessary using the Organization Chart tools. (A list of our favorite formatting tips is described below.)

7 Once your organization chart is completed, you must update your slide and return to PowerPoint so that your presentation will include the organization chart. To do this, choose Exit And Return To Presentation from the File menu.

> **NOTE**

> Oganization charts are not saved separately in their own files; rather, they reside in your PowerPoint presentation. When you save your presentation, you save the organization chart with it.

8 Click Yes when you're asked if your want to update your organization chart object, so that your new chart is copied to the slide. If you don't want to paste the chart (for example, if you want to discard the work you've done), click No to delete the organization chart and return to PowerPoint.

> **WARNING**

> **Discarded Chart Objects Are Lost!** Think carefully before you click No in the Update Object dialog box. If you choose to discard your organization chart, PowerPoint will delete it and you won't be able to undo the command.

Formatting Tips

You'll probably need to change the four-box organization chart template that PowerPoint gives you. Most management structures have more than four people, and most change from time to time as staffing changes occur. Restructuring your organization chart is a lot easier than restructuring your company, however. It's a breeze to add, delete, copy, and move boxes, as well as to change the information in the boxes. Here are some formatting techniques that we recommend:

- After you return to PowerPoint, you can reedit an organization chart by double-clicking the chart on the slide. When the Organization Chart utility opens, it automatically loads your organization chart, ready for formatting.

- When new people are hired, you'll need to add them to the chart. To add boxes, click one of the buttons on the Organization Chart toolbar (Subordinate, Left Co-worker, Right Co-worker, Manager, Assistant), shown below, and then click the box to which you want to attach the new hire's box. The new box is added, its contents are highlighted, and the box is ready for you to enter the new information.

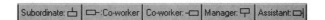

- When people leave the company for one reason or another, you'll need to delete their boxes. To delete a box, click the box and press the Delete key.

- Sometimes it's quicker to duplicate an existing box and make a few changes to it than it is to create a new box. Just click the box that you want to copy and use the Copy command to copy the box. Then click the box to which you want to attach the copied box, and use the Paste Boxes command. (The Cut and Paste Boxes commands are found on the Edit menu or on the shortcut menu that appears when you right-click on a box.) If you want to change the relationship (for, example, from subordinate to co-worker), move the box after pasting it.

- As people move up or down the ladder of success, you'll need to move boxes around. Use the drag and drop technique to move the boxes into their new places on the chart. To do this, drag a person's box *over* his or her new manager or co-worker. The box you're dragging over will highlight when it is selected. The mouse pointer changes shape while you're dragging, indicating the relationship between the box you're moving and the highlighted box.

- To change the information in a box, click the box, select the text that you want to change, and then type the new information over the selected text.

Customizing Your Organization Chart

In addition to rearranging chart elements and formatting, you can customize the structure and shape of an organization chart's design elements to make your chart slides more appealing and easier to interpret. To get started, point to Select on the Edit menu and use the submenu to specify which boxes you want to customize (you can choose all the boxes, or just a particular category of employee).

If you're tired of the garden-variety organization chart with its boxes arranged horizontally, you can modify the layout style by clicking the Styles menu and selecting a new arrangement. To add pizzazz to your text, you can use the commands on the Text menu to make changes to the font, color, and alignment.

How about those boxes? You can use the commands on the Boxes menu to change the color, add a drop-shadow effect, and change the border style, color, and line style of the boxes. To enhance the lines that connect the boxes, choose commands from the Lines menu to change the thickness, style, and color.

Finally, if the background color of the chart isn't what you want, choose Background Color from the Chart menu to customize the color. Just remember that you don't have to use all the options just because they're there. It's usually a good idea to keep your organization chart simple and easy to read—like the ones produced by the default settings.

Inserting a Table

Adding tables to your slide presentation is an excellent way to show important trends and relationships among groups of data. You can use tables to summarize facts and figures—for example, a two-column table with your competition's product features in one column and your product features in the other. It's a good idea to keep the table nice and simple, with no more than two or three columns and three or four rows, as shown in Figure 27-2. (When you want to illustrate the patterns in more complex data, you can insert a graph instead, as discussed later in this chapter.)

FIGURE 27-2.
When a Word table is active on a PowerPoint slide, the PowerPoint menus and toolbars are replaced by Word's menus and toolbars.

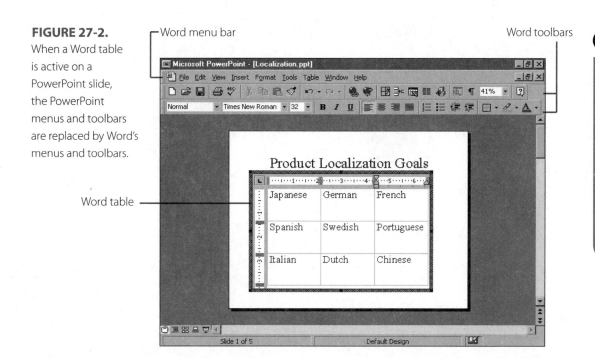

Word menu bar

Word toolbars

Word table

IV

Microsoft PowerPoint

Don't Table Tables

PowerPoint's table feature comes from Microsoft Word, the formatting king of word processing programs. Yet, in our experience, many Word and PowerPoint users resist using tables because they suspect that learning them will be difficult and that the process will only take valuable time away from their projects. (Rather than use tables, they enter data in columns using the "Tab technique," doing their best to line up text using Tab and Spacebar keys.) However, tables are truly useful organizational structures that will pay handsome formatting dividends if you use them wisely. In addition, tables make adding, editing, and deleting entries much easier than the "brute force" Tab method. Take the time to learn this feature in Word and PowerPoint, and you'll save yourself time down the road.

You can create a Word table that has numbers, words, or both in a PowerPoint slide. Follow these steps to see how it works:

1 Display the slide in which you're going to create the table.

2 Click the Insert Microsoft Word Table button on the Standard toolbar.

3 In the table grid, drag right and down to select the number of columns and rows that you need. When you release the mouse button, the blank table is inserted into the current slide.

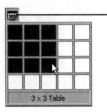

———— Insert Microsoft Word Table button

3 x 3 Table

4 In your blank table, click in each cell and enter the data. You can also move from cell to cell by using the Tab key or the arrow keys. (When you reach the bottom of the table, pressing Tab adds additional rows to the table.)

5 Since the table you've inserted comes directly from Word, notice that the menu bar and toolbar now contain Word commands, as shown in Figure 27-2 on the preceding page. (This will be the case whenever the table is active on your slide.) Feel free to use Word's formatting commands—especially the commands on the Table menu—to further customize your table.

6 When you're finished, click the slide background to close the table.

Insert
New Slide

Slide in a Table

Another way to add a table to your presentation is to add a table slide. Simply click the Insert New Slide button on the Standard toolbar or the New Slide button on the Common Tasks toolbar and choose the Table AutoLayout. Double-click the table placeholder in the center of your slide, and specify the number of columns and rows that you need in the Insert Word Table dialog box. Voilà! There's your table.

If you need to edit your table, double-click within the table area and make your changes. You can make any adjustments to your table, from the simplest change (correcting a typo) to the more involved (inserting and deleting rows and columns, changing the format, column width, row height, and so on).

Use the Tab key or the arrow keys to move from one cell to another within the table. To correct typos and make simple changes to the data, use the standard editing conventions such as overtype, insert, delete, copy, and move.

? SEE ALSO
To learn more about working with Word tables, see "Using Tables," page 228.

If a column is too narrow or too wide, move the mouse to the column border until the pointer changes to a double vertical bar with left and right arrows, and then drag the column border to change the width. You can do the same for a row to make the row shorter or taller.

Inserting a Chart

Many slide presentations include a set of numbers of some kind—projected sales figures for next year, for example, or comparisons of market trends. Rows of numbers are excruciatingly boring to look at and—worse—difficult to understand, especially in the short time your audience has to grasp their meaning. A chart can provide quick visual cues to the trends and comparisons that you want your audience to understand, and is a more suitable choice for conveying complex data than a simple table.

The first thing that you need to do to use a chart on a slide is to select a slide layout that has an appropriate placeholder. PowerPoint offers three choices, as shown in Figure 27-3. You can insert a new slide and select the slide layout from the New Slide dialog box. You can also convert an existing slide by choosing Slide Layout from the Format menu or by using the Slide Layout button on either the Standard or Common Tasks toolbar and using the Slide Layout dialog box.

FIGURE 27-3.
Any of these slide layouts let you add a graph to your slide.

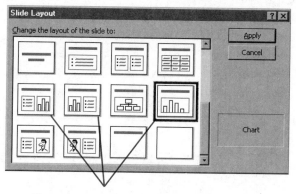

These three slide layouts include a chart.

After you've selected a slide layout containing a chart placeholder, you can add a chart to the slide two different ways. The first is to use Excel to create the chart, copy it to the Clipboard, and then paste it onto your slide. The advantage of this technique is that you can use *all* of Excel's tools for managing your data and creating your graph. In addition, you can use existing charts that have already been created and saved in Excel workbooks.

The second approach is to use Microsoft Graph 97, a utility program (like Organization Chart) that's included in Office 97. To open Microsoft Graph, you simply double-click the chart placeholder on your slide, or click the Insert Chart button on PowerPoint's Standard toolbar.

Insert
Chart

When Microsoft Graph opens in PowerPoint, you'll see a new menu bar, a new toolbar, and a datasheet (like a spreadsheet) that contains "dummy" (placeholder) words and numbers for your chart. Beneath the datasheet will be a column chart, as shown in Figure 27-4.

To customize this chart with your own information, modify the dummy chart one cell at a time, or click the Select All button in the upper left corner of the datasheet, press Delete to clear all the dummy information, and rebuild the whole chart. (We recommend that you modify the

FIGURE 27-4.
The Microsoft Graph utility opens a "dummy" datasheet when you open a chart in PowerPoint.

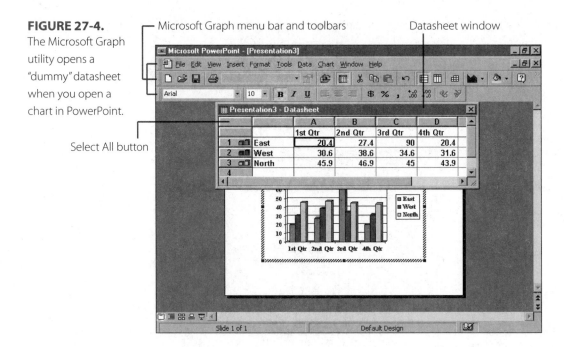

Microsoft Graph menu bar and toolbars

Datasheet window

Select All button

IV

Microsoft PowerPoint

? SEE ALSO
Using Microsoft Graph
and its various tools
is also discussed in
Chapter 39, "Sharing
Data Among Office
Applications."

datasheet one cell at a time until you're comfortable with the placement of the row and column labels.) Like magic, you see the chart
change each time you enter new data in a cell.

Using the buttons on the Graph toolbar, you can import data from
Excel worksheets, change the chart type, hide the datasheet window,
and modify the chart colors. (For more charting commands, explore
the Graph menus.)

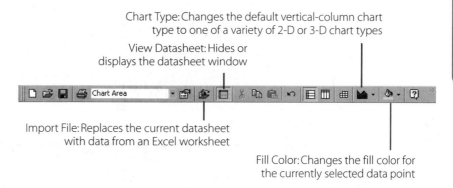

Chart Type: Changes the default vertical-column chart
type to one of a variety of 2-D or 3-D chart types

View Datasheet: Hides or
displays the datasheet window

Import File: Replaces the current datasheet
with data from an Excel worksheet

Fill Color: Changes the fill color for
the currently selected data point

Adding Clip Art

You can add excitement and visual interest to your slide presentation
by choosing an evocative piece of clip art. PowerPoint's clip art library
contains more than a thousand professionally prepared pictures that
will enhance a wide range of topics. Figure 27-5 on the following page
shows one example, added to new text.

There are two slide AutoLayouts that you can use to insert clip art onto
a slide. As with other graphics, you can add a new slide (by using the
New Slide command on the Insert menu or the New Slide button on
either the Standard or Formatting toolbars), *or* you can convert an existing slide (using the Slide Layout command on the Format menu or the
Slide Layout button on either the Standard or Formatting toolbars).
Both of these approaches can be used to create a slide with a clip art
placeholder. You can then double-click the placeholder to start the
Microsoft Clip Gallery.

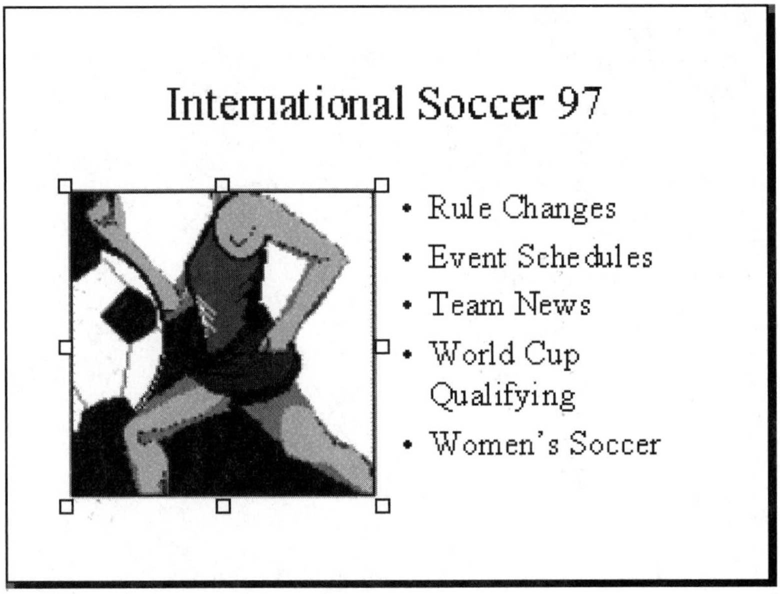

FIGURE 27-5.
Placing a clip art object next to bulleted text adds visual interest to your presentation.

NOTE

Run the Microsoft Office Setup again to install the Microsoft Clip Gallery and popular clip art images if necessary. If you installed Microsoft Office 97 from the CD-ROM, when you run the Clip Gallery you may see a dialog box asking if you want to preview additional clips available on the CD-ROM. You can insert the Microsoft Office 97 disc and click OK to see the clips or turn off the dialog box.

To use the Clip Gallery, follow these steps:

1 Display the slide that contains the clip art placeholder. If necessary, add a new slide with the Insert New Slide button or convert an existing slide with the Slide Layout command on the Format menu.

2 Double-click on the clip art placeholder to display the Microsoft Clip Gallery dialog box, shown on the facing page.

3 The clip art image appears surrounded by handles, and you can move it or resize it to fit your presentation needs. The Picture toolbar also appears when you insert clip art, and you can use its buttons to refine the color and presentation of the image considerably.

IV

Microsoft PowerPoint

1 Select the category of image here. **2** Click on the image to select it.

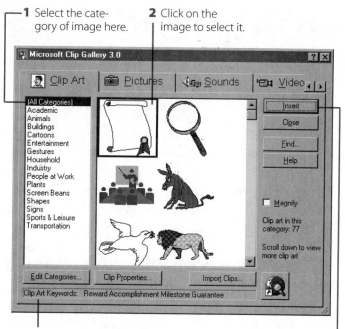

3 A description of the image appears here if one is available.

4 Click here to add the clip art to your slide.

Insert Clip Art

You can also add a clip art image to your slide by clicking the Insert Clip Art button on the Standard toolbar to open the Microsoft Clip Gallery dialog box.

 TIP

If you want to, you can add a piece of clip art to your Master Slide so that every slide in your presentation contains the same image.

SEE ALSO
Working with different types of images is discussed in "Adding Graphics," page 314.

Images Galore!

If you want more images to choose from, you can buy packages of clip art (in black-and-white or color) from software stores and mail-order catalogs. These clip art "libraries" are packaged by topics such as animals, business, holidays, music, people, and so on. If you want more professional artwork, look for photo collections, which are usually sold on CD-ROMs.

Drawing a Graphic Object

Despite the huge variety of wonderful clip art that's available, you *still* might not be able to find that perfect image. Or perhaps you'd just prefer to create your own art. In either case, you don't have to be a talented artist to create vibrant, eye-catching graphics.

By default, the Drawing toolbar appears at the bottom of the PowerPoint window. This toolbar is also available in Word and Excel, so once you learn how to use it in one application, you'll have the skills necessary to use it in all the Office programs. (If the Drawing toolbar isn't visible, display it by pointing to the Toolbars command on the View menu, and then clicking the Drawing toolbar.)

Working with Drawing Objects

We've already covered the Drawing toolbar in Chapter 10, so we won't repeat that detailed information here about creating Drawing illustrations. (To review these instructions, see "Creating Drawings in Word," page 320.) If you only have a few minutes to experiment with creating drawing objects, we recommend that you spend it browsing the shapes and drawing tools on the AutoShapes menu on the Drawing toolbar. With AutoShapes, you can create a variety of predefined shapes, including flowchart symbols, arrows, banners, and action buttons, and you can also create your own free-form drawings by selecting one of the pen shapes in the Lines category. For example, we created the shapes shown in Figure 27-6 with a few of the more popular tools from the AutoShapes menu. (The figure also shows an example of Word Art, as well as the Line, Rectangle, and Oval tools.)

When you create an image on your slide with the Drawing toolbar, it becomes an object that you can resize, copy, move, format, and delete. As with other objects on a PowerPoint slide, drawing objects are surrounded by selection handles when they're selected. (In Figure 27-6, a rectangle object has been selected.) Before you can change an attribute of a drawing object, it must be selected.

After you create your illustration, you can use commands on the Drawing toolbar's Draw menu to format or edit your object. For example, if you created one AutoShape on your slide and you want to exchange it

FIGURE 27-6.
The Drawing toolbar lets you create your own electronic art-work for presentations.

Banner AutoShape

Drawing toolbar

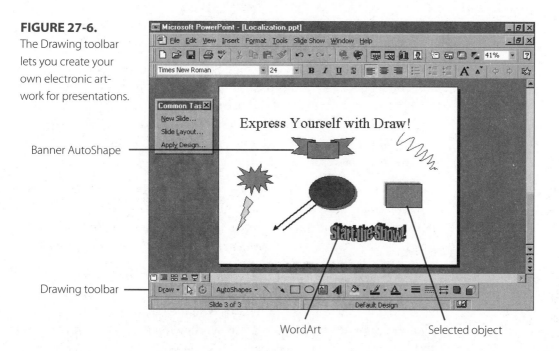

WordArt   Selected object

for another, simply select the object, click the Draw menu on the Draw-ing toolbar, point to Change AutoShape, and choose a new AutoShape from the submenu. Or, if you want to change the orientation of an object (in other words, if you want to spin the object on its axis), select the object, point to Rotate Or Flip on the Draw menu, and choose one of the rotate or flip commands from the submenu.

Perhaps the most useful set of commands on the Draw menu are those that let you create groups of objects. By creating a group, you can use a single command to change all the objects at once. For example, when you want to perform an action, such as adding a fill color, to more than one object at a time, select the first object, and then hold down the Shift key while selecting additional objects. Next, choose Group from the Draw menu. The objects are now grouped together into one object. After that, you'll notice that there is only one set of siz-ing handles for all the objects in the group.

⭐ TIP

If you change your mind and no longer want to group a collection of objects, select the objects and choose Ungroup from the Draw menu.

Drawing Objects Reside in Layers

Like the numerous bands of soil and artifacts that collectively compose an archeological site, each drawing object that is placed on a slide exists on its own *layer*. This means that some drawing objects (including those closer to the top of the pile) can appear to cover up parts of other objects (those toward the bottom of the pile). If you plan the order in which you create your drawing objects, you can use this feature to create interesting combination effects.

New objects are always drawn at the very front of the slide (on the top of the pile). Because objects toward the front of the slide can cover up those toward the back, it is often necessary to change the order of the objects. Fortunately, there are commands on the Drawing toolbar's Draw menu for just that purpose.

If you want an object to appear behind all the other objects (so that those objects can hide part of the object in the back), select the object, open the Draw menu, point to Order, and then choose the Send To Back command from the submenu. By contrast, if you want an object to appear at the very front of the slide (so that all of it is visible and it covers up parts of the objects behind it), select the object and then choose the Bring To Front command. If you're setting the order for a large number of objects, you can fine-tune the sequence with the Send Backward and Bring Forward commands, which move objects through the pile one step at a time. Since text doesn't look very good when it's partially obscured, you should do your best to create it last, so that it always remains on the top of the pile.

Advanced Text and Graphics Formatting

In addition to the commands on the Drawing toolbar, which deal specifically with drawing objects, you can also control the general appearance of the text and graphic objects on your slides with a new dialog box that creates interesting formatting effects. You can display this dialog box with either the Colors And Lines command or the last command on the Format menu (labeled AutoShape, Picture Text Box, and so forth, depending on what's selected). In either case, a dialog box appears with five formatting tabs. The name of the dialog box and what you can do with it depends on the type of object you selected before running the command. In some cases, all the tabs and options are available—in others, only a few. We will refer to the dialog box generally as the Format AutoShape dialog box.

The following sections describe each of the formatting tabs of the Format AutoShape dialog box.

Colors and Lines

When you choose the Colors And Lines command from the Format menu, the Format AutoShape dialog box appears with the Colors And Lines tab visible, as shown in Figure 27-7. The purpose of the Colors And Lines tab is to let you modify the type of line used in the object you've selected and (if applicable) modify the fill color and arrow styles. If a text placeholder is highlighted, you can only select a fill color for the interior of the text box, plus the characteristics of the border around the text box. If a line is highlighted, you can make it an arrow, change the thickness of the line, or vary the line color.

FIGURE 27-7.
The Colors and Lines tab of the Format AutoShape dialog box.

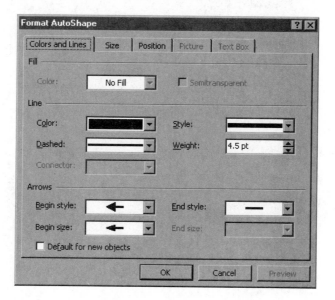

Size

If you choose the Colors And Lines or Picture command from the Format menu when a piece of clip art or other electronic artwork is highlighted, the title of the dialog box changes to Format Picture, and you can modify the artwork's size and scale with the Size tab, shown in Figure 27-8. Since most clip art has been designed to be resized, you can often create well-proportioned effects by adjusting the Height and Width options in the Scale area of the dialog box to shrink or expand the image. If the Lock Aspect Ratio check box is turned on (the default), all the Height and Width text boxes will change in tandem if you modify one of them, preserving the relative dimensions, or "aspect ratio," of the image.

If you're formatting text placeholders or AutoShape graphics, you should also consider using the Rotation option to change the orientation of the object in relative degrees around an imagined circle. (The Rotation spin buttons adjust the orientation in one-degree increments, starting at 0 and moving up to 360.) Using this feature, you can create text boxes that tilt at an angle—a compelling effect if used judiciously.

FIGURE 27-8.
The Size tab of the Format Picture dialog box.

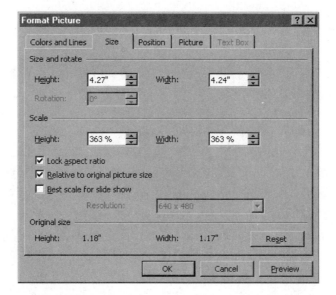

Position

The Position tab, shown in Figure 27-9, is a relatively straightforward feature that controls the placement of an object on the slide. It lets you specify a horizontal measurement and a vertical measurement for the object from the edge of the slide. To help you fine-tune your alignment, this tab lets you also specify the place in the object that the measurement is taken from. The default setting is the top left corner, though

FIGURE 27-9.
The Position tab of the Format AutoShape dialog box.

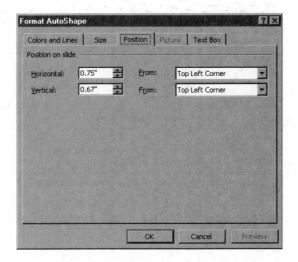

you can also measure from the center of the object, a useful location when you're trying to center an object on a slide.

Picture

The Picture tab, shown in Figure 27-10 on the following page, is a sophisticated editing tool for clip art, photographs, and other images. To trim or crop the highlighted picture, use the Left, Right, Top, and Bottom text boxes in the Crop From portion of the dialog box. Crop measurements are taken from the edge of the picture; positive measurements trim the image in from the edge, while negative measurements add white space to the picture.

The Image Control portion of the dialog box lets you control the color, brightness, and contrast of the picture you're including in your presentation. The Color drop-down list box contains four options especially useful for people who want to prepare their images for different types of presentations. The Automatic option is the default setting, which displays the image in its original representation. Gray Scale converts a color picture to shades of black-and-white (each color converts to an equivalent grayscale level). Black & White converts a picture to true black-and-white or "line art," which can be printed by devices that are incapable of grayscale printing. Finally, Watermark converts a picture to a bright, low-contrast image that looks good when placed behind everything else on a slide. (Some of the PowerPoint templates use Watermark images.)

FIGURE 27-10.
The Picture tab of the Format Picture dialog box.

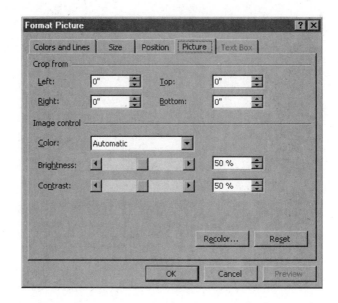

Text Box

Last, the Text Box tab, shown in Figure 27-11, is an advanced formatting option designed for text placeholders and Draw AutoShapes that can hold text (such as the Banner AutoShapes). Other drawing objects, such as those created by the Oval and Rectangle tools, don't support text automatically, so you need to create labels separately with the Text Box command on the Insert menu. The Text Anchor Point drop-down list box lets you adjust the center point for text within a placeholder. PowerPoint also lets you set the anchor point to the top or bottom of the placeholder, and you can further adjust the placement of text by choosing one of the centered anchor points or by using the alignment buttons on PowerPoint's Formatting toolbar.

The Text Box tab lets you set the internal margins of a text box, which is especially useful for text boxes containing bulleted lists. In addition, you can control how text flows inside an AutoShape object (such as a banner) by using the Word Wrap, Resize AutoShape, and Rotate Text check boxes in the Text Box tab.

FIGURE 27-11.
The Text Box tab of the Format AutoShape dialog box.

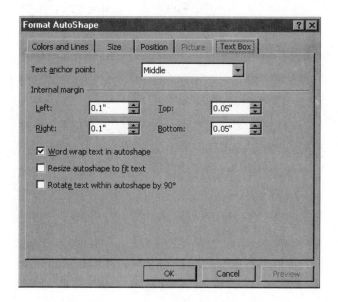

Although working with PowerPoint's many text and graphic formatting options takes a little practice, your efforts will pay big dividends in your presentations. PowerPoint slide shows have become popular and recognizable, so a few special effects are likely to impress your audience and bring admiring comments and questions afterwards: "Wow! Good show!" and "How did you *do* that, anyway?"

CHAPTER 28

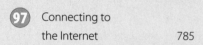
Adding Special Effects and Internet Links

PowerPoint's basic formatting effects create solid, compelling presentations. But if you really want to grab your audience's attention, you should consider adding one or more multimedia elements to your presentation. In this chapter, we'll explore the most compelling special effects you can create in a PowerPoint presentation. You'll learn how to add animation effects, such as objects that move and flashy slide transitions, and you'll learn how to insert video, sound, and narration clips in your show. In addition, you'll learn how to create action buttons that let you move to a specific slide or supporting presentation, or even a home page on the World Wide Web. By carefully balancing this combination of special effects—video, music, sound, animation, and Internet resources—you can make your slide show explode with life and energy.

769

Adding Animation

PowerPoint enables you to add animation effects to your slides and to use transitions between slides. Both of these make your slides appear more interesting and more energized. By using animation you can have each word fly in from one side of the slide, each paragraph seem to dissolve from the slide background, or any of a variety of other effects. When you use transitions, you can have one slide dissolve into another, make one slide appear to "iris" open like a camera lens, or choose from several other intriguing transition options.

Animation
Effects

Many of the standard PowerPoint effects are designed to animate text objects (although they can work with clip art or other images as well). You can begin in Slide view: Move to the slide that contains the text object that you want to animate, select the text object, and then click the Animation Effects button on the Formatting toolbar. PowerPoint displays the Animation Effects toolbar, which contains 11 buttons and 1 list box that you can use to control the animation effects on your slide. (See Figure 28-1.)

The Preset Animation command on the Slide Show menu contains a collection of animation effects similar to (but slightly larger than) what you'll find on the Animation Effects toolbar. The designers of Power-Point 97 have endeavored to make animating objects easier by organizing the effects into three different collections, with significant overlap among the three sets. The most basic animation effects are listed on the Animation Effects toolbar, a larger number is listed on the Preset Animation submenu, and the Custom Animation dialog box (opened with the Custom Animation command on the Slide Show menu or the Custom Animation button on the Animation Effects toolbar) gives you the ability to create your own effects by varying the animation timing, sound, and other settings. (You'll learn more about this feature later in the chapter.)

To create a slide with animation effects in your presentation, complete the following steps:

1 Create your slide content first, using text and graphic objects as you normally would. (For example, create a title, a bulleted list, and a piece of clip art on your slide.) You can't create animation effects until your slide content is finished.

FIGURE 28-1.

The Animation Effects toolbar provides access to the most common animation effects.

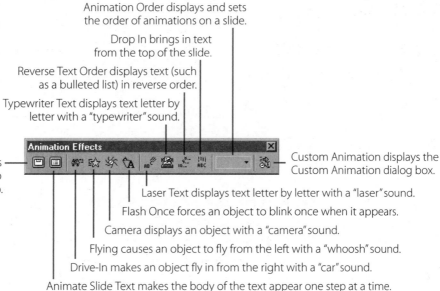

Animation Order displays and sets the order of animations on a slide.

Drop In brings in text from the top of the slide.

Reverse Text Order displays text (such as a bulleted list) in reverse order.

Typewriter Text displays text letter by letter with a "typewriter" sound.

Animate Title causes the title on a slide to appear from the top.

Custom Animation displays the Custom Animation dialog box.

Laser Text displays text letter by letter with a "laser" sound.

Flash Once forces an object to blink once when it appears.

Camera displays an object with a "camera" sound.

Flying causes an object to fly from the left with a "whoosh" sound.

Drive-In makes an object fly in from the right with a "car" sound.

Animate Slide Text makes the body of the text appear one step at a time.

2   Select the first object on your slide that you would like to animate.

3   Click the Animation Effects button on the Formatting toolbar. (The Animation Effects toolbar appears.)

4   Click the button on the toolbar corresponding to the effect you want to create. (See Figure 28-1.) If you don't see the effect you want on the Animation Effects toolbar, search the Preset Animation submenu on the Slide Show menu or create a custom effect with the Custom Animation dialog box.

5   Continue selecting objects one at a time on your slide and adding animation effects to them.

6   When you're finished, repeat the process on the remaining slides in your presentation, and then click the Animation Effects button again to close the Animation Effects toolbar.

7   Now click the Slide Show button or choose the View Show command from the Slide Show menu, and preview all your animation effects!

⭐ **TIP**

Practice Your Animation

In addition to reviewing an animation full screen in Slide Show view, you can also preview the animation without leaving Slide view by choosing the Animation Preview command from the Slide Show menu. When you run this command, PowerPoint opens a slide miniature in the workspace and runs the slide show with all the sound and animation you've specified. You can click the slide miniature to replay the animation. When you're finished previewing the animations, click the Close button on the slide miniature's title bar to remove it.

Using Slide Sorter View

You can also use Slide Sorter view to create animation effects on your slides. While Slide Sorter view doesn't let you animate the individual objects on a slide, it does give you control of both the *transition effects* (the way in which one slide changes to another) and the text animation displayed when bulleted lists appear (formerly called *build effects*). These two options are controlled by the Slide Transition Effects and Text Preset Animation drop-down list boxes on the Slide Sorter toolbar, as shown in the following illustration:

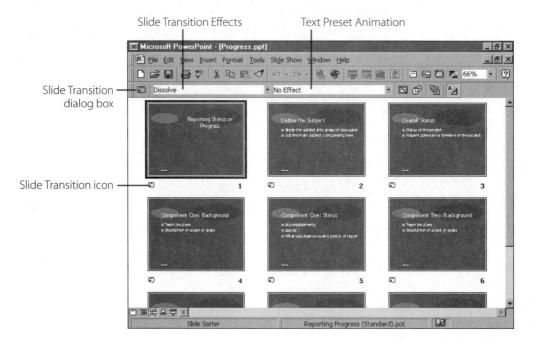

Selecting Transitions

The purpose of a transition is to add visual interest as you move from one slide to the next.

To create a transition from one slide to the next, follow these steps:

1 Click the Slide Sorter View button at the bottom left of the screen to switch to Slide Sorter view, and then select the slide the transition is to reveal.

TIP

You can create transitions for multiple slides by first selecting them as a group. To do so, hold down the Shift key and click each slide in Slide Sorter view.

2 Select a transition from the Slide Transition Effects list box or click the Slide Transition button to open the following dialog box:

4A Click here to apply the transition to all slides in your presentation.

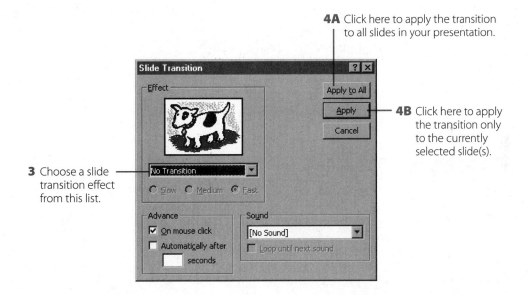

3 Choose a slide transition effect from this list.

4B Click here to apply the transition only to the currently selected slide(s).

After you specify a transition for a slide, a tiny icon appears below the slide in Slide Sorter view, identifying the slide transition. To preview the transition, click the icon.

Controlling Bulleted List Animation

You can also control how PowerPoint displays bulleted lists while you're in Slide Sorter view. Bulleted lists are special text elements that often form the cornerstone of a presentation. To allow you to draw out your points and give them the proper emphasis, PowerPoint lets you control how each line of a list appears with the Text Preset Animation drop-down list box. If you use this effect properly, your presentation ends up looking like it took several slides to show the bulleted list—not just one. The most popular text animation effects include Appear (in which your bullets simply appear on the screen), Fly From Right (bullets slide in from the right side of the screen), Blinds Horizontal (horizontal sections of the line "materialize" in place), and Checkerboard Across (bullets appear through a checkerboard mesh).

To select a text animation effect for a slide containing a bulleted list, follow these steps:

1 Click the Slide Sorter View button at the bottom left of the screen to switch to Slide Sorter view, and click the slide that contains the bulleted-list placeholder.

2 From the Text Preset Animation list box, choose the effect that you want.

3 To preview the effect, click the Slide Show button.

Don't Act Randomly in a Crowded Room

In most cases, we suggest that you stay away from the Random Effects animation option, which can be distracting, and the No Effect option, which is dull. As mentioned elsewhere, don't use *all* the effects just because they're there, unless you want a very chaotic presentation. Remember, you'll be giving this presentation in front of people you want to impress and persuade, not make seasick.

Customizing Your Animation

To maintain greater control over how the text and objects on a slide behave during an animation sequence, use the Custom Animation command on the Slide Show menu when the slide is visible in Slide view. You'll see the following dialog box:

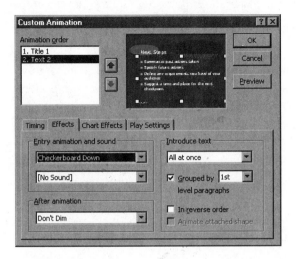

The Custom Animation dialog box contains an Animation Order list box, which you can use to set the order in which the objects on your slide are animated. (For example, you might want to display the title first, a piece of clip art second to plant a visual image in viewers' minds, and a bulleted list third to flesh out the image with text.) The dialog box also contains a preview window, which you can use to see the object you're working with, plus four tabs that control advanced aspects of the animation sequence you're customizing.

The Timing tab lets you identify objects on your slide that don't currently have animation effects associated with them, as well as control options that time each animation. (You can move objects when you click the mouse, or after a specific time interval.)

The Effects tab lets you set the special effect you see when you run the animation and the sound you hear while it happens. You can also use the Effects tab to control both how the textual elements in an animation are grouped together and the order in which they appear.

The Chart Effects tab is designed specifically to let you animate the charts in your presentation. You can display the chart elements all at once, or one at a time to highlight important trends. You can also specify a particular sound (such as a cash register!) to play when important values such as a great bottom-line are displayed.

Finally, the Play Settings tab lets you control how a video object is played during a slide show. You have the option of pausing the slide show while the video rolls, or continuing on with your slides as the video runs its course in a window. You can also stop playing the video after a specified number of slides have passed—a useful feature if your video is only relevant to a particular part of the presentation, like an entertainment preview for an upcoming event.

Inserting Video

You can insert one or more video objects into any slide. You might want to play a video quote from your product manager, for example, or run a short documentary movie for a fund-raising event. You could even create a video for product tutorials and educational materials. The following illustration shows one frame of a basketball video clip.

When presenting, you can play the video clip or movie—or you can have PowerPoint play it for you.

Before you insert any video objects, make sure that you have necessary hardware (such as a sound card, speakers, and an enhanced video card) for playing the multimedia items during your presentation. Once you do, adding media objects is the same as adding any other object to your slides, and the special effects are truly exciting.

 TIP

Check Out a Video
The multitude of videos and movies that come with Microsoft Office are stored on the Office CD. You can also click the Connect To Web For Additional Clips button in the Clip Gallery to connect to Clip Gallery Live—a Web site where you can preview and download picture, sound, and movie clips. If you still can't find the right video clip, you can find plenty of video software packages in your local software store. Since videos and movies occupy a lot of space on your hard disk, you might want to install only those you intend to use.

To insert a video object into a slide, follow these steps:

1   Move to the slide where you want to place the new video clip or add a new slide by choosing New Slide from the Insert menu or clicking the New Slide button on either the Common Tasks or Standard toolbar. Don't worry about the slide layout or the placeholders on the slide. Video clips are always inserted directly onto the slide, not into a placeholder.

2   If you want to browse the Clip Gallery for a movie clip, insert your Office CD into the CD-ROM drive, point to Movies And Sounds on the Insert menu, and then choose the Movie From Gallery command from the submenu. Then double-click the movie you want to add to your slide on the Videos tab of the Clip Gallery.

3   Alternatively, if you want to insert a movie from an existing movie file with an MMM or AVI extension on your hard disk, point to Movies And Sounds on the Insert menu, and then choose the Movie From File command from the submenu. Select the movie file in the dialog box that appears, and then click OK.

4   To customize how your video is presented, select the video object on the slide, choose the Custom Animation command from the Slide Show menu, and use the options on the Play Settings tab.

> **NOTE**
>
> You can also use the Object command on the Insert menu to insert a video clip, though it's usually more efficient to use the Movies And Sounds submenu. The Object command gives you access to all types of objects on your system (sounds, animation, documents from other programs, and so on) as well as to the tools available for creating new objects (generally the various programs installed on your system). The Clip Gallery and the Movie From File commands, by contrast, list only video clips that exist on your system. There's no need to define what type of object you're inserting, and PowerPoint assumes that the video clips already exist.

When you insert a video clip, you'll see a sample frame called a *poster*, which is usually the first frame of the clip. Are you ready to play your video? Lights! Action! Camera! Double-click the poster in Slide view or click on it in Slide Show view. Make some popcorn, sit back, and enjoy the action. The video will play during your slide show until either the clip ends or you move to the next slide.

> **NOTE**
>
> If you have any problems playing your videos, make sure that the video and media player settings are correct. Open the Windows Control Panel and choose Multimedia. Check the sound device, the hardware setup, and the sound setup—and check all cable connections. Also check the volume control by double-clicking the Sound icon on the taskbar.

Inserting Sounds

> **CAUTION**
>
> Before you add sound to your show, make sure that your sound card is Windows-compatible and that sound files are available on your system. Otherwise, PowerPoint can't play or record sounds. To record sound, you'll also need a microphone or other type of input device.

Sound effects, such as music and voice recordings, can add another level of professionalism to your slide presentations. You could play the airplane sound effect to make your animated airplane sequence more amusing or persuasive. You could play a movie theme song as background music for several slides. Or you could play a voice recording that contains advertising slogans or radio jingles.

You can find sound files in several places—the Media folder installed by Windows 95, the Office 97 ValuePack on the Office CD, and the folder created by your sound card. There are two primary types of sound files—wave and MIDI. After you add a wave sound to a slide, you'll see the following icon:

Here are the steps for adding sound to your slide show:

1 Display the slide to which you want to add sound.

2 If you want to browse the Clip Gallery for a sound file, insert your Office CD into the CD-ROM drive, point to Movies And Sounds on the Insert menu, and then choose the Sound From Gallery command. Then on the Sounds tab in the Clip Gallery, double-click the sound you want to add to your slide.

3 Alternatively, to insert a sound from an existing WAV, MID, or RMI file on your hard disk, point to Movies And Sounds on the Insert menu, and then choose the Sound From File command. The Insert Sound dialog box appears, as shown in Figure 28-2. Select the sound file that you want, and then click OK.

 NOTE

If you have problems using sound, make sure that the audio and MIDI settings are correct. Open the Windows Control Panel and choose Multimedia. Check the sound device, the hardware setup, and the sound setup. Also click the Sound icon on the taskbar to check the volume control.

FIGURE 28-2.
PowerPoint lets you add a variety of sounds to your presentations, which you can play by clicking tiny icons.

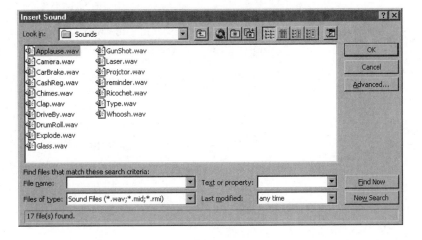

Recording Narration

PowerPoint 97 lets you add voice narration to a slide show so that you can prepare a final presentation in advance, complete with your own voice. If you're building a slide show for presentation in a kiosk or over the network, you'll find this feature especially useful.

 NOTE

> To record a voice narration, you'll need a sound card, a microphone, and a set of speakers.

Complete these steps:

1 From the Slide Show menu, choose Record Narration.

You'll see the Record Narration dialog box, showing the amount of free disk space and the number of minutes you can record.

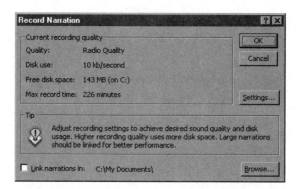

2 If you want to customize the recording or playback, click the Settings button and use the options in the Audio tab.

3 To begin recording, click OK in the Record Narration dialog box.

4 Record voice content for each slide in your presentation, clicking to move from one slide to the next.

If you want to stop the narration for any reason, right-click and then click Pause Narration on the shortcut menu. When you're ready to resume, right-click and then click Resume Narration.

Adding Embedded Documents

PowerPoint lets you add data from another Windows-based application and embed the data as an object that will appear as an icon on a slide. You can double-click the object during the slide show to "drill down" to the information and display the data in its original form. For example, you can embed a Word document or an Excel spreadsheet as an embedded document. In addition to Word and Excel files, you can embed files created in any Windows-based application that can provide OLE objects for use in PowerPoint.

To embed an existing object, choose the Object command from the Insert menu. Choose the Create From File option in the Insert Object dialog box, and then use the Browse feature to find the file that was created in another application. Select the file and click OK. When you return to the Insert Object dialog box, choose the Display As Icon option and click OK. You'll see an icon on the slide representing the type of object you inserted—generally, the icon that's used to represent documents of that type.

⊗ CAUTION

Because you can't record and play sounds at the same time, while you're recording you won't hear other sounds you inserted in your slide show.

5 When you're finished with the recording, click Yes to save it along with the timings you specified. To save only the narration, click No.

A sound icon appears in the middle of each slide that has narration.

When you run the slide show, the narration will automatically play with the show. To run the slide show without narration, choose Set Up Show from the Slide Show menu, and then turn on the Show Without Narrations check box.

Creating Action Buttons

By adding action buttons to a slide, you can branch to a specific slide or to a presentation from within another slide show, as well as launch another application or visit a site on the World Wide Web. You click an action button to move around within your show or to temporarily exit your slide show. Using this tool, you can create an interactive training or informational presentation. Within the presentation, the action buttons appear as icons on a slide—and you just click the button to jump to a new location.

Moving to a Slide or File

Perhaps you're showing slides about sales revenue, and at a certain point during the show you want to give yourself the option of moving to a particular slide that contains a pie chart showing sales expenses. You can create an action button that will let you branch to a specific slide, as shown in Figure 28-3.

FIGURE 28-3.
This slide's action button lets you jump to another location in your slide show during your presentation.

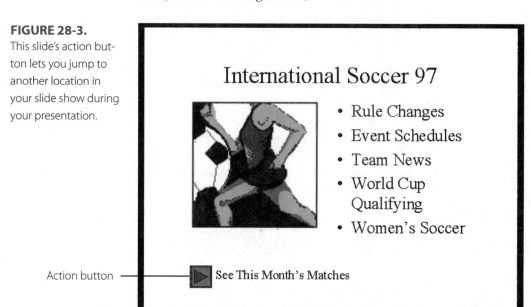

Action button ——

When you create an action button on a slide, you specify the button you want to use, identify the mouse movement you want to trigger the action, and then specify where you want to jump to. When you run the presentation in Slide Show view, the buttons are enabled, and when you click one, PowerPoint immediately jumps to that specific location. Jumping to a slide works the same way as the Go To feature in Word. In Office 97, however, the jumps are called *hyperlinks*.

To create a jump to a specific slide or file, follow these steps:

1 In Slide view, display the slide on which you want to create the jump.

2 From the Slide Show menu, point to Action Buttons and choose one of the action buttons on the submenu. PowerPoint supplies several intuitive shapes for the different type of jumps you might want to make. (Different shapes are especially useful when you're adding more than one button to a slide.)

 TIP

To clarify what the button does, add some explanatory text with the Text Box command on the Insert menu or the Text Box button on the Drawing toolbar. For example, you could insert a text box and type *Facts and Figures* or *On the Web* to give yourself a little reminder.

3 Drag the mouse on the slide to create the action button. When you release the mouse button, the Action Settings dialog box appears:

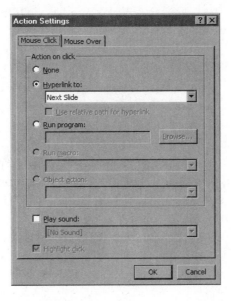

4 If you want to activate the jump with a mouse click, use the Mouse Click tab. If you'd rather activate the link by simply placing the mouse over the button, click the Mouse Over tab. (Both tabs have identical controls.)

5 In the Hyperlink To drop-down list box, choose the jump option you want to create for your action button. Select the Slide option if you want to jump to another slide in the current presentation, or the Other PowerPoint Presentation option if you want to open a presentation stored on disk. You can also specify a different type of file with the Other File option, or a valid Internet address with the URL option. In each of these cases, you'll be prompted for the location of the hyperlink you want to establish.

6 If you want to play a sound during the jump, turn on the Play Sound check box and select a sound in the drop-down list box.

7 When you're finished configuring the action button, click OK.

During your show, you can click the action button or move the mouse pointer over it to move to the specified slide or file location. If your hyperlink takes you to the Internet or another application, the Web toolbar (described below) will appear, helping you navigate from one link to the next.

Running Another Program

If you want to open a Windows-based application without loading a specific file, you can click the Run Program option in the Action Settings dialog box and use the Browse button to select the name of an application program (EXE file) on your system. You might find this technique useful if you want the ability to respond to audience requests during a presentation, such as demonstrating an application feature during a training session. Earlier in this chapter, the "Adding Embedded Documents" sidebar (page 781) explained how to create an embedded application object to run a Windows-based application. You can also use an action button for the same results. With an action button, however, you can control the look of the object that opens the application.

To create a button that starts an application on your system, follow these steps:

1 In Slide view, display the slide on which you want to create a jump to another application.

2 From the Slide Show menu, point to Action Buttons and choose one of the action buttons on the submenu.

3 Drag the mouse on the slide to create the action button. When you release the mouse button, the Action Settings dialog box appears.

4 Click the Mouse Click or Mouse Over tab, depending on how you want to start the application.

5 Click the Run Program option button, and then the Browse button. Use the navigation buttons to highlight the program file you want to run, and then click OK.

6 When you're finished configuring the action button, click OK.

 TIP

You'll find handy shortcuts for all the Office 97 programs in the \Program Files\Microsoft Office folder. You might even want to print these out and post on your office wall.

When you activate the action button during your show, you'll launch another application. To return to your presentation at the current slide, exit the application as you would any other.

Connecting to the Internet

In the last section, you learned how to create an action button on a slide and use it to open a PowerPoint slide, a Windows-based application, and an address on the Internet. In PowerPoint 97, you can also format a text placeholder so that it'll automatically establish an Internet connection if you have the necessary hardware and software installed on your computer. In Office terminology, such formatting is called a *hyperlink*, and the process of creating one is very similar to the one you've used throughout this book to create hyperlinks to the Internet and other documents in your Office applications.

In this section, you'll learn how to connect to the Internet with text hyperlinks, and how to jump back and forth between Web sites with the new Web toolbar. You'll also learn about the online templates included with PowerPoint that have been designed for Internet development.

Creating an Internet Hyperlink

Internet hyperlinks provide a simple way for you to display slides and other useful supporting documents that currently reside on the Internet World Wide Web—rather than having them occupy precious space on your hard drive. You can also use hyperlinks to display a home page on the Web as a resource for the people viewing your presentation. Hyperlinks are created with the Hyperlink command on the Insert menu or the Insert Hyperlink button on the Standard toolbar. The Insert Hyperlink dialog box then prompts you for the name of the Internet address or *URL* of the document you want to open on the Web, and the part of the document you want displayed, if it isn't the beginning. After you specify an Internet location, the Hyperlink command underlines the text placeholder on your slide that was selected when you ran the command. (The underlined word appears in a special color and looks similar to linked topics that appear in the Office online Help.) After a hyperlink has been established to another document, you can activate it by clicking the underlined word on your slide when your presentation is running.

Hyperlinks Can Be Local, Too

You can also use the Hyperlink command to open other documents on your system, provided that you have the Windows 95–based application necessary to open the document on your computer. (This makes it a nice complement to the Action Buttons command.) For example, if you have Microsoft Office Professional Edition installed, you can create a hyperlink to any Word, Excel, PowerPoint, Access, or Outlook document, and PowerPoint will automatically open it when you click the underlined "hyperlink" in your presentation. Similarly, if you have Microsoft Internet Explorer or another Windows 95–based Internet browser, you can create a hyperlink to any resource on the Internet that you have permission to use (and the proper address).

The following steps show you how to create a hyperlink in your presentation that connects to the Web:

1 Select the text placeholder on your slide with which you want to associate the hyperlink. It usually works best if that word or phrase is a descriptive label that describes the purpose of the link, so that users can see what they're connecting to. For example, "Sweet Peas Home Page" or "Check Scores on the Web."

Insert
Hyperlink

2 From the Insert menu, choose the Hyperlink command. (You can also click the Insert Hyperlink button on the Standard toolbar.) The Insert Hyperlink dialog box appears, shown in Figure 28-4, prompting you for the name of the file that will open when the hyperlink is activated. If you wish, you can specify a particular location in the file that should appear on the screen; if not, the document simply opens at the beginning.

FIGURE 28-4.
The Insert Hyperlink dialog box lets you establish a link between your slide and a document on your hard disk or the Internet.

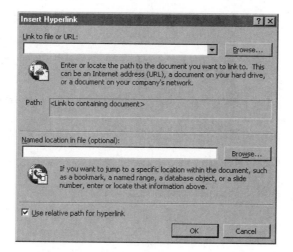

3 Type the address of the Web page in the Insert Hyperlink dialog box, or click the Browse button to search for an Internet shortcut on your hard disk. Addresses usually are in the format *http://www.xxxx.com*, where *xxxx* is the name of the business or service provider. For example, the address of InfoWord Electric (a free publication) is *http://www.infoworld.com*.

4 Click OK to add the hyperlink to your slide. When the Insert Hyperlink dialog box closes, the text in the highlighted cell appears in underlined type.

When you run your presentation, the hyperlinks will appear in underlined type, and you can activate them with a click. When you do this, Office automatically starts the application associated with the document and loads the linked document. If the hyperlink contains an Internet address, Office will start the default Internet browser on your system and ask you for a username and password. After you complete the necessary connection details, you'll see the Internet document you requested.

Using the Web Toolbar

Web
Toolbar

The Web toolbar lets you switch back and forth between open hyperlinks, establish additional Internet connections, or run special Web-related commands. Figure 28-5 shows the Web toolbar and the purpose of its buttons. To display the toolbar, click the Web Toolbar button on the Standard toolbar.

FIGURE 28-5.
The Web toolbar lets you switch back and forth between your open documents and Internet connections.

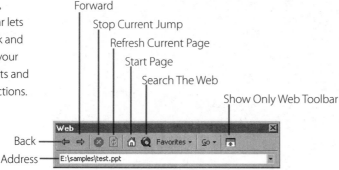

? **SEE ALSO**
For more information about using and configuring the Web toolbar, see "Linking Up with the World Wide Web," page 97.

The hyperlink navigation buttons are the essential tools on the Web toolbar. To display the last open document or Web page, click the Back (left-pointing) button. To display the next open document or Web page, click the Forward (right-pointing) button. If you want to open one of your favorite hyperlinks, click the Favorites drop-down list box and select it from the list. To see a list of the recent Internet addresses you've used, click the Address drop-down list box.

Using PowerPoint's Online Templates for Web Pages

In Chapter 24, you learned how to use PowerPoint's presentation templates to create slide shows based on predesigned "boilerplate" presentations. If you're posting information often on the Web, take a moment to scan the list of presentation templates again to see if one of the prepackaged designs might work for your organization. PowerPoint includes two types of templates—standard and online—that you can use to create presentations. Both are listed side-by-side on the Presentations tab of the New Presentation dialog box (see Figure 28-6), which is displayed when you choose the New command from the File menu.

FIGURE 28-6.

If you're responsible for creating online Web pages, check out the online presentation templates in the New Presentation dialog box before you create your own from scratch. Many of them are quite useful.

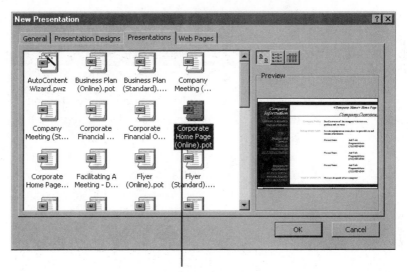

Online template

PowerPoint's online templates have been specially designed to be presented in a Web environment that uses hypertext markup language (HTML). Online templates include hyperlinks, navigation arrows, electronic mail jumps, and other features that are commonly used for home pages and other Web documents. For example, the Corporate Home Page (Online), shown in Figure 28-7 on the following page, is a well-organized presentation containing several useful screens of information that could quickly be adapted for a business in need of a Web home page.

FIGURE 28-7.
The Corporate Home Page template is an example of the presentations that have been designed for use on the Web.

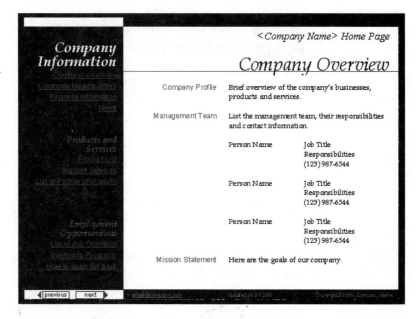

If you do create a presentation destined for the Web, test your links thoroughly, perhaps have a few colleagues call up the page from their computers and critique it for you, and then save your final copy of the presentation as an HTML document with the Save As HTML command on the File menu. The Save As HTML command starts the Save As HTML Wizard, which helps you customize your presentation with animations, frames, transitions, and other interactive settings. In no time you'll be a Web expert!

Perfecting Your Presentation

Perfecting your presentation is an important part of creating a slide show. This chapter discusses how you can fine-tune your presentation before you run your slide show. You'll find that PowerPoint's speaker's notes are invaluable as constant reminders of the slide you're talking about and what you're going to say about it. You can run the Spelling feature to eliminate the risk of any humiliating misspellings that would be magnified on a large screen.

You will probably print audience handouts in black-and-white rather than in color. (Remember that room lighting might not be very bright, especially if your handouts are to be consulted while your show is running.) To see how objects on your slides will appear when printed in black-and-white, you can use either the Black And White View option to see a full-size version or the Slide Miniature command to see a miniature version of a slide.

Finally, you can easily make last-minute changes, such as adding, deleting, or reordering slides, in Slide Sorter view. This view shows you miniatures of all slides, displaying several slides on the screen at one time. Hiding slides that contain confidential material or skipping over slides that you don't want to show to a particular audience is another last- minute change that you might want to consider.

By learning how to perfect your presentation in this chapter, you can be confident about the quality of your slide show while you're running it.

Adding Speaker's Notes

Unless you enjoy ad-libbing at a podium in front of an expectant audience, you've probably devised some way of reminding yourself of what you want to say. For example, you might number your slides and then make notes on correspondingly numbered index cards or papers. With PowerPoint, you have room to type speaker's notes for each slide. Even better, when you print them, you see the slide at the top of the page and the notes at the bottom. Figure 29-1 shows a note added to a slide.

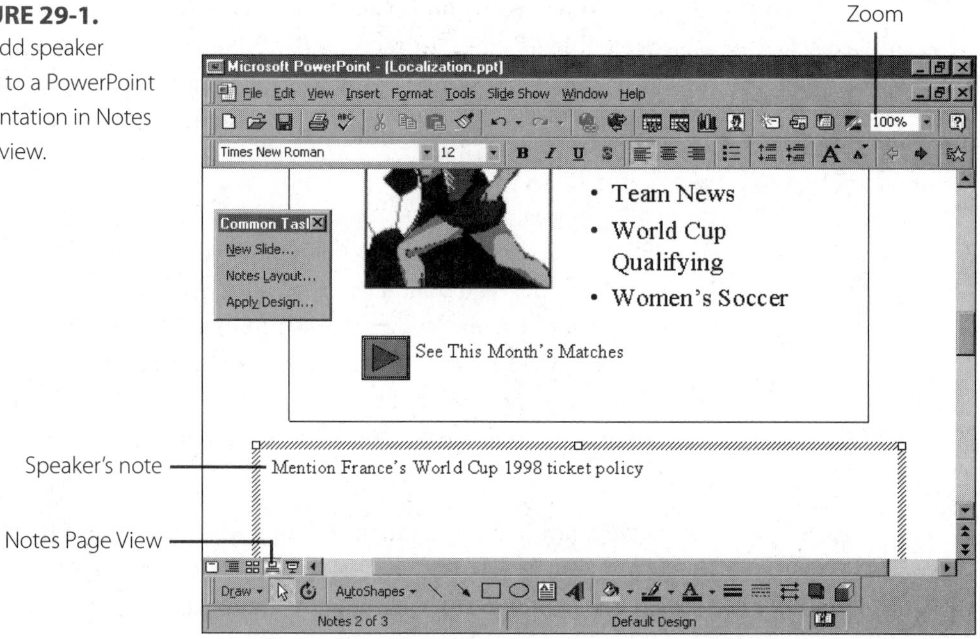

FIGURE 29-1.
You add speaker notes to a PowerPoint presentation in Notes Page view.

Of course, notes are not always necessary for every presentation, but it doesn't hurt to have a few cue cards in case you forget your lines or get caught up in the Q&A of the meeting. Another advantage of speaker's notes is that you can make your notes immediately after you create each slide, while the decisions you made when you created it are still fresh in your mind. You can add speaker's notes to any slide at any time by following these steps:

1 In Slide view, display the slide to which you want to add notes.

2 Choose Notes Page from the View menu or click the Notes Page View button at the bottom left of the screen.

3 Click within the notes area, and type whatever you want.

 TIP

Enlarge the notes area by choosing 100% in the Zoom box on the Standard toolbar. Now you can see what you're typing. Click the document window's scroll bars to see more of the note area or to view your slide.

4 When you've finished, choose Slide from the View menu or click the Slide View button to return to working with your slides and to hide the notes.

If you enlarged your slide with the Zoom box to see your note text close up, you may want to click the Zoom box again and select Fit to return your slide to normal size.

Whenever you need to revise your notes, all you have to do is display the slide to which you added the notes, and click the Notes Page View button or choose Notes Page from the View menu.

Checking Your Spelling

A presentation that contains spelling mistakes reflects poorly on the speaker. Misspellings loom even larger when your slide show is projected onto a big screen. How embarrassing! Before you take center stage, be sure to check the spelling throughout your presentation—perhaps on printouts as well as on screen, to be absolutely correct.

PowerPoint's Spelling feature will find and highlight for correction any misspellings in your outlines, speaker's notes (less important, since they're not being projected), and text on slides, such as titles and bulleted lists. Spelling's first line of defense is to check your spelling as you type. If this feature is active (the default), you'll see the Spelling icon on the right side of the status bar as you begin typing. If you don't see the Spelling icon, you can turn on this feature by choosing Options from the Tools menu. Then click the Spelling tab, turn on the Spelling option under Proofread As You Type, and click OK. As you type, PowerPoint will mark any misspelled words with a wavy red underline. To correct the spelling at that moment, right-click on the word and choose an option from the shortcut menu:

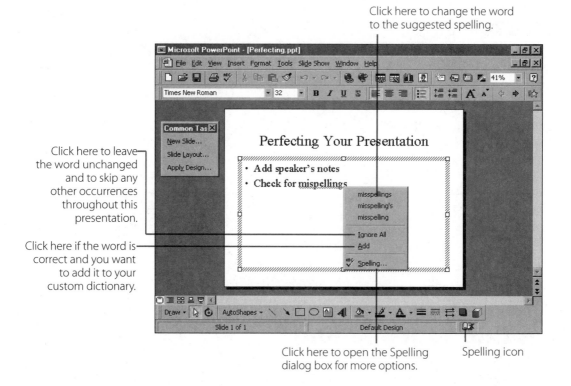

Click here to change the word to the suggested spelling.

Click here to leave the word unchanged and to skip any other occurrences throughout this presentation.

Click here if the word is correct and you want to add it to your custom dictionary.

Click here to open the Spelling dialog box for more options.

Spelling icon

You can use the Spelling icon on the status bar to review and correct your spelling. Each time you double-click the icon, PowerPoint will find and highlight the next misspelled word in your presentation and open the shortcut menu.

IV

Microsoft PowerPoint

You can also check your entire document by clicking the Spelling button on the Standard toolbar. To check your spelling with this method, do the following:

1 Click the Spelling button on the Standard toolbar.

Spelling

2 When PowerPoint finds a word that it can't match in its dictionary or in the custom dictionary, the Spelling dialog box opens.

 **SEE ALSO**

For more on using the Spelling feature and custom dictionaries, see Chapter 9, "Using Word's Proofing Tools." To learn more about AutoCorrect, see "Using the AutoCorrect Feature," page 135.

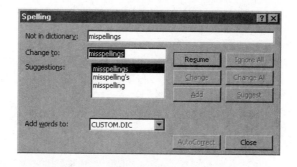

Your options are as follows:

- Click Ignore to skip the word this time.

- Click Ignore All to skip this word throughout this presentation—that is, not to stop on this word again.

- Click Add if the word is correctly spelled and you want to add it to your custom dictionary.

- Select a word from the Suggestions list to replace the selected word, and then click Change to change this occurrence of the word. Click Change All to change all occurrences throughout this presentation.

- If Spelling can't suggest a correct spelling, type the correct word in the Change To box, and then click Change or Change All.

- Click Close to exit the spelling check without making a change.

3 When Spelling is complete, click OK.

Fixing Mistakes with AutoCorrect

In an attempt to smooth out your writing and typing shortcomings, Power-Point's AutoCorrect feature catches and corrects common spelling, capitalization, and punctuation mistakes *as you type!* For example, if you type two initial caps at the beginning of a sentence or proper name, AutoCorrect automatically lowercases the second letter. AutoCorrect ensures that there are no inconsistencies in the way you use capitalization; it simply makes the changes in case as you type. If you tend to type the names of the days of the week without initial capital letters, PowerPoint can capitalize those for you. If there's a word whose spelling eludes you—for example, each time you type the word *receive,* you ask yourself, "Is it spelled *ie* or *ei?*"—you don't have to guess any more. AutoCorrect can also replace abbreviations with the entire word—when you type *adv,* AutoCorrect can replace it with *advertising.*

Here's how to have AutoCorrect do the job for you: Choose AutoCorrect from the Tools menu. You'll see the following dialog box:

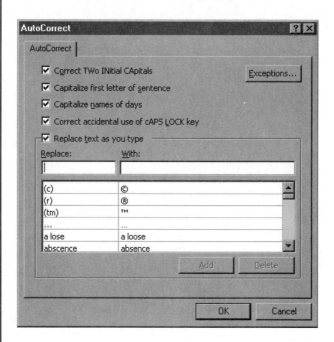

In the Replace box, type an abbreviation or a word that you often misspell, and then type the correct spelling of the word in the With box and click Add. You can leave the other options turned on, or you can turn them off. Finally, you can specify individual exceptions to the capitalization rules by clicking the Exceptions button and typing any special cases.

TIP

Hey Kids, Let's Make Our Own Dictionary!
PowerPoint's dictionary doesn't contain many proper nouns, such as names of people and places. It's a good idea to add your own proper nouns and technical terms to the custom dictionary. This custom dictionary is shared with other Office applications.

TIP

Don't Like Being Watched?
If you feel that your sixth-grade English teacher is standing behind you while you type, waiting to pounce on you when you make a mistake…or if you're using foreign words or terms that are consistently not in PowerPoint's proofing dictionary…you can disable PowerPoint's as-you-type spell-check feature by choosing the Options command from the Tools menu, clicking the Spelling tab, and turning off the Spelling check box. After you disable as-you-type spell-checking, you'll still be able to review your spelling with the Spelling command, but PowerPoint will no longer underline misspelled words with red as you type.

However, we can't help you with that uncanny feeling that Miss Thistlebottom is still back there, watching.

Viewing Black-and-Whites

When you want to see how the text and objects on color slides will look in black-and-white, display the slide and click the Black And White View button on the Standard toolbar (see Figure 29-2 on the following page) or choose the Black And White command from the View menu. Power-Point displays the black-and-white version on the screen, and shows the color version in a tiny preview window so that you can compare the two slides.

This view is useful when you want to see what your audience handouts will look like in black-and-white. The text should be legible and there should be a strong contrast between it and the background of the slide. The clip art and chart objects should print clearly and distinctly and should not blend in with the background color. Figure 29-2 shows a slide

FIGURE 29-2.
In Black And White view, color slides are displayed as they will be printed. A slide miniature in color also appears, letting you compare the two versions.

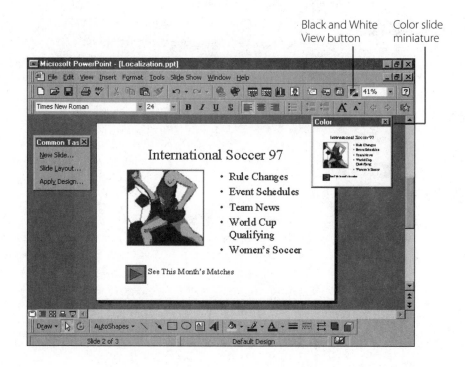

Black and White View button

Color slide miniature

in Black And White view (just as it will be printed), with an accompanying slide miniature in color so that you can compare the versions. (Admittedly, some of this detail is lost in our gray-scale screen shot.)

After you display a slide in Black And White view, you can make changes to the way PowerPoint displays any of the objects listed in Table 29-1. Just right-click the object, point to Black And White on the shortcut menu, and choose the shading you want from the submenu.

Table 29-1 lists the objects and how they first appear in Black And White view. Look for the objects used in your presentation and see whether the default appearances will work for you.

When you're finished using Black And White view, switch back to Color view by clicking the Black And White View button on the Standard toolbar. (This button is a toggle.) You can also use the Slide Miniature command on the View menu to display your slide in a tiny preview window as you work. When you're working in Color view, the slide miniature will be in black-and-white. When you're working in Black And White view, the slide miniature will be in color.

TABLE 29-1.   Objects in Black and White View

Object	Appearance
Text	Black
Text shadows	Hidden
Embossing	Hidden
Fills	Grayscale
Frame	Black
Pattern fills	Grayscale
Lines	Black
Object shadows	Grayscale
Bitmaps	Grayscale
Slide backgrounds	White

Using Slide Sorter View

Before the age of personal computers, graphics professionals used a light table to organize slides for presentations. A light table is a box with a light inside and a translucent plastic top. When you put slides on the lighted surface, the backlighting illuminates the contents of the slides. Well, the good news is that you don't have to go out and buy a light table or start taping slides in rows on your patio's sliding glass door. You have a much handier solution right in PowerPoint.

The Slide Sorter looks and works just like a light table, as shown in Figure 29-3 on the following page. It displays a miniature version of every slide in your presentation—and in the proper order. The number of slides that you can view at one time depends on your video card, video driver, and monitor, as well as the zoom percentage used and the size of the presentation window. You can view more slides at a glance if you lower the zoom percentage. If you view your slides at a high zoom percentage, such as 100%, you will see very few slides at one time, though in greater detail.

FIGURE 29-3.

Slide Sorter view showing miniatures of six slides.

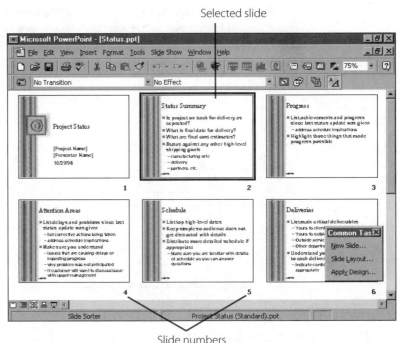

Selected slide

Slide numbers

To switch to Slide Sorter view, click the Slide Sorter View button at the bottom left of the screen. You can also choose the Slide Sorter command from the View menu.

With Slide Sorter, you get a thumbnail view (as if holding a slide up to the light at arm's length) of some or all the slides in your presentation. It doesn't matter that the text isn't very readable. You really want to look at the slides as a *whole*, focusing on layout consistency and perhaps contrast from one slide to the next, rather than the details.

As you can see in Figure 29-3, the slide number appears near the bottom right corner of each slide. One slide is currently selected (number 2) and surrounded by a dark border.

? SEE ALSO

To find out about slide transitions and animation effects, see Chapter 28, "Adding Special Effects and Internet Links."

You can't edit slides in Slide Sorter view; you must make changes to the content of slides in Slide view or Outline view. Slide Sorter view *does* let you do the following tasks: add and delete slides, rearrange the order of slides, add transitions and builds, hide slides, and rehearse your presentation. The Slide Sorter toolbar makes it a snap for you to perform these tasks.

⭐ **TIP**

> To get a closer look at a slide, double-click it. PowerPoint shifts to Slide view and displays the slide in full-slide view, enabling you to see the slide in detail. To return to Slide Sorter view, click the Slide Sorter View button.

Adding and Deleting Slides

PowerPoint lets you add slides one at a time or delete one or more slides from your presentation. When working with a single slide, you can work either in Slide view or in Slide Sorter view; the techniques are the same.

To add a slide, click in the space between the slides. A vertical bar appears between the slides to mark the location where the slide will be inserted, as shown in Figure 29-4. Because inserting a new slide is such a routine requirement, PowerPoint offers a number of ways of choosing the command. You can choose the New Slide command from the Insert menu, use the shortcut key (Ctrl+M), click the Insert New Slide button on the Standard toolbar, or click the New Slide command

FIGURE 29-4.
The vertical bar marks the current location for insertion.

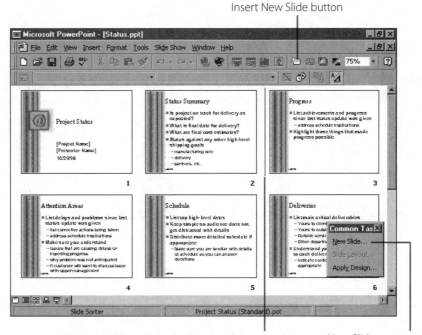

Insert New Slide button

This vertical bar marks the location for a new slide.   New Slide command on the Common Tasks toolbar (which typically appears as a floating window in the workspace).

To delete a slide, you must first select the slide and then choose the Delete Slide command from the Edit menu or press the Delete key.

Before you add or delete any slides in Slide Sorter view, you need to know the various ways to select slides in Slide Sorter view.

- Use the arrow keys to highlight a slide, or click the slide that you want to select. A selected slide is surrounded by a bold outline.

- Press Ctrl+Home to select the first slide in a presentation; press Ctrl+End to select the last slide.

- To select multiple slides, hold down the Shift key while clicking all the slides that you want to select.

- To select multiple slides using the mouse, hold down the left mouse button while dragging an outline around the slides that you want to select.

- To cancel a selection, click in any blank area of the Slide Sorter view window.

CAUTION

If you mistakenly delete a slide from your presentation, you can restore it in Slide Sorter view, Slide view, Outline view, or Notes Page view. Simply use the Undo command on the Edit menu immediately after you delete the slide.

To copy a slide, right-click it to select it and display the shortcut menu. Choose Copy from the shortcut menu, right-click in the space between the slides where you want to copy the slide, and choose Paste from the shortcut menu. Another quick way to duplicate a slide is to select it and choose Duplicate from the Edit menu or press Ctrl+D. The duplicate slide will appear at the right of the original slide. Then you can move the duplicate slide wherever you want. For more information on moving slides, see the next section, "Rearranging Slides."

Rearranging Slides

Slide Sorter view gives you a panoramic view of all your slides in the current order. This view lets you get an overall perspective of the presentation, as if every slide were laid out in a certain order on a light table. If you want to improve on the flow by changing the order of your slides, just select a slide and drag it to a new location. A vertical bar marks the location where the slide will be inserted when you release the mouse button. The slide numbers are changed to accommodate the new arrangement.

You can also move multiple slides within your presentation. For example, if you want to move slides 5 and 6 to the beginning of your presentation, simply select slides 5 and 6 and drag them to the left of the first slide in the presentation. PowerPoint automatically renumbers the reordered slides.

Hiding Slides

In certain cases, some slides might contain material that you'd rather not discuss with a particular audience due to time constraints or the sensitivity of the material. For instance, you might not want to announce in a general company meeting that your controller had vanished with $10 million in cash—but if asked about it you wouldn't want to lie, either. You can prepare a slide and hope that the news hasn't leaked out; if it has, you're covered. More common is the situation where you want to use similar presentations for different audiences. By hiding slides, you can change one presentation to match the needs of more than one group, or can speed up your presentation on the spot if time is running short (you can label a number of slides "Optional" on your speaker's notes, as a reminder that they can be cut).

? SEE ALSO
See "Revealing Hidden Slides," page 824, to learn how to display a hidden slide while presenting your slide show.

PowerPoint lets you create hidden slides to include in your presentation but to show *only* at your discretion. In Slide Sorter view, a hidden slide appears with its number enclosed in a box with a line across it.

To hide a slide, make sure that you're in Slide Sorter view. Select the slide that you want to hide, and click the Hide Slide button on the Slide Sorter toolbar. Notice that the slide doesn't disappear from the Slide Sorter. You see the slide, but its number is surrounded by a box with a diagonal line through it, as shown in the illustration on the following page.

Hide Slide button

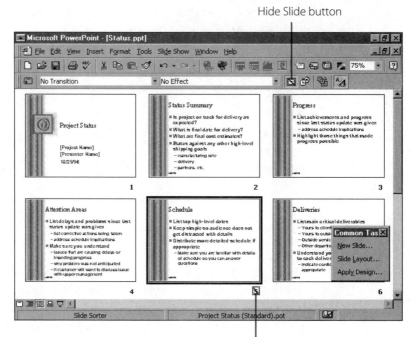

This slide is marked hidden.

> **NOTE**
>
> The Hide Slide button is only available in Slide Sorter view. In Slide view, you can hide a slide by choosing Hide Slide from the Slide Show menu, though there's no indication that the slide is hidden.

This chapter showed you how to add speaker's notes, check your spelling, view black-and-whites, look at miniature slides, use the Slide Sorter, and hide slides. These are just a few of the things you can do to polish your slide show. The next chapter will teach you how to plan and rehearse the slide show so that it's picture-perfect when you take a deep breath and walk into that crowded room.

Setting Up and Rehearsing the Slide Show

O nce you've created your slide show and perfected it as much as possible, you should rehearse your presentation so that you become comfortable with the content, flow, and timing of your material. Then decide on the type of media that you'll use to present your slides. If your audience will be a small one, you can go the inexpensive route and print all your slides, speaker's notes, and handouts on paper—and then use your desktop computer to run an electronic slide show. If you're going to use an overhead projector, you can set up your slides as transparencies. For a larger audience, go the extra mile and set up your presentation as 35mm slides. Send the presentation files to a service bureau and have them make professional 35mm slides for you. If you travel, and want to run your slide show from your portable computer, just use the Pack And Go Wizard to compress your presentation and copy it to disks. Then you or any other presenter can use PowerPoint Viewer to run the slide show from the portable computer. This chapter will help you set up and polish your presentation to meet professional standards.

Picking a Show Type

PowerPoint 97 includes a number of new presentation options to let you customize the type of slide show you're creating. You can set up your show to be presented full screen by an individual (you or a colleague), in a window with navigation controls, or at an automated kiosk. In addition, you can control which slides are included in the final presentation, how narration and animation are used, and how the slides advance.

To pick the show type, complete the following steps:

1 From the Slide Show menu, choose Set Up Show. You'll see the following dialog box:

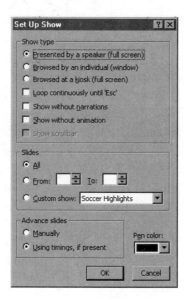

2 Specify the show type; either speaker (full screen), individual (window), or kiosk (full screen).

- If you choose the first option (the most common method), you'll have complete control of the slide show from beginning to end. You can skip slides, stop the presentation, add meeting minutes, and so on.

- The second option is designed for presentations that you want to distribute to co-workers or send out over a network. It runs the slide show in a smaller window, and includes menu commands for navigating the slide show, printing slides, and other useful options.

- The third option creates a self-running presentation suitable for a kiosk or trade show demonstrations. It disables most of the PowerPoint controls so that viewers can't modify the presentation, and it repeats the show over and over again automatically.

3 Specify which slides you want included in the show. You can include all the slides (the default), a slide range (in case you have to shorten your show on the spot), or a custom slide show that you've previously defined with the Custom Shows command on the Slide Show menu. (For more information about custom shows, see the sidebar on the next page.)

4 Finally, under Advance Slides specify whether you want to advance the slides manually or using timings if they're present. (Slide timings are created with the Rehearse Timings command on the Slide Show menu, as you'll see in the next section.)

5 When you're finished setting up the show, click OK. To see how your choices have affected the presentation, choose View Show from the Slide Show menu or click the Slide Show button and watch it run!

Creating a Custom Show

The Custom Shows command on the Slide Show menu lets you create a short list of alternate slide shows based on the slides in your presentation. Although in the past you could create custom shows by hiding slides or saving different versions of presentations in different files, the new Custom Shows command lets you manage all your slide show's variations *in one place*. For example, you might want to drop out a few slides for sales reps in your organization that don't need to know your production staff's editorial policies. After you create a custom show, you can then specify it when you're configuring your show's presentation options in the Set Up Show dialog box (described earlier).

When you choose the Custom Shows command, a dialog box appears, listing your current collection of custom shows (if any). You can edit, remove, copy, or show one of these presentations by clicking buttons in the dialog box. To define a new custom show, click the New button, give your custom show a name, and then specify the slides you want to include by highlighting the slide titles and clicking the Add button. The following illustration shows this process in action:

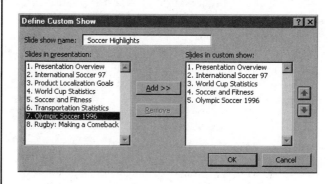

Rehearsing the Show

When you go to the theater to see a play, you probably don't think about the hours of rehearsal that made everything run smoothly—but rehearsals are the backbone of any professional production, whether it's a Broadway play or a company slide show. You need to rehearse your presentation so that you know what to say and when to say it, as well as to make sure that you don't run over or under your allotted time. You don't want to have to improvise if you run short, or race through your material if you run long. Even worse, at a busy conference, you could be asked to leave the podium if you run over your time limit.

PowerPoint can time your presentation so that it fits precisely into the allotted time. There are two ways to rehearse timings: automatically and manually.

Setting the Timings

Having PowerPoint automatically time your slide show is the best method for rehearsing your timing. That way, you can have PowerPoint determine the length of time to display each slide. PowerPoint will also calculate the length of the entire show for you. This is a great feature and one that you should use every time to get your timing perfected. (In the next section, you'll learn how to set the timings manually.) To use the Rehearse Timings feature, follow these steps:

1 Open the presentation that you want to rehearse, and use the Set Up Show command to specify the slides that you want to include. (Or you can just use some practice slides to see how this feature works.)

2 Click the Slide Sorter View button to switch to Slide Sorter view.

Rehearse
Timings

3 Click the Rehearse Timings button on the Slide Sorter toolbar, or choose Rehearse Timings from the Slide Show menu.

4 When the full-screen version of your first slide appears on screen, rehearse exactly what you'll tell your audience about this slide. You'll see the Rehearsal dialog box counting the seconds that the slide remains on screen.

Keep It Short

Your audience's attention can wander if you spend too much time on a slide. If you intend to spend more than two or three minutes on the topic covered on one slide, make two or three slides for this subject.

You can perform the following actions in the Rehearsal dialog box to rehearse timings:

- When you're ready to move to the next slide, click the Advance button to advance the slides manually. This resets the counter on the right (which measures the time spent on the current slide).

- To pause a slide and temporarily stop both time counters, click the Pause button. When you want to continue, click the Pause button again. (You might want to pause a slide if you lose your train of thought or if the phone rings.)

- To start over with a slide, click the Repeat button. (You might repeat a slide if you change your mind about what you want to say.)

- To stop rehearsing and return to Slide Sorter view, click the Close (X) button in the Rehearsal dialog box.

5 After you've finished with the last slide, the timing information box appears, giving you the total elapsed time for your presentation and the option to display the new timings in Slide Sorter view.

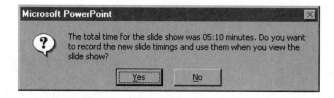

6 If you choose to accept the timings, click Yes. If you want to rehearse again to get the timings to fit into an allotted time, click

IV

Microsoft PowerPoint

No. If you're prompted to view your slide timings in Slide Sorter view, click Yes. You'll see the timing beneath each slide in Slide Sorter view, as shown in Figure 30-1.

FIGURE 30-1.
The rehearsal timings in Slide Sorter view.

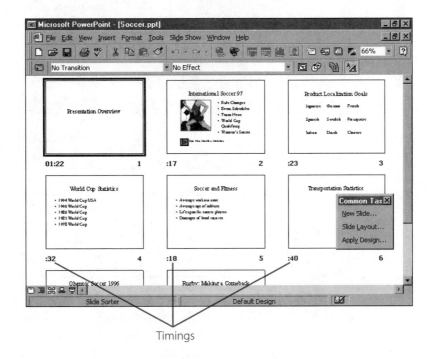

Timings

Setting Timings Manually

When you want tight control over the pace of your presentation, the manual method for rehearsing your slide show timings lets you enter the exact amount of time that you want each slide to remain on the screen. For example, you might want your title slide to appear for 45 seconds, the second slide for 2 minutes, the third slide for 1 minute and 30 seconds, and so on. To manually set slide timings:

1 Select the slide in Slide Sorter view.

Slide
Transition

2 Click the Slide Transition button on the Slide Sorter toolbar. You'll see the Slide Transition dialog box. If you had already set a timing for the slide (with the Rehearse Timings command or the Slide Transition dialog box), you'll see a timing in the dialog box, as shown on the following page.

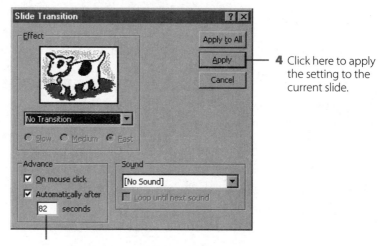

4 Click here to apply the setting to the current slide.

3 Specify the number of seconds before the slide should automatically advance.

5   Repeat the above steps for each slide in your show.

NOTE

If you click the Apply To All button, the timing you specified will be used for *all* the slides in your presentation. (This is a useful, but powerful feature—but it might hypnotize your audience if you have many slides each on-screen for the same period.)

TIP

Fly on Autopilot, or Grab the Controls?

After you rehearse the timings for your slide show, either you can run the show with the timings, as described in Chapter 31, "Running the Slide Show," or you can remove the slide timings and advance the slides manually. To do the latter, select those slides you want to control manually in Slide Sorter view, click the Slide Transition button on the Slide Sorter toolbar, and select On Mouse Click and deselect Automatically After in the Advance section of the Slide Transition dialog box. If *both* Advance options are selected, the slides will advance automatically after the specified number of seconds have elapsed; if you want to advance the slide sooner, do so manually by clicking the mouse.

Printing Slides, Notes Pages, and Handouts

In many cases you'll want to print your entire presentation, including your outline, slides, speaker's notes, and audience handouts. Even if you're presenting your material electronically, as described in the next chapter, you'll probably want to print your notes and handouts to rehearse with or pass around to colleagues for a critique or to fill information gaps. (The handouts contain printed copies of two, three, or six slides per page. These printouts support your presentation and help your audience to follow along with you.)

The process for producing the actual material for your presentation is the same, no matter what type of output you choose. The first step is to determine which printer you want to use. (You might be exposing film, for example, for which you wouldn't be using the draft laser-printer down the hall.) Next, you open the presentation that you want to print. Then you set up your slides by choosing the output medium (paper or transparencies, for example) and orientation, such as portrait or landscape. Finally, you start producing the material.

For a more professional look, you can print your presentation on inkjet or laser transparencies. If you're giving your presentation at an informal meeting, you can print your material in black-and-white on paper.

To print your presentation, follow these steps:

1 Open the presentation that you want to print.

2 Choose Page Setup from the File menu, and select the appropriate size for your medium in the Slides Sized For drop-down list. Click OK.

3 Choose Print from the File menu. The Print dialog box opens, as shown on the following page.

4 Specify the slides that you want to print in the Print Range area. You can print your entire presentation, the current slide, selected slides, a custom show, or a particular slide range (just as with Word, use commas to separate slides and hyphens to specify ranges).

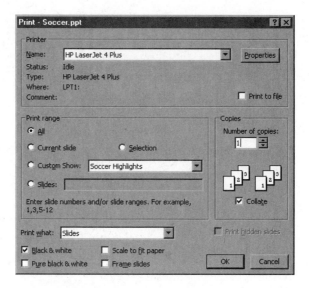

5 Select the material to be printed in the Print What drop-down list. Your options are slides, handouts, notes, or an outline of your presentation.

6 Click OK to begin printing the selected portion of your presentation.

Print

If you just want to print all your slides quickly, click the Print button on the Standard toolbar. PowerPoint will print your entire presentation immediately, bypassing the Print dialog box.

Using Transparencies

If you have an inkjet or laser printer, you can load the printer's paper tray with transparencies made especially for such printers. Some of the transparency products on the market include 3M Inkjet Printer Transparencies (for Hewlett-Packard DeskJets) and 3M Scotch Laser Printer Transparencies. Before you print your slides on overheads, you must change a few options. Choose Page Setup from the File menu to open the Page Setup dialog box, shown here:

To set the dimensions of your slides for overhead transparencies, select Overhead here before printing.

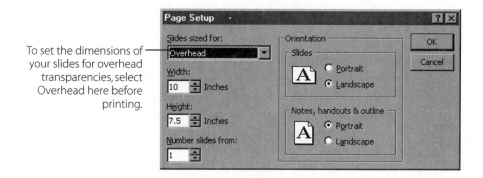

By default, slides are set to print in landscape orientation. However, if you print your slides in landscape orientation, you might find that certain overhead projectors will clip off the sides of your transparencies. Think about setting up your slides to print in portrait rather than landscape orientation. To change the orientation, choose Portrait in the Slides area of the Page Setup dialog box. If you change the slide orientation, be sure to review your slides before printing and adjust the placement and sizing of objects on the slides as necessary.

You can print your slides in black-and-white or color on transparencies, just as if they were paper. When you're ready to print, choose Print from the File menu. To print your color presentation in black-and-white, select the Black & White option in the Print dialog box. This option uses the settings from the Black And White view of your slides (described in "Viewing Black-and-Whites," page 797) to enhance your black-and-white transparencies. To print your color presentation on transparencies using a color printer, choose a color printer from the Name list in the Printer section of the Print dialog box. The result is a set of high-quality transparencies that you can project on an overhead projector.

Ordering 35mm Slides

The best way to deliver a presentation to a sizable audience is to project 35mm slides onto a large screen. Make sure that the room in which you're going to use a slide projector can be darkened as much as possible. To create 35mm slides, you'll need to copy your presentation to a floppy disk (never send your only original file!) and send the disk to a service bureau. Before you do so, contact the service bureau and ask for the special driver file that you'll need. Your service bureau will provide the file, together with instructions for preparing your files.

In the Page Setup dialog box, choose the 35mm Slides option in the Slides Sized For drop-down list so that your slides are the correct dimensions for making 35mm slides. There might be other options that you'll need to apply; your service bureau will tell you what they are.

If you live in North America and you have a modem attached to your computer, you can send your presentation file directly to Genigraphics Corporation. This service bureau will transform your slides into colorful 35mm slides, digital color overheads, large display prints, or posters. Genigraphics gives you a fast turnaround, too. You can send your files via modem at any time during the day and you'll get your presentation materials back via overnight delivery.

NOTE

If you don't see the Send To Genigraphics command on the File menu, you didn't install the Genigraphics Wizard on your computer. Simply run Setup again to install the option.

To prepare to send your file to Genigraphics, ask yourself the following questions:

- Which file do I want Genigraphics to output?
- What type of presentation output do I want?
- How fast do I want my order processed?
- Do I have my shipping and billing information ready?

Here's how to set up your presentation file for output by Genigraphics:

1 Open the presentation that contains the slides you want to send to Genigraphics.

2 Choose Send To Genigraphics from the File menu.

3 Follow the instructions in the Genigraphics Wizard dialog boxes.

Using Pack and Go

Many presenters run their presentations on a portable computer that they take with them on their travels. Even if you can't install Microsoft Office with PowerPoint on your portable computer because of limited hard disk space, you can still use your notebook or laptop computer to deliver your presentation. With PowerPoint's Pack And Go feature, you can compress and save your presentation with all its multimedia files, as well as copy a small portion of PowerPoint called the PowerPoint Viewer onto floppy disks or directly onto your portable computer if it's connected to your desktop system. The PowerPoint Viewer is a mini-application that lets you run your slide show from a computer that has limited hard disk space.

NOTE

Be prepared. Make sure that you have several formatted floppy disks on hand before you start the Pack And Go Wizard.

To pack up your presentation to go, follow these instructions:

1 Open the presentation that you want to compress and save to floppy disks.

2 Choose Pack And Go from the File menu.

3 Follow the instructions in the Pack And Go Wizard dialog boxes.

TIP

To ensure the maximum portability, be sure to turn on the Include Linked Files and Embed TrueType Fonts options when prompted by the Pack And Go Wizard. If you don't turn on these options, you might need to copy additional files for your presentation to run smoothly.

This chapter showed you how to print material using various output media for your slide show. The next chapter will tell you how to run your slide show electronically.

Running the Slide Show

You've designed, created, embellished, and planned your presentation down to the last precisely timed second. Now, it's *show time!* You can deliver your electronic slide show using Slide Show view—one of the best ways to give a presentation. (Most alternatives involve printing your slides, as discussed in Chapter 30.) If you created action buttons to branch to other places in your show, this is the time to use them. PowerPoint provides many useful features to facilitate your on-screen presentation.

You can use the Slide Navigator tools to quickly locate and move to specific slides during your show. If you're called on to display any hidden slides, this is where you'll learn how to reveal them. With PowerPoint's useful Meeting Minder, you can record action items, take written minutes of the discussion or action points, and even schedule appointments with Outlook during the slide show. You can also write and draw (temporarily) on your slides to reinforce a point. Last but not least, with presentation conferencing, you can deliver your presentation without gathering your audience into a single room—by making the presentation across a network. Your show can be run and viewed simultaneously by people in a variety of different locations.

Preparing Electronic Presentations

A professional-looking electronic presentation can impress a small or large audience. A computer slide show fills the screen with your slides, using various special effects such as builds, transitions, and timings. For an audience of only three or four viewers, you can use a desktop computer. For a larger audience, you'll need a larger monitor or projection technology such as a projection panel—that is, a transparent color computer display designed to fit on top of an overhead projector.

To make sure that your slide show will be effective and enjoyable, use these guidelines to critique your slides before you set up for your electronic presentation:

■ Builds and transitions should emphasize your points and *not overwhelm* your audience with special effects. See Chapter 28, "Adding Special Effects and Internet Links."

■ A sound effect, narration, or some music during a build or transition will grab your audience's attention. Don't overdo the sound effects, though—they can divert your audience's attention away from the points you want to make. See Chapter 28.

■ Set the timing for your show so that it's neither too fast nor too slow. If you rush through it, you'll exhaust your viewers (and yourself). If you drag it out, you'll put them to sleep! See the section "Rehearsing the Show," page 808, in the previous chapter.

■ As you rehearse your timing, study your presentation's visual and informational impact. A good rule to remember is "Keep it simple"—too many words or pictures on a slide can be confusing and annoying. Your viewer doesn't know what to look at first, and becomes too overloaded with information to remember any of it. See Chapter 25, "Entering and Editing Text" for other guidelines.

Use the Set Up Show command on the Slide Show menu to finalize the show type and display features of your slide show, and use the Page Setup command on the File menu to adjust the size of your slides. That's all you have to do! Now you're ready to run your slide show on a computer.

Using Slide Show View

You've rehearsed and polished your presentation, and now it's time to get on with the show. Any butterflies that you might be feeling will fly away after the first minute or two of your presentation. With Slide Show view, you can pull your show off without a hitch. You can move instantly to the next slide or to the previous slide; you can pause a slide to answer questions; you can use the Go feature to go to any slide in this presentation; and you can "branch" to other slides, documents, or even a Web page with the action buttons that you created in Chapter 28. Make sure that you have printed copies of your speaker's notes. If you have a sudden attack of stage fright, and can't remember your lines, those notes are your "memory" on paper. It's also a good idea to print more audience handouts than you need, just in case there are some unexpected participants.

OK, relax, take a deep breath, and come on stage from any of several wings:

- From the Windows Explorer, right-click the PowerPoint presentation file, and choose Show from the shortcut menu. During the presentation, your slides appear in Slide Show view. When you finish the show, you're returned to the Windows Explorer.

- Within PowerPoint, you can switch to Slide view and move to the slide that you want to show first, or you can switch to Slide Sorter view and select the slide that you want to begin with. To start, click the Slide Show button at the bottom left of the window.

- To start your show with a command, choose the View Show command from the Slide Show menu, or choose Slide Show from the View menu.

> NOTE

The amount of time PowerPoint waits before moving through slides is set through the Rehearse Timings feature, which is covered in Chapter 30. You set up the timing for each slide and specify how long you want the slide to remain on screen. You can also use the automatic timing method but still advance some slides manually when you need to.

Whichever method you use to start your slide show, the first slide appears on screen. You'll talk about your first slide, and then, if your show is automatically timed, the slide will be erased from the screen, using the transition effect you've specified, and the next slide will appear immediately. If your show doesn't have timings, simply click the slide when you've finished with it and advance to the next slide.

During your show, an icon with an up arrow button appears in the lower left corner of your screen as soon as you move the mouse. When you click this button, you see a pop-up menu. (You can also open this menu by right-clicking on a slide.) This menu appears only in Slide Show view, and has been specifically designed to give you fast access to all the commands you'll need while a show is running.

The simplest way to move manually to the next slide in sequence is to click the slide. If you prefer to use the keyboard to move to the next slide, you can press one of the following keys: the letter N, the Spacebar, the Down arrow, the Right arrow, or the Page Down key. To go back to the previous slide, press P, the Backspace key, the Up arrow, the Left arrow, or Page Up. If you prefer to use the pop-up menu, choose Next or Previous from it. To move to a specific slide, type the slide number and press Enter.

TIP

> A fast way to return to your first slide is to hold down both mouse buttons for two seconds.

The mouse pointer arrow appears on the screen when you move the mouse, but you can change its color or remove it by using commands on the Pointer Options submenu. The arrow is useful for pointing to various text and objects on your slides, so you'll probably want to keep it.

If you don't want the arrow pointer or the pop-up menu button to appear on screen, you can hide both of them. You can press Ctrl+H to hide the pointer and button for as long as you'd like. To make them reappear, move the mouse. You also can press Ctrl+L to hide the pointer and button for the entire show. Even with the pointer hidden, you can still click your mouse to move to the next slide.

TIP

> **Call for "Help!" with F1**
> If, in the middle of delivering your presentation, you suddenly forget which slide-show controls to use—for example, the actions and keys for moving between slides, or for hiding and displaying the arrow pointer, button, or hidden slides—all you have to do is press the F1 key. This displays a list of controls anytime during your presentation.

Using Slide Navigator

Navigate your way through a slide show with ease by using the handy Slide Navigator. As discussed in the preceding section, you can click on a slide or use keyboard shortcuts to move to slides in sequence or to a specific slide. However, to find a particular slide that you want to discuss with your audience, use Slide Navigator. From Slide Show view's pop-up menu, point to Go, and then choose Slide Navigator from the submenu. You'll see the dialog box shown on the following page.

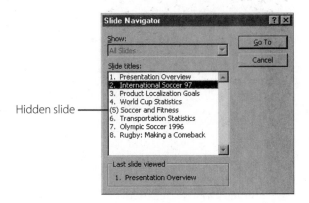

Hidden slide

Slide Navigator contains a list of all the slides in your show and displays the name of the last slide shown. Notice that the slide number for a hidden slide is enclosed in parentheses. To jump to a slide that's out of sequence, find the slide in the Slide Titles list, and double-click it.

Revealing Hidden Slides

If an audience member probes you enough for sensitive or confidential information that you've got tucked away on a hidden slide, you might have to disclose it. PowerPoint gives you several ways to reveal a hidden slide. If you're on the slide immediately *before* a hidden slide, reveal it by choosing the Hidden Slide command from the Go submenu of Slide Show view's pop-up menu. To reveal a hidden slide that appears *elsewhere* in your presentation, choose it from Slide Navigator's Slide Titles list. Choose Slide Navigator from the Go submenu of Slide Show view's pop-up menu, find the slide whose slide number is in parentheses, and double-click it.

There's a third way to reveal your hidden slides. First jot down a note as to where your hidden slides are going to appear in the slide show. To find this out, switch to Slide Sorter view and look for the slides whose slide number is inside a box that has a diagonal line through it. Then, from the slide that precedes it, just press H to unveil a hidden slide. This is the smoothest way to do it—no menu appears, so your audience won't realize that you're actually displaying a hidden slide.

Closing the Show

At the end of your show, you can display a black slide to indicate that the presentation is over. A black slide is similar to seeing "The End" at the end of a movie (plus, it gives your viewers' eyes a chance to adjust). Before you run the slide show, choose Options from the Tools menu, click the View tab, and select the End With Black Slide option.

As you learned in the last chapter, you can also run your show in a continuous loop, rather than ending with the last slide. For example, if you're demonstrating a new product at a trade show, you might want to run the show continuously on a computer in your booth. To do so, choose Set Up Show from the Slide Show menu and turn on the Loop Continuously Until 'Esc' option in the Set Up Show dialog box. When you decide to stop the slide show, press Escape.

NOTE

At any time, you can press Escape or choose End Show from the Slide Show view pop-up menu to stop the slide show.

Branching with Action Buttons

After creating those action buttons (see Chapter 28, "Adding Special Effects and Internet Links"), you need to know how to use them in your slide show. When you arrive at a slide that contains an action button, just click the button to branch to another slide, to begin another presentation, to start another Office 97 program, or to connect to the Internet. If you created an action button on the slide to which you branched, click that button to return to the original slide or to move to a different slide. If you branched to another presentation, PowerPoint automatically returns you to the slide from which you branched in your original presentation at the end of the second presentation. If you launched an application, you can edit the document "live" for your audience. For example, you can demonstrate the effects of a "what-if?" scenario in a budget created on an Excel worksheet, and your audience can watch the changes reflected in an Excel chart. When you're ready to move to the next slide, choose Exit from the application's File menu.

Using Meeting Minder

PowerPoint's Meeting Minder is a helpful reminder tool that lets you create action items and record minutes of the meeting, as well as schedule appointments in Outlook, while you're delivering your presentation. During an informal slide show, you might want to create a list of action items based on the feedback you're getting on the slides. For example, at a staff meeting, you might discuss a certain topic that triggers a new idea, task, or question that you need to deal with later.

You can also take minutes during a slide show. Perhaps you're giving a presentation at a quarterly budget meeting, and you're the one responsible for recording the minutes of the meeting. Use Meeting Minder to record the minutes as the meeting progresses, typing up the important points or items to be acted on, After the meeting, transfer your minutes to your note pages or to a new Word document. From there, you can print them and distribute copies to all the attendees and to those people who couldn't attend.

Finally, you can start Outlook from the Meeting Minder to update your schedule or handle other administrative tasks. To select this option, you need a working copy of Outlook on your system that has a copy of your schedule.

Follow these steps to work with Meeting Minder:

1 During your show, right-click a slide, and choose Meeting Minder from the pop-up menu. You'll see the following dialog box:

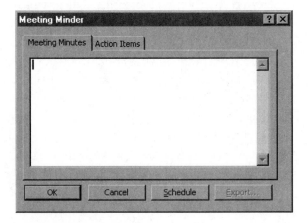

IV

2 Click the appropriate tab that indicates what you'd like to do, or click Schedule to start Outlook.

3 If you're adding an action item or meeting minute, type it in the space provided.

4 To export action items and meeting minutes to a Word document, click Export, and select the Send Meeting Minutes And Action Items To Microsoft Word option. Then click Export Now.

5 When you're finished, click OK.

Action items are added to a new slide at the end of the current presentation. You can refine this information into a finished slide, or print it the same way that you print other note pages and slides, as discussed in Chapter 30, "Setting Up and Rehearsing the Show."

 TIP

Update Your Speaker Notes

You can also amend your speaker notes during a presentation by choosing the Speaker Notes command from Slide Show view's pop-up menu. You might find this command useful if you find a mistake in your notes while you're giving a presentation, or if you think of a new analogy for explaining a tricky point. Your edits will appear in Notes Pages view the next time you need them.

Marking with the Pen

Amazingly, you can actually annotate your PowerPoint slides with the Pen feature during an electronic slide show, just as you would use a marking pen on overhead transparencies. You can even choose from a large assortment of pen colors.

To use the Pen feature during a show, right-click a slide and choose Pen from the pop-up menu or press Ctrl+P. This will change the pointer to an on-screen pen. Hold down the mouse button as you write or draw on a slide.

 NOTE

The writing or drawing that you add during a show to a slide is a temporary overlay; it doesn't stay on the slide once you've moved on to another slide in your show.

If you dislike the pen color, you can change it. To do so, right-click a slide, point to the Pointer Options submenu, point to the Pen Color submenu, and pick a new color.

To return to the regular cursor, choose Arrow from the pop-up menu or press Ctrl+A.

Running a Presentation Across a Network

PowerPoint's clever presentation conferencing innovation enables you to run a slide show on a network. While you take notes using Meeting Minder and operate the slide show using Slide Navigator on a single monitor, your audience watches the show on various computers across the network—you could call an emergency meeting for your entire sales force, seated at their own desks, scattered among several buildings! What's even more exciting is that participants can annotate the slides with the pen during the show.

If you're the presenter, it could be your responsibility to organize the network connections, similar to setting up a conference phone call. In that case, you must first make sure that all the participants are running PowerPoint, have access to the network you're using, and have joined the presentation as audience members.

To participate in presentation conferencing, each audience member must follow these steps:

1 In PowerPoint, choose Presentation Conference from the Tools menu.

2 Follow the on-screen instructions in the Presentation Conference Wizard and select the Audience option.

3 Click Finish when done and wait for the presentation to begin.

When the conference begins, the presentation will appear on screen. If desired, annotate the slides by moving the mouse, and then drawing with the pen. The other participants can see your annotations. To take notes, use Meeting Minder.

Of course, the presentation doesn't begin until the presenter steps up to the podium and activates the slide show. The first step is to invite each member of the audience to join the presentation. To do that, you must know the computer name or Internet address used by each audience member. (Ask each audience member for this information ahead of time.) Once you've collected that information, you can establish your connections and begin the show. To run a presentation conference, make sure the audience is ready and then:

1 Open the presentation that you want to run across a network.

2 Choose Presentation Conference from the Tools menu.

3 Follow the on-screen instructions in the Presentation Conference Wizard dialog boxes to select the Presenter option and what controls will appear on your screen during the presentation and to invite your audience members to the conference.

4 When you are ready to start the presentation, click Finish.

When the slide show begins, you'll see the Stage Manager tools that you can use to control the presentation conference. You can review notes, monitor timings, add action items, and take minutes.

PART V

Microsoft Access

CHAPTER 32

Databasics

J ust as Word is designed to work with documents containing text and images and Excel is designed for use with worksheets containing numbers and charts, Access is designed to manage data. *Data* consists of a collection of information; data becomes useful information when it's organized in a meaningful way. Of the Microsoft Office 97 applications, Access is the tool that you use to provide that organization.

A *database* consists of a collection of tables, forms, queries, and reports that are used to manage and present the data. In Access, you manage these database objects through the Database window. The process of creating a database involves these basic steps:

1   Create a database by designing and building tables to hold data.

2   Enter the data.

3   Develop additional database objects for viewing, editing, and printing the information.

The Database Foundation

Before you can begin working with your database, you must establish some vessel to hold your data. In Access, the *table* object holds the data. Separate tables can be used to hold related information. For example, one table might hold information about students, and another table might hold information about the classes in which the students are registered. Relationships must be defined between these tables so that they can work together. This combination of all the tables and their relationships makes up the foundation of your database.

Fields and Records

When you look at an Access table like the one shown in Figure 32-1, one of the first things you'll notice is its resemblance to an Excel worksheet (providing you've consulted Part III of this book). Both are organized into rows and columns, with the actual values entered into the cells that are created by the gridlines. What makes an Access table different from an Excel worksheet, however, is that in Access each column in a table represents a *field,* which is a category of information, while each row in the table consists of a single *record,* which holds all the information for one item in the table.

FIGURE 32-1.
The fields and records in an Access table.

Each column is a field.

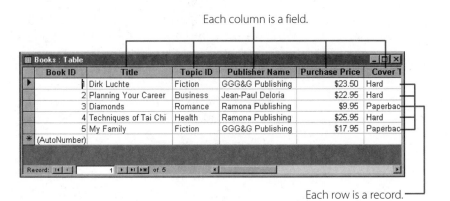

Each row is a record.

This is more than just a difference in terms. Unlike a column in Excel, in Access each field can contain only one type of data—text or numbers or dates, and so on. In Access, each record contains the information about a single item (for example, everything you're tracking about one student or everything you're tracking about one class).

When you work with information from the database, you often work with a single record at a time. Specifically, when using a *form* to view the data in a table, you will generally see only one record at a time; and when you generate a *report*, each line that is printed usually represents a single record. (When you design a form or a report, you determine which fields will be included from the record.)

Access is very flexible in the types of data that it lets you define for your fields. Any kind of text, numbers, dates, times, and amounts of money can be entered. In fact, Access includes a special field type, OLE, which allows you to insert an object from another Windows program, such as a picture, an animation, a sound, or even a movie clip (see Chapter 39, "Sharing Data Among Office Applications," for more information on using OLE objects). In general, however, most database work is done with the text, number, and date field types that are the focus of the chapters in this part of the book.

If you're familiar with the other Microsoft Office applications, you'll find a number of differences in the way that Access stores its information. For example, in Word, each document is stored separately and stands alone. In Excel, each workbook might contain several different worksheets, yet there are no restrictions on the type of information that you can put into any part of the workbook. In PowerPoint, each file holds an entire presentation, although a presentation can contain different types of slides and various kinds of information.

In Access, however, there is a uniform structure for each database table, and everything must be placed into its appropriate storage compartment. If a field for a given record is left empty, Access displays that space even though there is currently no information in it.

The "Relational" in a Relational Database Management System

Database applications can be divided into two basic types: those that create *flat-file* databases and those that create *relational* databases. Flat-file databases have been around for many years. Among the current programs that create them are Microsoft Works and Microsoft Excel. In a flat-file database, all related information must fit into a single table. This means that any information that is common to several records will be repeated for each of those records. For example, a table with a

FIGURE 32-2.

In a flat-file database, duplicate information is common.

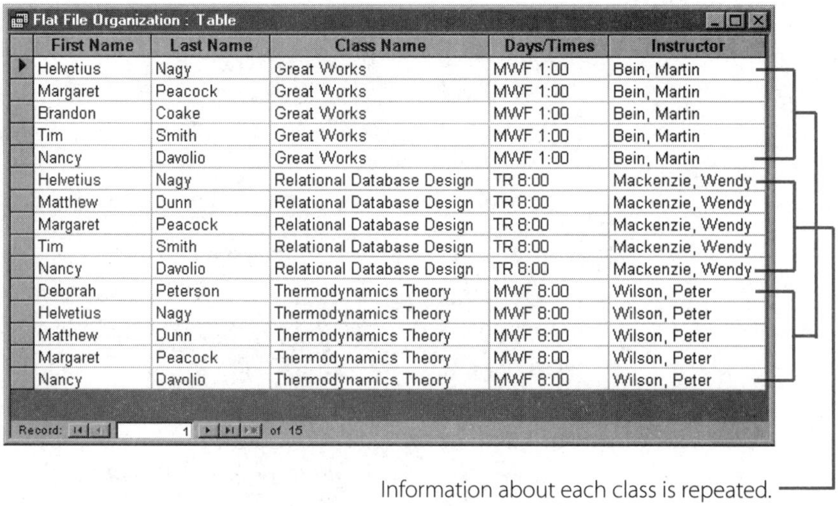

Information about each class is repeated. ────

collection of records, several of which contain duplicate information, is shown in Figure 32-2.

As computerized databases evolved in recent years into more sophisticated tools, it became obvious that a flat-file database was an inefficient way to store large quantities of data—and thus the idea of a relational database developed. This is the type of database created in Access. In a relational database, several different tables are used with *relationships* between the tables. A relationship lets you enter information into one table and connect that information to a record in another table via an identifier. Figure 32-3 shows the same information as Figure 32-2, but in the later figure the information is organized into two related tables, Enrollment and Classes. The Class ID field of the Enrollment table is linked or *related to* the Class ID field of the Classes table. Notice that the class information that was repeated in Figure 32-2 only needs to appear once in Figure 32-3, in the second table.

There are a number of advantages to structuring your data in a relational format:

■ You'll save considerable time by not having to enter the same data again and again across many records.

■ Your database will be smaller, often a small fraction of the size of a flat-file database, saving space on your system and making the database more portable if you want to share it with others.

FIGURE 32-3.
In a relational database, repeated information can be entered once in a separate table.

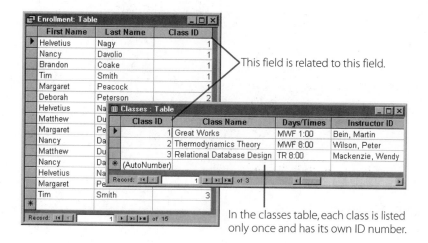

This field is related to this field.

In the classes table, each class is listed only once and has its own ID number.

- Data entry errors will be greatly reduced. Imagine entering the same data for a large number of records. How many times can you type *Thermodynamics Theory* into the Class Name field without error? If the repeated data is stored in a related table, you need to enter the correct information only once in the related table; then, in the original table, you enter only the identifier of the information—usually a short numeric or alphanumeric code—each time the repeated data occurs. (You can even set up the field so that you can simply select the identifier from a list, without typing anything!)

Updating data, such as a new instructor for one of the classes in the example that was just given, is a one-step process if you've stored the instructor names in a separate "Classes" table. If instead you had included the instructor names in the Enrollment table for each enrollment, you would have to manually update the name for every enrollment.

To see how multiple tables in an Access relational database are related, you can choose the Relationships command from the Tools menu in Access or, when the Database window is active, you can click the Relationships button on the Database toolbar to see the Relationships window shown in Figure 32-4 on the following page. Using the Relationships window is described in detail in the next chapter.

Relationships

FIGURE 32-4.
Access provides
an overview of
the relationships
among your tables.

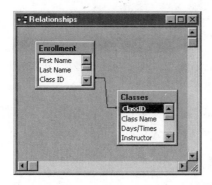

 NOTE

A next step in consolidating the example database shown in Figure 32-3 on the preceding page would be to place the First Name and Last Name fields of the Enrollment table (and any other information on each student) within a separate related table, because the student information is also repeated in several records. Then, the Enrollment table would need to store only a short identifier for each student who is referenced.

While relational databases have a number of advantages as far as speed and efficiency are concerned, understanding the theory isn't crucial for understanding how Access works. What you *do* need to understand is that a field is a category of information, an entry is the information that goes into a field for a single record, a record consists of the related entries for an individual item in the database (and fills up a row within a table), and you can set up relationships between separate tables so that repeated information need be entered only once.

The Database Window

Access stores all the objects belonging to a single database in one database file. This database file is what you open and work with when you use the Access program. The different objects belonging to a single database can include the tables that contain the actual data; the forms and reports that you use to present the data; queries, which you use to ask questions of the data; and modules and macros, which you use to automate tasks within the database. All the objects within a database are organized by their object type, and are displayed on tabs in the Database window as shown in Figure 32-5.

FIGURE 32-5.
The Database window organizes the objects that make up your database.

Reports tab

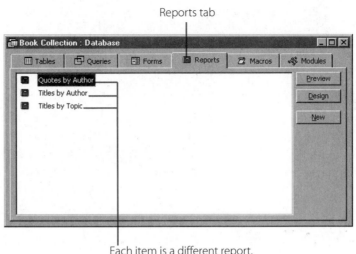

Each item is a different report.

Each tab at the top of the Database window represents a different kind of object within the database. Each item listed on a tab represents a distinct object.

> **NOTE**
>
> When you close the Database window, Access also closes all the associated database objects. If you have made changes to the *design* of the database objects but haven't saved the changes, Access asks whether to save those changes. Rest assured that any changes to the *data* stored in the database are automatically saved the moment you make them.

Moving to the Database Window

As you work with the different objects in your database, you might sometimes need to return to the Database window. You can do so in these ways:

■ Choose it from the Window menu. The Database window is always listed as the name of the database that you're working with, followed by a colon and the word *Database*. For example, if you're working with the Book Collection database, the menu item would be *Book Collection : Database*.

V

Microsoft Access

Database
Window

- Click the Database Window button at the right side of the toolbar.

- Click anywhere within the Database window if it's visible on your screen.

 **NOTE**

> You can use the various commands on the Edit menu to work with database objects themselves. To delete an object, select it in the Database window and then choose Delete from the Edit menu. To make a copy of an object, select it, choose Copy from the Edit menu, and then choose Paste from the Edit menu. Access prompts you for a name for the copy, and might require additional information about exactly what's to be copied. For example, with a table, you can copy the structure, copy both the structure and the data, or append the data to an existing table.

An Alternative—the Switchboard

When you create a database using a Database Wizard (described later in the chapter), in addition to the standard Database window for the database, you also get a Switchboard window like the one shown here:

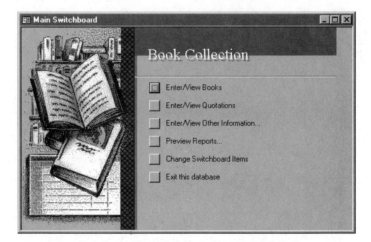

The Switchboard is basically a fancier and more automated Database window. It controls access to many of the various elements of the database environment created by the wizard, including forms for entering the data, collections of reports, and often a command for exiting the database. You have the option of working with the database only through the Switchboard, only through the Database window, or through a combination of the two. If your database has a Switchboard, it will probably appear in place of the Database window when you first open the database, and the Database window will be minimized at the bottom left corner of the Access window. To bypass the Switchboard, click its Minimize or Close button and click the Restore button in the Database window.

Database Objects

Access provides much more than just a container for a collection of data—it provides the tools you need to present meaningful information. You'll find that the various forms, reports, and queries that make up a database file can be as important as the tables used to hold your actual data.

 TIP

See What Objects Are in Your Database

You can determine the various objects that are in your database by choosing the Database Properties command from the File menu and then clicking the Contents tab. You can display the same information by right-clicking the title bar of a Database window and choosing Database Properties from the shortcut menu.

Working with Access database objects involves two key modes or phases of operation. We can summarize them as a *design phase* and an *editing phase*.

Before your database can manage your information, it must be designed. More than opening a new file in Microsoft Word or opening a blank worksheet in Microsoft Excel, in Microsoft Access each and every object within the database—including the tables that hold the data—must be designed. This is the process of initially creating the object and then customizing it to your needs. In most cases, you work in Design view, which offers you tools for making changes. Figure 32-6 on the following page shows a table in Design view and Figure 32-7 shows a form in Design view.

In both cases, the design of the object controls what you see when you work with data using that object. For example, the design of a table determines the type of data that you can enter into the table.

FIGURE 32-6.
Creating or modifying a table in Design view.

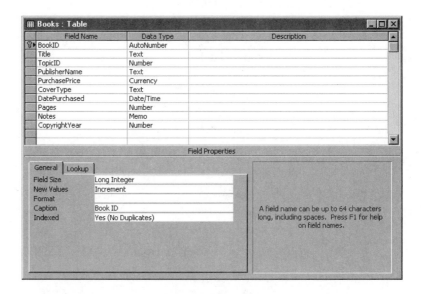

FIGURE 32-7.
Creating or modifying a form in Design view.

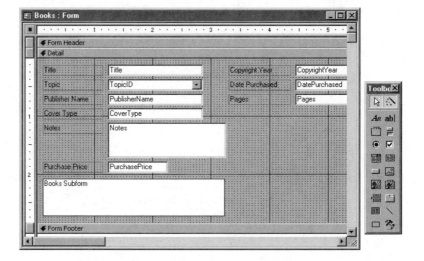

After the design phase, you use the various database objects to enter information, edit that information, query the database to retrieve the specific information you want, and print reports that present your data exactly the way you want. In these ways raw data is organized into meaningful information.

In the second or editing phase, Design view is traded for Datasheet or Form view, where data can be entered, edited, and managed, which we will discuss next.

While it might seem confusing at first, one of the truly helpful features in Access is that as you work with different types of database objects and switch between designing and using those objects, the menus and toolbar also change to reflect the tasks you need to perform. The commands that become available as different windows are activated are the ones that make sense for you to use in the current window.

TIP

If you have difficulty locating a command in Access, make sure that the proper object's window is active and that you're in the right view—that is, you're either using an object or designing one.

Tables

SEE ALSO

For more information on tables, see Chapter 33, "Creating Tables and Relationships." For details about datasheets, see Chapter 34, "Entering and Viewing Data with Datasheets."

As previously mentioned, the structure of a table is defined using Design view. Entering and editing the table's data is commonly done using Datasheet view. Datasheet view resembles an Excel worksheet, organized in rows and columns. In Access recall that each row represents a single record and each column a single field. Figure 32-8 shows an example of viewing the data in a table through Datasheet view.

You can sort and filter a table's data through the datasheet, as well as rearrange the layout of the datasheet itself. You can then print the datasheet, which will display the data exactly as it appears on the screen.

FIGURE 32-8.
Datasheet view is useful for displaying several records at a time.

Book ID	Title	Topic ID	Publisher Name	Purchase Price	Cover Type
1	Dirk Luchte	Fiction	GGG&G Publishing	$23.50	Hard
2	Planning Your Career	Business	Jean-Paul Deloria	$22.95	Hard
3	Diamonds	Romance	Ramona Publishing	$9.95	Paperback
4	Techniques of Tai Chi	Health	Ramona Publishing	$25.95	Hard
5	My Family	Fiction	GGG&G Publishing	$17.95	Paperback

Books : Table — :oNumber) — Record: 1 of 5

NOTE

As you'll learn later, you can also display an Access form or query in Datasheet view.

Microsoft Access

Forms

When you work with a form, you have much greater control over how the information is arranged than you have when working with tables in Datasheet view.

Forms are intended primarily for working with your data on screen. Figure 32-9 shows a typical Access form displayed in Form view. Form view typically displays only one record at a time and allows for text boxes, command buttons, pictures, and other objects that make the data easy to view and manage. If you want to see multiple records at a time, you can display a form in Datasheet view. Compare the presentation of data in Form view as shown in Figure 32-9 with the Datasheet view shown in Figure 32-8 on the preceding page.

FIGURE 32-9.
Form view makes it easy to view and enter data for a single record at a time.

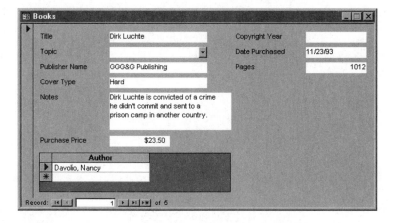

? SEE ALSO

Using forms and creating them with a wizard is covered in Chapter 35, "Entering and Viewing Data with Forms."

A powerful feature of using a form object is the ability to pull in data from more than one table. The form in Figure 32-9 displays information from two tables simultaneously. The data at the top of the form comes from a table containing specific information about each book. The data at the bottom of the form, labeled Author, comes from a separate table that stores the names of the authors of the books. (This arrangement lets you enter more than one author for a single book).

Reports

You use reports solely for printing information from the database. Designing a report not only lets you print information in an attractive

? **SEE ALSO**

Creating and using reports is treated in Chapter 37, "Generating Reports with Wizards," and modifying both reports and forms is covered in Chapter 38, "Formatting Forms and Reports."

and effective format; it also—like a form—lets you combine data from more than one table and organize data from one table based on the data from other tables, all in the same report. You design a report on screen using Design view, and you have to use your imagination to envision what the final report will look like. You design the report by adding visual objects known as *controls* to the design grid. Each control both displays an item of information and specifies the source of that information within the database, as well as its position on the printed report and its printed appearance. When you print your report, the facts and figures from your tables are neatly organized and summarized to create a report like the one shown in Figure 32-10. (This figure shows the report as displayed on screen using the Print Preview command, which lets you see how the report will look when printed.)

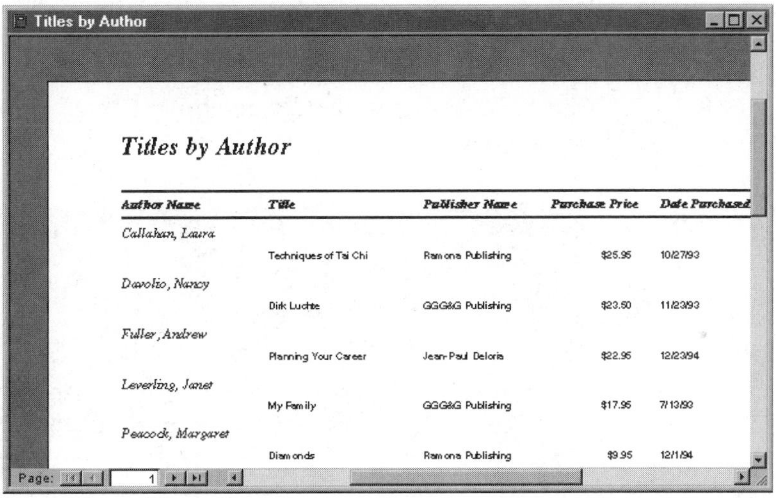

FIGURE 32-10.
Unlike other database objects, reports are intended to be printed rather than viewed on screen.

V

Microsoft Access

Queries

After you have created your tables and entered your data into them, the most important type of database object might be the query. It is through queries that you can gather selected information from your database and organize it either for use in reports or for viewing on screen through Datasheet or Form view.

You design a query in Design view, using it to ask a question of your database. The answer displays in Datasheet view, which looks exactly like Datasheet view for a table. The primary difference between a datasheet for a table and a datasheet for a query is that the query's datasheet can combine information from multiple tables, based on their related fields.

> To include the query results in forms or reports, you must first make sure the query design is saved. You then select the query object in place of a table object for your form or report design.

Each query consists of one or more criteria that you use to create a pattern or rule for selecting matching records. For example, if you use the criterion <30 in your Purchase Price field, the query will match only records for which the value in the Purchase Price field is less than 30. Figure 32-11 shows the design grid in Design view that you use to set up a query.

FIGURE 32-11.
Use Design view to ask for specific data.

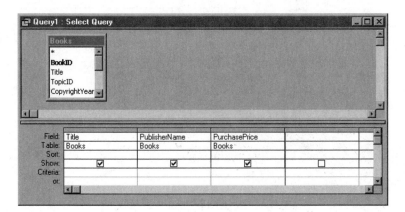

The data in each record is compared to the query criteria, and if the information in the record matches the criteria (for example, the price is less than $30), the record is included in the query's datasheet. Each query can contain multiple criteria. The criteria can be organized so that all must be true for a record to be included, or so that any single matching criterion is sufficient for including the record.

SEE ALSO
Queries are described in greater detail in Chapter 36, "Getting Answers with Queries."

In addition to asking questions, Design view can be set up to provide summary information about your data, as well as to group and organize the information in your database. These techniques rely on the use of a Total row, which can be added to the query design grid, and provide an on-screen alternative to generating and printing a report.

Programming Tools

Access also provides tools similar to those in Word and Excel for creating macros, as well as complete access to the Visual Basic for Applications (VBA) language. With these tools, you can automate many of the common tasks that you might want to perform with your database. Examples of this automation include the construction of complete databases through the Access Database Wizards. Going further, you can develop database systems that interact with data stored on other computer systems and that offer functions not available in the standard Access environment. These topics, however, fall within the realm of programming and are beyond the scope of this book.

Saving Data and Objects

Because the data is the most important thing in your database, Access automatically saves any changes that you make to your tables' contents the moment you make them.

On the other hand, the designs of various *objects* that you create for your database must be saved individually. For example, if you create a report to summarize the data in several of your tables, you must save that report within the database. When you do, Access asks you to provide a name for the report, and the name then appears within the Database window on the Reports tab. In general, you save the objects within the database while designing them, and Access takes care of saving the data while you work with the various objects.

Working with a Database

The first step in using Access is to create a database. Your starting place is the Microsoft Access dialog box (shown on the following page) that appears when you start Access.

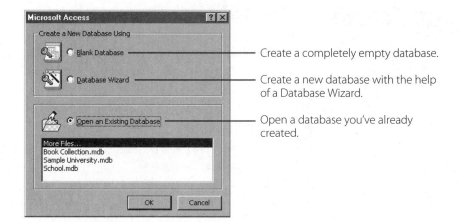

Create a completely empty database.

Create a new database with the help of a Database Wizard.

Open a database you've already created.

If you've already created a database, or if you want to examine a sample database supplied with Access, select the Open An Existing Database option and select a database file at the bottom of the Microsoft Access dialog box.

Creating a Blank Database

A blank database is just that—it contains neither tables, forms, reports, nor any other objects of any kind. You create each and every database object yourself. If you choose the Blank Database option when you first start the program, Access prompts you for the new database name by displaying the File New Database dialog box, shown in Figure 32-12. Enter the name and location for Access to use when storing the database, and click the Create button. Access will create the new database and open the Database window. You can then begin adding database objects using the techniques that will be given in the following chapters.

FIGURE 32-12.
The first step is always to name your database, using the File New Database dialog box.

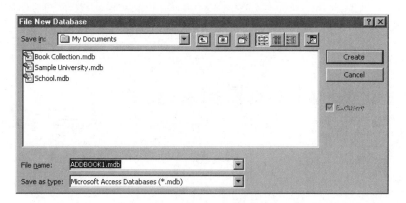

If you've already started Access, you can create a blank database by choosing the New Database command from the File menu, clicking the General tab in the New dialog box, and then double-clicking the Blank Database icon. The next section supplies more information on the New Database command.

Creating a Database with a Wizard

Another option for creating a new database is to use a Database Wizard. If you've just started Access, simply select Database Wizard in the Microsoft Access dialog box and click the OK button. Or, if you're already working in Access, you can choose the New Database command from the File menu, press Ctrl+N, or click the New Database button on the toolbar.

New Database

Whichever method you employ, Access opens the New dialog box; you should click the Databases tab, shown in Figure 32-13.

FIGURE 32-13.
The Databases tab of the New dialog box lists the Database Wizards.

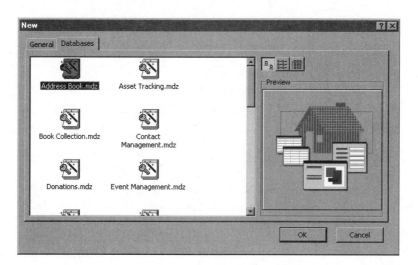

From the Databases tab, you can select the appropriate Database Wizard to use to build a database for you. (As you saw, the Blank Database icon on the General tab is for creating a blank database, forgoing the assistance of a wizard.)

Microsoft Access

⭐ **TIP**

You can also get to the various Database Wizards by choosing the New Office Document command from the Start menu or by clicking the New Office Document button on the Office Shortcut Bar. When the New Office Document dialog box appears, click the Databases tab.

Notice that when you click the icon for a particular Database Wizard, graphic information on the database appears in the Preview area to help you make your selection. Access provides wizards for creating databases that serve a wide variety of purposes, ranging from managing a collection (such as Music Collection, Picture Library, Video Collection, and Wine List) to organizing your diet and fitness (Recipes and Workout), and to tracking business accounts (such as Asset Tracking, Inventory Control, and Ledger). Select whichever wizard generates a database that meets your needs most closely. In the remaining chapters in this part of the book, you'll learn how to modify the database to match your needs exactly.

To start a Database Wizard, simply double-click the icon (scroll down to view additional icons). Access will then display the File New Database dialog box (see Figure 32-12, page 848), where you give the new database a name and save the database file on your hard disk.

The File New Database dialog box is similar to the Save As dialog box used in other Office programs—in fact, the only difference is its title. For general instructions on using this dialog box, see "Using the Save As Command," page 81. When you have specified a name and location for your database, click the Create button to have Access store the database file. The wizard will then open the Database window and begin its process of helping you design and create a complete database.

With most Database Wizards, the wizard's opening screen provides an overview of the tables that it will create. Figure 32-14 shows an example. When you click the Next button, you're generally given control over which fields from these tables the wizard will add to the database. You make these decisions in a dialog box similar to the one shown in Figure 32-15.

FIGURE 32-14.
The opening dialog box displayed by the "Book Collection" Database Wizard.

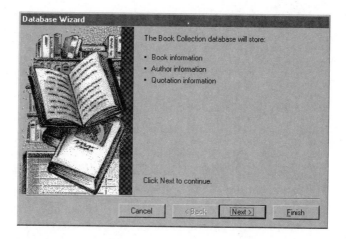

FIGURE 32-15.
The next dialog box shown by a Database Wizard generally lets you specify which fields to include in your new database tables.

These tables are included in the database.

These fields are included in the selected table.

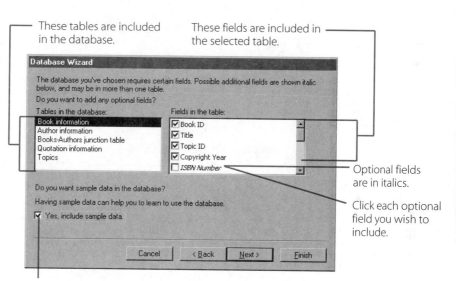

Optional fields are in italics.

Click each optional field you wish to include.

Click to include sample data to get you started.

NOTE

If you turn on the Yes, Include Sample Data option at the bottom of the Database Wizard dialog box, Access loads the database with a small *sample* of data records for you to experiment with. The various examples we present throughout this part of the book were created using this sample data. To follow along with any of the examples, simply create the appropriate database and turn on the Yes, Include Sample Data option. The fields included in our database examples are the same ones that Access selects by default.

V

Microsoft Access

The remaining dialog boxes displayed by the Database Wizard prompt you for the patterns for various types of objects, such as the background you want to use for screen displays on your forms, or the style you'd like for your reports. When you've made all your selections, click the Finish button, and Access will create the database with all the appropriate tables, forms, reports, and queries. Of course, you have the option of adding to these items and modifying them later.

Opening an Existing Database

Once a database has been created, there are several ways to open it from within Access. The first, which becomes available when you start Access, is the bottom portion of the Microsoft Access dialog box, shown here:

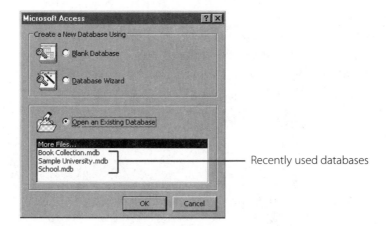

Recently used databases

The list at the bottom of the dialog box contains your most recently used databases. To open one, double-click its name. If a database that you want to use isn't included in this list, double-click the More Files option at the top of the list to display the Open dialog box, shown in Figure 32-16.

Open
Database

You can also display the Open dialog box by choosing Open Database from the File menu or by clicking the Open Database button on the toolbar.

The Open dialog box works the same way in Access as in the other Microsoft Office applications. In this dialog box, locate the folder that

FIGURE 32-16.
The Open dialog box displays all the databases on your system, folder by folder.

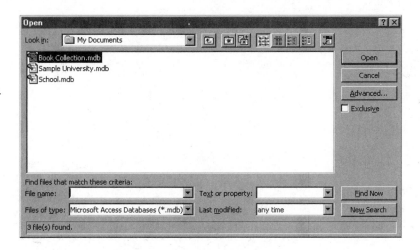

contains your database file and double-click the database file name to open it. You can use the file search features to help find a specific database. For instructions on searching for files, as well as general information on using the Open dialog box, see "Opening an Existing Document," page 66.

 TIP

> You can also open an Access database by choosing the Open Office Document command from the Start menu or by clicking the Open Office Document button on the Office Shortcut Bar. In the Files Of Type list at the bottom of the Open dialog box, you can select Microsoft Access Databases so that other types of files won't be displayed.

Many of the items created by the Database Wizards contain tools for simplifying your data entry and your work with the database. And as you work with your databases, you'll likely decide to build forms and reports of your own. In the remaining chapters of this part of the book, you'll gain an understanding of how these items work, and you'll acquire the skills for making your own modifications.

V

Microsoft Access

CHAPTER 33

Creating Tables and Relationships

The organization of the tables and the relationships among them determine how you'll be able to access the information contained in your database. When you generate a database using one of the Database Wizards, Access creates the tables and the relationships for you. If, however, you want to go beyond what Access can do for you, you need to learn how to design, create, and modify your own tables and their relationships.

Designing Your Database Foundation

One of the least understood aspects of creating a database—and what makes it different from using any other type of application—is that much of the work must be done away from the computer, *before* you start working in Access. Whereas you can sit down at a word processor and start drafting a memo to be edited later, or start typing numbers into a spreadsheet, intending to divine your formulas at the last minute, it's less efficient to design your database on the computer than away from it.

The process of designing your database consists of several distinct steps. You might be best served by sitting down with a pad of paper and several sharp pencils with erasers; or, if you prefer, you can use Word for this step, creating and maintaining an electronic version of a design document.

Decide on the content of your fields.   The first step is to identify what fields of information you want to include in your database. You should try to identify every element that you might ever want to store and access. For example, if you're creating a database about books, you would obviously want to include the book's title, author, and subject. But you might also want to consider including the publication date, the publisher's name, whether or not the book contains figures, the book's page count, its price (domestic and overseas, if applicable), whether it's paperback or hardcover, and so on.

How Much Data Is Enough?

It's essential to balance the usefulness of having lots of information against the difficulty of managing it. While it might be tempting to design a database that includes every possible fact, you'll quickly tire of filling in all the necessary fields when it's time to enter your data. Therefore, you must include only the information that you really think you'll use. Still, it's better to include too many fields than too few. You'll find it easier to stop filling in some of your less-essential fields than to go back later and add fields that require you to update every record manually. Imagine cataloging an extensive music collection and then realizing you forgot to include a field telling whether each item was on CD, tape, or LP album!

Decide on the type of information for your fields.   Next you need to identify the type of information that will go into each field. Your primary choices are text, numbers, and dates, although Access provides several other options. (The various data types for fields are described later in this chapter in "Working with the Design of a Table," page 863.)

Design your database framework.   The process of designing the framework of the database involves taking the field names and data types and deciding how to organize them within your database. This means deciding which fields should appear within a given table, and in what order. When the database is organized and set up properly, you'll be able to arrange the fields in your reports and on screen in almost any manner conceivable.

Relate your tables to one another.   Another design consideration is whether to relate tables to one another, which is desirable if the information in some fields in a table is repeated in several records. By moving these fields into a separate table and setting up a relationship between the two tables, you can save considerable space and improve the accuracy of your data. For example, you might have a Books table that lists information on each book in a collection, and many of these books likely will have the same publisher. You might therefore consider placing the information on each publisher (its name, address, and so on) in a separate table, perhaps named "Publishers," giving each publisher an identifying ID, and establishing a relationship between the two tables. Then, in your Books table, you would simply type the ID for each publisher rather than having to type the publisher's name and other information each time it occurs. The process of organizing and arranging your fields into one or more tables and creating relationships to eliminate duplicated information is called *normalization*. Access provides some assistance with this rather complex process by providing a Table Analyzer Wizard, described in the sidebar "Analyzing an Existing Table," page 878, in the last part of this chapter.

Designate your fields as primary keys or indexes.   Another important concept is that of designating fields in your tables as *primary keys* or as *indexes*. A primary key consists of one or more fields that uniquely identify each record in a table. Designating a field as an index (that is, "indexing it") increases the speed of searches or sorts performed with that field. A field designated as a primary key is automatically indexed, but you might want to index additional fields that you'll use frequently for searches or sorts. Primary keys and indexes should be part of your planning process and are usually defined as each table is created. They're discussed more fully later in the chapter. Identifying relationships between data in separate tables, understanding when it's best to split information into two or more tables, and determining primary keys and indexes are the skills that underlie quality database design.

Start building your database on the computer. At this point, you can begin creating your database on the computer. You now know the definitions that you need for each table and the relationships between the tables. However, there's still planning to be done. You should consider how you want the data entered. Will you be importing it from another source that's already computerized, copying it from a list, or entering each item separately? Some questions to consider are these:

- Are there certain tables that should be completed first? Would it be worthwhile, for example, to develop a list of all the publishers, assign them IDs, and have that list available as you enter book information?

- Are there default values that you might consider having Access assign for you? This is particularly common for address databases where most of the addresses are within a single city or state.

- Are there additional fields that you might want to include for asking particular types of questions, or for creating reports? In general, these types of fields consist of information that might be used to group the records. For example, you might decide to include information in your Book Collection database indicating where each book is located.

 TIP

Let Access Perform Your Calculations

If there are values that can be derived by performing math on other fields in your tables, they shouldn't be part of a table's structure. Fields whose values are the result of calculations can be added to forms, queries, or reports without being a part of a table. This allows Access (rather than the data entry person) to perform the calculation and eliminates storing unnecessary information. For example, if you want to display an inventory of office supplies, your table only needs two fields: Units On Hand (for example, number of boxes of pencils), and Measure Of Unit (for example, 12 pencils to a box). Access can do the multiplication and display it in a field on a form or print it in a report.

Creating a Table Using the Table Wizard

? SEE ALSO

For information on working with datasheets, see Chapter 34, "Entering and Viewing Data with Datasheets." For information about defining the table's structure, see "Working with the Design of a Table," page 863. For help in importing a table, see "Importing Data," page 874.

As with other database objects in Access, you have the option of using a wizard to help you create a new table. In Access, the Table Wizard will walk you through the process of creating a table based on a table in one of its Database Wizards. You simply choose the table that most closely matches the kind of data you need to track, and then select the specific fields that you want to include.

Before you can use a wizard to help you create a database object, the database file that's to receive the new object must already exist and be open, even if it's a completely empty database created using the Blank template. Our sample Sales database already contains two tables, Customers and Products. See "Working with a Database," page 847, for more information about creating a database. The following is the procedure for using the Table Wizard to create a new table:

1 Select the Tables tab in the Database window, and click the New button, as shown in Figure 33-1. Access will display the New Table dialog box, which is shown in Figure 33-2 on the following page. This dialog box lets you choose from a variety of different ways to create a new table. In this procedure, however, you'll create the table using the Table Wizard.

2 Select the Table Wizard option from the list in the New Table dialog box and click OK. Access will then display the first Table Wizard dialog box, which is shown in Figure 33-3 on the following page.

V

Microsoft Access

FIGURE 33-1.
Click the New button on the Tables tab to start creating a new table.

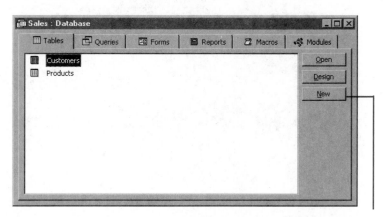

Click here to create a new table.

FIGURE 33-2.
Access offers several different methods for creating a new table.

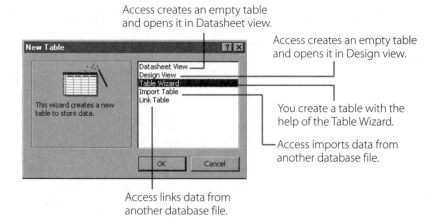

Access creates an empty table and opens it in Datasheet view.

Access creates an empty table and opens it in Design view.

You create a table with the help of the Table Wizard.

Access imports data from another database file.

Access links data from another database file.

3 Scroll through the Sample Tables list box until you find one that seems similar to what you need, and then select it. We selected Orders in our example.

4 Now check the associated fields in the Sample Fields list box. If your table selection was appropriate, the sample fields should provide you with what you need for your new table. Use the four buttons shown in Figure 33-3 to copy the fields you want to the Fields In My New Table list box.

FIGURE 33-3.
The first Table Wizard dialog box lets you select the fields for your new table.

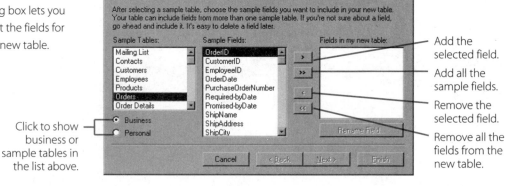

Add the selected field.

Add all the sample fields.

Remove the selected field.

Remove all the fields from the new table.

Click to show business or sample tables in the list above.

It is possible to include fields from more than one sample table in your new table. Simply select different tables from the Sample Tables list as you're compiling your list of fields on the right.

5 Once you have added a field, you can rename it. Simply select the field name in the Fields In My New Table list box and click the Rename Field button. Access opens a small dialog box in which you type the new name and click OK.

6 When you've finished selecting fields, click the Next button and the second Table Wizard dialog box will appear (see Figure 33-4). Here you can change the default name for your table and decide whether to let Access select the primary key for you. If you're not sure how to select a key, let Access do it for you, or read the section "Designating a Primary Key," page 873. Click the Next button.

7 If your database contains more than one table, the dialog box shown in Figure 33-5 on the following page appears and lets you set relationships between your new table and any of the existing tables in your database. The wizard might be able to suggest one or more relationships for you, and will list them in the dialog box. To add, change, or remove a relationship with a table, select the table from the list and click the Relationships button. You'll learn more about defining relationships in the section "Relating Your Tables," page 875. Click Next to continue.

FIGURE 33-4.
The second Table Wizard dialog box lets you specify the table name and decide whether to let the wizard set the primary key.

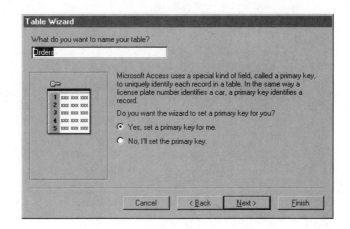

FIGURE 33-5.
This dialog box appears only if your database already contains other tables.

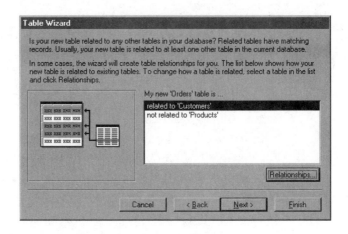

SEE ALSO
For more information on entering data through Datasheet view, see Chapter 34, "Entering and Viewing Data with Datasheets." For details about using forms, see Chapter 35, "Entering and Viewing Data with Forms."

8 The final dialog box of the Table Wizard (Figure 33-6) gives you the following choices about what to do after Access creates your table:

- Modify the table design (this takes you directly to Design view, where you can work with the table's structure).

- Enter data directly into the table using Datasheet view.

- Have the wizard create a form for you to use to enter data.

If you'll be entering data from the keyboard, consider having Access create the form for you. After making a choice, click the Finish button and Access will complete your table.

TIP

Let Access Define Your Table
After you have selected the fields you want in the first Table Wizard dialog box, click the Finish button anytime during the remainder of the creation process to have the wizard create the table using any settings you've already made (plus the default choices for all the remaining settings). If you accept *all* the default choices, the wizard gives the table a standard name, defines the primary key, automatically assigns any relationships it finds, and opens the new table in Datasheet view for you to begin entering data.

FIGURE 33-6.
The final Table Wizard dialog box lets you choose how to begin working with your new table.

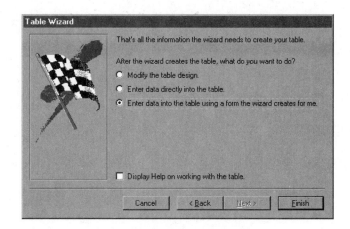

Working with the Design of a Table

To define or modify the structure of a table, you use Design view. This view lets you add, remove, or rearrange fields; define the name, the data type, and other properties of each field; and designate a primary key for the table. You can use Design view to create a new table or to modify an existing one.

The following are several different ways to open a table in Design view; you should choose the one that's most appropriate for your current stage in working with the table:

- If you've created a new table using the Table Wizard, refer back to step 8 of the previous section. At this point you should select the Modify The Table Design option. Access will open the newly generated table in Design view.

- To create and open a new, blank table, click the New button in the Database window and in the New Table dialog box select the Design View option. Access will open the table in Design view.

- To modify the design of a table you've already created, select the Tables tab in the Database window, select your table, and then click the Design button.

View

■ If your table is already open in Datasheet view, you can switch to Design view by choosing the Design command from the View menu, or by clicking the View button at the left end of the toolbar.

Figure 33-7 shows the Books table from the Book Collection sample database in Design view. The top half of the window lists the table's fields, data type, and an optional description. If you're using Design view to create a new table, this list will initially be empty. The bottom half of the window shows the properties for the currently selected field and lets you modify them, with the help provided in the lower right text box for each property you click on.

FIGURE 33-7.
Design view lists all of the table's fields and their properties.

Primary key field   Each row is a field; click to select a field.

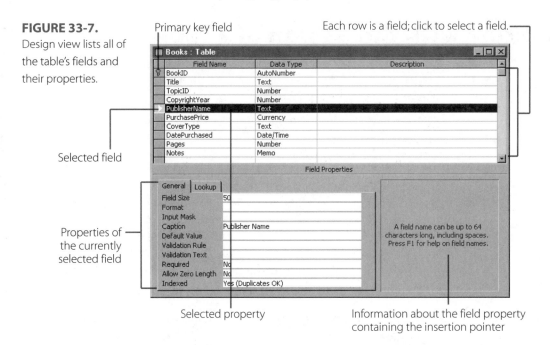

Selected field

Properties of the currently selected field

Selected property   Information about the field property containing the insertion pointer

Adding, Removing, and Rearranging Fields

Using Design view, you can add new fields to a table, remove fields, and move or copy fields from one position in the list of fields to another.

Adding a Field

To create a new field for the table, click in the Field Name column of the first blank row in the grid at the top of the Table Design window and enter a field name. You can type up to 64 characters for the field name, including spaces. Ideally, however, you should make the name short and descriptive of the contents of the field. You should then proceed to set any of the field properties that you want to change from their default values, following the instructions that will be given later (in the section "Setting the Field Properties").

To insert a new field between two existing fields, do any of the following:

- Select the lower field, and then choose the Rows command from the Insert menu.

Insert
Rows

- Select the lower field, and then click the Insert Rows button on the toolbar.

- Select the lower field, and then click the right, or secondary, mouse button. A shortcut menu appears. Choose the Insert Rows command.

- Select the entire lower row by clicking in the column at the far left. The entire row is selected. Press the Insert key.

	Field Name	Data Type	Description
🔑	BookID	AutoNumber	
	Title	Text	
▶	TopicID	Number	
	PublisherName	Text	
	PurchasePrice	Currency	

⊞ Books : Table

This row was selected by clicking here.

 NOTE

The order in which the fields are listed in Design view (from top to bottom) is the same order in which they'll be shown in Datasheet view (from left to right). Arranging the fields in a certain order might be more logical and make it easier to enter or modify the data. The field order in Design view, however, *doesn't* affect the order of the fields on forms, queries, or reports.

V

Microsoft Access

Removing a Field

To remove a field from the table, click anywhere in the field's row and do one of the following:

■ Choose the Delete Rows command from the Edit menu.

Delete
Rows

■ Click the Delete Rows button on the Table Design toolbar.

■ Click the right mouse button. Choose Delete Rows from the shortcut menu.

■ Select the entire row by clicking in the leftmost box, and then press Delete.

You won't be able to delete a field that's used to create a relationship with another table; you must first remove the relationship.

⚠ **WARNING**

> If your table already contains data, Access will ask for confirmation before actually deleting a field. Be aware that deleting a field will delete its data for *every record of your table*.

Moving or Copying a Field

To move a field to a different position in the list, first select the entire row by clicking in the box at the left of the row. Then do one of the following:

■ Use the mouse to drag the box up or down to the new position.

Drag this box to move
field up or down in list. ——

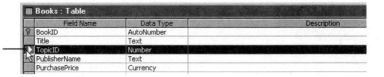

■ Choose the Cut command from the Edit menu. Then select the row where you want the field inserted. Choose Paste from the Edit menu.

■ Click the right mouse button to display the shortcut menu and choose Cut. Select the row where you want the field inserted. Right-click the mouse and choose Paste.

■ Press Ctrl+X to cut the field. Select the row where you want the field inserted and press Ctrl+V.

> If you want to copy both a field and its properties, use the Copy command or Ctrl+C key combination instead of the Cut command in the above steps. After the field is copied, click on the field name and type in a different, unique name.

Setting the Field Properties

Each of the fields in a table is described by a set of *properties*. The properties of a field determine how the field's data is stored, handled, or displayed. They include the field name, the data type, the description, and other features such as the field size, format, and caption. You can view and set a field's properties within the boxes in the Table Design window (both in the grid at the top of the window and on the tabs in the bottom portion). (See Figure 33-7, page 864.) Note that when the insertion point is within a property box, Access displays information about that property in the lower right corner of the window, and you can get more detailed information by pressing F1.

As you saw in the previous section, when you create a new field in Design view, you must enter a name for it. Initially, each of the other properties of the new field will have a default value. Sometimes the default is no setting at all, and the property box will be blank. You can modify any of these properties, or you can simply accept the default.

Renaming a Field

To change the name property of a field, simply click in the box containing the name (which is in the Field Name column) and type in the name you want. Changing the field name doesn't affect any of the existing table relationships or change anything within your database.

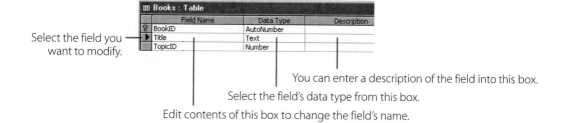

Select the field you want to modify.

You can enter a description of the field into this box.

Select the field's data type from this box.

Edit contents of this box to change the field's name.

Despite what you would expect, changing a field's name might not even change the name that appears at the top of the field columns in Datasheet view. This is because the field name displays in Datasheet view only if you haven't entered a more customized name in the Caption property, one of the field properties you can set in Design view. This property will be described in more detail later.

Setting the Data Type

The data type determines the kind of data that can be entered into a field. As previously mentioned, each field in an Access table must be assigned a data type. Access provides a variety of data types, as described in Table 33-1. The default type is Text.

To enter or change the data type for a field, click in the Data Type column for the field that you want to change, and select a new data type from the drop-down list:

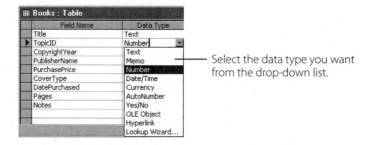

Select the data type you want from the drop-down list.

Setting Other Field Properties

If you wish, you can enter a description for a field into the Description column.

The remaining field properties are set through the General and Lookup tabs in the bottom half of the Design view window. To set additional properties for a field, do the following:

1 Make sure you've selected the field you want in the top half of the table window.

2 Click the General tab in the lower half of the table window, or select Lookup to change the properties of a lookup field.

TABLE 33-1.   Data Types Used in Access

Data Type	Usage
Text (default)	Holds any type of characters, either letters or numbers. The number of characters that can be stored depends on the value (0 to 255) assigned to the Field Size property (described later). Even if you set the characters to 255, Access will use only the amount of memory required by each entry.
Memo	Similar to Text but holds up to 64,000 characters.
Number	Holds a numeric value that you can use to perform mathematical calculations or comparisons. The size and type of number you can store is determined by the current setting of the Field Size property (described later).
Date/Time	Holds valid calendar dates for the years 100 through 9999 and clock times in both 12- and 24-hour formats. This data type lets you sort and calculate data chronologically.
Currency	Most accurate way to enter monetary values for use in financial calculations.
AutoNumber	A field that increments itself automatically as each new record is added. Numbers aren't reused when you delete records, and you can't change the value of an AutoNumber field.
Yes/No	Most efficient way to store a single value that indicates yes or no, on or off, true or false, and so on. The field can be set through a check box on a form.
OLE Object	Holds an OLE object (such as an Excel spreadsheet, a Word document, or a picture, sound, animation, or video clip) that is inserted via the Object command on the Insert menu. See Chapter 39, "Sharing Data Among Office Applications," for information on OLE objects.
Hyperlink	Holds a *hyperlink*—that is, the *location* of another database object, an Office document, or a page on the World Wide Web. You insert the hyperlink into the field via the Hyperlink command on the Insert menu. You can then open the target object, document, or Web page by clicking the hyperlink in the field.
Lookup Wizard	This adds a drop-down list box, from which you can click the entry for the field from a scrolling list of data from another table or list that you've created beforehand. For instance, you could have a book publisher lookup field that drops down a scrolling list of publishers, allowing you to merely click the correct publisher rather than type in the full name. (The list that appears when you click in the Data Type property box is itself a lookup field.)

V

Microsoft Access

3 Click on any property you want to modify and enter the new value. Use the help window on the right, or press F1 for detailed information about the current property.

The set of additional properties that you can apply to a field depends on the field's data type. In general, these properties control the way data is entered, stored, and displayed in the field, and they also provide a means of enforcing the integrity and consistency of your data. The following sections describe most of the important properties.

Field Size Property

The Field Size property lets you determine how much space is available for a particular field. It is available only for a field with the Text or Number data type. For a Text field, the Field Size specifies the maximum number of characters that can be stored in the field; you can enter a value between 0 and 255 (the default value is 50). For a Number field, you choose a value from the drop-down list that determines the type of number that can be stored:

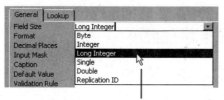

Select a value from the drop-down list to specify the type of value that can be stored in a Number field.

For example, you can choose the default Long Integer value to store whole numbers ranging from -2 million to +2 million, or the Double value to store numbers with decimal components (such as 3.14).

Format Property

The Format property determines the way the data is displayed on the screen or is printed. Choose the format that you want from the drop-down list. For example, for a field with the Date/Time data type, you could choose to display the date as 30-Jun-97, 6/30/97, and so on.

Decimal Places Property

The Decimal Places property lets you choose the number of decimal places that are displayed for a field with the Number or Currency data type. (It affects only the *way* the number is displayed, not the *precision* of the value that is stored internally.) Choose a specific number of decimal places from the drop-down list, or choose Auto (the default value) to display the number of decimal places specified by the Format property.

Input Mask Property

With most data types, you also have a choice of defining an *input mask* (by default, there is no input mask). An input mask controls how information can be entered into the field. Assigning an input mask can make it easier to enter data into the field, and can help ensure that the data is entered in the proper format. Figure 33-8 shows an input mask for a date field in the Book Collection database.

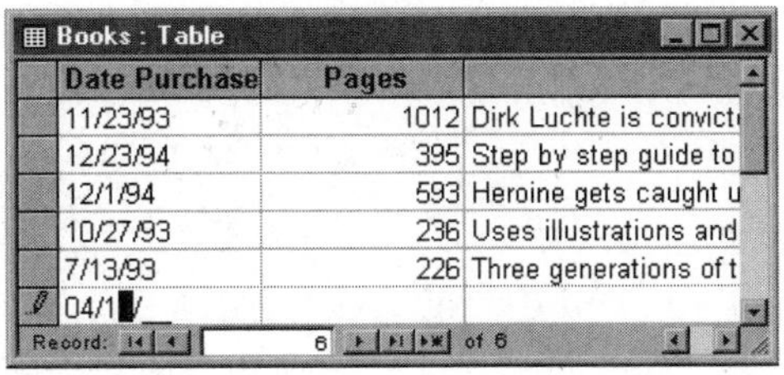

FIGURE 33-8.

This input mask encourages you to enter the date in numeric format.

Date Purchase	Pages	
11/23/93	1012	Dirk Luchte is convict
12/23/94	395	Step by step guide to
12/1/94	593	Heroine gets caught u
10/27/93	236	Uses illustrations and
7/13/93	226	Three generations of t
04/1		

Books : Table

Record: 6 of 6

An input mask is created by using a series of codes as placeholders. For example, the input mask for the date in Figure 33-8 is specified as 99/99/00. The *9* means only a number can be entered, but is not required; the *0* means only a number can be entered and *is* required; and the / (slash) marks are passed through as constants. For a complete description of the input mask codes, press F1 while the insertion point is in the Input Mask property box.

NOTE

> Access provides the Input Mask Wizard to guide you in setting up an input mask without entering codes manually. Activate it by clicking the Build button, the ellipsis (…), at the right side of the Input Mask property box.

Caption Property

If you enter text into the box for the Caption property, Access will use this text to label the field in Datasheet view, as well as on forms and reports. If you leave the Caption box empty (the default value), Access labels the field using the field name. This give you flexibility in how you want your fields to appear for those viewing your database or entering data into it, without your having to change the actual field name.

V

Microsoft Access

Default Value Property

Another item that you might want to change is the Default Value. If you're creating a database in which a field usually contains the same value—for example, the City field in an address database with most of the addresses in the same city—you can assign that value to the Default Value property. Then, whenever Access creates a new record, it will insert the value into the field for you (for example, *New Orleans*). Of course, you can then change the value if you need to enter another city. To assign a default value, type the information into the Default Value property box. Or, click the Build button (with three dots) that appears to the right of the box to get help in building a complex expression.

Required Property

If you select Yes in the Required property box, Access will *require* that a value be entered into the field when the record is created or modified. If you choose No (the default value), the field can be left empty.

Indexed Property

You can also determine whether a field is indexed. Indexing a field significantly speeds up searching or sorting operations, as well as queries done on the field, but it requires more space for storing the information and can make adding, deleting, or updating records slower. The primary key for a table (discussed in the next section) is automatically indexed. These are the choices available from the Indexed drop-down list:

- Yes (Duplicates OK)—The field will be indexed and you'll be able to enter the same value into more than one record.

- Yes (No Duplicates)—The field will be indexed and you must enter a unique value into the field for each record so that the index will always be able to retrieve a single record based only on the information in this field.

- No—The field won't be indexed. This is the default.

Indexes

To see a list of all the indexed fields in a table, choose Indexes from the View menu or click the Indexes button on the toolbar.

Designating a Primary Key

While a primary key isn't required, every table should be assigned one. The primary key consists of one or more fields that Access can use to uniquely identify and organize the records contained within the table. When you designate a field (or several fields) as the primary key, the field's Indexed property is automatically set to Yes (No Duplicates), and you won't be able to change this setting. Thus, the records can be quickly sorted or retrieved by the primary key field, and you'll be barred from entering duplicate values into this field. Also, when you enter or modify the data in a record, Access doesn't let you leave a primary key field blank.

In most cases, just a single field is used as the primary key, though in situations where the data in a single field can't be unique for each record, two or more fields might be designated. In this case, the data in all the primary key fields combined must be unique for each record. (For example, an inventory table might contain a part number field and a subpart number field; neither is unique by itself but, when taken together to form the complete part number, *are* unique.)

If you used the Access Table Wizard to create your table as we described earlier in this chapter, you probably had Access create the primary key for you. If not, or if you want to change the primary key Access selected, you can set it now by clicking the field that you want to use as the primary key. Choose Primary Key from the Edit menu or click the Primary Key button on the toolbar.

Primary
Key

To designate multiple fields as the primary key, you must select *all* the fields before choosing the Primary Key command or clicking the Primary Key button. Recall that to select a field, you click on the button at the far left of the row containing the field (the entire field will then be highlighted). To select several fields, select the first one and then select each additional one while holding down the Ctrl key.

Saving the Table Design

Whenever you create or modify a table's definition in Design view, you must save your work before you can enter or edit data. Access will give you the opportunity to save your changes when you close Design view. If you're making extensive changes, however, you should also periodically save your work by choosing Save from the File menu, by pressing Ctrl+S, or by clicking the Save button on the toolbar.

Save

If the table has no data, Access quickly saves the table's structure and lets you either continue working on the table design or switch to Datasheet view to begin entering data. If there's data already stored in the table, however, Access checks to see if the new structure can hold the old data or if the changes would cause a conflict.

If your design changes caused a problem, you'll see an error message. You should then write down the design changes you want to make (so that you can implement them later), abandon the changes you made by closing the table *without* saving the changes, and then open the table in Datasheet view and make any necessary modifications. For example, if you change the Indexed property of a field to Yes (No Duplicates), Access can save this design modification only if the field contains no duplicates. If the field *does* contain duplicates, Access advises you to go to the table and modify the contents of the field to eliminate the duplicates. (An easy way to find the duplicates is to sort the table on that field, as described in the section "Sorting Your Information," page 892.)

Importing Data

You can create a new table in an Access database by importing data from another database file. You can import data from a database file that was created by the current version of Access, by a previous version of Access, or by another program (such as Excel, dBASE, or Paradox).

To create a new table by importing data, follow these steps:

1 Create or open the database that will receive the imported data.

2 On the Tables tab of the Database window, click the New button to display the New Table dialog box.

3 Select the Import Table option, and click OK to start the Import Wizard. The Import Wizard will begin by displaying the Import dialog box, shown in Figure 33-9.

FIGURE 33-9.
The first step in importing data is to locate it.

5 Select the data file.

6 Click to start the Import Wizard.

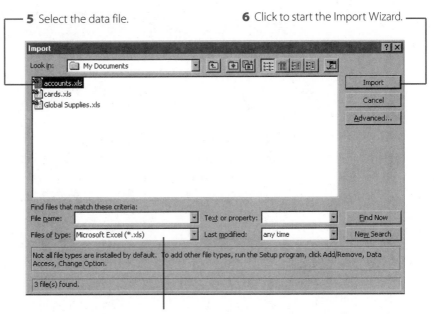

4 Select the file type of the program the data is coming from.

7 The next dialog box that you see in the wizard varies, depending on the type of program that was used to manage the data you're importing. An Access database or Excel spreadsheet will be displayed with its fields or rows and columns and let you specify how to import the data, while a dBASE file will be imported in its entirety without any choices made by you.

8 Make the choices you want in all the dialog boxes the Import Wizard displays. When you click the Finish button, the Wizard will create a new table that will contain the imported data. If some of your records fail to import correctly, Access creates an Error table listing any problems. If this happens it's usually best to go back to your original data file, correct the errors, and then import the table again.

Relating Your Tables

We have already explained the advantages of separating repetitive information in your database into additional, related tables. (To review these advantages, see the section "The 'Relational' in a Relational

---

Linking Data

When you import data, a *copy* of the data is brought into the new table, where it becomes an integral part of the database and is indistinguishable from data entered using Access. As an alternative, you can create a new table by *linking* it to data within another database file. When you link to data, the data is *not* copied into the new table, but rather remains within the original database file. Access, however, stores a connection to this file so that you can view or modify the data using an Access table. (You can also view or modify the data using the database program that originally created the file.)

To create a new table by linking, follow the same basic procedure as when importing data, except choose the Link Table option rather than the Import Table option in the New Table dialog box.

Database Management System," page 835.) Although *you* might be aware of the connection between a field in one table and a field in another table, it's important that the connection be explicitly defined within Access. Such a definition is known as a *relationship*, and each of the fields is said to be *related to* the other field. The tables containing these fields are also said to be related. Once a relationship has been designated, Access can help you maintain the integrity of the related data and can make it easier to access related data (for example, a lookup column, described in Table 33-1, page 869, can let you choose a valid linking value from a related field rather than having to remember it and type it in manually.) Relationships also allow you to create queries, forms, and reports that display information from several tables at once (queries, forms, and reports are discussed in the following chapters).

To see the existing relationships among tables in a database, open the database and choose the Relationships command from the Tools menu, or, if the Database window is active, click the Relationships button at the right end of the toolbar. Access will open the Relationships window, as shown in Figure 33-10, and add the Relationships menu to your menu bar.

The lines between the table lists indicate relationships between specific fields. The symbols at the ends of some lines represent the type of relationship and will be explained later in this section.

FIGURE 33-10.
By moving the table lists, you can make the relationships easier to see.

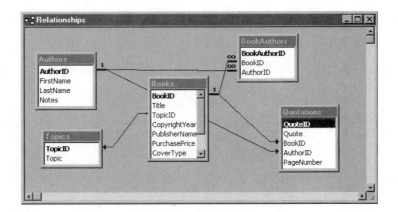

It's important when working with the Relationships window to arrange your table lists so that the relationship lines can be seen clearly. You can move a table list in the Relationships window by using the mouse to drag its title bar. Do this to untangle the relationship lines and make them easy to see and understand.

When a scroll bar appears at the right side of the table list, it indicates that only some of the field names are visible. (Notice the Books list in Figure 33-10.) To remove the scroll bar and to see all the fields at a glance, you can increase the height of the table list by dragging the top or bottom edge of its list box. Likewise, you can increase the width of the table by dragging the sides so that the complete field names are visible. Figure 33-11 on the following page displays the same relationships as Figure 33-10, but with the tables arranged more neatly.

 NOTE

> If you used a Database Wizard to create your database system, Access will create all the necessary relationships among your tables. Also, when you create a new table using the Table Wizard, you can have the wizard create relationships between the new table and existing tables in the database (see step 8 in the section "Creating a Table Using the Table Wizard," page 859). At any time you can have the Table Analyzer Wizard (see the sidebar on the following page) suggest relationships between tables. In general, it's easier to let Access creates relationships for you. You might, however, need to modify or remove a relationship, or add a new one. The instructions given in the remainder of this section will show you how.

FIGURE 33-11.
The relationship lines are untangled, and the Books table list has been enlarged to show all its fields.

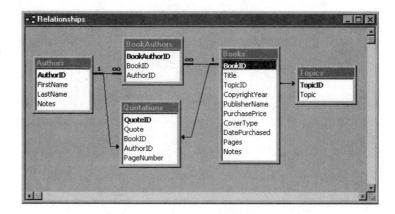

You'll now learn how to add, modify, or remove individual relationships. In a typical relationship, the field in *one* of the two tables has a unique index. That is, Access requires that you enter a different value into the field for each record. A unique field would be a primary key field or any field whose Indexed property is set to the value Yes (No Duplicates). The other table's field in a typical relationship has a nonunique index; that is, its Indexed property is set to No or to Yes (Duplicates OK). The table containing the unique field is commonly known as the *primary* table, and the table containing the nonunique field is commonly known as the *related* table. Because a field in the primary table can match several fields in the related table, the relationship between these fields is called a *one-to-many* relationship.

Analyzing an Existing Table

Say you have a table that was created from a source outside Access, or you realize that a table you've created using Access contains several fields with information that repeats regularly. It's a good idea to let Access analyze such a table, to determine whether it would be best to split it into a series of related tables.

To start this process, choose Analyze from the Tools menu and then choose Table from the submenu that appears. The Table Analyzer Wizard starts and guides you through its various steps. The first time you use this wizard for a given database, it describes the purpose for analyzing the table and the process of reducing repetitive data. In general, if a table contains one or more fields that contain repeated data, the wizard will give you the option of putting those fields into one or more separate tables that are related to the original.

To illustrate a one-to-many relationship, consider the example tables discussed in Chapter 32 and shown here in Figure 33-12. In the primary table, Classes, each class is listed once; therefore, each class's ID, the primary key, occurs only once, making it a unique field. In the secondary table, Enrollment, many people enroll in the same class; therefore, the related Class ID field often contains the same value, making it a nonunique field and completing the one-to-many relationship.

FIGURE 33-12.

In a one-to-many relationship, one record in the primary table can match several records in the related table.

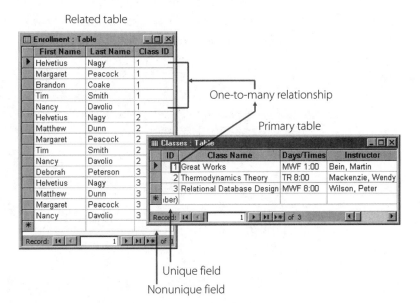

Related table

One-to-many relationship

Primary table

Unique field

Nonunique field

> **NOTE**
>
> Although it rarely occurs, *both* fields in a relationship can be unique; in this case, the relationship is known as *one-to-one*. It's also possible to indirectly create a *many-to-many* relationship by using a third, related table. These types of relationships are less common than the one-to-many relationship and are not discussed in the book. For more information, look up "relationships" in the Access online Help Index.

To create a relationship between two tables, follow these steps:

1 Make sure the database is open but that all tables are closed.

Microsoft Access

2 Open the Relationships window. Be sure that all the tables that you want to relate are included in the window.

Show
Table

3 To add one or more tables to the Relationships window, choose Show Table from the Relationships menu or click the Show Table button on the toolbar, and then click the Tables tab.

4 Select a table you want to add and click the Add button. When you're done adding tables, click the Close button. (The Show Table dialog box appears automatically when you choose the Relationships command if the Relationships window is empty.)

TIP

You can remove a table list from the Relationships window by clicking anywhere on it and pressing the Delete key. Doing so *won't* remove any relationships that are associated with this table, but will merely hide the table and its relationships from view.

5 To create the relationship, simply drag one of the fields you want to relate and drop it on the other field. For example, to create the relationship shown in Figure 33-12 on the preceding page, do the following:

To create the relationship,
drag this item...

...and drop it here.

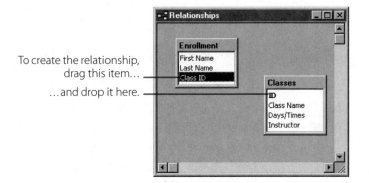

In this example, you could also drag the ID field and drop it on the Class ID field; the effect would be the same. Access will immediately open the Relationships dialog box, as shown here:

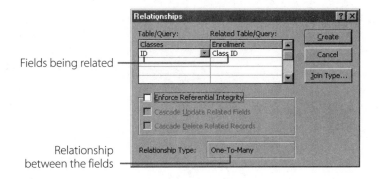

Fields being related —

Relationship between the fields —

V

Microsoft Access

6 The Relationships dialog box lists the names of the fields involved in the relationship and lets you set several options. Access identifies the category of the relationship in the Relationship Type box at the bottom of the dialog box. If neither field is unique, the text box will display Indeterminate. You shouldn't create an indeterminate relationship because it would have limited usefulness. If you select the Enforce Referential Integrity option, Access will make sure that as you enter or modify the data, the correspondence between the related fields is maintained. See the "Enforcing Referential Integrity" sidebar on the following page.

7 When you have set the options you want in the Relationships dialog box, click the Create button. Access will return you to the Relationships window, which will now display a line indicating the relationship you just defined, as in the following:

Infinity symbol marks the related table
(the "many" table in a one-to-many relationship).

"1" marks the primary table (the "one" table
in a one-to-many relationship).

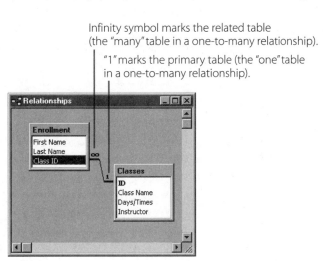

> NOTE

If you click the Join Type button in the Relationships dialog box, you can specify which records will be displayed by default when you create a query that is based on the related tables. Queries are discussed in Chapter 36, "Getting Answers with Queries."

Enforcing Referential Integrity

You can select the Enforce Referential Integrity option when relating two tables to tell Access to make sure that the correspondence between the tables is maintained as you enter data and work with the database. Specifically, it ensures that each record in the related table will properly match a record in the primary table. To select this option, the data types of the related fields must be the same and the relationship can't be indeterminate. If the option is enabled, Access will control changes you attempt to make to the related fields, in the following ways:

- Access won't allow you to enter a value into the related table field that lacks a matching value in the primary table field. You can, however, leave the related table field blank (indicating that it doesn't refer to any record). In the example tables shown in Figure 33-12 on page 879, Access would let you enter only *1, 2,* or *3* into the Class ID field, or leave this field blank.

- Access won't permit you to change the value in the primary table field if there are already matching records in the related table field. In Figure 33-12, you wouldn't be able to change the value of the ID field in *any* of the records in the Classes table because each of the ID values is already used in the Enrollment table. (Actually, you couldn't change this field anyway because it has been assigned the AutoNumber data type.) However, you could select the Cascade Update Related Fields option in the Relationships dialog box, and then Access will let you change the primary table field and will automatically update all the matching values in the related table field so that referential integrity is maintained between the two tables.

- Access won't let you delete a record in the primary table if there are matching records in the related table. In Figure 33-12, none of the Classes records could be deleted because each one has matching records in the Enrollment table. However, you could select the Cascade Delete Related Records option in the Relationships dialog box, and then Access will enforce referential integrity by deleting all the matching records in the related table for each record you delete in the primary table.

Access will draw a thick line with the infinity and "1" (numeral one) symbols only if you enabled the Enforce Referential Integrity option. Otherwise, it will draw a thin line without the symbols.

You can modify options for an existing relationship by double-clicking the line representing the relationship to reopen the Relationships dialog box. You can delete a relationship by clicking on the line to select it and then pressing the Delete key. You can also perform either of these actions by clicking the relationship line with the right mouse button and choosing Edit Relationship or Delete from the shortcut menu that appears.

When you have finished working with relationships, close the Relationships window. If you have modified the layout of the window (that is, the tables that are included and their arrangement), Access will ask if you want to save the layout (rest assured that the relationships themselves have already been saved). Be sure to click the Yes button if you want to reuse this same layout.

V

Microsoft Access

Entering and Viewing Data with Datasheets

I n Datasheet view, information is arranged in rows and columns. Datasheet view is the most common way of viewing a table or a query. You can also view a form in Datasheet view, though you almost always work with forms in Form view. (Tables were discussed in Chapter 33; forms will be discussed in Chapter 35, "Entering and Viewing Data with Forms," and queries in Chapter 36, "Getting Answers with Queries.")

Figure 34-1 shows a table displayed in Datasheet view. In this view, each column represents a single field in your database and each row represents a record. Even though its organization is simple, a datasheet is quite flexible and you can use it in a variety of ways that you might think would require designing a form or report. You can use the datasheet to do the following:

- View and edit data in a variety of ways.

- Customize the layout of Datasheet view to change the size of rows and columns and rearrange the order of columns.

- Add, delete, and rename the fields in a table.

- Add, remove, and edit the records in a table quickly and easily.

- Sort your records.

- Find specific field entries.

- Filter the data so that you see only the records you want.

FIGURE 34-1.
Datasheets provide an easy way to work with the data stored in your database.

Book ID	Title	Topic ID	Publisher Name	Purchase Price	Cover Type
1	Dirk Luchte	Fiction	GGG&G Publishing	$23.50	Hard
2	Planning Your Career	Business	Jean-Paul Deloria	$22.95	Hard
3	Diamonds	Romance	Ramona Publishing	$9.95	Paperback
4	Techniques of Tai Chi	Health	Ramona Publishing	$25.95	Hard
5	My Family	Fiction	GGG&G Publishing	$17.95	Paperback

Books : Table

Record: 1 of 5

Viewing a Datasheet

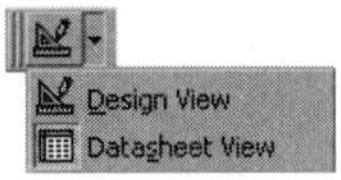

View button
drop-down menu

When you open a table or query through the Database window, it will be displayed in Datasheet view. (Remember that you open a table from the Database window by selecting the Tables tab and double-clicking the table object you want to open.) When you open a form through the Database window, however, it is displayed in Form view. Whenever you want to switch to Datasheet view from another view, you can choose Datasheet View from the View menu. You can also click the down arrow on the View button at the left end of the toolbar and select Datasheet View from the drop-down menu.

Making Changes to Datasheet View

In this section, you'll learn several ways to modify the design of a datasheet. Some of the changes you can make affect only the layout of Datasheet view and don't alter other views or the underlying structure of the table, query, or report. These changes include adjusting the column width or row height, and rearranging the order of the columns. Other changes affect the underlying structure of a table, and will alter the way the table appears in other views such as Design view. These changes include renaming, adding, and deleting fields (you can make these changes only to a table viewed in Datasheet view, *not* to a query or form). Note that many of the techniques for modifying the design of a datasheet resemble techniques used in Microsoft Excel worksheets. For instance, you can change the width of a column by dragging its border, as shown below:

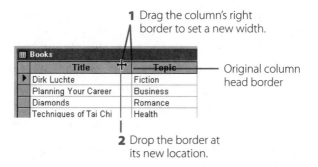

1 Drag the column's right border to set a new width.

Original column head border

2 Drop the border at its new location.

You can change the height of a row using a similar technique with the row heading:

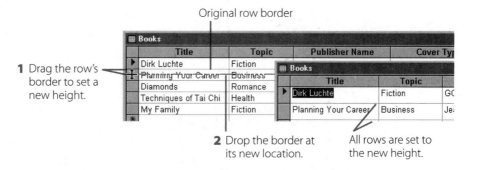

Original row border

1 Drag the row's border to set a new height.

2 Drop the border at its new location.

All rows are set to the new height.

TIP

Let Access Size Your Columns for You

You can have Access determine the most appropriate width for the column by double-clicking the right border of the column heading. Access will then adjust the column width to the smallest possible size that displays all the information contained within that column (including the caption in the column heading).

You can also change the arrangement of the columns in a datasheet. To move a particular column, select the column by clicking the column heading and releasing the mouse button. Then, click the column heading again and drag it right or left to the new location. (If you don't release the button after you first click the column heading, dragging will simply select multiple columns.) Note that changing the order of columns in a datasheet does *not* change the underlying order of the fields as displayed in Design view or other views.

In an Access datasheet, the caption displayed in each column heading is normally the name of the field. However, if you have assigned text to the field's Caption property, that text will be displayed rather than the field name. In the Datasheet view of a table, you can change the field name by double-clicking the column heading, typing a new name, and pressing Enter. If you've assigned text to that field's Caption property, that text will be removed (the property will be set to blank).

You can also add or delete columns in the Datasheet view of a table. To add a column, select the column to the right of the position where you want the new column by clicking in the column heading, and then choose the Column command from the Insert menu. Access will create a new column and will assign it an initial name; it will name the first column you add *Field1*, the second column *Field2*, and so on. You can then change the field name as described previously.

WARNING

Keep in mind that when you delete a column, you're permanently removing a field—together with all its data—from the table. If you delete a column and then realize later that you should have left that information where it was, you'll have to re-create the field and reenter that field's information *for every record in the database, perhaps thousands*! In short, be very careful about deleting a column, and always keep a backup copy of your database.

To delete a column, simply select it by clicking the column heading, and then choose Delete Column from the Edit menu. You'll have the opportunity to confirm your action.

You can also temporarily *hide* one or more columns by selecting them and choosing Hide Columns from the Format menu. You can later make one or more hidden columns visible again by choosing Unhide Columns from the Format menu and selecting all columns you want to reappear.

Access automatically saves any changes that affect the *underlying struc-ture* of a table (renaming, adding, or deleting a field, as well as edits to each record). If, however, you adjust the datasheet *layout* (the column width, row height, or column arrangement), you must save your changes by using the Save command from the File menu. If you haven't saved your layout changes, you'll be asked whether you want to do so when you close Datasheet view. If the changes aren't neces-sary, click No and the next time Datasheet view is opened, it will be displayed in its original layout.

Entering and Editing Data in a Datasheet

The last row of a datasheet is available for adding new records, and is marked with an asterisk in the row heading at the left end of the row to indicate where the new record goes. You can quickly move to the last row by clicking the New Record button on the toolbar.

New
Record

To enter data into a new record, or to modify any record in the table, you can use the mouse to click the field that you want to fill in or mod-ify. If you prefer using the keyboard, you can press the Enter or Tab key to move from left to right through the columns in a record. To move back a column, press Shift+Tab.

You can enter or modify text in a field using the standard editing meth-ods provided by all Office applications. For example, you can use the Left or Right arrow keys to move the insertion point to the position in the text that you want to edit; you can use the Backspace key to delete the previous character or the Delete key to delete the following character;

Microsoft Access

and you can select text and use the Copy or Cut command and the Paste command on the Edit menu (or the equivalent keystrokes) to copy or move blocks of characters.

As soon as you begin entering or changing information in a record, the row heading to the left of the row displays a pencil with two dots, indicating that the record is being edited, as shown in Figure 34-2. When you first enter data into a new record in the last row, Access immediately creates a new blank row below the one that you're editing.

FIGURE 34-2.

As soon as you enter or edit a field in a record, Access automatically stores your changes.

Pencil symbol indicates that record is being edited.

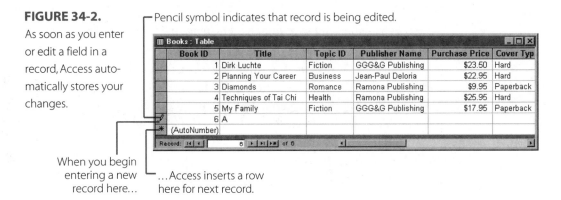

When you begin entering a new record here...

...Access inserts a row here for next record.

Some fields might have been designed to display a preset list of choices in a drop-down list box or combo box. When the insertion point is within such a field, a button with a down arrow is displayed at the right of the field. Click this button or press Alt+Down arrow to display the list. The choices in this list are created beforehand by the Lookup Wizard and are usually set up as the only valid entries for that field. To enter the data, either select one of the choices or type the entry as listed.

Using Formatted Fields

If a specific format has been assigned to a field's Format property, all you have to do is enter the value that goes into that field and press Tab to move to another field. Access will immediately format the entry for you. For example, if a numeric field is formatted for currency, when you type *2.1* and press Tab, Access converts the information in the field to $2.10.

For information on the Format and Input Mask field properties, see "Setting Other Field Properties," page 868.

A field with an input mask, such as a date field, will display a template for you to fill in with the actual values, as shown here:

Date Purchased
11/23/93
12/23/94
12/1/94
10/27/93
7/13/93
/ /

Deleting a Record

Delete Record

To delete a record, select it by clicking in the row heading to the left of the row, and then choose the Delete Record command from the Edit menu, press the Delete key on the keyboard, or click the Delete Record button on the toolbar.

The record is removed from view and a dialog box appears, telling you exactly what you're deleting. If you realize that you're deleting something by mistake, click the No button to stop the deletion process. To proceed with the deletion, click the Yes button.

WARNING

Once you delete a record and click the Yes button to confirm your action, you won't be able to restore the record. You *can't* undo a record deletion using the Undo command on the Edit menu. If you ever want to restore a deleted record, you'll have to reenter it from scratch.

Keep in mind the distinction between deleting a row (record), which is all the fields of information about a single entry (a customer, for instance), and deleting a column (a field), which is a category of information (the Address field, for instance) for every record in the table. While you don't want to delete either by mistake, and while neither deletion can be undone by Access, it's *generally* easier to reenter a record (*all* the information about a single customer) than a field (the Address for *every* customer).

You can also select a group of records to delete, if necessary. To select the records, click the row heading of one record and drag the highlight up or down over the other records in the group.

When you delete a record in a table that's related to another table, Access might need to delete one or more records in the related table

V

Microsoft Access

SEE ALSO

For a discussion on referential integrity and cascading deletions, see the sidebar "Enforcing Referential Integrity," page 882.

(to enforce referential integrity). Before doing so, it will display a message similar to the one shown in Figure 34-3. At this point, you must determine whether you want Access to delete the additional records, which you can't currently see. If you're the least bit uncertain about what associated information is about to be deleted, click No to stop Access from making the deletions. Then determine what related information was about to be deleted and decide whether to go back and make the original deletion. You might want to use the Relationships window to help you find the related data.

FIGURE 34-3.
Deleting one record can result in a "cascade" of deletions in related tables.

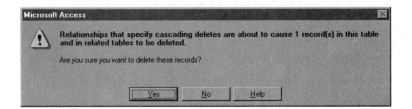

Sorting Your Information

The easiest way to sort the records in a datasheet is to select a single column of information to use as the sort key. To begin, select the column by clicking the column heading. Then, to sort the records by the values in that column, choose Sort from the Records menu and choose Ascending on the submenu that appears, or simply click the Sort Ascending button on the toolbar. This organizes the records from the smallest to the largest value. In the case of numbers, for example, that means from least to greatest (-3, 0, 1, 2, 10); for date fields, from earliest to most recent (1/19/48, 6/15/94, 3/15/97, and so on); and for text, alphabetical order (A to Z).

Sort
Ascending

TIP

Shortcuts Are a Mouse Click Away
Many times the next action you want to perform can be found on the special shortcut menu that appears when you press the right (or secondary) mouse button. The menu changes with the context of your actions, so check it often for possible shortcuts to accomplish your tasks more quickly.

To sort in reverse order, follow the above procedure but choose the Descending command from the Sort submenu or click the Sort Descending button on the toolbar. Access will reorganize your information based on that field from greatest to least for numeric fields, from most recent to earliest for date fields, and from Z to A for text fields.

Sort
Descending

For greater control over organizing your records, you can create a query and use the sorting instructions that are part of the query design grid, as described in "Sorting," page 934.

Finding Information

At times all you need to do in your database is locate an entry in a field that contains a particular item of information. This could be text, a number, or a date. The easiest way to locate the item is to choose the Find command from the Edit menu or press Ctrl+F, either of which displays the dialog box shown in Figure 34-4.

FIGURE 34-4.
You can use the Find dialog box to locate matching entries in your database.

To try out the Find command, follow these steps:

1 Click any field that you'd like to search, for instance the Cover Type field in the Books table shown in Figure 32-2, page 836.

2 Type the text of your search in the Find What text box, perhaps *Paperback* to see which books are available in that format.

3 Click the Find First button. Access will search from the first record of the table and highlight the first match that it finds (or display a message that it found no matches).

V

Microsoft Access

4 If a first match was found, click the Find Next button to find each subsequent match. You can also close the Find dialog box and continue the search by pressing Shift+F4 to find the next match.

The following sections discuss how you can customize the search.

Controlling Where Access Searches

When you first choose the Find command, the name of the dialog box caption includes the name of the *current field*, as shown in Figure 34-4 on the preceding page (unless you've selected fields in more than one column). The current field is the one corresponding to the column that contains the insertion point or selection. This means that the search will be restricted to that field only. If you want Access to search *all* your fields, turn off the Search Only Current Field option at the bottom of the dialog box. The Find dialog box will now look like this:

CAUTION

Using the Find First button always causes Access to start searching from the beginning of the database toward the end, regardless of the setting in the Search list box. To use the Search setting, always click the Find Next button rather than the Find First button.

The Search drop-down list box in the Find dialog box controls the direction in which Access searches the table. When Search is set to All, Access looks through every record in the table, from the beginning to the end. When Search is set to Down, Access searches from the current location to the end of the table. When Search is set to Up, Access searches from the current location to the start of the first record. Unlike Microsoft Word, Access doesn't offer the opportunity to loop around to the beginning or the end of the file with the Down or Up option.

Controlling What Access Matches

The choices in the Match list box determine how Access searches the contents of each field; that is, the criterion for finding a match within a field. The choices are described in Table 34-1.

TABLE 34-1. Effects of Changing the Match Settings of the Find Dialog Box

Match Option	Match Criterion	Example	Will Match	Will Match
Any Part of Field	Your search text might be contained anywhere within the field.	new	Newton renewal Agnew new	
Whole Field	Your search text must match the field contents exactly.	new	new	Newton renewal Agnew
Start of Field	The field must begin with your search text, but this text might be followed by any additional text.	new	Newton new	renewal Agnew

You can use the other controls in the dialog box to determine how precisely Access matches information. When you turn on the Match Case option, Access will find only those instances where the text matches the specified capitalization. For example, with the Match Case option turned off, *Query Grid* matches *query grid*, *Query grid,* and *Query Grid* or any other form of capitalization. With the Match Case option turned on, *Query Grid* will match only *Query Grid*.

The Search Fields As Formatted option requires some explanation. Recall from Chapter 33 that the values for fields with certain data types (such as Date/Time) can be set to display in different formats. The particular format is applied according to the setting of the field's Format property (such as 30-Jun-97 or 6/30/97 for a Date/Time field). If the Search Fields As Formatted option is off, you could search for a date such as 30-Jun-97 by entering it in *any* valid date format (such as 6/30/97, June 30, 1997, or 06/30/1997). (For this to work, you must also select Whole Field match and turn on Search Only Current Field.) However, if you turn on the Search Fields As Formatted option, the only way you could find the entry 30-Jun-97 would be to enter the same text in the Find What box: *30-Jun-97*.

V

Microsoft Access

> The options you select in the Find dialog box can affect the speed at which Access searches your data. Turning on the Search Fields As Formatted option, turning off the Search Only Current Field option, or selecting Any Part Of Field from the Match list each tend to slow down the search process.

Replacing Data

As in Microsoft Word, you can have Access replace data in a table that matches a text string, number, or date that you specify. To replace data, choose the Replace command from the Edit menu or press Ctrl+H. Access will open the Replace dialog box, which is similar to the Find dialog box and is shown in Figure 34-5. Then follow these steps:

1   Enter the data you want to find in the Find What box (this is the data you'll be replacing).

2   Enter the replacement data in the Replace With text box.

3   To start replacing from the beginning of the table, click the Find First button. When Access finds a match, it will highlight the text (or it will display a message indicating that it can't find a match).

4   Click the Replace button to replace the text and have Access look for the next match; or click the Find Next button to look for the next match without replacing the current one.

TIP

Replace All—Quick and Permanent
If you're sure your search will match only data that you want to change, you can select Replace All and Access will make all the replacements without showing them to you or asking for your confirmation. You'll save time, but make sure your search is set up correctly, because you can't undo this operation once you confirm it. Only the total number of replacements made will be shown on the status bar.

SEE ALSO
For more general information on finding and replacing text, see "Finding and Replacing Text," page 151.

The options in the Replace dialog box are similar to those in the Find dialog box that were just discussed. Turning on the Match Whole Field option in the Replace dialog box has the same effect as turning on the Whole Field option in the Match list of the Find dialog box. *Not* turning

FIGURE 34-5.
You can use the Replace dialog box to locate and replace matching entries in your database.

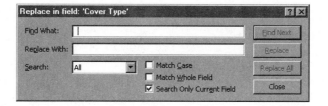

on Match Whole Field has the same effect as turning on Any Part Of Field in the Match list. (See Table 34-1 on page 895 for an explanation of the Match options.)

The Match Case and Search Only Current Field options, as well as the choices in the Search list, work just as they do in the Find dialog box.

Filtering Records

Although the Find command can be useful for moving from one match to another, at times you might want to display *only* the records that match your criteria, rather than displaying *all* the records in the table. Access provides a way to do this through the use of a filter.

Using Filter By Selection

The easiest way to filter records is by finding a field in a record that contains the information you want to use as a filter criterion, and then telling Access to list only those records that contain the same entry in that field. For example, in the Book Collection database, you might want to list all the hardcover books in your collection. To do so, you first locate a record containing the entry that you want to use to select your records—in this case, a record with the entry Hard in the Cover Type field, as shown in Figure 34-6.

FIGURE 34-6.
To start a Filter By Selection, you must first select the information that you want to use as a filter criterion.

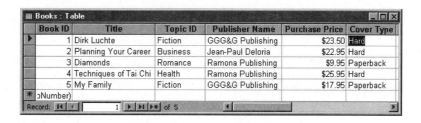

V

Microsoft Access

Filter By
Selection

Either click anywhere within the field *or* select the whole entry to tell Access to match the field's entire contents. Then, choose Filter from the Records menu and choose Filter By Selection from the submenu that appears. Or, just click the Filter By Selection button on the toolbar. Access will then show only the records that meet the filter criterion. The datasheet shown in Figure 34-6 on the preceding page will appear as shown in Figure 34-7, where only hardcover books are displayed.

FIGURE 34-7.
When a filter has been applied, only those records that match the filter criterion are displayed.

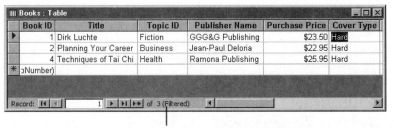

Indicates that a filter has been applied and therefore not all records are displayed.

Apply
Filter

To return to viewing all your records, choose the Remove Filter/Sort command from the Records menu or click the Apply Filter button on the toolbar. (The Apply Filter button actually toggles the filter settings on and off each time you click it, so it both applies and "un-applies.") Access always remembers your last filter settings, so you can apply and remove them as often as you like.

If you select a *portion* of a field entry before issuing the Filter By Selection command, Access will use only that selected text in determining which records to display. For example, in the Books table shown in Figure 34-6 on the preceding page, if you select the word *Publishing* in one of the entries in the Publisher Name field, and then apply Filter By Selection, both the books by GGG&G Publishing and those by Ramona Publishing will be included in your list. This is similar to the way the Any Part Of Field option works in the Find dialog box.

To filter records using the entries from *several* fields in a record, first be sure that the fields with the values you want to use are next to each other (move columns in the datasheet if necessary). Then, select all the entries to be used for the match and issue the Filter By Selection command. To select several adjoining field entries in a record, click on the left end of one entry to select it (click when the pointer becomes a large plus sign) and drag the highlight over the other entries, as shown below:

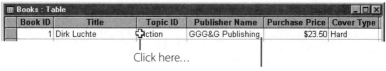

Click here...

...and then drag selection highlight through here.

In the above example, after you issue the Filter By Selection command, only the records for fiction books published by GGG&G Publishing will be listed (that is, all records except 1 and 5 will be filtered out).

Finally, you can select field entries across adjoining records, rather than fields, and then use the Filter By Selection command. In this case, Access will list records that match *any* of the selected field values. For instance, if you had dragged a selection from the top of the Fiction entry in the Topic ID column downward across the Business entry below it (as shown next), Access would display all books categorized as business or fiction. In other words, if you select horizontally across fields, only items matching *all* the fields are shown; but if you select down through rows, items matching *any* of the selected fields will be shown.

Click here to select this entry...

Books : Table					
Book ID	**Title**	**Topic ID**	**Publisher Name**	**Purchase Price**	**Cover Type**
1	Dirk Luchte	Fiction	GGG&G Publishing	$23.50	Hard
2	Planning Your Career	Business	Jean-Paul Deloria	$22.95	Hard

...and then drag highlight to here to include this entry in the selection.

Using Filter By Form

While filtering one value or adjacent values is quick and easy using Filter By Selection, it becomes awkward when you want to filter your data using several values that might not be contiguous (neighboring). A better approach is to use Filter By Form.

If you'd like to learn how to use this powerful filtering method, follow the steps on the next page, which use the sample data in the Books database created by the Access Table Wizard, or adapt these steps using your own database.

V

Microsoft Access

Filter By
Form

1 Click the Filter By Form button on the toolbar or choose the Filter By Form command from the Filter submenu of the Records menu. Your datasheet will disappear and the Filter By Form window will take its place.

2 The Filter By Form window displays a single, blank row in the same format as one of your records. At the bottom of the screen the Look For tab is selected. You can now enter values into any fields you want to use to filter your data. In our example, we want a list of fiction and romance books in paperback format. We begin by clicking the blank field labeled Topic ID. A down arrow appears. Click on this arrow and a drop-down list appears of all the values in this field for the records in the table. Select Fiction. Then follow the same procedure to select Paperback from the Cover Type field:

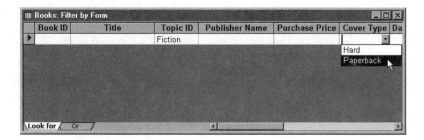

3 Because we also want to include romance books, and because we've already selected fiction books in the Topic ID field, we need to add a new row. Do this by clicking the Or tab at the bottom of the Filter By Form dialog box. In the new row that appears select Romance for the Topic ID field and Paperback for the Cover Type field:

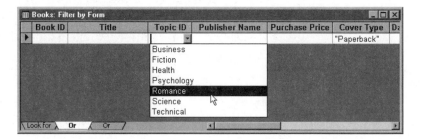

4 To view the filtered list, click the Apply Filter button, and Datasheet view returns, with a filtered list of books:

5 The list shows two paperback books, one fiction and one romance. Suppose we decide that our interest is not so much in paperback books as it is in books that cost less than $25. Rather than selecting an exact value for a field, it's possible to filter values by comparing them to a relative value we enter in the field. This is done by typing an expression containing a comparison operator. The six standard comparison operators are shown in Table 34-2.

TABLE 34-2. Standard Comparison Operators

Operator	Definition
>	Greater than
<	Less than
=	Equal to
<=	Less than or equal to
>=	Greater than or equal to
<>	Not equal to

6 To try out a comparison operator, return to the Filter By Form dialog box (click the Filter By Form button). With the Or tab next to the Look For tab selected, delete the Paperback entry for romance books and click instead in the Purchase Price field. Enter <25, the limit we want to spend for a book. Then click the Look For tab and repeat the same steps for fiction books.

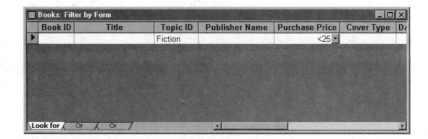

7 Click the Filter By Form button to apply this new filter. Now the list displays three books, including one hardcover book costing $23.50:

Book ID	Title	Topic ID	Publisher Name	Purchase Price	Cover Type	Da
▶ 1	Dirk Luchte	Fiction	GGG&G Publishing	$23.50	Hard	11
3	Diamonds	Romance	Ramona Publishing	$9.95	Paperback	12
5	My Family	Fiction	GGG&G Publishing	$17.95	Paperback	7/
*	ɔNumber)					

Record: ⏮ ◀ 1 ▶ ⏭ ⏭* of 3 (Filtered)

> With Filter By Form, there's no easy way to tell Access to look for matches be-
> tween two values. For example, you can't find any books with prices above $20
> but below $40. For that, you need to use a query as described in Chapter 36,
> "Getting Answers with Queries."

If you enter a comparison and then decide that you don't really want
to use it, you can delete the entry, remove the entire tab, or clear the
entire filter. To delete a single entry, select it and press the Delete key.
To remove a tab that you've created, select it and then choose the
Delete Tab command from the Edit menu. The order of the tabs
doesn't matter. You can clear all the entries in the filter by choosing the
Clear Grid command from the Edit menu, or by clicking the Clear Grid
button on the toolbar.

Clear
Grid

To remove the filter and display all records, choose the Remove Filter/ Sort command from the Records menu, or click the Apply Filter button on the toolbar. You can later reapply your most recently defined filter by simply choosing Apply Filter/Sort from the Records menu or by clicking the Apply Filter button again.

Using Advanced Filter and Sort

If you want to filter *and* sort the records in a table, rather than performing the two-step process of first applying a filter and then sorting the records, you can use the Advanced Filter/Sort command on the Filter submenu of the Records menu. This command opens a special query window that's associated with the table you're working with. In this single window, you can define criteria for sorting and filtering the records in the table, using one or more fields. The use of this window is discussed in "The Simplest Grid—Advanced Filter/Sort," page 928.

Entering and Viewing Data with Forms

A form is a tool that makes it easy to enter, modify, and view the information stored in one or more tables in a database. A form consists of a window filled with a collection of *controls*. A control is a visual object used for displaying information, entering or modifying information, performing an action, or decorating a form; examples of controls include labels, text boxes, command buttons, and graphics such as lines and boxes.

Keep in mind that a form doesn't store the information itself; it simply provides a convenient way to access the information that is stored in one or more tables. Each control on a form typically accesses one field within a table (though some controls don't access fields at all). Working with a form, rather than accessing data thorough the Datasheet view of a table or query, offers several advantages:

- A form allows you to focus on a single record at a time, because typically a form uses its window to display all the fields of a single record, unlike a datasheet that displays several records but usually requires you to scroll the window to see all the fields for those records.

- The controls in a form can be arranged in a logical manner that makes it easy to read and access the data.

- The individual form controls provide many features that facilitate entering or modifying specific items of information.

- Advanced database objects such as pictures, animations, sounds, and video clips can be displayed or run in Form view, but not in Datasheet view.

Using a Form

All the databases created by the wizards included with Microsoft Access and most other commercial databases contain forms for entering information or for reviewing the information stored in the tables of the database. Once you've opened a database, open a particular form by clicking the Forms tab in the Database window and double-clicking on the name of a form.

The techniques for using forms are very similar to those for moving through and entering information into standard Office 97 dialog boxes, with just a few differences. How easy the form is to use depends in large part on how well its designer was able to predict your needs.

If you want to work with an actual form while you read this chapter, have the Access Database Wizard create a new database based on the Membership database, and then open the Members form. The form you see will have all the controls that are discussed here, plus some additional ones that were removed from the form shown in Figure 35-1 to simplify this discussion.

Figure 35-1 shows an example form named Members, which was designed for entering information on the members of an organization. Figure 35-1 shows the Members form ready to accept a new record. In this section, you'll learn how to work with the controls in this typical Access form. You can use these techniques either for defining a new record (as shown in Figure 35-1) or for modifying an existing record. (In the next section, you'll learn how to access existing records.)

FIGURE 35-1.
An example form named Members, ready to accept a new record.

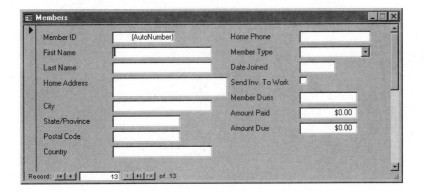

To define or modify the information in a particular control, you can simply click on the control to activate it and then perform any additional action necessary for the specific type of control, such as typing text into a text box or selecting an item from a list. If you want to enter information into the controls in sequence, activate the first control by clicking it, and then press Tab or Enter to move to each subsequent control. (Press Shift+Tab to move back to a previous control.) Generally, a form is designed so that pressing Tab or Enter moves you through the controls in a logical order. For example, in the Members form the Tab or Enter key moves you down through the controls in the first column and then down through the controls in the second

? SEE ALSO

The data types of fields in tables are discussed in "Setting the Data Type," page 868. Setting formatting control properties is discussed in Chapter 38, "Formatting Forms and Reports."

column. When you get to the last control, Tab or Enter moves you back to the first control. Note that when you press Tab or Enter to move to a text box control, the control's entire contents are selected. You can then replace these contents by simply typing the new text. If you need to start a new line in a text box (which would be appropriate only for the Home Address text box), press Ctrl+Enter.

The remainder of this section provides a brief tour of the controls in the Members example form:

- The first control, labeled Member ID, is a *text box* with two peculiarities. First, the table field that it accesses has the AutoNumber data type. As a result, the text box initially displays the value (AutoNumber), but as soon as you enter any data into the new record the value changes to the next incremental record number. Second, the control's Enabled property is set to No. You therefore can neither activate the text box nor change its value.

NOTE

If you delete a record that has an AutoNumber field, that field's number will *not* be reused. There is no easy way to reassign that number to a new record.

- The remaining controls in the first column, as well as the Home Phone control at the top of the second column, are standard text boxes, and each of these controls accesses a field that has the Text data type.

- The Postal Code and Home Phone text boxes each have a *mask* assigned using the Input Mask property, to assist you in entering properly formatted information.

NOTE

A control "inherits" certain properties from the field that it accesses, while other properties must be explicitly set for the control. For example, if the Required property of a field in a table is set to Yes, any control that accesses this field will require data input. By contrast, assigning an input mask to a field's Input Mask property doesn't affect controls that access the field; rather, you must assign an input mask to the Input Mask property of the control itself. For information on setting field properties, see "Setting the Field Properties," page 867.

- The Member Type control is a *combo box*. You normally click the down arrow and select a value from the list that drops down. If the list doesn't contain the value you want, however, you can double-click the text box at the top of the list to open another form, which lets you enter a new member type into the table that stores the list of member types. Once you select a value in the Member Type control, Access automatically enters the appropriate dollar amount into the Member Dues control (different member types pay different dues).

> **NOTE**
>
> You can define a control so that whenever a specified event affects the control, Access will perform another specific action. For example, the Member Type control was defined so that whenever the control is double-clicked, Access opens another form; and whenever the control is updated, Access inserts a value into another control.

- The Member Dues control is a text box that accesses a field with the Currency data type. Although this field is automatically filled in when you make an entry in the Member Type control, you can optionally change the value by entering a new one directly in the text box.

- The Date Joined control is a text box that accesses a Date/Time field. Like the Postal Code and Home Phone controls, it has a mask assigned to its Input Mask property, which assists you in entering a properly formatted date.

- The Send Inv. To Work control is a *check box* that is associated with a field of the Yes/No data type. Checking the box sets the field to Yes, and clearing the box sets the field to No. When you use the Tab or Enter key to move to a check box control, a dotted line is drawn around the control's label to indicate that the control has been activated. You can then press the Spacebar to check or clear the box. If you prefer to use the mouse, you can simply click the box to check or clear it in a single step.

- The Amount Paid and Amount Due text boxes are used only for *displaying* information. You can't edit the contents of these

Microsoft Access

controls, because the Enabled property of each control is set to No. All the controls in the Members form, *except* Amount Paid and Amount Due, are directly associated with a field in the table of this database that is set up to store member information. (In this database the table itself is also named Members, but form and table names don't have to be the same.) The Amount Paid field derives the information it displays from another table of the database that stores payment records (the Payments table). The Amount Due control subtracts the value in the Amount Paid control from the value in the Member Dues control and displays the result. The Format property of both of these controls is set to Currency so that the results are displayed as monetary values.

Spelling

Did You Spell Your Data Correctly?

You can check the spelling of the text you have entered into the controls in a form by choosing Spelling from the Tools menu, pressing F7, or clicking the Spelling button on the toolbar. The Spelling command works the same way it does in other Office applications. For general instructions, see "Checking Your Spelling," page 265. You can also have Access automatically make text replacements as you type by using the AutoCorrect feature; to set it up, choose AutoCorrect from the Tools menu. For information on this feature, see "Using the AutoCorrect Feature," page135.

Figure 35-2 shows the Members form after all the fields have been assigned values. Later in the chapter, you'll learn about other types of controls that can be added to forms.

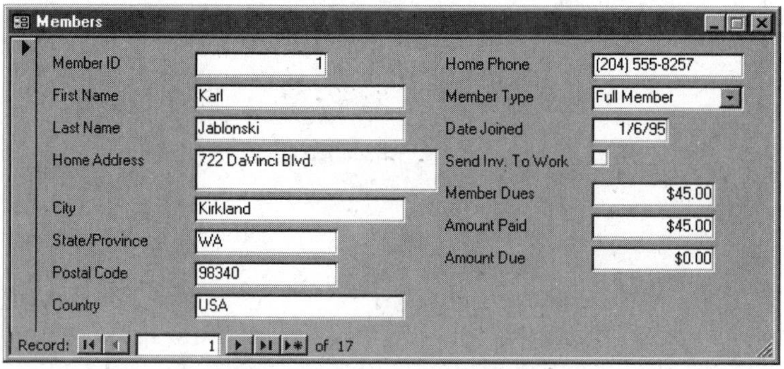

FIGURE 35-2.
The Members form with information entered into each of the fields.

Members	
Member ID	1
First Name	Karl
Last Name	Jablonski
Home Address	722 DaVinci Blvd.
City	Kirkland
State/Province	WA
Postal Code	98340
Country	USA
Home Phone	(204) 555-8257
Member Type	Full Member
Date Joined	1/6/95
Send Inv. To Work	
Member Dues	$45.00
Amount Paid	$45.00
Amount Due	$0.00

Record: 1 of 17

NOTE

When you finish defining or modifying a record and move on to a new record (using one of the methods that will be described later), Access automatically saves the record's new contents. You can also save the current record's contents at *any* time by choosing the Save Record command from the Records menu, or by pressing Shift+Enter.

You can reverse any changes you made to the value in a control by choosing the Undo command from the Edit menu, or by clicking the Undo button on the toolbar. If you just modified and saved a record (by moving to another record), you can issue the Undo command to reverse *all* changes you made to that record.

Undo Current
Field/Record

Printing a Form

Although the primary use of forms is to view and work with data on your computer screen, you do have the option of printing a form and its contents. As with the other Microsoft Office programs, you use the Page Setup, Print Preview, and Print commands on the File menu. Of special interest is the Print Data Only option on the Margins tab of the Page Setup dialog box. This option lets you print the data from the on-screen form directly onto a preprinted paper form, without printing the labels and lines that make up the form itself. This is advantageous if, for example, your data tracks employment applicants and you want to print the data on preprinted application forms. You simply design a form on screen to match the paper form, but you put the application forms in your printer's paper tray and use the Print Data Only option when printing.

Working with Records

A form is always associated with a specific table or query in the database, which is known as the *record source*. Most of the controls in a typical form directly access fields belonging to the record source (controls, however, can be used for other purposes). In a form's window, you can view any of the records belonging to the record source, and you can add new records to the record source or delete records from it. Access provides a small toolbar permanently positioned in the lower left corner of the form window, which can be used to navigate through the existing records or to add new records:

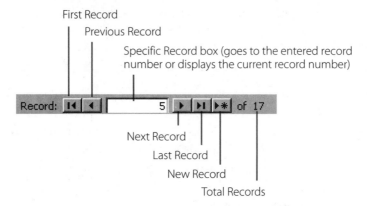

First Record
Previous Record
Specific Record box (goes to the entered record number or displays the current record number)
Next Record
Last Record
New Record
Total Records

If you prefer to use the keyboard rather than the mouse, press Page Down to move forward a single record or Page Up to move back a single record. To jump to the start of the first record, press Ctrl+Home, and to jump to the end of the last record press Ctrl+End. (If Ctrl+Home or Ctrl+End moves the insertion point within a field instead of moving between records, press the Tab key once and try again.)

To view a specific record in a table, you can click the Specific Record box, type in the record number, and press Enter. You can also go to a record that contains specific text in one of its fields by choosing Find from the Edit menu, pressing Ctrl+F, or clicking the Find button on the toolbar.

Find

Likewise, you can replace the contents of matching fields by choosing Replace from the Edit menu or by pressing Ctrl+H. For instructions on using the Find and Replace commands, see "Finding Information," page 893.

New
Record

To create a new record, click the New Record button in the toolbar at the bottom of the form window (pictured above), or click the New Record button on the main toolbar. The new record will be added to the end of the table or query, and will be displayed in the form window so that you can enter information into it (as shown in Figure 35-1 on page 907).

Rather than entering mostly repetitive information for a new record, you can copy the data from another, similar record into the new record, and then modify only the data necessary. You can also copy information from one record over another record's data, replacing the original contents of the target record. To copy a record, do the following:

1 Select the record that is the source of the information by displaying that record in the form window and clicking in the vertical bar at the left of the form window (this bar is equivalent to the row heading you see in Datasheet view):

Click anywhere in this bar to select the entire record.

2 Choose the Copy command from the Edit menu. (If you want to move the source record's contents, choose Cut instead.)

3 Display the target record in the form window and choose the Paste command from the Edit menu. The value of every control in the source record will be copied into the equivalent control in the target record, *except* for any control that accesses a primary key field or other field that must have a unique value, such as the Member ID field in our sample form.

Delete
Record

To permanently delete a record, display the record in the form window, and then choose the Delete Record command from the Edit menu or click the Delete Record button on the toolbar. Access requires that you confirm the deletion before the record can be removed. If the deletion will result in additional cascading deletions in related tables, a dialog box will inform you of that and give you an opportunity to stop. Just as when you delete a record in Datasheet view, once you confirm a deletion the data is permanently lost—it *can't* be restored with the Undo button, and you'll have to manually reenter it if you want to restore it later.

> You can sort or filter the records viewed in a form in the same way that you sort or filter records when you view a table or query in Datasheet view. For instructions, see "Sorting Your Information," page 892, and "Filtering Records," page 897.

Note that you can also display a form in Datasheet view. Each row in the Datasheet view of a form displays the controls for a particular record, one per row. Although Datasheet view is generally much less convenient for working with a form than Form view, it has the advantage of allowing you to view multiple records at a time. To switch to Datasheet view, choose Datasheet View from the View menu.

Creating a Form

You can create a form in several ways, but for most purposes the best way is to start with the New button on the Forms tab of the Database window. When you click the New button, Access opens the New Form dialog box:

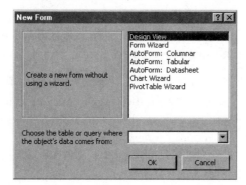

In the list in the New Form dialog box, you can choose from a variety of different ways to create your new form:

- Select the Design View option to create the form yourself, by adding controls one at a time in Design view (which is described in the next section, "Modifying a Form," and in Chapter 38, "Formatting Forms and Reports").

- Select the Form Wizard option to have Access create the form for you, according to your specifications. The Form Wizard option lets you choose the specific fields to include, which might belong to one or more tables or queries.

- Choose one of the three AutoForm options, to have the Form Wizard generate the form for you; however, rather than asking for your specifications, it quickly creates and opens a specific type of form—a columnar, tabular, or datasheet form—using the default options. (You can also create any of these three types of forms using the Form Wizard option, which will be discussed later in this section.) Also, a form created via an AutoForm option always includes controls for *all* the fields of a *single* table or query.

- The Chart Wizard option causes Access to take information from a database table or query and create a chart using Microsoft Graph, which is discussed in Chapter 39, "Sharing Data Among Office Applications."

- The PivotTable Wizard option takes information from a table and creates a pivot table, which is covered in "Creating a Pivot Table," page 626, as an Excel feature.

In general, it's easiest to use the Form Wizard or one of the AutoForm options to create at least a rough draft of your form. You can then customize the form, using the techniques described in the next section and in Chapter 38, "Formatting Forms and Reports."

Design View Option

If you selected the Design View option, click OK to open the form in Design view and begin adding controls (you don't need to select an item from the list at the bottom of the New Form dialog box).

AutoForm Options

If you selected any of the AutoForm options, you must choose a table or a query from the drop-down list at the bottom of the New Form dialog box, and then click the OK button. The wizard will immediately create and open the new form, which will contain a control for each field in the selected table or query.

Using the New Object Button

You can quickly create a simple form that includes controls for all the fields belonging to a single table or query, with all controls placed in a single column. To do this, click the Tables or Queries tab in the Database window and select the table or query on which you want to base your form. Then, click the down arrow next to the New Object button on the Access toolbar and choose the AutoForm item from the menu that drops down:

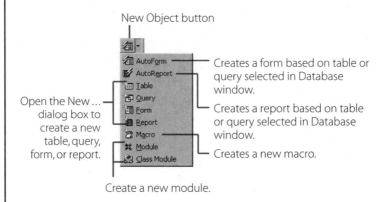

Notice that you can also use the New Object button to quickly create a new report based on the selected table or query, or to open the New Table, New Query, New Form, or New Report dialog box to create one of these database objects. Finally, you can use it to create a new macro or module.

Form Wizard Option

If you selected the Form Wizard option, you can simply click the OK button to run the wizard, without selecting an item from the list. The wizard will then display a series of dialog boxes. The first dialog box, which is shown in Figure 35-3, asks you to select the fields that you want to include in your form. The resulting form will contain a separate control for accessing each of the fields that you pick.

In the Tables/Queries list, select a table or query that has one or more of the fields that you want to include in your form. All the fields belonging to the selected table or query will be displayed in the Available Fields list. Then, gather the specific fields that you want into the Selected Fields list, using the four buttons shown in Figure 35-3.

FIGURE 35-3.

Begin by selecting all the fields you want to access in your new form.

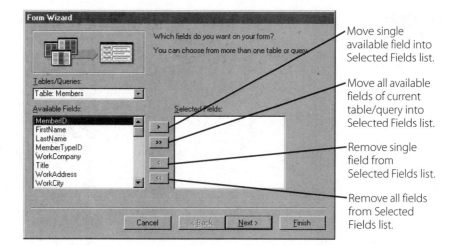

Move single available field into Selected Fields list.

Move all available fields of current table/query into Selected Fields list.

Remove single field from Selected Fields list.

Remove all fields from Selected Fields list.

> **NOTE**

You might get the impression that you're moving fields from a table into your form, but of course the fields and their data remain in the table; you're instead creating a *link* to those fields by symbolically moving the field name into the Selected Fields list box.

You can then select one or more additional tables or queries and move the fields you want from each one into the Selected Fields list. When the Selected Fields list has all the fields you want, click the Next button to display the second Form Wizard dialog box.

The second Form Wizard dialog box, shown in Figure 35-4 on the following page, lets you choose the basic arrangement of the controls on the form. To make your choice, click on each option and observe the way the selected layout will look on your form, as shown in the dialog box. The Columnar layout is the most common, and usually enables you to view a complete, single record at a time in Form view (the example form in Figure 35-1 on page 907 uses this layout). The Tabular layout lets you view multiple records at the same time in Form view, while the Datasheet layout generates a form that is intended to be displayed in Datasheet view. The Justified layout arranges the form's object to fill the form window. When you've selected the layout you want, click the Next button.

FIGURE 35-4.
Then choose the arrangement of the controls on the form.

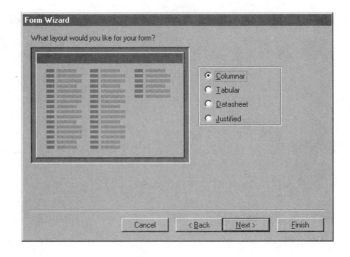

In the third Form Wizard dialog box, shown in Figure 35-5, you choose the style of your form—the background color or pattern, the fonts, the look of the controls, and so on. Again, to help you make your choice, the dialog box shows how the form will look with each style option. (You can later change the style by displaying the form in Design view, clicking the AutoFormat button on the toolbar, and selecting a new style in the AutoFormat dialog box.) When you've made your choice, click the Next button to open the final dialog box, shown in Figure 35-6.

Auto-
Format

FIGURE 35-5.
Choose the style of the form, including a variety of backgrounds.

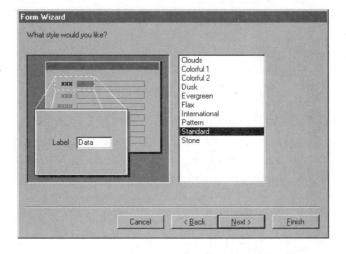

FIGURE 35-6.

Finally, choose a name for your form and the view in which it will open.

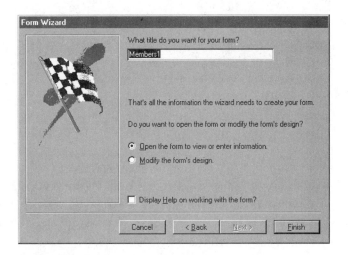

The final dialog box in the Form Wizard lets you assign a name to the form and choose the way the form is initially opened. If you select the first opening option, the form will be opened in Form view (or Datasheet view if you selected the Datasheet layout) so that you can immediately begin using the form to view or modify data, as discussed at the beginning of this chapter. If you select the second opening option, the form will open in Design view so that you can modify its design, as described next.

When you've made all your choices, click the Finish button to have Access create the form. (As with the other Access wizards, you can click the Finish button within any of the dialog boxes to create the form using the options you've set and the default choices for the options you *haven't* set.)

Modifying a Form

You can make changes to a form quite easily by switching to Design view. You have the option of moving directly to Design view after creating a form with the Form Wizard. If you're already working with data in a form in Form view, you can switch to Design view by choosing the Design View command from the View menu or by clicking the View button on the left end of the toolbar and choosing Design View from the drop-down menu, as shown on the following page.

Alternatively, you can open any form in Design view by selecting it on the Forms tab of the Database window, and then clicking the Design button.

Figure 35-7 shows the same form shown in Figure 35-1 on page 907 in Design view rather than the standard Form view. Design view lets you add, remove, or modify the controls that make up a form, which you'll recall include text boxes, labels, list boxes, option buttons, command buttons, lines, and more.

FIGURE 35-7.

Design view provides a wide variety of tools for modifying a form's layout and controls.

Toolbox toolbar

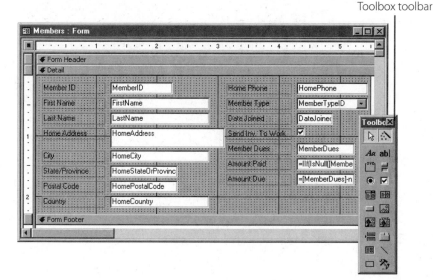

When you open a form in Design view, Access displays the Toolbox toolbar with tools for adding and working with many different types of controls. (If the Toolbox isn't currently displayed, either choose Toolbars from the View menu and choose Toolbox from the submenu that appears, or click the Toolbox button on the toolbar.)

Toolbox

The Toolbox buttons are shown and described in Figure 35-8. A selected button will appear "pressed in" or recessed compared to the other Toolbox buttons.

FIGURE 35-8.
The Toolbox buttons and their functions.

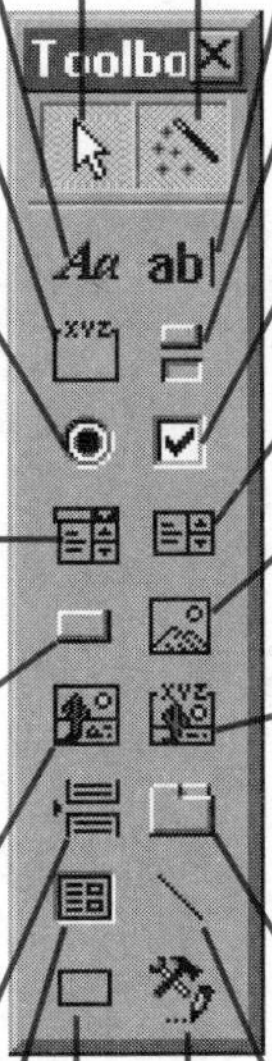

Select Objects Select single control by clicking it or multiple controls by pressing Shift while clicking each one (or drag a selection rectangle around the object).

Label Descriptive text to label a control or provide instructions. Labels are automatically attached to most controls you add.

Option Group Create a set of controls that you can select among and that assign a numeric value to a field.

Option Button Round button usually used in a group of mutually exclusive options (for example, male or female). Selected button contains a black dot.

Combo Box Add a control that consists of a text box with a list box below it. You can either type text into the text box or select an item from the list.

Command Button Add a rectangular button that can be clicked to perform an action (such as OK or Close).

Unbound Object Frame Display OLE object, such as an Excel spreadsheet. The object is constant; it doesn't change with each record.

Page Break Divide a form into multiple screens (or multiple pages for printing).

Subform/Subreport Add information from an additional table to a form, so that you can view or modify its data.

Rectangle Draw a rectangle on a form to group or emphasize controls.

Control Wizards When selected, Access will guide you through the process of creating a new control—a good idea until you've mastered the intricacies of form design!

Text Box Add a box for displaying, entering, or modifying data.

Toggle Button Add a rectangular push button that can be used to turn an option on or off. Appears "pressed" when the option is on.

Check Box Add a small square box that can be used to turn an option on or off. Contains a check mark when the option is on.

List Box Add a control that displays a list box from which you select an item.

Image Add a constant picture to a form (doesn't change when you change records).

Bound Object Frame Display OLE objects that are stored in the records of a table, such as employee photos. The object will change as you view various records.

Tab Control Allows you to divide the form into separate tabs, like those you see in tabbed dialog boxes.

Line Draw a single straight line on a form to separate or emphasize controls.

More Controls Add from a list of additional controls supplied with Office. These controls are displayed on a menu when you click this tool.

V

Microsoft Access

When you switch to Design view, the Property Sheet appears as well. You will use the Property Sheet later in "Adding a Control Using the Toolbox," page 923. If it obstructs your view of the form, you can close it until you need it.

When you're working in Design view, the Standard toolbar near the top of the application window provides commands that are useful for designing a form. In Design view Access also displays the Formatting toolbar, which contains a wide variety of commands for modifying the appearance of the form and the controls it contains. The Formatting toolbar is discussed in detail in Chapter 38, "Formatting Forms and Reports." Depending on the size of your window, your Formatting toolbar might not display all these buttons:

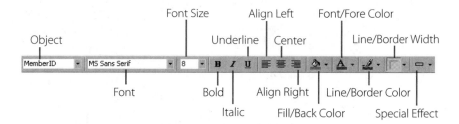

Adding a Bound Control

A *bound* control is one that is associated with a field belonging to the table or query being used as the record source for the form. A bound control lets you view or modify the value of the associated field, and is the most common type of control (in the next section, you'll learn about controls that aren't bound). You can quickly add a bound control to your form by using the *field list*, a window that lists all the fields contained in the record source. The following is the field list for the Members form used as an example in this chapter:

Field
List

To display the field list, choose the Field List command from the View menu or click the Field List button on the Form Design toolbar.

To add a control to your form that is bound to a particular field, simply drag the field name from the field list and drop it at or near the desired position on the form. Access creates an appropriate control based on the data type of the field that you dragged to the form. For example, if you dragged a text field or a numeric field, Access creates a text box together with a label, as shown here:

Controls bound to the FirstName text field

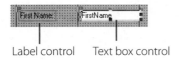

Label control   Text box control

Similarly, if you drag a Yes/No field, Access creates a check box control, and if you drag a field that has been assigned a lookup column, Access creates a combo box. (Recall from Table 33-1 on page 869 that a field with a lookup column is one that displays a list of values.)

> To delete a control from a form, make sure that the Pointer button on the Toolbox is selected (that is, "pressed"). Click on the control to select it, and then press the Delete key.

Adding a Control Using the Toolbox

You can use the Toolbox to change the type of control that Access creates when you drag a control from the field list. For example, if you drag a control with the Yes/No data type, Access will normally create a text box control together with a label. If you would rather have a check box control, click the Check Box button on the Toolbox immediately *before* you drag the field from the field list, and Access will create a check box instead. Clicking a button on the Toolbox will have an effect only if the type of control you click is appropriate for the data type of the field that you drag to the form (for instance, selecting Command Button will have no effect if you drag a text field, because you can't access a text field with a command button).

You can also use the Toolbox to directly add a control to your form. To do this, click the Toolbox button for the control you want to add, and then click on the form at the approximate location where you want to display the control. Access will add the control, assigning it a default size; you can later adjust its size or position.

If the Control Wizards Toolbox button is selected and if the field you select is one that requires multiple steps to complete—an option group, a combo box, or a list box, for example—Access starts a wizard to guide you through the steps. During this process the wizard generally asks you which field you want to associate with the control, and the resulting control will be bound to that field.

If, however, the field you select is a simple one—such as a label, text box, or option button—Access will simply create it directly on the form without running a wizard. In this case, the control *won't* be bound to a field. You can use a control that isn't bound to a field to display the results of a calculation (such as the Amount Due control in the Members example form), or to display instructions or other information.

If you do want to bind the control to a field so that it can be used to access the field, you'll need to use the Property Sheet, which opens automatically when you enter Design view. If it's not currently displayed on your screen, you can open it in several ways:

- Double-click the control on the form.

- Right-click the control and choose Properties from the shortcut menu.

- Choose Properties from the View menu.

Then follow these steps:

1 Select the All tab, which is shown on the facing page.

2 You can set any of the selected control's properties. To bind the control to a field, click in the Control Source box and select the field you want from the drop-down list.

3 You can change the name of the control by typing a new value into the Name property box (though this won't change the label that appears next to it).

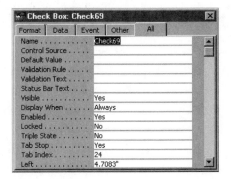

4   You can also assign a default value to the control by entering the value into the Default Value property box. Chapter 38, "Formatting Forms and Reports," provides more information on setting control properties.

Changing a Control

Once you've created a control, you can convert it to another type of appropriate control by choosing the Change To command from the Format menu, and choosing the new type of control you want from the submenu that appears. Note that you'll be able to choose only a control type that's similar to the original control type (that is, one that would be suitable for accessing the same data types). For example, you can change a text box only to a label, list box, or combo box. Figure 35-9 shows the Change To submenu as it appears for several different types of controls.

FIGURE 35-9.

The available choices on the Change To submenu depend on the type of control selected; for example, a text box (A), a combo box (B), or a check box (C).

A

B

C

Copying a Control

Rather than creating a new control, you can save a bit of effort by making a copy of another control already on the form and then modifying it:

- Make sure that the Select Objects button on the Toolbox is selected and then click on the control you want to make a copy of. Access will draw a border with sizing handles around the selected control.

- Choose the Copy command on the Edit menu and then choose the Paste command. The copy of the control will appear near or perhaps on top of the original control.

- Move the copy where you want it to be on the form. To move a control, select it by clicking on it, if necessary. Then move the pointer near an edge of the control and the pointer will become a small hand. Drag the control to its new location.

See Chapter 38, "Formatting Forms and Reports," for more information on moving controls.

The other types of changes you can make to a control include moving the control, changing the control's size or shape, altering the color or style effects of a control, and setting additional control properties (you already saw how to change several of the properties). These topics are discussed in Chapter 38, "Formatting Forms and Reports."

> NOTE

You might sometimes be confused as to whether to work with the control itself or with the label next to it. Some controls, such as a toggle button, have a Caption property that can be used to add text directly to the control. In general, however, the label for the control exists as a separate control on the form.

Creating your own forms—and designing them for ease of use—can be a very complex process, yet a very rewarding one. This chapter has provided a general introduction to get you going. The best way to learn how to create controls is to add bound controls using the field list and then experiment with changing their formats and properties.

Getting Answers with Queries

A query is the tool you use to get information from your database in response to specific questions. Rather than presenting every record in a table, the results of a query show only those records that are relevant. With a query, you set up a condition describing the types of records you want Access to include. When you run the query, Access produces a datasheet containing just those matching records.

Queries can be simple—for example, the results of a query can list all records in which the purchase price of a book is more than $100—or complex, involving a series of comparisons among fields and alternative conditions strung together—for example, the results of a query can list all records in which the purchase price of a book is less than 85 percent of the cover price if the book was purchased in a state with no sales tax or less than 80 percent of the cover price if purchased elsewhere.

? SEE ALSO

The results of a query are always displayed in Datasheet view. For more information about rearranging columns, sorting records, and making other changes to datasheets, see Chapter 34.

All queries are based on the contents of a *design grid*, which provides a row-and-column structure for organizing the fields that are used in the query and for entering the query conditions. In this chapter, you'll learn how to use the Advanced Filter/Sort command, which displays a design grid and offers many of the features of a true query object. You'll then learn how to create a full-fledged query object, which employs a design grid with many additional options. Because of the similarities of these two methods, the chapter uses the general term *query* to refer both to an Advanced Filter/Sort operation as well as to a true query.

The Simplest Grid—Advanced Filter/Sort

If you're working with a table in either Datasheet or Form view and want to develop a query that creates a list of only a subset of the records in that table, you can use the Advanced Filter/Sort command on the Filter submenu of the Records menu. When you choose this command, a window similar to the one shown in Figure 36-1 appears.

FIGURE 36-1.

The Advanced Filter/ Sort command displays a design grid for entering your conditions.

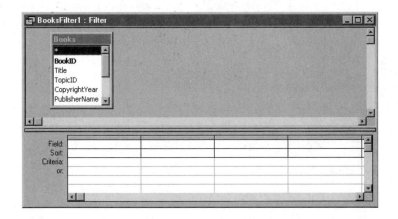

★ TIP

If you want to work with the database that was used for the examples in this chapter, use the Database Wizard to create a database from the Book Collection database included with Access. Be sure to have the wizard include sample data. Information on the Database Wizard is given in Chapter 32.

Take note of several limitations to using the Advanced Filter/Sort command rather than creating a true query:

- Only the fields that are present in the table that is active when you select the Advanced Filter/Sort command are available for you to use in creating the query.

- Some features of the actual query design grid are not available. (See "Features of the Query Design Grid," page 942.)

Still, everything that you do with the Advanced Filter/Sort command is also necessary for creating a true query, so it's a good place to start.

Defining the Conditions

Queries consist of a series of conditions, or *criteria*, that are combined to narrow down which records are displayed. In many ways this process resembles an archaeologist's using a finer and finer mesh screen to filter out the undesired bits (or records in this case), leaving only the objects wanted.

Each condition consists of three elements:

- The field that will be used for the comparison

- The operator, which describes the type of comparison to be performed

- The value, which specifies exactly what the field will be compared to

For example, if you want to list all records in which the cover price of a book is less than $50, the field would be PurchasePrice, the comparison operator would be the less-than symbol (<), and the value would be 50. To create the condition, you would enter this information in the design grid, as shown on the following page.

1 First select the name of the field that will be used in the condition. There are several ways to select the field name. One is to simply click on an empty column in the Field row of the filter

V

Microsoft Access

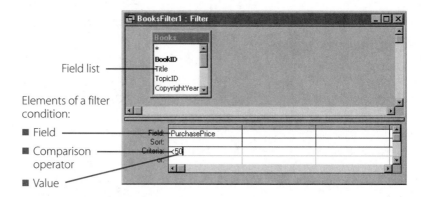

Field list

Elements of a filter condition:

- Field
- Comparison operator
- Value

design grid. On the right side of the column an arrow appears that drops down a list of all the fields in your table when clicked. Scroll through the list, if necessary, and click the field name you want to use. Alternatively, you can click on the name in the field list that appears in the top half of Design view and drag the name down to the Field row in the grid at the bottom.

 TIP

* Stands for "All"

The asterisk (*) at the top of the field list and at the top of the drop-down list just below the table name is a shorthand notation to include *all* fields in the table. This notation isn't necessary with the Advanced Filter/Sort command, but it's useful when you're constructing a query that you want to have return all the information in the table. The primary key field(s) for each table are indicated in **bold** in the field list.

2 Click on the Criteria row of the design grid, and type the operator and the value. If you want to use the Expression Builder, right-click on the Criteria row and choose Build from the shortcut menu. (The Expression Builder feature lets you select the different components of your condition from a complex dialog box instead of simply typing them in.) To define additional conditions, add fields as necessary and then add the criteria for those fields (using multiple criteria is discussed later, in the section "Combining Conditions").

You can use the commands on the Edit menu to delete entries from grid rows, to delete entire grid rows or columns, or to clear the grid

Clear
Grid

completely. You can also clear the entire grid by clicking the Clear Grid button on the toolbar.

Viewing the Results

Apply
Filter

To see the results of your Advanced Filter/Sort, choose the Apply Filter/Sort command from the Filter menu or click the Apply Filter button on the toolbar. Access immediately switches back to your original view—Datasheet or Form—with only those records that match your conditions listed. The record indicator at the bottom of the window in Datasheet or Form view will indicate that a filter is currently in place (provided that you didn't use the Advanced Filter/Sort command merely to *sort* your records, as described later). Datasheet view's record indicator is shown here:

Indicates that a filter has been applied, so not all records will be listed

Close

To return from the Advanced Filter/Sort window to Datasheet or Form view *without* applying the filter, simply close the Advanced Filter/Sort window or click the Close button on the toolbar.

After you've applied a filter to a table in Datasheet or Form view, you can remove the filter and view all the records again by choosing Remove Filter/Sort from the Records menu, or by clicking the Remove Filter button on the toolbar (the Apply Filter button will toggle to Remove Filter and back each time you click it).

Combining Conditions

The advantages of using an Advanced Filter/Sort or a true query, rather than the Filter By Form or Filter By Selection commands (discussed in Chapter 34), include the following:

■ You can more easily combine separate filtering conditions.

■ You can combine conditions in ways that aren't possible using the simpler filter methods.

■ You can sort the records at the same time that you filter them.

For example, you might want to list those books for which the price is less than $50 *and* the type is hardcover. In this case, your query would resemble the one shown here:

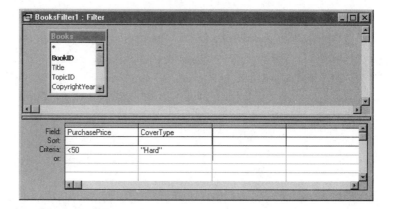

Notice that both criteria are entered into the same row. This tells Access to list only those records that match *both* requirements. If, on the other hand, you want to list those books for which the price is less than $50 *or* the cover is hard, you would put the second condition into the separate "Or" row, as shown here:

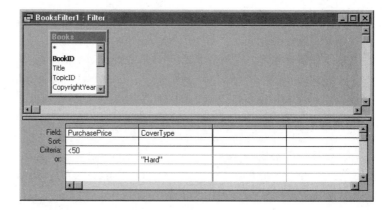

In this case, your query would produce many more matches—all the books costing less than $50 and all the hardcover books would be listed. The only books that wouldn't be included are those that meet neither criterion.

Under certain circumstances you might want to specify more than one condition for the same field. Suppose you want to find all occurrences of a value that's between two extremes. For example, to list all the books with a purchase price between $10 and $50, you need to break the condition into two parts. The first part is that you want books with a purchase price greater than or equal to $10, but you also want to further restrict the books found to those with a purchase price less than or equal to $50. There are two methods that could be used in the design grid to pose this condition. The first would be to add the field to the design grid twice—once for each part of the condition. You can see a sample of the method using the same field twice displayed here:

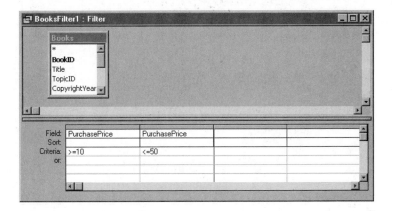

Another method would be to enter both conditions into a single Criteria box with the word *and* between them; for example, *>=10 and <=50*. Or, you could use the words *Between* and *And*; for example, *Between 10 And 50*, for equivalent results. In this case, you would need to add the field to only a single column in the design grid.

> **NOTE**
>
> Although in conversation people might typically say they want those books with a purchase price greater than or equal to $10 *but* less than or equal to $50, this is in reality an *and* condition. We want those records that are greater than or equal to $10 *and* that are less than or equal to $50.

At times, you might want to enter alternative comparisons into separate cells in a single column. For example, in a table that tracks authors, you might want to obtain information on all authors who belong to a particular set of authors. In this case, all conditions can be entered into the "Or" cells in the same column because the criteria involve only a single field (LastName) and are to be combined using *or* logic (that is, each record you want to see will have information on author A *or* author B *or* author C, and so on). The following example shows how the filter could be set up for two authors:

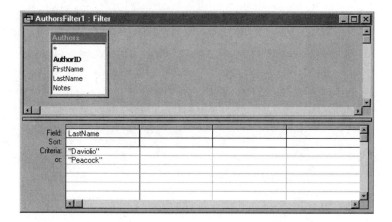

> You'll notice in the graphic above that no operator has been used and that quotation marks surround the names entered. When you want an exact match, you can use the equal operator (=), or, if you use nothing, the equal sign is assumed. Access inserts the quotation marks for you when you're working with conditions in text fields. They imply that the value is to be used literally.

Sorting

The Sort row of the query design grid can be used to organize the information that appears in Datasheet and Form views. When you click on a box in the Sort row, a down arrow appears at the right side of the box. Clicking on that down arrow reveals a list with the choices Ascending, Descending, and (Not Sorted). Select either Ascending or Descending to have Access sort the records using the values in the field selected in that column. Select (Not Sorted) to have Access ignore that field when sorting. For instance, to sort the records in the Books table in alphabetical order by title, you would select Title in the Field row and Ascending in the Sort row, as shown here:

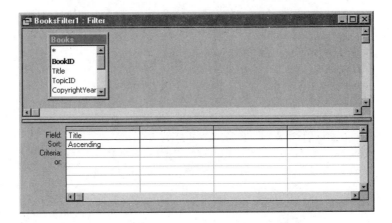

SEE ALSO

For more information on how Access sorts information, see "Sorting Your Information," page 892.

You can also sort information using multiple fields. Access always sorts on the fields from left to right, so your most important sort field should be to the left of any other sort field. When a sort is based on multiple fields, each field to the right of the first one is used for sorting *only* if records have identical information in the sort fields to its left. For example, you could sort the Authors table so that the authors are arranged by last name, and if several authors have the same last name their records are further sorted by the first names. The following example shows how this sort could be set up:

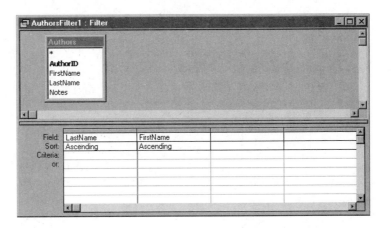

Microsoft Access

Creating a Simple Query

At times you might find the design of the Advanced Filter/Sort command inadequate to answer the questions you have for your database:

■ When you need to ask questions that depend on fields stored in more than one table

■ When you want to create a query that displays some, but not all, the fields in a table

In these cases, the solution is to use the formal query features of Access.

You have available a number of ways to create a new query. The easiest is to select the Queries tab of the Database window and click the New button. Alternatively, you can choose Query from the New Object drop-down menu at the right end of the toolbar:

With either method, the New Query dialog box appears, which is shown here:

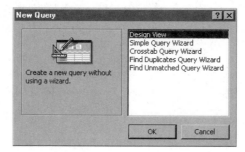

Housecleaning Wizards

No, Access doesn't offer the power to turn your computer into a home mainte-nance device. Rather, Access includes two wizards designed to help you main-tain the integrity of the data in your tables.

The Find Duplicates Query Wizard goes through a selected table or query and lists all records that contain duplicate values for a given field. This wizard can be useful for identifying all customers who live in a particular city or for finding all books in your collection on a particular topic. The Find Duplicates Query Wiz-ard is also a powerful tool for when you want to create a relationship between two fields. You can also use this wizard to determine whether the primary field in the primary table has duplicate values. (Recall from Chapter 33 that the primary field in the primary table in a relationship must have unique values.)

The Find Unmatched Query Wizard is used to compare two tables and locate any records in the first table that lack related records in the second. This wizard can be useful simply for locating special cases within your data (for example, finding students who aren't enrolled in any classes). It can be crucial if you're redesigning your database and want to define a one-to-many relationship be-tween two tables in which referential integrity is to be enforced (that is, there should be no record in the related table without a matching record in the pri-mary table). For more information about relationships, refer to Chapter 33.

To use either query wizard, open the Database window, select the Queries tab, click the New button, and then select the wizard from the New Query dialog box.

This dialog box lets you choose the type of query you want and the way you want to create it:

- Design view is one way to use a standard query-design grid. Choose Design View if you want to create your query from scratch in Design view, which is described in the section "Doing Without the Simple Query Wizard," later in the chapter.

- The other way to use a standard query design—and the easiest way to create a new query—is to select the Simple Query Wizard option to have Access assist you in designing the query.

- The Crosstab Query Wizard option is discussed in "The Crosstab Query," later in this chapter.

■ The Find Duplicates Query Wizard and Find Unmatched Query Wizard options run special-purpose wizards that can help you maintain your data; they are discussed in the "Housecleaning Wizards" sidebar on the preceding page.

If you'd like to create a query for one of your own databases or for the Book Collection database supplied with Access, follow the steps presented below:

1 Select the Simple Query Wizard from the New Query dialog box.

2 The Simple Query Wizard will start and the first dialog box that appears will instruct you to select all the fields (from any combination of tables in your database) pertinent to your query. This dialog box is shown in Figure 36-2.

FIGURE 36-2.
Selecting fields in the first Simple Query Wizard dialog box.

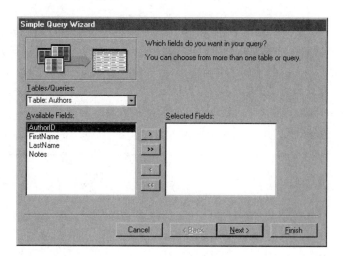

3 Select a table or query that has one or more fields that you want to include in your new query from the Tables/Queries drop-down list at the top left of the dialog box. To include a field, move it from the Available Fields list to the Selected Fields list using the four buttons arranged vertically between the list boxes. You can include fields from more than one table or query by selecting additional tables or queries from the Tables/Queries drop-down list. When you finish selecting fields, click the Next button to open the second wizard dialog box.

> Be sure to include all the fields that are to be displayed in the query datasheet, to be used for setting the conditions of the query, or to be used for sorting the results of the query.

4 The second wizard dialog box, shown in Figure 36-3, asks you to choose either a *detail* query or a *summary* query. A detail query lists all records that match the conditions you specify. A summary query performs calculations using values from the matching records. Summary queries are discussed in the section "Summarizing Your Records," later in this chapter.

FIGURE 36-3.
The second Simple Query Wizard dialog box lets you choose the type of query you want.

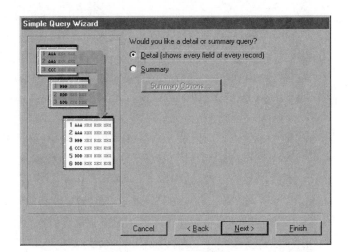

5 When you click the Next button, you're taken to the final dialog box of the Simple Query Wizard (see Figure 36-4 on the following page). If you're ready to view your query, you can choose the Open The Query To View Information option to immediately open the query in Datasheet view (see "Viewing the Results of a Query," later in this chapter). Usually, however, you'll want to examine and possibly modify the query design before you view the results. In this case, choose the Modify The Query Design option to open the query in Design view, which is discussed next.

Microsoft Access

FIGURE 36-4.
The final Simple Query Wizard dialog box.

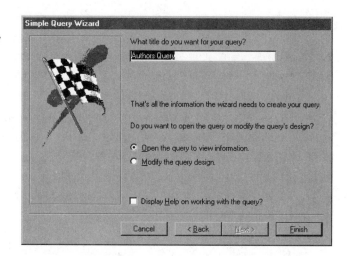

Doing Without the Simple Query Wizard

The main advantage to using the Simple Query Wizard is that it automatically adds to the upper portion of your Design view the required field lists (tables or queries) that you need to use in your query, and it adds the fields themselves to the grid in the bottom portion of the window, as shown in Figure 36-5.

FIGURE 36-5.
When you use the Simple Query Wizard, Access adds the field lists and field names to Design view for you.

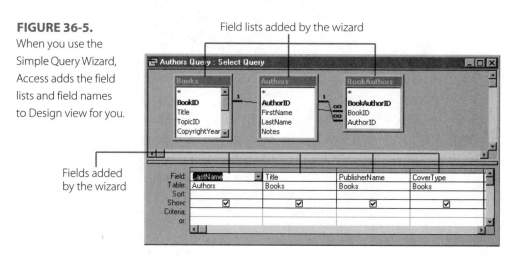

Field lists added by the wizard

Fields added by the wizard

NOTE

> The Simple Query Wizard adds a field list to the Design view for each table from which you selected fields in the first wizard dialog box (the one shown in Figure 36-2, page 938). It also adds a field list for any table that's needed to establish a relationship between the fields you selected. For example, when the query shown in Figure 36-5 was designed, fields were selected only from the Books table and the Authors table. However, there's no direct relationship between these two tables; they're related only indirectly through the BookAuthors table. The wizard, therefore, included a field list for the BookAuthors table. Including the BookAuthors table allows the query to match the appropriate book or books to each author whom it lists.

Instead of using the Simple Query Wizard, if you select the Design View option from the New Query dialog box (click the New button on the Queries tab of the Database window to open the New Query dialog box), Access displays the Show Table dialog box, shown in Figure 36-6. In this dialog box, you select the tables or queries that contain the fields you want to include in your new query. (You should also select any table needed to establish an indirect relationship between fields, as explained in the previous note.) To select a table or query, simply double-click on its name, or select it and click the Add button.

FIGURE 36-6.
Use the Show Table dialog box to add a table or query to Design view.

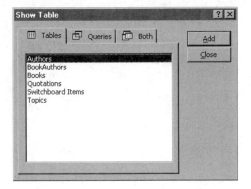

When you've finished adding tables or queries, click the Close button. Access will bring you to Design view, which will display a field list for each table or query that you selected. You then need to add to the query design grid the fields that you want included in the results, either by clicking on the Field row and selecting the field names from the drop-down list that becomes available, or by dragging the names from the field lists, as described in the section "Defining the Conditions," earlier in this chapter.

Features of the Query Design Grid

The design grid in Design view offers additional options not available using the Advanced Filter/Sort command.

■ Perhaps the most useful feature is the Show row, which offers a check box for each field that controls whether that field is displayed in the resulting datasheet. By clearing the check box, you can include a field as part of a condition, though that field won't appear in the datasheet. For example, the query shown in Figure 36-7 would list the author's last name, title, and publisher for those books that sell for over $30, but won't list the purchase price for the books. (In this figure, the field lists have been rearranged from their initial layout to make the relationships easier to see.)

FIGURE 36-7.
With a query, you can use fields in your conditions without displaying them in the datasheet.

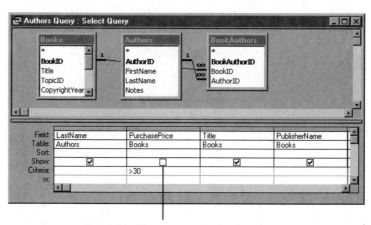

This field will not appear in the datasheet.

■ As with the Advanced Filter/Sort command, you can sort based on any field in the query by specifying either Ascending or Descending in the Sort row. Access sorts using the Sort row entries it encounters while moving from left to right through the fields, and it uses additional fields only when it finds exact matches in the first field used for sorting. However, when you're working in Design view, you don't have to display the sort fields in your datasheet.

Show
Table

- You can add a field list to the Design window at any time by choosing the Show Table command from the Query menu or by clicking the Show Table button on the toolbar. The Show Table dialog box is then displayed, which was described in the previous section and was shown in Figure 36-6, page 941. And, of course, you can add fields from any table or query in the database.

  When more than one field list is added to Design view, Access will draw lines to indicate any relationships between fields (these lines are the same as those shown in the Relationships window). You can add or alter the relationships yourself. But if you run a query without valid relationships, the query will likely not show the results you expected, or Access might display a message indicating that it can't process the query. For information on relationships, see "Relating Your Tables," page 875.

- Use the Table Names command on the View menu to control whether the Table row is included in your query design grid. If it's included, this row lists the table name for each field included in the grid, which can be helpful when you're creating more complex queries.

- To remove a field list from Design view, simply click on it, and choose Remove Table from the Query menu or press the Delete key.

Viewing the Results of a Query

When you're designing a query, you often need to switch between Design view and Datasheet view. Fortunately, you have a number of easy ways to do this. From the View menu, you can choose Design View or Datasheet View as appropriate. Also, from Design view, you can click the Run button on the toolbar to view the results of the query in Datasheet view. (Note that switching to Datasheet view automatically *runs* the query—that is, shows the results that correspond to the current query definition.) Additionally, you can switch between various

Run

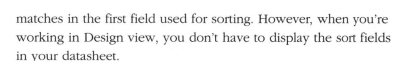

V

Microsoft Access

views by clicking the down arrow on the View button at the left of the toolbar and choosing the view you want from the drop-down menu:

As a shortcut, you can simply click on the View button, without opening the drop-down menu, to switch between Datasheet and Design views, because the default selection will alternate between these two views as you do.

> Both the View menu and the View button offer a third option: viewing the SQL (structured query language) information associated with your queries. This view is useful primarily when you use Access to work with data managed by certain other database systems. You needn't worry about this view if all your data is stored within Access itself.

Top-Value Queries

Access has one nifty feature that goes a bit beyond sorting and lets you look at the highest or lowest values for a field when using an actual query. For example, in a query that lists books (such as the example Authors Query shown in the previous figures), you might be interested in looking at only the five least expensive titles. To do that in Access, follow these steps:

1 Display the query in Design view.

2 Sort on the field you want to use to organize your list. In this example, the field would be Purchase Price. To look at the lowest values in the list, sort by selecting Ascending in the Sort row. To look at the highest values on the list, sort by selecting Descending in the Sort row.

3 In the Object list box on the toolbar, select the number of top or bottom values you want to see. If the number you want isn't listed, enter your own number into the box at the top of the list:

Object list box (the first three matching queries will
be shown in the order of the sort)

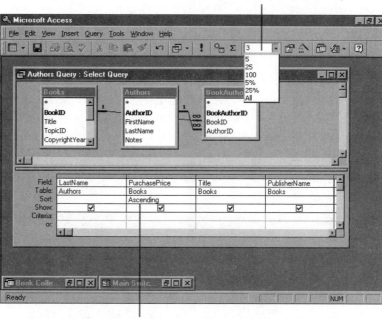

Sorting direction (Ascending starts with the lowest prices)

🌟 **TIP**

The Object list also lets you select or type a *percent* rather than an absolute
actual number of records to be displayed. For example, in a query listing students and their test scores, you could select a Descending sort on the score field
and enter *15%* into the Object list to retrieve a list of students in the top 15 percent of the class (perhaps the ones who get A's).

4 To view the results of the query, use any method to switch into
Datasheet view. The following datasheet shows the results of the
query defined in the example above:

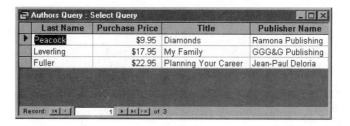

Summarizing Your Records

In addition to providing a list of records that match a set of conditions, a query can also be used to summarize the information contained in those matching records. This is accomplished through the use of a Total row in the query design grid. To add the Total row to your grid, you must be working with a Select query (the standard type of query), and the query must be open in Design view. Choose the Totals command from the View menu, or click the Totals button on the toolbar.

Totals

Figure 36-8 shows a query design grid with the Total row added and the drop-down list showing a variety of calculations to perform on the totaled field.

FIGURE 36-8.

Selecting options in the Total row summarizes values within the datasheet.

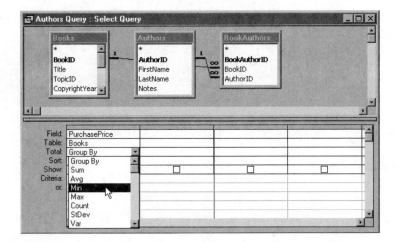

To use the Total row, you must have at least one field in your query design grid that contains values that can be summarized. Usually this would be a field with the Number or Currency data type. If you want to summarize that field for all the records in the table, simply select the type of summary calculation to be performed from the drop-down list. The items on this list resemble the functions used in Microsoft Excel and are briefly described in Table 36-1. If a field can't be summarized numerically, such as a text field, the only choice available is Count, which will give you the number of matches that have any value in that field.

TABLE 36-1. The Aggregate Functions in the Total Row

Function	Description
Sum	Adds up all the values within the group
Avg	Finds the average for all the values within the group
Min	Finds the lowest value within the group
Max	Finds the highest value within the group
Count	Determines the number of values within the group
StDev	Determines the standard deviation for the population defined by the group
Var	Determines the variance for the population defined by the group
First	Lists the first value encountered in the group
Last	Lists the last value encountered in the group

If all you do is select a summary function for a single field (as shown in Figure 36-8), the resulting datasheet will look similar to the one shown here:

Notice that the datasheet contains only an answer to your query with a column heading identifying the function and field that were used—in this case, MinOfPurchasePrice (the minimum—lowest—value in the PurchasePrice field).

In addition to providing overall summaries for the datasheet, these tools can also be used to perform calculations on *groups* of values within the records. To do this, you need to add a field to the grid that will be used to group the records and select the Group By option in its

Total box. For example, you might want to determine the average price of hardcover books versus paperback books. You would need to have two fields in your data group: the CoverType field, which is used for grouping the records, and the PurchasePrice field, which is used for the calculation, as shown here:

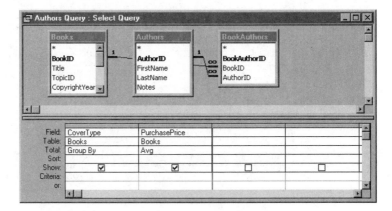

When you run this type of query, Access lists each group together with the calculation result for the values within that group, as shown next:

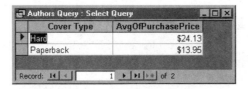

As you might imagine, you can control the order of the records in the datasheet by using the Sort row to display the records in ascending or descending order.

In addition to the Group By option in the Total row, you can also select the Where option in the Total row drop-down list. The Where option lets you add a field to the query design grid that is to be used only for including a condition for selecting records. In this case, the field isn't used to group records, nor is it displayed. It is used simply to determine which records will be included in the group to be summarized. When you use the Where option, you must provide a condition in the Criteria row.

> **NOTE**

The Expression option on the Total row drop-down list is used to create more complex calculations based not only on the values within fields but also on the values resulting from *aggregate* operations on fields, such as sum, average, or standard deviation.

Calculating New Values

Sometimes you might need to calculate the results for information contained within each record, rather than summarizing across records. To do that, the best approach is to create a calculated field. You can create such a field within a query, on a form, or within a report. For example, perhaps you'd like to see the purchase price of books if their prices were all increased by 15 percent. To include this information in a query, you would create a field in the query design grid that would perform this calculation. This new field is called a calculated field because it performs a calculation and isn't a regular field from a table.

? **SEE ALSO**

For information on creating formulas in Excel, see Chapter 19, "Crunching Numbers with Formulas and Functions."

To create a calculated field, click in the Field row in a blank column in the query design grid and enter the expression for calculating the value. Rather than typing the name of a field to be used in your calculation, you can click the down arrow to the right of the text box and select the field name from the list; you would then type the remainder of the expression. Formulas for calculating fields are similar to formulas entered into cells in Excel spreadsheets—the main difference is that rather than referring to cell addresses, you refer to field names. The formula will be calculated for every record.

Figure 36-9 on the following page shows an expression to calculate a 15 percent increase in the purchase price of books. Because Access doesn't allow you to express values in terms of a percentage, the formula multiplies the current price by 1.15—the equivalent of 115 percent.

When you run this query, you see the results shown in Figure 36-10 on the following page. Notice that the field name consists of the letters *Expr* followed by a digit, indicating the sequence in which the calculated field was created, and that the results of the calculation aren't formatted.

Fortunately, you're not stuck with the default format used by Access. It's quite easy to change both the name of the calculated field and its

V

Microsoft Access

FIGURE 36-9.
A calculated field contains a value that is computed from the values of other fields.

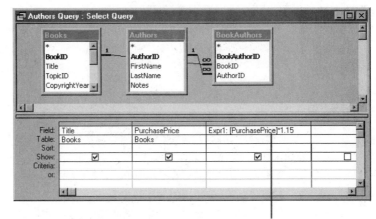

Expression typed in to create a calculated field in the query.

FIGURE 36-10.
Calculated fields can be displayed within the query datasheet.

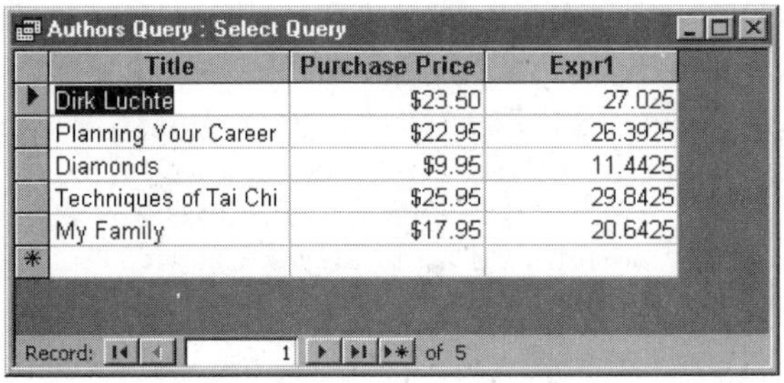

formatting. If you return to Design view, you'll notice that the expression you originally typed into the Field box for the calculated field (in the example, *PurchasePrice*1.15*) has been reformatted to include a field name. In the example, the expression would now appear as follows:

*Expr1: [PurchasePrice]*1.15*

To change the field name, simply highlight the text before the colon, and type the new name. For instance, in this example you could replace *Expr1* with *Expected Price*.

To format the calculated field, right-click anywhere in the column for the field in the query design grid, and choose Properties from the shortcut menu that appears. On the General tab, click on the Format box, and from the drop-down list that appears, select an appropriate format. For this example, you would choose Currency. Now when you switch to Datasheet view, the information will be much more in keeping with the format of the other material in your database, as shown here:

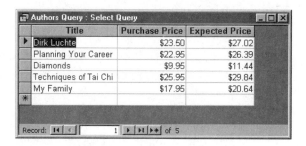

The Crosstab Query

All of the queries discussed so far are known as *Select* queries. A Select query is the routine type of query that passively displays a list of records or calculates summary values. Now we will discuss a second category of query, the Crosstab query. Sometimes you'll have organized the information in your database by two or more different grouping categories, and you'll have included important information based on the subsets of these groups. Imagine, for example, that you've collected some test results from a group of students. The students can be grouped based on gender (male or female) as well as on factors such as their age (15, 16, or 17). It might be useful to know the average test score for each of the possible subsets (15-year-old boys, 15-year-old girls, 16-year-old boys, 16-year-old girls, and so on), to consider whether your teaching is equally effective for both genders. This is best accomplished through a statistical matrix called a cross-tabulation. In Access, you can generate a cross-tabulation by creating a Crosstab query. The results of a Crosstab query for the test score scenario just described are shown here:

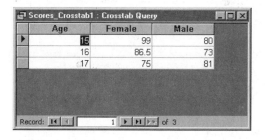

To create your own Crosstab query, or to review an example using the Book Collection database, follow these steps:

1 In the Database window, select the Queries tab, and then click the New button.

2 In the New Query dialog box, select the Crosstab Query Wizard, which guides you through the steps of designing your Crosstab query.

3 Select the table or query containing the fields you want to include. In our example we'll select the Books table.

4 Select from one to three fields to be used for row headings (for our example, select the Cover Type field).

5 Select a single field to be used for the column headings (for this example choose the PublisherName field).

6 Now choose the field and the function for which you want the cross-tabulation generated. In this example, choose the PurchasePrice field and choose the Avg function. You can also choose to display a value at the beginning of each row that summarizes all the values in that row (the average of all values if you chose the Avg function, the sum of all values if you chose the Sum function, and so on). Click Next, and then click Finish to view the results of the Crosstab query:

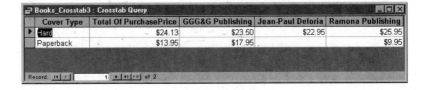

You might find it interesting to compare this result with the graphic at the top of the preceding page. The Crosstab query has all the information that was contained in that figure, plus it includes an entire second dimension of information that breaks out the average purchase price of hard cover and paperback books by publisher. The sample database contains so little data that these figures aren't really meaningful, but in a working database you could analyze the expense of books from different publishers by cover type and apply other calculations such as the standard deviation, maximum, minimum, or simple count of books in each crosstab cell.

> **From Query to Crosstab**
>
> You can also convert an existing query to a Crosstab query. To do this, open it in Design view, choose the Crosstab option from the Query menu, and designate the row and column heading fields, as well as the function to be used in the calculations, by selecting values in the Crosstab and Total rows of the query design grid.

Queries that Change Things

We have now discussed two major types of queries, the Select query and the Crosstab query. But there is another important category of query, with four subtypes, that actually changes your data. These last four query types rely on the conditions defined in the query design grid to identify which records should be changed, and they use other information that you provide to determine what sort of changes to make. When you're working with a query in Design view, you can convert the query to one of these types by choosing a query type from the Query menu or by clicking the down arrow on the Query Type toolbar button and choosing from the drop-down menu, as shown here:

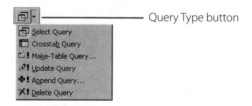

Query Type button

When you convert a query to a different type, the rows in the query design grid change according to the type of information that must be specified. For two of the query types (Make-Table and Append), Access displays a dialog box to obtain more information before returning you to the Design window.

Delete Query

The most dangerous of these four queries is the Delete query, which removes from your tables all records that match your conditions. This can be useful for housekeeping—for example, you might choose to eliminate from your database all old records with dates prior to January 1, 1996—but it can be tragic if you make a mistake in defining your conditions. Always use the Select query type *first*, using the conditions you plan to use for deleting records, so that you can first display the records to confirm that you've got the right subset of your database. *Only then* go ahead and switch to the Delete query type to remove them *permanantly*.

Make-Table Query

As the name implies, the Make-Table query type creates a new table of all the information your query returns. The Make-Table query type can be particularly useful for backing up your information. For example, in the case above, before you delete all records prior to January 1, 1996, you might want to use the Make-Table query type to make a separate table containing that information. Your first step would be to use the Select query type to specify all records prior to 1996. Then you would use the Make-Table query type to create a new table of just these older records. Finally, you would use the Delete query type to delete the older records from your more recent ones.

Append Query

Like the Make-Table query type, the Append query type copies records from one table (or from a collection of tables) to a new location. The Append query type doesn't create a new table, but instead adds the fields your query retrieves to an existing table. This query is often used for adding a new batch of records to update an existing table or database; for instance, you might receive a table or database of new books published in 1997 that you want to integrate with your existing books database.

Update Query

The fourth query subtype, the Update query, provides a powerful way to change the value of any fields in your database for those records that match the conditions you specify. When you use an Update query, Access adds an Update To row to the query design grid. You can then use that row to specify a value or an expression that indicates how the value in the field should be changed. You create expressions using the same general guidelines you follow when creating calculated fields as we described earlier in the "Calculating New Values" section.

You'll remember from that section that we created a new field, increasing the PurchasePrice field value of all the books in the Books table by 15 percent. This calculated value wasn't part of the database and didn't change any data in the database. But if you were to decide that you needed to raise the price of books by 15 percent (because of increased overhead, for example) you might use the Update query to physically change the value in every PurchasePrice field in the Books table to 115 percent of its previous value, permanently changing the data in your database.

While the Select and Crosstab queries helped you view and understand your data, the careful use of these four query types (Make-Table, Update, Append, and Delete) will prove to be the most powerful way to change your data.

Generating Reports with Wizards

Reports are the means that Access provides for displaying the information in your database. You probably won't find it very efficient to try to interpret the information presented in a report on your computer screen, for reports are really meant to be printed. (For working on screen with the information in your database, forms are generally preferable. They're discussed in Chapter 35.)

Access includes a number of items under the category of report, including generating address or other types of labels (Access provides the Label Wizard to assist you) and charts (which can be created using the Chart Wizard). Like the standard type of report, these take information from the fields in your database tables and then organize and summarize that information in meaningful ways. The Chart Wizard is shared by the Microsoft Office products and is discussed in "Using Graph," page 1022.

This chapter gets you started creating standard reports with the Report Wizard and shows you how to make simple changes to the report design once the report has been created. You'll also learn how to create labels using the Label Wizard.

Creating a Standard Report

Standard reports come in two basic varieties: columnar and tabular. A *columnar report*, as shown in Figure 37-1, resembles the layout of a simple form. Each field is presented in a separate row with the field name on the left and the contents of the field on the right. Depending on the number of fields in your database, each record might fit on a single sheet of paper or might extend onto several sheets; you might even be able to fit several records on one page.

 TIP

> If you want to work with the database used for the examples in this chapter, use the Access Database Wizard and select the Asset Tracking icon from the Databases tab of the New Database dialog box, as described in Chapter 32. Remember to ask the wizard to include sample data so that you have something to work with.

A *tabular report*, as shown in Figure 37-2 on page 960, organizes the information with each field in its own column and each record represented as a single detail line—this resembles viewing a table in Datasheet view. Summaries (subtotals, averages, and so on) can also be included at various levels of the report structure. The tabular report more closely resembles the format typically used for various types of business reports.

As with other types of database objects, the easiest way to begin a new report is to perform these initial steps:

- Open the database you want to report on.

- Open the Database window.

- Select the Reports tab.

- Click the New button.

FIGURE 37-1.
A columnar report prints the information for a single record in rows arranged in a column.

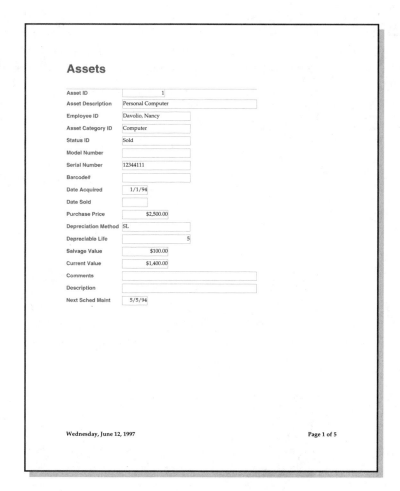

The New Report dialog box appears, as shown here:

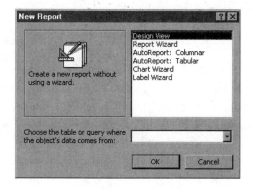

FIGURE 37-2.
A tabular report puts an entire record's information in one row and might print best in landscape orientation.

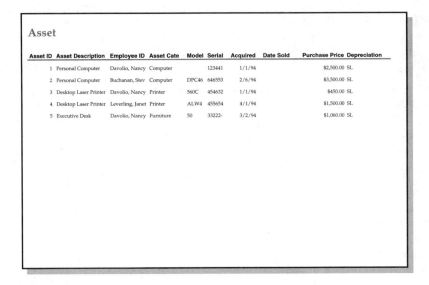

Asset

Asset ID	Asset Description	Employee ID	Asset Cate	Model	Serial	Acquired	Date Sold	Purchase Price	Depreciation
1	Personal Computer	Davolio, Nancy	Computer		123441	1/1/94		$2,500.00	SL
2	Personal Computer	Buchanan, Stev	Computer	DPC46	646553	2/6/94		$3,500.00	SL
3	Desktop Laser Printer	Davolio, Nancy	Printer	560C	454632	1/1/94		$450.00	SL
4	Desktop Laser Printer	Leverling, Janet	Printer	ALW4	455654	4/1/94		$1,500.00	SL
5	Executive Desk	Davolio, Nancy	Furniture	50	33222-	3/2/94		$1,060.00	SL

Note that you can also open the New Report dialog box by clicking the arrow on the New Object toolbar button and choosing Report from the drop-down menu:

In a moment we'll be stepping through the report-creation process using the Report Wizard option, but first you might like to know about the other report types shown in the New Report dialog box:

- Use the Design View option if you want to create a report from scratch using Design view. We describe this method in "Modifying the Report Design," later in the chapter.

- Select the AutoReport: Columnar or AutoReport: Tabular option to quickly create a columnar report (as shown in Figure 37-1 on page 959) or a tabular report (as shown in Figure 37-2). Either report will include *all* the fields belonging to the table or query that you select in the list box at the bottom of the New Report dialog box.

- Select the Chart Wizard option to create a chart using the Microsoft Graph program, as described in the section "Using Graph," page 1022.

- Select the Label Wizard to create mailing or other types of labels. We discuss this procedure in "Making Labels" at the end of this chapter.

Now select the Report Wizard option to create a report with the help of this Access wizard. We focus here on using the Report Wizard because it's the easiest way to design a report and yet is quite flexible. Although selecting one of the AutoReport options is a faster way to create a columnar or tabular report based on the fields in a single table or query, you can create these same types of reports using the Report Wizard with much greater flexibility in the choice of fields and in the report design.

 TIP

> You can quickly create a simple unformatted report, with a columnar arrangement, by selecting a table on the Tables tab of the Database window or by selecting a query on the Queries tab, and then choosing AutoReport from the New Object drop-down menu shown on the facing page.

To run the Report Wizard, select the Report Wizard option in the New Report dialog box and click the OK button. You don't need to select a table or query in the list at the bottom of the dialog box.

The first Report Wizard dialog box appears and asks you to identify the fields to be included in the report, as shown in Figure 37-3 on the following page. As with other Access wizards, you have the option of selecting from several tables or queries. Be sure to include all the fields that have

Microsoft Access

FIGURE 37-3.
In the first Report Wizard dialog box, you select all the fields to be used in the report.

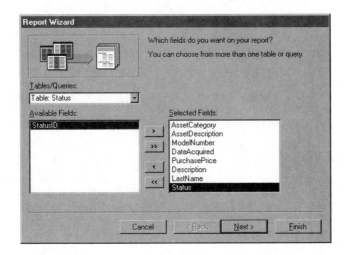

any relevance to your report, whether the values are to be displayed in each detail line, summarized, or used as values by which to group the records.

To access fields from different tables or queries, simply select the tables or queries from the Tables/Queries drop-down list. This list includes all the tables and queries defined in your database. Move the fields you want from the Available Fields list into the Selected Fields list box using the four buttons located between the list boxes. When you've finished selecting fields, click the Next button to display the next Report Wizard dialog box.

Grouping Records

The dialog box shown in Figure 37-4 appears only if you selected fields from more than one table in the previous step. This dialog box lets you choose one table for grouping the information in your report. In the example shown in Figure 37-4, fields were selected in the first dialog box from the Asset Categories, Assets, Employees, and Status tables (all of which are related through one-to-many relationships). We'll choose Asset Categories here, which will group the records on the report by asset category—that is, the report will list all Asset records that match the first asset category (which is Computer), then all records that match the second category (which is Printer), and so on through each of the remaining categories.

FIGURE 37-4.
If this dialog box appears, you need to choose a table to be used for grouping the records on the report.

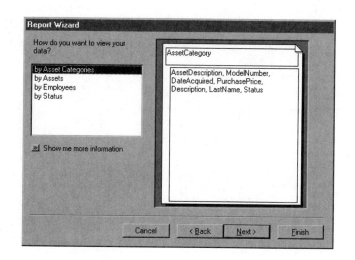

> In the example database, the Asset Categories, Employees, and Status tables are all *primary* tables in one-to-many relationships with the Assets table. Therefore, each record in the Asset Categories, Employees, or Status table can match *many* records in the Assets table and thus can easily be used for grouping records in the Assets table. This isn't true for the Assets table, however, because it constitutes the *related* table in all the relationships. Accordingly, if you select the Assets table, the wizard won't attempt to group your records for you. In the next wizard dialog box, however, you'll have the opportunity to specify grouping on the basis of individual fields. For information on relationships and the differences between primary and related tables, see "Relating Your Tables," page 875.

After selecting the grouping table we want, we click Next and open the third Report Wizard dialog box, shown in Figure 37-5 on the following page. In this dialog box, you can further define the grouping of records in your report by selecting one or more specific fields to be used to group the records. In the example shown in Figure 37-5, because the Asset Categories table was selected in the previous dialog box, the field from this table, AssetCategory, is already selected as the main grouping field. (If the Assets table had been selected in the previous dialog box, *no* grouping field would be selected.) You could then add one or more fields to create additional grouping levels.

FIGURE 37-5.
Add additional levels to the grouping of your records by selecting more grouping fields.

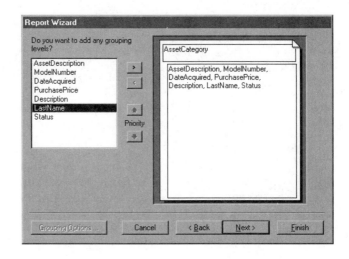

For instance, if you added the LastName field, records would be grouped by asset category, and then records within each asset category would be grouped by the last name of the holder of the asset. This grouping would be shown in the report model at the right of the dialog box (see Figure 37-6). To see how the resulting report will look, see Figure 37-10 on page 969.

FIGURE 37-6.
The third Report Wizard dialog box after an additional grouping field has been added.

Top grouping level (wizard added this field based on choice in previous dialog box)

Move selected grouping field (LastName) to higher level.

Move it to lower level.

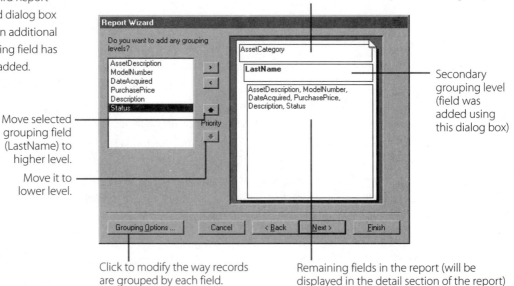

Secondary grouping level (field was added using this dialog box)

Click to modify the way records are grouped by each field.

Remaining fields in the report (will be displayed in the detail section of the report)

> ### Why Use Grouping Levels?
>
> Deciding which fields to group and which to leave in the *detail section* of your report can be a confusing process at first. You might recall from earlier chapters that tables and queries can be sorted by any number of fields in a left-to-right order. You can do the same thing with a report, using just the detail section. But the powerful advantage of placing one or more fields into grouping levels (beyond making those fields visually stand out in your report), is that summary calculations can be made on one or more of the numeric fields that fall within each grouping level you set up.
>
> For instance, if all your assets were sorted only on detail lines by asset category first and by last name second, the order of the data in your report would be the same as in the report we're creating in this section of the chapter. But how would you find the total cost of all the computer equipment vs. all the furniture? Or, how would you compare the average cost of computer equipment used by Buchanan with that used by Davolio? With an undifferentiated listing of your data, you could only calculate a grand total for the Purchase Price field for the entire report.
>
> But by *grouping* the report by Asset Category first (computers, and so on) and by Last Name second, you'll be able to perform aggregate (sum, maximum, minimum, or average) calculations on the numeric fields in the detail section of the report. You'll be able to break down the cost of assets by category and by individual. And you can still have a Grand Total line at the end of the report giving you the total value of *all* assets.

To add a grouping field, click the top button to move the field onto the report model at the right; if you decide to remove a field, use the next button to move it back to the left. You can add up to three fields, which when combined with an initially selected grouping field, would generate up to four grouping levels in your report. You can change the priority level of a grouping field that you've chosen by clicking on the field name at the right of the dialog box and then clicking the up-arrow or down-arrow Priority button.

When you've finished defining the grouping of your records, click the Next button to move to the fourth Report Wizard dialog box.

Sorting Fields

The fourth Report Wizard dialog box, shown in Figure 37-7 on the following page, lets you choose the sorting order for the detail section in

FIGURE 37-7.
Choose how to sort the detail lines in your report.

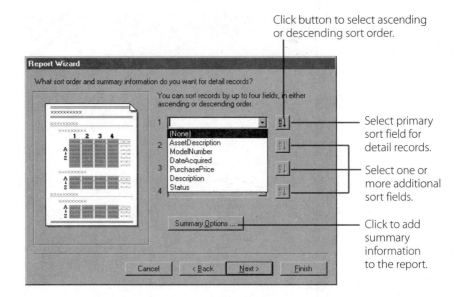

Click button to select ascending or descending sort order.

Select primary sort field for detail records.

Select one or more additional sort fields.

Click to add summary information to the report.

the report. Note that the report *groups* are automatically sorted on the fields used for grouping. In this dialog box, however, you can choose one or more fields that will be used for sorting the detail lines falling *within* each group. Choose the primary sort field by selecting it from the top list (labeled 1); you can then choose one or more additional sort fields in the remaining lists. (Note that each list contains the names of only those report fields that are *not* used for grouping.)

Setting Summary Options

One button in the fourth Report Wizard dialog box is crucial but easy to overlook: the Summary Options button. Click this button to open the Summary Options dialog box, shown in Figure 37-8. This dialog box lists each of the numeric or currency fields included in the detail section of your report. In this example, only the PurchasePrice field qualifies as a summary field, being of the Currency type.

You can choose to have Access summarize the values in one or more of these fields for each group in the report. If you want a summary to appear in your report, simply check one of the summary value functions for the field that you want to summarize. Access can determine the sum, average, minimum, or maximum value.

FIGURE 37-8.

In the Summary Options dialog box, specify how Access summarizes numeric information for each group.

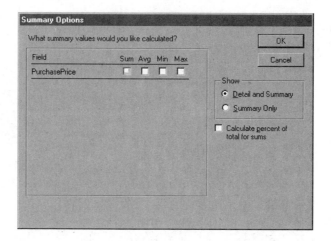

You can also specify whether the records within each group will be shown, or only the summary information will be shown. In general, the first time you produce a report you'll probably want to leave this option set to Detail And Summary so that you can see clearly how Access is organizing the information. Later, you might want to hide the detail information so that your report is more concise and contains fewer distractions.

You can also turn on the Calculate Percent Of Total For Sums option to have Access calculate the percent of the grand total represented by each group total. In this example, you could determine what percentage of total cost of assets was spent on computers as compared to printers or furniture, and even break it down further by employee. This can be useful for seeing how group values contribute to the overall result. When you've finished setting the summary options, click OK to return to the fourth Report Wizard dialog box. Verify that the sorting options are the ones you want, and click Next again to move to the fifth dialog box of the Report Wizard.

Selecting a Layout

The fifth Report Wizard dialog box, shown in Figure 37-9 on the following page, lets you select the layout and orientation of your report. Each of the layout options in this dialog box specifies how much of the database information is repeated at each level of the report. When you

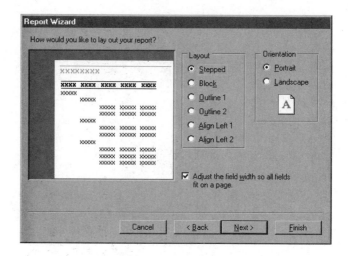

select an option, the model at the left of the dialog box gives you an idea of how your report will look:

- The Stepped layout (shown in Figure 37-10) places each new group heading in its own section of the report, with no other information on the same line.

- The Block layout compresses the information for the group heading onto the same line as the information for the first detail listing in that group. This makes for a more vertically compact report, but often it's somewhat difficult to find the information you need.

- The Outline 1 and Outline 2 layouts overlap the columns used for the grouping values but keep the text for each on a separate line. This is useful when you have a report that's too wide to fit comfortably on a single page. Alternatively, you can consider changing the page orientation from the Portrait option to the Landscape option, which gives you a wider page to work with.

- Finally, the Align Left 1 and Align Left 2 layouts position the grouping values and detail records beginning at the left margin. This provides the largest area across your page for your detail records, though it can be difficult to determine whether a header has in fact changed. The Aligned Left 1 layout is shown in Figure 37-11 on page 970.

FIGURE 37-10.
The stepped layout keeps each field in its own column.

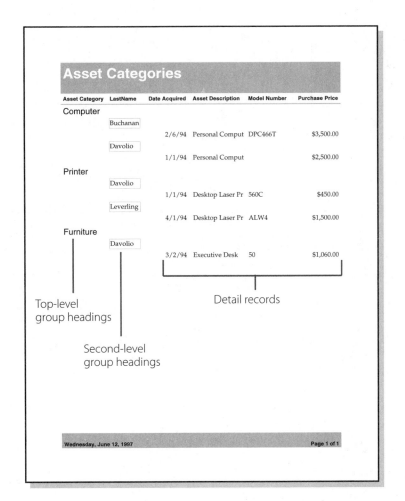

When you're done setting options in the fifth Report Wizard dialog box, click the Next button to go to the sixth dialog box.

Selecting a Style

The sixth dialog box of the Report Wizard, shown in Figure 37-12 on page 971, lets you choose a format style for your report. These format styles automatically apply fonts, borders, and spacing to your report design. In general, the simpler the design, the better your system's performance in producing the report. Complex designs involving a lot of graphics or shading might take significantly longer to create and, subsequently, to print out.

V

Microsoft Access

FIGURE 37-11.
The Aligned Left 1 layout displays the fields used for creating the groups as headers and starts each detail line at the far left.

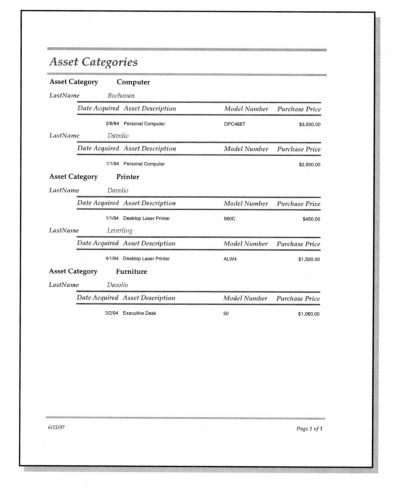

When you're done selecting the style, click the Next button to move on to the final dialog box.

Wrapping It Up

In the seventh and final Report Wizard dialog box (see Figure 37-13), you can name your report and choose whether to immediately preview the printed appearance of the report or open the report in Design view so that you can modify its design, which we'll do next.

FIGURE 37-12.
Choose the style
of the elements in
your report.

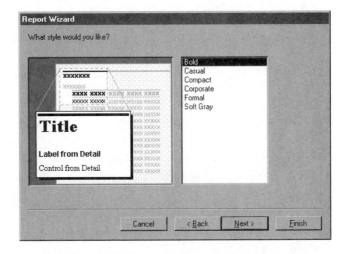

FIGURE 37-13.
Decide on a report
name and choose
how to open the
report to finish.

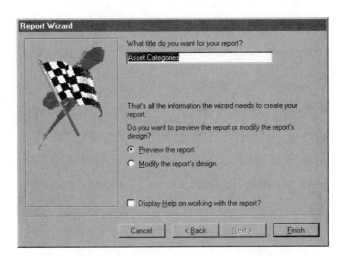

Modifying the Report Design

Once Access has created your report, you might discover that there are
a number of changes you need to make. For example, Access is often
unable to fit an entire field name into the available column width, and so
it might cut off letters from the start or the end of the name as necessary.
These problems are generally cosmetic and are best solved by changing

the font or the font size or by simply editing the text used for the label. See Chapter 38, "Formatting Forms and Reports," for a discussion of working with the fonts in your reports.

To work with the design of the report, you must be in Design view. As you saw in the previous section, you can have the Report Wizard open the report in Design view as soon as it has finished generating it. You can also open an existing report in Design view at any time. One of the easiest ways to accomplish this is by opening the Database window, selecting the Reports tab, selecting the report you want to work with, and clicking the Design button. Alternatively, if you're previewing the report, you can choose Design View from the View menu, or simply click the Close button on the Print Preview toolbar to go directly to Design view.

Close

Figure 37-14 shows a report in Design view.

FIGURE 37-14.
To make changes to your report, you must be in Design view.

Labels are displayed exactly as they will print.

Report sections

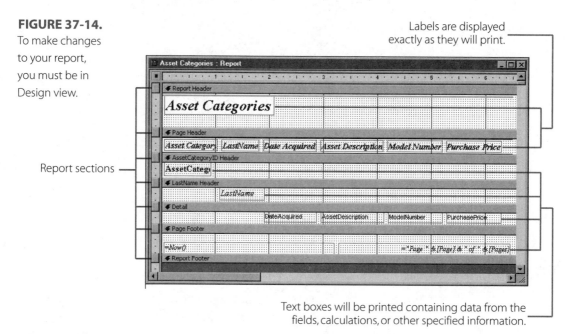

Text boxes will be printed containing data from the fields, calculations, or other specified information.

The design of a report consists of a number of controls. These include label controls used for titles, headings, and field labels; and text box controls used for the fields themselves, which represent the data that will be printed. The horizontal bands (labeled Report Header, Page Header, and so on) mark the different sections of the report—namely, the headers, the footers, and the detail section. Rest assured, the bands aren't printed on the actual report.

Figure 37-14 shows the design that was used to create the Stepped layout report shown in Figure 37-10 on page 969. Notice that all the labels in the design window appear exactly as they do on the actual report, but that the text box for each of the fields in the design window is replaced with the field contents on the report. Furthermore, the text is positioned without gaps even though in the design window the controls for the actual fields are organized into separate sections.

The changes that you most commonly need to make to a report design include changing the positions, sizes, or formats of the labels or text boxes, and perhaps changing the contents of the labels. To change a label's contents, simply click on it to select it; then click on the position within the text where you want to make the change (the pointer will be an I-beam) and edit the text. Techniques for changing the position, size, or format of a control are given in Chapter 38, "Formatting Forms and Reports."

Figure 37-15 shows the design screen that was used to create the Aligned Left 1 report in Figure 37-11 on page 970. The primary difference between the report designs shown in Figures 37-14 and 37-15 lies not in which controls appear on the screen, but in how those controls are *arranged*. The location of the controls in Design view determines the location of the information in the printed report.

FIGURE 37-15.
The Aligned Left 1 layout report shown in Design view.

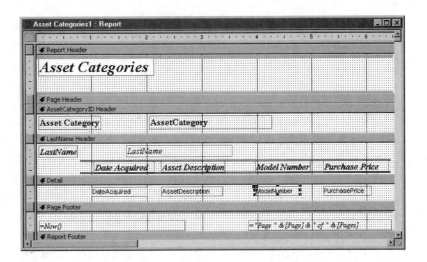

Report Sections

As you can see in Figures 37-14 and 37-15 on pages 972 and 973, Design view divides the report into separate sections. The information defined within each section will appear at a specific position on the printed report. The Report Header information appears at the beginning of the first page, and the Report Footer information appears at the end of the last page. The contents of the Page Header section appears at the top of each page, and the contents of the Page Footer section at the bottom of each page.

If you chose to group your report using one or more fields (in the second and third Report Wizard dialog boxes), there will also be a header section for each of these fields. Also, if you chose to calculate summary values for one or more fields (through the Summary Options button in the fourth Report Wizard dialog box), there will be a footer section corresponding to each of the group header sections; these footer sections are described in the next part of the chapter. Later in this chapter in "Controlling the Groupings" you'll learn several ways to modify the group headers and footers in your report.

Finally, the information contained in the Detail section is displayed for each detail record printed on the report. You can study Figure 37-16 to see where the different sections displayed in Design view will appear on a printed report. This figure shows the printed appearance of the report shown in Design view in Figure 37-14 on page 972.

Working with Summary Controls

The footer sections of reports often contain summary information. In a report created with the Report Wizard, summary information can be displayed for each group used in the report, as shown in Figure 37-17. (This report is the same as the example report given previously, except that the Sum summary function was assigned to the PurchasePrice field, via the Summary Options button in the fourth Report Wizard dialog box.) To eliminate the summary information for one of the groups, simply delete the summary controls from that group's footer and close up the space. You can adjust or completely close the space within a report section by simply dragging—up or down—the top part of the band below that section.

FIGURE 37-16.
A report based on the design shown in Figure 37-14 (page 972), showing the location of each of the report sections on the printed report.

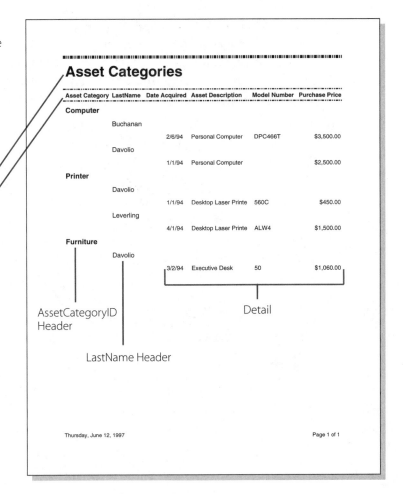

Report Header
Page Header

AssetCategoryID Header

LastName Header

Detail

FIGURE 37-17.
The controls in report footers usually summarize values in one or more numeric fields.

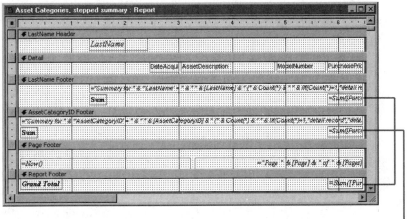

Text boxes containing the Sum function

V

Microsoft Access

Each control has its own set of properties that you can use to adjust the way it looks and acts in the report. To access a control's properties, simply right-click the control and choose the Properties command from the shortcut menu. This is true of all controls but particularly important for summary controls.

Figure 37-18 shows the Data tab of the Properties dialog box for one of the controls used to calculate the sums in the example report. Notice that the Control Source option on the Data tab is a mathematical function based on the field that it summarizes. In this case, the Sum function is used to add all the values contained in the preceding group for the PurchasePrice field. To change the function used, simply highlight the function name, and type a new one. The standard summary functions, Sum, Avg, Min, Max, and Count, are all available. See Table 21-1 on page 624 for a description of these and other functions.

FIGURE 37-18.
The properties of a control used to sum the PurchasePrice field.

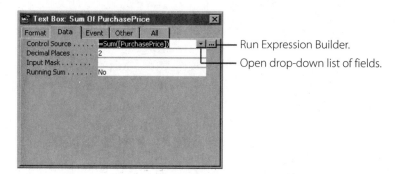

To change the field being summarized, simply highlight the field name and type a new one, or select a new field from the drop-down list. Alternatively, you can get help in constructing an expression by clicking the Expression Builder button at the right of the Control Source row.

You can use the Format tab of the Properties dialog box to change the way in which the values are formatted. In this case you would want to use the Currency format. Note that the number of decimal places is controlled on the Data tab, unless you change this setting to Auto, in which case the number of decimals displayed will be according to the Format type—Currency, in this case. The Decimal Places setting represents only the number of decimal places displayed, *not* the internal accuracy of the data itself. (This is controlled by the field's FieldSize property. See Chapter 33 for information on setting field properties.)

To display complete information on any property from the Access online Help, place the insertion point in the relevant Property dialog box field and press F1.

Controlling the Groupings

The organization of the groups used for your report and the sorting of the records in the Detail section are controlled by the Sorting And Grouping command on the View menu. Choose this command to reveal the Sorting And Grouping dialog box, shown here:

Fields used for grouping records

Records within each group are sorted by this field.

In the example report, the AssetCategoryID and LastName fields were designated as grouping fields in the second and third Report Wizard dialog boxes. The DateAcquired field was chosen for sorting detail records within each group through the fourth Report Wizard dialog box.

By changing properties for the items in the Field/Expression column, you can modify the group headers and footers that appear in the report. You can remove a group header or group footer by selecting the name of the grouping field in the Field/Expression column and changing the Group Header or Group Footer property setting at the bottom of the dialog box to No. You can also specify the sort order for any field by selecting Ascending or Descending in the Sort Order column.

The Group On property setting is one of the most important options available in this dialog box. Group On controls whether the report creates a new group for every distinct record value (the default, as described previously) or whether a different grouping interval is used. To change to a different grouping interval, click the Group On row and select the type of grouping interval to be used from the drop-down list.

The display of the Page Header, Page Footer, Report Header, and Report Footer sections is controlled by options on the View menu. To remove both the Page Header and the Page Footer, turn off the Page Header/Footer option on the View menu. Use the Report Header/Footer option to control the display of the Report Header and Report Footer. If you turn off these displays, you'll also delete any controls in them! Access will ask you for confirmation first.

Different field data types offer different grouping interval options. For example, date fields provide a set of options for Year, Month, Day, and so on.

When working with text, you set the number of characters used to create each group in the Group Interval text box. For example, to group all records by the first letter (*A, B, C, D*), you would set Group On to Prefix Characters and Group Interval to 1. To group the same information in smaller groups (*Aa, Ab, Ac*), you would set Group On to Prefix Characters and set Group Interval to 2. Access doesn't generate a group if no records are contained within that group.

If you want to display all the records contained in a single group on a single page of the report and start each new group on a new page, assign the Whole Group setting to the Keep Together property. Bear in mind, however, that some groups will be too large to fit on a single page—in which case, Access will use as many pages as necessary to finish the group and start a new page for the next group.

More often, you'll want to save space by letting new headings start anywhere on a page. In this case you'll want to design the report so that the headings for a group remain with at least the first detail record that follows the headings. This avoids having a new heading appear at the bottom of a page with no data below it, moving the headings over to the next page if necessary. To do this, assign the With First Detail setting to the Keep Together property.

As with field properties, you can obtain detailed information on any group property by placing the insertion point within the property's box in the Sorting And Grouping dialog box and pressing F1, the help key.

Making Labels

Because databases are so often used to store information about a company's customers or physical inventory, small wonder that one of the most common uses of database information is to produce labels. Whether these labels are then affixed to envelopes for bulk mailing, used as name tags for a conference, or placed on equipment for inventory control, Access considers these labels a kind of report, and the creation process is very similar.

Link Your Data Between Word and Access

In addition to creating labels directly in Access, you can also use the Office Links submenu of the Tools menu to move information from Access to another program. The Publish It With MS Word command on this submenu lets you translate your report or form into a document file that retains all the formatting information. This file can then be opened within Microsoft Word, and you can change the appearance and, if appropriate, the formatting of the form or report. When working with a query or table datasheet, you can use the Merge It With MS Word command on the Office Links submenu of the Tools menu to have Access use the information from a database to create a Word table. You can then use Word's Mail Merge features to reference that table as your data document, as described in Chapter 13.

Creating labels is something that's best done within Access itself—since Access provides the Label Wizard specifically for this purpose. To get started, open the New Report dialog box, either by opening the Database window, selecting the Reports tab, and clicking the New button, *or* by clicking the New Object button on the toolbar and choosing Report from the drop-down menu:

1 Select the Label Wizard option from the New Report dialog box, and then in the drop-down list at the bottom, specify the table or query that's to be used for generating the labels. For Access to generate labels, all the fields must appear on a single datasheet. If you need to combine information from more than one table, you must construct a query combining the fields from the various tables as described in Chapter 36. To follow our example screens, use the Employees table from the Asset Tracking database we've been using in this chapter. Click OK.

V

Microsoft Access

2 Access now starts the Label Wizard. The first Label Wizard dialog box (see Figure 37-19) prompts you to select the type of labels that you'll be using, by product number or dimensions. The built-in list of labels is quite comprehensive. Changing a unit of measure in the first dialog box or changing the label type changes the list of labels displayed. There are four separate label lists: English Sheet Feed, English Continuous, Metric Sheet Feed, and Metric Continuous. In case you don't find the label layout that matches your labels, click the Customize button to create a custom label layout.

FIGURE 37-19.
Specify the type of label you're printing on.

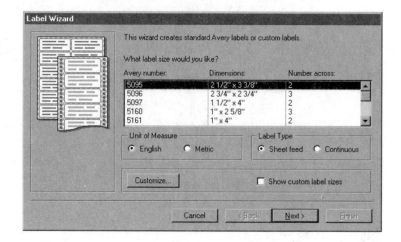

3 Once you've specified the layout of your labels, click the Next button to move to the second dialog box of the Label Wizard (see Figure 37-20), where you can select the font and color to be used for the text on your labels. This dialog box gives you access to the fonts installed on your system and lets you specify not only the text color but also the font weight. Most programs let you choose a regular or bold weight (making them more readable), but you'll find many more choices in this list. This font will be applied to all the text contained in the labels.

4 In the third dialog box, shown in Figure 37-21, you specify the fields to be included in the labels. The number of characters that will fit in the Prototype Label area is determined by the size of the label you selected in the first dialog box and the size of the font you selected in the second. If you find that you don't have enough lines to organize the information the way you want, use

FIGURE 37-20.
Specify the appearance of the text to be printed on your labels.

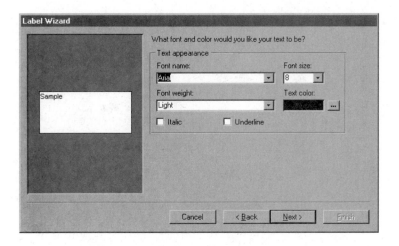

the Back button to change either the size of your labels or the font that you've chosen.

You design your label by working within the Prototype Label area. To define a particular line within the prototype, simply click on the line and Access will highlight it in light gray. To add a field to the highlighted line in the prototype, select the field name in the Available Fields list and click the button with the arrow between the two boxes; or, simply double-click the field name. If you move a field that you later decide you don't want, select it and press the Delete key. You don't have to use every line; to leave a line blank, simply skip over it and add text to the next line. To move to the next line, you can click it, or press the Enter or Down arrow key.

FIGURE 37-21.
The Prototype Label area is where you arrange the fields for your label.

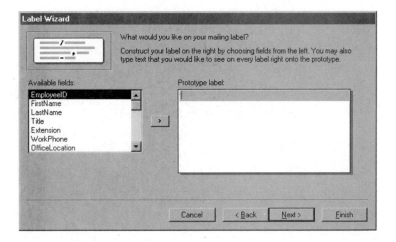

Microsoft Access

V

FIGURE 37-22.
The label is created with a combination of fields and fixed text.

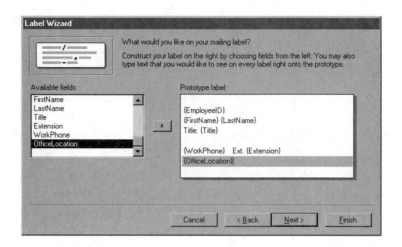

Position the various fields as you want them to appear on the label. Type any fixed text (text that should appear on *every* label, such as *Priority Mail* or *Confidential*) directly into the Prototype Label area. Figure 37-22 shows a sample label for identifying equipment belonging to a particular employee. The words *Title:* and *Ext:* are examples of fixed text, as are the spaces between fields.

If you don't care about the order in which your labels appear, click the Finish button. If you want to sort your labels, click the Next button, and in the fourth dialog box select the fields to be used for sorting. Remember that the *first* field you add to the list of sort fields is used to make the initial sort. Only when values within that field match are any additional fields used for sorting.

In the fifth and final Label Wizard dialog box, you can modify the report name that the wizard has assigned, and you can choose to either preview the printed appearance of the labels, or go to Report Design view to modify the label design.

Look at the report in Design view, and you'll notice that several functions were added by the Label Wizard, to eliminate spaces within fields and to add spaces and text where necessary in the labels. Access also customizes your page setup to ensure that the labels print correctly.

Print

To print the labels, choose the Print command from the File menu, or click the Print button on the toolbar. You can print the labels either when you're previewing them, or from Design view.

Formatting Forms and Reports

Forms and reports provide ways to display the information contained in your database, plus they share another important feature: both use the same techniques and tools to format their controls. (Each control represents an element, such as a field or piece of text, that appears on the forms or reports.) The controls on an Access form or report are placed in layers, similar to the objects that you create in Microsoft Word or with Microsoft PowerPoint. For a discussion of how these layers can affect your work and of how to use the Bring To Front and Send To Back commands on the Format menu, see "Working with Drawing Objects," page 760.

Techniques for formatting your controls include methods for moving and aligning the various controls, for changing the font style, and for changing the color, border, and shading effects used for different elements.

To work with the controls on a form or a report, you must be in Design view. If you have an existing form or report to work with, follow these steps:

- Open the database whose forms or reports you want to design.

- Open the Database window.

- Select a form listed on the Forms tab or a report listed on the Reports tab.

- Click the Design button.

Moving Controls

Often, one of the first things you want to do with a form or report is reposition the various controls on it. This can be done either by moving individual controls or groups of controls, or by selecting one or more controls and aligning them.

The examples in this chapter are drawn from the form used in Chapter 35. This form was created by modifying the Members form from the Membership database created by the Access Database Wizard. To make the controls easier to see in the figures, the grid (marked with lines and dots on the form background) was hidden by turning off the Grid option on the View menu.

To move an individual control, follow these steps:

1 Select the control by clicking on it. When selected, the control has eight visible handles around its perimeter:

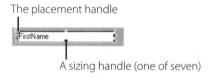

The placement handle

A sizing handle (one of seven)

If the control contains the insertion point, you'll have to select the control by clicking on one of its *edges*. If you click *within* the control, you'll only move the insertion point.

2 Move the mouse over the border of the control (but not over one of its handles) until the pointer changes to an open hand.

3 Drag the control to its new location.

In many forms and reports, you'll discover that what appear to be two separate controls are a linked set—most often, a label control is connected to the control it's labeling. In this case, when you select one of the controls, the placement handle for the second control also appears, as shown here:

Placement handles

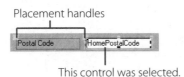

This control was selected.

These placement handles can be used to change the relative positions of these two controls. When controls are joined like this, moving one to a new location using the method described above always moves the other. However, when the mouse is positioned over the placement handle rather than over the border of the control, the pointer turns into a hand with an extended index finger, and dragging the placement handle moves just that one control and *not* the attached control.

To work with a group of controls, select the group by dragging a rectangle through all the controls you want to group. This is particularly useful when you're working with the options on the Align submenu of the Format menu. If the controls aren't arranged in such a way that you can draw a rectangle around them, you can still select multiple controls by clicking to select the first one and then holding down the Shift key while you click each of the others.

To reset the form so that no controls are selected, click on an area of the form with no controls, such as the form background.

Even though two controls are attached, it's possible to select only one of them. A control that has its placement handle visible but not the seven sizing handles is *not* selected. It will move with its attached control, but *formatting* commands will have no effect on it.

Microsoft Access

> Particularly when working with reports, keep in mind that the position of a control might influence how the data within that control is presented. For example, if you move a control from one section of a report to another, you might inadvertently change the order in which the values of the control are displayed and summarized.

Aligning Controls

Using the Align commands, you can move a group of controls so that their edges—left, right, top, or bottom—are all aligned along a single axis, making them more readable or attractive in reports. The Align commands won't allow the selected controls to overlap one another, however.

For example, to right-align a group of controls, follow these steps:

1 Select the controls, as shown here:

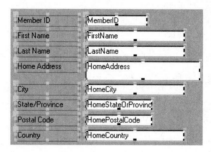

2 Choose the Align command from the Format menu or from the shortcut menu (click the right mouse button while the pointer is over one of the selected controls). This displays the Align submenu, as shown here:

3 Choose Right from the submenu. This command rearranges the various controls, as shown next:

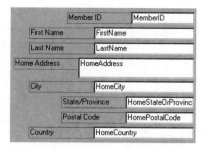

The Right command causes the rightmost controls to align along their rightmost edges, and it moves the other controls as far to the right as possible.

TIP

If you've selected a group but want to exclude just one or two controls from the group and format the rest, hold down the Shift key and click on each control you want to "unselect." Only items left with eight handles showing (seven sizing handles plus one placement handle) will be affected by menu commands.

Using the Grid

In Design view, forms and reports have a background grid to help you align controls, whether or not the grid is visible on screen. This handy grid is turned on and off by choosing the Grid command from the View menu or from the shortcut menu. When visible, the grid appears as solid lines at 1-inch intervals with a fine mesh of dots spaced evenly in between.

One way to use the grid is to choose the Snap To Grid command from the Format menu. Every control that's subsequently moved or resized (discussed below) will jump or *snap* to the closest gridline or point (whether or not the grid is visible). When the Snap To Grid option is not selected, you can position a control anywhere you want without regard to the grid.

A second way to use the grid is to realign controls. If you placed controls while Snap To Grid was turned off, you can later align them to the nearest grid point by selecting the controls and choosing the To Grid command from the Align submenu of the Format menu.

Spacing Controls

Not only can you align controls along one edge, but you can also distribute controls evenly within an area on a form or report, for clarity and appearance. If you select a group of controls that are randomly spaced and choose an option on either the Horizontal Spacing or the Vertical Spacing submenus of the Format menu, Access positions the objects according to your instructions. You can proportionally increase or decrease the distance between selected controls, or you can equalize the space between a selected group of controls.

For example, to make the vertical spacing between a group of controls even, follow these steps:

1 Select all the controls to be positioned, being sure in this case to include their labels, as shown here:

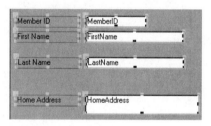

2 Choose Vertical Spacing from the Format menu to display the submenu shown here:

3 From the Vertical Spacing submenu, choose the Make Equal option. The result is shown next:

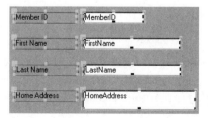

The first and last controls of a group don't move when you use the Make Equal command—only the controls in between are adjusted to even the spacing. However, if you use the Increase or Decrease command, all the controls move proportionally.

Changing the Size of a Control

To make room for data or its labels, you can change the size of a control on an Access form or report by following these steps:

1 Click on the control to select it and to display the sizing handles. (If the control contains the insertion point, you'll have to select it by clicking on one of the *edges* of the control.)

2 Position the mouse over one of the sizing handles (not the placement handle) so that a two-headed arrow—rather than a hand—appears, as shown here:

3 Drag that side of the control to its new location. If you're dragging a corner, the two adjoining sides will be repositioned. (If you hold down the Shift key while dragging a corner, it will move only horizontally or only vertically, whichever direction you first start moving it.)

The Size submenu on the Format menu provides a series of commands for changing the size of the selected control or group of controls:

Only two commands are available if a single control is selected: To Fit and To Grid. *All* commands are available if multiple controls are selected:

- To Fit sizes controls until they're just large enough to show the information they contain. Note that controls whose contents will vary can't be set with this option. You can set the label of a text box, because the label is constant, but you can't set a text box that displays a data field, because the amount of data can change from record to record.

- To Grid adjusts selected controls so that all four corners and sides align on the nearest grid. This makes it easier to move or align them later and gives your form or report a more consistent look.

- To Tallest, To Shortest, To Widest, and To Narrowest resize groups of controls so that each control is the same size as the tallest, shortest, widest, or narrowest control in the selected group. When Access does this kind of sizing, it pays no attention to whether such a change will allow sufficient space to display the contents of a control—so be careful, especially when you adjust to narrowest width or shortest height.

Changing the Color and Effects of a Control

Each kind of control, including text boxes, has a set of colors assigned to it. One color is assigned to the background of the control, while the other is assigned to the text. In addition, most controls have a border of some sort, which can be displayed in a separate color.

Fill/Back
Color

To change the background color used for a control, simply select the control and click the down arrow to the right of the Fill/Back Color button on the Formatting toolbar.

This displays the palette of available colors from which you choose the color you want. The Transparent button causes the control to acquire the color of the form, report, or any object underneath the control. To change the background color for an entire form or report, click on the background itself, and select the desired color. Each section of a form or a report can have a different background color, placing different emphasis on your various blocks of information.

Font/Fore
Color

To change the color of the text associated with a control, select the control and click the down arrow to the right of the Font/Fore Color button on the Formatting toolbar.

From the color palette that appears, select the color you want for the text. There is no transparent setting, otherwise the text would just disappear. Of course, if you intentionally want to hide text from view without actually deleting the control, you can set the control's Visible property to No. Or, if you want the control to be visible, but not the text in the control, just set the text color to match the background color.

 TIP

> The most recent color applied by the Fill/Back Color, Font/Fore Color, and Line/Border Color buttons appears on each button. To reapply those colors to a new control, you can simply select the control and click the relevant button without dropping down the color palette.

Line/Border
Width

Formatting borders is a bit more complex than simply applying background and text colors, because borders also have widths (thicknesses) and special effects. First select the control whose border you want to change, and then click the down arrow to the right of the Line/Border Width button on the Formatting toolbar to display the drop-down list of border widths.

The first width is a thin hairline border. The other widths are measured in points ranging from 1 point through 6 points (72 points = 1 inch). The greater the width of the border, the more noticeable will be the control as well as the color you apply to it.

Line/Border
Color

To change the color of the border, simply select the control, and click the down arrow to the right of the Line/Border Color button on the Formatting toolbar to display a palette of colors.

You can then select the color you want for the border. As with the Fill/Back Color button, the Line/Border Color button provides a Transparent option for hiding the border. You could also choose the same color as the control's Fill/Back Color if you want the border to blend with the background of the control.

Finally, you can apply a special effect to a control's border. To do this, select the control or controls you want to change, click the down

Special
Effect

arrow to the right of the Special Effect button on the Formatting toolbar, and then select the effect you want from the drop-down list that appears. The six styles of borders are illustrated in Figure 38-1.

FIGURE 38-1.
Applying a special effect to a control affects how its border appears against the background.

TIP

Add your own embellishments to a form by using the Line and Rectangle tools on the Toolbox (shown in Figure 35-8, page 921). A line or rectangle that you draw on a form functions as a control and can be assigned any of the properties discussed here.

Changing the Look of the Text

Access gives you mastery over the way your forms and reports look, by letting you format the text. We just discussed how you can change the color of your text, though you can format *more* than just the text's color. Each control's text can be formatted independently of another's, but any single control must have all its text formatted the same. To format the text in a control, select the control and then use any of the controls on the Formatting toolbar that are labeled here:

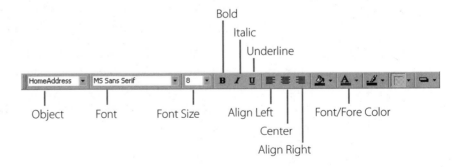

The first drop-down list, Object, shows any currently selected control and lets you select any other control currently on the form, even if that control isn't visible. Simply scroll through the list until you find the item you're looking for. In general, however, it's easier to simply click directly on the control on the form. If you've selected a group of controls, the Object list box will be blank, indicating that you're formatting more than one object simultaneously.

The second drop-down list, Font, is used to designate the font used in a control. This list displays all the fonts installed on your system. The third drop-down list, Font Size, lets you set the size of the characters in points. To change the font or the character size, simply select new settings from these drop-down lists, or type in a setting directly.

You can also set text to bold, italic, underline, or any combination of the three. To do so, select the control you want to change, and then click the Bold, Italic, or Underline buttons as you wish.

⭐ TIP

Line Up Your Controls for Emphasis

You might sometimes want to have a label with two different text formats, for example a label reading: "*First* Name." You can't have multiple text formats appear in a field containing data, though you can simulate the above effect in a label field by creating two label controls that are lined up to appear as if they were only one. Since each word is in a separate control, you can assign different formats to each.

You can also control how Access aligns the text within a control. This is especially useful when working with labels or text boxes. The Align Left, Center, and Align Right buttons are used to specify where in the control the text will appear. For most controls you'll want the text to align left or align right. One common format, shown in Figure 38-2 on the following page, aligns the labels to the right and their related text box controls to the left. This minimizes the amount of blank space that the eye must track over in moving from the label to the attached information.

V

Microsoft Access

FIGURE 38-2.
Aligning text closer
together makes it
easier to read.

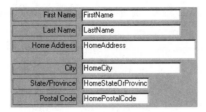

Using Control Properties

All the formatting options in this chapter are also available as property
entries in each control's Properties dialog box. To display the Properties
dialog box for a control, right-click on the control and choose Properties
from the shortcut menu that pops up, or simply double-click the control.
Different types of controls have different properties. Most of the options
discussed in this chapter affect various settings on the Format tab. Here's
the Format tab of the Properties dialog box for a label control:

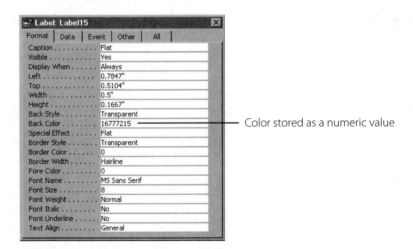

Color stored as a numeric value

You might notice that the Back Color for the label is listed as *16777215*—
not very informative! Don't despair. When you click in the box for a property that sets a color, a button with three dots appears at the far right.
Click this button and you'll open the familiar color palette, from which
you can select a color in the usual way or even define your own custom

color. A few advanced formatting options, such as setting a custom color, are available only from the Properties dialog box. Here are some more examples:

- Add scroll bars to a control to view text that wouldn't otherwise display—such as a three-line address in a one- or two-line address box.

- Set a report control that holds a memo field with variable amounts of text to grow or shrink when printing each record—to be able to show extra text on paper and save space when there's only a little text.

- Set a control's border line to solid, transparent, or several choices of dashed or dotted lines—for emphasis and flair.

 TIP

"Hmmm . . . What Does *This* Property Do?"
To learn how the many properties listed in the Properties dialog box affect different types of controls, select a control, open the Properties dialog box, and click in any property box you're curious about. Press F1, the help key, and Access's online Help system will take you directly to a complete explanation of the property. You can also choose the What's This? command from the Help menu—the pointer will change to an arrow and a question mark. Click the question mark on a property box you're interested in.

Using the formatting tools provided in Access and your own creativity, you can design functional, attractive, and highly professional reports and forms.

PART VI

Integrating Microsoft Office Applications

Sharing Data Among Office Applications

In the previous parts of the book, you learned how to copy and move data within a single document and among separate documents within a single Office program. In this chapter, you'll learn the different ways of exchanging data among separate Office applications. The chapter also describes the Office Tools—a set of programs designed for creating and embedding various types of information within Office documents.

Different Ways to Share Data

This section provides a general overview of the three basic ways to exchange data among separate Office applications:

- Static copying or moving of data

- Linking of data

- Embedding of data

This discussion will help you choose the most appropriate method. The following sections will discuss the techniques for performing each method.

In *static copying* or *static moving*, the data that you insert becomes an integral part of the receiving document and retains no link or connection with the document or program from which it was obtained. This is the type of copying or moving that you normally perform when you're working within a single document or program, using the techniques discussed in previous chapters. When you statically copy or move data from one application to another, you might or might not be able to edit the data within the receiving document. If the data can be converted to a format that the receiving program understands, you'll be able to edit it—for example, when you copy text from a Microsoft Excel worksheet and paste it into a Word document. If, however, the data can't be converted into a format native to the receiving program, the data can be displayed and printed but can't be edited in the receiving program—for example, when you copy bitmapped graphics from some drawing programs into a Word document.

In *linking*, the data that you insert retains its connection with the document and the program from which it was obtained. In fact, a complete copy of the data is stored only within the source document; the receiving document stores only the linking information and the data required to *display* the data. When the data in the source document is edited (by you or someone else), the linked data in the receiving document can be updated automatically or manually to reflect the changes.

In *embedding*, the data that's inserted retains its connection with the source program but not with the source document. In fact, there might not even *be* a source document, because you can create *new* embedded data. The receiving document stores a complete copy of the information, just as it does with statically copied data. However, because of the connection between this data and the source program, you can use the source program's tools to edit the data.

You should use linking rather than embedding when you want to store and maintain data within one document and merely display an up-to-date copy of the data in one or more other documents. Linking is especially useful in the following situations:

- You want to display only part of the source document within the receiving document. For example, you want to display only a totals line from a large Excel worksheet within a Word document. (If you *embed* the data, the entire workbook will be copied into the receiving document.)

- You maintain a single master document that you want to display in several other documents—for example, a Word document containing instructions that you want to display within several other Word documents or PowerPoint presentations.

- You want to minimize the size of the receiving document. (In linking, the receiving document stores only the linking information plus the data required to display the item.)

 SEE ALSO

For information on using the Binder program to combine entire documents created by Office applications, see Chapter 40, "Using the Office Binder Program."

You should use embedding rather than linking when you want to store an independent block of data as an integral part of the document in which it's displayed. Maintaining documents that contain embedded data is simpler than maintaining documents that contain linked data, because you don't have to keep track of source documents. (To update linked data, the source document must be present in its original location under its original filename.) You can easily share a document containing only embedded data with other users—without having to provide linked source documents along with it.

Using Drag and Drop or the Paste Command

In previous parts of the book, you learned how to copy or move data *within* an Office application using the drag and drop technique, as well as by using the Cut or Copy command followed by the Paste command.

VI

Integrating Applications

On occasion, you'll also find it extremely handy to use drag and drop to exchange data *among* separate Office applications. If the source and receiving documents are both open and visible on the Windows screen, you can move a block of data by simply selecting it in the source document within one program and then dragging it to the receiving document in another program. (As usual, hold down the Ctrl key to copy rather than move.) If the receiving document is open but *not* visible—if, for example, the source program is maximized on the screen—you can move or copy the data as follows:

1 Select the data in the source document.

2 Drag the data to the Windows taskbar button for the receiving program and hold the pointer over the button without releasing the mouse button. In a second or so, Windows will activate the receiving program.

3 Drag the data to the receiving document and drop it at the desired location.

When you exchange data among separate Office applications using the drag and drop method—or the Cut or Copy and Paste commands—the data might be copied or moved statically, or it might be embedded in the receiving document, depending on the nature of the data and the specific applications involved. In the following sections, you'll learn how to use the Copy or Cut command followed by the Paste Special command to precisely control the format and the manner in which data is transferred.

 TIP

Create Hyperlinks Using Drag and Drop or Paste As Hyperlink
Instead of statically copying data from one application or file to another, you can create a hyperlink to the source document. Follow the above steps for using drag and drop, but use the *right* mouse button instead of the left to drag the selection to the receiving file. Then choose Create Hyperlink Here from the short-cut menu that appears when you release the right mouse button. You can also copy and paste text as a hyperlink by first copying the text and then choosing the Paste As Hyperlink command from the Edit menu. The text you copy must be from a saved file.

Static Copying and Moving

To copy or move data statically from one Office application to another, as described above, do the following:

1 Select the data in the source program and choose the Cut or Copy command from the program's Edit menu.

2 Switch to the receiving program and place the insertion point at the position in the receiving document where you want to insert the data.

3 Choose Paste Special from the receiving program's Edit menu. The program will open the Paste Special dialog box, as shown in the example in Figure 39-1.

FIGURE 39-1.
Statically pasting data using the Paste Special dialog box.

5 Select the desired data format from the As list. You can choose any format description except one containing the word *object*. (Selecting an object format would *embed* the data.) The formats listed depend on the source program and the nature of the data.

4 Select the Paste option.

6 When you select a format from the As list, a description of that format appears here.

Linking Data

You can transfer and link many kinds of data among Office applications. The following are some examples:

■ You can insert and link part or all of an Excel worksheet or an Excel chart into a Word document or a PowerPoint slide.

■ You can insert and link part or all of a Word document into an Excel worksheet or a PowerPoint slide.

VI

Integrating Applications

- You can insert and link a PowerPoint slide into a Word document or an Excel worksheet.

> You can't link data from the Office Tools programs (such as Equation Editor). These programs can be used only for embedding data.

You can transfer and link either a selected part of a document or an entire document. To transfer and link part of a document, do the following:

1 Select the data in the source document and choose the Copy command from the source program's Edit menu *(don't choose Cut!)* to copy the data to the Clipboard.

Link a Slide to Another Document

To link a PowerPoint slide to another document, you must be in Outline or Slide Sorter view (choose Slide Sorter from the View menu), and you must select a single slide.

2 Place the insertion point at the position in the receiving document where you want to insert the data, and choose the Paste Special command from the receiving program's Edit menu.

3 In the Paste Special dialog box, select the Paste Link option and then select the desired data format in the As list.

> If the Paste Link option is not available, this means that the data in the Clipboard—or the selected format—can't be linked or the source program doesn't support linking.

If you want to link an entire document, you can select the whole document in step 1 above, *or* you can use the following alternative method:

1 Place the insertion point at the position in the receiving document where you want to insert the data.

2 Choose the Object command from the receiving program's Insert menu, and click the Create From File tab in the Object dialog box. (In PowerPoint and Access, Create From File is an option you click, rather than a tab.)

3 Select the Link To File option, and in the File Name box enter the name of the document you want to insert. (In PowerPoint and Access, the option is simply called Link.) Click the Browse button if you need help locating the file. See Figure 39-2.

FIGURE 39-2.
Inserting and linking an entire document.

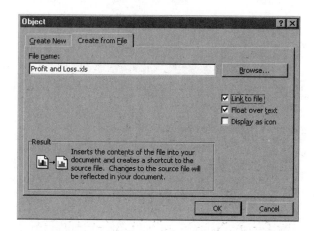

 TIP

Display Your Data as an Icon, or Float It over the Text

If you select the Display As Icon option in either the Paste Special or the Object dialog box, the receiving program displays an icon representing the linked data rather than displaying the data itself. Also, when you print the document, only the icon is printed. To view the linked data within the source program, use one of the methods for editing linked data, which will be described next. Using icons to display linked data is a convenient way to present various types of information in a compact format within a document that's intended to be viewed on the screen.

In a Word document, when you link certain types of data in certain formats (for example, an Excel worksheet in the Picture format), the Float Over Text option is available in both the Paste Special and Object dialog boxes. If you select this option, the data will be displayed in a box outside the normal flow of text, and you'll be able to position it anywhere on the page. For more information on the Float Over Text option, see "Using Text Boxes to Position Text on the Page," page 309; the Picture format is discussed in "Importing Pictures," page 314.

VI

Integrating Applications

You must edit linked data by making the changes within the *source* document. To do this, you can use one of the following methods:

- Run the source program and open the source document.

- Select the entire block of linked data in the receiving document, or simply place the insertion point anywhere within the data. Then, choose Linked *Item* (where *Item* is an actual description of the selected data, such as Worksheet Object) from the Edit menu, and choose either Open Link or Edit Link from the submenu that appears:

    The source document will then be opened in the source program and you can edit the data. (The commands that appear on this submenu depend on the source program and the nature of the data.)

- For some types of linked data formats (for example, *picture* or *bitmap* in a Word document), you can open the source document in the source program by simply double-clicking the linked data in the receiving document.

You can modify one or more links within a document by choosing the Links command (in Access, the OLE/DDE Links command) from the Edit menu to open the Links dialog box, which lists all the links contained in the active document. The appearance of the dialog box varies among Office applications; Figure 39-3 shows how it looks in Word. To modify a link, select it in the list. To simultaneously modify several links, select them by pressing the Ctrl key while clicking each link. You can now do one or more of the following—but note that not all these actions are available in all Office applications:

⊗ **CAUTION**

Although you might be able to edit certain types of linked data directly within the receiving document (for example, Unformatted Text in a Word document), your changes will be overwritten the next time the data is updated! However, formatting changes (such as applying the bold or italic format to text) will generally be preserved when the data is updated.

FIGURE 39-3.

Modifying links in the active document.

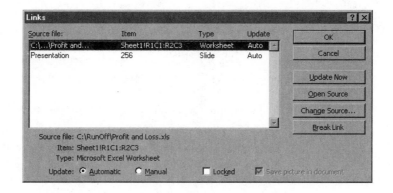

- You can make a link either automatic or manual by selecting the Automatic or Manual option at the bottom of the dialog box. By default, a link is automatic, which means that the data is automatically updated whenever the receiving document is opened, and whenever the data is modified in the source document while the receiving document is open. If you make a link manual, it won't be updated until you explicitly issue a command. You might want to make links manual to avoid slowdowns while working with a document that contains many links or linked data whose source is modified frequently.

- If the selected link is manual, you can update it by clicking the Update Now button.

- To change the name or location of the source document for the linked data, click the Change Source button. (You might also be able to change the description of the data location within the source document—for example, the range of cells in a spreadsheet.) You would need to do this to reestablish a link after the source document has been moved or renamed. When you click the Change Source button, it opens the Change Source dialog box. To specify a new source document, enter the filename into the File Name box. To select a new data location within the source document, enter the description into the Item box. For a Word document, you would enter a bookmark name. For an

VI

Integrating Applications

Excel workbook, you would enter the name of the worksheet and the row and column range within this worksheet, as in the following example:

Sheet1!R1C1:R2C2

■ To open the source document within the source program, click the Open Source button. This has the same effect as using one of the techniques for editing linked data, which were described above.

■ To remove the link, click the Break Link button. The data will become an integral part of the receiving document, just as if you had copied it statically. After doing this, you won't be able to restore the link.

■ In Word, to prevent the link from being updated, turn on the Locked option.

Keep Your Source Document Available

To help ensure that the source document is always available to maintain the link, place both the source document and the receiving document together within the same folder.

A Linking Example

Consider that you've created an Excel worksheet containing the daily prices for a commodity—wheat—together with a chart illustrating those prices for a period of 25 days (see Figure 39-4). You now want to write a report in Word describing the price action over that period. To link a copy of the Excel chart to your report, you would perform the following steps:

1 In the Excel worksheet, click the chart to select it, and choose the Copy command from Excel's Edit menu.

2 In the Word document containing your report, place the insertion point at the position where you want the chart, choose Paste Special from Word's Edit menu, and complete the dialog box as shown in Figure 39-5. The resulting report is shown in Figure 39-6 on page 1010.

FIGURE 39-4.
An Excel worksheet,
together with a chart.

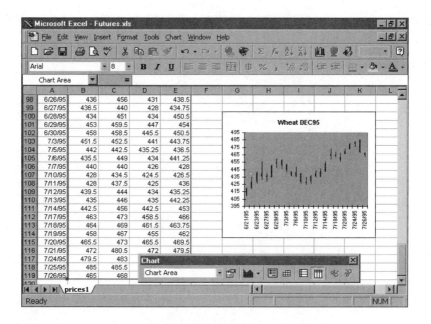

FIGURE 39-5.
Linking the Excel
chart to a Word
document.

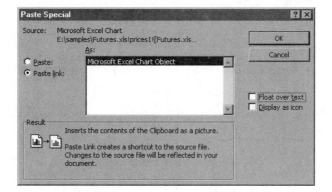

The following are some advantages of *linking* this chart rather than
embedding it:

■ Only the link and the information required to draw the chart are
copied into the receiving document. If you *embedded* the chart,
the entire workbook, including all the price data, would be copied into the receiving document, significantly increasing its size.
(Although you would see only the chart, the workbook data is
also stored in the document so that you can edit both the data
and the chart.)

FIGURE 39-6.

The Excel chart shown in Figure 39-4 (on the preceding page) linked to a Word document.

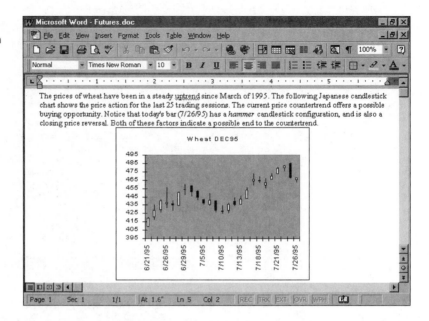

■ The same chart can be linked to additional Word documents, PowerPoint presentations, or other documents. The chart will then be updated within all receiving documents whenever you change the price data in the Excel worksheet.

Embedding Data

A block of embedded data is known as an *embedded object*. In an Office document, you can embed data that you have created in another Office application, in an Office Tools program (as described later in the chapter), or in any other Windows-based program that's been designed to be a source of embedded data. There are three ways to create an embedded object, which differ in the way that you obtain the data for the object.

First, you can obtain the data for an embedded object from a portion of an existing document, as follows:

1 Select the data in the source document, and choose the Copy or Cut command from the source program's Edit menu.

2 Place the insertion point at the position in the receiving document where you want to add the embedded object, and choose Paste Special from the receiving program's Edit menu.

3 In the Paste Special dialog box, choose the Paste option, and in the As list, choose the first format description that contains the word *object*. (See Figure 39-7.)

FIGURE 39-7.
Embedding an Excel worksheet object.

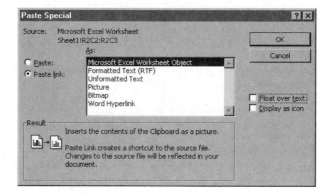

The second way to create an embedded object is to use an entire existing document as the source of the data, as follows:

1 Place the insertion point at the position in the receiving document where you want to embed the object, choose Object from the receiving program's Insert menu, and click the Create From File tab (or option button) in the Object dialog box.

2 Make sure that the Link To File (or Link) option is *not* selected, and enter the name of the source document into the File Name box (see Figure 39-8).

FIGURE 39-8.
Embedding an entire document.

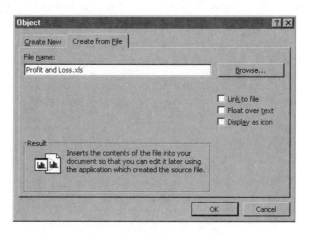

VI

Integrating Applications

The third way to embed an object is to create *new* data for the object, using the source program's tools, as follows:

1 Place the insertion point at the position in the receiving document where you want to embed the object, choose Object from the receiving program's Insert menu, and click the Create New tab (or option button) in the Object dialog box.

2 In the Object Type list, select the type of object that you want to embed. This list contains one or more items for every installed Windows-based program that can be the source for an embedded object. Click OK, and one of two things will then happen:

   • The source program's window will be opened, and will display a blank working area.

   • A blank working area will appear within the receiving document, and the source program's menus and buttons will be displayed within the receiving program's window. The source program's keyboard commands will also be available.

3 In either case, use the source program's commands to enter the data for the embedded object into the working area.

4 When you've finished entering the data, exit the editing mode. If you're working in the source program's window, do this by choosing the Exit command from the File menu (or using any other method to quit the program), and selecting Yes in the dialog box if the source program asks you whether you want to update the object. If you're working in the receiving program's window, simply click in the receiving document *outside* the object.

> **NOTE**
>
> With the Office Tools programs (described later), you must use this third method for creating an embedded object, because these programs can't create independent documents.
>
> When you use any of these three methods for embedding an object, you might be able to select the Display As Icon option or the Float Over Text option in the dialog box. For an explanation of these two options, be sure to see the tip "Display Your Data as an Icon, or Float It over the Text," page 1005.

To edit an embedded object, simply double-click it. The object will then be opened for editing either within the source program or, more commonly, within the receiving program.

> For some types of embedded objects, double-clicking the object does *not* open it for editing. For example, if you double-click an object containing a sound or video clip, the clip will be played. To edit the object, you must use the alternative method, given next.

Alternatively, you can select the object by clicking it, and then choose *Item* Object (where *Item* is a description of the selected object, such as Worksheet) from the receiving program's Edit menu to display the submenu shown here:

Choose one of the following commands from this submenu:

■ The Edit command, if present, which normally lets you edit the object within the receiving program's window using the menus and toolbars of the source program

■ The Open command, if present, which normally lets you edit the object within a separate window provided by the source program

The actual commands that appear on the submenu—and their actions—depend on the source program and the nature of the embedded data.

When you've finished editing the object, exit the editing mode. If you're editing in the source program, do this by exiting from the source program and selecting Yes in the dialog box if the source program asks whether you want to update the object. If you're editing in the receiving program, click in the receiving document *outside* the object.

VI

Integrating Applications

Convert Objects to the Format You Prefer

If the Object submenu includes a Convert command, you can choose it to change the data format of the embedded object so that it can be edited by a different source program. You might do this if the original source program isn't available.

An Embedding Example

Imagine that you're preparing a PowerPoint presentation and that you want to include a table of numeric values in a slide. By embedding an Excel Worksheet object, you can use all the features provided by Excel for creating the table. You could do this as follows:

1 Run Excel, open a new document, and enter the data into a worksheet.

2 Select the worksheet cells that you want to display in the Power-Point slide, as shown in Figure 39-9, and choose the Copy command from Excel's Edit menu.

3 Open the slide in the PowerPoint presentation in which you want to display the worksheet cells. (You must be in PowerPoint's Slide view; to switch to this view, choose Slides from PowerPoint's View menu.)

4 Choose Paste Special from PowerPoint's Edit menu, and in the Paste Special dialog box, choose the Paste option and select the Microsoft Excel Worksheet Object item in the list, as shown in Figure 39-10.

After you've pasted the worksheet cells into the slide, you can either save or discard the original Excel document. Note that the embedded object was created by copying cells from an Excel document—rather than choosing Object from PowerPoint's Insert menu to create new data—because the copying method lets you specify the exact number of cells to display in the slide and makes it easier to scale the worksheet within the PowerPoint slide.

FIGURE 39-9.
Selecting cells in
an Excel worksheet.

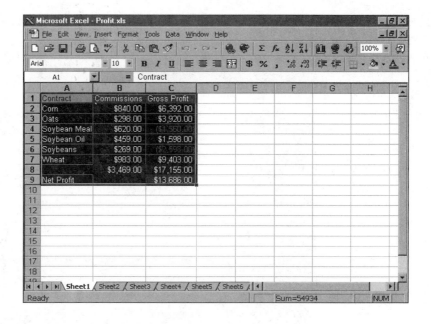

FIGURE 39-10.
Embedding the Excel
worksheet cells shown
in Figure 39-9 into a
PowerPoint slide.

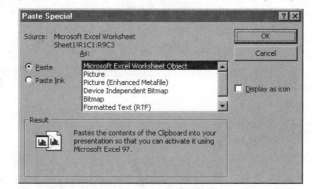

The resulting PowerPoint slide is shown in Figure 39-11 on the following page.

After embedding the worksheet into the slide, you can edit it within PowerPoint by double-clicking it, as shown in Figure 39-12 on the following page. Notice that the Excel menu and toolbar are displayed within the PowerPoint window to let you edit the object.

FIGURE 39-11.
Excel worksheet cells embedded in a PowerPoint slide.

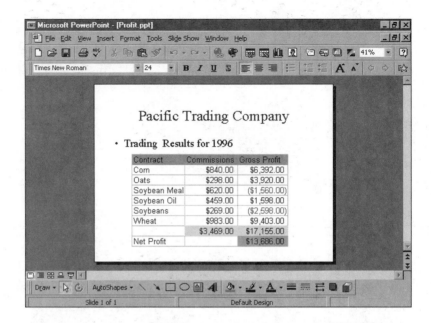

FIGURE 39-12.
Editing Excel worksheet cells embedded in a PowerPoint slide.

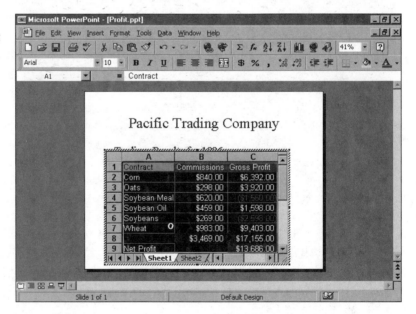

Using the Office Tools

When you install Office, you have the option of installing one or more of a group of Office Tools programs. These programs are designed to generate various types of information that you can embed in your Office documents. The Office Tools programs can't be run independently, nor can they create their own documents. You can run them only from an application, and the data they generate can be stored only as embedded objects.

> **NOTE**
>
> Not all the Office Tools are part of the Typical installation of Office. You can install any of the Office Tools you're missing by rerunning the Office Setup program.

To run an Office Tools program, perform the following general steps:

1 Place the insertion point at the position in the receiving Office document where you want to insert the embedded object.

2 Choose Object from the receiving program's Insert menu, and click the Create New tab.

3 Select the appropriate object description in the Object Type list and click OK. Table 39-1 lists each of the standard object descriptions for the Office Tools programs.

TABLE 39-1. The Office Tools Programs

Office Tools Program	Object Description Displayed in the Object Dialog Box	Purpose of Program
Clip Gallery	Microsoft Clip Gallery	Finds clip art pictures and inserts them into your documents
Equation Editor	Microsoft Equation 3.0	Enters mathematical expressions into your documents
Microsoft Graph	Microsoft Graph 97	Creates charts for displaying data
Organization Chart	MS Organization Chart 2.0	Creates organization charts and other types of hierarchical charts

VI

Integrating Applications

4 Use the commands of the Office Tools source program to enter the data for the embedded object into the working area provided. The working area will be either within the receiving program window or within a separate window displayed by the source program. (With the Clip Gallery program, you choose a picture in a list rather than entering your own data.)

5 Exit the editing mode. If you're working in the receiving program's window, exit editing mode by clicking in the program window *outside* the embedded object. If you're working in the source program's window, exit editing mode by choosing Exit from the source program's File menu or by closing the source program window; to save your work, answer Yes when asked whether you want to update the object.

Try Another Way to Run Office Tools Programs

Some of the Office applications let you quickly run one or more of the Office Tools programs by choosing a command from the Picture submenu of the Insert menu. For example, in Excel you can run the Clip Gallery by choosing Clip Art from this submenu or you can run the Organization Chart program by choosing Organization Chart. Likewise, in Word you can run the Clip Gallery by choosing Clip Art or you can run Microsoft Graph by choosing Chart.

To edit an object embedded by an Office Tools program, use any of the methods discussed previously in the chapter under "Embedding Data," starting on page 1010. Note that when you "edit" a Clip Gallery object, you replace the current picture with another one, rather than actually editing the picture data.

The following sections introduce you to each of the Office Tools programs. Keep in mind that each program provides extensive online Help from which you can learn the details of using the program's commands.

Using the Clip Gallery

The Clip Gallery program can help you to find and organize clip art, pictures, sounds, and videos and to insert them into your Office documents. When you select the Microsoft Clip Gallery item in the Object dialog box from the Insert menu and click OK, the Clip Gallery program is displayed

FIGURE 39-13.
The Clip Gallery
program.

2 Click the preview image of the
picture that you want to insert
(scroll for more pictures).

3 Click here to insert
the clip art picture.

1 Choose a category
of pictures to
preview.

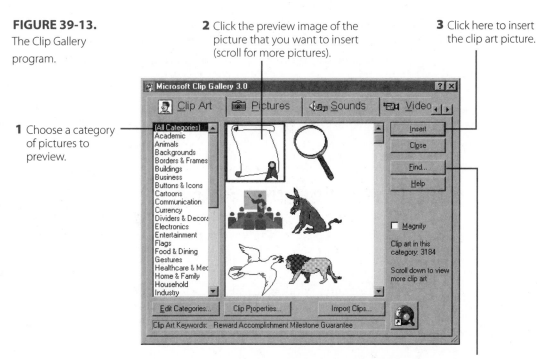

4 Click here to search for pictures that have a
specified description, filename, or file format.

in a separate window, shown in Figure 39-13. The Clip Gallery displays
all the clip art files that have been added to the program. If, when you
ran Setup, you installed the Clip Gallery program as well as the popular
clip art provided with Office, the Office clip art will already have been
added and will be displayed in the Clip Gallery window. Additional clip
art is available on the Office CD-ROM disc. Insert the disc into your
CD-ROM drive if you want to preview these clip art images as well. The
four tabs in the Clip Gallery window allow you to preview clip art
images, pictures, sounds, and videos and insert them into your document.

You can organize and update the images in the Clip Gallery window
by doing one or more of the following:

- Click Import Clips to add new clip art pictures to the Clip Gallery
  program. You need to do this if you've installed additional clip art
  images on your hard disk that you want to access through the
  Clip Gallery.

- Right-click in the previews area and choose Update Clip Previews to update the preview images that the Clip Gallery displays. You might need to do this if you've modified one or more clip art pictures.

- Click Clip Properties to change the description or category of the currently selected picture.

- Click Edit Categories to add, rename, or delete a picture category.

Using the Equation Editor

The Equation Editor lets you add mathematical expressions to your documents. When you select the Microsoft Equation 3.0 item in the Object dialog box and click OK, a working area is inserted into the receiving document and the Equation menu and toolbar are displayed within the receiving program's window. See Figure 39-14.

FIGURE 39-14.
Embedding an Equation Editor object in a Word document.

Working area—enter equation here.

Equation toolbar

Symbols

Templates

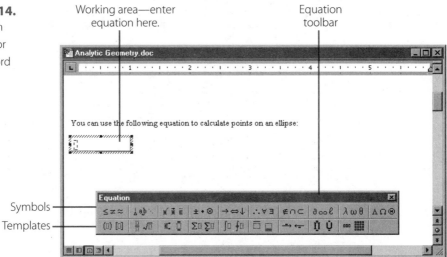

To create a mathematical expression, do the following:

- To enter numbers or variables, simply type them using the keyboard, as in the following example equation:

- To enter a mathematical operator that appears on the keyboard, such as +, -, or =, you can simply type it. For instance, you could add an equal sign to the example equation:

- To enter an operator or symbol that doesn't appear on the keyboard, click the appropriate button on the top row of the Equation toolbar, and then click the desired symbol on the drop-down palette of symbols. For example, you would click the following

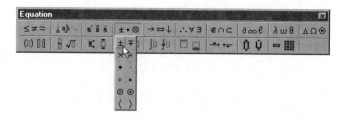

to add a ± symbol to the example equation:

- To enter an expression such as a fraction, a square root, an exponent, or an integral, click the appropriate button on the bottom row of the Equation toolbar, and then choose one of the templates on the drop-down palette. For example, you would click the following template

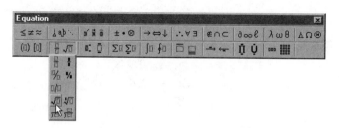

VI

Integrating Applications

to add a square-root expression to the example equation:

Then enter the desired numbers and variables into the area marked by dotted lines within the template. For example, you could type the following into the radical expression in the example equation:

$$y = \pm\sqrt{1+a}$$

You can insert templates within other templates to create nested operator expressions, such as a fraction within a square-root operator.

The Equation Editor won't let you enter space characters when you're typing an expression because it automatically sets the spacing between the numbers and symbols that you enter (for consistency). You can adjust the spacing or alignment of symbols, however, by selecting symbols from the Spaces And Ellipses palette, as shown below, or by choosing commands from the Format menu.

You can also modify the font, font size, or format (that is, the normal, bold, or italic features) of characters or symbols by choosing commands from the Style and Size menus.

Using Graph

Using the Graph program, you can insert charts into your Office documents. Graph supports a wide variety of chart types, and provides a handy alternative to using Excel charts. The easiest way to create a chart with the Graph program is to use a Word table, as follows:

1 Insert a table into a Word document, enter into this table the data that you want to graph, and then select the entire table. An example is shown in Figure 39-15.

FIGURE 39-15.
Selecting a Word table containing the data that you want to graph.

Contract	Gross Profit
Corn	6,392.00
Oats	3,920.00
Soybean Meal	-1,560.00
Soybean Oil	1,598.00
Soybeans	-2,598.00
Wheat	9,403.00

2 Choose Object from the Insert menu, click the Create New tab, select the Microsoft Graph 97 Chart object type, and click OK. Alternatively, you can simply choose the Chart command from the Picture submenu of the Insert menu. Graph will immediately embed a chart into the document that depicts the data contained in the Word table. Graph will also display a *datasheet* containing the chart data. See Figure 39-16.

FIGURE 39-16.
Embedding a Chart object in a Word document. This chart is based on the Word table shown in Figure 39-15.

Table entered into the Word document in step 1

Menu commands and toolbar buttons provided by Microsoft Graph

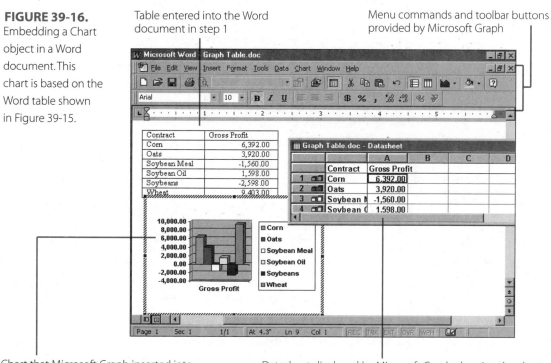

VI

Integrating Applications

Chart that Microsoft Graph inserted into the document as an embedded object

Datasheet displayed by Microsoft Graph, showing the chart data (which was copied from the table in the document)

3 The datasheet contains a copy of the data from the original Word table that you selected. If you want to change the values plotted on the chart, you must edit the numbers within the datasheet, *not* within the original table. (Once the chart is inserted, a copy of the data from the Word table is stored independently within the embedded chart object. Changing the table data won't affect the chart; in fact, you can delete the table if you want to.)

4 If you want, you can now make modifications to the chart using the menu commands and toolbar buttons provided by the Graph program. You can access detailed online information on using the Graph commands through the Help menu.

5 To change the size or the proportions of the chart, drag the sizing handles displayed around the embedded object.

6 When you've finished modifying the chart, click in the Word document *outside* the chart and the datasheet. The datasheet and the Graph commands on the menu and toolbar will disappear, leaving the chart embedded in your document.

If you later want to modify the chart, simply double-click on the embedded chart object. The Graph commands will return and you can change the features of the chart. To change the numbers on the chart, choose the Datasheet command from the View menu or click the View Datasheet button on the Graph toolbar to display the datasheet. If you want to display the chart within *another* Office document (for example, in a PowerPoint presentation), select the Chart object, cut or copy it, and then paste it into the other document.

? SEE ALSO
For information on Word tables, see "Using Tables," page 228. For details on creating charts in Excel, see "Creating a Chart," page 570.

Note that if you embed a new Graph object within a program other than Word (via the Object command from the program's Insert menu), or if you embed a new Graph object in a Word document without first selecting a table containing valid chart data, Graph will create an example chart displaying example data. You'll then need to enter the actual data, as well as the row and column headings, into the Graph datasheet.

Using Organization Chart

You can use the Microsoft Organization Chart program to add organization charts and other types of hierarchical (that is, in a ranked series) charts to your Office documents. When you select the MS Organization

Chart 2.0 object type in the Object dialog box and click OK, the Organization Chart program opens a separate window, which displays a template for a new chart, as shown in Figure 39-17.

FIGURE 39-17.
The Organization Chart program window, when you first start the program.

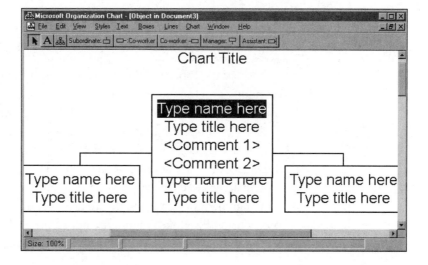

The following are the basic procedures for creating an organization chart:

■ To select a box, click the Select button on the toolbar (if it's not already "pressed"), and then click on the box.

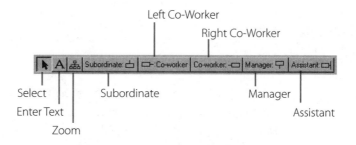

■ To add a new box, click one of the following buttons on the toolbar and then click on the box to which you want to attach a new box that has the desired relationship: Subordinate, Left Co-Worker, Right Co-Worker, Manager, or Assistant.

■ To delete a box, select it and press the Delete key.

VI

Integrating Applications

- To move a box, click the Select button (if necessary) and then drag the box and drop it onto another box. Where you position the box before dropping it determines its relationship to the other box.

- To add or modify text in a box or in the chart title, click the Enter Text button on the toolbar and then click on the text at the position where you want to add or edit characters.

- To modify the format of the chart, first select the part that you want to modify and then apply a formatting command. To select a single box, click the Select button and then click the box. To select text, click the Enter Text button and then highlight the text by dragging over it. To select groups of boxes or various chart elements, choose the Select or Select Levels command from the Edit menu. You can then change the chart type using the Styles menu, the formatting and alignment of text using the Text menu, the appearance of boxes using the Boxes menu, the appearance of lines using the Lines menu, or the chart background color using the Chart menu.

- You can draw lines and rectangles on the chart using the drawing buttons. To show these buttons, choose Show Draw Tools from the View menu.

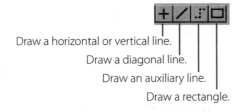

Draw a horizontal or vertical line.
Draw a diagonal line.
Draw an auxiliary line.
Draw a rectangle.

SEE ALSO

For information about using an organization chart in PowerPoint, see "Inserting an Organization Chart," page 748.

When you've finished creating the chart, choose the Exit And Return To *Document* command (where *Document* is the name of your Office document) from the File menu, and answer Yes when asked if you want to update the object in the document. The organization chart will be inserted into your Office document.

CHAPTER 40

Using the Office Binder Program

I n the preceding chapter, you learned how to add blocks of data derived from other documents and programs to an Office document. In this chapter, you'll learn how to use the Office Binder program to combine several entire documents in an Office binder. A binder is like an electronic paper clip—you can use it to store a set of related documents as a collection. Consider, for example, that you've prepared a report that consists of a Word document, an Excel workbook, and a PowerPoint presentation. You can use the Binder program to combine a copy of each of these documents within a single binder. (You can also create new documents within the binder.) All the documents in a binder are stored within a single disk file, and once you've created a binder, you can do the following:

- View, edit, and format all the documents directly within the Binder program window.

- Print the entire set of documents, with consecutive page numbers and uniform headers or footers, by issuing a single print command.

For information on sharing documents electronically over a network, see "Sharing Documents in a Work-group," page 92.

■ Take the report on the road or share it electronically with co-workers by copying, sending, or routing a single disk file. (You'll never again accidentally omit an essential document.)

You can include Word, Excel, or PowerPoint documents in a binder. You can also add documents created in programs from other software companies that have been designed to support the Binder.

Bring in Information from Access and the Office Tools Programs

You can also include data from Access or from the Office Tools programs (discussed in Chapter 39) in a binder, by pasting, linking, or embedding the data within a Word, Excel, or PowerPoint document that's contained in the binder.

Throughout this chapter, the term *Binder* (with a capital B) refers to the Microsoft Office Binder program, and the term *binder* (lowercase) refers to a collection of documents created by the Binder program.

Creating and Saving a Binder

To run the Binder program, choose Microsoft Binder from the Programs submenu of the Windows Start menu.

Alternatively, you can double-click a Microsoft Binder shortcut within a Windows folder or in the Windows Explorer. The Binder window is shown in Figure 40-1. Notice that the Binder window is divided into two panes: the *contents pane* (also known as the *left pane*) displays an icon for each document contained in the binder, and the *document pane* (also known as the *right pane*) displays the active document, allowing you to view and edit it. If the contents pane isn't visible, you can open it by clicking the Show/Hide Left Pane button to the left of the File menu. (If neither the contents pane nor the button is visible, choose Binder Options from the File menu and turn on the Show Left Pane And Left Pane Button option.)

FIGURE 40-1.
The Binder program window, displaying a new, blank binder.

Show/Hide Left Pane

Contents pane

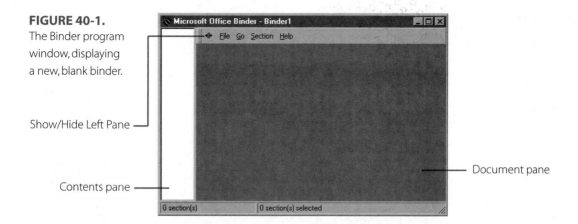

Document pane

TIP

Try Other Ways to Run the Binder Program
You can also run Binder and create a new, blank binder by choosing the New Office Document command from the Windows Start menu, or by clicking the New Office Document button on the Office Shortcut Bar. Then, in the New Office Document dialog box, click the General tab and double-click the Blank Binder icon. Alternatively, you can right-click within a blank area in a Windows folder or the Windows Explorer, choose Microsoft Office Binder from the New submenu, and then double-click on the new binder filename or shortcut icon that's created.

CAUTION
When using the drag and drop method to add a document to a binder, be sure *not* to drop the icon in the Binder document pane. Doing so would embed the document within the section currently displayed in the document pane, rather than adding the document to the binder.

When you run the Binder program, it creates a new, blank binder. The next step is to add documents to this binder. A document that you add to a binder is called a section. (Throughout this chapter, the terms *document* and *section* will be used synonymously when referring to a document that has been added to a binder.) You can add a document that you've already created with an Office application (Word, Excel, or PowerPoint), or a new, empty document to which you'll add information.

To add an existing document to a binder, do *either* of the following:

■ Choose Add From File from the Section menu in the Binder program, and in the Add From File dialog box (see Figure 40-2 on the following page), select the document that you want to add and click the Add button. Note that if you select several documents (by holding down the Ctrl key as you click each one), they'll all be added to the binder simultaneously as separate sections. To list all

VI

Integrating Applications

FIGURE 40-2.
The Add From
File dialog box.

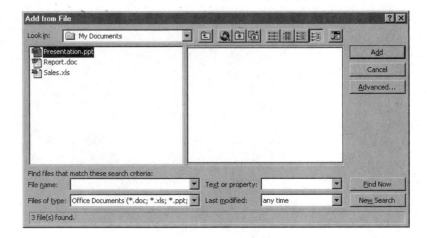

your Office files, be sure that the Office Documents item is selected in the Files Of Type list in the Add From File dialog box.

■ Drag a document icon from a Windows folder or from the Windows Explorer and drop it in the contents pane of the Binder window. If you select and drag several document icons, all the documents will be added to the binder simultaneously.

When you add a document to a binder, the binder stores a *copy* of the document, leaving the original document file. Although the document within the binder has the same name as the source document file, there is no link between the two.

If you drag a binder file—rather than an Office document—and drop it in the contents pane of the Binder program, a copy of each of the documents contained in the binder file is added to the open binder. You can use this technique to merge the contents of separate binders.

When Binder Is Hidden, Drag

If the Binder program is running but its window isn't visible when you begin dragging a document icon from a folder or from the Explorer, drag the icon over the Binder's button on the Windows taskbar and hold the pointer over the button without releasing the mouse button. Within a second or so, Windows will activate the Binder window and you can complete the drag operation.

To add a new, empty document to a binder, choose Add from the Section menu to display the Add Section dialog box (see Figure 40-3). To create a blank document, select one of the icons on the General tab (for example, to create a blank Word document, choose the Blank Document icon). Notice in Figure 40-3 that you can choose to create an Excel worksheet *or* an Excel chart. In either case, an Excel workbook document is added to the binder. If you choose the Excel worksheet, the workbook will contain a single blank worksheet, while if you choose the Excel chart, the workbook will contain an example chart plus a worksheet with the data for the chart.

FIGURE 40-3.
The Add Section dialog box.

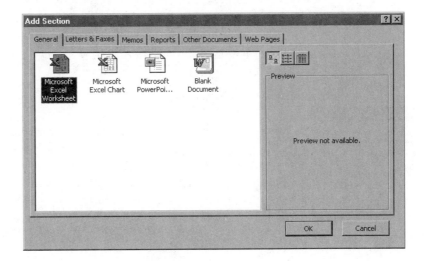

To base the new document on a template, select one of the other tabs in the Add Section dialog box and select the icon for the template that you want (for example, to create a business memo, you could click the Memos tab and select the Professional Memo.dot icon).

You can create an additional new binder by choosing New Binder from the File menu (or by pressing Ctrl+N), clicking the General tab in the New Binder dialog box, and then double-clicking the Blank Binder icon to create a blank binder. (The Binders tab will be discussed in the next section.) The current binder is left open and the new binder is displayed in an entirely separate Binder program window.

VI

Integrating Applications

NOTE

In other Office programs, a new document is opened in a separate child window within the program window. With Binder, however, a new binder is opened within a separate running copy of the Binder program.

Using a Binder Template

Rather than opening a new, blank binder and then adding documents to it, you can get a head start creating certain kinds of binders by basing a new binder on the Report Binder *template* provided by Office. When you create a new binder based on the template, the binder will have an initial set of documents (that is, sections), each of which will contain a basic framework of data and example information. You can then add, remove, or edit the documents as necessary, using the techniques discussed in this chapter.

NOTE

If the Report Binder template is not available on your computer, you must rerun the Office Setup program and select the Microsoft Binder Templates option of the Microsoft Binder component. If you have the Office CD, additional Binder templates are also available in the ValuPack\Binders folder on the CD. To use the templates, copy them to your hard disk to the Binders folder in the Templates folder, which is within the folder in which you installed Office.

To create a new binder based on a template, you first open the New dialog box. The following are several different ways to do this:

- Click the New Office Document button on the Office Shortcut Bar.

- Choose the New Office Document command from the Windows Start menu.

- With the right mouse button, click within a blank area in a Windows folder or in the Windows Explorer, then point to the New submenu and choose the Other Office Documents command:

SEE ALSO

For information on modifying binder templates as well as creating your own templates, see "Modifying and Creating Binder Templates," page 1043.

- If a Binder program window is currently open, you can choose New Binder from the File menu or press Ctrl+N. (In this case, the dialog box that appears will be titled New Binder.)

In the New Office Document (or New Binder) dialog box, click the Binders tab, select the template by clicking it, and click the OK button. (See Figure 40-4.) Notice that when you select a template, a preview image appears in the Preview area, showing the first page of the first document in the template. The name of the template suggests its purpose. After you click OK, the Binder program window appears, displaying the new binder.

FIGURE 40-4.
Selecting a template for creating a new binder.

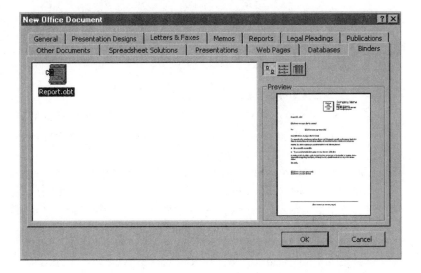

VI

Integrating Applications

Saving a Binder

You can save the entire binder within a single file in *either* of the following two ways:

- To save the binder under its current name, if any, choose Save Binder from the File menu or press Ctrl+S. (If you haven't previously saved the binder, the Save Binder As command will automatically be activated.)

- To save a copy of the binder under a different filename, choose Save Binder As from the File menu and specify the name and location of the file in the Save Binder As dialog box. Be sure that the Binder Files item is selected in the Save As Type list.

SEE ALSO
For information on saving a copy of an individual binder document, see "Managing Binder Sections," page 1039. For a general discussion on Office document properties, see "Working with Property Sheets," page 88.

A binder file is normally saved with the OBD file extension. However, you don't need to include this extension in the filename that you enter because the Binder does it for you. (You won't see the file extensions if you've chosen to hide MS-DOS file extensions within Windows.)

 TIP

> **Change Binder or Document Properties to Suit Your Fancy**
> You can set the properties of the binder itself by choosing Binder Properties from the File menu in the Binder program. You can set the properties of an individual document within the binder by activating that document (click its icon in the contents pane) and choosing Section Properties from the Section menu.

Closing a Binder

After you've saved a binder, you can close it by choosing Close from the File menu. Note that this also exits the Binder program. (This command is equivalent to using one of the standard ways for exiting a program, such as clicking the Close box in the upper right corner of the window.) By contrast with the technique you use in other Office programs, you can't close the document and leave the Binder program running.

Opening a Binder

You can open a binder that you've saved on disk by double-clicking the icon for the binder file within a Windows folder or in the Windows

Explorer. A binder filename will include the OBD extension if you've chosen to show MS-DOS file extensions in Windows. You can also recognize a Binder file by its binder-clip icon, as shown here.

Book.obd

Also, if you've recently opened the file, you can choose it from the Documents submenu of the Windows Start menu.

Alternatively, you can open a binder using the Open dialog box. To display the Open dialog box, use any of the following methods:

- Click the Open Office Document button on the Office Shortcut Bar.

- Choose the Open Office Document command from the Start menu.

- If a Binder program window is currently open, you can choose Open Binder from the File menu or press Ctrl+O. (In this case the dialog box will be titled Open Binder.)

Choose the binder file you want to open and click OK. The Binder program window will appear, displaying the binder.

If you open a binder using the Open Binder command on the File menu of the Binder program, the Binder Files item in the Files Of Type list must be selected. Also, when the specified binder is opened, it will be displayed in a *separate* Binder program window, and the current binder will remain displayed in the original Binder window. (If, however, the current binder is empty and unnamed, it will be discarded and the newly opened binder will be displayed in the *same* window.)

Editing Binder Sections

You can edit a document within a binder using the commands (that is, the menu commands, toolbar buttons, and shortcut keys) provided by the source program. The *source program* is the application that was used to create the document—typically, Word, Excel, or PowerPoint.

To edit a document, simply click the document's icon in the contents pane of the Binder window. If the contents pane isn't visible, click the

Show/Hide Left Pane button at the left of the File menu. If the document icon isn't visible in the contents pane, use the buttons at the top or bottom of the contents pane to scroll the icon into view:

Click here to jump to the
icon for the first section.

Click here to scroll
one section up.

Clicking the document icon *selects* (that is, highlights) the icon. More importantly, clicking the icon *activates* the document. When a document is activated, the following occurs, as shown in Figure 40-5:

- A right-pointing arrow is displayed next to the document's icon in the contents pane.

- The document is displayed in the document pane.

- The source program's menus are displayed in addition to the Binder program's menus—that is, the menus of the two programs are merged.

- The source program's toolbars, if any, are displayed.

- The source program's shortcut keys become available.

You can also activate a particular section by choosing Next Section or Previous Section from the Section menu to activate the next or the previous section in the order in which they're listed in the contents pane.

Show the Status Bar and Set Other Binder Options

If you don't see the Binder status bar shown in Figure 40-5, you can display it by choosing Binder Options from the File menu and turning on the Show Status Bar option in the Binder Options dialog box. You can also use this dialog box to specify the default location for your binder files and to set other options discussed in this chapter.

FIGURE 40-5.

The Binder program window, displaying a binder containing several sections. The Word document "Chapter 4" is currently activated.

Close/open contents pane

Scroll buttons

Word menus (merged with Binder menus)

Selected, activated document (section)

Document (section) icons

Selected (but not activated)

Scroll buttons

Binder program status bar

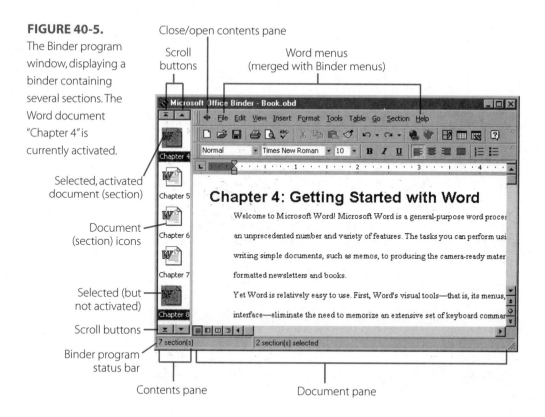

Contents pane

Document pane

You can now use the source program's commands to edit and format the document, following the instructions given in previous chapters. The following, however, are some general ways that editing within the Binder program differs from editing within the source program (that is, within Word, Excel, or PowerPoint):

■ In Binder, the commands on the File menu affect the binder as a whole, not just the activated document.

■ In Binder, the Section menu provides several of the commands that are normally found on the source program's File menu, and these commands affect only the activated document. Specifically, the Page Setup command on the Section menu is equivalent to the

VI

Integrating Applications

Page Setup command on the source program's File menu, Print Preview is equivalent to Print Preview, Print is equivalent to Print, Save As File is equivalent to Save As, and Section Properties is equivalent to Properties.

- The source program's status bar isn't displayed. It is replaced with Binder's status bar. This makes certain features unavailable, such as the Excel AutoCalculate feature.

- You can run macros while editing within Binder, but you can't record or edit macros.

 TIP

Get Help

While you're working with a document in a binder, the Help menu lets you access online Help both for the Binder program itself and for the program that's the source of the activated document. Just choose commands from the appropriate menu or submenu.

? SEE ALSO

For a discussion on Word document templates, see "Modifying and Creating Document Templates," page 215. For details on Excel templates, see "Creating Templates," page 494. PowerPoint templates are discussed in "Using a Template," page 686.

While you're editing a document within a binder, you can move data from one binder document to another using the following drag and drop technique:

1 Select the data in the source document.

2 Drag the data to the icon for the receiving document within the contents pane, and without releasing the mouse button, press the Alt key to activate the receiving document.

3 Continue dragging the data to the target location in the receiving document.

To copy rather than move the data, hold down the Ctrl key while dragging. If you don't press the Alt key and position the mouse pointer in the document pane before releasing the mouse button, the selected material is inserted as a new section.

TIP

Remember to Copy Word Templates

As you learned in Chapter 7, Word macros, AutoText entries, and custom inter-face configurations are stored within document templates. If a binder contains a Word document and you move the binder to a computer other than the one on which the document was created, macros and other template items might be unavailable when you edit the document. The easiest way to make these items available is to copy the template or templates containing them into the same folder on the destination computer into which you copy the binder file.

Editing Within the Source Program Window

Rather than editing a binder section within the Binder window, you can edit it within a separate window provided by the document's source program (such as Word, Excel, or PowerPoint). You might want to do this so that *all* of the source program's commands are available or so that you can work in the more familiar environment provided by the source program.

To edit a binder section within the source program, do the following:

1 Activate the document by clicking its icon in the contents pane.

2 Choose View Outside from the Section menu. The source pro-gram will open a separate window displaying the document.

3 When you have finished editing, exit the source program. If you are asked whether you want to update the document within the binder, click Yes in the dialog box. The modified document will appear in the binder.

You might have noticed that this procedure is similar to that for editing an embedded object within the source program, as described in Chapter 39.

Managing Binder Sections

You can use commands on the Binder's Section menu to delete, rename, rearrange, duplicate, hide, and save individual binder sections. You can also use drag and drop techniques to perform most of these operations.

VI

Integrating Applications

For the majority of the section operations, you first need to select the section that you want to act on. You select a section by clicking its icon in the contents pane of the Binder window. Clicking the icon also activates the section—that is, displays it in the document pane.

For some of the section operations, you can select several sections to operate on simultaneously. Only one of the selected sections will be activated. You can select multiple sections using any of the following methods:

- Click the first section of the group that you want to select, and then click each of the other sections while pressing the Ctrl key.

- To select a group of adjoining sections, click the first one and then click the last one in the range while pressing the Shift key.

- To select all the sections in a binder, choose Select All from the Section menu. To deselect all the sections except the activated one, choose Unselect All from the Section menu.

To deselect a specific section from a group of selected sections, click the section's icon while pressing the Ctrl key. (To deselect the activated section, you must first activate *another* section within the selected group by clicking its icon.)

To delete one or more sections, first select the section or sections and then choose Delete from the Section menu. If you've selected more than one section, the command will be labeled Delete Selection.

⭐ **TIP**

Use the Shortcut Menu

If you click in the contents pane with the right mouse button, you can choose any of the following commands from the shortcut menu that pops up, rather than from the Section menu: Add, Add From File, Delete, Duplicate, Rename, and Section Properties. The Delete, Duplicate, Rename, and Section Properties commands will be available only if you right-click on a section icon, and these commands will affect only the clicked section, regardless of which section or sections are selected. The Add and Add From File commands will insert a new section below the currently activated selection.

To rename the activated section, choose Rename from the Section menu. The insertion point will be placed within the label below the section's icon and you can type the new name. Alternatively, you can rename any section by clicking on its label (you might need to click twice).

To rearrange the order of the sections in a binder, choose Rearrange from the Section menu—you don't need to select a section. In the Rearrange Sections dialog box (see Figure 40-6), highlight a section that you want to move and click the Move Up or Move Down button. Alternatively, you can move a section by simply selecting and then dragging its icon to a new position within the contents pane. If you select several icons, you can move the whole group.

FIGURE 40-6.
The Rearrange
Sections dialog box.

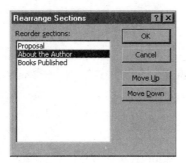

To duplicate a section, select it and choose Duplicate from the Section menu. Then, in the Duplicate Section dialog box (see Figure 40-7), select the section after which you want to insert the copy of the section. If you select several sections, you can duplicate them all at once; in this case, the menu command will be labeled Duplicate Selection. Alternatively, you can duplicate a section by dragging its icon to a new location in the contents pane while holding down the Ctrl key. If you select several icons, you can copy all of them.

FIGURE 40-7.
The Duplicate
Section dialog box.

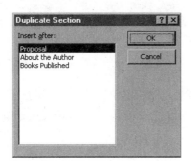

VI

Integrating Applications

> **Move or Copy a Section to Another Binder**
>
> You can move a section into another binder by dragging its icon to the contents pane of the other Binder window. To copy rather than move the section, press the Ctrl key while dragging. If you select several sections, you can move or copy the entire group.

You can also hide one or more sections in a binder. A hidden section won't appear in the contents pane, it can't be activated, and it won't print when you print the binder (as described later). To do this, select one or more sections and choose Hide from the Section menu. To show a section again, choose Unhide Section from the Section menu, select the section in the Unhide Sections dialog box, and click OK.

Earlier in the chapter you learned how to save the entire binder within a single disk file. You can also save a copy of an individual binder section within a separate disk file. To do this, select the section that you want to save and choose Save As File from the Section menu. Then, in the Save As dialog box, specify a name and location for the file.

Alternatively, you can simply drag a section icon from the Binder program directly to the folder in which you want to save the document. In this case, a copy of the section will be saved under its original file-name. If you select several sections, you can drag them all at once. In the next topic, you'll learn how to save a copy of *all* sections in a binder with a single operation. Note that none of the techniques removes the section from the binder.

> **Drag an Icon to a Hidden Window**
>
> When dragging an icon from a binder to a folder or to another binder, recall that if the target window is open but isn't visible, you can activate it by holding the pointer over the window's icon on the Windows taskbar without releasing the mouse button.

A Binder Unbound!

You can save a separate copy of *all* sections in a binder, using the following method:

1 With the right mouse button, click the name of the binder file within a Windows folder or in the Windows Explorer. (A binder file will have the OBD extension if you've chosen to show MS-DOS file extensions in Windows.)

2 From the shortcut menu, choose Unbind.

A copy of each section in the binder will be saved within a disk file under its original name. The files will be placed within the same folder that contains the binder file, and Windows will warn you before over-writing a file with the same name. Note that unbinding a binder only makes *copies* of the sections; the sections aren't removed from the binder.

  TIP

Create a Copy of a Binder and Open It in a Single Step
If you choose New from the shortcut menu that's displayed when you click a binder file with the right mouse button, a Binder window displaying a copy of the clicked binder will be opened.

Modifying and Creating Binder Templates

Previously, you learned how to create a new binder based on a template. If you frequently create a particular type of binder, you can save time by preparing a template that contains all the basic elements of this binder. You can prepare such a template by modifying an existing template or by creating a new one.

You can modify an existing template to suit your needs, using the following procedure:

1 In the Binder program, choose Open Binder from the File menu or press Ctrl+O.

2 In the Files Of Type list in the Open Binder dialog box, select Binder Templates, and then choose the binder template that you want to modify and click Open. Note that Binder templates are stored in the Binders folder in the Templates folder, which is within the folder in which you installed Office.

VI

Integrating Applications

3 Modify the template as necessary. You can add or remove sections, edit sections, or perform any of the other operations discussed in this chapter.

4 When you've finished changing the template, choose Save Binder from the File menu to save the modified template under its original name. To store the modified template under a *new* name, so that the original template version is left intact, choose Save Binder As from the File menu and specify a new filename (make sure that Binder Templates is selected in the Files Of Type list).

You can create a new Binder template as follows:

1 Use any of the methods for creating a new binder that were discussed earlier in the chapter under "Creating and Saving a Binder," page 1028.

2 Add documents and data to the binder so that it will serve as a good starting point for the type of binders that you want to create.

3 Choose Save Binder As from the File menu to display the Save Binder As dialog box.

4 In the Files Of Type list, select the Binder Templates item to save your work as a binder template rather than as a binder document.

5 Specify a name and location for the template, and click the Save button. Note that you should save the template within the Templates folder of your Office folder, or within one of the subfolders within this folder (usually Binders). If you don't store your template in one of these locations, it won't be displayed in the New Binder dialog box when you create a new binder.

> **NOTE**
>
> A Binder template normally has the OBT file extension. You won't see the extensions, however, if you've chosen to hide MS-DOS file extensions in Windows.

Printing a Binder

You can print an entire binder, or print one or more individual sections within a binder, using commands provided by the Binder program. You can also print a single binder section using the more specialized commands provided by that section's source program.

Printing an Entire Binder or a Group of Sections Within a Binder

You can use commands on the File menu of the Binder program to define headers or footers for the binder, to preview the printed appearance of the binder, or to print the binder. You can apply these commands to the entire binder or to one or more binder sections.

To create headers or footers, choose Binder Page Setup from the File menu and click the Header/Footer tab in the Binder Page Setup dialog box. As shown in Figure 40-8 on the following page, you can define a header, a footer, or both; and you can apply the header or footer to all sections in the binder or to one or more sections that you select.

On the Print Settings tab of the Binder Page Setup dialog box, shown in Figure 40-9 on page 1047, you can specify which sections are to be printed, and you can control the page numbering. The options you select on this tab will be used as the default values whenever you print the binder. When you print, however, you can override these settings by choosing different ones in the Print Binder dialog box, as explained shortly.

Before you print, you can preview the printed appearance of the binder by choosing the Print Preview command from the File menu. For more information on previewing documents, see "Previewing and Printing Documents," page 330.

When you're ready to print, proceed as follows:

1 If you want to print specific sections, rather than the entire binder, select those sections.

2 Choose Print Binder from the File menu or press Ctrl+P. The Print Binder dialog box will be displayed (see Figure 40-10 on page 1047).

FIGURE 40-8.

Defining headers
or footers for one
or more sections
in a binder.

To create a header, select a predefined header from this list...

...or click this button to define a custom header.

Header that you create will be be displayed here.

To apply headers or
footers to all sections,
select this option.

To apply headers
to one or more
specific sections,
select this option...

...and then select
sections in this list.

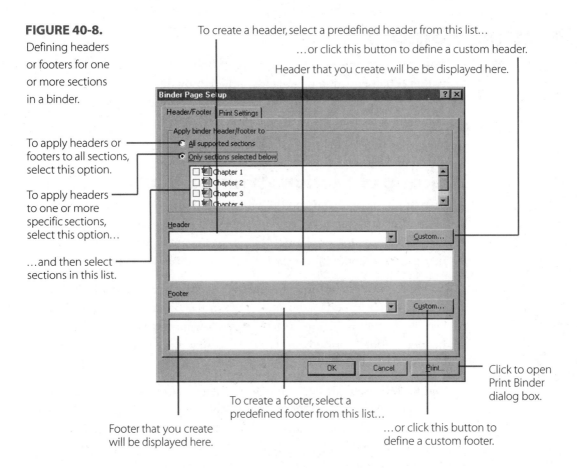

Click to open
Print Binder
dialog box.

To create a footer, select a
predefined footer from this list...

...or click this button to
define a custom footer.

Footer that you create
will be displayed here.

Although you can control page numbering in the Print Binder dialog box, page numbers won't appear on the pages of your binders unless you've defined headers or footers that *include* page numbers. Note that the numbering sequence you select in the Print Binder dialog box will override any starting page numbers you might have specified for an individual document within the binder.

Quick-Print a Binder

You can also print a binder by using the right mouse button to click a binder file within a Windows folder or in the Windows Explorer, and then choosing Print from the shortcut menu that pops up. The Binder program will begin running and will immediately print the document. It will print all visible sections, using consecutive page numbering starting at 1. The program will terminate when it's finished printing the binder.

FIGURE 40-9.
Setting default
printing options.

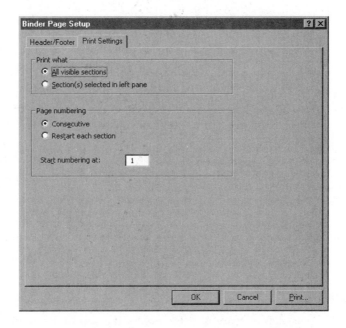

FIGURE 40-10.
Printing an entire
binder or selected
binder sections.

1A Choose this option if you want to print the whole binder (not including any sections you've hidden).

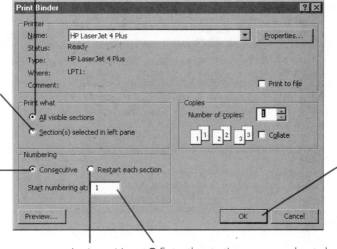

1B Choose this option if you want to print only those sections you selected in step 1.

2A To print a continuous sequence of page numbers, select this option.

2B To restart page numbering with each section, select this option.

3 Enter the starting page number to be used for the first page of the first document in the binder.

4 When you're finished selecting any desired print options, click here.

Printing a Single Section

The method that was just given would let you print a single section by selecting it alone in step 1, and then choosing the Sections Selected In Left Pane option in the Print Binder dialog box. Alternatively, you can preview and print a *single* section using commands on the Section menu. The advantage of this alternative method is that you'll be using the more specialized and feature-rich commands provided by the source program, rather than the general-purpose commands provided by Binder. For example, if you print a single section using the Print command on the Section menu, the source program's Print dialog box might provide options that aren't available in the Print Binder dialog box. For instance, the Word Print dialog box provides options for printing the selected text only, for printing a range of pages, and for printing specific document elements such as comments, styles, and AutoText entries.

The first step is to activate the section you want to print. If you wish, you can define headers or footers for the section using the commands provided by the source program. For example, to define headers or footers for a Word document, you could use the Header and Footer command on the View menu. If you want to preview the document before you print it, choose the Print Preview command from the Section menu.

When you're ready to print the activated section, choose Print from the Section menu. The section's source program will then display its usual Print dialog box, in which you can select print settings and click OK to begin printing.

② SEE ALSO

For a general discussion on printing Office documents, see "Printing Documents," page 57. For information on adding page numbers, headers, or footers to a Word document, see "Adding Page Numbers," page 290, and "Adding Headers and Footers," page 293.

Managing Information with Microsoft Outlook

Microsoft Outlook is a new application provided with Office 97. It combines the features of the Microsoft Exchange Inbox, Schedule+ (provided with Office 95), and the Windows Explorer, all within a single, tightly integrated program. With it, you can manage many different types of information and perform a great variety of useful tasks, such as the following:

- Send and receive e-mail and fax messages.

- Maintain your personal calendar.

- Schedule meetings with your co-workers.

- Store information about your business and personal contacts.

- Set up dates for personal or group projects.

■ Keep a record of important events.

■ Jot down miscellaneous notes.

■ Access the programs and document files on your computer or on a network.

An Overview of Outlook

You can run Outlook by choosing the Microsoft Outlook command from the Programs submenu of your Windows Start menu. Alternatively, because Outlook is useful for so many purposes, you might want to have it start automatically whenever you run Windows and leave it running all the time. To do this, you must place a shortcut for the Outlook program within your StartUp folder. (For instructions on doing this, choose Help from the Windows Start menu, click the Index tab, and select the topic "shortcuts, adding to the StartUp folder.")

Figure 41-1 shows the Outlook program window as it appears when the program first begins running. As you can see, the main part of the Outlook window is divided into two panes: the Outlook bar and the Information Viewer.

FIGURE 41-1.
The Outlook program displaying the Inbox folder.

Click one of these three buttons to display the different default groups of folders in the Outlook bar.

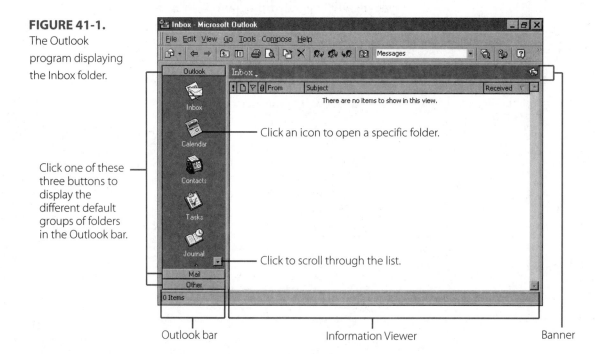

Click an icon to open a specific folder.

Click to scroll through the list.

Outlook bar   Information Viewer   Banner

Each of the different types of information that you manage in Outlook is kept in a separate *folder*. Your first step in working with a particular type of information is to *open* the appropriate folder by clicking its icon within the Outlook bar. For example, to manage appointments and meetings, you would open the Calendar folder by clicking on the Calendar icon in the Outlook bar. When you open a folder, its contents are displayed in the Information Viewer pane; also, the Outlook toolbar buttons and menu commands change to provide the commands that are needed to manage the type of information kept in the folder.

 NOTE

The instructions given in the following sections assume that you've already opened the appropriate folder. For example, the instructions given in the "Contacts" section for working with your list of contacts assume that you've already opened the Contacts folder.

Before You Install Outlook

Make sure that you've already installed the Microsoft Exchange component of Windows 95 before you install Outlook, because Outlook requires features provided by Exchange. If you don't see an icon on your Windows 95 desktop titled Inbox, then you haven't installed Exchange and you must do so by double-clicking the Add/Remove Programs icon in the Windows Control Panel, selecting the Windows Setup tab, and turning on the Microsoft Exchange item in the list. If you have a fax modem installed on your computer and if you select the Microsoft Fax item in addition to the Microsoft Exchange item, you'll be able to send and receive fax messages using Outlook.

After Exchange is installed, a wizard guides you through the process of setting it up. Outlook will use this same setup. (You can later change the setup through the Services and Options commands on Outlook's Tools menu.) Also, if you've been using Exchange for a while and have stored messages or other information in your personal folders, Outlook will allow you to access any of this information (Exchange and Outlook use the same set of personal folders).

Note that although you must have *installed* Exchange to use Outlook, Exchange doesn't need to be running when you use Outlook. That is, you *don't* need to open the Exchange Inbox or run the Exchange program before running Outlook. This is because Outlook *replaces* the user interface provided by Exchange with an environment that's much more feature-rich.

VI

Integrating Applications

You can click one of the three buttons in the Outlook bar—Outlook, Mail, or Other—to display different groups of folders. In Outlook, you can work with two types of folders: *personal folders* and *file folders*. Personal folders store the information that is managed by Outlook or Exchange (for instance, e-mail messages or appointments). All the personal folders, together with the information they contain, are actually stored within a single file on your hard disk (this file has a PST file extension and is usually stored in the Exchange folder). To access the personal folders, click either the Outlook or the Mail button in the Outlook bar. The Outlook group contains the general Outlook folders; the following sections discuss each of these in detail. The Mail group contains folders used specifically for managing e-mail and fax messages.

File folders are the folders that contain the files that are stored on your computer or network—for instance, the Windows folder on your hard drive (these folders are managed by the Windows file system). You access the file folders by clicking the Other button in the Outlook bar. The file folders are discussed in the final section of this chapter, "Accessing Files," page 1088.

Folder
List

You can also display a hierarchical folder list to make it easy to find specific folders. This list is similar to the one shown in the left pane of Windows Explorer. You can open a permanent folder list by clicking the Folder List toolbar button, or you can open a temporary one by clicking at the left end of the banner above the Information Viewer. A permanent folder list is displayed in a separate pane and remains displayed until you click the Folder List button again. A temporary folder list overlaps the information in the Information Viewer and disappears as soon as you use it to open a folder. Figure 41-2 shows a folder list and indicates how it's opened. Note that if you currently have a personal folder opened, the folder list will show all your personal folders; and if you have a file folder open, it will show all your file folders.

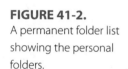

FIGURE 41-2.
A permanent folder list showing the personal folders.

Click here to show or hide a permanent folder list.

Click here to show or hide a temporary folder list.

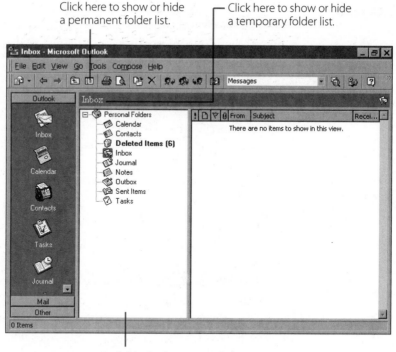

Folder list (permanent)

 TIP

Try Yet Another Way to Open a Folder
You can also locate and open a specific folder by choosing the Go To Folder command from the Go menu to open the Go To Folder dialog box. In the Look In list, choose the Outlook item if you want to open a personal folder, or choose the File System item if you want to open a file folder. Then select the folder in the Folder Name list and click the OK button.

Because Outlook is so replete with features and options, this chapter can't discuss all of them. To help you locate additional information, the following sections include references to specific *books* within the Outlook online Help. To access a particular book, choose the Contents And Index command from Outlook's Help menu and then click the Contents tab in the Help Topics window.

VI

Integrating Applications

> **Making the Most of This Chapter**
>
> To get the most out of this chapter, you should read it through from the begin-
> ning, even if you aren't planning to use some of the folders. Earlier sections
> explain general techniques and provide general tips that are useful for working
> with *any* folder but that aren't repeated in later sections. Also, be sure to read *all*
> the sidebars—because they cover important techniques that you can use when
> working with any of the personal folders.

Inbox

The Inbox folder allows you to receive, view, and send *messages*. These
messages can be e-mail messages that are transmitted directly over a network attached to your computer, e-mail messages that you send and
receive using a modem and an online service or other remote connection, or faxes carried through a fax modem installed on your system.
When you initially set up Microsoft Exchange, as described in the previous section, you select the types of messages you want to process (you
can later change this information through the Services and Options commands on Outlook's Tools menu). If your system doesn't support any of
these message mechanisms, you won't find much use for the Inbox, but
you'll certainly be able to use the other Outlook components.

Reading Messages

When a new message comes in, Outlook displays a letter icon at the
right end of the Windows taskbar:

Indicates that a new message has arrived in your Inbox

You can also have Outlook notify you of the receipt of a new message
by displaying a dialog box, playing a sound, or changing the mouse
cursor. To select notification options, choose Options from the Tools
menu and click the E-Mail tab.

NOTE

If you're connected to a network, faxes and e-mail messages will arrive in your Inbox automatically. If you use a modem and an online service or other remote connection to send and receive e-mail, you'll need to decide how Outlook should handle your mail. Using the Services and Options commands on the Tools menu, you can have Outlook automatically connect to your online provider at preset intervals and send and receive all your pending faxes and e-mail. Or, you can work offline and use Remote Mail to save online costs by receiving only the headers of messages waiting for you and then choosing offline which you want to download in their entirety. You can also compose your messages while offline and then connect manually to take care of all your mail at once, using the Connect button on the Remote toolbar (selected from the Toolbars submenu of the View menu). For more information about setting up and using Remote Mail, choose the Contents and Index command from the Help menu, select the Index tab, and then type *Remote Mail* in the text box.

To read your new message or messages, open the Inbox folder in Outlook, and you'll see a list of your new messages, plus any messages you've already read that are still stored in the Inbox. See Figure 41-3.

FIGURE 41-3.
The Inbox displaying three e-mail messages and a fax.

Each column displays a different field of information on the messages (source, subject, date received, and so on).

Indicates that the Inbox contains 3 unread messages

If message is unread, it's displayed in bold…

…and (for an e-mail message) can include a preview.

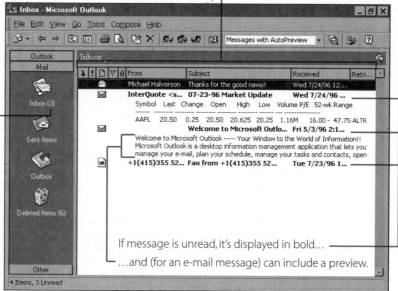

VI

Integrating Applications

Using Different Views

You can work with an Outlook folder using different *views*, which affect—often radically—the way information is organized on the screen as well as the amount of detail that's shown. For example, the Inbox in Figure 41-3 on the preceding page shows the Messages With AutoPreview selection from the Current View submenu of the View menu. It displays the messages in a simple list and includes a preview of the contents of each unread message. (Preview information isn't available for faxes.) You can hide or show the preview information by choosing the AutoPreview command from the View menu or clicking the AutoPreview button on the toolbar.

To change the view, simply select another item from the Current View drop-down list on the toolbar:

Available views for the Inbox folder. Change the view of the folder by selecting an item from the list.

Alternatively, you can choose an option from the Current View submenu of the View menu.

Note that you can modify the view for any of the Outlook personal folders, not just the Inbox. Later in the chapter, you'll learn ways to modify the features of a view. You can even save your modifications as a custom view, so that you can reuse it whenever you wish. For complete information on the views available for each of the personal folders, and detailed instructions on working with views, see the Outlook online Help book "Working with Views."

To read a specific message, simply double-click it within the Inbox, and Outlook will open the message within a Message window, as shown in Figure 41-4. You can then view the message text (or modify it, if you wish). As you can see in Figure 41-4, you can also view or modify fields of information that are associated with the message—for example, the message importance (low, normal, or high; also known as its priority) and the message tag (a comment such as *Call* or *Follow up* attached to the message; also known as a flag). Additionally, the

Message window provides commands for replying to the message, printing it, moving it to a different personal folder, or deleting it. You can also open other messages, create new messages, and perform additional operations. Most of these tasks are discussed later in the chapter.

FIGURE 41-4.
Reading a message in a Message window.

Show message header.

View other messages.

Delete message.

Move message to another folder.

Flag message.

Cut, copy, or paste text or attach a file.

Print message.

Reply to or forward this message.

Assign importance level or category to the message.

Message header

Message text

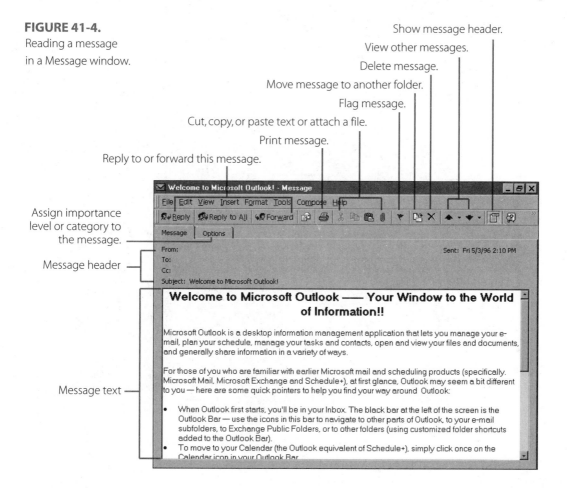

NOTE

If you open a *fax* message, it will be displayed in the Fax Viewer window, as shown in Figure 41-5 on the following page, rather than in the usual Outlook Message window that's shown in Figure 41-4. The Fax Viewer window lets you view the fax at various levels of magnification, print the fax, and manipulate the image in several different ways.

VI

Integrating Applications

FIGURE 41-5.

Viewing a fax message in the Fax Viewer window.

Save any changes you made to fax.

Print fax.

Mouse will drag the fax within the window.

Mouse will select areas of the fax.

Zoom in.

Zoom out.

Zoom to percent.

Zoom fax to fit window width.

Open a thumbnail view of each page.

Rotate fax 90 degrees to left.

Rotate fax 90 degrees to right.

Open a fax stored in a file.

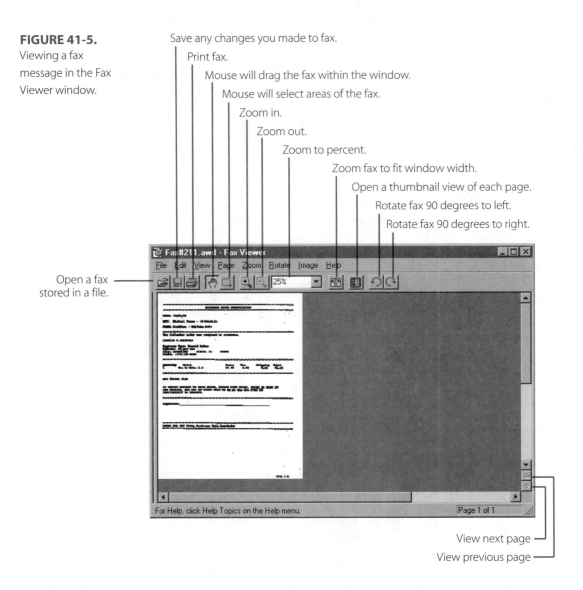

View next page

View previous page

To return to the Inbox, close the Message window (or Fax Viewer window). You'll notice that once you've read the message, it's no longer displayed in bold and, for an e-mail message, the preview text is no longer shown. Also, if in the Message window you've set the message importance to high or low priority, tagged the message with a flag, or inserted a file into the message text, the change you made will be indicated in the appropriate column (see Figure 41-6).

FIGURE 41-6.
The default message fields displayed in the Inbox.

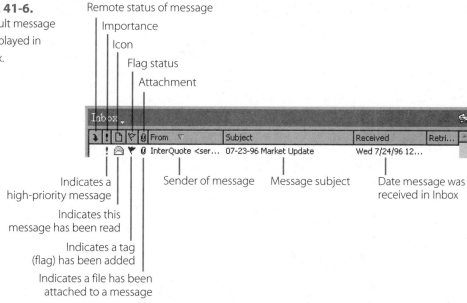

Remote status of message
Importance
Icon
Flag status
Attachment

Indicates a high-priority message

Sender of message

Message subject

Date message was received in Inbox

Indicates this message has been read

Indicates a tag (flag) has been added

Indicates a file has been attached to a message

Printing Information Stored in Outlook

Outlook lets you print the information stored in any of your personal folders. For example, you can print a message in the Inbox, a day or a range of days in the Calendar, or one or more contacts in the Contacts folder. Outlook provides a variety of methods for printing. The following is a flexible, general procedure you can use for printing any kind of information:

1 Open the folder containing the information you want to print.

2 If you want to print one or more specific items—for example, messages in the Inbox or days in the Calendar—select the item or items. To select an item, click on it; to select additional items, press Ctrl while you click each one.

3 Choose the Print command from the File menu to open the Print dialog box, which is shown in Figure 41-7 on the following page.

4 In the Print Style list in the center of the dialog box, select a style to specify the general way the information will be organized on the printed copy and the level of detail that will be shown.

VI

Integrating Applications

Printing Information Stored in Outlook *continued*

5   If you want to modify the selected print style, click the Page Setup button to open the Page Setup dialog box, which allows you to modify the fonts, paper size, headers or footers, and other features of the printed pages.

6   Change other print options in the Print dialog box, as necessary. The specific options that are available depend on the folder you opened and the items you selected before opening the dialog box. For example, if you opened the Contacts folder, you can choose whether to print all contacts or only the contact or contacts that you selected before opening the Print dialog box.

7   To preview the appearance of the printed output, and see the effect of all the options you've selected, click the Preview button.

8   To begin printing, click the Print button in the Print Preview window or the OK button in the Print dialog box.

For more information on printing, see the "Printing" book in the Outlook on-line Help.

FIGURE 41-7.

The Print dialog box, opened after selecting a message from the Inbox.

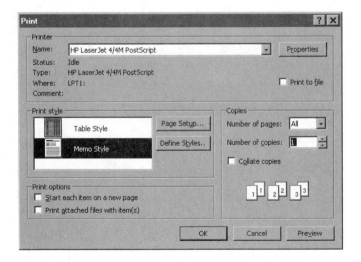

Sending Messages

To send a message, you can either base the message on an existing message that you've received, or you can send a new message not related to an existing one. To base the message on an existing one, first select the message in the Inbox and then click one of the following three buttons on the Outlook toolbar:

Reply
Reply to All
Forward

If you click Reply, a new message will be sent back to the sender of the selected message. If you click Reply To All, a message will be sent to the sender and to all other recipients of the selected message (as you'll see, a message can be sent to more than one person). If you click Forward, a copy of the received message will be sent on to the person or persons that you specify.

To send a new e-mail message that isn't related to an existing one, choose New Mail Message from the Compose menu, or simply press Ctrl+N. To send a new fax message, choose New Fax from the Compose menu.

Whichever of these methods you use for sending a message, Outlook will now open a Message window, which you can use to create and send your message, as shown in Figure 41-8 on the following page. (Note, however, that if you choose the New Fax command from the Compose menu to send a new fax message, Outlook will run a wizard to help you compose your fax, rather than displaying the Message window.) Notice that the Message window shown in Figure 41-8 is quite similar to the Message window that's displayed when you view a message you've received (which is shown in Figure 41-4 on page 1057). The primary differences are that the Message window for sending a message normally contains a Formatting toolbar for formatting the message text that you enter, and the header contains text boxes that allow you to enter or modify the header information (that is, the message recipients and subject).

VI

Integrating Applications

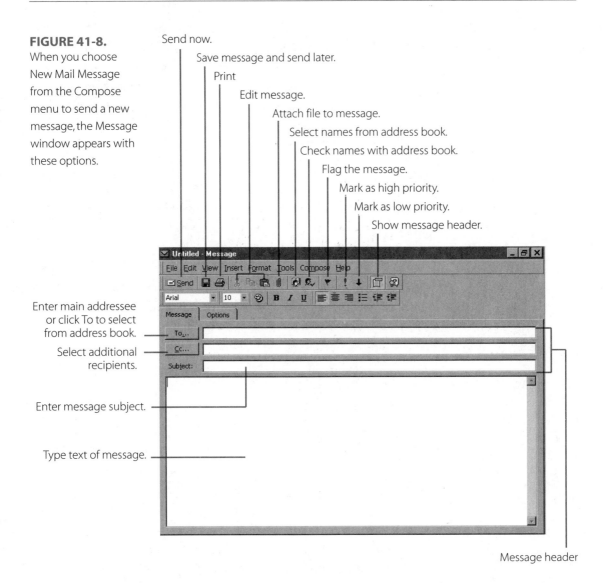

FIGURE 41-8.
When you choose New Mail Message from the Compose menu to send a new message, the Message window appears with these options.

Send now.

Save message and send later.

Print

Edit message.

Attach file to message.

Select names from address book.

Check names with address book.

Flag the message.

Mark as high priority.

Mark as low priority.

Show message header.

Enter main addressee or click To to select from address book.

Select additional recipients.

Enter message subject.

Type text of message.

Message header

If, instead of creating a new message, you reply to or forward an existing message using the Reply, Reply To All, or Forward command, the message text box in the Message window will contain the text of the original message you selected. This provides the recipient with a copy of the message that you're replying to or forwarding. You can then enter your reply in the message text box (or add your own comments if you're forwarding a message).

Organizing Messages

As you begin to accumulate messages in your Inbox, you might want to do some housekeeping. First, you might want to delete some of your older messages. To delete a message, select it and press the Delete key or click the Delete button on the toolbar.

Delete

 CAUTION

If you delete an item from the Deleted Items folder, it *will* be permanently removed and unrecoverable.

When you delete a message from the Inbox, or delete an item from another personal folder such as a contact in the Contacts folder, the item is actually moved into the Deleted Items folder. You can later restore the item by moving it from the Deleted Items folder back to the original folder (moving items will be discussed next).

⭐ **TIP**

> **Archive Items in Your Personal Folders**
>
> You can manually move old items to a storage file by choosing the Archive command from the File menu. You can also have Outlook automatically archive or delete items when they reach a specified age. For complete information on these techniques, see the Outlook online Help book "Archiving Items."

You might also want to store some of your messages in a different mail folder. For example, you might wish to create a folder named Saved Email, move to this folder all the e-mail messages you want to save, and delete the others.

The following is a way to move one or more Inbox messages to another folder. Note that you can use this same general method to move items stored in other personal folders, as well as messages from the Inbox:

1 Select one or more of the messages or items that you want to move.

2 Click the Move To Folder button on the toolbar and choose the Move To Folder command from the drop-down menu that appears:

VI

Integrating Applications

Sorting, Filtering, and Grouping Items in Personal Folders

Recall from the previous sidebar "Using Different Views" (on page 1056) that you can modify the basic way information is displayed in a personal folder by changing the view. You can further refine the way information is displayed in a particular view by sorting, filtering, or grouping the items in the folder.

You can use the Sort command on the View menu to sort the information in a personal folder, provided that the current view displays the items in a simple list (as in the default view of the Contacts folder), or in a table consisting of rows and columns (as in the default views of the Inbox and Tasks folders). You can sort the items in either ascending or descending order, and you can sort by the values of one or more fields.

When you open a folder, Outlook normally displays all items stored in that folder. However, you can use the Filter command on the View menu to display only those items that meet a specified criterion. For example, you could display only those messages in the Inbox that contain the word *manuscript* in the message text, or only those messages that are marked as high priority.

You can use the Group By command on the View menu to group items by the values of one or more fields, rather than displaying the items in a simple list. For example, if you grouped the messages in your Inbox by the Importance field, Outlook would list all high-priority messages in one group, followed by all normal-priority message in a second group, followed by all low-priority messages in a third group. This is different than merely sorting, because the groups are arranged in an outline view fashion from which you can open and close each group to focus on just those you want to view.

You can also use the Categories command on the Edit menu to assign categories to items in your personal folders. For example, you might assign some messages to the Business category and others to the Personal category. You can then sort, filter, or group the items based on their categories. (You can also locate items that belong to a given category using the Find command, which is discussed in the next sidebar.)

For complete details on the techniques discussed in this sidebar, see the book "Organizing and Viewing Items in Outllook" in the online Help. This book also explains how to reorganize the information in a folder by adding, removing, resizing, rearranging, or formatting the columns that display each field of information.

Outlook will open the Move Items dialog box, which is shown here:

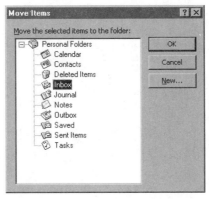

3 If you're moving messages to an existing folder, click the destination folder for your selected messages and click OK. If you want to move messages to a new folder, click the New button and continue on to steps 4 through 7.

4 In the Create New Folder dialog box, name the new folder in the Name box, and select the type of information it will contain in the Folder Contains box.

5 In the Make This Folder A Subfolder Of list, select an existing folder if you want your new folder to be a subfolder of another, or else select Personal Files to put the new folder on an equal basis with your other personal folders.

6 Click OK in the Create New Folder dialog box. The Move Items dialog box will reappear and your new folder will be selected.

7 Click OK in the Move Items dialog box and the selected messages will be moved to your new folder.

> If you want to place a *copy* of a message in another folder, choose Copy To Folder from the Edit menu instead of clicking the Move To Folder button in step 2 of the above procedure.

VI

Integrating Applications

Streamline Your Copy and Move Operations

You can more quickly move or copy an item by selecting the item and:

- Choosing Cut from the Edit menu to move it or Copy to copy it, opening the destination folder, and choosing Paste from the Edit menu; or

- Pressing Ctrl+X to move the item or Ctrl+C to copy the item, opening the destination folder, and pressing Ctrl+V to paste the item; or

- If the destination folder is visible in the Outlook bar, you can drag the item and drop it on the icon of the destination folder in the Outlook bar to move it, or drag the item while pressing the Ctrl key to copy it to a destination folder (you'll see a small plus sign to indicate that the item is being copied).

Finding Items in Personal Folders

You can use the Outlook Find Items command to search for items within a single personal folder; for example, you could search for all messages in the Inbox that were sent by a given person. You can also search for items within all personal folders; for instance, you could search for all items in all personal folders that are assigned a particular category, such as Business or Personal. Finally, you can search for regular files in your Windows file system; that is to say, you could search for all Word document files stored on your hard disk that contain a specific word or phrase.

To use the find feature, choose Find Items from Outlook's Tools menu. Alternatively, you can click the Start button on the Windows taskbar, click Find on the Start menu, and then choose Using Microsoft Outlook from the submenu that appears:

Finding Items in Personal Folders   *continued*

The second method lets you use Outlook's Find command even if you aren't running the Outlook program.

Whichever method you use, Outlook will open the Find window and you can proceed to define and carry out your search as shown here:

Select type of item to search.

Select any number of folders from file list.

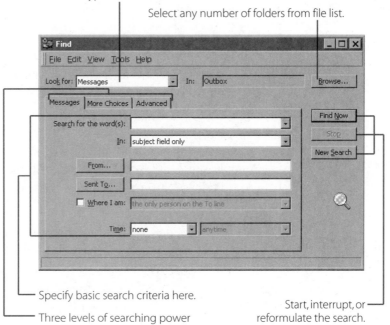

Specify basic search criteria here.

Three levels of searching power

Start, interrupt, or reformulate the search.

Note that the options appearing on the tabs of this window depend on the type of item you're searching for (which you select in the the Look For list).

After you click the Find Now button and the search is completed, Outlook will display all matching items or files in a list that's added to the bottom of the Find window. You can open an item in a personal folder, or a file, by double-clicking it within this list. You can save the results of a search in a file by choosing the Save Search command from the File menu in the Find window. You can later view these results again by choosing the Open Search command from the File menu. Note that you can leave the Find window displayed while you work in the main Outlook window.

For complete information on using the Find command, see the book "Finding Items and Files" in the Outlook online Help.

VI

Integrating Applications

You can delete a personal folder that you created by selecting it and then choosing the Delete *Folder Name* command (where *Folder Name* is the name you assigned the folder) from the Folder submenu of the File menu. Rather than permanently deleting the folder, Outlook will move it so that it's a subfolder of the Deleted Items folder.

Calendar

You can use the Calendar folder to schedule appointments, events, or meetings. In Outlook, an *appointment* is an activity that consumes a block of your own time; for example, an interview that you're planning to conduct next Wednesday morning from 9 to 9:30. An *event* is an occurrence that lasts for at least 24 hours but doesn't necessarily fully consume your time; for example, your birthday next May 21. A *meeting* is similar to an appointment but involves other people and resources; for example, a meeting with your team of programmers, which will be held next Friday from 1 to 2:30 and will require reserving a conference room and a projector.

Figure 41-9 shows the default Day/Week/Month view that appears when you first open the Calendar folder in Outlook. The Task Pad area of the window is actually a view of the Tasks folder, *not* the Calendar folder; it's included in the view of the Calendar folder to help you schedule time for working on your pending tasks. Tasks will be discussed in the "Tasks" section later in the chapter.

Go To
Today

To view or modify your schedule for a particular day, simply click the date in the monthly calendar in the upper right corner of the Information Viewer area. To quickly view today's schedule, click the Go To Today button.

You can also click the Day, Week, or Month button to modify the amount of detail shown in the Calendar:

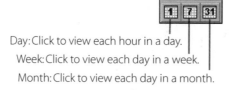

Day: Click to view each hour in a day.
Week: Click to view each day in a week.
Month: Click to view each day in a month.

FIGURE 41-9.

The Calendar folder before information is added, in the default Day/Week/Month view.

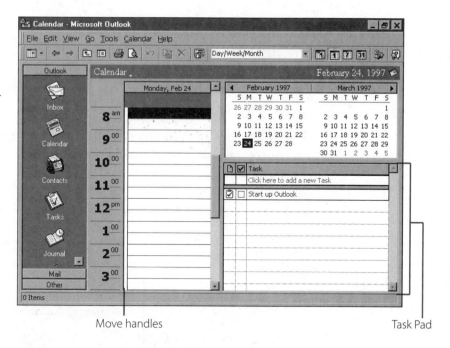

Move handles   Task Pad

Additionally, you can change the overall view by selecting an item in the Current View drop-down list on the toolbar:

For a general discussion on views, see the sidebar "Using Different Views" on page 1056.

 NOTE

To take advantage of all the features of the Calendar folder, you need to be connected to a network on which the Microsoft Exchange Server has been installed. If Exchange Server is *not* available, you can still schedule your personal appointments and events. However, you won't be able to access other people's calendar information, nor can they access yours. Also, you won't be able to use the Meeting Planner to schedule meetings that involve other people and resources.

VI

Integrating Applications

Scheduling Appointments

You can schedule either a one-time appointment or a *recurring* appointment. A recurring appointment is one that occurs at regular intervals, such as a basketball game you play every Friday at 4 PM.

To schedule a one-time or recurring appointment, begin by clicking on the day and time of the appointment (this step is optional, because you can set the day and time later). Then, choose the New Appointment command from the Calendar menu, or press Ctrl+N, and fill out the Appointment window as shown in Figure 41-10. Consult Table 41-1 to help you complete the appointment.

FIGURE 41-10.
Defining an appointment in the Appointment window. See Table 41-1 for more help.

Invite Attendees to a meeting (don't use this for an appointment).

Recurrence—click here to set up a regularly recurring appointment.

Delete appointment.

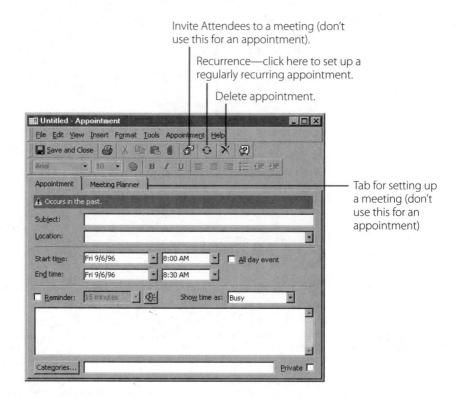

Tab for setting up a meeting (don't use this for an appointment)

TABLE 41-1.   Creating an Appointment in Outlook

Appointment Item	Purpose
Subject box	Appointment subject that's displayed in Calendar view.
Location box	Where the appointment is to take place.
Start Time, End Time	Set starting and ending dates and times.
All Day Event check box	Convert an appointment to an all-day event.
Reminder items	Turn on the check box to have Outlook sound an audible reminder for the appointment. Set the length of time before the appointment begins that you want the reminder to sound. Click the speaker button to set the sound that will be used as the reminder.
Show Time As list box	Select an item to specify how the appointment time appears to other people on an Exchange Server network.
Large text box	If you wish, you can type a note for the appointment here.
Formatting toolbar	Use the toolbar to format note text for the appointment.
Categories button	Click to assign appointment to one or more categories. The categories you select will appear in the text box.
Private check box	Turn on the check box to prevent other people on an Exchange Server network from reading the appointment.
Save And Close button	Click this button when you've finished defining the appointment.

To create a recurring appointment, click the Recurrence button on the Appointment window toolbar. Outlook will display the Appointment Recurrence dialog box, shown on the following page, in which you specify the appointment time and indicate the frequency of the recurrence and how long it's to continue.

VI

Integrating Applications

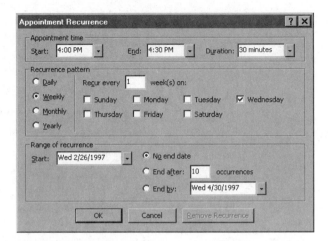

When you click OK, Outlook will return you to the Appointment window, which will now be labeled Recurring Appointment and will no longer include the appointment time fields (because, for a recurring appointment, the times are set through the Appointment Recurrence dialog box).

When you close the Appointment window, the newly defined appointment will be displayed within the appropriate box in the Information Viewer area:

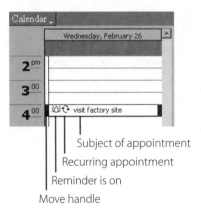

Subject of appointment

Recurring appointment

Reminder is on

Move handle

To move the appointment to another time, use the mouse to drag the move handle at the left edge of the appointment to the desired time slot. To copy the appointment, press Ctrl while you drag. To delete an appointment, select it by clicking on its move handle, and then press the Delete key.

To open an appointment so that you can view or modify the appointment information, double-click the move handle. For a one-time appointment, Outlook will immediately open the Appointment window. For a recurring appointment, however, Outlook will first display the following dialog box:

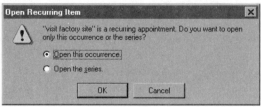

If you choose Open This Occurrence, you'll be able to change the specific appointment that you selected, without affecting the other appointments in the recurring series. If, however, you choose Open Series, you'll be able to modify the features of the entire recurring series of appointments.

Scheduling Events

To schedule an event, choose the New Appointment command from the Calendar menu, or press Ctrl+N. When Outlook displays the Appointment window, turn on the All Day Event option to define an event rather than an appointment. When you turn on this option, the title of the window changes from Appointment to Event. Also, the starting and ending hour fields are removed—leaving only the starting and ending day fields—because an event is always assigned to one or more whole days. Finally, the default value in the Show Time As field changes from Busy to Free, because the time occupied by an event is normally marked as free (unlike an appointment, an event generally doesn't fully consume your time). Note that the Show Time As field affects the way your time is marked when other people on an Exchange Server network view your schedule. Complete the remaining fields in the Event window as described in Table 41-1 on page 1071.

Recurrence

To create a recurring event, which is analogous to a recurring appointment, click the Recurrence button and fill in the times. For example, you might want to mark your partner's birthday as a recurring yearly event.

VI

Integrating Applications

When you close the Event window, you'll notice that the event is displayed in a banner at the top of the list of appointments:

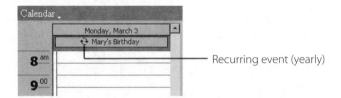

Recurring event (yearly)

Scheduling Meetings

If your computer is attached to a network with Microsoft Exchange Server, you can use the Outlook Meeting Planner to schedule a meeting at a time when all attendees are free and all required resources (for example, a conference room and a projector) are available. You can also send invitations to all attendees and requests for all resources, and you'll receive the replies to these invitations and requests in your Inbox.

The following is a summary of the method for scheduling a meeting:

1 Open the Calendar folder and choose Plan A Meeting from the Calendar menu. Outlook will open the Plan A Meeting window.

2 In the Plan A Meeting window, enter a list of meeting attendees and required resources, and choose a meeting time when all attendees and resources are available, as shown here:

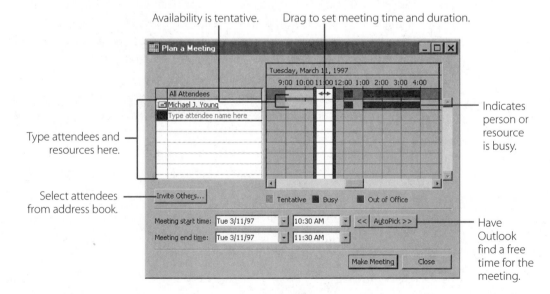

When you click the Make Meeting button in the Plan A Meeting dialog box, Outlook will open the Meeting window, which is similar to the Appointment window shown in Figure 41-10 on page 1070.

3 In the Meeting window, enter the subject and location for the meeting, and enter or revise other information as necessary (refer to Table 41-1 on page 1071). To create a recurring meeting, which is analogous to a recurring appointment, click the Recurrence button and enter the times into the Appointment Recurrence dialog box.

4 Click the Send button in the Meeting window to send an invitation to all meeting attendees and to issue a request for the needed meeting resources.

The new meeting will be shown in your Calendar folder in the same way as an appointment, and you can use the techniques that were described for appointments to open, move, copy, or delete it.

Contacts

You can use the Contacts folder to store names, addresses, and other information about your business or personal contacts. To add a new contact, open the Contacts folder and then choose New Contact from the Contacts menu, or click Ctrl+N. Outlook will open the Contact window. Enter the information for your contact as shown in Figure 41-11 and described in Table 41-2.

TABLE 41-2.   Adding a New Contact to Outlook's Contacts Folder

Contact Item	Purpose
Full Name button and text box	Click the button for help in properly formatting the name, or type the name directly in the text box.
File As text box	Select how to file the contact (for example, *Cruz, Maria* or *Maria Cruz*).
Address button and text box	Click the button for help in properly formatting the address, or type it directly in the text box.

(continued)

TABLE 41-2. *continued*

Contact Item	Purpose
E-mail addresses	Click the list box to designate up to three e-mail addresses, and then type each in the text box, or click the address book button to select the address from your address book.
Web Page	If the contact operates their own Web page, enter the complete Web address (for example, http://www.microsoft.com).
Categories button and text box	Click the button to assign one or more categories to the contact, and they'll be displayed in the text box.
Private check box	Turn on this check box to prevent other people on an Exchange Server network from viewing the contact information.
Phone list and text boxes	Enter up to four phone numbers for each contact, selecting the type of phone number in the list box and then entering the number itself in the corresponding text box.

FIGURE 41-11.

Defining a new contact in the Contact window. See Table 41-2 for more information.

Save contact and define another contact.

Click here to view Journal entries related to this contact.

Select the Address category you're entering for the contact (Home, Business, or Other).

AutoDialer: Start new call, redial, or speed dial.

Open contact's Web page.

Send message to contact.

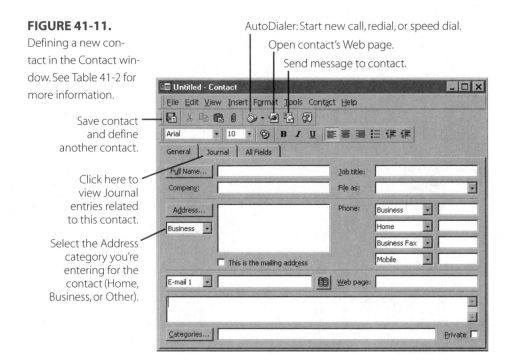

Get a Head Start in Creating Another Contact from the Same Company
If you want to enter a new contact that has the same company information as a contact you previously entered, select the previous contact in the Contacts folder and then choose New Contact From Same Company (rather than New Contact) from the Contacts menu. When the Contact window is opened it will already contain the company information.

Figure 41-12 shows the Contacts folder in the default Address Cards view, displaying three cards that have been added (in this view, a contact item is termed a *card*). To locate a specific contact, you can scroll through the cards in the window (click a button on the right side of the window to go to a specific alphabetical grouping), or you can choose the Find command from the Tools menu (for information on this command, see the sidebar "Finding Items in Personal Folders" on page 1066).

To view all the information for a contact—or to edit this information—open the contact's card by double-clicking the card's heading. The contact information will again be displayed in the Contact window shown in Figure 41-11. If the Allow In-Cell Editing option is enabled, you can also edit any of the information that is displayed on a card in the Contacts folder by simply clicking on the text (to set this option, choose Format View from the View menu).

FIGURE 41-12.
The Contacts folder in the default Address Cards view.

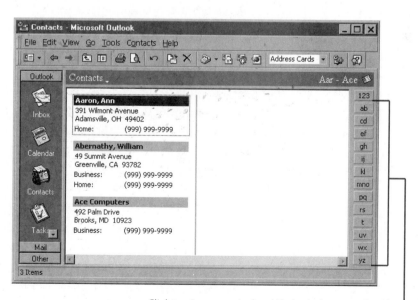

Click to view a particular alphabetical group of cards.

If you have a modem attached to your computer, you can also have Outlook dial a number by clicking the AutoDialer toolbar button and choosing an appropriate command from the drop-down menu:

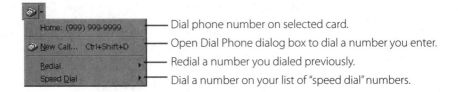

Home: (999) 999-9999 ——— Dial phone number on selected card.
New Call... Ctrl+Shift+D ——— Open Dial Phone dialog box to dial a number you enter.
Redial ——— Redial a number you dialed previously.
Speed Dial ——— Dial a number on your list of "speed dial" numbers.

To configure Outlook for your modem, or to define one or more "speed dial" numbers, choose the Options command from the Tools menu and select the Dialing Options button on the General tab.

Explore
Web
Page

Finally, if you've installed a Web browser on your system and if you've entered a Web page address for a contact (see Figure 41-11, page 1076), you can use Outlook to open that Web page. To do this, select the contact's card by clicking on it and then click the Explore Web Page button.

Tasks

You can use the Tasks folder in Outlook to track short jobs that you need to complete or even large projects that you're managing. You can manage tasks for yourself, or—if your computer is connected to an Exchange Server network—you can manage tasks that involve other people in your workgroup.

To start tracking a new task, open the Tasks folder and choose the New Task command from the Tasks menu or click Ctrl+N. Outlook will open the Task window. You can then enter information for the task on both the Task tab and the Status tab, as shown in Figures 41-13 and 41-14. Some of the information on these tabs (primarily the Status tab) indicates the progress you've made toward completing the task; you obviously won't be able to supply this information until later.

FIGURE 41-13.
Entering task informa-
tion on the Task tab of
the Task window.

Send status report.

Assign task.

Mark task as complete.

Mark task as recurring.

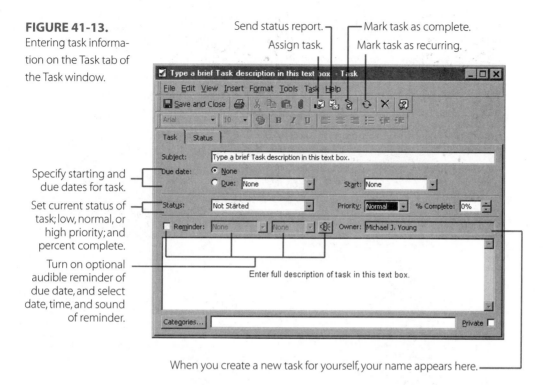

Specify starting and
due dates for task.

Set current status of
task; low, normal, or
high priority; and
percent complete.

Turn on optional
audible reminder of
due date, and select
date, time, and sound
of reminder.

When you create a new task for yourself, your name appears here.

FIGURE 41-14.
Entering task informa-
tion on the Status tab
of the Task window.

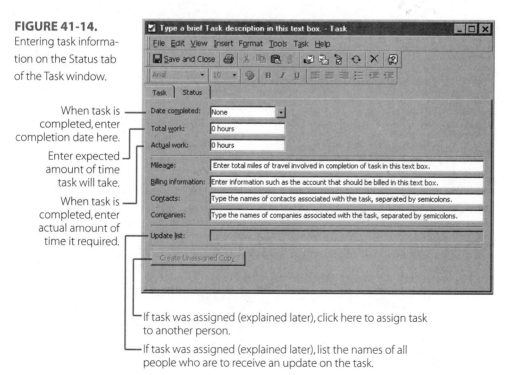

When task is
completed, enter
completion date here.

Enter expected
amount of time
task will take.

When task is
completed, enter
actual amount of
time it required.

If task was assigned (explained later), click here to assign task
to another person.

If task was assigned (explained later), list the names of all
people who are to receive an update on the task.

VI

Integrating Applications

AutoPreview

Figure 41-15 shows the Tasks folder, in the default Simple List view, after several tasks have been defined. In this view, you can also display the first three lines of the Notes field of each task (see Figure 41-13 on the preceding page) by clicking the AutoPreview button on the toolbar.

FIGURE 41-15.
The Tasks folder in the default Simple List view.

Completed task shows subject and date with line drawn through it.

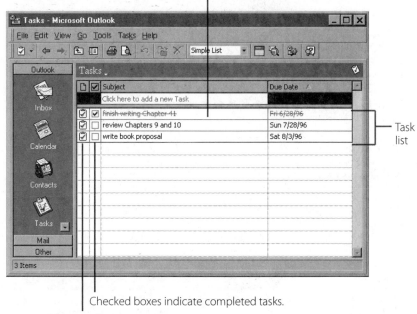

Task list

Checked boxes indicate completed tasks.
Double-click to open task.

Note that the task list that you see in the Simple List view of the Tasks folder is also displayed within the default view of the Calendar folder, as was shown in Figure 41-9 on page 1069.

Define a Task Quickly
You can quickly define a task by clicking in the box at the top of the Subject column, which is labeled "Click here to add a new Task." (See Figure 41-15.) Type the task subject into the Subject box, enter the due date into the Due Date box, and press Enter to add the task to the task list. You can later open the task in the Task window (as explained next) to key in additional information.

To view the complete information on a task, or to update this information, you can open the task in the Task window (shown in Figures 41-13 and 41-14, page 1079) by double-clicking the task's icon in the task list. You might need to do this, for example, to update the status of a task.

You can also directly edit any of the information for a task that appears in the task list, without opening the task. Specifically, you can change the task subject by editing the text in the Subject box, you can mark the task as completed by checking the box to the left of the Subject box, or you can change the due date by clicking in the Due Date box and choosing a new date from the drop-down calendar:

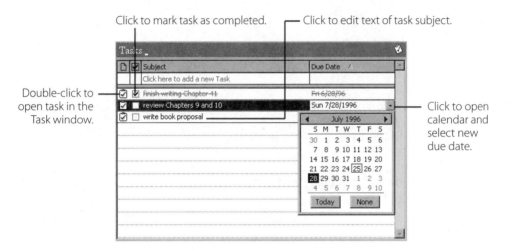

Click to mark task as completed.

Click to edit text of task subject.

Double-click to open task in the Task window.

Click to open calendar and select new due date.

Note that to change information directly within the task list, the Allow In-Cell Editing option must be turned on. To set this option, choose the Format View command from the View menu.

To delete a task, click its icon in the task list and press Delete. To move a task to a different position in the list, drag the icon. To make a copy, hold down the Ctrl key while you drag.

If you want to see your tasks in a timeline arrangement, you can choose the Task Timeline view from the Current View drop-down list on the toolbar (see the sidebar "Using Different Views" on page 1056). When in this view, you can control the amount of detail that is shown by clicking the Day, Week, or Month toolbar button.

VI

Integrating Applications

Figure 41-16 shows the Tasks folder as it appears in the Task Timeline view, with the Week button pressed (this figure shows the same tasks that are listed in Figure 41-15 on page 1080).

FIGURE 41-16.
The Tasks folder in the
Task Timeline view.

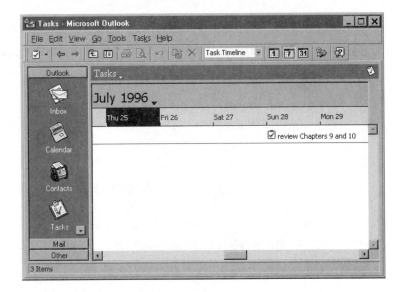

Assigning a Task

If your computer is connected to a Microsoft Exchange Server network, you can also use Outlook to assign a task to a co-worker. After you assign a task to another person, you'll receive back in your Inbox either an acceptance or a refusal of the task. A person who accepts a task assignment becomes the task *owner* (if you create a task for yourself, as described in the previous section, you're the owner).

To create a task and assign it to another person, choose the New Task Request command from the Tasks menu, or press Ctrl+Shift+U. Outlook will display the Task window; fill it out as shown in Figure 41-17 and then click the Send button.

FIGURE 41-17.

Assigning a task to another person in the Task window.

Click here to send task assignment to assignee.

Enter task status information (see Figure 41-14 on page 1079).

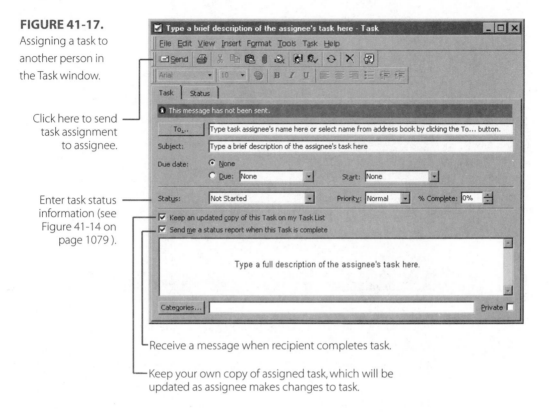

Receive a message when recipient completes task.

Keep your own copy of assigned task, which will be updated as assignee makes changes to task.

Journal

The Journal folder allows you to keep a record of events and to view these events according to the times they occurred. You can have Outlook automatically create journal entries for certain types of events—for example, receiving an e-mail message from a particular person or sending a task request to a specific individual. You can also manually record *any* type of event—for example, a telephone conversation you had or an interview you conducted.

To have Outlook begin creating journal entries automatically, choose Options from the Tools menu and click the Journal tab of the Options dialog box, which is shown at the top of the next page.

You must now select one or more Outlook items; Outlook will create a journal entry whenever you receive or send one of these items. You must also select one or more people from your list of contacts (kept in the Contacts folder, as explained previously in the chapter); Outlook

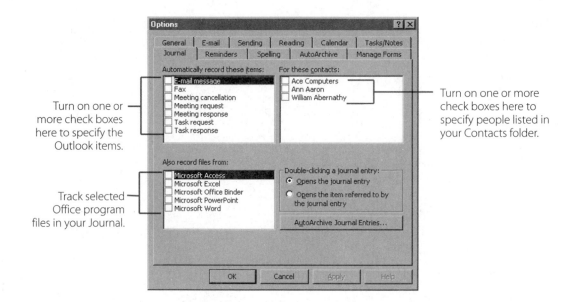

Turn on one or more check boxes here to specify the Outlook items.

Turn on one or more check boxes here to specify people listed in your Contacts folder.

Track selected Office program files in your Journal.

will create a journal entry only for items that are associated with the people you select. For example, if you select the E-Mail Message and Fax items and the Ann Aaron contact, Outlook will automatically create a journal entry whenever you send or receive an e-mail message or a fax to or from Ann Aaron.

You can also manually create a journal entry for *any* type of event. To do this, choose the New Journal Entry command from the Journal menu, or press Ctrl+N. Then, complete the Journal Entry window as shown here:

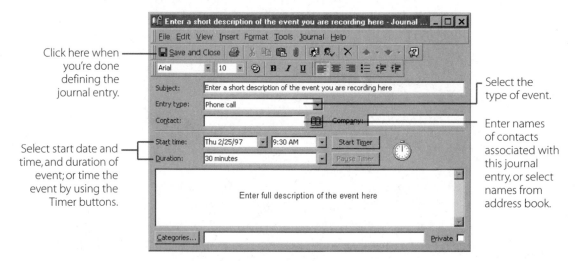

Click here when you're done defining the journal entry.

Select start date and time, and duration of event; or time the event by using the Timer buttons.

Select the type of event.

Enter names of contacts associated with this journal entry, or select names from address book.

The default view used in the Journal folder, By Type, shows the journal entries arranged in a timeline (similar to the Task Timeline view in the Tasks folder, discussed previously) and grouped according to the type of the event (phone calls, e-mail messages, and so on). You can select the amount of detail shown in this view by clicking the Day, Week, or Month toolbar buttons.

Figure 41-18 shows the Journal folder in the default By Type view, with the Week button selected.

FIGURE 41-18.
The Journal folder in
the default view, By
Type, with the weekly
level of detail selected.

Weekly level of detail selected

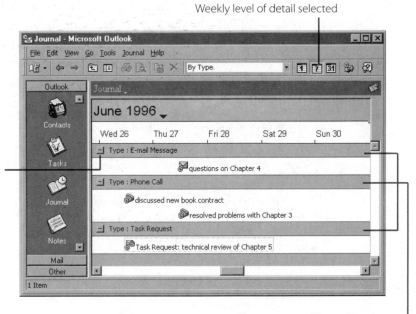

Click to hide/show
entries belonging
to this type.

Three groups of Journal entries

To open a journal entry in the Journal Entry window, so that you can view or modify any of the entry information, simple double-click the entry within the Journal folder.

> **NOTE**

If the journal entry you're opening was automatically recorded and if the Opens The Item Referred To By The Journal Entry check box is turned on (on the Journal tab of the Options dialog box), double-clicking the item will open the original Outlook item that the entry is based on (for example, an e-mail message) *rather* than open the journal entry itself.

VI

Integrating Applications

As in other folders, you can delete a journal entry by selecting it and pressing Delete. To move a journal entry to another location in the timeline, however, you *can't* simply drag it using the mouse. Rather, you must open the entry and change the start time or duration.

Notes

You can use the Notes personal folder to store and organize miscellaneous bits and pieces of information. You might want to store information that doesn't fit into any of the categories provided by the other Outlook folders (for example, a list of supplies to purchase for your meeting). You might also want to use the Notes folder to temporarily store information that you'll later place in the appropriate folder (for example, you could quickly jot down a name and address that you'll later store in the Contacts folder).

Once you open the Notes folder, you can create a new note by choosing the New Note command from the Notes menu, by pressing Ctrl+N, or by simply double-clicking a blank spot within the Information Viewer area. Outlook will then open a Notes window into which you can type the text for your note, as shown here:

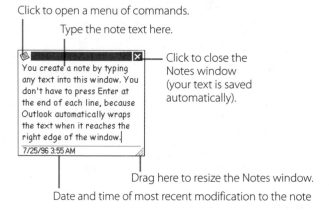

Click to open a menu of commands.

Type the note text here.

You create a note by typing any text into this window. You don't have to press Enter at the end of each line, because Outlook automatically wraps the text when it reaches the right edge of the window.

7/25/96 3:55 AM

Click to close the Notes window (your text is saved automatically).

Drag here to resize the Notes window.

Date and time of most recent modification to the note

You can click the icon in the upper left corner of the Notes window to open a menu of commands for changing the color of the note or performing other tasks. This menu is shown here:

When you're done typing the text for your note, you can close the window by clicking the Close box in the upper right corner, or you can simply switch back to the Outlook window and leave the Notes window open. In either case, the new note will be added to the Notes folder. You can display the notes as large or small icons, or as a list.

Hi, I'm a note!

If you choose the By Color view from the Current View drop-down list on the toolbar, your notes will be grouped according to their colors. You already saw how to change the color of a note when it's open in the Notes window. You can also change a note's color (say, blue for casual information, yellow for a cautionary note) by right-clicking the note in the Notes folder; a menu will appear that allows you to change the color of the note or perform other actions:

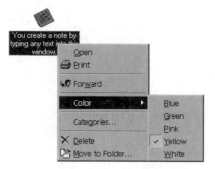

You can select various ways of sorting your notes using the Sort dialog box (choose Sort from the View menu). You can change the way the notes are arranged and whether sorting is turned on by choosing the

Format View command from the View menu and entering your choices into the dialog box that's displayed:

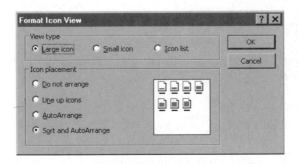

You can open a note in the Notes window, so that you can add or modify its text, by double-clicking the note in the Notes folder. To delete a note, select it by clicking on it and then press the Delete key.

Change the Default Features of Notes to Suit Your Fancy

You can modify the default color, size, font, and other features for all new notes that you subsequently create by choosing the Options command from the Tools menu and selecting the Tasks/Notes tab.

Accessing Files

You can also use Outlook to access any of the files that are located on your computer or on a network attached to your computer. For example, you can access programs, Office documents, and other types of data files. You can use Outlook to open, move, copy, rename, print, or delete files as well as file folders. You can also create new file folders and shortcuts to files. The Outlook file interface is quite similar to Windows Explorer. If you've used the Explorer, you'll already be familiar with most of the file access features of Outlook. (If you aren't familiar with the Explorer, see the "Windows Explorer" topic in the Windows manual or online Help.) This section focuses on the features that are unique to the Outlook file interface.

To access files, begin by using the Outlook bar to open a specific folder, as follows:

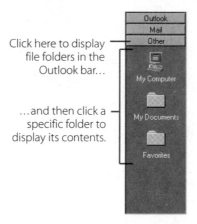

Click here to display file folders in the Outlook bar...

...and then click a specific folder to display its contents.

The My Computer folder lets you access folders on any of the disk drives on your computer. The My Documents folder is generally located on your hard drive and is the default folder for storing your Office documents. If you've installed a Web browser, the Favorites folder will store the addresses of sites on the Internet that you've visited frequently; you can double-click an icon in this folder to start your browser and open a Web site. You can also add or remove frequently used file folders from the Outlook bar.

Folder
List

If you click the Folder List button on the Outlook toolbar, Outlook will display your folders in a hierarchical list. This list is similar to the one shown in the left pane of the Explorer and will make it easier for you to navigate through your folders and files (see Figure 41-19 on the following page).

You can now use the same techniques that you employ in Explorer to view the contents of folders; to open files or run programs; to copy, move, rename, or delete files or folders; or to print files. Several techniques, however, vary slightly from those used in Explorer. For example, to use Outlook to create a new file folder, you choose the Folder command from the New submenu of the File menu. Also, to create a shortcut for an application, drag its filename to the folder in which you want it to appear, or to the desktop.

VI

Integrating Applications

FIGURE 41-19.
The My Computer folder opened in Outlook, with the folder list displayed.

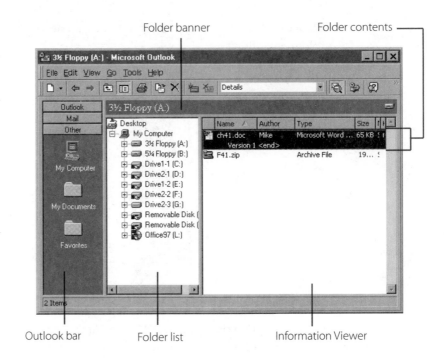

Folder banner

Folder contents

Outlook bar

Folder list

Information Viewer

To make it easier to open file folders you use frequently, you can add these folders to the Outlook bar. To add a folder to the Outlook bar, right-click on the folder you want to add in the folder list. Choose Add To Outlook Bar from the menu that appears, and the folder will be displayed in the Outlook bar.

To remove a folder from the Outlook bar, right-click the icon for the folder within the Outlook bar and choose the Remove From Outlook Bar command from the menu that pops up. Adding or removing folders from the Outlook bar will *not* affect the actual folders in your file system. *However,* don't *select a folder and press the* Delete *key. Just as in Explorer, you* will *delete the folder and send all its files to the Recycle Bin!*

Index

IMPORTANT—READ CAREFULLY BEFORE OPENING SOFTWARE PACKET(S). By opening the sealed packet(s) containing the software, you indicate your acceptance of the following Microsoft License Agreement.

MICROSOFT LICENSE AGREEMENT

(Book Companion CD)

This is a legal agreement between you (either an individual or an entity) and Microsoft Corporation. By opening the sealed software packet(s) you are agreeing to be bound by the terms of this agreement. If you do not agree to the terms of this agreement, promptly return the unopened software packet(s) and any accompanying written materials to the place you obtained them for a full refund.

MICROSOFT SOFTWARE LICENSE

1. GRANT OF LICENSE. Microsoft grants to you the right to use one copy of the Microsoft software program included with this book (the "SOFTWARE") on a single terminal connected to a single computer. The SOFTWARE is in "use" on a computer when it is loaded into the temporary memory (i.e., RAM) or installed into the permanent memory (e.g., hard disk, CD-ROM, or other storage device) of that computer. You may not network the SOFTWARE or otherwise use it on more than one computer or computer terminal at the same time.

2. COPYRIGHT. The SOFTWARE is owned by Microsoft or its suppliers and is protected by United States copyright laws and international treaty provisions. Therefore, you must treat the SOFTWARE like any other copyrighted material (e.g., a book or musical recording) except that you may either (a) make one copy of the SOFTWARE solely for backup or archival purposes, or (b) transfer the SOFTWARE to a single hard disk provided you keep the original solely for backup or archival purposes. You may not copy the written materials accompanying the SOFTWARE.

3. OTHER RESTRICTIONS. You may not rent or lease the SOFTWARE, but you may transfer the SOFTWARE and accompanying written materials on a permanent basis provided you retain no copies and the recipient agrees to the terms of this Agreement. You may not reverse engineer, decompile, or disassemble the SOFTWARE. If the SOFTWARE is an update or has been updated, any transfer must include the most recent update and all prior versions.

4. DUAL MEDIA SOFTWARE. If the SOFTWARE package contains more than one kind of disk (3.5", 5.25", and CD-ROM), then you may use only the disks appropriate for your single-user computer. You may not use the other disks on another computer or loan, rent, lease, or transfer them to another user except as part of the permanent transfer (as provided above) of all SOFTWARE and written materials.

5. SAMPLE CODE. If the SOFTWARE includes Sample Code, then Microsoft grants you a royalty-free right to reproduce and distribute the sample code of the SOFTWARE provided that you: (a) distribute the sample code only in conjunction with and as a part of your software product; (b) do not use Microsoft's or its authors' names, logos, or trademarks to market your software product; (c) include the copyright notice that appears on the SOFTWARE on your product label and as a part of the sign-on message for your software product; and (d) agree to indemnify, hold harmless, and defend Microsoft and its authors from and against any claims or lawsuits, including attorneys' fees, that arise or result from the use or distribution of your software product.

DISCLAIMER OF WARRANTY

The SOFTWARE (including instructions for its use) is provided "AS IS" WITHOUT WARRANTY OF ANY KIND. MICROSOFT FURTHER DISCLAIMS ALL IMPLIED WARRANTIES INCLUDING WITHOUT LIMITATION ANY IMPLIED WARRANTIES OF MERCHANTABILITY OR OF FITNESS FOR A PARTICULAR PURPOSE. THE ENTIRE RISK ARISING OUT OF THE USE OR PERFORMANCE OF THE SOFTWARE AND DOCUMENTATION REMAINS WITH YOU.

IN NO EVENT SHALL MICROSOFT, ITS AUTHORS, OR ANYONE ELSE INVOLVED IN THE CREATION, PRODUCTION, OR DELIVERY OF THE SOFTWARE BE LIABLE FOR ANY DAMAGES WHATSOEVER (INCLUDING, WITHOUT LIMITATION, DAMAGES FOR LOSS OF BUSINESS PROFITS, BUSINESS INTERRUPTION, LOSS OF BUSINESS INFORMATION, OR OTHER PECUNIARY LOSS) ARISING OUT OF THE USE OF OR INABILITY TO USE THE SOFTWARE OR DOCUMENTATION, EVEN IF MICROSOFT HAS BEEN ADVISED OF THE POSSIBILITY OF SUCH DAMAGES. BECAUSE SOME STATES/COUNTRIES DO NOT ALLOW THE EXCLUSION OR LIMITATION OF LIABILITY FOR CONSEQUENTIAL OR INCIDENTAL DAMAGES, THE ABOVE LIMITATION MAY NOT APPLY TO YOU.

U.S. GOVERNMENT RESTRICTED RIGHTS

The SOFTWARE and documentation are provided with RESTRICTED RIGHTS. Use, duplication, or disclosure by the Government is subject to restrictions as set forth in subparagraph (c)(1)(ii) of The Rights in Technical Data and Computer Software clause at DFARS 252.227-7013 or subparagraphs (c)(1) and (2) of the Commercial Computer Software — Restricted Rights 48 CFR 52.227-19, as applicable. Manufacturer is Microsoft Corporation, One Microsoft Way, Redmond, WA 98052-6399.

If you acquired this product in the United States, this Agreement is governed by the laws of the State of Washington. Should you have any questions concerning this Agreement, or if you desire to contact Microsoft Press for any reason, please write: Microsoft Press, One Microsoft Way, Redmond, WA 98052-6399.

Register Today!

Return this
Running Microsoft® Office 97
registration card for
a Microsoft Press® catalog

U.S. and Canada addresses only. Fill in information below and mail postage-free. Please mail only the bottom half of this page.

1-57231-322-6A   ***RUNNING MICROSOFT ® OFFICE 97***   *Owner Registration Card*

NAME

INSTITUTION OR COMPANY NAME

ADDRESS

CITY   STATE   ZIP

Microsoft®*Press*
Quality Computer Books

For a free catalog of
Microsoft Press® products, call
1-800-MSPRESS

BUSINESS REPLY MAIL
FIRST-CLASS MAIL   PERMIT NO. 53   BOTHELL, WA

POSTAGE WILL BE PAID BY ADDRESSEE

NO POSTAGE
NECESSARY
IF MAILED
IN THE
UNITED STATES

MICROSOFT PRESS REGISTRATION
RUNNING MICROSOFT® OFFICE 97
PO BOX 3019
BOTHELL WA   98041-9946

Michael and Michael's Top 50 Productivity Tips...

Microsoft Excel *(continued)*

25. To repeat a command that you just executed on a new range of cells, select the cells and choose the Repeat command from the Edit menu or press Ctrl+Y. This is especially powerful if the command you used involved several steps, such as formatting a label or changing number formats. See page 451.

26. To change the default number of worksheets in a new Excel workbook, choose the Options command from the Tools menu, and then specify a new number on the General tab. See page 506.

27. Use Excel's new Data Map feature to add accurate and customizable regional maps to your worksheets and reports. To add a map, choose the Map command from the Insert menu and specify the map's features. You can even fill your map with spreadsheet data! See page 601.

28. Here's the best tip to impress your friends: If you get tired of the pictures on your toolbar buttons, you can edit them to customize their look. Choose Toolbars from the View menu, and then choose Customize from the submenu. On the appropriate toolbar, right-click on the button you want to edit, choose the Edit Button Image command, and then edit the bitmap. See page 536.

29. Rather than reinventing the wheel, be sure to use functions to guide your calculations. To compute the future value of an IRA when you retire, use the FV function. (This is Excel's most popular financial function.) See page 568.

30. You can use the Goal Seek command to rapidly determine the unknown value in a forecasting scenario, but if you want to watch it make its calculations one iteration at a time, you can do that too. See page 638.

31. Here's a cool charting tip: Spruce up your chart's looks by adding a color or a background graphic to it. Click the chart to select it, choose the Selected Chart Area command from the Format menu, click the Patterns tab, and then select a color or click the Fill Effects button to pick a background graphic. See page 598.

Microsoft Powerpoint

32. To create a basic PowerPoint presentation, even if you don't know much about PowerPoint, use the AutoContent Wizard. See page 684.

33. To dramatically format the shape, size, and presentation of key text in your slide show, use the WordArt feature. Simply choose the Picture command from the Insert menu, click WordArt, and type your text. See page 716.

4. Spicing up your presentation with rows and columns is often useful and persuasive. To add a Word table to a slide, click the Insert Microsoft Word button on the Standard toolbar. See page 752.

To record voice narration to accompany your slide show, choose the Record Narration command from the Slide Show menu. See page 780.

'ring a presentation, you can jump quickly to the first slide in your presentation by holding down both se buttons for 2 seconds. See page 823.

a professional touch to your slide show, use transitions to dissolve one slide into another. Click 'e Sorter View button at the bottom left of the screen, and then select a transition from the Slide n Effects list. See page 773.

38. To quickly rearrange the slides in your presentation, click the Slide Sorter View button at the bottom left of the screen, and then drag slides from one location to another. See page 799.

Microsoft Access

39. Why reinvent the wheel? You can create several useful databases automatically by choosing the New Database command from the File menu and selecting one of the Database Wizards on the Databases tab. See page 849.

40. To have Access automatically determine the most appropriate width for a datasheet column, double-click the right border of the column heading. See page 888.

41. Trust us: To create a customized form for data entry, start by using the Form Wizard. Click the New button on the Forms tab in the Database window, and then double-click the Form Wizard option. See page 916.

42. To sort your database using multiple fields, use the Advanced Filter/Sort command on the Filter sub-menu of the Records menu. You can even tell Access to limit the number of records it displays in the list. See page 928.

43. To generate labels for a customer mailing list or inventory control system, select the Label Wizard in the New Report dialog box and start customizing your labels. See page 978.

44. To align controls on your form along one axis (so they look neat and tidy), select the controls as a group and choose the appropriate command from the Align submenu of the Format menu. See page 986.

Microsoft Outlook

45. To quickly open a specific personal or file folder, choose the Go To Folder command from the Go menu. Then select the Outlook item if you want to open a personal folder, or select the File System item if you want to open a file folder. See page 1053.

46. Get old Outlook items out of the way by choosing the Archive command from the File menu. See page 1063.

47. Quickly copy an Outlook item to a different folder by choosing Copy To Folder from the Edit menu. See page 1065.

48. In the Outlook Contact Folder, enter a new contact that has the same company information as a contact you previously entered by choosing New Contact From Same Company from the Contacts menu. See page 1077.

49. In the Outlook Tasks folder, quickly define a task by clicking in the box at the top of the Subject column. See page 1080.

Microsoft Office Binder

50. Organize all of your related documents into a single binder to make them easier to manage. To print all the documents in a binder, choose the Print Binder command from Binder's File menu. See page 1045.